PENGUIN

GEORGE ELIOT

'Eliot's is a remarkable story, told by Ashton with sensitivity and flair, of a mind locating its natural energy and undergoing a dramatic expansion from narrowness and timidity to an imaginative moral sympathy unequalled by any other writer of the age' Elizabeth Lowry, *Spectator*

'Ashton argues that Eliot's brilliance, proud prickliness, need, and dignity were the sources of her best writing. The result is a lively and nuanced portrait of the sort that Eliot herself so rigorously drew, in which human complexity produces its own singular reward' *New Yorker*

'Ashton is good on the powerful tensions that give Eliot's life its lasting sheen . . . This is a model introduction to Eliot – well researched' D. J. Taylor, *Independent*

'It is one of the many strengths of this accomplished biography that Rosemary Ashton deals so feelingly with [George Eliot's] pain, and with the sad, discomfiting coda to her life when, after Lewes's death, she married a man 20 years her junior . . . Her comments on the novels – entirely free of academic jargon – are inspiriting, but what most readers will value more, I suspect, is the insight she gives into what it cost George Eliot to create "some of the most wonderful works of fiction ever written"' Stephen Gill, *Daily Telegraph*

'Ashton exhibits a sure feel for her subject in her engaging new book . . . a pleasure to read: limpidly written with a nicely understated wittiness' Merle Rubin, *Christian Science Monitor*

'Reflects Rosemary Ashton's immense scholarship and her deep love of Eliot. It is rigorously sourced and fluently written' Kathryn Hughes, *Literary Review*

GEORGE ELIOT

A Life

ROSEMARY ASHTON

PENGUIN BOOKS

For Ben, Kate and Tom

PENGUIN BOOKS

Published by the Penguin Group
Penguin Books Ltd, 27 Wrights Lane, London W8 5TZ, England
Penguin Putnam Inc., 375 Hudson Street, New York, New York 10014, USA
Penguin Books Australia Ltd, Ringwood, Victoria, Australia
Penguin Books Canada Ltd, 10 Alcorn Avenue, Toronto, Ontario, Canada M4V 3B2
Penguin Books (NZ) Ltd, 182–190 Wairau Road, Auckland 10, New Zealand

Penguin Books Ltd, Registered Offices: Harmondsworth, Middlesex, England

First published by Hamish Hamilton 1996
Published in Penguin Books 1997
3 5 7 9 10 8 6 4 2

Copyright © Rosemary Ashton, 1996
All rights reserved

The moral right of the author has been asserted

Printed in England by Clays Ltd, St Ives plc

CONTENTS

CONTENTS

LIST OF ILLUSTRATIONS

FRONTISPIECE George Eliot, drawing by Sir Frederic William Burton, 1865.

ILLUSTRATION ACKNOWLEDGEMENTS

The author and publishers gratefully acknowledge permission to use the illustrations in this book, as follows:

Warwickshire County Libraries, 1; The National Portrait Gallery, London, 2, 12, 13, 30; Coventry City Libraries, 4, 5, 11; Coventry City Libraries, Photograph by Geoff Russell, 6, 8; City of Nottingham Museums: Castle Museum and Art Gallery, 9; Herbert Art Gallery and Museum, Coventry, 10, 15; Staatsbibliothek, Berlin, Photograph BPK, Berlin, 14; The Mistress and Fellows, Girton College, Cambridge, 16, 27; Department of Manuscripts, MS Add 34020, folio 1, The British Library, 17; The Beinecke Rare Book and Manuscript Library, Yale

University, 18, 32; The Royal Collection © 1996 Her Majesty Queen Elizabeth II, 19, 20; London Borough of Camden from the Collections at Keats House, Hampstead, Photograph by Keith Wynn, 21; Mrs Ursula Cash, 22, 23; The Trustees of The British Museum, 24; S. P. Avery Collection, Miriam and Ira D. Wallach Division of Art, Prints and Photographs, The New York Public Library, Astor, Lenox and Tilden Foundations, 28.

A NOTE ON SPELLINGS

Victorian spelling and punctuation are sometimes irregular. I have not modernized spellings or corrected punctuation, and have avoided using [*sic*] except in cases where the spelling is really strange, as in the letters of Robert Evans and John Chapman. Otherwise, when I quote from letters and journals, I follow the originals without comment. Thus the reader can expect to see 'Shakespeare' sometimes spelt 'Shakspeare', 'don't' spelt 'dont', 'honour' spelt 'honor', and so on. George Eliot writes 'surprize', and when she quotes from French or German, her spelling and accents are sometimes irregular.

LIST OF ABBREVIATIONS

Some of the most frequently occurring references are given in abbreviated form, as follows:

BL	British Library
BM	British Museum
Cross	J. W. Cross, *George Eliot's Life as Related in her Letters and Journals*, 3 vols. (London, 1885)
GE	George Eliot
GEL	*The George Eliot Letters*, ed. Gordon S. Haight, 9 vols. (New Haven, Connecticut, 1954–5, 1978)
GHL	George Henry Lewes
Haight	Gordon S. Haight, *George Eliot: A Biography* (Oxford, 1968, reprinted 1969)
LSE	London School of Economics
NLS	National Library of Scotland
UCL	University College London

PREFACE

All George Eliot readers and scholars owe a huge debt of gratitude to the late Professor Gordon S. Haight, editor of *The George Eliot Letters* (*GEL*), 9 volumes (New Haven, Connecticut, 1954–5, 1978). This edition, originally published in seven volumes, with two supplementary volumes added in 1978, is meticulously researched and full of useful information in footnotes and apparatus. Moreover, Haight printed not only George Eliot's letters but also many by her partner G. H. Lewes, and several letters to George Eliot from her friends and, above all, from her publisher John Blackwood. The result is an extraordinarily rich collection of material, invaluable to the critic or biographer of George Eliot.

In addition to the great work on the letters, Gordon Haight published a widely acclaimed documentary life of George Eliot (Oxford, 1968, reprinted 1969), as well as other books and articles on George Eliot and Lewes (see Bibliography). Haight's biography presents the facts of George Eliot's life, researched by him in the course of editing the letters, in a fair and scholarly way. It has for long stood as the definitive life.

The present biography is indebted to Haight's work, and does not seek to supersede it as a piece of scholarship, though some new letters have come to light since the Haight edition of *GEL*, including a small collection of George Eliot's letters to John Chapman (see Bibliography under Ashton) in the Huntington Library at San Marino, California, and some new information about Lewes. Much of this new material appeared in my biography of Lewes, *G. H. Lewes: A Life* (Oxford, 1991).

My debt to Gordon and Mary Haight in the researching of the biography of Lewes is expressed in the Preface to that book. A new collection of Lewes's letters has recently been published by William Baker (see Bibliography).

The present *Life* of George Eliot is intended to be a critical biography rather than a purely documentary one. I proceed on the assumption that the reader is interested in George Eliot the writer as well as George Eliot the woman. Since writing is what she did for a living, I discuss her writing both from the point of view of its origins in her life and from the point of view of the reader responding to the works. I also discuss her works in the context of the nineteenth-century novel, both in England and in Europe, with reference to writers like Walter Scott, Goethe, Jane Austen, Balzac, George Sand, and Tolstoy. And I deal with her relations, intellectual, literary, and social, with the great writers and thinkers she knew – they were mostly men – including Dickens, Darwin, Huxley, Tennyson, and Browning.

No more interesting subject could present itself than that of a young woman from the provinces, living in Victorian times, who broke with convention in more ways than one. As a young woman she lost her faith and defied and alienated her family by refusing to go to church. In her early thirties she moved alone to London to pursue an independent career as a journalist and translator. She met, and lived among, a most interesting set of progressive thinkers, most of them free-thinking and some of them free-living. Her journey to Weimar in 1854 with G. H. Lewes, a married man, and her subsequent partnership with him until his death in 1878, made her a sort of internal exile in most social circles. Even after Lewes's death she caused an outcry by marrying John Cross, nearly twenty years her junior.

With her formidable intellect, her wide-ranging knowledge of languages, literatures, philosophy, and science, she was the greatest woman of the century. She was also one of the luckiest. For she was fortunate indeed to meet with a man – Lewes – who returned her love, recognized her genius, and fought against her diffidence and self-doubt to encourage her to express her genius in fiction. Her happiness with Lewes was, however, tempered by the painful social position their relationship put her in. While Lewes was still invited to dinner, for many years George Eliot was not an acceptable guest except in exclusively male, or in unusually daring female, company.

Out of these extraordinary elements in her life and personality – proud yet sensitive, rebellious yet longing for the approval of those she could not help offending – came some of the most wonderful works of fiction ever written. In the narrative which follows, I seek to tell the story of their genesis, to point out some of their most interesting and original literary qualities, and to assess the contemporary response to them, presenting a picture of the woman, the works, and the age in which the woman lived and the works were written.

Though a wealth of materials is available in the published and unpublished sources on which I have drawn, there are some gaps in the record. Most notably, no letters survive between George Eliot and Lewes. She took his letters with her to the grave. Though both George Eliot and Lewes kept journals or diaries for most of their lives, those before their liaison in 1854 have disappeared, hers being presumably destroyed by John Cross after he had selected passages for quotation in his biography of George Eliot (1885). Haight has published passages from the surviving journals in *GEL*; I refer to *GEL* when quoting these. For Lewes's journals I quote from the manuscripts in the Beinecke collection at Yale, and for extracts from George Eliot's not published by Haight I have been able to quote from a typescript prepared for forthcoming publication by Margaret Harris and Judith Johnston of the University of Sydney, Australia, from the manuscripts in the Beinecke Library at Yale and – in the case of George Eliot's diary for 1879 – in the Henry W. and Albert A. Berg Collection at the New York Public Library. I am indebted to Professor Harris and Dr Johnston, and to Josie Dixon of Cambridge University Press, for allowing me to consult the typescript. Jonathan Ouvry, Lewes's great-great-grandson, has been generous with permissions to quote from the GE and GHL manuscripts at Yale.

Others who have helped me with material, information, and suggestions are: Bill and Kathleen Adams of the George Eliot Fellowship; Peter Beal, FBA, of Sotheby's; Andrew Brown; Sally Brown and Christopher Date of the British Museum; Ursula Cash; Andrew Franklin; Christina M. Gee, Curator of the Keats House Museum; Vincent Giroud of the Beinecke Library; Philip Horne, Dan Jacobson, Danny Karlin, John Sutherland, David Trotter, and Henry Woudhuysen of University College London; Kate Jones of Hamish Hamilton; Alexandra Pringle; John Rignall of the University of Warwick; Clyde de L.

Ryals of Duke University; Ronald C. Speirs of Birmingham University; Tilli Tansey of the Wellcome Institute; Ina Taylor; Kathleen Tillotson; Rosemary VanArsdel; Susan Womersley; Gabriel Woolf.

I wish to thank the archivists and trustees of the following libraries for permission to consult and quote from their manuscript holdings: Beinecke Rare Book and Manuscript Library, Yale University; British Library; British Library of Political and Economic Science at the London School of Economics; British Museum; Cambridge University Library; Coventry City Libraries; Girton College, Cambridge; Henry E. Huntington Library, San Marino, California; Herbert Art Gallery and Museum, Coventry; London Library; National Library of Scotland, Edinburgh; New York Public Library; Nuneaton Library; Somerset House; University College London Library; Warwickshire County Record Office and Lord Daventry; Dr Williams's Library, London.

I am indebted to the Leverhulme Trust for a Research Fellowship awarded in 1995 to enable me to finish the research and writing of the book. My greatest debt is to my husband, Gerry Ashton.

INTRODUCTION

On Monday 3 May 1852 Dickens sent a brief note to the radical London publisher John Chapman about a meeting scheduled for the next day at Chapman's bookselling business and family home, 142 Strand. 'I have a previous appointment', he wrote, 'but will be with you as early as I can, and before the general hour.'[1] The meeting in question had been called by Chapman, owner and nominal editor of the *Westminster Review*, the quarterly periodical set up in 1824 by Jeremy Bentham and James Mill to support political reform, and publisher of books of a radical tendency in politics, philosophy, and religion. The object of the meeting, which Dickens was to chair, was to protest against the practice of fixing book prices. More specifically, the protesters were targeting the Booksellers' Association, a grouping of large booksellers which had set prices, prohibiting smaller businesses like that of Chapman from offering discounts over 10 per cent. Dickens's publishers Bradbury and Evans had protested against the Association, and Dickens was only one of a number of leading writers to support Chapman in his bid for free trade in books.

The April number of the *Westminster Review* had carried an article by Chapman, 'The Commerce of Literature'. In it he accused the Association of adding to the 'taxes on knowledge' represented by duty on paper and the Stamp Tax on newspapers – which was not abolished until 1855 – by its price fixing. A wider debate was sparked off, with the letters page of *The Times* printing arguments for and against loosening the regulations governing the sale of books.

The meeting on 4 May attracted support for the cause from a large number of luminaries. Thomas Carlyle, John Stuart Mill, and the Anti-Corn Law agitator Richard Cobden sent letters which Dickens read out. Those present at 142 Strand included Wilkie Collins, the social phil-osopher Herbert Spencer, and the medical lecturer and practitioner Edwin Lankester. Among the speakers were Richard Owen, naturalist, designer of dinosaur models for Crystal Palace, and prime mover in the establishment of the Natural History Museum in South Kensington; Francis Newman, brother of John Henry Newman and professor of Latin at University College London; and Charles Babbage the inventor. The meeting endorsed several resolutions to be sent to Lord Campbell, the Lord Chief Justice, who was chairing a committee set up to arbitrate between the free traders and the protectionists. Also there was George Henry Lewes. He was co-founder and editor of the *Leader*, a radical weekly newspaper, and a frequenter of Chapman's regular soirées for authors.

Another man of note was Henry Crabb Robinson, ageing literary man, erstwhile friend of Wordsworth, Coleridge, and Lamb, and in-defatigable diarist from 1811 until his death in 1867. Crabb Robinson not only attended the meeting, but noted the occasion in his diary. According to him, the best speakers were the playwright Tom Taylor and Professor Owen, who 'spoke feelingly'. Some booksellers 'on the other side' also spoke, but 'were not listened to'.[2]

Not everyone spoke. Lewes did not, nor did Herbert Spencer, though he did a lot of backroom work, helping Chapman draft parts of his address.[3] Neither did the person who has left the most detailed account of the proceedings. This was not Dickens or Crabb Robinson or Spen-cer, but Marian Evans, Chapman's editorial assistant on the *Westminster Review*, who lodged in one of the upper rooms at 142 Strand which Chapman let to his assistants, and to visiting authors and business ac-quaintances. She had moved into Chapman's house in January 1851, having left Warwickshire at the age of thirty-one to make an independ-ent living as a journalist in London. Marian Evans was in fact much more than Chapman's assistant. She was the actual editor of the *West-minster*, though unofficially so.

The account she sent on 5 May to her Coventry friends Charles and Cara Bray conveys her excitement at being involved in a cause embraced by so many of the leading writers and thinkers of the day:

Dearest Friends

The meeting last night went off triumphantly, and I saluted Mr. Chapman with 'See the Conquering Hero Comes' on the piano at 12 o'clock, for not until then was the last magnate except Herbert Spencer out of the house. I sat *at* the door for a short time, but soon got a chair within it and heard and saw everything.

Dickens in the chair – a position he fills remarkably well, preserving a courteous neutrality of eyebrow, and speaking with clearness and decision. His appearance is certainly disappointing – no benevolence in the face and I think little in the head – the anterior lobe not by any means remarkable. In fact he is not distinguished looking in any way – neither handsome nor ugly, neither fat nor thin, neither tall nor short.

The reference to benevolence and anterior lobes was directed at Charles Bray's interest in phrenology, the 'science' of reading character by means of observing the contours of the head in the belief that certain faculties resided in different parts of the cranium and could be assessed in terms of the relative size and shape of those parts. Like Crabb Robinson, Marian thought that Professor Owen's speech was 'remarkably good', adding for Bray's benefit, 'Owen has a tremendous head and looked, as he was, the greatest celebrity of the meeting.'[4]

As it happens, Marian Evans's own head had also more than once been pronounced tremendous. She had accompanied Bray to London in 1844, when she had a cast made of her head by James Deville of the Strand. The cast was taken by the country's leading phrenologist, George Combe of Edinburgh, for a man's.[5] When Combe subsequently met Marian at Rosehill, Bray's hospitable house in Coventry, in August 1851, he studied her head in the flesh, noting its unusual size and drawing on his conversation with her as well as his experience of feeling her head to report that she was 'the most extraordinary person of the party' gathered at Rosehill. 'She has a very large brain, the anterior lobe is remarkable for length, breadth, and height, the coronal region is large, the front rather predominating', Combe wrote admiringly in his journal.[6]

The phrenologists were not alone in their astonishment at the size of Marian Evans's brain. Herbert Spencer, her closest companion in 1852, wrote in April that year that she was 'the most admirable woman, mentally, I ever met'. He was working with her in preparation for the 4 May meeting, making multiple copies of the resolutions to be put by

Chapman, and later recalled the speed with which she wrote in her large, free handwriting.[7] She had not yet written a line of fiction; no one knew her outside the small but important circle of progressive men of letters clustered around Chapman. But she was known to them – to Chapman, for whose charms she had fallen in 1850; to Spencer, with whom she was in love in 1852; to Lewes, with whom she was to live happily for twenty-five years; to Dickens, whose pre-eminence among novelists she was to challenge in 1859 with the publication of *Adam Bede* – as a most remarkable woman.

Her presence at the meeting on 4 May, attended by all these men, each of whom played such an important part in her life then and later, was itself remarkable. For Marian Evans was the only woman there. The unusualness of her position as a young woman pursuing an independent career in the radical free-thinking man's world of London in 1852 can hardly be overestimated.

Two contemporaries who knew her well in these years before she achieved fame recalled her early days in London in striking terms. Bessie Rayner Parkes (later Madame Belloc, mother of Hilaire) frequently saw Marian Evans, nearly ten years her senior, at dinner parties given at the London house of her father, Joseph Parkes, a radical lawyer from Birmingham:

On these occasions, from 1851 to 1855, she used to wear black velvet, then seldom adopted by unmarried ladies. I can see her descending the great staircase of our house in Savile Row (afterwards the Stafford Club), on my father's arm, the only lady, except my mother, among the group of remarkable men, politicians, and authors of the first literary rank. She would talk and laugh softly, and look up into my father's face respectfully, while the light of the bright hall-lamp shone on the waving masses of her hair, and the black velvet fell in folds about her feet.[8]

And William Hale White, known as 'Mark Rutherford' from the two pseudonymous volumes of semi-fictional 'autobiography' he published in the 1880s, described her in even more arresting detail. He lodged in the same house, 142 Strand, for two years from 1852. Like her, he was employed as an assistant by Chapman. In 1885 Hale White remembered Marian Evans, with whom he had been half in love but too diffident to express his feelings at the time, in the following words:

She was really one of the most sceptical, unusual creatures I ever knew, and it

4

was this side of her character which to me was the most attractive. She told me that it was worth while to undertake all the labour of learning French if it resulted in nothing more than reading one book – Rousseau's 'Confessions'. That saying was perfectly symbolical of her, and reveals more completely what she was, at any rate in 1851–54, than page after page of attempt on my part at critical analysis. I can see her now, with her hair over her shoulders, the easy chair half sideways to the fire, her feet over the arms, and a proof in her hands, in that dark room at the back of No. 142.[9]

Sceptical, unusual, a working woman, admirer of Rousseau, the only unmarried woman to attend dinner parties and agitation meetings with the leading authors and politicians of radical London – Marian Evans was already a striking figure some half-dozen years before she published her first work of fiction. She was not quite the only single woman pursuing a career in London in the 1850s. Eliza Lynn, later Linton, was a minor novelist and free spirit who followed a similar path, even lodging in the Chapman household for a time. She, nettled at George Eliot's far greater success as an author, looked back with less admiring eyes than Bessie Parkes or Hale White, describing Marian Evans on her arrival in London, rather meanly, as 'under-bred and provincial'.[10]

There were, of course, other women writers. There was Harriet Martineau, author of political economy tracts disguised as fiction, who lived in the Lake District but often visited London as a celebrity; there was Elizabeth Gaskell, who lived with her husband, a Unitarian minister, in Manchester; and the last surviving Brontë, Charlotte, was writing her passionate novels while keeping house for her father at the vicarage at Haworth. But Marian Evans was different in that she struck out, leaving house and family to follow her own devices at a time when unmarried women of no fortune kept house for their fathers or lived with married siblings as useful aunts. No university degrees were then awarded to women, and consequently none of the professions was open to them. Marian Evans took up the only career in which something like equal rights for women prevailed, that of writing. Moreover, she did so among an unconventional, progressive, in part Bohemian set of men.

The distinctiveness of George Eliot's life – the particular turns it took, the successive milieus she inhabited, the shock waves caused in respectable, orthodox social circles by some of her actions – needs to be stressed. Nowadays few bat an eyelid at young people, and young women in particular, professing no religious faith, pursuing studies and careers in bedsits, living with men to whom they are not legally married. Marian Evans did all these things, yet as others observed of her, and as she herself recognized, her temperament was at bottom one which sought approval and desired to conform. Herbert Spencer saw that though intellectually she threw off her early beliefs, religious and political, 'her natural feeling was a longing to agree as far as possible'.[11]

This paradox, a tension between the urge to criticize, and if necessary to rebel against, established ideas and practices, and the counter-urge to belong securely in the family and social group, is at the heart of George Eliot's life in all its stages. It informs her novels too. From Maggie Tulliver in *The Mill on the Floss* (1860) to Dorothea Brooke in *Middlemarch* (1871–2), her protagonists struggle against limiting social conditions, the stifling effect of the practical rule that 'sane people did what their neighbours did, so that if any lunatics were at large, one might know and avoid them'.[12]

In her life, such tensions brought her some uneasiness and ensured that many of her achievements and fulfilments were hard won. In the novels, they are followed through the lives of whole communities, as well as individuals, with extraordinary insight, variety, complexity, and a dramatic humour that has been likened by her most perceptive readers to that of Shakespeare. Marian Evans, as much as her more politically-minded contemporary Karl Marx, was *déracinée*, an intellectual at odds with her cultural background.[13] She might almost be called an internal exile, and though she voluntarily took the step of removing herself from her home, she chafed at what she saw as in some senses a forced decision. Like many an exile, forced or not, she can be observed being liberated into a career of imaginative writing which takes a loving as well as critical look back at the past from which she has fled. Most of her novels are set back in time; many of them fit the description offered by the subtitle of *Middlemarch*, 'A Study of Provincial Life'. As James Joyce could write fluently about Dublin life only while living outside Ireland, so George Eliot is the novelist *par excellence* of middle England, though not one of her works of fiction was written while she lived in the Midlands.

By 'middle England' more is meant, of course, than a mere accident of geography. The society George Eliot renders with such wit and imagination, as well as accurately observed detail, was politically and socially middling: quiet, conservative, decent but narrow; as slow to be set on fire, as she wrote pungently in a letter to Cara Bray's sister Sara Hennell in 1854, 'as a *stomach*'.[14] All her novels except *Romola* picture English life in the nineteenth century; all trace the fate of individuals caught up in a process of change, sometimes momentous change, which finds them in some way out of step with their immediate surroundings. It is Dorothea's misfortune, for example, to be born on the one hand too late, and in a society too secular, for her to be able to channel her idealism into the founding of a religious order like St Teresa of Avila, with whom she is compared, and on the other hand too soon (since *Middlemarch* is set around 1830) to enjoy the equal educational opportunities for women going forward at the time George Eliot was writing the novel, from 1869 to 1872. Girton College was founded by her friend Emily Davies in 1869. The following year saw the passing of two Acts of Parliament of far-reaching significance. One was the Education Act, which legislated for elementary education for all children, rich or poor, boy or girl. The other was the Married Women's Property Act, which removed the injustice by which women and their wealth became the property of their husbands upon marriage.

Not only George Eliot's fictional women, but also several of her men, find that for them the time is out of joint. Lydgate is a doctor with progressive ideas for medical reform who is hampered by the caution, the ignorance, the petty rivalries, and understandable fear of redundancy of his fellow practitioners in Middlemarch. Mr Tulliver in *The Mill on the Floss*, by contrast, suffers from his inability to adapt to a changing world in which sleepy old family mills are being superseded by large mill-owning, banking concerns in the early decades of the nineteenth century. Two of the novels, *Felix Holt, the Radical* (1866) and *Middlemarch*, are set in the years immediately leading to the first great Reform Bill, passed in 1832. *Felix Holt* was written during the agitation which culminated in the second Reform Bill of 1867, which further removed anomalies and extended the franchise. Both works illuminate the lives of individuals, among whom some help to instigate major changes, some suffer and survive them, and others fail to adapt and go under.

All ages – or stretches of time which we more or less arbitrarily define as ages – embrace change. Discoveries are made, inventions patented, laws passed. Wars change boundaries, travel opens up trade routes, and ordinary lives are affected in a thousand ways by such public or corporate events. More subtly, more slowly, and in ways difficult to define, attitudes and customs change, so that what is acceptable or respectable at one time and in one place, ceases to be so at another. The fashion in dress is at different times more or less revealing, more or less formal, more or less restrictive of free movement. Social and sexual ethics go through periods of relative freedom and relative intolerance. Moreover, the beliefs expressed in many societies may be at variance with the ways in which people actually behave.[15]

Much has been said about Victorian prudery and hypocrisy. The popular image – reinforced by the buttoned-up dress of the period and the sombre stare with which even the most liberal and light-hearted subjects were fixed in those early days of slow-exposure photography – is of a repressed and repressive society. Certainly, some subjects were not discussed widely in public. Yet sexual prudery is a relative thing. And as a matter of fact, among the novelists Thackeray, George Eliot, and Trollope all deal boldly with sexual relations. Becky Sharp in *Vanity Fair* (1848) becomes a courtesan, and Thackeray's characteristic irony of presentation tends to play this fact up rather than down. Trollope's reply to Thackeray himself in November 1860, when the latter had refused to publish a Trollope short story in the *Cornhill Magazine* on the grounds that it was 'indecent', was to refer Thackeray to the 'naughtiness' of Hetty Sorrel's giving birth to an illegitimate child in *Adam Bede*. He named Walter Scott, Thackeray himself, *Jane Eyre*, and *Adam Bede* as examples of a lack of squeamishness, concluding pleasantly, 'I do not approach them in naughtiness any more than I do in genius.'[16]

At any moment in time there are those who are deemed to be in some aspect of their beliefs or behaviour 'ahead of their age' or, conversely, 'behind the times'. But a man (or woman) who breaks the code of, say, monogamy, may be conformist in other ways, such as voting and church-going. And the atheist or agnostic – the latter word was coined in 1869 by T. H. Huxley to describe his own stance (it was George Eliot's too) – does not necessarily vote for a radical Member of Parliament or live a promiscuous life.

The Victorian age is like any other in presenting a bewildering number of facets, in being characterizable only in complex, paradoxical terms. It was an age known for both reverent faith and gnawing doubt; for imperial expansion and for increased democracy; for political and social reform and for retarding bureaucracy; for scientific progress and for entrenched refusals to accept the conclusions suggested by that progress. Perhaps it stands out among other ages for the sheer pace of change in the industrial and political spheres. Railways and Reform Bills made tremendous, irreversible differences to the lives of all citizens, though not all at once or in equal measure. The same is true of social reforms such as the improved sanitation achieved under Edwin Chadwick's leadership and the introduction of anaesthetics and antiseptic conditions in surgery in the late 1840s by men like James Simpson and Joseph Lister.[17]

If any one writer of the age captures sympathetically the discontinuities, contradictions, and bewilderments of the Victorian age and its immediate predecessor, it is George Eliot, born, as it happens, in the same year as Queen Victoria herself. More than any other novelist – even Dickens – she gives imaginative expression to the excitement and the pain of being caught up in a society in flux. Her career as a novelist began relatively late, when she was in her late thirties. By that time she had lived an already rich and extraordinary life, moving from provincial piety to metropolitan scepticism, from scholarly spinsterhood to stimulating partnership, from sexual frustration to sexual fulfilment, from Church-and-State Toryism to liberalism of a conservative kind.[18]

When Marian Evans Lewes, as she liked to be known, sat down in September 1856 to write fiction under the pseudonym George Eliot, she had all those upheavals in her personal life to draw on. We can note with the benefit of hindsight that George Eliot changed her name often, and at significant moments in her life. She was at different times Mary Ann, Marian, Pollian, Polly; she signed herself first Evans, then Lewes, then Cross, and sometimes 'George Eliot'. The name with which she began, when she was born in Warwickshire on 22 November 1819, was Mary Anne (with an *e*) Evans. It is to the early life of Mary Anne Evans that we now turn.

CHAPTER ONE

A Warwickshire Childhood
1819–41

George Eliot's father, Robert Evans, came from a Derbyshire family of Welsh ancestry. Born in 1773, the fourth of eight children, he received a rudimentary schooling and was apprenticed with his four brothers to their father's trade, carpentry. He became agent to Francis Parker, a landowner who inherited the large estate centred on Arbury Hall, on the outskirts of Nuneaton in Warwickshire, when Parker's cousin, Sir Roger Newdigate, died childless in 1806. Sir Roger had rebuilt the Tudor building in extravagant Gothic style, turning the main reception rooms into fantastic fan-vaulted shrines full of white and gold tracery and bosses.[1] Francis Parker took the name Newdigate, and brought with him from Derbyshire his trusted agent Robert Evans.

Evans settled at South Farm on the Arbury Estate with his wife Harriet Poynton and their two children, Robert, born in 1802, and Frances (known as Fanny), born in 1805. His work on the Newdigate Estate was both miscellaneous and specialized. He surveyed land and buildings, found respectable tenants for the various farms on Newdigate's land, collected rents, discussed and oversaw repairs, negotiated for the sale and purchase of land, and was actively involved in the arrangements for road-building, timber-cutting, and the coal-mining which went on beneath the estate. George Eliot described her father's work in a letter of 1859, when she had been somewhat rattled to hear Robert Evans spoken of as an artisan who rose to be a farmer.

It was not the description of her father as an artisan which upset her, rather that of him as a 'mere farmer':

Now my Father did not raise himself from being an artizan to be a farmer: he raised himself from being an artizan to be a man whose extensive knowledge in very varied practical departments made his services valued through several counties. He had large knowledge of building, of mines, of plantation, of various branches of valuation and measurement – of all that is essential to the management of large estates. He was held by those competent to judge as *unique* amongst land-agents for his manifold knowledge and experience, which enabled him to save the special fees usually paid by landowners for special opinions on the different questions incident to the proprietorship of land.[2]

It is entirely characteristic of George Eliot that her pride should have been hurt less by snobbery about the lowly class to which her father belonged than by ignorance of his accomplishments and acquisition of wide and important expertise. Robert Evans's own journals and surviving letters, most of them written on estate matters to Francis Newdigate, son of Francis Parker Newdigate and resident for most of the year in Blackheath outside London, give ample support to her claim. His employers gave him an unusually free hand in the making of important financial decisions, as well as in the day-to-day running of the estate.[3] In due course Robert Evans was employed by neighbouring landlords in addition to the Newdigate family.

Mrs Evans died in 1809, and in 1813 Robert Evans married again. His second wife was Christiana Pearson, daughter of a respectable farmer at Astley, near South Farm. The children of this marriage were Christiana, known as Chrissey (born in 1814), Isaac Pearson, called after his mother's uncle (born in 1816), and Mary Anne, named after two aunts on her mother's side. She was baptized in the nearby parish church of Chilvers Coton. In the spring of 1820, when Mary Anne was a few months old, the family moved from South Farm to a large brick house known as Griff, situated just off the main Nuneaton to Coventry road. This was to be her home until she was twenty-one.

Griff was a large, comfortable building, easily spacious enough to accommodate the Evans family of five. (Twin sons were born in March 1821, but died when they were only ten days old.) There were stables, outbuildings, a dairy and farmyard, fruit trees and flower beds in this quiet corner of what George Eliot later called 'fat central England'.[4] But the countryside was not entirely lush and rural, even in George Eliot's childhood. Coaches between Stamford and Birmingham passed up and down the Coventry Road twice a day before the extension of the railway network in the 1830s and 1840s. Near the road was the Coventry Canal, used for moving coal from Griff Colliery, which was less than a mile from Mary Anne's home. Most of the local villagers worked in the pits and lived in poor cottages strewn around that part of the Newdigate Estate. Just across the Coventry Road from Griff House were quarries, to which the shrewd Robert Evans turned his attention in 1833, recommending to Francis Newdigate that 'a hard road' be made between Griff Colliery and Attleborough quarry to facilitate the sale of land.⁵ In July 1836 a fatal accident occurred at the colliery. Robert Evans reported laconically to his employer that a man had been killed 'in a second' by a load of timber falling on him, 'and his Brains lay on the *Ground*'.⁶

When George Eliot looked back late in life on her Midlands childhood, she described her 'early affectionate joy in our native landscape' of villages and markets, 'tree-studded hedgerows', elms, buttercups, and 'little wayside vetches' (wild herbs). But she acknowledged too the 'heavy barges' seen in the distance and the small boys in corduroys 'hungrily eating a bit of brown bread and bacon'.⁷ In her last work, *Impressions of Theophrastus Such* (1879), a collection of sketches of human nature characterized according to type, she gave a thinly-veiled picture of her own youth. While alive to the fact that 'this England of my affections is half visionary', Theophrastus nevertheless looks back lovingly to 'that elder England' of his childhood in the days of 'frankly saleable boroughs'. The landscape itself, both timeless and yet rapidly being industrialized, seems to Theophrastus symbolic of the recent history of England itself: 'Is there any country which shows at once as much stability and as much susceptibility to change as ours?'⁸

George Eliot's father – changed in *Theophrastus Such* to 'a country parson', but recognizable as Robert Evans – seemed to her of a piece with his surroundings, their geography and their history during his lifetime. Throughout the Reform agitation of the 1820s, the debating of the Catholic Question, the clamour for extension of the franchise and for freedom of speech and of the press, Mr Evans maintained his stubborn Tory 'Church and State' views. Theophrastus Such offers a slightly exaggerated, ironic view of Robert Evans's opinions:

To my father's mind the noisy teachers of revolutionary doctrine were, to speak mildly, a variable mixture of the fool and the scoundrel; the welfare of the nation lay in a strong Government which could maintain order; and I was accustomed to hear him utter the word 'Government' in a tone that charged it with awe, and made it part of my effective religion, in contrast with the word 'rebel', which seemed to carry the stamp of evil in its syllables, and, lit by the fact that Satan was the first rebel, made an argument dispensing with more detailed inquiry. I gathered that our national troubles in the first two decades of this century were not at all due to the mistakes of our administrators; and that England, with its fine Church and Constitution, would have been exceedingly well off if every British subject had been thankful for what was provided, and had minded his own business – if, for example, numerous Catholics of that period had been aware how very modest they ought to be considering they were Irish.[9]

Mild caricature though this is, it shows a response no more gloomy than that expressed by Wordsworth, for example, who seriously contemplated leaving the country when the first Reform Bill was passed, or Southey, who predicted civil war in Ireland as a result of Catholic Emancipation.[10]

Like the rest of the country, Warwickshire was caught up in Reform fever during 1831 and 1832. In the election of December 1832 the county returned ten MPs, only two of whom were Tories, the rest being liberals and pro-Reform candidates. Against the trend, Nuneaton returned a Conservative, W. S. Dugdale, whom Robert Evans supported. Dugdale's election was not without its drama, which thirteen-year-old Mary Anne witnessed.[11] Naturally enough, accounts of what happened varied according to political allegiance, but all agreed that on the first day of the poll, 21 December 1832, a row broke out between the supporters of Dugdale and those of the Radical candidate, Dempster Heming. Windows were broken, the Tories called in the militia, a regiment of Scots Greys rode into Nuneaton, the Riot Act was read from an upper window of the Newdigate Arms, the poll was suspended, and one unfortunate man, Joseph Glover, died in the affray. According to the *Coventry Herald*, a paper which was strongly pro-Reform, the jury at the Coroner's Inquest held at the Queen's Head public house at Newton Regis, fifteen miles north of Nuneaton, returned a verdict of accidental death, though the reformers believed he had been the victim of a cavalry charge.[12] George Eliot was able to draw on her memories of this exciting event when she wrote *Felix Holt*.

Robert Evans took a cautiously favourable view of social reforms such as the New Poor Law of 1834, by which the administration of poor relief was removed from parishes and put under the authority of an elected Board of Guardians.[13] He told Newdigate in September 1834 that he thought parish officers had not always made a distinction between an 'industrious good man' and 'an idle bad man' when doling out relief.[14] But he always voted Conservative with his master. In the election of August 1837, following the coronation in June of Queen Victoria, he even became involved in the ubiquitous practice of treating voters, though not so shamelessly as the agents at Eatanswill in *Pickwick Papers*, published in the same year, where, as Dickens slyly observes,

everything was conducted on the most liberal and delightful scale. Excisable articles were remarkably cheap at all the public-houses; and spring vans paraded the streets for the accommodation of voters who were seized with any temporary dizziness in the head – an epidemic which prevailed among the electors, during the contest, to a most alarming extent, and under the influence of which they might frequently be seen lying on the pavements in a state of utter insensibility.[15]

Robert Evans was pragmatic. There was, he told Newdigate in July, 'a strong party against us, Sir'. With his characteristic forthrightness (and idiosyncratic spelling), he continued, 'I intend giving the Arbury & Astley Tenants a Breakfast on the morning of the election to get them together as we must not loose a Vote if we can help it if the Opposite party are doing all they can.'[16]

Well might George Eliot write, in the person of Theophrastus Such, that 'our midland plains have never lost their familiar expression and conservative spirit for me',[17] since the days when she had been allowed as a child to accompany her father on some of his rides around the district. Mary Anne no doubt observed his firm – sometimes even harsh – management of the farms and their tenants on the one hand, and his obedient respect for his superiors on the other. But she also knew her father's independence and stubbornness. He was not always obsequious towards the Newdigate family. A strong streak of self-righteousness and a forceful sense of right and wrong could overcome his tendency to obey authority.

In 1834, when as a prominent member of the Chilvers Coton Parish Council he undertook to raise subscriptions for the enlargement of the church, he wrote bluntly to Francis Newdigate: 'Your Father Gives £100', 'the Bishop £50', the local Tory MP Mr Dugdale £25, and other worthies £20 or £15. Robert Evans himself had pledged £20, on which he commented with satisfaction:

I was very pleased with my days work which you will perceive as I put down more for myself than I should have done if I had considered my Station in Life but I find it is every Churchmans duty to do all they can to support that Church which I hope will never fall – now Sir, we are waiting for your Mite to say what you intend to Give, your Father told me that his sun [*sic*] wd Give something . . .[18]

And, conservative though he was, his strong sense of social justice outweighed his awareness of his 'station in life' when he saw people suffering through no fault of idleness or stupidity. He lost no time in telling Newdigate that the poor wheat crop of 1834 was causing crippling hardship to the Astley tenants. Newdigate's father, the old man at Arbury Hall, had been reluctant, when Evans applied to him, to return a percentage of the rents to his tenants, and Evans appealed to Francis to authorize him to give them back enough to live on. The younger Newdigate's draft reply was that Evans should go ahead and make 'whatever allowance you think I ought to make them', without troubling his father further.[19] It was this aspect of her father's character, his love of fair play and his plain speaking in support of it, that George Eliot brought to her fictional carpenter Adam Bede, whose employers Squire Donnithorne and his grandson Arthur have in common with the two Newdigates a meanness on the part of the older landlord and a spirit of generosity on the part of the younger.

While Mary Anne was still very young, her half-brother Robert moved to the estate in Derbyshire where his father had begun his work as land agent, taking Fanny, Mary Anne's half-sister, with him to keep house. Chrissey was sent to board at a school in nearby Attleborough, and Isaac and Mary Anne attended a day school run by a Mrs Moore just across the road from Griff. Isaac and Mary Anne were playmates; theirs was a very close relationship, with Isaac, stubborn and stern like his father, inclined to dictate to his younger sister, who alternated between 'puppy-like' submission and rebellious self-assertion.[20] She later remembered having tried to impress the servant with her accomplishment on the piano, which she played at the age of four without knowing a note.[21] And when Isaac was not with her she indulged in heroic fantasies, encouraged by whatever books she was given by family and friends. As she told her teacher and friend, Maria Lewis, in 1839:

When I was quite a little child I could not be satisfied with the things around me; I was constantly living in a world of my own creation, and was quite contented to have no companions that I might be left to my own musings and imagine scenes in which I was chief actress. Conceive what a character novels would give to these Utopias. I was early supplied with them by those who kindly sought to gratify my appetite for reading and of course I made use of the materials they supplied for building my castles in the air.[22]

In 1824 Mary Anne joined Chrissey at Miss Lathom's school in Attleborough, where she remained for three years. Isaac went to a boarding school in Coventry. George Eliot told her husband John Cross in 1880 that her chief memory of boarding school was of being cold in winter and unable to get near the fire. Like many another child removed from the parental home at such an early age, she suffered from dreadful night terrors.[23]

We do not know why the children went away to school. It was common for middle-class parents to send their children away to board, of course, and there was at this time no regular provision of state education. Whether Mr and Mrs Evans intended to do the genteel thing, or were merely seeking an education for their children where it could be had, is not clear. Probably the latter motive predominated, since the schools attended by Chrissey, Isaac, and Mary Anne were only a few miles from home, and the two girls were close enough to one of Mrs Evans's sisters, Aunt Evarard, to visit her frequently.

The children came home for holidays, when they rambled about the dairy and fields, played down by the canal and near the quarry, and got into the usual scrapes. They also read the usual books: Aesop's *Fables*, *Pilgrim's Progress*, and jest books, but though Mary Anne's fondness for reading was indulged, the family was not a specially bookish one. Mr Evans, already middle-aged when his last three children were born, often took them on his rounds of the estate. Isaac was groomed in the same business as his father, becoming in due course land agent to Francis Newdigate's successor, his cousin's son, Charles Newdigate Newdegate.[24]

Of Mrs Evans little trace remains. She is scarcely mentioned in George Eliot's surviving letters and journals, and when she does make an appearance there, we learn nothing of what she was like. When travelling with Lewes in August 1859 George Eliot noted in her journal that they stayed overnight at the Swan Hotel in Lichfield, adding the neutral remark that it was the same hotel 'where I remember being with my mother and father when I was a little child'.[25] This was in May 1826, when she was six and a half, on the way back from a visit to Robert Evans's relations in Derbyshire and Staffordshire. She told Sara Hennell in October 1859 that visits between her own family and these 'northerly relatives' were few and far between. She had made this one journey 'to see my uncle William (a rich builder) in Staffordshire', but her 'uncles and aunts and cousins from my father's far-off native country' seemed strange 'to my childish feelings'.[26]

We catch a glimpse of Christiana Evans in a letter of her husband's to Francis Newdigate in December 1833 describing a recent fire on the estate. 'Mrs Evans kept up her Spirits wonderfull [sic] while the fire lasted, and that was the case with myself, for I had the presents [sic] of mind to Act and direct in every point were [sic] there was the most danger, and my courage never failed me during the day & night.'[27] We do not know when Christiana first became ill, but by April 1835 Robert was confiding to his employer that she had breast cancer and saying in his laconic, stoical way, 'I am now afraid she will not have much more comfort.'[28] She lingered on for another ten months in her hopeless condition.

Meanwhile, Mary Anne was away at school, first at Miss Lathom's in Attleborough, then from 1828 as a boarder at Mrs Wallington's school in Nuneaton, and from 1832 to 1835 at a school in Coventry run by the sisters Rebecca and Mary Franklin. Chrissey went with her to Mrs Wallington's school, where there were about thirty boarders. An Irish governess at the school, Maria Lewis, was to become Mary Anne's first close friend. When after George Eliot's death a passionate friend of her last years, Edith Simcox, visited the Midlands in search of memories of George Eliot, she interviewed Miss Lewis in Leamington. Edith recorded this meeting with the best friend of George Eliot's youth, adding some shrewd comments of her own:

A nice little fair old lady, with one eye gone, which they say was an ugly squint in youth. She was governess at the Nuneaton School and had evidently been the superior person of that period: the virtuous cultivated young lady whom Mrs Evans held up as a model for imitation to her aspiring little daughter. Miss Lewis used to visit at Griff – remembered going to see Polly [George Eliot] and Chrissy in bed with measles, was 'like an elder sister' to them. Spoke of the child as very loveable, but unhappy, given to great bursts of weeping; finding it

impossible to care for childish games and occupations: it is of course significant that as a mere child, the governess should have been her friend rather than
any schoolfellow.[29]

It is worth noting that Edith Simcox takes it for granted here – we do
not know on what authority – that Mrs Evans did have genteel aspirations for her children. She also notices that Mary Anne, not unusually
for the youngest child in a family, was inclined to look for friendship to
someone older than her peers.

On Mary Anne's tenth birthday, 22 November 1829, Robert Evans
visited the school to take her home for the day. Miss Lewis came too
and, since it was Sunday, attended Chilvers Coton Church with the
Evans family.[30] She belonged to the Evangelical wing of the Church of
England, and had a Puritan distrust of pleasure and leisure with which
she infected Mary Anne. Some of the latter's earliest extant letters are to
Miss Lewis, to whom she pours out scriptural echoes, piety, and severe
disapproval of all triviality. Mary Anne signed herself Polly, the familiar
form of Mary which was also used later by the Brays and Sara Hennell,
and later still by Lewes. Sara Hennell converted Polly to Pollian, pun-
ning on Apollyon, the monster in Revelation and 'foul fiend' which
meets Christian in the Valley of Humiliation in *Pilgrim's Progress*. It may
be that Mary Anne attached the name to herself in wry allusion to her
plain looks, as she was later to call herself a fright, and a *Medusa*, among
other unflattering things. In her mid-to-late teens she took her pious
severity to extremes, neglecting her dress and appearance and going
about 'like an owl', as she told another Coventry friend, Mary Sibree, in
1842, 'to the great disgust of my brother'. Moreover, she expressed her
disapproval to Isaac himself of what she later acknowledged were 'quite
lawful amusements'.[31]

Religious dissent was strong in the Midlands during George Eliot's
childhood. Not only was Evangelical Anglicanism well represented;
there were also chapels of every kind of dissent: Unitarian, Baptist,
Wesleyan, Quaker, Presbyterian, Congregationalist. Mary Sibree's
father, an independent minister, published in 1855 an account of the
local dissenting congregations, *Independency in Warwickshire*. According to
this, there were in the ribbon-weaving district of Foleshill, to which
Mary Anne and her father moved in 1841, no fewer than twelve places
of Wesleyan worship alone.[32]

George Eliot thus grew up with inward knowledge of a variety of types of faith and of worship. Her father was an undogmatic traditional Anglican, suspicious alike of Roman Catholics, who finally gained full civil rights in 1829, and of dissenters with their fanaticism and enthusiasm. His own brother Samuel had converted to Methodism in the 1790s in Derbyshire. In his account of his conversion, Samuel Evans tells of hearing a travelling preacher when he was a young man of eighteen and of feeling that 'the Lord in great mercy broke in upon my soul, pardoned my sins and made me happy in His love'. He remembered how his older brothers Thomas and Robert teased him about his new-found zeal: 'They were High Church in their sympathies and despised the Methodists, and tried hard to argue, to baffle and confound me.' Samuel's wife Elizabeth was a Methodist preacher, though women were prohibited from preaching, except under special dispensation, by the Methodist Conference of 1803. For a time Samuel and Elizabeth Evans joined a separatist branch of the church, so that she could continue to preach.[33] They and their Warwickshire relations paid a few mutual visits while George Eliot was a child. As is well known, she drew on her first-hand acquaintance with a woman preacher, her aunt Elizabeth, when creating Dinah Morris in *Adam Bede*.

Mary Anne soon came into contact with another dissenting family. In 1832, aged twelve, she moved from Mrs Wallington's school in Nuneaton to Mary and Rebecca Franklin's school in Coventry. Their father was minister of the Cow Lane Baptist Chapel. The curriculum at the school was not a narrow one, though the atmosphere was as religious as that in Nuneaton. Mary Anne learned English, French, history, arithmetic, music, and drawing. A schoolmate remembered her as clever, musical, but agonizingly shy and apt to rush out of the room in tears, as Miss Lewis recalled her doing at Nuneaton.[34] She won the school prize for French, and excelled in English composition, though the sample essay to be found in her school notebook for 1834, on 'Affectation and Conceit', is not remarkable except for the ponderousness of its prose. Her moral severity is uncompromising, particularly on the vanity of women:

She [the vain woman] is so used to admiration that she finds it impossible to live without it, and as the drunkard turns to his wine to drown his cares, she the former beauty, finding all that before naturally attracted gone, flies to artificial means, in order she vainly hopes and believes to secure still her usual meed of adulation – She affects a youthful walk, & a youthful manner, upon all occasions, and at the age of fifty may often be seen clothed in the girlish fashion of sixteen totally forgetting that her once rounded neck and shoulders which at the latter age, were properly uncovered, are now pointed & scraggy and would be much better hidden from sight by a more matronly habiliment.[35]

Thus the plain, sensitive, censorious girl of fifteen.

The school notebook also contains pages of poems copied out by Mary Anne from the popular annual publications of the time, volumes like the *Keepsake* and the *Literary Souvenir*. These were miscellanies published at Christmas by editors who pestered famous writers – Scott, Wordsworth, and Coleridge, for example – for unpublished scraps and fragments, and reprinted poems and stories – usually, but not always, with permission – from their collected editions.[36] Mary Anne copied out various romantic and sentimental verses about forsaken maidens and unwilling brides.

She also wrote in the notebook a fragment of a story, 'Edward Neville', set in Cromwell's day, and drawing heavily on Walter Scott and his imitators in the genre of historical fiction. Like many a Scott novel and many more by his popular imitator G. P. R. James, Mary Anne's story begins with a useful stranger arriving on the scene:

It was on a bright and sunny morning towards the end of Autumn of the year 1650 that a stranger mounted on a fine black horse descended the hill which leads into the small but picturesque town of Chepstow. Both horse and rider appeared to have travelled far for besides their both being covered with dust, the poor animal bore the marks of the spur in his reeking sides, and notwithstanding the impetuosity with which his master still urged him on, he seemed almost unable to proceed even at a foot pace.[37]

The schoolgirl falls readily into all Scott's narrative habits, though without his subtlety, panache, and humour. Detailed descriptions of dress, of surroundings, of castles and manorial buildings, a 'mystery' with clues dropped here and there about the stranger's identity, all the secrecy, disguise, and intrigue required by the story's being set in stirring times of wars and plots, a love interest for the young hero, whose beloved is at first forbidden to him – these are the ingredients she used.

They all belong to the master's recipe for fiction, as adapted in *Waverley* (1814), *Old Mortality* (1816), and *Ivanhoe* (1819), to name but three.

Also in the notebook are religious verses, reflecting the influence on the serious girl of Miss Lewis and the Coventry Baptists among whom she was now living. Though she never converted officially to any dissenting sect, her brand of faith was, as is not uncommon in adolescent girls, severe and self-denying. One of the last poems in the school notebook is unattributed; we may reasonably suppose it to be an original composition. Like the historical romance 'Edward Neville', it is unfinished. Entitled 'On Being Called a Saint', it expresses the delicious self-satisfaction to be had from self-denial and a ready sense of martyrdom:

> A Saint! Oh would that I could claim
> The privileg'd, the honor'd name
> And confidently take my stand
> Though lowest in the saintly band!
>
> Would though it were in scorn applied
> That term the test of truth could bide
> Like kingly salutation given
> In mockery to the King of Heaven.
>
> . . .
>
> Oh for an interest in that name
> When hell shall ope its jaws of flame
> And sinners to their doom be hurl'd
> While scorned saints 'shall judge the world'.
>
> How shall the name of Saint be prized
> Tho' now neglected and despised
> When truth

And there the poem breaks off.

Mary Anne left school at Christmas 1835, aged just sixteen. She went home to a series of domestic crises. Her mother was getting weaker, and by the beginning of January 1836, as Mary Anne reported to Miss Lewis in her earliest surviving letter, 'suffered a great increase in pain'. 'We dare not hope', she continued, 'that there will be a permanent improvement.'[38] Robert Evans had been taken ill on 31 December 1835 while

away from home on estate business with what he described as an in-
flammation of the kidneys.[39] Mary Anne gave Miss Lewis an idea of the
seriousness of the attack and the fright it had caused at home, coming
on top of her mother's worsening state:

Our anxieties on her account though so great have been since Thursday almost
lost sight of in the more sudden and consequently more severe trial which we
have been called to endure in the alarming illness of my dear Father. For four
days we had no cessation of our anxiety, but I am thankful to say that he is now
considered out of danger, though very much reduced by frequent bleeding and
very powerful medicines.[40]

To add to his troubles, Robert Evans had heard from his brother
Thomas, who managed Francis Parker Newdigate's estate at Kirk
Hallam in Derbyshire. Thomas had got into debt and was 'obliged to
assign over his Effects to his Creditors & to absent himself from
Hallam'. Robert's solution was to take over responsibility himself for
the tenancy of Thomas's farm. '*I will stock it well*', he assured Francis
Newdigate, 'and pay you rent as it becomes due. If you will grant me
this Favour, I have no doubt but I can provide Bread for him by him
and his Boy working upon the Farm.' Newdigate replied that he would
'most willingly take you Tenant for your Brother Thomas's Farm'.[41]
Other problems which beset Mr Evans at this time concerned his
own work on the Arbury Estate. Old Francis Parker Newdigate had
died in 1835, but young Francis had not inherited. The Hall went to his
cousin's wife Mrs Newdigate and her son Charles (who was to be Isaac's
employer, as Francis was Robert's). Robert was continually caught between the two branches of the family. Francis Newdigate would direct
him to settle the rents of the Arbury tenants, and Mrs Newdigate would
prevent him from doing so. In April 1835 Robert had had to tell Francis
that Mrs Newdigate was preparing to sue him for destruction of part of
the land.[42] Robert Evans's life was plagued by these disagreements. The
only good effects of this change of authority at Arbury Hall were that
Isaac began work in 1836 for Charles Newdigate Newdegate, eventually
replacing his father when the latter retired in 1841 at the age of sixty-
seven, and that Mrs Newdigate kindly offered Mary Anne the use of the
magnificent library at Arbury Hall.[43]
Mr Evans recovered from his painful illness, though on 3 January
1836 he recorded a terrible day and night which he thought he would

not survive. But his wife's health deteriorated. At 5 am on 3 February 1836, Christiana Evans died after 'a Dreadfull night of pain', as her husband noted in his journal.[44] He wrote in a stoical spirit to his sympathetic patron a few weeks after her death: 'I have gone through a great deal of pain and Greif, but it is the work of God therefore I submit to it chearfully as far as Human Nature will *permit*.'[45] He was soon back at work, paying one of his regular visits to oversee Newdigate land in Kent in April. He wrote to Chrissey, now mistress of the house at the age of twenty-two, reporting on his satisfactory settling of the tenants' accounts there, and asking her to send the gig to Coventry to meet him when he returned home in a few days.[46] (Owning a gig – a two-wheeled carriage – had been taken as a sign of middle-class respectability since the testimony of a witness at the much-reported Thurtell murder trial of 1824; Carlyle seized on the idea and coined the word 'gigmanity' to signify narrow-minded, self-satisfied respectability, or philistinism.[47])

All three children were now at home. Isaac was helping his father with the estate business, Chrissey was chief housekeeper, and Mary Anne, at sixteen, helped Chrissey until the latter's marriage in May 1837. She took the Anglican communion for the first time at Chilvers Coton Church on Christmas Day 1836, though she had by no means lost her enthusiasm for the more spiritual forms of worship practised by Miss Lewis and the Misses Franklin.[48]

Nor had she lost her severity. After Chrissey's wedding on 30 May 1837 to Edward Clarke, a doctor from Meriden, a few miles outside Coventry, Mary Ann – as she chose to spell her name in the marriage register, perhaps thinking it a more grown-up form and hence suitable for a young woman who would soon be eighteen – was now mistress of the house at Griff. Her father went to Derbyshire later in the year and brought back his sister-in-law Elizabeth Evans to stay for a few weeks. Mary Ann relished her discussions with her Methodist aunt. She told Sara Hennell in 1859 that she was then 'strongly under the influence of Evangelical belief, and earnestly endeavouring to shape this anomalous English-Christian life of ours into some consistency with the spirit and simple verbal tenor of the New Testament'.[49]

Looking back, she acknowledged how narrow and intolerant her views had been, and how she had clashed with her gentle aunt. Her analysis of her youthful behaviour gives an idea of the serious differences on points of doctrine between the two kinds of Christianity, as

well as mercilessly laying bare the human unattractiveness of the opinions she had embraced in adolescence:

I had never talked with a Wesleyan before, and we used to have little debates
about predestination, for I was then a strong Calvinist. Here her superiority
came out, and I remember now, with loving admiration, one thing which at the
time I disapproved: it was not strictly a consequence of her Arminian belief,
and at first sight might seem opposed to it, yet it came from the spirit of love
which clings to the bad logic of Arminianism. When my uncle came to fetch
her, after she had been with us a fortnight or three weeks, he was speaking of a
deceased minister, once greatly respected, who from the action of trouble
upon him had taken to small tippling, though otherwise not culpable. 'But I
hope the good man's in heaven for all that', said my uncle. 'Oh, yes', said my
aunt, with a deep inward groan of joyful conviction. 'Mr. A's in heaven – that's
sure.' This was at the time an offence to my stern, ascetic views – how beautiful it is to me now![50]

This reminiscence helps to explain how it was that the sceptical, free-
thinking author of the novels could take for her subject the life of
country people, both dissenters and traditional church-goers, and show
generosity towards their superstitions, aspirations, and limitations.
Having embraced an unforgiving, damnation-conscious form of religion in her youth, she experienced its shedding as a liberation into
tolerance. That tolerance covered the many kinds of faith she had
encountered, from unattractive Calvinism, which rejected the idea that
salvation might follow from attempts to live a moral life, to more attractive Arminianism, which accepted the possibility of salvation for all.
Dorothea in *Middlemarch*, when unhappily married to Mr Casaubon but
trying to give him comfort in his lonely fear of death and of the critical
ridicule of his fellow Biblical scholars, speaks for her creator when she
associates her new-found undogmatic belief in doing good with an
advance in true religious feeling over the narrow views of her Puritan
girlhood. 'I have always been finding out my religion since I was a little
girl', she tells Will Ladislaw. 'I used to pray so much – now I hardly ever
pray.'[51]

But as mistress of her father's house from 1837, when her life consisted of dealing with servants, making jam, organizing everything to do
with the house and dairy while her father and Isaac were out on the
estate, and visiting the poor with secondhand clothes, Mary Ann prayed

a great deal. Her letters to Maria Lewis, now living as a governess with a clergyman's family in Northamptonshire, are fulsomely pious. Announcing the birth of Chrissey's first child, Edward, to her friend in May 1838, she drew a solemn lesson from the happy event:

Truly may change be called our only certainty; may our experience of the fact lead us feelingly to join in that beautiful collect which closes with praying that amidst all the changes of this transitory life, our hearts may *surely* there be fixed, where true joys are to be found.[14]

When she heard in August 1838 that an acquaintance of Maria Lewis was to be married, eighteen-year-old Mary Ann took a gloomy view, the insufferable sonorousness of which is only lightened – prophetically, we may say with the wisdom of hindsight – by a salutary strain of ironic self-criticism:

I trust that the expected union may ultimately issue in the spiritual benefit of both parties; for my part when I hear of the marrying and giving in marriage that is constantly being transacted I can only sigh for those who are multiplying earthly ties which though powerful enough to detach their heart and thoughts from heaven, are so brittle as to be liable to be snapped asunder at every breeze. You will think I need nothing but a tub for my habitation to make me a perfect female Diogenes, and I plead guilty to occasional misanthropical thoughts, but not to the indulgence of them: still I must believe that those are happiest who are not fermenting themselves by engaging in projects for earthly bliss, who are considering this life merely a pilgrimage, a scene calling for diligence and watchfulness, not for repose and amusement. I do not deny that there may be many who can partake with a high degree of zest of all the lawful enjoyments the world can offer and yet live in near communion with their God; who can warmly love the creature, and yet be careful that the Creator maintains His supremity in their hearts; but I confess that in my short experience and narrow sphere of action I have never been able to attain this; I find, as Dr. Johnson said respecting his wine, total abstinence much easier than moderation.

Thank goodness for that ironic reference to herself as a female Diogenes – from the Greek philosopher who was so disgusted with all the things of this world that he took to living in a tub – and the relatively light-hearted (and literary) allusion to Dr Johnson.

Ever watchful for her own sinfulness, she confesses immediately after this pronouncement:

But I am as usual becoming egotistical, and you by the bye have naughtily encouraged the habit. I am in danger of imitating the frog in the fable vainly imagining herself a rival for the ox, and such pride generally has a similar catastrophe to hers.[53]

In the same letter of 18 August 1838 Mary Ann told Miss Lewis about a trip to London she had recently undertaken with Isaac. She concentrated on her experience of a service at St Paul's:

I grieve to say my strongest feeling was that of indignation (I mean during the sermon) towards the surpliced personages, chapters I think they are, who performed the chanting, for it appears with them a mere performance, their behaviour being that of schoolboys, glad of an opportunity to titter unreproved.[54]

Isaac recalled late in life that during this London visit she had refused to go to the theatre with him, as she disapproved of such idle entertainment. While Isaac bought as a souvenir of their visit a pair of hunting sketches, she chose a copy of Josephus' *History of the Jews.*[55]

Miss Lewis was the chief recipient of all her youthful opinions. She discussed her reading, particularly of spiritually improving works like the letters of Hannah More, the life of Wilberforce, and Archbishop Leighton's commentary on St Peter, the seventeenth-century work which Coleridge had taken as the basis of his influential *Aids to Reflection* (1825). In May 1839 she wrote comparing several works of differing doctrinal import. She had read the independent minister John Hoppus's *Schism as Opposed to Unity of the Church* (1839), which she thought 'ably expresses the tenets of those who deny that any form of Church government is so clearly dictated in Scripture as to possess a Divine right'. In other words, it was an attack on established churches like the Church of Rome and the Church of England.

This she compared with Joseph Milner's *History of the Church of Christ* (1794–7), with its 'moderate evangelical episcopalian' view, in favour of government by bishops but not implacably opposed to dissenters. And she was reading too the famous Oxford *Tracts for the Times* as they came out between 1833 and 1841, written by High Church Anglo-Catholics including John Henry Newman (before he converted to Rome). Predictably, Mary Ann expressed hostility to these attempts 'to give a romish colour to our ordinances' and 'to fraternize with the members of a church carrying on her brow the prophetical epithets applied by St. John to the Scarlet beast, the Mystery of iniquity' in Revelation.[56]

The girl who was to begin her writing career only five years later by translating a learned sceptical work of Biblical criticism from German wrote self-deprecatingly in November 1838 of this intense course of reading in religious controversy:

Of course I mean only such studies as pigmies like myself in intellect and acquirement are able to prosecute; the perusal and comparison of Scripture and the works of pious and judicious men on the subject.[57]

In fact this 'pigmy' was already employing her intellect in quite sophisticated ways. Her religious views required her to distrust imaginative literature, particularly fiction, as frivolous and even dangerous, being a form of lying. But she liked reading Scott and Shakespeare, and was adding to these writers the works of a great many more, explaining ingeniously to Miss Lewis that it was acceptable, even desirable, to read certain 'standard works whose contents are matter of constant reference, and the names of whose heroes and heroines briefly and therefore conveniently describe character and ideas'. Such were, for example, *Don Quixote*, Samuel Butler's *Hudibras*, *Robinson Crusoe*, Gil Blas, 'Byron's poetical romances', Southey's poetry, and, of course, Scott's novels and poems and Shakespeare. She was severe on religious novels, which were 'more hateful to me than merely worldly ones', being 'a sort of Centaur or Mermaid'. 'Like other monsters that we do not know how to class [they] should be destroyed for the public good as soon as born.' 'The weapons of the Christian warfare were never sharpened at the forge of romance', she concluded firmly.[58]

These convenient distinctions freed her to read quite miscellaneously without fearing for the state of her soul. By September 1839 she could describe the contents of her mind in an interesting, if somewhat clumsily expressed, metaphor:

I have lately led so unsettled a life and have been so desultory in my employments, that my mind, never of the most highly organized genus, is more than usually chaotic, or rather it is like a stratum of conglomerated fragments that shews here a jaw and rib of some ponderous quadruped, there a delicate altorelievo of some fernlike plant, tiny shells, and mysterious nondescripts, encrusted and united with some unvaried and uninteresting but useful stone. My mind presents just such an assemblage of disjointed specimens of history, ancient and modern, scraps of poetry picked up from Shakspeare, Cowper, Wordsworth, and Milton, newspaper topics, morsels of Addison and Bacon,

Latin verbs, geometry entomology and chemistry, reviews and metaphysics, all arrested and petrified and smothered by the fast thickening every day accession of actual events, relative anxieties, and household cares and vexations. May I hope that some pure metallic veins have been interjected, that some spiritual desires have been sent up, and spiritual experience gained?[59]

On the same principle on which she disapproved of religious fiction, Mary Ann could not reconcile herself to the oratorio she heard in St Michael's Church, Coventry, in 1838 with her old teacher Rebecca Franklin. 'I think nothing can justify the using of an intensely interesting and solemn passage of Scripture, as a rope-dancer uses her rope,' she wrote to another friend, her fellow pupil at Miss Franklin's school, Martha Jackson.[60] She went so far as to tell Maria Lewis that it 'would not cost me any regrets if the only music heard in our land were that of strict worship'.[61] This extreme position was not held for long. Two years later she reported to Miss Lewis that she had heard and enjoyed the *Messiah* at Birmingham; and in February 1849 she told Sara Hennell she had not touched the piano for two months since her father was ill, but was 'determined to play a mass before the piano is utterly baked out of tune again'.[62] How her younger self would have shuddered at such profanity.

Mary Ann sent two poems to Miss Lewis. One, described by the modest author as 'some doggrel lines, the crude fruit of a lonely walk', has the distinction of being her first published work. She sent it to Miss Lewis in July 1839, and it was published over the signature 'M. A. E.' in the *Christian Observer* for January 1840. Taking as its text the phrase from the Second Letter of Peter, 'Knowing that shortly I must put off this tabernacle', the poem begins:

> As o'er the fields by evening's light I stray,
> I hear a still, small whisper – "Come away!
> Thou must to this bright, lovely world soon say
>   Farewell!"

> The mandate I'd obey, my lamp prepare,
> Gird up my garments, give my soul to pray'r,
> And say to earth and all that breathe earth's air
>   Farewell![63]

The second poem is a sonnet included in a letter of 4 September 1839. It is undistinguished, but perhaps significant for its melancholy theme and tone. The last five lines run:

> But ever, at the wished-for place arrived,
> I've found it of those seeming charms deprived
> Which from the mellowing power of distance rose:
> To my poor thought, an apt though simple trope
> Of life's dull path and earth's deceitful hope.

Conventional though this is, it expresses Mary Ann's habitual low spirits, against which she had to struggle all her life. The sonnet is followed by a telling reply to a reproach from her correspondent, Miss Lewis, about a remark in a previous letter which Miss Lewis took to be sarcastic. 'Why did you think I did any other than envy your vivacity', writes Mary Ann; 'instead of ironically blaming it I only desire to catch a portion of your mercury to render my character more malleable'.[64] The offending remark may have been the comment on 17 July, prefacing her poem on the text from St Peter, that 'my attempt at poetry will serve to amuse you, if no more, and you love a laugh so well that it would be ungenerous to withhold the occasion of one'.[65] This is more the awkward expression of authorial diffidence than an accusation of frivolity in poor Miss Lewis.

Mary Ann's uncertainty of tone, and an unclearness about her own aspirations at this time, find expression also in a letter to her Methodist aunt. She felt guilty about her behaviour during her aunt's visit to Griff in 1839, accusing herself of a 'lack of humility and Christian simplicity that makes me willing to obtain credit for greater knowledge and deeper feeling than I really possess':

Instead of putting my light under a bushel, I am in danger of ostentatiously displaying a false one. You have much too high an opinion my dear Aunt, of my spiritual condition and of my personal and circumstantial advantages. My soul seems for weeks together completely benumbed, and when I am aroused from this torpid state, the intervals of activity are comparatively short.[66]

Some excitement intruded into 'life's dull path' in November 1839, when Queen Adelaide, the widow of William IV, passed through Nuneaton. She was met at Griff by Isaac's employer, Charles Newdigate Newdegate, and a number of tenants on horseback, among them Robert Evans, who recorded in his journal that the Queen 'passed by Griff about half past 12 o'clock and we esscorted [*sic*] her through Nuneaton to the Turn to Weddington'.[67] In contrast to the splendour of this occasion, Mary Ann noted that 'the distress of the lower classes in our neighbourhood is daily increasing from the scarcity of employment for weavers'.[68] As early as December 1831 the *Coventry Herald* had reported a 'Memorial from Foleshill', a plea by the ribbon weavers of that district for relief from the dropping off of the trade since an Act passed in 1826 had permitted the import of cheap ribbons from France.[69]

A publishing plan formed in her mind at this time. This was a chronological chart of ecclesiastical history, which she hoped to finish by November 1840. Some of the profits arising from the sale would go to the building of Attleborough Church, and Mrs Newdigate opened the great library of Arbury Hall to her, allowing her to visit whenever she wanted in search of books to assist her.[70] The work was given up, however, when she found in August that a similar chart had just been published, 'only 7s. far superior in conception to mine', as she humbly acknowledged.[71]

Her reading was becoming ever wider. Though her letters to Maria Lewis were still full of scriptural allusions, these were increasingly joined by quotations from, and references to, secular literature. She read Carlyle's *Chartism* (1839), with its sympathetic account of the artisans of Glasgow, to whom the world 'is not one of blue skies and a green carpet, but a world of copperas-fumes, low cellars, hard wages, "striking", and gin'. She quoted Wordsworth and Shakespeare, Byron and Madame de Staël.[72] And at her request her father hired a language teacher from Leamington, Joseph Brezzi, to come to the house and teach her Italian and German. The lessons began in March; by October she was translating a German poem about roses without thorns, and reading Schiller's tragedy *Maria Stuart* and Goethe's *Tasso*.[73] She also found her tutor 'anything but uninteresting, all external grace and mental power', as she fancifully expressed her crush to Miss Lewis in May. But, she added, '"Cease ye from man" [Isaiah 2:22] is engraven on my amulet.' This was her second heart-fluttering; in March she had hinted mysteriously at a 'beloved object' she had given up. She told Miss Lewis, half-sorrowfully, half-proudly, that she believed she was 'a negation of all that finds love and esteem'.[74]

Love and marriage were in the air. In 1840 Isaac became engaged to Sarah Rawlins of Birmingham. It was decided that he and his wife would live at Griff; Robert Evans would retire as agent to the Newdigates, and he and Mary Ann would look for another house. The thought produced some anxiety and resentment in her. She went on a reluctant visit to Birmingham to meet Sarah Rawlins in September, and at one of the concerts she attended there she apparently burst into hysterical sobbing.[75] With forebodings that she herself would not find someone to love and be loved by, and in a state of confused conscience about the propriety of seeking happiness for herself, she set about helping her father find a house. They settled on one 'very pleasantly situated' at Foleshill, within five minutes' walk of Coventry.[76]

In a letter written in Biblical style to her Methodist aunt and uncle she confessed, not for the first time, to the sin of ambition:

I desire to be entirely submissive and without care for the morrow, to be so intent on the improvement of present time and present blessings as to allow myself no leisure for dreaming about my *worldly* future; but nevertheless I find an increased uncertainty respecting that future to unhinge my mind a little. I earnestly desire a spirit of childlike humility that shall make me willing to be lightly esteemed among men; this is the opposite of my besetting sin, which is an ever struggling ambition.[77]

Shortly before the move, which took place on 19 March 1841, she told her old schoolfriend Martha Jackson that leaving the home she had known all her life was 'deeply painful', 'like dying to one stage of existence'.[78]

On 8 March she wrote to Miss Lewis, whom she now addressed in the 'language of flowers' as Veronica, signifying fidelity in friendship (she herself was Clematis, or mental beauty, and Martha was Ivy, for constancy). As if some sixth sense told her that the move to Foleshill would herald great changes for her, she asked for her friend's blessings and prayers 'that my spirit may not become warped by intercourse with earthly trifles and considerations of worldly interest, but may rather be urged to cling closely to heavenly hopes'.[79]

Though things turned out rather differently, there is no doubt that the move to Coventry was momentous for twenty-one-year-old Mary Ann Evans.

CHAPTER TWO

Coventry, Rebellion, and The Life of Jesus *1841–6*

The removal to Foleshill, on the outskirts of Coventry, took Robert and Mary Ann Evans only five miles from their previous home at Griff. They were near Mary Ann's half-sister Fanny, who lived two miles away at Baginton with her husband, Henry Houghton, and five miles from Chrissey and Edward Clarke at Meriden. Mary Ann's dim view of the matrimonial state was intensified when she contemplated poor Chrissey's troubles, with an increasing family to bring up on the precarious income her husband earned as a general practitioner in competition with other doctors who were longer established in the neighbourhood. As Mary Ann put it in a letter of October 1841 to Miss Lewis, 'the troubles of married life seem more conspicuously the ordinance of God, in the case of one so meek and passive' as Chrissey.[1]

Isaac's wedding to Sarah Rawlins took place in Birmingham on 8 June 1841, with Mary Ann as bridesmaid. The couple went off to the Lake District and Scotland on their honeymoon. On their return, Isaac settled into doing all his father had done before him on the Newdigate Estate. He was to live at Griff until his death in 1890, serving his employer with the same cool respect and thoroughness his father had shown towards Francis Newdigate. His letters to Charles Newdigate Newdegate reveal more accurate spelling than his father's, but the handwriting is remarkably similar, as is the attention to detail and the independence and relishing of responsibility he exhibits.

A real friendship seems to have grown up between the two men, who were exact contemporaries.[2] In 1855 Isaac sent a present to his employer in gratitude for 'the confidence you have always placed in me, and the many kindnesses conferred upon me in various ways for a period of more than 20 years'.[3] When a difference occurred between them, however, Isaac was at least as forthright as his father before him. Indeed he resigned from the service in February 1880 after finding that Newdegate had advertised the letting of three farms without consulting him. Isaac wrote firmly that this made it 'impossible for me to continue the Agency with benefit to you or credit to myself'.[4]

Coventry was a pleasant town of some 30,000 inhabitants, of whom about 5,000 were employed as ribbon weavers. Most of the philanthropic ventures were undertaken by men who had made their fortunes in the industry, and it was these people whom Mary Ann got to know. There was, for example, Joseph Cash, a Quaker member of the family firm whose name continues to be associated with the manufacture of name tapes. Cash built an Infants' School in his garden at Sherbourne House in 1835, which he allowed a group of Wesleyans to use for worship.[5] Mary Ann's next-door neighbour, Abijah Pears, who served as Mayor of Coventry in 1842–3, was a wealthy ribbon manufacturer, as was his wife's brother, Charles Bray, who became Mary Ann's first close male friend.

The atmosphere in which she moved was still predominantly Evangelical and dissenting. Miss Rebecca Franklin, excited at the prospect of her brightest former pupil coming to live in Coventry, visited her friends the Sibrees in Foleshill to tell them of Miss Evans's imminent arrival, dwelling 'with much pride' on her 'mental power' and her 'skill in music', as the daughter of the house, Mary Sibree, recalled.[6] John Sibree was an Independent minister; his son – also John – was preparing to follow in his footsteps; and Mary, aged sixteen in 1841, became an eager friend and student of Mary Ann, who taught her German.

But these new friendships did not come all at once. The first few months at Foleshill were uneventful, even lonely. Mary Ann worried about the effect of the change on her father, so used up to now to an active life with extended visits away from home on business. By May 1841, however, she was able to report to Martha Jackson that Robert Evans was happily settled.[7] He had become active in the local church, Holy Trinity, holding a collection plate on Easter Day.[8] The minister, John Howells, held the lease on the Evans house, and was welcoming, though Mary Ann, at least, thought poorly of his preaching. 'Though we hear the truth', she told her uncle Samuel in October, 'yet it is not recommended by the mode of its delivery.'[9]

Mary Ann was soon busy, becoming involved, with her neighbour Mrs Pears, in setting up a clothing club for the poor and unemployed in the district of Coventry known as the Pudding-Pits.[10] But in August she confessed to her faithful friend Maria Lewis that she was '*alone* in the world' in the sense that she had 'no one who enters into my pleasures or my griefs, no one with whom I can pour out my soul, no one with the same yearnings and the same temptations the same delights as myself'.[11] She was longing for Maria to visit at Christmas, and was active in trying to find a position in a school or family at Coventry for her friend, who did, in fact, take up a post in a school in Nuneaton in January 1842.[12]

During 1841 Mary Ann's correspondents remained the same as before: Miss Lewis, Martha Jackson, her Methodist aunt and uncle. The tone of her letters remains the same too – earnest, pious (though with fewer direct allusions to the Bible), often despondent. But a change was occurring which would seem revolutionary to these same friends, though it evolved more gradually than Mary Ann could express in letters, since her correspondents were the very people who would be most horrified by it. The change was nothing less than a growing religious doubt which became, by January 1842, a rejection of Christianity as practised in the Church of England to which she belonged.

Even as she wrote of her desire to see Miss Lewis, she was inevitably preparing to shock her spiritual friend. In October she put an end to Clematis and Veronica. 'May I call you Maria?' she wrote. 'And restore to me Mary Ann.'[13] In November she let her friend know that she was 'engrossed in the most interesting of all enquiries', that of investigating historical criticism of the Bible, though she stopped short of telling Miss Lewis so. She contented herself with hinting at the probable conclusion of her studies – had she in fact already drawn it? – as 'possibly one that will startle you, but my only desire is to know the truth, my only fear to cling to error'. (Note the suggestion that her previous views, to which she had hitherto 'clung', might be wrong.) The most she could say was that she longed 'to have a friend such as you are I think I may say alone to me, to unburthen every thought and difficulty'.[14] There is something hesitant, gingerly, about this, suggesting that she feared her friend would be alienated by the change in her opinions, and might even end their friendship. Mary Ann asks Miss Lewis in this letter if there is

35

'any *conceivable* alteration in me that would prevent your coming to me at Christmas?'

Miss Lewis came to Foleshill. She was still there on Sunday 2 January 1842 when Mary Ann refused to go to church, putting her father in a rage and, as she had anticipated, losing her the friend of so many years' standing. The correspondence with Maria Lewis was not broken off immediately. Mary Ann wrote a few more letters after her friend's departure for Nuneaton, but the tone of these is uneasy, proud, defensive. She now gave only general news, saying vaguely that 'some day or other' the friends would meet and talk again, and protecting herself against an expected snub by saying she knew Maria was so busy at her new school that she would not be able to write 'just yet'.[15] When Edith Simcox visited Miss Lewis over forty years later, the old woman insisted that it was not she who instigated the breach. Asked for her views as to how the great change had come about in her friend, she replied that she thought it 'due to the over excitement, fostered by the Methodist Franklins, and the Aunt, leading to a reaction'.[16]

There is probably some truth in this. But another reason is the very thoroughness and studiousness Mary Ann brought to her reading in literature relating to religious belief. She was already accomplished at comparing High Church with Low Church views, and both with various forms of dissent, and it was inevitable that books critical of religious belief of all colours should come her way and be devoured with the rest. One such was Charles Hennell's *Inquiry concerning the Origin of Christianity* (1838), the second edition of which was published in August 1841. Mary Ann's copy has her name inscribed on the flyleaf with the date 'Jany 1st 1842',[17] a most suggestive date since it was the very next day which she chose for her rebellion against church-going. She may, however, have read Hennell's book sooner than this. Charles Bray, Hennell's brother-in-law, recalled that she had bought it by the time she was introduced to him in November 1841 by his sister Mrs Pears.[18]

The *Inquiry* was an extraordinary work to have emanated from a young man like Charles Hennell. Born in 1809 the son of a Unitarian merchant, he followed his father in both profession and religion. His belief was therefore not orthodox, since Unitarianism denied the co-eternal divinity of Christ and the Atonement. When Hennell's sister Caroline, known as Cara, married Charles Bray in 1836 and was distressed by her husband's immediate onslaught (on their honeymoon in Wales) on her simple devout faith, she turned to her brother for support.

Charles Hennell spent two years investigating the Bible for evidence of the truth of the accounts of miracles in the Gospels. As he confessed frankly in the Preface to the *Inquiry*, what began as a search for evidence in favour of at least 'the principal miraculous facts supposed to lie at the foundation of Christianity' ended in 'a gradually increasing conviction that the true account of the life of Jesus Christ, and of the spread of his religion, would be found to contain no deviation from the known laws of nature'.[19] It was the conclusion David Hume had come to in his *Enquiry concerning Human Understanding* (1748), but Hume's approach was through investigation of the faculties of the human mind, not of the Bible. The German Biblical critic David Friedrich Strauss had reached the same views in his thorough, scholarly work *Das Leben Jesu, kritisch bearbeitet* (*The Life of Jesus, Critically Examined*, 1835–6), but Strauss's work had not yet been translated into English and was unknown to Hennell when he first published his *Inquiry* in December 1838.

Hennell proceeded clearly and logically by taking each Gospel in turn and discussing its probable date of composition, the character of its author, and the events it relates, comparing all four records in order to 'weigh the probability in favour of the real occurrence of a fact, considered in reference to the ascertained history of the time, with that in favour of its invention by the author or some intermediate narrator'.[20]

At the end of this careful sifting and weighing of evidence, he concluded that Jesus was 'a noble-minded reformer and sage, martyred by crafty priests and brutal soldiers', but that there is insufficient evidence, as well as 'notable discrepancies' between the four Gospels, on the question of Christ's supernatural birth, miraculous works, resurrection, and ascension. Hennell finishes his work with an optimistic turning to the possibility of moral (and social) improvement in *this* life, despite there being no assurance of a future state for us (which follows from the rejection of the ascension of Jesus). He stops short of atheism, or even agnosticism, but thinks we should not go on seeking out 'the hidden things of God' but rather 'enjoy fully our present lot' on 'this beautiful planet'.[21]

In the Preface to the second edition, which Mary Ann owned, Hennell added that since the first edition was published, he had read 'the celebrated Leben Jesu of Dr. Strauss, which contains a most minute and searching analysis of the various stories, anecdotes, and sayings, which mainly make up the Gospels'. Strauss's work was much more detailed and scholarly than his own, and more sceptical about the 'historical reality' of the Gospels; Hennell recommended this 'elaborate and erudite work' to his readers. He also noted with pride that Strauss had taken a 'sincere interest' in Hennell's first edition of 1838, 'which at that time had found but few readers in its own country'.[22]

Indeed, Strauss had arranged for Hennell's book to be translated into German, and wrote a generous preface for it, marvelling at the achievement of a layman, and an Englishman to boot, in undertaking such a study without knowledge of the works done by learned German theologians and historians 'since Schleiermacher's work on Luke'. Summing up the different approaches of the two types, the German *Gelehrter* and the English self-taught man, Strauss is evenhanded in his praise of their two different methods and achievements:

These elevated views, which the learned German appropriates as the fruit of the religious and scientific advancement of his nation, this Englishman, to whom most of the means at our command were wanting, has been able to educe entirely from himself ... An Englishman, a merchant, a man of the world, he possesses, both by nature and by training, the practical insight, the sure tact, which lays hold on realities. The solution of problems over which the German flutters with many circuits of learned formulæ, our English author often succeeds in seizing at one spring ... To the learned he often presents things under a surprisingly new aspect; to the unlearned, invariably under that which is the most comprehensible and attractive.[23]

This translated extract from Strauss's German preface was published in 1852 by Mary Ann Evans, who had by that time translated *The Life of Jesus* itself.

It is not surprising that Hennell's work appealed to Mary Ann. Though serious and learned in its way, it is attractively robust, clear, and positive, even optimistic in tone. Nor is it destructive of religious belief; rather it supports a practical and sentimental Christianity of good works and unquestioning faith in God, while discarding much of the ritual and dogma of the various Christian sects. It undoubtedly struck a chord with Mary Ann, even as it soothed the woman for whom the task was first undertaken, Hennell's sister Cara Bray.

Cara and her unmarried sister Sara rapidly became Mary Ann's closest female friends. They shared her seriousness and propensity to piety. Cara insisted on her right to go to church when she wanted, telling a local clergyman in 1845 that though she was 'certainly not orthodox' in her views, she had 'with careful study endeavoured to ascertain what Christ himself taught & if he were again on earth I think I may say I would leave all to follow him'.[24] Her Commonplace Book, begun in 1836 shortly before her marriage and continuing to 1892, reads like a *Who's Who* of Victorian faith and doubt. It contains prose and verse extracts from a range of writers who troubled themselves about questions of belief and of social and practical morality. Coleridge, Carlyle, Emerson, Kingsley, Harriet Martineau, Tennyson, and in due course George Eliot herself figure frequently.[25] Cara's own minimal but vital faith is characterized by the idea of God as an invisible force helping one through life as expressed in the lines from Tennyson's late poem, 'Crossing the Bar', which she copied out on the day of the poet's death, 6 October 1892:

> Sunset and evening star,
>   And one clear call for me!
> And may there be no moaning of the bar,
>   When I put out to sea.
>
> . . .
>
> For though from out our bourne of Time and Place
>   The flood may bear me far,
> I hope to see my Pilot face to face
>   When I have crost the bar.[26]

Late in life, Cara was angered by the suggestion, frequently made by early biographers and critics of George Eliot, that it was contact with the 'unbelieving' Brays which had unsettled Mary Ann and led to the loss of her faith and the consequent breach with her father. Cara rebuked her correspondent and fellow animal rights campaigner Frances Power Cobbe in 1895 for remarking on George Eliot's 'rapid change of creed', protesting that Mary Ann had 'for some time before she knew us been changing her religious opinions'. She added firmly:

She did not distress her poor Father or her Evangelical friends, Miss Lewis or Mrs Pears, by imparting to them her doubts, and it was not until she came amongst congenial minds that her religious sense expanded into a higher and purer atmosphere.[27]

Mary Ann's schoolfriend and correspondent, Martha Jackson, like Miss Lewis, understandably took a different view. She remembered in 1884 the 'deep regret' and 'astonished grief' among 'Miss Evans's early Christian friends' that she should 'stray away into the dark regions of infidelity'. In her opinion, 'pride of intellect' made Mary Ann 'an easy prey to the flattering temptations to which she was subjected' when 'thrown into the – to her – fascinating society of certain enlightened friends whose rationalistic metaphorical minds had carried them altogether beyond the revealed word of God'.[28]

The description fits Charles and Cara Bray rather well. While Cara was quiet and temperamentally inclined to piety, her husband was an unabashed iconoclast, revelling in his status as oddity, and in the fact that he could ignore the outrage of his fellow men because of his independent means, inherited from his father's ribbon firm and increased by his own management of the business. He was also unusually self-confident and convinced of his own rightness. His robust autobiography, *Phases of Opinion and Experience during a Long Life*, written during the last three years of his life and published immediately after his death in 1884, gives cheerful witness to his irrepressible attitude to life. When asked by others who noticed he was not a church-goer whether he did not need forgiveness of sins, he tells us he replied that he only believed in punishment which was 'reformatory, that is, for my good'. He did not call himself an atheist, but rather expressed an easy belief in a God who required no worship; Bray's view of prayer was that it was unnecessary, since 'God will always do what is right *without asking* and not *the more for asking*'. 'It was reported', he writes proudly, 'that I believed in neither God nor devil, and I pleaded guilty to the latter impeachment, – because I believe in God I do not believe in a devil.'[29]

This Panglossian nonesuch was as different as could be from anyone Mary Ann had yet seen in her twenty-two years. She was taken by Mrs Pears to visit the Brays on 2 November 1841. According to Bray himself, Mrs Pears hoped 'this superior young lady of Evangelical principles might be beneficial to our heretical minds'. The influence, of course, went the other way, though Bray, like his wife, insists that Mary Ann's mind 'was already turning towards greater freedom of thought in religious opinion' by the time they became acquainted. He remembered being impressed by her 'modest demeanour' and her 'measured, highly-cultivated mode of expression, so different from the usual tones of young persons from the country'.[30]

The house to which Mary Ann now found entry was Rosehill, a large comfortable residence which Bray boasted was unique in Coventry at the time, a claim which can readily be granted him. He describes the house, situated about a mile from the centre of Coventry and the same distance from Mary Ann's home at Foleshill, and its large garden with lawn, trees, and in particular 'a fine old acacia, the sloping turf about whose roots made a delightful seat in summer time':

We spread there a large bear-skin, and many friends have enjoyed a seat there in that wooded retreat, far enough from the town for country quiet, and yet near enough to hear the sweet church bells and the chimes of St. Michael's, with the distant hum of the city, which gave a cheerful sense of the world being alive on week-days, and the peaceful lull which told that it was enjoying its respite on the Sunday. There was a free-and-easy mental atmosphere, harmonizing with the absence of all pretension and conventionality, which I believe gave a peculiar charm to this modest residence . . . [It] is still associated with the flow of talk unrestrained, and the interchange of ideas, varied and peculiar according to the character and mood of the talkers and thinkers assembled there; for every one who came to Coventry with a queer mission, or a crotchet, or was supposed to be a 'little cracked', was sent up to Rosehill.[31]

The Midlands had seen nothing like this since the days of the 'Lunaticks', or Lunar Society of radicals, scientists, doctors, and industrialists who met regularly at the full moon to discuss contemporary affairs in the 1770s and 1780s – men like Thomas Beddoes, Josiah Wedgwood, Joseph Priestley, Erasmus Darwin, and James Watt.[32] Cara's engagement diary tells of visits to Rosehill by many eminent men of the mid-nineteenth century, usually holding radical or liberal views, and active in politics, social philosophy, philanthropy, or journalism.

Visitors included Robert Owen (the opening of whose experimental Harmony Hall Bray attended in 1842), John Chapman, J. A. Froude, Ralph Waldo Emerson, the phrenologist George Combe and his wife, Herbert Spencer, Harriet Martineau (the only eminent woman) and her collaborator H. G. Atkinson. In this liberated atmosphere Mary Ann met most of these friends of the Brays over the next few years, when she was the most frequent visitor of all. Mary Sibree, who also made her way there with her brother John, recalled Mary Ann's expressing the debt she owed to her friends at Rosehill:

Mr and Mrs Bray and Miss Hennell, with their friends, were *her* world, – and on my saying to her once, as we closed the garden door together, that we seemed to be entering a Paradise, she said, 'I do indeed feel that I shut the world out when I shut that door.'[33]

Though Charles Bray was a generous host and snapper up of eccentrics, he was more than that. He was a philanthropist and social philosopher. A wonderful example of that class of do-gooder who refused to preach religion and morality at those he was seeking to help, he set up an Infants' School in opposition to one founded by local Anglicans, who had insisted that the catechism be taught. Bray objected that children of Dissenters would be excluded, set up his own school, and acknowledged pleasantly that 'we consequently had two good schools instead of one'. He agitated for sanitary improvements in Coventry, never letting the subject drop, as he said, until 1848, when 'the Health of Towns Act enabled us to save four people's lives in every thousand, that is, 160 lives a year of the 40,000 in Coventry'. For forty-five years he was a member of the committee of the Provident Dispensary, established in 1831 to provide medical care for the wage-earning poor who preferred to pay a small amount towards their medicines rather than depend entirely on charity.[34]

Bray's active involvement in such schemes was supported by a series of publications. In 1837 he produced a pamphlet, *The Education of the Body*, designed to help the poor improve their health and hygiene. In October 1841, shortly before Mary Ann visited Rosehill for the first time, the first volume of his *Philosophy of Necessity* was published; the second volume appeared in December. In Volume I, which contains the theoretical matter, Bray inquires into 'the nature of the constitution of man', drawing on his mentor George Combe's famous work, *The Constitution of Man*, first published in 1828 and reprinted several times. He traces 'the Law of Consequences' and points to 'the *good of Evil*'. Evil is to be regarded as 'remedial'; Bray believes in the 'advance of the race towards the perfection of which it is capable'. Absurdly optimistic but convinced of the correct tendency of his views, he hopes to bring home 'to every heart the all-cheering conviction that "WHATEVER IS, IS RIGHT"'.[35]

In the second volume Bray turns to actual social conditions – not at all RIGHT – as described rhetorically by Carlyle and statistically by Archibald Alison, and looks to social reforms – sanitation, drainage, education – to bring down the rates of crime, illness, death, and poverty in Britain's cities. He puts his faith in the Co-operative Movement, according to which 'men shall live together as one family'.[36]

During the time Mary Ann knew him, Bray initiated several more schemes, including a Co-operative Society for Coventry labourers in 1843, for whom he provided, with Joseph Cash, allotments at a pepper-corn rent, and a Working Man's Club in 1846. Later he would give a paper at the first meeting of the British Association for the Advancement of Social Science in 1857.[37] Whatever might be said of his lack of intellectual rigour – and it was later attacked by Lewes and other critics, one of whom addressed Bray aggressively with 'Fitly art thou called Bray, my worthy friend!'[38] – his energy and generosity in action were admirable.

With Cara Bray and her sister Sara Hennell, Mary Ann widened her reading even more than she had already begun to do on her own. They provided congenial female company both socially and intellectually. With Bray and his famous male visitors she soon conversed and disputed as an equal. Bray remembered going on 'long frequent walks' with her. (Miss Lewis, who met the Brays before settling into the mutual estrangement from Mary Ann, told Edith Simcox that they had walked about 'like lovers'.[39]) She knew 'everything', Bray recalled, but had 'little self-assertion'. She was also 'frequently very depressed – and often very provoking, as much so as she could be agreeable'.[40] Though she continued to be liable to fits of depression, the society of the Brays did much to lighten her life.

Mary Ann needed all the support she could get from the Brays in the next few months. On her refusing to go to church on 2 January 1842, her father treated her with 'blank silence and cold reserve', '*cooled* glances, and exhortations to the suppression of self-conceit'.[41] He got Isaac to '*school*' her on 24 February, and went as far as to put the lease of the house in the hands of an agent, since he no longer wished to remain there.[42] Isaac apparently told Mary Ann, or, as she put it, 'more than insinuated', that the house at Foleshill had only been taken 'to give me a centre in society' as a respectable young woman living with a father who might either continue to keep her in comfort or hand her over in marriage if a suitable person came along. Now he intended to move to a cottage on Lord Aylesford's estate, though whether with or without his daughter remains unclear.[43] She wrote to him, since all her efforts at conversation had failed, a brave letter in which she proudly gave up any claim to his munificence at the expense of her siblings. 'I could not be happy', she declared, 'to remain as an incubus or an unjust absorber of your hardly earned gains which might be better applied among my Brothers and Sisters with their children.'[44]

The letter, written on 28 February 1842, is a strong, brave, but also conciliatory one. Mary Ann explains that she has not become a Unitarian, as he has feared. Rather – and worse, from his point of view – she no longer believes in the divine authority of the Old and New Testaments:

I regard these writings as histories consisting of mingled truth and fiction, and while I admire and cherish much of what I believe to have been the moral teaching of Jesus himself, I consider the system of doctrines built upon the facts of his life and drawn as to its materials from Jewish notions to be most dishonourable to God and most pernicious in its influence on individual and social happiness.

Since she 'could not without vile hypocrisy and a miserable truckling to the smile of the world for the sake of my supposed interests, profess to join in worship which I wholly disapprove', she would not attend church with him and take the sacrament as before.

Strength, and uncompromising rectitude not unlike Robert Evans's own, mingle in the letter with expressions of dutifulness and diffidence. 'I fear nothing but voluntarily leaving you', she says, and assures him she would be happy to move with him to any cottage of his choosing. She finishes the letter with an expression of love, a plea for understanding, and a promise (which her father might construe, however, as a threat) to act according to her own lights, whatever the consequences:

As a last vindication of herself from one who has no one to speak for her I may be permitted to say that if ever I loved you I do so now, if ever I sought to obey the laws of my Creator and to follow duty wherever it may lead me I have that determination now and the consciousness of this will support me though every being on earth were to frown upon me.[45]

The appeal failed, as it was bound to do. Robert set about preparing to leave Foleshill, still unreconciled to his daughter. She saw nothing else for it but to seek employment elsewhere. On 12 March she told Cara that her 'guardian angel', Mrs Pears, would accompany her to Leamington to find a teaching post. Expressing herself doubtless more bravely than she felt, she assured Cara that the only 'woe' was 'that of leaving my dear Father'. 'All else, doleful lodgings, scanty meals, and *gazing-stockism* are quite indifferent to me.'[46]

It did not come to that. Isaac thought his father too harsh, and persuaded him to reconsider. Meanwhile, Isaac and Sarah invited Mary Ann to stay with them at Griff for a few weeks, until her father came round. This she gratefully did, and by 17 March Cara was reporting to her sister Mary that it looked as though things would be resolved. Mary Ann now had 'a face very different from the long dismal one she has lately worn'; Mr Evans had cancelled his order for the letting of his house; and 'we quite expect that his daughter will be reinstated and all right again'.[47]

Mary Ann was grateful to Isaac. She wisely bided her time at Griff, though she was irritated at having been placed, as she told Cara with some bitter irony, 'on the very comfortable pedestal of the town gazing-stock' and 'made a fool of' by the announcement that she had been sent away from home.[48] She put up with her excommunication, glad to have the Brays to complain to and grateful for Cara's frequent notes cheering her on. Still, it was not until the end of April or beginning of May that peace was restored and she returned to Foleshill. On 15 May she attended church once more, but on the understanding with her father that she could think as she pleased. The 'Holy War' thus ended in a draw.[49]

Though her letter to her father was dignified, it was thoroughly determined, and in conversation she may well have been more determined than dignified. Even in the midst of the row she confessed to Mrs Pears that she regretted her 'impetuosity both of feeling and judging'; John Cross reported her saying in the last year of her life that 'few things had occasioned her more regret than this temporary collision with her father, which might, she thought, have been avoided by a little management'.[50]

If her father's feelings had been roused more by the shame of having a free-thinking daughter than by fear for the state of her soul or a desire to understand what her beliefs now were, there were others anxious to find these out. Her friends the Sibrees were upset by her loss of faith, and asked a Birmingham professor of theology, the Revd Francis Watts, to speak to her. According to Mary Sibree, he returned from one conversation with her on the critical study of the Bible saying, '*She* has gone into the question.' Miss Rebecca Franklin, whom Robert Evans visited on 24 March, asked a Baptist minister of her acquaintance to speak to the renegade. He, too, emerged defeated, saying 'there was not a book that I recommended to her in support of Christian evidences that she had not read'.[51]

Mary Ann was once more living quietly with her father, but her life had changed radically. She continued to visit the Brays as often as she could, though she displeased her father by doing so.[52] His attention was taken up during the summer of 1842 with Chrissey's difficulties. A baby daughter, born in February 1841, died in May 1842; Chrissey's husband was ill and in debt. In July the Clarkes moved away from Meriden temporarily to Barford, near Warwick, with a loan of £800 from Mr Evans.[53]

It was in July that Mary Ann first met Sara Hennell, on one of her frequent visits to the Brays from Hackney, where she lived with her mother. Sara and Mary Ann were immediately attracted to one another, and began a correspondence which would last many years. Mary Ann was unashamedly gushing in her first letter to Sara when the latter had returned to London in August. 'I begin to think that cold dignity is only becoming to wise people and suits me about as ill as would the Lord Chancellor's wig', she wrote; 'so I shall go on being sentimental and Liebsehnende [i.e. yearning for love] in defiance of the march of reason and propriety.'[54]

Cara was doing a small watercolour portrait of Mary Ann, which she finished in September. As the sitter herself reported to Sara, the painter's 'benevolence extends to the hiding of faults in my visage as well as my character'.[55] The portrait shows a demure young woman with abundant ringleted hair, a large forehead, and a nose and chin flatteringly shorter than those of the breathing original.

Mary Ann went on with her reading, telling Francis Watts she had finished a work by Friedrich Tholuck written as a critical response to

Strauss's *Das Leben Jesu*, and remarking diplomatically that she was indebted to it for 'some important thoughts'. But she was not shaken out of her new-found rationalism, as Mary Sibree recounted with sorrow to her brother John, now studying theology with Tholuck himself at Halle in Germany.[56]

In October Mary Ann met Rufa Brabant, who was visiting the Brays at the same time as Charles Hennell, to whom she was unofficially engaged.[57] Rufa was translating Strauss's *Das Leben Jesu* with the approval of her father, Dr Robert Brabant of Devizes. Brabant had been Coleridge's doctor during the latter's stay in Wiltshire in 1815–16, while he wrote *Biographia Literaria*; it was Coleridge who had given the child Elizabeth Rebecca Brabant the nickname Rufa, on account of her golden red hair.[58] Coleridge had also introduced Brabant to the study of German theology. Brabant read *Das Leben Jesu* and became acquainted with Strauss; he also read Hennell's *Inquiry* and invited him to visit. Since he was interested in medical and political reform as well as in radical theology, he was naturally invited in turn to Rosehill. Having examined Hennell and found his lungs unsound, he refused permission for Rufa to marry him, though his opposition was eventually ignored when Rufa was left some money, and the couple were married in November 1843.[59] Hennell then persuaded Mary Ann to take over the task of translating Strauss from Rufa, who had done only part of the first volume.

Mary Ann was the obvious person. She was the most learned member of the Bray–Hennell circle, and had made a particular study of the Bible, first as ardent Evangelical, then as historical critic. She knew German. Indeed, her reading since December 1842 had been predominantly in German literature. With Cara she read Schiller's *Wallenstein* trilogy, Lessing's *Nathan der Weise*, a dramatic homily about religious tolerance, and Goethe's *Wilhelm Meister*.[60] In January 1843 Dr Brabant sent the Brays a copy of one of Spinoza's works, which Mary Ann began translating from Latin. Spinoza was a forerunner of German Higher Criticism; his philosophical works had been neglected until Lessing and Goethe, and German Biblical critics from Johann Gottfried Eichhorn in the 1790s to Strauss, drew attention to Spinoza's rigorous logic and demythologizing of religion.[61] Mary Ann was keen to undertake serious work, and her friends recognized her need and her ability for such tasks as translating Spinoza and Strauss.

She also hoped to fall in love, and was in fact liable to become enthusiastic where her feelings were not returned. Interestingly enough, her brother Isaac was also keen that she should marry, but he viewed the case as hopeless, since she was so much in the Brays' company. Cara told Sara Hennell in February 1843 that he had tried to make trouble with Mr Evans about Mary Ann's visits to Rosehill:

It seems that brother Isaac with real fraternal kindness thinks that his sister has no chance of getting the one thing needful – i.e. a husband and a settlement, unless she mixes more in society, and complains that since she has known us she has hardly been anywhere else; that Mr. Bray, being only a leader of mobs, can only introduce her to Chartists and Radicals, and that such only will ever fall in love with her if she does not belong to the Church. So his plan is to induce his father to remove to Meriden where being away from us and under the guardianship of her sister she may be brought back to her senses. M. A. says there is no interested motive in it, but a pure zeal for her welfare. But Mr. Evans says he does not wish to leave Coventry, and does not mind her coming here; so Isaac must be quiet again for the present.[62]

What would Isaac say if he could see his sister in November 1843, on a visit to Dr Brabant's home in Devizes after attending Rufa's wedding to Charles Hennell in London on 1 November? Her letters to her friends show her pleasure in the flattering attention being paid to her by Dr Brabant, now in his early sixties and with a wife who was blind. Cara received the news that he had christened Mary Ann 'Deutera, which *means* second and *sounds* a little like daughter', and that she was 'in a little heaven here, Dr. Brabant being its archangel'. She and the doctor 'read, walk and talk together, and I am never out of his company'.[63] Perhaps Cara warned her to be careful. On 24 November Mary Ann assured her that 'he really is a finer character than you think', though she joked ominously about the findings of the phrenological reading of her head Bray had done: 'I have some very bad propensities and my moral and animal regions are unfortunately balanced.'[64] A week later she wrote more soberly that she was returning to Coventry two weeks earlier than expected.

She had behaved impulsively and indiscreetly, and Dr Brabant himself had been weaselish, as his daughter Rufa, who returned from her honeymoon to witness the goings-on in her parents' house, told John Chapman some years later. Chapman wrote down her version of events, which he said exactly corresponded with Mary Ann's own account to him:

In 1843 Miss Evans was invited by Dr Brabant (she being then only 22 [actually almost 24]) to visit his house and to fill the place of his daughter (then just married) she went, the Doctor liked her extremely, and said that so long as she had no home she must consider his house as her permanent home. She in the simplicity of her heart and her ignorance of (or incapability of practicing [*sic*]) the required conventionalisms gave the Doctor the utmost attention; they became very intimate, his sister in law Miss S. Hughes became alarmed, made a great stir, excited the jealousy of Mrs Brabant, Miss Evans left. Mrs B vowed she should never enter the house again, or that if she did, she Mrs Brabant would instantly leave it. Mrs Hennell says Dr B. acted ungenerously and worse, towards Miss E. for though he was the chief cause of all that passed, he acted towards her as though the fault lay with her alone. His unmanliness in the affair was condemned more by Mrs Hennell than by Miss E. herself when she (a year ago) related the circumstances to me.[65]

Dr Brabant's sister-in-law Miss Hughes found it necessary to tell this cautionary tale to another young literary lady who stayed in Devizes in 1847. This was Eliza Lynn Linton, who told Herbert Spencer in 1885 that she, too, had been the object of Dr Brabant's flattery. He was, she said, 'more antipathetic than any man I have ever known, and his love-making more purely disgusting'. How Mary Ann Evans could have liked him 'was to me a marvel!'[66] In her peculiar autobiographical fiction, also of 1885, *The Autobiography of Christopher Kirkland*, Eliza Lynn Linton was even more critical of both Dr Brabant, to whom she refers sarcastically as 'that learned and fastidious Dr. Devise', and George Eliot, of whom she says: 'One of our greatest celebrities, when in the Ugly Duck stage of her existence and before she had joined her kindred Swans, had wanted to dedicate her life to him', but 'the friendship came to a stormy end, after a more than ordinarily ardent beginning'.[67]

Chapman was right about Mary Ann's simplicity and 'incapability of practicing the required conventionalisms' on such occasions. He knew – none better – how easily the diffident, physically plain but emotionally and intellectually passionate Mary Ann Evans could fall for men who showed her some kindness or admiration. Hers was a difficult lot, to be so intelligent as to attract the amazed attention of men, but to find that her attraction for most of them was purely intellectual, not physical.

One young man did come forward to ask for her hand during the long months when she was working at Strauss, translating at the rate of six pages a day.[68] Very little is known about him. He was 'a young artist' and picture-restorer of Leamington, who met Mary Ann through her half-sister Fanny and proposed to her in March 1845 through her brother-in-law, Henry Houghton, after knowing her for only a few days. Mary Ann was 'brimful of happiness', according to Cara, though unsure whether she loved him. On meeting him again, she decided that he was not as interesting as she had thought, and broke off the relationship before an engagement had been arranged.[69] She told Sara Hennell simply, 'My unfortunate "affaire" did not become one "du coeur" but it has been anything but a comfortable one for my conscience.' She added, making light of the matter, that she now kept the episode 'recorded in my book of reference, article *"Precipitancy, ill effects of"*'.[70]

But she was shaken by her own intensity and impetuosity followed by alarmed withdrawal. Years later Cara Bray told Herbert Spencer that she had forgotten the young man's name, had never met him, and indeed had not been told very much by Mary Ann. Mary Sibree had apparently found her 'in distress' one day, saying she had given him too much encouragement. She was upset to find that her letter to him ending the relationship had crossed with one from the young artist to Mr Evans asking his permission to marry her.[71] As Cara wrote at the time, 'poor girl, everything seems against the grain with her'.[72]

Mary Ann worked on at the Strauss, the cost of which was being borne by Joseph Parkes, the wealthy Birmingham radical who had first suggested the work be translated. He contributed £150, and John Chapman, publisher of unorthodox and heterodox books, fixed with Charles Hennell for '½ expense and ½ profit'.[73] No one expected the translation to sell, of course, and Mary Ann certainly did not hope for either financial gain or celebrity. The work was hard, but she kept her spirits up as well as she could, encouraged by Cara and especially Sara, who acted as her first reader and editor, scrutinizing the manuscript as it grew.[74] Cara reported on 14 April 1845, with the love affair just over, that 'Dr. Pollian', Sara's nickname for the learned translator of the learned German author, 'looked in high spirits this morning'. Mary Ann herself wrote two days later that she was displeased with her efforts, 'but I have not courage to imitate Gibbon – put my work in the fire and begin again'.[75]

Strauss took her just over two years to complete. She turned his two long volumes into three English volumes. No translator could have been more careful and thoughtful. Her letters to Sara Hennell, who was generous in her support, reveal anxieties about translating not only Strauss's difficult German, but his Greek and Hebrew as well. In March 1846 she threw out a set of questions – half-rhetorically, for she had already decided more or less how to proceed – which are typical of the problems she faced:

I am not altogether satisfied with the use of the word Sacrament as applied specifically to the Abendmahl. It seems like a vulgarism to say, *the* Sacrament, for one thing, and for another, it does not seem *aboriginal* enough in the life of Jesus: but I know of no other word that can be substituted. I have altered passover to paschal meal, but τὸ πάσχα is used in the New Testament of the eating of the lamb, par excellence. You remember in the title of the first § in the Schluss [Conclusion] which I had been so careless as to omit, the expression is 'Nothwendiger Uebergang der Kritik in das *Dogma*'. Now Dogmatism will not do, as that would represent *Dogmatismus*. Dogmatik is the idea I believe – i.e. positive theology.[76]

(She translated 'Abendmahl' variously as 'the Christian supper', 'the Lord's supper', and 'the ritual supper', and the title of § 144 as 'Necessary Transition from Criticism to Dogma'.)

As Hennell indicated in the Preface to the second edition of his *Inquiry*, Strauss's work presents a detailed examination of the Gospels from a critical standpoint. That is, much as Kant proceeded in his three philosophical *Critiques* of the 1780s and 1790s – of Pure Reason, of Practical Reason, and of Judgment – Strauss subjected each story to rational scrutiny. Hence the subtitle 'kritisch bearbeitet', which Mary Ann rightly insisted be prominent in the translated title – *The Life of Jesus, Critically Examined* – because of Strauss's emphasis on his philosophical method.[77] As he said in the Preface, he was taking the eighteenth-century rationalism of writers like Lessing and Eichhorn, who read the life of Jesus as natural, rather than supernatural, history, one logical step further, by means of his Kantian investigative technique:

The exegesis of the ancient church set out from the double presupposition: first, that the gospels contained a history, and secondly, that this history was a supernatural one. Rationalism rejected the latter of these presuppositions, but only to cling the more tenaciously to the former, maintaining that these books present unadulterated, though only natural, history. Science cannot rest satisfied with this half-measure: the other presupposition also must be relinquished, and the inquiry must first be made whether in fact, and to what extent, the ground on which we stand in the gospels is historical.[78]

Having set out this aim, Strauss proceeds to investigate every episode as told in all four Gospels, looking first at traditional interpretations, then at historical explanations, and finally offering an argument for reading each episode mythically. That is to say that he finds for such miraculous stories as that of the annunciation of the birth of John the Baptist to an aged mother a precedent in the Old Testament, in this case the common theme of long barrenness in Hebrew poetry and the birth of Samson to elderly parents. His conclusion is that John the Baptist was belatedly 'glorified' by a grafting of this ancient myth on to the story of his life.[79]

The method is exhaustive, and leads to inevitable repetition. As Mary Ann complained to Sara in March 1846, 'the last 100 pages have certainly been totally uninteresting, considered as matter for translation', since Strauss has already 'anticipated in the earlier part of his work all the principles and many of the details of his criticism, and he seems fagged himself'. She was aware, too, of the pitfalls of his inclusive method, the danger that he might interpret everything in terms of his mythical approach, whereas some episodes might have historical truth. 'I am never pained when I think Strauss right', she wrote, 'but in many cases I think him wrong, as every man must be in working out into detail an idea which has general truth, but is only one element in a perfect theory, not a perfect theory in itself.'[80]

Early in 1846, when she was finishing this enormous task, her father became ill, and Cara reported to Sara that Mary Ann was 'Strauss-sick – it made her ill dissecting the beautiful story of the crucifixion, and only the sight of her Christ-image and picture [a cast of Thorwaldsen's figure of the risen Christ and an engraving] made her endure it'. Cara pitied her 'pale sickly face and dreadful headaches, and anxiety about her father'.[81] It could hardly be a completely congenial task for the recently pious Christian to retell as translator the passion of Christ, analysing it in the cool, neutral, unsensational yet necessarily destructive tones of the critical Strauss. Mary Ann mustered some wry humour when she heard, as her two-year work finally reached completion, that an old schoolfellow of hers, a Miss Bradley Jenkins, was thinking of exchanging the life of a governess for that of a translator. 'She thinks she could sit from morn till noon, from noon till dewy eve,' she told Sara, echoing Milton in *Paradise Lost*, 'translating German or French without feeling the least fatigue.' Mary Ann hoped Sara might help her get that 'maggot' out of the poor woman's brain. 'There are not even the devil's wages for a translator – profit and fame.'[82] The translation was published anonymously in three volumes on 15 June 1846 by John Chapman. Mary Ann received £20 in payment.[83]

During her two years of hard work Mary Ann had some short periods of respite, mainly thanks to the Brays. Charles Bray took her to London in July 1844. This short trip was very different from her first visit to the capital, when she had declined to go to the theatre with Isaac. Now she had a phrenological cast made of her head, which the keen amateur Bray rapidly interpreted, later describing his conclusions in his autobiography. It was a reading of her character which her behaviour, at least as much as the contours of her head, dictated to him. Bray's analysis clearly contains much that is incontrovertible, but leans too far, I think, in the direction of stressing her vulnerability at the expense of her indomitableness:

In the Feelings, the Animal and Moral regions are about equal; the moral being quite sufficient to keep the animal in order and in due subservience, but would not be spontaneously active. The social feelings were very active, particularly the adhesiveness. She was of a most affectionate disposition, always requiring some one to lean upon, preferring what has hitherto been considered the stronger sex to the other and more impressible. She was not fitted to stand alone.[84]

Maybe so. But her life was by no means the submissive one this might suggest. She needed her father's love and approval, but she had already shown that she would not compromise her beliefs simply to retain that love and approval, though her half-sister Fanny, who apparently agreed with her religious conclusions, took a different and easier course of action, simply keeping quiet about her doubts.[85] And so it proved with Mary Ann's later relationships and choices, when contradictory needs, desires, and duties came into collision.

In the summer of 1844 Mary Ann accompanied the Brays to the Lake

District, where she met the large family of the liberal Unitarian minister
James Martineau, brother of Harriet. Martineau's wife was a cousin of
Cara's. At their house Mary Ann met W. B. Hodgson, a liberal edu-
cationalist who tried mesmerizing her. According to Cara, he nearly
succeeded, 'to the degree that she could not open her eyes, and begged
him most piteously to do it for her, which he did immediately by
passes'.[86] Hodgson himself wrote to a friend that he had 'partially mesmerized a Miss Evans' who 'reads Greek, Latin, French, Italian,
German'. As for Bray, said Hodgson, 'a fine, jolly fellow he is, and we
had a delightful talk till twelve at night'.[87] There was much talk of
mesmerism once more in April 1845, when Mary Ann, again in the
company of the Brays, met the redoubtable Harriet Martineau.[88]

In October 1845 Mary Ann was again included in a trip taken by the
Brays and Sara, this time to Scotland. Mary Ann almost did not go. Her
brother-in-law Edward Clarke was declared a bankrupt, and she was
needed at home to support her father and Chrissey. But she was so
disappointed at the thought of missing the trip that Bray stepped in and
persuaded Robert Evans that she must be allowed to go, otherwise her
health would suffer.[89] The party set off on 14 October to Liverpool,
then north to Glasgow, and on to Loch Lomond, Stirling, and finally
Edinburgh. Mary Ann read her favourite novelist, Scott, on the way, and
the visit to his home at Abbotsford was the high point of the tour. But
the weather was bad, all the party caught colds, and when they reached
Edinburgh on 25 October Mary Ann's 'ecstasies' were dampened by a
letter from Isaac saying her father had broken his leg and asking her to
come home as soon as possible.[90]

The only remaining record of Mary Ann's impressions of this journey is a versified account by Sara Hennell copied into Cara's Commonplace Book. She describes the group's first sight of Edinburgh, focusing
particularly on Mary Ann's excitement:

> But oh, when we enter the glorious city –
> (To have seen it by daylight the first were a pity)
> It seems to our wondering eyes a delusion,
> For houses up there and down here in confusion.
> And windows & windows in multiplied row –
> Stars gleaming above, & lamps gleaming below –
> We scarcely ourselves or our own level know.
> – Dear Pollian, thy pulses beat wild with delight –

> 'Tis an hour of excitement – existence – this night.
> But e'en now on thy joy is impending a sorrow –
> Alas! that must call us all homewards tomorrow.[91]

After the last proofs of the Strauss had been corrected, Mary Ann paid another visit to London. She visited Sara Hennell and her mother at Clapton, where they now lived, at the end of May 1846. The contrast between her younger, forbidding self and her new enthusiastic embracing of London's pleasures is striking. She instructed the Brays, who were due to visit London too, to 'come in a very mischievous, unconscientious, theatre-loving humour'.[92]

The day after their return to Coventry on 9 June 1846, Cara wrote in her diary, 'Brought home Elinor.'[93] This was a reference to the Brays' adoption of a baby known as Nelly. The Brays had no children of their own, but Nelly appears to have been the second child brought into the household. In May 1845 Mary Ann had written to Cara, then on holiday in Hastings, 'Of Baby you shall hear to-morrow, but do not be alarmed. You will not have to chant "O ever thus" over her.' And, two days later, 'The Baby is quite well and not at all triste on account of the absence of Papa and Mamma.'[94] A month later Cara's diary reads mysteriously, 'Took our child back to Hampton Station.' No more is heard of Baby; the Census of March 1851 shows the household at Rosehill to consist of Charles and Cara Bray; Harry Bray, 'nephew, aged 19, assistant to ribbon manufacturer'; Mary Ann Evans, 'visitor'; a housemaid; a cook; and Elinor Mary, 'adopted daughter, aged 5'.[95]

It seems that both Baby, who for some reason did not remain with the family, and Nelly, who did, were Charles Bray's children by another woman. When George Combe paid one of his regular visits to Rosehill in September 1851, he analysed Bray's head, noting in his journal that his subject had 'an enormous cerebellum' which revealed 'excessive activity'. The cerebellum is the base of the brain, where the 'animal' qualities were held by phrenologists to be located. On discussing this with Bray, Combe learned something which he recorded in a shorthand of his own. Deciphered, the entry reads:

At twelve years of age he was seduced by his father's Cook and indulged extensively in illicit intercourse with women. He abstained from 18 to 22 but suffered in health. He married and his wife has no children. He consoled himself with another woman by whom he had a daughter. He adopted his child with his wife's consent and she now lives with him. He still keeps the mother of the child and has another by her. I strongly objected to his being cooped up and recommended to him to lower his diet and increase his exercise and by every means lessen the vigour of his amativeness and be faithful to his wife.[96]

There is some evidence to suggest that Bray was unable, or unwilling, to follow Combe's advice, for he may have fathered four more children outside his marriage to Cara, who remained childless but for the adopted Elinor.[97] If John Chapman is to be believed, Cara herself was in love with a friend, Edward Noel. Rufa Hennell apparently told him in the course of the same conversation in which she described Mary Ann's Devizes escapade with her father, that 'Mr Bray promotes her wish that Mr Noel should visit Rosehill as much as possible, and that she in return tries to promote his happiness in any way that his wishes tend.'[98]

It is not clear how much Mary Ann knew at this time, or later, about the Brays' marriage arrangements. What is likely is that she observed her friends closely and respected their right to make mutually convenient decisions. Bray himself joined in the debate among Victorian psychologists and doctors about the best way for men to channel their sexual needs. In his autobiography he wrote that the strongest of human feelings is 'the sexual feeling or Amativeness, and this is therefore the largest consumer of force in the whole system, and requires the most careful regulation and restraint'. The solution to the problem of how best to achieve this is marriage:

Matrimony is the law of our being, and it is in that state that Amativeness comes into its proper use and action, and is the least likely to be indulged in excess; and it is there also that the feeling, as it ought to do, acts only in association with the social and higher feelings.[99]

Bray was the first, but not the last, man of Mary Ann's acquaintance whose practice did not quite live up to his theory, who was 'simply a man whose desires had been stronger than his theoretic beliefs, and who had gradually explained the gratification of his desires into satisfactory agreement with those beliefs', as she was to write of a character in *Middlemarch*, the banker Mr Bulstrode.[100]

CHAPTER THREE

Father's Illness and Death; Interlude
in Geneva 1847–50

After her first few tentative letters of friendship to Cara and Sara when they were becoming acquainted early in 1842, Mary Ann had settled into an increasingly free and relaxed tone with them. Gone was the religious matter and religiose tone of those letters to Miss Lewis. Her expanding social circle, thanks to the Brays, her increasingly secular reading – Goethe and George Sand were favourites, both noted, even notorious, for their frankness about sexual relations – and perhaps, too, the confidence she had gained from achieving a piece of published writing, albeit only of translation, all these fed into her epistolary style. In October 1846 she tried out on Charles Bray a *jeu d'esprit* which gives the first indication that Mary Ann Evans's *métier* would turn out to be novel writing, and humorous novel writing at that. A great deal of wit and some impressive learning lightly worn are in evidence in the comic scene she creates, turning her experience of translating Strauss to playful account:

The other day as I was sitting in my study, Mary [Sibree] came with a rather risible cast of expression to deliver to me a card, saying that a gentleman was below requesting to see me. The name on the card ran thus – Professor Bücherwurm, Moderig University [Professor Bookworm of Musty University]. Down I came, not a little elated at the idea that a live professor was in the house, and, as you know I have quite the average quantity of that valuable endowment which spiteful people call assurance, but which I dignify with the name of self possession, you will believe that I neither blushed nor made a nervous giggle in attempting to smile, as is the lot of some unfortunate young ladies who are immersed in youthful bashfulness.

And whom do you think I saw? A tall, gaunt personage with huge cheek bones, dull grey eyes, hair of a very light neutral tint, un grand nez retroussé, and very black teeth. As novel writers say, I give you at once what was the result of a survey carried on by degrees through a long interview. My professor's coat was threadbare enough for that of a first-rate genius, and his linen and skin dirty enough to have belonged to the Emperor Julian. A profound reverence. I begged him to be seated, and this very begrimed professor began in sufficiently good English, 'Madam, you can form no preconception of my design in waiting on you.' I bowed. 'About a fortnight ago I came to London to seek – singular as it may seem to you – a *wife*.' (Surely, thought I, this poor man has escaped from a lunatic asylum, and I looked alternately at the door and the poker, measuring my distance from the two.) 'But', my professor continued, 'there were certain qualifications which were indispensable to me in the person whom I could receive into that relation. I am a voluminous author – indeed my works already amount to some 20 vols. – my last publication in 5 vols. was a commentary on the book of Tobit. I have also written a long dissertation on the Greek Digamma, a treatise on Buddhism shewing that Christianity is entirely derived from this monstrous oriental superstition, and a very minute inquiry into the date, life and character of Cheops. My chief work, however, and that by which I hope to confer a lasting benefit on mankind is yet on hand. It is a system of metaphysics which I doubt not will supersede the latest products of the German philosophic mind.'

The professor then comes to the point:

'I am determined if possible to secure a translator in the person of a wife. I have made the most anxious and extensive inquiries in London after all female translators of German. I find them very abundant, but I require, besides ability to translate, a very decided ugliness of person and a sufficient fortune to supply a poor professor with coffee and tobacco, and an occasional draft of schwarzbier, as well as to contribute to the expenses of publication. After the most toilsome inquiries I have been referred to you, Madam, as presenting the required combination of attributes, and though I am rather disappointed to see that you have no beard, an attribute which I have ever regarded as the most unfailing indication of a strong-minded woman, I confess that in other respects your person at least comes up to my ideal.'

To complement this portrait of a solemn, preposterously egotistical professor, Mary Ann proceeds to give a mock analysis of her feelings as the recipient of this magnificent proposal:

I said that I was taken by surprize, having long given up all hope of such an application as the present, but that I was decidedly pleased with the business-like tone of my suitor, and I thought no woman had been wooed in a more dignified manner since the days of the amazons, who were won with the sword. I thought it possible we might come to terms, always provided he acceded to my irrevocable conditions. 'For you must know, learned Professor', I said, 'that I require nothing more in a husband than to save me from the horrific disgrace of spinster-hood and to take me out of England.'

She promises 'to be a dutiful wife so far as the task of translation is concerned', and 'to give to the English a lucid idea of your notions respecting Cheops and Tobit etc'. Finally, 'As to my want of beard I trust that defect may be remedied' with 'creams and essences', and 'it is an interesting physiological experiment yet to be tried, whether the feminine lip and chin may not be rendered fertile by this top-dressing'.[1]

So Mary Ann turned into a fine joke her anxiety about her physical appearance and her genuine apprehension, as she approached twenty-eight, about remaining a spinster. What is remarkable, too, is the ease with which she illustrates her narrative by means of analogies and metaphors drawn from the world of learning, using arcane knowledge to universally comprehensible comic effect, as in the reference to 'the days of the amazons' and the professor's 'notions respecting Cheops and Tobit etc'. Her seemingly innocent remark about novel writers giving 'the result of a survey carried on by degrees through a long interview' is a sly dig at minor novelists who could not manage sustained dialogue or description.

She was also beginning to pass interesting critical comments on novels she was reading. Of Disraeli's *Tancred* (1847) she wrote with self-assured disrespect in May 1847, complaining that while 'writing himself much more detestable stuff than ever came from a French pen', he 'can do nothing better than bamboozle the unfortunates who are seduced into reading his Tancred than speak superciliously of all other men and things, an expedient much more successful in some quarters than one would expect'.[2] This scores a palpable hit on Disraeli's clumsy, pretentious, yet popular writing.

The idea of creating a comic learned German probably came from Carlyle, who invented Professor Diogenes Teufelsdröckh (Devil's Dung) in *Sartor Resartus* (1836), which Mary Ann had read in December 1841, declaring then to Martha Jackson that Carlyle was 'a grand favourite of mine', though not 'orthodox'.[3] Her reading between 1843 and

1847, often shared with Cara and Mary Sibree, included more Carlyle (*Past and Present*, 1843), a lot of George Sand, Rousseau's *Nouvelle Héloïse*, Goethe's *Faust*, *Werther*, and *Die Wahlverwandtschaften* (*Elective Affinities*), Novalis's *Heinrich von Ofterdingen*, and the whimsical work of Jean Paul Richter, *Blumen-, Frucht-, und Dornenstücke, oder Ehestand, Tod, und Hochzeit des Armenadvokaten Fr. St. Siebenkäs*. This last work, translated as *Flower, Fruit and Thorn Pieces; or, the Married Life, Death and Wedding of the Advocate of the Poor, Firmian Siebenkäs* by Cara's friend Edward Noel in 1845, Mary Ann read with Cara in December 1844.[4]

Increasingly Mary Ann's reading was in secular and imaginative literature. Her mind, liberated, in her words, 'from the wretched giant's bed of dogmas on which it has been racked and stretched ever since it began to think', absorbed 'the bracing air of independence'.[5] No wonder Sara Hennell thought in September 1846 that Mary Ann 'must be writing her novel'.[6] She wasn't – yet. But she was about to compose her 'German professor' letter, and she was also about to write her first review. This was a short criticism of works on Christianity and the Jesuits by Jules Michelet and Edgar Quinet which she completed for the *Coventry Herald* of 30 October 1846.

The *Herald*, long the radical newspaper in the city, had been bought by Bray in June. The first edition under his proprietorship appeared on 17 July, sporting an 'Address from the New Proprietary to the Public', in which readers were assured that the *Herald* would continue to be 'devoted to the advocacy of LIBERALISM' and advised, with Bray's customary optimism, that 'the irresistible tendency of society is FORWARD'.[7] Naturally, Bray invited Mary Ann to try her hand at writing for this progressive organ. She wrote five short sketches between December 1846 and February 1847, none of them as good as her spoof letter, where she was more at ease. They take the form of little homilies supposedly found in a trunk full of manuscripts.[8]

The best of them, 'Hints on Snubbing', though rather heavily written on the whole, carries something of the irony and breadth of reference of her later writing, both journalistic and fictional. Mary Ann characterizes the sorts of people who can afford to snub others, but only if they choose their victims with care. Such are 'any who have been elevated in society'; these may snub 'their former familiars' with impunity. Another sort are 'ladies who go to parties', who may target 'the plain and ill-dressed'. Who knows whether the next class of snubbers anatomized here was not one within Mary Ann Evans's own recent experience? These are 'ladies of decidedly orthodox sentiments' who deliver 'the snub religious':

All such ladies, we say, may snub any man not marriageable, and any woman not an heiress, though as full of talents or of good works as a Sir Philip Sidney or a John Howard, if he or she be suspected of diverging in opinion from that standard of truth which is lodged in the brain of the Rev. Amylatus Stultus, who keeps the key of these same ladies' consciences. But let every one beware of snubbing on religious grounds in quarters where there is wealth, or fashion, or influence. In such cases all aberrations from the standard are to be regarded as amiable eccentricities, which do not warrant an uncharitable construction. On the whole it must be admitted that the snub religious is a most valuable agent in society, resembling those compensating contrivances by which nature makes up for the loss of one organ by an extraordinary development of the functions of another.[9]

Such writing has the animus of personal experience of a painful sort transformed into generalized wit.

At this time Mary Ann was also sharpening her wit privately at the expense of one who had made a fool of her. Three years after the episode with Dr Brabant at Devizes, she wrote sharply, and not entirely truthfully, that she had 'offered incense to him' because there was 'no other deity at hand, and because I wanted some kind of worship pour passer le temps'. Really, she now told Sara, she had 'laughed at him in my sleeve'.[10] We may take this half-truth and unkindness as a token of her much increased self-confidence since she had worshipped her false god in 1843.

By a quirk of circumstance pleasing to the biographer, the letter in which Mary Ann thus puts Dr Brabant in his place goes on to tell Sara not to judge too harshly a new acquaintance Sara has made in London. This was none other than Eliza Lynn, then living at Chapman's house in Clapton (he had not yet moved to 142 Strand), and making something of a stir as a 'literary lady' with her historical novel, *Azeth the Egyptian* (1846). Not only was Eliza thus preceding Mary Ann herself as a boarder of the charming Chapman – 'How many more young ladies is he going to have?' asked Cara Bray in innocence of future events – but she was about to follow Mary Ann briefly into the clutches of the doctor of Devizes himself.[11]

That other figure from the past, Maria Lewis, stepped briefly back into Mary Ann's life, when she came to stay at Foleshill in the New Year. Cara wrote brutally on 3 January 1847 that Mary Ann was 'going to have a stupid Miss Lewis visitor for a fortnight, which will keep her at home'.[12] In stark contrast, the important future friend, John Chapman, began to figure in Mary Ann's life. She had met him in the early summer of 1846 when she stayed with Sara in Clapton and he was bringing out *The Life of Jesus*. In February 1847 she mentioned him rather slightingly in a letter to Sara, a sure sign that she was intrigued by him. She was asking for information about the print run of Strauss:

My strong impression was, that the first 250 copies were to be Mr. C's, the second 250, the subscribers'. We have a dispute here as to the number of copies printed. Was it 1000 or 2000? I hope Mr. Chapman will not misbehave, but he was always too much of the *interesting* gentleman to please me. Men must not attempt to be interesting on any lower terms than a fine poetical genius.[13]

In April 1847 Mary Ann was herself in London once more, attending a concert of Mendelssohn's *Elijah* and hearing Bellini's *I Puritani*. Sara Hennell came to Coventry in June and reported to her mother that her friend 'grows better and wiser every time I see her'.[14] Mary Ann's expanding character is increasingly evident in the frankness and confidence with which she now wrote to her friend. Her proper Evans pride, somewhat emphatically deployed, was expressed in September, when she scolded Sara for not reminding her of a debt of two shillings. 'Pray have the generosity another time', she demanded, 'to save me from the pain of finding that I have neglected to pay *even* my money debts, when there are so many others which I am unable to defray.'[15]

She tells Sara in this letter that she has been reading Charles Hennell's *Inquiry* again, concluding that the book is so clever, candid, and generous that 'he ought to be one of the happiest of men that he has done such a life's-work'. 'I am sure', she adds, 'if I had written such a book I should be invulnerable to all the arrows of all spiteful gods and goddesses.'[16] One can hear in this her desire, whether she yet acknowledged it to herself or not, to be a writer.

Perhaps she would have begun now if it had not been for her father's declining health. The Strauss had been reviewed favourably, with Charles Wicksteed praising the 'faithful, elegant, and scholarlike translation' in the Unitarian *Prospective Review*. 'Though the translator never obtrudes himself upon the reader with any notes or comments of his own,' he wrote, 'yet he is evidently a man who has a familiar knowledge of the whole subject.'[17] This was music to the ears of the surprisingly learned young *woman* who had completed the task without having enjoyed the university education which the reviewer took for granted. She did ponder a book or essay in October 1847, something she told Sara would be called 'the superiority of the consolations of philosophy to those of (so-called) religion'.[18] But this startling work was not written. Her father's long decline was to preoccupy her for many months of lonely nursing and worrying at Foleshill.

All her great intellectual energies – and a great deal of nervous energy too – seem to have gone into her letter writing at this time. There was no stopping her once she had begun on a magisterial, if humorous, rebuke. In February 1848 she chided Sara for complaining that she never wrote:

I can only say that if you were clairvoyante you would see the proof of that possibility [that she could go on loving Sara even if she did not write to her] in my heart or stomach or bowels or pineal gland or adhesiveness or cerebral mass in toto.

Very well, she continued:

Behold me ready to tear off my right hand or pluck out my right eye (metaphorically of course – I speak to an experienced exegetist, comme dirait notre Strauss) or write reams of letters full of interesting falsehoods or very dull truths – anything so you will revoke those cruel words.[19]

To add to her ever bolder, more dominant letters to Sara came a new correspondence. This was with Mary Sibree's brother John, now returned from Germany and studying at a theology college for Independent ministers in Birmingham. Sibree was reading Strauss and having doubts about his vocation. With great self-confidence, Mary Ann took it upon herself to encourage his critical inquiry. He needed a dose of the 'critical, logical character' of Strauss – 'just the opposite of his own', she told Sara in November 1847.[20]

Mary Ann's letters to Sibree show her taking the lead in their friendship, presuming to instruct him and presuming also to flirt with him in a lofty, defensive way. On 11 February 1848 her long letter ranges over various subjects. These include Hannah More, whom she once admired but now pronounces detestable, a blue-stocking, 'a monster that can only exist in a miserably false state of society, in which a woman with but a smattering of learning or philosophy is classed along with singing mice and card playing pigs'. Then she dissects Disraeli and his theory of Jewish superiority, and touches on Handel's music, Hegel's aesthetic philosophy, and the visual arts. She seems determined to impress Sibree with her wide culture. To cover her embarrassment at thus putting herself forward in a letter to a young man she takes refuge in a humorous reference to the windy Welshman in *The Merry Wives of Windsor*: 'I hate bashfulness and modesties as Sir Hugh Evans would say, and I warn you that I shall make no apologies.'[21]

In her next letter she confesses that 'my fluid nature is always stirred by the idea that any heart beats just a little quicker because of me'.[22] She has been reading George Sand's *Lettres d'un Voyageur*; perhaps the frank Frenchwoman has encouraged her to write more openly than she might naturally have done. She is also fighting the deepening depression of living alone with a beloved but difficult father who may die at any moment or may live on gloomily and painfully for an indefinite period.

Another long letter went off to Sibree on 8 March, full of excitement about the February revolution in Paris. Mary Ann had no time for those who pitied 'Louis Philippe and his moustachioed sons', who had been smuggled out of France and into England with the help of the British Consul. Sounding like Carlyle at his righteous best, she declared, 'for heaven's sake preserve me from sentimentalizing over a pampered old man when the earth has its millions of unfed souls and bodies'. (Compare Book III, chapter seven, of *Past and Present*, entitled 'Over-Production': 'Too many shirts? Well, that is a novelty, in this intemperate Earth, with its nine-hundred millions of bare backs!') She did not anticipate an uprising in Britain:

Our little humbug of a queen is more endurable than the rest of her race because she calls forth a chivalrous feeling, and there is nothing in our constitution to obstruct the slow progress of *political* reform.[23]

Sure enough, while other European cities saw uprisings and riots, London stayed calm. The famous Chartist meeting scheduled for 10 April 1848 had the authorities enrolling thousands of 'special constables' (including the exiled Louis Philippe himself), but the meeting passed off peacefully.[24] Mary Ann probably exaggerated her enthusiasm for revolution in inverse proportion to what she perceived to be the likelihood of its spreading to Britain.

There is something excitable, even febrile, about several of her letters at this time, particularly those to Sibree. She asked him to burn them, so that there would be 'no risk of a critical third pair of eyes getting a sight of them' (let alone the many pairs of eyes of curious posterity), 'which would certainly be a death blow to my reputation for gravity and wisdom – not that I am very careful in this matter – for this lump of cautiousness with which nature has furnished me is of very little use to me'. She confessed that she felt 'hardly able to write rationally'.[25]

During the next few months she suffered from dreadful headaches, and on 11 April Cara 'found her well nigh out of her senses with toothache'. Cara sent for a dentist, who, attended by Robert Evans's doctor, Dr John Bury, administered chloroform before taking out the offending tooth. The dentist insisted on having a doctor present for two reasons. First, chloroform was new, its anaesthetic properties having been discovered only late in 1847 by James Simpson, the Edinburgh surgeon, who performed his first operation with its help in November of that year.[26] Second, Mary Ann had already reacted with 'violent screaming' to a previous dose of chloroform, and the dentist, Mr Wright, intended administering 'a second extra-strong dose' to render her unconscious.[27]

All this time Robert Evans grew worse. Mary Ann wrote to Fanny Houghton, giving bulletins and asking her to visit if she could. He rallied a little towards the end of April, which cheered her up, 'though the poor thing looks as thin as a poker', according to Cara on 30 April.[28] Mary Ann kept going, enjoying her reading aloud to her father of Scott's novels. Naturally, quotations from his novels began to pepper her letters. She dreamed of a different life. On hearing that John Sibree was planning to visit Germany again, she exclaimed, 'O the bliss of having a very high attic in a romantic continental town, such as Geneva.'[29] But there was no respite. Though her father was fit enough to be taken on holiday to St Leonard's, near Hastings, at the end of May, she was worried and lonely, telling Sara that she felt 'a sort of madness' growing on her, 'so entirely am I destitute of contact'.[30] To Charles Bray she wrote, 'for the present my address is Grief Castle, on the river of Gloom, in the valley of Dolour'. She had been reading Scott's *Tales of a*

Grandfather, in which Castle Campbell is called 'the castle of Gloom', being situated on 'the brook of Grief' in 'the parish of Doulour or Dollar'.[31]

While still at St Leonard's she read *Jane Eyre* (1847), on which she commented:

All self-sacrifice is good – but one would like it to be in a somewhat nobler cause than that of a diabolical law which chains a man soul and body to a putrefying carcase. However the book *is* interesting – only I wish the characters would talk a little less like the heroes and heroines of police reports.[32]

This is an interesting remark, showing her belief that marriage (Rochester's) to a lunatic should not be indissoluble – did she know that Thackeray was suffering in this way, with his wife in an asylum? – and expressing a fellow-feeling with those who sacrifice their own interest in a good cause. It is hard not to think that she felt she was sacrificing her own pleasures and plans for the sake of giving her full day-by-day attention to her father in his very long decline.

Back in Coventry in July 1848, she had the rare pleasure of meeting someone new. Ralph Waldo Emerson was in Britain and of course he stayed with the Brays for a few days. Mary Ann was impressed by his calm nobility, and he was struck – like all Bray's visitors – by her intelligence. He asked her what book had been most formative in her mental life, and she answered 'Rousseau's *Confessions*', to which he replied that Carlyle had given the same response.[33]

Not that Rousseau was in any way a moral example to her, as she explained in a letter to Sara in February 1849:

The writers who have most profoundly influenced me – who have rolled away the waters from their bed raised new mountains and spread delicious valleys for me – are not in the least oracles to me. It is just possible that I may not embrace one of their opinions, that I may wish my life to be shaped quite differently from theirs. For instance it would signify nothing to me if a very wise person were to stun me with proofs that Rousseau's views of life, religion, and government are miserably erroneous – that he was guilty of some of the worst bassesses that have degraded civilized man. I might admit all this – and it would be not the less true that Rousseau's genius has sent that electric thrill through my intellectual and moral frame which has awakened me to new perceptions, which has made man and nature a fresh world of thought and feeling to me – and this not by teaching me any new belief. It is simply that the rushing mighty wind of his inspiration has so quickened my faculties that I have been able to shape more definitely for myself ideas which had previously dwelt as dim 'ahnungen' [presentiments] in my soul – the fire of his genius has so fused together old thoughts and prejudices that I have been ready to make new combinations.[34]

The same could be said of George Sand, she went on. 'I should never dream of going to her writings as a moral code or text-book.' 'I don't care whether I agree with her about marriage or not' – George Sand advocated freedom for married couples to pursue their happiness outside marriage – since she 'delineates human passion and its results' with such 'tragic power' and 'loving gentle humour'. In *Jacques*, for example, she gives a truthful 'psychological anatomy' of the early married life of the theoretical hero and his naïve young bride, making of it 'an everyday tragedy', as Mary Ann observes.[35]

These are strong critical responses to books which may well have saved her from complete despair, as her father approached his end. We do not know whether Isaac or her other siblings visited much at this time. Only some letters to Fanny Houghton survive, in which Mary Ann appeals to her to come. To Sara Hennell she confessed in February 1849, 'My life is a perpetual nightmare' under her father's moans of pain, and in May, 'I am living unspeakable moments.'[36] Cara had reported several months earlier that Mary Ann looked like a ghost. In September 1848 she told Sara:

The doctors expect his death to take place suddenly, by a suffusion of water on the chest; and poor M. A., alone with him, has the whole care and fatigue of nursing him night and day with this constant nervous expectation.

When Isaac told his father he might die suddenly, Robert took the news calmly, 'and he takes opportunities now of saying kind things to M. A., contrary to his wont', Cara reported.[37]

By May 1849 it was clear that at last her father would die. Mary Ann told Charles Bray that 'strange to say I feel that these will ever be the happiest days of life to me. The one deep strong love I have ever known has now its highest exercise and fullest reward.'[38] She may have felt that by her devotion to his needs she had more than made up for the pain she had caused him by her religious rebellion. On the evening of 30 May she wrote to the Brays that Dr Bury had said Robert Evans would not last till morning. Her half-brother Robert would be sleeping at Foleshill that night. In her strange circumstances she feared life without her father:

What shall I be without my Father? It will seem as if a part of my moral nature were gone. I had a horrid vision of myself last night becoming earthly sensual and devilish for want of that purifying restraining influence.[39]

She had been putting his needs before her own for so long that it frightened her to contemplate the change of focus which was about to come. Robert Evans died during the night. What would his daughter do now?

Robert Evans was buried in Chilvers Coton churchyard, next to his wife, on 6 June 1849. Under his will the properties he owned were divided between his sons Robert and Isaac; Fanny and Chrissey, who had each been given £1,000 when they married, received another £1,000 on his death, together with items of furniture and possessions. Mary Ann was left £2,000 in trust and some household items. The invested sum would yield her an income of something over £90 a year in interest, payable in half-yearly amounts through the three trustees, her brothers Robert and Isaac and the family solicitor, Vincent Holbeche.[40] It was enough to make her consider living independently, but not quite enough to live on in the longer term.

The solution to the problem of what to do next was offered by the Brays, who invited Mary Ann to accompany them on a continental tour. She was exhausted in mind and body by her long stint of nursing, and this was just what she needed. At first it was thought that Edward Noel would join them, as well as another new acquaintance, J. A. Froude, who stayed at Rosehill early in June. Froude was exactly the sort of person to be courted by Bray, since he had caused a stir in February 1849 by publishing a novel, *The Nemesis of Faith*, in which the hero, a newly ordained clergyman, reads German Biblical criticism and Carlyle and loses his belief in the Thirty-Nine Articles of the Church of England, writes 'Confessions of a Sceptic', and, for good measure, falls in love with a married woman when visiting Italy.[41] Since Froude was a Fellow of Exeter College, Oxford, and the book was instantly taken to be both autobiographical (which it partly was) and immoral, he had to resign his fellowship before it was taken away from him. His notoriety was great; as he told his friend A. H. Clough on 28 February:

Oxford grows rapidly too hot for me. I have *resigned*. I was *preached* against Sunday in Chapel, denounced in Hall, and yesterday *burnt* publicly (by Sewell [Sub-Rector of the College]) before two Lectures.[42]

Froude was cast into the wilderness. Naturally, Bray took him up.

Froude's publisher was, of course, John Chapman, who sent a copy of the novel to Mary Ann. She wrote the author a note of thanks, signed only 'The Translator of Strauss', and she reviewed the book enthusiastically in the *Coventry Herald* of 16 March. Conceding that the novel has its faults, she nevertheless hails the author as 'a bright particular star', and rather boldly uses Biblical language to describe the effect of reading this troubled, sceptical work. It seems to be written, she says, by a spirit

who is transfusing himself into our souls, and so vitalizing them by his superior energy, that life, both outward and inward, presents itself to us in higher relief, in colours brightened and deepened – we seem to have been bathing in the pool of Siloam, and to have come forth seeing.

Expanding into sympathy with her fellow iconoclast, she continues:

Its trenchant remarks on some of our English conventions, its striking sketches of the dubious aspects which many chartered respectabilities are beginning to wear under the light of this nineteenth century, its suggestive hints as to the necessity of re-casting the currency of our religion and virtue that it may carry fresh and bright the stamp of the age's highest and best ideas – these have a practical bearing which may well excite the grave, perhaps the alarmed attention of some important classes among us.[43]

In the end, neither Froude nor Noel accompanied them abroad. Just Charles, Cara, and Mary Ann made the journey, setting off from Folkestone to Calais on 12 June, and thence in leisurely fashion to Paris, the south of France, Genoa, Milan, Como, Geneva, and Vevey, which they reached on 21 July.[44] Mary Ann was a difficult companion, exhausted, depressed, given to fits of weeping. She reminded Cara eleven years later how 'wretched' she had been on this trip, 'how peevish, how utterly morbid! And how kind and forbearing you were under the oppression of my company!'[45] She was reacting to the months of self-sacrifice behind her and anticipating with dread the uncertain future ahead.

But however badly she behaved, however helpless she felt, she did take a brave decision. When the Brays set out for home on 26 July, they left Mary Ann behind, having settled her in a *pension* in Geneva, the city of her dreams, where she intended to spend the winter recovering her strength and deciding what to do next. Once more a stubborn independence of spirit did battle with her fear of loneliness and insecurity, and won. What she was doing was unusual, particularly when she left her initial haven, the Campagne Plongeon with its view of the Jura mountains across Lake Geneva, to go into private lodgings in the city.[46]

She found that 'the Swiss ideas of propriety are rigid to excess', and that 'as long as people carry a Mademoiselle before their name, there is far less liberty for them on the Continent than in England'. She had thought, she told the Brays frankly on 28 August, that her 'old appearance would have been a sufficient sanction and that the very idea of impropriety was ridiculous', but was finding out her mistake.[47] Still, she could not afford to stay longer than two months at the Plongeon, and after spending the late summer months observing and describing her fellow guests as if she were preparing to write a Balzac novel – and in 1877 or thereabouts she did use some of the names of these guests in notes for a novel which was never written[48] – she was lucky enough to find a respectable family with whom to lodge for the winter.

Early in October she moved into the house of François D'Albert Durade. As she told Fanny Houghton:

He is a highly respectable artist, a man I am told of *beaucoup d'esprit*, fond of music and possessing a circle of superior friends. His wife is a very pleasing lady-like person with a most kind face. I shall be their only pensionnaire and I am to have a nice apartment with an alcove, that continental device for turning a bedroom into a sittingroom. Everything is to be provided for me except firewood for 150f. i.e. £6 per month. One of the advantages of being in Geneva is that people of a really high tone of manners and education receive pensionnaires – the fruit of the revolution I believe, which has reduced many fortunes.[49]

M. D'Albert Durade was 'not more than 4 feet high with a deformed spine – the result of an accident in his boyhood – but on this little body is placed a finely formed head', she wrote to the Brays.[50] He and his wife had musical parties, in which she joined in on the piano she hired, and she became very fond of them and their two teenage sons. By 26 October she was able to report to Sara Hennell that she was snugly settled several floors up in her apartment, where 'one feels in a downy nest high up in a good old tree'. Her dream of a high attic in a continental city had come true. 'I have always had a hankering after this sort of life and I find it was a true instinct of what would suit me.'[1]

She filled her time with walking, playing the piano, learning mathematics, and reading Voltaire, who had spent his last years in Geneva, and no doubt also her favourite Rousseau, who had been born there. Before her father's death she had begun translating Spinoza's *Tractatus Theologico-Politicus* with the idea that Chapman would publish it, but she now told the Brays she had given it up, thinking 'a true estimate of his life and system' was needed more than a translation of his works.[2] (G. H. Lewes had already done something to fill this gap; his 1843 *Westminster Review* article on Spinoza's life and works had been reprinted as a pamphlet.[3]) In December she attended a course of lectures on experimental physics at the University; otherwise she appears to have spent her eight months at Geneva chiefly in improving her health and taking stock.

She was still very thin, she told the Brays in September, and her hair was falling out, 'so how much will be left of me by next April I am afraid to imagine'. She joked imaginatively about this, but the joke had a defensive sting: 'I shall be length without breadth – quite bald and without money to buy a wig – but Mr. Hennell will think that I am fancying myself unhappy.'[4] This was a sharp reference to a comment she had received from Sara Hennell quoting her brother Charles's remark about Mary Ann having a morbid character, 'with a dwelling on yourself and a loving to think yourself unhappy'. At first she was upset by this criticism, especially as she was conscious of having tried to avoid complaining too much in her letters to the Brays and Sara.[5] Then she turned the matter over and decided that they had put her in an impossible position. If she wrote that she was lonely or unhappy, they taxed her with morbidity; if she sent only cheerful news, they accused her of forgetting them. Her forensic mind worked on the problem, and she soon took verbal revenge on all three friends:

Henceforth I tell you nothing whatever about myself, for if I speak of agreeables and say I am contented, Mr. Bray writes me word that you are all trying to forget me. If I were to tell you of disagreeables and privations and sadness, he would write that he should like me to go to hell for a few months that I might learn to be contented – also Sara would write, 'If you are unhappy now, you will be so à fortiori ten years hence.' Now since I have a decided objection to doses sent by post which upset one's digestion for a fortnight, I am determined to give you no pretext for sending me either blue pill or bitters. You shall not know whether I am well or ill, contented or discontented, warm or cold, fat or thin.[56]

Her isolated position high up in her foreign attic, poised between a past life of much frustration and under-achievement and an unknown future, encouraged her *penchant* for thorough analysis and turned it inward. Sara had worried about her state of mind and her ability to cope alone. Mary Ann replied that she did quite enough worrying on her own account. Solicitude which expressed itself in criticism was not helpful:

I want encouraging rather than warning and checking. I believe I am so constituted that I shall never be cured of any faults except by God's discipline – if human beings would but believe it, they do me most good by saying to me the kindest things truth will permit – and really I cannot hope those will be superlatively kind.[57]

Never was a more ingenious case made for special treatment, or an extreme sensitivity to criticism clothed in such self-knowing irony. She could not know it, but she was to receive just such special treatment from two men, the partner of her life and the publisher of her novels.

Meanwhile, she subjected others as well as herself to critical scrutiny. Mary Sibree's father had blamed her for unsettling both Mary and John, and Mary asked her friend to write to her not at home, but care of the Brays at Rosehill. The Evans pride and dislike of secrecy rose up at this, and Mary Ann wrote firmly to the Brays, asking them to tell Mary that 'I cannot carry on a correspondence with anyone who will not avow it.'[58] She ventured to criticize Mary for the 'strong leaven of Sibreeanism in her which I have tended to nourish by shewing a very strong interest in her':

Sibreeanism is that degree of egotism which we call bad taste but which does not reach to gross selfishness – the egotism that does not think of others, but would be very glad to do them good if it did think of them – the egotism that eats up all the bread and butter and is ready to die of confusion and distress after having done it.[59]

In these studies of her own and her friends' characters we can see her expressing a knowledge of human nature in its weaknesses and complexity which would bear abundant fruit in her novels. One thinks here, for example, of the spoilt but amiable Arthur Donnithorne in *Adam Bede*, or the child Maggie Tulliver eating up her (larger) half of the jam puff she is sharing with her brother, then struck with remorse at not having offered to swop it for the smaller portion.

Like anyone spending a period away from home and family, Mary Ann felt she was living a double life:

I possess my dearest friends and my old environment in my thoughts – and another world of novelty and beauty in which I am actually moving – and my contrariety of disposition always makes the world that lives in my thoughts the dearer of the two – the one in which I more truly dwell![60]

She did not hear much from her family. Fanny Houghton wrote occasionally, but not Isaac. Mary Ann told Fanny on 6 September that his wife Sarah had 'written to me once and I answered her immediately. I hoped to hear again from Isaac before this, but I find I must moderate my expectations.'[61] The letter from Sarah had contained bad news of Chrissey. The third oldest of her seven surviving children, Clara, had died of scarlet fever, aged seven. 'My heart aches', Mary Ann told the Brays, 'to think of Chrissey with her children ill of scarlet fever – her husband almost frantic with grief and her own heart rent by the loss of this eldest little daughter.'[62] Foleshill was on her mind too, the empty house in which she had spent her young adulthood. 'How beautiful all that Foleshill life looks now – like the distant Jura in the morning.'[63]

England had suffered from a cholera epidemic in the summer of 1849; Cara noted in her diary for September, 'cholera at Coventry'. It had spread across Europe, but Mary Ann assured her friends that 'the medical men say [Geneva] is cholera-proof'.[64] Bray had financial troubles, due to fluctuations in the ribbon trade, and indeed he was to give it up in 1856.[65] Mary Ann sympathized with him and with all her family in England, especially Chrissey, who wrote to say what a sad Christmas she had had.[66] Meanwhile, Geneva was lost in mists for two months. Mary Ann kept snug in her attic and became ever more intimate with the D'Albert Durades, who called her Minie. She was soon addressing Mme D'Albert Durade as 'maman' and being treated like her own child, 'and I am baby enough to find that a great addition to my happiness'.[67] In February 1850 she sat to M. D'Albert Durade for her portrait; he kept the original and made three copies, one of which he gave to his subject.[68] The painting shows a modest, pensive, heavy-eyed but pleasant-looking Mary Ann Evans aged thirty.

With winter over and the roads becoming passable, Mary Ann made plans to return to England in March 1850. M. D'Albert Durade accompanied her to London, the first part of the journey being by sledge across the Jura.[69]

By 30 March Mary Ann was staying with Isaac and Sarah in her childhood home at Griff. If she had thought even for a moment while in Geneva that she might settle with them as a maiden aunt – the usual step for unmarried sisters with no parental home – she soon saw the impossibility of that idea. She felt 'more of an outcast here than at Geneva', she told Fanny Houghton on 30 March. To Sara Hennell she could be more expansive. Writing from Griff on 11 April, she declared:

O the dismal weather and the dismal country and the dismal people. It was some envious demon that drove me across the Jura to come and see people who don't want me. However I am determined to sell everything I possess except a portmanteau and carpet-bag and the necessary contents and be a stranger and a foreigner on the earth for ever more.[70]

She had more or less decided to go to London, and she asked Sara to find out how much Chapman charged his lodgers at 142 Strand, where he now lived and had his publishing business.

But first she left Isaac and Sarah to stay for a week or two with Chrissey at Meriden. Here she was made more welcome than at Griff, but she was sure she could not settle down with or near any of her relations, from whom she felt more alienated than ever, now that her father was no longer alive to act as a link. She wrote somewhat bitterly to Cara:

Dear Chrissey is much kinder than any one else in the family and I am happiest with her. She is generous and sympathizing and really cares for my happiness. But I am delighted to feel that I am of no importance to any of them, and have no motive for living amongst them. I have often told you I thought Melchisedec the only happy man and I think so more than ever.[71]

Melchisedec is described in Hebrews 7:3 as being 'without father, without mother, without descent, having neither beginning of days, nor end of life'.

Her stay in Geneva had stiffened her nerve, and she was preparing to try a similar life in London. But she was in no hurry to put herself to the independence test once more. The Brays invited her to stay with them indefinitely, and by 4 May she had gratefully installed herself at Rosehill. D'Albert Durade, who was still in England, came to stay for four days. As usual, Sara Hennell came from London in July; Edward Noel was at Rosehill on a visit with his daughter at the same time. On 2 September Charles Hennell died of the tuberculosis Dr Brabant had diagnosed eight years before. The Brays went to London for the funeral.[72]

Chapman came to Rosehill in October with Robert William Mackay, author of a learned work of comparative religious history, *The Progress of the Intellect, as Exemplified in the Religious Development of the Greeks and Hebrews*. Chapman, its publisher, was keen that Mary Ann, as the transla-tor of Strauss, should review it. She agreed, and her review appeared in the January 1851 number of the *Westminster Review*. It is a piece of great interest. Of all the scholars in Britain, this unknown young woman was best equipped by expertise and temperament to appreciate Mackay's book, which may be described as an amalgam of Strauss's critical and historical method with the practical, optimistic, forward-looking approach of Hennell (and Bray) as applied to the Hebrew and Greek religions. As Mary Ann wrote in her enthusiastic review:

England has been slow to use or to emulate the immense labours of Germany in the departments of mythology and biblical criticism; but when once she does so, the greater solidity and directness of the English mind ensure a superiority of treatment.[73]

Mackay's work, though critical, is not destructive of all religious belief. Rather, it takes a progressive view of the history of thought and belief, maintaining that divine revelation is 'co-extensive with the his-tory of human development, and is perpetually unfolding itself to our widened experience and investigation, as firmament upon firmament becomes visible to us in proportion to the power and range of our exploring instruments', as Mary Ann puts it. Drawing on her knowledge of recent philosophy, of scientific treatises such as Charles Lyell's *Prin-ciples of Geology* (1830–3), and of the optimistic materialism of Bray and Hennell, she aligns herself with their progressive view of history. 'The master key to this revelation', she writes, 'is the recognition of the presence of undeviating law in the material and moral world – of that invariability of sequence which is acknowledged to be the basis of physical science, but which is still perversely ignored in our social organization, our ethics and our religion.' The problematic questions about God's purpose and the precise nature of his revelation, with all the attendant difficulties of scriptural and church creeds and practices, are put to one side by this adroit shift of emphasis to the recent history and future progress of human endeavour in the intellectual and moral spheres.

Mary Ann Evans here enunciates the philosophical standpoint from which she would never deviate. As George Eliot, she would embody imaginatively, through plot development and character analysis, the ideas expressed here about 'the inexorable law of consequences' in all branches of human knowledge and activity. Her comparative habit of intellect, in evidence here, would become ever richer and more varied in its application when she turned to writing fiction. She even exhibits the beginning of that intellectual tolerance which, though always in tension with a temperamental inclination to intolerance, is the hallmark of the novelist George Eliot. One hears the distinctive narrative voice already:

Every past phase of human development is part of that education of the race in which we are sharing; every mistake, every absurdity into which poor human nature has fallen, may be looked on as an experiment of which we may reap the benefit. A correct generalization gives significance to the smallest detail, just as the great inductions of geology demonstrate in every pebble the working of laws by which the earth has become adapted for the habitation of man.[74]

When she came to write fiction, George Eliot found she was as gifted at imagining and understanding the 'smallest details' as she undoubtedly was at comprehending the 'great inductions' of science and philosophy.

At the end of November 1850 Mary Ann was in London briefly, staying at 142 Strand, attending Chapman's soirées – at one of which she met the 'literary lady' Eliza Lynn herself – and planning to return after Christmas at Meriden with Chrissey to become one of Chapman's female boarders and, did she but know it, to begin her hesitant progress towards becoming herself the greatest 'literary lady' of the age.[75]

CHAPTER FOUR

Marian Evans in London:
142 Strand 1851–3

Mrs. Chapman's Terms

BOARD AND RESIDENCE AT 142 STRAND.

10 doors west of Somerset House.

	per wk.
Visitors occupying First class Bed rooms............	2 10 0
Visitors occupying Second class Bed rooms.........	2 5 0
For a Second Person in any of the Rooms...........	1 10 0
Fires in Bed Rooms...............................	3 6
Boot Cleaning and Attendance	3 6
Exclusive of Wines, Spirits and Malt Liquors.	

Friends introduced to dinner 3/-.

Breakfast hour ½ past 8 o'clock.
Luncheon 1 o'clock. Dinner at 6 o'clock.
Tea ½ past 8 o'clock.

So ran Susanna Chapman's advertisement for lodgers at 142 Strand. In addition to these details, her card described the house and its attractions to guests, especially Americans who might wish to 'add to their Libraries while in London'. For these John Chapman would be able to use 'his long experience as an extensive purchaser of all kinds of Old and New Books for Exportation' to help them acquire books 'on the most advantageous terms'.[1]

On the other side of the card is written:

Visitors to London are respectfully informed that the House occupied by Mr. John Chapman, Publisher, being a very large and superior one, and having been recently built for a First Class Hotel, has been furnished and the requisite arrangements effected with a view of affording to Ladies and Gentlemen either for a few days or for a longer period, the advantages of an Hotel, combined with the quiet and comfort of a Private Residence. The number of Visitors is limited to ten or twelve persons, and the Sleeping Rooms are all quite free from noise.

The central position of the House (midway between the City and West End, near the Theatres and Houses of Parliament, and within reach of the Thames Steamers and of Omnibuses to all parts of the Metropolis) affords peculiar facilities to Strangers and to all who wish to economise their time.

This central situation was especially attractive early in the year 1851, when London was preparing for its largest influx of visitors ever, the six million who would come between May and October to see the extraordinary Great Exhibition of the arts and industry of the world, for which Joseph Paxton's Crystal Palace was under construction in Hyde Park. The capital was an exciting place to be in, the most advanced city in the world. From 1 May, when the Exhibition was opened by Victoria and Albert, it would be a showcase to an admiring world.

But London was also, as Carlyle, Dickens, and Henry Mayhew in his *Morning Chronicle* articles on 'London Labour and the London Poor' (1849–50), reminded complacent readers, a city of cruel contrasts. When Mary Ann Evans arrived on 8 January, she came by train to Euston Station, which had been completed in 1837. Nearby, King's Cross Station was being built; the Strand itself was being repaved. But not far away were some of the notoriously overcrowded and insanitary slums known as 'rookeries', one of which Dickens describes with powerful rhetoric as 'Tom All-Alone's' in *Bleak House*, begun in November 1851:

It is a black, dilapidated street, avoided by all decent people; where the crazy houses were seized upon, when their decay was far advanced, by some bold vagrants, who, after establishing their own possession, took to letting them out in lodgings. Now, these tumbling tenements contain, by night, a swarm of misery. As on the ruined human wretch, vermin parasites appear, so, these ruined shelters have bred a crowd of foul existence that crawls in and out of gaps in walls and boards; and coils itself to sleep, in maggot numbers, where the rain drips in; and comes and goes, fetching and carrying fever, and sowing more evil in its very footprint than Lord Coodle and Sir Thomas Doodle, and the Duke of Foodle, and all the fine gentlemen in office, down to Zoodle, shall set right in five hundred years – though born expressly to do it.[2]

The cholera outbreak of 1849 had galvanized the authorities into action on sanitary matters. But it was many years before London had a proper sewerage and drainage system; in 1852 *Punch* carried a cartoon of a slum with the caption 'A Court for King Cholera', and in 1855 the same magazine showed a disgusting monster rising out of a filthy Thames.[3]

142 Strand backed almost directly on to the Thames, which must have been pleasant enough at that point, for John Chapman had acquired a key to a gate at the back of nearby Somerset House leading on to a private terrace, where he and his boarders could walk up and down away from the London crowds.[4]

Chapman's house was in more than one way the London equivalent of Rosehill. If Bray presided over two domestic households and humoured his wife's fondness for Edward Noel – though it appears that Cara's love was not returned, and there was almost certainly no sexual relationship between her and Noel[5] – Chapman's household combined two relationships under one roof. He and his wife Susanna, who was fourteen years older than the twenty-nine-year-old Chapman, lived with their children and the children's governess, Elisabeth Tilley. Miss Tilley was Chapman's mistress, presumably accepted in that role by Susanna Chapman.

Chapman himself was handsome, often compared to Byron, and known, according to Eliza Lynn, as 'the Raffaelle bookseller'.[6] He was at least as self-confident and optimistic as Charles Bray, though financially much more precarious. Herbert Spencer called him 'a sanguine speculative man', and William Hale White, his helper and lodger in the early 1850s, gave a psychological study of him in his *Autobiography of Mark Rutherford*. There the radical bookseller Wollaston is described as 'a curious compound, materialistic yet impulsive, and for ever drawn to some new thing'. Though holding 'liberal' notions about the relationship between the sexes, he was, according to Hale White, 'without love for anybody particularly, as far as I could see, and yet with much more general kindness and philanthropy than many a man possessing much stronger sympathies and antipathies'.[7]

Chapman kept an intimate diary at this time, in which he recorded the minutest details of his relations with his wife and his mistress. By an extraordinary chance, his diary for the year 1851 survives, having turned up on a bookstall in Nottingham in 1913 and found its way in 1930 to the library of Yale University. Though several pages have been cut out at some time, and some passages have been so heavily deleted as to be indecipherable, enough remains to give a fascinating picture of Chapman's doings at 142 Strand.[8]

The opening entry, for 1 January 1851, gives a flavour of that 'curious compound', caught between two women, and with a third, Miss Evans, about to join the household as a boarder:

Wednesday 1 January 1851
I open the record of this new year with a sad retrospect of the last one, – sad in regard to the trying difficulties I have gone through pertaining to my business, sad in regard to the wretchedness I have endured through my affections, sad that I have wasted much time and seem to have made no intellectual progress, – and saddest of all that I have made *others* sad, and have not at all profited by this year, in the very vigour of my manhood, to become a better man.[9]

Mary Ann Evans features prominently in the diary from 8 January, the day Chapman met her at Euston and took her to 142 Strand. As she had done before at a decisive moment – her sister's wedding in 1837 – she marked this important new departure in her life by changing the spelling of her name. Though for a while she continued to sign herself 'Mary Ann' to family and friends in the Midlands, varying it as before with 'Polly' and – to the Brays and Sara – 'Pollian', to Chapman and her London acquaintances she now became known by the more urbane name of Marian Evans.[10]

142 Strand was a metropolitan mecca for a wide range of progressives and free thinkers, along with a good many religious dissenters, who also used Chapman as their publisher. As Herbert Spencer later pointed out, Chapman was 'the only respectable publisher through whom could be issued books which were tacitly or avowedly rationalistic'.[11] Here Marian renewed her acquaintance with people she had met at the Brays' Midlands haven, among them Spencer, Harriet and James Martineau,

the Combes, Froude, Robert Owen, Mackay, W. B. Hodgson, who was lodging at Chapman's when she arrived, and Rufa Hennell and her derided father Dr Brabant. She also met for the first time a great many more people – mostly men – associated with radical causes and, in particular, the *Westminster Review*.

During the spring of 1851 Chapman was negotiating to buy the *Review* from W. E. Hickson, who had bought it in 1840 from its most famous proprietor, John Stuart Mill. Under the younger Mill the periodical's early reputation for influential political articles and good literary reviewing, established by James Mill and Jeremy Bentham in the 1820s, had continued. But by 1850 the *Westminster Review* was declining in sales, in interest, and in the quality of its contributors. Chapman's decision to buy was bolstered by the support, psychological and financial, of leading progressives who wanted a journalistic outlet for their views. The purchasing of the *Westminster Review* was a momentous event not only for Chapman, but also for his newest lodger, who became at once the most distinguished and the most reticent editor in the history of the journal. Negotiations between Chapman and Hickson, and Chapman's chief financial supporter, a wealthy eccentric living in Florence, Edward Lombe, were protracted, so that the deed of sale was not signed until 8 October 1851.[12] The first number to appear under the new ownership of Chapman and the (anonymous) editorship of Marian Evans was that for January 1852.

When Marian first arrived at 142 Strand early in 1851, negotiations for the *Review* had not yet begun. She came simply with the intention of making an independent life for herself, possibly by doing more translation, and, she hoped, by reviewing works of a progressive tendency in religion, politics, and history. Chapman sought to help by sending her *Westminster* article on Mackay's *Progress of the Intellect* to William Empson, editor of the *Edinburgh Review*, with the suggestion that he ask Miss Evans to review Harriet Martineau's *Letters on the Laws of Man's Nature and Development*, written with H. G. Atkinson and just published by Chapman.[13] She also hoped to review another Chapman book, *The Creed of Christendom* (1851), by William Rathbone Greg, for the *Westminster*. But this review appeared instead, thanks to Chapman, in the *Leader*, a progressive weekly paper run from offices in Wellington Street, just across the Strand from Chapman, by Thornton Hunt and G. H. Lewes.[14] She seems to have been the author also of two articles in the

Leader on the Martineau–Atkinson book, for which the witty Douglas Jerrold had proposed the motto 'There is no God, and Harriet Martineau is his prophet', as Marian gleefully reported to the Brays in February.[15]

Marian's excitement is palpable in the letters from London to her close friends in Coventry. Though she struck new acquaintances as provincial and dowdy (Eliza Lynn) or, more charitably, as 'thoughtful, somewhat severe', and wearing clothes with a 'certain quaint solemnity of cut' (Bessie Parkes[16]), she was ready, after her experience of the Brays and their circle, to absorb the even greater freedom of radical London. She attended Chapman's Friday evening soirées and was invited out by all sorts of interesting new people. Mr Mackay asked her and the Chapmans to dinner on Sunday 26 January. At his house she met Dr Neil Arnott, a prominent medical and social reformer, and the painter Charles Robert Leslie. Chapman took her to lectures by Michael Faraday at the Royal Society and by Francis William Newman at 'the Ladies' College', i.e. Bedford College, founded for women in 1849.[17] On 11 March Marian went with Chapman to see an exhibition of Turner drawings. The Unitarian Henry Crabb Robinson, the close friend of Wordsworth (who had died in April 1850), and earlier of Coleridge and Lamb, visited Chapman on 8 February and 'there saw Miss [Evans], translator of Strauss – no recommendation to me certainly, but the contrary'. 'And yet', he added, 'there was something about her which pleased me much both in look and voice.'[18] The something was probably the quiet, serious demeanour noticed by Bessie Parkes, which she characterized with some shrewdness as being 'the living incarnation of English Dissent'.[19]

Not that Marian was, or ever had been, a dissenter, as we know. But she had retained, since her loss of faith nine years previously, a moral seriousness and a disinclination to embrace atheism outright. Like Charles Hennell, she was content to leave aside questions about the nature of God, and such evidence as there is suggests that she never denied the *possibility* – no more than that – of the existence of God. Certainly her articles on Harriet Martineau's *Letters* in the *Leader* show a distinct lack of sympathy with that work's 'studiously offensive' expression of atheism, as Henry Crabb Robinson reported her describing it to him when he met her on 8 February.[20] On 1 March she wrote in the first of the two short reviews of the Martineau and Atkinson book that she admired the authors' truthfulness, while dissenting 'unequivocally' from their opinions. She states her position as that which Huxley would later define as agnostic. 'While science teaches us that we are profoundly ignorant of *causes* and *realities*', she writes, 'it becomes us not to dogmatize upon what we *cannot* know.' 'In plain language: as it is confessed we cannot have direct immediate knowledge of God, so neither can we know that he is not.'[21]

In the second article Marian dissects the *Letters*, mercilessly showing the absurdity of the authors' dogmatic insistence on atheism while they glory in a naïve alternative faith in clairvoyance and mesmerism. Harriet Martineau believed she had been cured of a life-threatening disease by the latter, and she evangelized enthusiastically – hence Jerrold's quip about her being 'no God's' prophet. 'Here is Miss Martineau,' writes Marian, 'who thinks belief in a God and immortality irrational, declaring that it is "only reasonable" to expect we may, some day, have "certain knowledge of things distant and things future"!' As for Atkinson, his absurdity is allowed to speak for itself, as when 'this new light is thrown upon Ghosts': 'When a Ghost appears on horseback and in armour,' Marian quotes Atkinson as remarking, 'we must conclude the horse and armour to have ghosts as well as men.'[22] Henry Crabb Robinson praised the review on the reasonable grounds that its author refused to join the ridicule of traditional belief so illogically expressed by Martineau and Atkinson.[23]

On 24 March Marian left 142 Strand to take refuge once more with the Brays at Rosehill, and there she stayed until 30 September. This was not how she had planned matters, but as Chapman's diary reveals, there was more drama going on in the rooms at number 142 than that concerning the negotiations to buy the *Westminster Review*. Chapman was getting into frequent hot water with his wife, and even more with the jealous and emotional Elisabeth Tilley, because of the attentions he paid to his new paying guest, Miss Evans. There may already have been some delicious flirtation away from the jealous eyes at 142 Strand when Chapman had visited Rosehill the previous October, for in his 1851 diary he takes the trouble to mention that when he met her at Euston at 3 pm on 8 January, 'her manner was friendly but formal and studied'.[24]

As had happened before, Marian found herself becoming less and less formal with a man who attracted and encouraged her. The very day after her arrival in London Chapman wrote in his diary an entry which he or someone else subsequently scored out very heavily:

Had a very painful altercation with Elisabeth the result of her groundless suspicions hence I have been in a state of unhealthy excitement all day. – She gave notice at the dinner table that she intended to leave in the Autumn. –

Miss Evans is very poorly, sat with her a short time and talked about Miss Lynn and her book.

For the next few weeks the incorrigible Chapman gave Elisabeth – and Susanna – ever more grounds for suspicion, while he protested his innocence to one and all. On 11 January he went out with Marian to choose a piano for her use; the next morning, he 'sat in Miss E's room while she played one of Mosart's [sic] Masses with much expression'. There followed 'a painful night' with his wife.[25]

In his diary Chapman indicated his sexual relations with Elisabeth Tilley by consecutively numbering the occasions he spent with her, from '1' written against the date Thursday 2 January to '66' written against Tuesday 7 October, after which he made very few entries to the end of the year. The entry for 26 August proves that his numbers refer to sexual intercourse with Elisabeth. He has added the number '53–4', and the entry reads, with the passage between ⟨ and ⟩ restored from heavy deletion:

Susanna was in an unhappy excitable mood, and made Miss Evans the subject on which she gave vent to it, and hence I had a miserable morning, ⟨ supplemental to Elisabeth's upbraidings before breakfast that I was not kind to her and that every time last night I met her coldly the dear! ⟩[26]

Detective work on the diary further reveals that Chapman also regularly noted when Elisabeth was menstruating, using the symbol +. At these times he appears to have returned to his wife, as he did on Sunday 12 January, after listening to Miss Evans playing Mozart.[27]

A week after this, the diary for Saturday 18 and Sunday 19 January indicates that he may have embarked on a sexual relationship with Marian. In two deleted notes he wrote cryptically 'M. P.M.' for 18 January and 'M. A.M.' for 19 January, noting also on the 18th that 'this has been a week of much painful experience'. We cannot be sure precisely what Chapman's note signifies, but in the context of his obsessive recording of his relations with Elisabeth, and in view of the subsequent events in the household, it appears likely that he and Marian came together briefly during that weekend in January.[28]

Nothing in Marian's remaining letters and papers indicates the turmoil at 142 Strand. Her letters to the Brays are full of news about visits to lectures and the theatre, and to Chapman's activities in connection with the *Westminster Review*, but of course she would not confide even to them her feelings for Chapman, let alone whether she had become sexually involved with him. Our only source of information is his diary, which though unusually explicit, was also rather cryptic, as well as having been tampered with at crucial points.

We therefore cannot know for sure what went on, but it is worth pausing to note that when Marian came to write about the relations between the sexes in her novels, she paid close and sympathetic attention to the difficulties and confusions of her characters' emotional lives. Maggie Tulliver loves both Philip Wakem and Stephen Guest, though in different ways, her love for the sensitive, crippled Philip being partly dictated by pity and that for Stephen being, against her conscious will, a physical, instinctual attraction. For much of the course of *Middlemarch*, Dorothea is unconscious of her growing sexual feelings for Will Ladislaw, though author and readers recognize the symptoms well enough through repeated references to Will's attractive smile and Dorothea's thirst to see him.

Susanna Chapman and Elisabeth Tilley certainly thought Chapman and Marian were having an affair in the early weeks of 1851. His diary reveals that he spent ever more time in her room; soon she was teaching him German, as well as sharing musical moments with him. Tiffs occurred about which of the three women should accompany him on walks in the park or to plays and lectures in the evenings. On 22 January Chapman ruefully recorded a bad, but not untypical, day of emotional tension among the four chief players in the drama – himself, Susanna, Elisabeth ('E'), and Miss Evans (sometimes referred to as 'M'):

Invited Miss Evans to go out after breakfast, did not get a decisive answer, E. afterwards said if I did go, she should be glad to go, – I then invited Miss Evans again telling her E. would go whereupon she declined rather rudely, Susanna being willing to go out, and neither E. nor S. wishing to walk far I proposed they should go a short distance without me, which E. considered an insult from me and reproached me in no measured terms accordingly, and heaped upon me suspicions and accusations I do not in any way deserve. I was very severe and harsh, said things I was sorry for afterwards, and we became reconciled in the Park.

Miss Evans apologized for her rudeness tonight, which roused all E.'s jealousy again, and consequent bitterness.[29]

By 18 February, after other events which were recorded but at some point cut out of the diary, Elisabeth and Susanna had decided to take joint action. As the diary records, with the matter between ⟨ and ⟩ restored from deletion:

I presume with the view of arriving at a more friendly understanding S. & E. had a long talk this morning which resulted in their comparing notes on the subject of my intimacy with Miss Evans, and their arrival at the conclusion ⟨that we are completely in love with each other. – E. being intensely jealous herself said all she could to cause S. to look from the same point of view, which a little incident (her finding me with my hand in M's) had quite prepared her for. E. betrayed my trust and her own promise. S. said to me that if ever I went to M's room again she will write to Mr Bray, and say that she dislikes her.⟩[30]

Some more skirmishing occurred, until Marian agreed to leave, which she did on 24 March, Chapman accompanying her to the station. Chapman recorded their final conversation in his blithe way:

M. departed today, I accompanied her to the railway. She was very sad, and hence made me feel so. She pressed me for some intimation of the state of my feelings, – ⟨I told her that I felt great affection for her, but that I loved E. and S. also, though each in a different way.⟩ At this avowal she burst into tears. I tried to comfort her, and reminded her of the dear friends and pleasant home she was returning to, – but the train whirled her away very very sad.[31]

The farcical aspect for observers of this affair, which all the parties themselves naturally took very seriously, is compounded by the fact that the *dramatis personae* were simultaneously involved in a critical judgement of a novel by Eliza Lynn, *Realities*, which she had offered to Chapman. On 11 January Chapman read in this bold portrait of the contemporary London theatre world with its loose morals 'a love scene which is warmly and vividly depicted, with a tone and tendency which I entirely disapprove'. He adds in his diary account, 'Miss Evans concurs with me, and Elisabeth and Susanna are most anxious I should not publish the work.'[32]

Miss Lynn would not take his no for an answer, whereupon Chapman sent her with her manuscript to Thornton Hunt, who told her 'it would be best for her welfare and reputation to throw the M.S. in the fire'.[33] This was rich, considering that Hunt, as well as being the political editor of the *Leader*, was also known in the Chapman circle to be the father of a child by his friend Lewes's wife Agnes. (This was Edmund Lewes, born in April 1850. Hunt was soon to be the father of a second child with Agnes – Rose, born in October 1851 – with two more children following in 1853 and 1857.[34])

But Chapman was untroubled by recognition of any discrepancy between his and his associates' professions of principle and their actions. Being, as Hale White recalled, a 'curious compound' of the impulsive and the calculating, he reckoned that precisely because he was 'the publisher of works notable for their intellectual freedom', it 'behoves me to be exceedingly careful of the *moral* tendency of all I issue'.[35] He did not publish *Realities*, which Eliza Lynn reluctantly took elsewhere.

Back in Coventry, Marian presumably gave her friends some explanation for her precipitate departure. There is no mention of the exciting events at 142 Strand in her surviving letters, and the journal she had begun to keep at Geneva later had the forty-six pages covering the years 1849 to 1854 cut out and destroyed by a solicitous John Cross.[36] From Coventry Marian wrote regularly to Chapman, sending letters about his negotiations for the *Westminster Review* which have survived and notes about more personal matters which have not.[37] That her pride was hurt is shown by one or two waspish remarks in letters which have not disappeared, such as the sarcastic comment on 9 May, when Susanna Chapman returned from a visit to Cornwall, having left 142 Strand to Chapman and Elisabeth for the duration: 'I should think you are right glad to have Mrs. Chapman again to enliven you all.'[38]

Chapman visited Rosehill for two weeks on 27 May, followed a few days later by Thornton Hunt, whose wife was already on a visit there.[39] Chapman 'found Miss Evans shy calm and affectionate'. On Friday 30 May the two of them visited Leamington, where Marian called on her sister Fanny, then Kenilworth Castle, where they talked of personal matters. Chapman's record of the outing suggests that he indicated that, however close they may have become at 142 Strand at the beginning of the year, Marian was not really physically attractive to him:

As we rested on the grass, I remarked on the wonderful and mysterious embodiment of all the elements of nature which man and woman jointly present. I dwelt also on the incomprehensible mystery and witchery of beauty. My words jarred upon her and put an end to her enjoyment. Was it from a consciousness of her own want of beauty? She wept bitterly.

By 5 June, when they had another walk together, they had 'made a solemn and holy vow which henceforth will bind us to the right', as Chapman noted. 'She is a noble being.'[40] She certainly was, since all the sacrifice was on her part.

While Chapman was with the Brays, the discussion was primarily about the *Westminster Review* and how to raise financial support and enlist good writers for the new management. It was also decided that Marian should edit the *Review*, though this fact was to be kept a secret from as many people as possible, probably at her request. She wrote to him the day he left, 9 June:

With regard to the secret of the Editorship, it will perhaps be the best plan for you to state, that for the present *you* are to be regarded as the responsible person, but that you employ an Editor in whose literary and general ability you confide.[41]

Because of her unfortunate start at 142 Strand, Chapman had to work hard over the summer to get Elisabeth and Susanna to agree that Marian could return in the autumn. As late as 26 August, Susanna 'made Miss Evans the subject on which she gave vent' to her unhappiness, as we have seen.[42] Marian was already showing what an invaluable adviser and editor she would be. Her intellectual maturity and tact are evident in her letters from June 1851 steering Chapman through difficulties with Hickson, who was slow to relinquish his hold on the *Westminster Review*, with J. S. Mill, whom Chapman hoped to induce to write for the periodical once more, and with James Martineau, who was fearful that the journal would become atheistic in its principles. She had clearly got the measure of Chapman's deficiencies of character and ability, for she continually advised caution and plain dealing, neither of which came naturally to him.[43]

In late July Marian went with Cara on a visit to Bishop's Teignton in

Devon, where Edward Noel lived with his children. From there she told Chapman she would do the regular summaries of new English literature in the *Westminster*, and agreed that 'Lewes would be likely to do an article on Modern Novelists very well.'[44] Marian and Lewes had not yet become acquainted but she knew his reputation as the chief critic of the *Leader*.

Marian and Cara passed through London on their way home from Devon, staying for a few days in Kensington with Mary Marshall, Cara's cousin. Chapman met them at the station and took Susanna to see them that evening. He extracted a promise from both Susanna and Elisabeth to allow Marian to return for the winter as his professional colleague. On the evening of 15 August Marian 'made a call' on Susanna to mend the breach.[45] She had spent the day with the Brays, Sara Hennell, and Chapman himself at the Great Exhibition in Hyde Park. The next day the 'Coventry party' returned home after a second visit to the Crystal Palace.[46] It was arranged that Marian would return to London at the end of September.

In late August George Combe and his wife made one of their regular summer visits to Rosehill. It was now that Combe had his private conversation with Bray about the latter's sexual activities, and he phrenologized Bray, finding him to have 'great Combativeness and Destructiveness and very deficient Concentrativeness'. Miss Evans struck him as 'the most extraordinary person of the party' with her many languages, her 'very large brain', her 'love of approbation' and large organ of Concentrativeness. He judged her to be 'near 40 apparently', though she was not quite thirty-one. In his discussions with her Combe found that she showed 'great analytic power and an instinctive soundness of judgment'. She was, in fact, 'the ablest woman whom I have seen'.[47] Combe agreed, perhaps because he had such admiration for Chapman's new editor, to become 'the first subscriber and the first advertizer [*sic*] to the Review' under Chapman's management.[48] By December Combe was wisely advising Chapman 'to use Miss Evans's tact and judgment as an aid to your own'. The phrenological vocabulary proved rather useful for telling Chapman the otherwise unpalatable truth that Marian Evans was his intellectual superior:

She has certain organs large in her brain which are not so fully developed in yours, and she will judge more correctly of the influence upon other persons of what you write and do, than you will do yourself.[49]

On 20 September 1851, shortly before Marian returned to London, her review of Greg's *Creed of Christendom* appeared in the *Leader*. She was able to respond warmly to this work of 'the New Reformation', since Greg seemed to her to be invigorating English Protestantism not by ignoring the work of historical critics of the Bible but by meeting it honestly and earnestly. She compares Greg to her old friend Hennell as a 'sensible, educated layman' who cannot compete as a scholar with learned Germans like Strauss or Schleiermacher, but can summarize 'salient facts and arguments' gathered from such critics for that class of readers which is 'struggling towards free religious thought amidst the impediments of critical ignorance and early artificial associations'.[50] Chapman, who had placed the review in the *Leader* for Marian, noted on 23 September that the paper's co-editor Lewes 'called in the afternoon to express his high opinion of Miss Evans' Article'.[51]

By the end of September Marian was back in London, and was soon writing to the Brays about the new people she was meeting in the course of seeking out with Chapman supporters and contributors for the first number of the *Westminster* under their joint management. One was Robert Chambers, the Edinburgh publisher and anonymous author of *Vestiges of Creation* (1844), a layman's book suggesting some of the evolutionary conclusions to which Darwin would give authority in his *Origin of Species* in 1859. Another was the famous Swedish novelist Frederika Bremer, who came to stay at Chapman's house early in October. Dr Brabant was there too, and 'very politely' took Marian to the Crystal Palace, the theatre, and the 'Overland Route', a moving diorama in Regent Street of the Overland Route to India.[52]

On Friday 3 October at Chapman's soirée she met Herbert Spencer, sub-editor of the *Economist*, which had its office just across the Strand from Chapman's house, and author of a book published by Chapman in 1850, *Social Statics, or the Conditions Essential to Human Happiness specified, and the First of Them Developed*. Spencer himself characterized the book as 'a kind of Natural-History ethics'. It has something in common with J. S. Mill's more famous *On Liberty* (1859), since it sets out the principle that 'every man is free to do whatsoever he wills provided he does not infringe the equal freedom of any other man'. And it embraces an evolutionary view of social and moral questions, using the language of organization, adaptation, and modification in the social sphere which Darwin was to make famous in his account of the origin and development of animal species.

'Man', writes Spencer, 'has been, and is, undergoing modifications of nature which fit him for the social state, by making conformity to these conditions [i.e. the laws of life at large and increase in numbers] spontaneous.' He goes so far as to draw the logical conclusion that the freedom he defines should be 'as fully recognized in women as in men', but stops short of suggesting they should be given completely equal political rights, since they cannot compare with men in the important function of defending the country in times of war.[13] His argument, outdated and cautious though it may seem now, was distinctly progressive in 1851, when the majority of *men* still had no vote.

Spencer was the most serious and weighty of the radical thinkers among whom Marian now moved. He was the same age as she was, and came from a somewhat similar background, having been born in Derby into a serious, middle-class but not wealthy family of nonconformist – in this case Wesleyan – background, the only surviving child of nine born to his parents. He had tried teaching, like his father, and had become an engineer, working on the extension of the Midlands railway network in the 1840s, then coming to London in 1848 to work on the *Economist*. By no means an enthusiast by temperament, he nevertheless became at least temporarily a 'believer' in phrenology, having attended lectures by one of the two instigators of the 'science'. Johann Kaspar Spurzheim, disciple and colleague of Franz Joseph Gall, had visited Derby in 1830 or so, as Spencer recalled. In 1842 Spencer had his head examined by an English phrenologist, J. Q. Rumball, who pronounced his organ of Combativeness to be 'rather full', his Love of Approbation large, his Self-esteem very large, but unfortunately his Wit and Amativeness only moderate.[14] In confirmation of the diagnosis he had written to a friend in April 1851 that, at nearly thirty-one, he was still a bachelor and had 'pretty well given up the idea' of marriage.[15]

Spencer had recently become a close friend of G. H. Lewes, who was becoming dissatisfied with the arrangement he had originally encouraged and condoned between his wife Agnes and Thornton Hunt. Agnes was to give birth to her second child by Hunt on 21 October; she already had three sons by Lewes and one by Hunt. Lewes remembered this period of his life as 'a very dreary *wasted*' one, and Spencer became a welcome companion on walking tours and in the literary *salons* they both frequented.[56] Spencer described his new friend in a letter to his father of 3 October 1851:

Lewes is about 34 or 35, of middle height, with light brown hair, deeply marked with small-pox, and rather worn-looking. He is very versatile. He is a successful novelist and dramatist, writes poems occasionally, is an actor, a good linguist, writes for the reviews, translates for the stage, is a musical critic, and is, you may suppose, deeply read in philosophy. He is a very pleasant companion. He is married and has three children.[57]

Lewes reviewed *Social Statics* admiringly in the *Leader*. Since both he and Spencer were obvious candidates to contribute to Chapman's *Westminster* – indeed Lewes had written articles for it since 1840, on subjects as diverse as French drama, Shelley, and Spinoza[58] – it was inevitable that Marian would soon meet Lewes too. She did, on 6 October, when she and Chapman called on the bookseller William Jeffs in the Burlington Arcade to ask him to lend French books for review.[59] 'I was introduced to Lewes the other day in Jeff's [*sic*] shop', Marian wrote to Bray on 8 October, adding in allusion to his famed ugliness, 'a sort of miniature Mirabeau in appearance.'[60]

Marian's life was full of excitement now. On 10 October she walked to Chelsea with Chapman and waited for him while he called on Carlyle in Cheyne Row, hoping to get the great man to contribute to the *Review*. Carlyle wrote to Robert Browning in Paris, describing Chapman in his curious insulting yet indulgent way as a 'Publisher of Liberalisms, "Extinct Socinianisms" [i.e. Unitarianism], and notable ware of that kind, in the Strand', 'really a meritorious, productive kind of man, did he well know his road in these times'. Chapman had told Carlyle he had 'capital "for four years' trial"', he says; an able Editor (name can't be given), and such an array of "talent" as was seldom gathered before'. The author of *Past and Present* wished him well but regretted that he could not help by contributing himself.[61]

Even without Carlyle, the *Westminster Review* for January 1852 did indeed include articles written by some of the most talented authors of the day. Lewes did one, though not on modern novels; James Martineau wrote on 'The Ethics of Christendom', Froude on Mary Stuart, F. W. Newman on French and German theories of legislation, the naturalist

Edward Forbes on shellfish, W. R. Greg on 'The Relations between Employers and Employed', and the Unitarian William J. Fox on 'Representative Reform', the essay which opened the volume. All the articles appeared anonymously, as did Marian Evans's contribution of short reviews of recent works in the section headed 'Contemporary Literature of England'.

The day after Chapman's visit to Carlyle, when his 'able Editor' stayed outside to preserve her anonymity, she went to the final ceremony of the Great Exhibition, where 'God Save the Queen' was sung by fifty thousand voices. She reported to Sara Hennell that Carlyle had amused Chapman by complaining that the Exhibition brought to his door a succession of bores, 'who present themselves by twos and threes in his study, saying "Here we are" etc. etc.'. Her buoyant mood is shown by the trenchancy with which she describes Greg's response to her review in the *Leader* of his book:

> Mr. Greg thought the Review 'well done, and in a kindly spirit,' – but thought there was not much in it – dreadful true, since there was only all his book. I think he did not like the apology for his want of theological learning – which however was just the thing most needed, for the Eclectic [*Eclectic Review*] trips him up on that score.[62]

Marian was at last in her element. It suited her to be meeting the leading liberal thinkers of the day, most of whom shared her views on religion and politics, but none of whom was – as she saw clearly enough – superior to her in intelligence or knowledge. She revelled in her backroom role of adviser and organizer, knowing that she could boss Chapman to good effect, and finding, too, that she had a store of tact which she could use successfully on Chapman and others. When he toyed with the idea of contributing an article himself to the *Westminster*, she adroitly argued him out of it. 'Miss Evans thinks I should lose power and influence by becoming a writer in the Westminster Review,' he wrote docilely in his diary on 21 September, 'and could not then maintain that dignified relation with the various contributors that she thinks I may do otherwise.'[63] It was actually she, not he, who maintained the dignity of the relationship she had so ingeniously invoked, as the three-way correspondence between her, Chapman, and such important but prickly contributors as Combe over the next few months was to prove.

Her life, though gratifyingly busy, was not composed entirely of work during the last months of 1851. On her thirty-second birthday, 22 November, Spencer invited her and Chapman to go to the theatre to see *The Merry Wives of Windsor*. In a grouping which cannot help being intriguing to us now, the three friends shared a box with Lewes, who was reviewing the play for the *Leader* in his *persona* of gay-dog bachelor and *bon viveur* 'Vivian'. Marian told Cara Bray that Lewes had 'helped to carry off the dolorousness of the play' by a running commentary of irreverent remarks.[64] The young woman who had so often been in despair about her future – emotional, social, and intellectual – thus sat thoroughly enjoying a bad performance of one of Shakespeare's lesser plays in the company of the three men who had been, or were shortly to be, in the closest possible relation to her in all three respects.

After spending the New Year with the Brays, Marian returned to London to hear what everyone thought of the January 1852 number of the *Westminster*. Marian's own contribution on this occasion went unnoticed, being merely the short reviews section. But a George Eliot watcher can spot her characteristic turns of phrase in the enthusiastic review of Carlyle's new work, *The Life of John Sterling* (1851). She sympathizes with Carlyle's motives in writing the life of his late friend, a man who had resigned his curacy on grounds of ill health and had become alienated from the Church altogether on reading Strauss. Another friend, Archdeacon Julius Charles Hare, had published in 1848 a biography of Sterling which stopped at the point of most interest to Carlyle (and Marian Evans), namely the moment when Sterling left the Church of England. Carlyle felt it his duty to put the record straight.

'Under the rich lights of Carlyle's mind', wrote Marian, the 'comparatively tame scenes and incidents gather picturesqueness and interest'. She castigates Hare for suggesting Sterling might have avoided his breach with orthodoxy, finding a characteristic analogy for this supposition of Hare, who apparently thought, she says, 'like that friend of [Dr] Arnold's who recommended a curacy as the best means of clearing up Trinitarian difficulties, that "orders" are a sort of spiritual backboard which, by dint of obliging a man to look as if he were strait [*sic*], end by making him so'.[65]

Chapman's financial situation in January was precarious, and got worse before it got better. In May Marian told Cara that 'the immediate difficulty' was to find enough money to pay the contributors to the July number – 'a sum of £250!'[66] The journal's chief backer, Edward Lombe, had died in March, and George Combe's support had to be kept up because he knew several men with large purses. Indeed, one of these, a Mr Bastard, saved matters in the short term in June with a gift of £60 to pay for articles.[67] Since January Chapman had been involved in his argument with the Booksellers' Association, which cancelled his ticket allowing him to buy books at a discount provided he did not in his turn sell the books on at a further discount. His stance was brave and determined, culminating in the great meeting of 4 May, when Dickens took the chair and the Booksellers' Association sustained a moral defeat, though Chapman's own bookselling business suffered throughout the affair.[68]

In spite of some ill health, mainly in the form of headaches, Marian went on expanding her circle of acquaintance, attending parties and meetings as well as wooing Combe and soothing his anxiety about the *Westminster*'s reputation in some quarters for atheism.[69] She met Harriet Martineau once more in January 1852, and found her 'kind and cordial', but disliked her 'looks and gestures'. Some of the European exiles from the aftermath of the 1848 revolutions came to 142 Strand. Pierre Leroux and Louis Blanc, two of the French revolutionaries, were in London, as was the veteran campaigner for Italian unification, Giuseppe Mazzini, who agreed to write on European 'Freedom v. Despotism' for the April number of the *Westminster Review*.[70] In February Marian attended a meeting at St Martin's Hall of the Association for the Abolition of the Taxes on Knowledge, where she heard the Anti-Corn Law agitator Richard Cobden; in March she went to a meeting of the Society of the Friends of Italy to hear Mazzini speak.[71]

Though Marian had not taken to Harriet Martineau, she did make some new female friends to add to all the male acquaintances she had accumulated. Joseph Parkes's daughter Bessie, who had met her the previous year at Rosehill, called and began a friendship with Marian, who was naturally invited to dinners and parties at Mr Parkes's home in Savile Row, where she impressed the men with her intelligence. 'Miss Parkes is a dear, ardent, honest creature, and I hope we shall be good friends', she told the Brays and Sara Hennell on 2 February.[72] Bessie, for her part, wrote to her friend and fellow feminist Barbara Leigh Smith on 6 March:

I don't know whether you will like Miss Evans. At least I know you will *like* her for her large unprejudiced mind, her complete superiority to most women. But whether you or I should ever *love* her, as a friend, I don't know at all.

On 27 March Bessie reported that she and Marian had an 'instinctive affection' for one another. 'As I know her better, the harsh heavy look of her face softens into a very beautiful tender expression.'[73] In due course Barbara met Marian Evans, and after a slow start became an even closer, and more lasting, friend than Bessie.

Clementia Taylor, wife of the radical politician and silk merchant Peter Taylor, who was chairman of the Society of the Friends of Italy, was another new acquaintance to whom Marian was attracted. She began to visit Clementia at her home in Sydenham in south London, and wrote rather confidingly to her on 27 March:

You know how sad one feels when a great procession has swept by one, and the last notes of its music have died away, leaving one alone with the fields and sky. I feel so about life sometimes. It is a help to read such a life as Margaret Fuller's. How inexpressibly touching that passage from her journal – 'I shall always reign through the intellect, but the life! the life! O my God! shall that never be sweet?' I am thankful, as if for myself, that it was sweet at last.[74]

A memoir of Margaret Fuller's life had just been published (with Emerson as one of the editors), telling the story of the American transcendentalist and feminist who had settled in Italy, living in hiding with her husband, the Marquis Ossoli, a follower of Mazzini. She and her husband and their child, born in 1848 a year before their marriage, had been drowned in 1850 while on their way to America. Margaret Fuller was a free spirit with whom Marian felt an affinity. Interestingly, Henry Crabb Robinson also read the memoir of her life, and commented in his diary for 12 February 1852:

These comet like phænomena are less alarming under an American than an English sky. Wild experiments are less offensive, where what is fixed is still a sort of novelty. No English woman known as a writer has yet borne testimony to her admiration of George Sand as Margaret Fuller does.[75]

His new acquaintance Miss Evans of the *Westminster Review* would be the Englishwoman to bear such testimony to her admiration of George

Sand and Margaret Fuller in due course; she would also be the 'comet-like phænomenon' to try in her own life what Crabb Robinson thought 'wild experiments'.

Perhaps inevitably, Marian was finding as she made new friends she could confide in that she needed Cara and Sara less and less in their old capacity as comforters. They began to be jealous of her exciting London life and her burgeoning new friendships. She rebuked Sara on 21 April for fancying that there was 'any change in my affection for you', repeating that 'it is impossible that I should ever love two women better than I love you and Cara':

Indeed it seems to me that I can never love any so well, and it is certain that I can never have any friend – not even a husband – who would supply the loss of those associations with the past which belong to you.[76]

The casual mention of a husband here is the second such remark; on 30 March Marian had written teasingly to Cara, 'I had two offers last night – not of marriage, but of music – which I find it impossible to resist.' One was an invitation from Herbert Spencer to hear *William Tell* at Covent Garden, the other a request from Bessie Parkes to accompany her to Exeter Hall to hear Haydn's *Creation*.[77]

Marian *was* thinking of marriage, and during April she thought Herbert Spencer was too. As he himself recalled in his *Autobiography*, he and she were seen so often in one another's company that spring, walking together on the terrace behind Somerset House and in the parks, and going to opera and theatre, for which Spencer often had press tickets, that soon 'there were reports that I was in love with her, and that we were about to be married'.[78] But Spencer was not in love with her. He admired her more than any other woman he knew, as he told his friend Edward Lott. 'I am very frequently at Chapman's', he wrote on 23 April 1852, 'and the greatness of her intellect conjoined with her womanly qualities and manner, generally keep me by her side most of the evening.'[79]

Marian showed once more that innocence of conventionalities which Chapman had noted in her, and embarrassed Spencer with her ardour. On 21 April she replied to a note he had sent which had clearly been intended to dampen the ardour; her pride and intelligence came once more to her aid:

Dear Friend

Not for the 'satisfaction of breaking a conventionalism', but for the sake of hearing Le Prophète and yet more of hearing it with you, I accept your kind proposal. I am not sure that I understand your note, or rather, I am sure that I do not. But prior to all further explanation, or, if you wish, to the exclusion of it, let me assure you that I never imputed to you an ungenerous thought. I felt disappointed rather than 'hurt' that you should not have sufficiently divined my character to perceive how remote it is from my habitual state of mind to imagine that any one is falling in love with me.[80]

A few days after she wrote in this way to Spencer, Marian told the Brays she had been once more to Covent Garden 'with my "excellent friend Herbert Spencer", as Lewes calls him. We have agreed that we are not in love with each other, and that there is no reason why we should not have as much of each other's society as we like.'[81] But she could not help wishing for more than his friendship and company, which was now constant, with their collaboration with Chapman over the Booksellers' Association meeting, frequent visits to the theatre, and in June an outing to Kew Gardens on a 'scientific expedition'. Her comment to Sara Hennell shows that her critical faculty and her wit were not in abeyance despite the intensity of her feelings. Spencer, she wrote, 'has all sorts of theories about plants – I should have said a *proof*-hunting expedition. Of course, if the flowers didn't correspond to the theories, we said, "*tant pis pour les fleurs*".'[82]

The Brays picked up her indirect hints and suggested inviting Spencer to Rosehill at the same time during the autumn as Marian was due to visit them. This was indeed what happened; Cara Bray's diary shows that on 26 October 'Marian came', and on 30 October 'Herbert Spencer came'. But by the time they were all together in Coventry it was too late for the Brays to try out their matchmaking skills. In July Marian had gone on holiday alone to Broadstairs, from where she sent Spencer some extraordinary letters, so extraordinary that he, mindful of her reputation and even more mindful of his own, went to inordinate lengths to keep them secret, though he did not, thank goodness, destroy them.[83]

The heat in July 1852 was a talking point in London. Part VI of *Bleak House*, published in August, evokes the actual conditions in London's Inns of Court that summer: 'It is the hottest long vacation known for many years'; 'in Mr. Krook's court, it is so hot that the people turn their houses inside out, and sit in chairs upon the pavement'.[84] Marian's first letter to Spencer from Broadstairs, written about 8 July, alludes to the heat she has left behind in the city, and jokes boldly about Spencer's contrasting coldness. Was ever another letter written by a woman to a man showing such frankness, pride, humility, vulnerability, commanding power, and wit?

The letter opens as follows:

Dear Friend

No credit to me for my virtues as a refrigerant. I owe them all to a few lumps of ice which I carried away with me from that tremendous glacier of yours. I am glad that Nemesis, lame as she is, has already made you feel a little uneasy in my absence, whether from the state of the thermometer or aught else. We will not inquire too curiously whether you long most for my society or for the sea-breezes. If you decided that I was not worth coming to see, it would only be of a piece with that generally exasperating perspicacity of yours which will not allow one to humbug you. (An agreeable quality, let me tell you, that capacity of being humbugged. Don't pique yourself on not possessing it.) But seriously and selfishness apart, I would like you to have the enjoyment of this pleasant place ... Do come on Saturday, if you would like it. There is a nice hotel where you can have a bed, and shant I be proud to do hospitalities once more? I think the Boat is better than the Excursion train – in spite of the shorter time of the latter. The heat and dust stretch 3 hours into 6.

Marian adds that she has been 'dreaming away' her time at Broadstairs. Risking a joke about her appearance, she says she will 'soon be on an equality, in point of sensibility, with the star-fish and the sea-egg – perhaps you will wickedly say, I certainly want little of being a *Medusa*' (i.e. a jellyfish, with allusion to the legendary monster which was so ugly that those who looked at it were turned to stone).[85]

Spencer did visit on Saturday 10 July, when we can assume that he made it absolutely clear that he did not love her. She then wrote again, conscious that she was doing something unusual, but unrepentant on that score:

I want to know if you can assure me that you will not forsake me, and that you will always be with me as much as you can and share your thoughts and feelings with me. If you become attached to some one else, then I must die, but until then I could gather courage to work and make life valuable, if only I had you near me. I do not ask you to sacrifice anything – I would be very good and cheerful and never annoy you. But I find it impossible to contemplate life under any other conditions ... Those who have known me best have always said, that if ever I loved any one thoroughly my whole life must turn upon that feeling, and I find they said truly. You curse the destiny which has made the feeling concentrate itself on you – but if you will only have patience with me you shall not curse it long. You will find that I can be satisfied with very little, if I am delivered from the dread of losing it.

I suppose no woman ever before wrote such a letter as this – but I am not ashamed of it, for I am conscious that in the light of reason and true refinement I am worthy of your respect and tenderness, whatever gross men or vulgar-minded women might think of me.[86]

Spencer's reply to this dramatic yet proudly subdued appeal, like all his letters to Marian, has disappeared. But it is clear that he could not meet her unusual request, except the part which pleaded with him not to marry someone else. He remained a bachelor all his long life. But to the credit of both, they remained good friends after this unfortunate episode. Marian wrote once more from Broadstairs at the end of July, inviting him to visit her there again and promising him 'such companionship as there is in me, untroubled by painful emotions'.[87]

Marian stayed on in her seaside lodgings. She must have seemed even more unorthodox here than in London, for it was certainly not usual for respectable unmarried women to take lodgings or holidays alone. As late as 1869, when Trollope published his novel about a contemporary marriage, *He Knew He Was Right*, he has one of his characters, Nora Rowley, propose to go into lodgings for a week or two. She is soon persuaded out of taking this reckless 'Bohemian' step by her solicitous mother.[88] And much later still, H. G. Wells's Ann Veronica, in his 1909 novel of that name, creates a tremendous stir when she decides to leave her father's suburban home for lodgings in London. It is likely that Marian relied, as she had hoped to do in Geneva, on her serious demeanour and her looking older than she was to save her from social embarrassment.

At the same time as she was negotiating emotionally with Spencer, Marian was sending helpful advice to Chapman, whose finances were in a very bad way and who was losing the confidence of important supporters like Combe.[89] She told Bray on 14 July that she was 'surprized that you and [Combe] think so ill of Mr. C's affairs. My impression was that the business was in a thoroughly promising condition apart from the need of temporary assistance in capital.'[90] Bray persuaded Combe not to withdraw his support, appealing to Combe's trust in Miss Evans's abilities rather than Chapman's.[91] With Combe and Bray mollified, the *Westminster Review* carried on.

Marian's stay in Broadstairs lasted till 28 August. During her two months there she was visited by the Brays. After they had left, she apologized to Cara for having been 'irritable and out of sorts', and said she now felt ' "plucky", a word which I propose to substitute for happy, as more truthful'.[92] Her letters have a subdued tone in the aftermath of the Spencer affair. A rare surviving letter to a member of her family, Fanny Houghton, of 22 August professes her affection but declares the difficulty of having 'positive communication with you' since 'I live in a world of cares and joys, so remote from the one in which we used to sympathize with each other.'[93]

Even as she resignedly withdrew her affections from Spencer, she began to see more of Lewes and to write about his doings to the Brays. She was aware that they did not like Lewes, finding him probably too free-thinking and free-living even for their liberal but cautious taste. After all, Bray's illegitimate family was kept a secret from the world at large, whereas the Hunt–Lewes marital arrangements were the talk of London. And Lewes had little time for what he saw as a prevarication in religious questions such as that which prevailed in the Bray–Hennell circle. There is no evidence that he had ever held a religious belief; certainly no heart-searching, painful conversion such as Marian's, or cautious sentimental positioning such as Cara's, had occurred in his life. He came of a theatrical family, had never known his father, was brought up in London, Jersey, and France by his mother and hated stepfather, and had made his own way into London literary life as a young man in the late 1830s. His background was as different as possible from Marian Evans's and the Brays'.[94]

Marian saw him frequently with Chapman and Spencer, on *Westminster Review* or *Leader* business and at the theatre. She liked him, though in June 1852, when she had hoped to come to an engagement with Spencer under the acacia tree at Rosehill and it appeared Lewes too might be a guest, she had told Charles Bray she would rather he did not invite Lewes when she was there – 'not that I don't like him – *au contraire* – but I want nothing so Londonish when I go to enjoy the fields and hedgerows'.[95]

Still, she was rather fascinated by him. On 2 September she wrote to Sara Hennell from the Strand, defending Lewes roundly against Harriet

Martineau's jeering at his *Leader* articles on the social philosopher Auguste Comte – Harriet had begun translating Comte's *Philosophie Positive* in June, having first read about the positivist philosopher in a book by Lewes himself, his *Biographical History of Philosophy* (1845–6).[96] Marian wrote to Bray on 18 September that she was 'in better spirits than I have generally been since I came back', adding casually, 'Lewes called on me the other day and told me of a conversation with Prof. Owen.'[97] Lewes was engaged in scientific study as preparation for a biography of Goethe he was writing, and frequently visited Richard Owen in his laboratory at this time. His impressive article on 'Goethe as a Man of Science' appeared in the *Westminster Review* in October 1852.

Because of the Brays' and Sara Hennell's dislike of Lewes, Marian could not be open about her own growing liking for him. Moreover, there was an insurmountable problem about her emotional entanglement with him, when it did come about, since, unlike Spencer, Lewes was a married man. There was no possibility of his ever getting a divorce, since he had under the law condoned Agnes's relationship with Hunt by registering Edmund and Rose as his own children. Some time during the course of the next year, probably in the spring of 1853 though it is impossible to say with certainty, she and Lewes became lovers. Meanwhile, her letters to her Coventry friends mention him increasingly as an important companion. She made sure to drop his name to them in her birthday letter on 22 November, telling them that Lewes had called on her that day, and sat talking for two hours.[98]

In October Marian spent some time in Edinburgh – 'this beautiful Auld Reekie' – as a guest of the Combes. There she submitted gracefully to being a conversational stooge for the eloquent phrenologist, having 'little to do but shape elegant modes of negation and affirmation like the people who are talked to by Socrates in Plato's dialogues – "certainly, that I firmly believe" etc.'[99] On the way back from Edinburgh she stayed for a few days with Harriet Martineau at Ambleside in the Lake District. 'Miss M. is charming in her own home', she told the Brays.[100]

Chapman's business troubles rumbled on. 'Mr. Chapman's affairs are just like the fog', Marian wrote to the Brays on 13 November. 'Instead of a *thousand*, he wants £1200 now! The Lord have mercy on him!'[101] She thought she would not be able to visit Coventry till after Christmas, so busy was she with *Westminster* proofs and problems, but on 20 December Chrissey's husband Edward Clarke died, leaving Chrissey with six young children and not much money. Marian went to Meriden on 23 December to help plan her sister's future.[102] Here she inevitably came into contact with Isaac and found that on the matter of making provision for Chrissey they were as far apart as they had long been on every other subject, from religion to politics to the proper thing for an unmarried woman to do with her life. Back in London on 31 December, Marian complained to the Brays:

> I had agreed with Chrissey that, all things considered, it was wiser for me to return to town – that I could do her no substantial good by staying another week, while I should be losing time as to other matters. Isaac, however, was very indignant to find that I had arranged to leave without consulting him and thereupon flew into a violent passion with me, winding up by saying that he desired I would never 'apply to him for anything whatever' – which, seeing that I never have done so, was almost as superfluous as if I had said I would never receive a kindness from him.[103]

Isaac's view that it was her duty to stay longer with Chrissey to comfort her versus her own sense that she should be back in London trying to make some money to help Chrissey financially was an example of precisely the kind of tragic family dissent which she created between Maggie and Tom Tulliver in her most autobiographical novel, *The Mill on the Floss*. Both parties could argue a duty where inclination was also a strong factor: it would free Isaac from daily responsibility for Chrissey if Marian stayed with her, while for Marian the personal choice between spending longer in the Midlands and returning to her exciting life in London was a clear one. The result of their discussion, however painful and bitter, was that Isaac made a financial arrangement for Chrissey, to which Marian hoped to 'add something', though she was living almost entirely on her half-yearly income from her father's legacy, since Chapman was unable to pay her a salary.

In January 1853 Marian told Bray she wanted to leave 142 Strand 'and get another home for myself'. 'Many reasons, besides my health, concur to make me desire this change', she added. By the end of February she had told Susanna Chapman she was going to leave, and hoped to do so by the beginning of April.[104] In fact, it was October before she found lodgings of her own. It is highly likely that her growing intimacy with Lewes during the year 1853 dictated her move away from curious eyes at

Number 142. Lewes himself had left his family home in Bedford Place, Kensington, some time after July 1852, never to return, though he made frequent visits to Agnes and his sons Charles, Thornie (named after Thornton Hunt in more harmonious days), and Herbert. Lewes seems to have borrowed a flat in Cork Street, off Piccadilly, from his bachelor friend, the *Times* correspondent and helpmate of Edwin Chadwick on sanitary commissions, F. O. Ward. From September 1852 to July 1853 Ward was in Brussels for an International Hygiene Congress and as an adviser on sewerage systems to the Belgian authorities. A lively, bachelorish, allusive letter from Lewes to Ward, written in the spring of 1853, suggests that he and Marian may already have been lovers, enabled to meet quietly at Cork Street rather than publicly at 142 Strand.

In his undated letter to Ward, known as FOW, Lewes alludes to Charlotte Brontë's *Villette*, published in February 1853 (in which Belgium is called Labassecour), uses sexual slang about Ward's 'private adventures' in Brussels, and slides effortlessly into French at suggestive moments. He describes himself as busy in the laboratory – as he often was with Professor Owen, working on science in relation to Goethe and Comte – and translating and adapting a French play for the Lyceum Theatre:

Of all your public doings in Labassecour I have heard. Your private adventures I hope to hear over snug cigarettes in Cork St. Profitez en, mon ami! . . .

Dear FOW its no use – I *shall* praise you for brilliancy as long as you deserve it! Why, que diable! is there no brilliancy but in tinsel; what say you to Diamond – and to me!!! As to your bread – bake it & let us eat forthwith – but even the loaves may have des formes gracieuses as well as our solid quartern [i.e. attractive women], hein?

Of news I dont know that there is any – at least not *writable* . . . May one ask when is Ward coming back? & Brussels answers When?

For myself I have been furiously dissecting Fishes and carrying a torch into unexplored regions of Biology tant bien que mal. I must now set to work & write a play to get some money. L'amour va son train.[105]

The last sentence refers, I suggest, to his relationship with Marian.

Lewes's letter gives a good idea of the man – racy, versatile, linguistically fluent, confident, sexually experienced, and many-sided in his professional activities. As Spencer had said in his letter to his father in 1851, Lewes at thirty-four had done a multitude of things. He had acted, both in Dickens's amateur company of 'strolling players' and professionally in the provinces in his own 'Spanish' tragedy, *The Noble Heart* (1849–50), and he frequently adapted French farces for the London stage. He was co-editor and chief literary and drama critic of the *Leader*, cultivating his flippant bachelor *persona* 'Vivian', a role which George Bernard Shaw declared had 'brilliantly' anticipated his own approach to theatre criticism, 'especially in his free use of vulgarity and impudence whenever they happened to be the proper tools for the job'.[106]

Lewes had also published two not very good novels, *Ranthorpe* (1847), about a young writer's struggles and mistakes and revival from the brink of suicide, and *Rose, Blanche, and Violet* (1848), a tortured tale of the fortunes in love of three young women. Though Charlotte Brontë, who was corresponding with Lewes about his reviews of her novels, found his fiction interesting, Jane Carlyle commented that *Rose, Blanche, and Violet* was 'execrable', and that she did not think 'the ape' – the Carlyles' nickname for Lewes – was capable of writing anything so silly.[107] Marian Evans took *Rose, Blanche, and Violet* to Broadstairs with her in July 1852, but forgot the third volume, and confessed to Spencer that – 'damaging fact, either for me or the novel!' – she did not care about the missing volume.[108] Lewes himself, realizing that fiction was not his strong point, did not attempt another novel.

Fluent in French, German, and Spanish, and with a knowledge of Italian, Latin, and Greek, Lewes had also published a book on *The Spanish Drama: Lope de Vega and Calderon* (1846), a *Life of Robespierre* (1849), and a great many articles on European subjects for journals including the *Athenaeum*, *Blackwood's Magazine*, the *British and Foreign Review*, the *Edinburgh Review*, the *Foreign Quarterly Review*, *Fraser's Magazine*, and the *Westminster Review*. His *Biographical History of Philosophy* (1845–6) was a clear, popularizing overview of philosophy from Thales and Pythagoras to Hegel and Comte; by 1857 it had sold 40,000 copies and a new revised edition was printed. Herbert Spencer recorded that it was reading Lewes's book which stimulated his own interest in philosophy and psychology.[109] In 1853 Lewes published in Bohn's Scientific Library series his account of the Positivist Philosophy, *Comte's Philosophy of the Sciences*, a copy of which he presented to Marian Evans in October 1853.[110]

This was the man with whom Marian Evans fell – at last requitedly – in love. They were both free thinkers, Lewes more uncompromisingly

so than Marian; both were well versed in European languages and literatures, with a special interest in German literature and Goethe in particular, for whose biography Lewes was now gathering materials; both were
acquainted with recent scientific progress, Lewes in a practising capacity
as well as a theoretical one; both were conversant with ancient and
modern philosophy and shared an enthusiasm for Comte's Positivist
Philosophy, which substituted social science for religious belief.
Comte's philosophy was known as the 'religion of humanity', since it
focused on the observation and classification of physical and psychological laws governing human life instead of asking what Lewes frankly
described as 'futile' questions about 'causes and essences' (i.e. God and
his purpose for mankind).[111]

The differences between Marian and Lewes turned out to be a
strengthening factor in their relationship. His careless, flippant attitude
to sexual and marital relations had ended in making him unhappy; as a
writer he was keen to make his mark as more than a versatile journalist
and writer for the theatre. Marian's intelligence, seriousness, and learning, leavened by a trenchant wit only in evidence when she felt confident
and at ease, appealed to him. Conversely, his raffishness and experience,
softened by his unhappiness in 1852, attracted Marian. Tom Trollope,
brother of Anthony, looked back on their relationship and suggested,
rightly, that part of Lewes's charm for Marian lay in that 'touch of
Bohemianism' about him:

It must have offered so piquant a contrast with the middle-class surroundings
of her early life. I observed that she listened with great complacency to his talk
of theatrical things and people. Lewes was fond of talking about acting and
actors, and in telling stories of celebrated theatrical personages, would imitate
– half involuntarily perhaps – their voice and manner.[112]

It is probable that Marian and Lewes were intimate by early 1853. Her
comments in letters to the unsympathetic Brays and Sara Hennell lag
behind events, gradually seeking to prepare them for the shock and
displeasure of discovering that she and Lewes were more than friends.
In March 1853 she mentions to Sara that Lewes 'has quite won my
liking, in spite of myself', being always 'genial and amusing'. By April
the Brays were being told that 'Lewes has been quite a pleasant friend to
me lately.' To Cara she wrote on 16 April that he was 'a man of heart
and conscience wearing a mask of flippancy'.[113] As previously with her

loss of faith and her correspondence with pious friends like Maria Lewis, so here she was restrained from giving full confidences by her expectation of disapproval on the part of her correspondents.

After a summer holiday in St Leonard's, where she had last spent time with her father in June 1848, Marian moved in October 1853 to lodgings in Cambridge Street, Hyde Park. She was helping Lewes correct proofs of the *Leader*, and told Sara in her usual birthday letter of late November that she began this year, her thirty-fifth, 'more happily than I have done most years of my life'.[14] She also revealed that she had told Chapman she wanted to give up editing the *Westminster Review*. She had agreed to translate another free-thinking German work, Ludwig Feuerbach's *Das Wesen des Christenthums* (*The Essence of Christianity*, 1841) for publication by Chapman. In December she wrote an uncharacteristically sharp letter to him about arrangements for publication – half profits having, as she said, more a 'conceptional existence' than a material one.[15] She had often been critical and commanding in her letters to Chapman, but one detects an extra toughness here, which suggests that she may have had at her elbow someone with experience of negotiating with publishers and the confidence to be frank, even rude, when he deemed it necessary – namely G. H. Lewes.

CHAPTER FIVE

Life with Lewes:
Weimar and Berlin 1854–5

The January 1854 number of the *Westminster* carried a hostile review of Lewes's book on Comte. Lewes's work was compared unfavourably with Harriet Martineau's abridged translation of the *Positivist Philosophy*, published by Chapman at the end of 1853, and Lewes was accused of being an amateur with 'mere book-knowledge' of scientific subjects. The author of this review, which annoyed Lewes and upset Marian, was T. H. Huxley, the rising star in London's scientific circles, whom Marian had met at Chapman's in February 1853.[1] Her last efforts in her unpaid job of editor – for though she gave Chapman her notice in November, he persuaded her to see the January number through the press – were made in an attempt to get Chapman to omit or alter Huxley's review, which she saw in proof and disliked.

Marian advised Chapman to leave the article out of the January number altogether, adding that it was hardly becoming for a Chapman book to be so praised at the expense of a rival book brought out by another publisher. 'Do you really think that if you had been the publisher of Mr. Lewes's book and Bohn the publisher of Miss Martineau's, Mr. Huxley would have written just so?' she asked. 'Tell that to the Marines.'[2]

She went even further in one of several letters to Chapman on the subject during December 1853. Marking this one '*Private*', she stands on her right as editor to influence policy in a matter on which she feels very strongly indeed:

I think I ought to have a voice in the matter, in virtue of the share in the management of the W R which I have had hitherto, & which does not cease till this number is out. My opinion is, that the editors of the Review will disgrace themselves by inserting an utterly worthless & unworthy notice of a work by one of their own writers – a man of much longer & higher standing than Mr. Huxley, & whom Mr. H's seniors in science & superiors both in intellect & fame treat with respect.[3]

She had in mind Richard Owen, who was soon involved in a bitter feud with the pugnacious Huxley. In spite of all her efforts, the offending article appeared in January 1854.

Marian began work on the translation of Feuerbach. *The Essence of Christianity* was a more congenial work than Strauss's *Life of Jesus*, as well as being easier to translate, Feuerbach being '*for a German* – concise, lucid, and even epigrammatic now and then', as she told Sara Hennell, who was once more acting as chief critic and proofreader.[4] Feuerbach built on the findings of Strauss and others to discuss religion as a psychological necessity for man, who in his awareness of his own imperfections posits perfection, then worships it as God. In so doing, he is really worshipping the perfection of his own species: '*Homo homini Deus est.*' Love and duty between human beings is at the heart of Feuerbach's religion of humanity:

The relations of child and parent, of husband and wife, of brother and friend, – in general, of man to man, – in short, all the moral relations are *per se* religious. Life as a whole is, in its essential, substantial relations, throughout of a divine nature. Its religious consecration is not first conferred by the blessing of the priest.[5]

This corresponded exactly with Marian's views. And when Feuerbach goes on to say of marriage that it is nothing more nor less than 'the free bond of love', 'sacred in itself', a matter of mutual love not requiring a religious ceremony to make it sacred, Marian could hardly have found herself translating a more congenial or apt idea. For during the early months of 1854, if not before, she and Lewes were quietly planning to take the step which would cause a social scandal but which they felt fully justified in taking. They were preparing to live together as man and wife. In July, when Chapman published *The Essence of Christianity*, the only work of hers to have the name 'Marian Evans' on the title-page, Marian Evans was poised to change that name to Marian Lewes.

In January 1854 Marian visited Chrissey at Meriden to help her sister with plans for her oldest boys, aged fifteen and fourteen. At one time Chrissey had thought of sending the eldest, Edward, to Australia, and even toyed with the idea of taking the whole family there.[6] The plan was dropped, and by December 1853 Chrissey and Isaac were disagreeing about what to do with the children. To Marian's relief, the two eldest boys were found situations by May 1854.[7] Marian could relax now that Chrissey's affairs seemed settled.

Chapman's affairs, on the other hand, looked worse than ever. He was embroiled in a protracted dispute with George Combe about the latter's article on prison reform for the *Westminster Review*. Marian did her best to hold the ring, but a sure sign of her having removed herself from the editorship came in March, when she was bold enough to tell Combe, whom she was used to humouring, not to make her 'a referee in any matters relating to Mr. Chapman, as I have nothing whatever to do with his affairs'.[8] Chapman was retrenching. 142 Strand was too big and too expensive for him to manage. In June 1854 he moved his household to Blandford Square and his publishing business to King William Street, off the Strand. At the same time, Elisabeth Tilley left the Chapman family.[9]

A little later Chapman survived an attempted ousting by two of his creditors, the Unitarians James Martineau and W. B. Hodgson, who disliked what they considered the determinedly atheistic tone of the *Westminster Review*. Harriet Martineau, at odds with her brother since he had reviewed her *Letters on the Laws of Man's Nature and Development* unfavourably in the *Prospective Review* in 1852, came to Chapman's rescue and simultaneously got her revenge on her brother by taking a mortgage on the *Westminster Review*.[10] Thus once more Chapman was enabled to carry on with the journal, despite its unprofitability.

Marian was more concerned with seeing the *Leader* through the press in April than she was with the management of the *Westminster*. 'Poor Lewes is ill', she told Cara, 'so I have something to do for him in addition to my own work'.[11] Lewes had headaches, toothache, and a singing in the ears which prevented him from working for two months. He went to visit his friend Arthur Helps in Hampshire, then in June he tried Dr Balbirnie's famous water cure in Malvern.[12] Marian took on his reviewing in the *Leader* for April and May. One reason why she had given up her unpaid editorial job on the *Westminster Review* was so that she could write regular articles in it for which she would be paid like other contributors. 'I am thinking of doing the Belles Lettres in the Contemporary Literature after this quarter', she told Bray in April. 'It would be £16.16 a quarter, so I think it would be worth while groaning over.'[13] She was manoeuvring herself into a position to make a regular income.

She and Lewes had decided to begin living together openly first in Germany, not England. Lewes needed to visit Weimar and Berlin to interview surviving friends of Goethe and consult German libraries for his biography. Once the Feuerbach translation was in the press and Marian disengaged from the day-to-day editorial work in London, they could set off. No doubt they were keen – especially Marian – to let tongues wag about their relationship while they were well out of earshot in Germany. Marian dropped little hints to the Brays about her plans for the summer. 'It is quite possible that I may wish to go to the continent or twenty other things', she told Bray on 27 May. More mysteriously still, she announced to Sara on 10 July that she was 'preparing to go to Labassecour'.[14]

When *Villette* came out in February 1853 Marian had been much struck by it, thinking it 'a still more wonderful book than Jane Eyre', with 'something almost preternatural in its power'.[15] Well might she respond sensitively to the feverish tale of Lucy Snowe's lonely, per-secuted life as a schoolteacher in Villette, in love with the fiery little master Paul Emanuel and fated to be unhappy. She would have em-pathized even more had she known not only that Lucy's experiences were closely based on Charlotte Brontë's own, but that Charlotte's be-loved schoolmaster was, unlike M. Emanuel, the *married* M. Heger. Marian was happier than Charlotte and her fictional *alter ego*; she found, as she had been delighted to know Margaret Fuller had finally found, that life could be sweet.

Marian took private verbal revenge on Herbert Spencer, on whom her hopes had centred two years before. She joked to Sara that Spencer would stand in the biographical dictionaries of a hundred years hence as:

'Spencer, Herbert, an original and profound philosophical writer, especially known by his great work x x x which gave a new impulse to psychology and has mainly contributed to the present advanced position of that science, com-pared with that which it had attained in the middle of the last century. The life

GEORGE ELIOT: A LIFE

of this philosopher, like that of the great Kant, offers little material for the narrator. Born in the year 1820 etc'.[16]

Spencer's reputation has not survived as prophesied here. George Eliot could not have known that Freud would live. Spencer's evolutionary psychology-cum-social science has become outmoded because of its general rather than specialized approach, though it was a notable forerunner and contemporary of Darwin's momentous work of evolutionary science – indeed it was Spencer who first used the phrase 'survival of the fittest' in Volume I of his *Principles of Biology* (1864), referring in his use of the phrase to Darwin's theory of natural selection in biology.[17]

After a visit to Rosehill – her last, as it turned out – from 17 to 26 June, Marian got ready to leave the country. She told Chapman and Bray, but not Cara and Sara, what she was about to do. On 19 July she sent a short note to Coventry which signalled an end and a beginning:

Dear Friends – all three

I have only time to say good bye and God bless you. Poste Restante, Weimar for the next six weeks, and afterwards Berlin.

Ever your loving and grateful

Marian.[18]

Marian's journals from 20 July 1854 have survived destruction by Cross. On that day she left for Weimar via Labassecour with her M. Emanuel:

I said a last farewell to Cambridge street this morning and found myself on board the Ravensbourne, bound for Antwerp about ½ an hour earlier than a sensible person would have been aboard, and in consequence I had 20 minutes of terrible fear lest something should have delayed G. But before long I saw his welcome face looking for me over the porter's shoulder, and all was well. The day was glorious and our passage perfect. Mr. R. Noel [Robert, brother of Edward] happened to be a fellow-passenger. The sunset was lovely but still lovelier the dawn as we were passing up the Scheldt between 2 and 3 in the morning. The crescent moon, the stars, the first faint blush of the dawn reflected in the glassy river, the dark mass of clouds on the horizon, which sent forth flashes of lightning, and the graceful forms of the boats and sailing vessels painted in jet black on the reddish gold of the sky and water, made up an unforgettable picture. Then the sun rose and lighted up the sleepy shores of Belgium with their fringe of long grass, their rows of poplars, their church spires and farm buildings.[19]

They took a leisurely journey to Weimar, stopping at Brussels, Cologne, Mainz, and Frankfurt among other places on the way. On the leg of the journey which took them to Cologne they were joined in the railway carriage by another acquaintance, none other than Dr Brabant. He 'very kindly exerted himself to procure me an interview with Strauss at Cologne', as Marian told Chapman on 6 August.[20] The meeting was a little awkward, since Strauss looked 'strange and cast-down', and Marian was conscious that her 'deficient German prevented us from learning more of each other than our exterior which in the case of both would have been better left to imagination', as she reported to Bray with her usual unsparing frankness about her appearance.[21]

Arriving in Weimar in the afternoon of 2 August, they settled into the Erbprinz for the night. The next day they set out to explore the town and look for reasonably priced lodgings, which they found in the Kauf-gasse. On 27 September Lewes wrote a charming letter to his two older sons, Charles, aged nearly twelve, and Thornie, aged ten, describing the town and his doings there, though not, of course, mentioning Marian:

Here I am in the capital of the Grand duchy of Weimar, about which you, Thornie, know something already, I have no doubt – or soon will. It is a very queer little place although called the 'Athens of Germany' on account of the great poets who lived here; one of them, the greatest of all, you know already by the portraits and little bust in our house – I mean *Goethe*. I am writing his Life, which work brought me to Weimar, to seek for materials. Fancy a little quiet town without cabs, omnibuses, very few carts and scarcely a carriage – with no gas lights for the streets, which are lighted (in winter only) by oil lamps, slung across the streets on a cord.[22]

Lewes gave a full account of their impressions of Weimar in his *Life of Goethe* (1855). Marian also described the place in loving detail in two articles published in *Fraser's Magazine* in June and July 1855, pieces which she worked up from her 'Recollections of Weimar 1854', written in her journal in Berlin in November. A passage from the 'Recollections' which Marian did not publish was her private apostrophe to the park in which they spent much time breathing in Goethe's spirit:

Dear Park of Weimar! In 1854, two loving, happy human beings spent many a delicious hour in wandering under your shade and in your sunshine, and to one of them at least you will be a 'joy for ever' through all the sorrows that are to come.[23]

Another unpublished recollection was her account of a day spent in Ettersburg, a summer residence of the Duke of Weimar where Goethe had organized 'private theatricals and *sprees*'. They took a picnic and Keats's poems, which they read aloud among the trees. Lewes also did one of his mimicking turns: 'G. made this place echo with his imitation of Kean's Othello for my amusement.'[24] It was undoubtedly an irreverent imitation, for Lewes had been locked in a battle of words with Charles Kean during his tenure as 'Vivian' of the *Leader*, when he regularly accused Kean of melodramatic rather than dramatic acting.[25] Then there was the day they went on an excursion to Ilmenau, where Goethe had had a little wooden house; Lewes told another theatrical story, about 'John Kemble jun. and his wife'. While they waited for a train back to Weimar 'G. beguiled the time by telling me of the fiasco he made with a lecture on Othello at Hackney.'[26] (Lewes had lectured on Shakespeare and on philosophy at Mechanics' Institutes in various towns when on his acting tour in 1849.[27])

Marian's happiness in the society of this lively, talented, beloved man shines out of her recollections, as it does out of some of her letters. She was, of course, unsure about how her action would be viewed by friends at home, but she could be reasonably open to both Bray and Chapman, to whom she had confided her plans before leaving England. Chapman was the first to write to her, and in her grateful reply on 6 August all her customary superiority towards him has disappeared. 'I was delighted to see your writing', she wrote, and 'opened it with all sorts of grateful, affectionate feelings towards you for having written to me so soon.'

She was also pleased that he had asked her to do an article for the *Westminster* on Victor Cousin's recent book on Madame de Sablé and other women of seventeenth-century France. She promised him 'an article piquant and fresh', and was as good as her word.[28] In another letter to Chapman on 30 August Marian was quite expansive about her happiness with Lewes:

I am happier every day and find my domesticity more and more delightful and beneficial to me. Affection, respect, and intellectual sympathy deepen, and for the first time in my life I can say to the moments 'Verweilen sie, sie sind so schön' [an echo of Goethe's *Faust*, meaning 'Let them last, they are so beautiful'].[29]

Marian wrote to Bray a little more diffidently, aware that Cara and

Sara would be looking over his shoulder and not at all sure what they would make of her new situation:

I hope you want to hear something of me though I confess I do not write to satisfy your wants but my own. It is a necessity to me to know how you all are, and I venture to hope that if I ask you for a letter you will send me one.

She went on to say that she had had 'a month of exquisite enjoyment, and seem to have begun life afresh'.[30]

To one other correspondent Marian unbent in gratitude for a letter sent voluntarily to her. This was brave Bessie Parkes, who went against her parents' wishes by writing to her friend. Marian's reply on 10 September talks of enjoying a life 'full of quiet happiness':

Liszt is here, as you know, and has been particularly friendly. He is a glorious creature in every way – a bright genius, with a tender, loving nature, and a face in which this combination is perfectly expressed. He has that 'laideur divinisée' by the soul that gleams through it, which is my favourite kind of physique.[31]

Well might she think so, for her phrase described Lewes's ugliness lit up by intelligence and good humour as much as it did Liszt's.

Liszt, who was the Weimar court's resident Kapellmeister and theatre director, thrilled Marian with his playing. 'For the first time in my life I beheld real inspiration', she enthused in her journal on 10 August; 'for the first time I heard the true tones of the piano'.[32] He was an inspiration in another way too, for he was living openly with the Princess Carolyne Sayn-Wittgenstein, whose husband had not yet divorced her. Marian made sure to tell Bray in her first letter to him that Liszt 'lives with a Russian Princess, who is in fact his wife, and he is a Grand Seigneur in this place'.[33] Not only did the Weimar court accept the relationship between Liszt and his princess; it made no fuss about the English visitors, Mr Lewes and Miss Evans. Even the resident Britons, James Marshall, private secretary to the Duchess of Weimar, and Thomas Wilson, whom Marian had met at 142 Strand in 1851,[34] were happy to meet Lewes and Marian socially.

But back home in England there was a great fuss in those circles where Marian and Lewes were known. At Rosehill, Cara and Sara were miserable because they disliked Lewes and disapproved of Marian going to live with him, hurt because Marian had not confided in them, and insulted by what they took to be coldness on her part. Not all the letters between Coventry and Weimar have survived, but a recently discovered letter to Marian from Sara throws a good deal of light on the complex emotions felt by Marian's oldest and best female friends. It seems she misjudged them, characteristically assuming that their disapproval would outweigh their fondness for her. In her first cautious letter to Bray on 16 August, she pictured them 'taking tea in the summerhouse and lying on the bearskin', but did not mention Cara and Sara by name, rather proudly taking refuge in a vague salutation – 'much love to all'. According to Sara, writing indignantly on 20 October, she and Cara both 'wrote to you just as usual' after Bray had received this first letter. 'Cara says hers was full of affection & I am sure mine was too.' These letters (now lost) should have shown Marian, says Sara, that the step she had taken, 'tho' as you knew we shd. do, we strongly disapproved of it, would not alter our affection and intercourse with you'.[35]

Marian had replied, but to Charles Bray only, anxiously refuting rumours which had reached her about Lewes's having 'run away' from his wife and family. Marian stoutly defended Lewes's fairness, even generosity, towards Agnes – 'she has had all the money due to him in London' – and reiterated her faith in his good will. As for herself, she knew 'many silly myths' were 'already afloat about me', but she did not care as long as Lewes was treated fairly. Then she added, fatally showing that she doubted her friends:

I am ignorant how far Cara and Sara may be acquainted with the state of things, and how they may feel towards me. I am quite prepared to accept the consequences of a step which I have deliberately taken and to accept them without irritation or bitterness. The most painful consequence will, I know, be the loss of friends. If I do not write, therefore, understand that it is because I desire not to obtrude myself.[36]

Sara picked up these words and quoted them back at Marian as a 'most unfeeling message – classing us in fact with the rest of your acquaintance, coldly & proudly defying us to give up our friendship & boasting with what serenity you can bear it'. 'Not to *obtrude* yourself,' expostulated Sara, 'when if you ever thought our friendship good for any thing, you must know how anxious we have been to hear from you!' Anger and hurt spill out, as does the jealousy Sara and Cara had already begun to feel when their protégée, so dependent on them for comfort and approval in the Coventry days, had spread her wings for London, independence, and a succession of interesting new acquaintances. 'So much for my own feelings of your treatment of us', continued Sara, 'a trifling subject indeed compared with that of your change of life – but on that I hardly dare to enter.'[37]

This heartfelt angry letter called forth a direct reply from Marian on 31 October. She opened by confessing to Sara that she was afraid she would 'only give rise to fresh misconceptions' whatever she wrote, yet she dreaded even more the effect of not writing at all. Then comes a spirited denial of the accusation of coldness:

When you say that I do not care about Cara's or your opinion and friendship it seems much the same to me as if you said that I didn't care to eat when I was hungry or to drink when I was thirsty. One of two things: either I am a creature without affection, on whom the memories of years have no hold, or, you, Cara and Mr. Bray are the most cherished friends I have in the world. It is simply self-contradictory to say that a person can be indifferent about her dearest friends; yet this is what you substantially say, when you accuse me of 'boasting with what serenity I can give you up', of 'speaking proudly' etc.

After some more undeniably proud words she moves into a more mollifying key, declaring her unchanged affection for her friends and appealing to their shared past:

Cara, you and my own sister are the three women who are tied to my heart by a cord which can never be broken and which really *pulls* me continually. My love for you rests on a past which no future can reverse, and offensive as the words seem to have been to you, I must repeat, that I can feel no bitterness towards you, however you may act towards me. If you remain to me what you have ever been, my life will be all the happier, and I will try not to be unworthy of your love so far as faithfulness to my own conscience can make me worthy of it.[38]

This letter went some way towards putting things right, at least with Sara, who replied on 15 November, signing herself 'your ancient friend', but showing her sense of inevitable alienation:

Your letter to Charles today seems to show you very happy now – but I have a strange sort of feeling that I am writing to some one in a book, and not to the Marian that we have known and loved so many years. Do not mistake me, I mean nothing unkind.[39]

Cara, however, having written once and received a reply (both now lost), stopped writing to her old friend. We can only speculate about her feelings towards Marian – did she perhaps resent Marian's taking for herself happiness with a married man when she, a married woman, had contented herself with loving the widowed Edward Noel platonically? Her own husband had a sexual relationship with another woman; did she share with society in general the view that such things were natural and forgivable – if regrettable – in a man, but utterly unforgivable in a woman?

The men of Marian's acquaintance present an interesting case of moral confusion and hypocrisy. Marian had written to Chapman on 6 August that 'any London news will be welcome'. But the news that finally came was not welcome. On 11 October Marian wrote in her journal the terse sentence, 'A painful letter from London caused us both a bad night.' Two days later Lewes wrote 'explaining his position' to two valued and respectable friends, Arthur Helps, who had spent a few days with them at Weimar at the end of August,[40] and Carlyle. Neither letter has survived, but a second one to Carlyle, written by Lewes on 19 October, thanks him for his kindness. Carlyle's response to his appeal for fair play had 'given me new courage':

I sat at your feet when my mind was first awakening; I have honoured and loved you since both as teacher and friend, and *now* to find that you judge me rightly, and are not estranged by what has estranged so many from me, gives me strength to bear what must yet be borne!

Lewes goes on to say that his separation from Agnes had taken place – though not publicly – before he and Marian left for Germany and was 'not caused by the lady named [Marian Evans] nor by any other lady'.[41]

In the face of gossip and scandal – much of which Lewes knew would relate to his own free-living past as well as to Agnes's relationship with Hunt – his course of action was to ensure that Marian was understood not to have been a factor in the breakdown of his marriage. Otherwise, as he nobly told Carlyle, 'on all private matters my only answer is *silence*'. He would not vilify Agnes or Hunt in order to save his own name. Unfortunately, Carlyle did not respond so generously to this letter as he had clearly done to the previous (lost) one. Carlyle was at first inclined to support Lewes. He wrote to Edward Fitzgerald on 19 October:

Have you heard about poor Lewes, 'hairy Lewes' as we sometimes call him? He has put away his Wife *at last*, and for right good cause; but the rest of the rumour about him I believe to be, in brief, *lies*. He is a good soul in several respects in spite of his hair.[42]

But on receiving Lewes's very fair account of 19 October about his relations with Marian, Carlyle annotated the letter as follows:

Alas! alas! – I had (at his request) approved unequivocally of parting *such a marriage*; and advised to contradict, if he could, on his word of honour, the bad rumours circulating about a certain strong minded woman and him. He assures me, on his word of honour, the strong minded did not *write* etc.: as well assure me her stockings are both of one colour; that is a very insignificant point! – No answer to this second letter.[43]

The nickname 'strong-minded woman' thus came to be applied to Marian in the Carlyle circle – how prophetic in an unexpected sense her spoof letter to Bray of October 1846 had turned out to be, though she sported no beard and though Lewes, while taking her as prophesied to Germany, was no pedantic German professor. Jane Carlyle was later reported to have said that when she heard that 'the strong minded woman of the *Westminster Review* had gone off with a man whom we all knew', it was as startling 'as if one heard that a woman of your acquaintance had gone off with the strong man at Astley's' – the famous theatre for equestrian entertainments.[44] The Carlyles, disappointingly for such independent spirits, did not accept Marian into their society, though Lewes continued to be a visitor at Cheyne Row. This was to be the pattern with all but a few acquaintances when the couple returned to England in 1855.

The letter by the 'strong minded', the existence of which Lewes strongly denied and on which Carlyle declined to take a view, was one which Marian was supposed to have written to Harriet Martineau. Marian wrote to Chapman on 15 October after hearing that this mythical letter was said to have been shown at the Reform Club: 'It is hardly necessary to tell you that I have had no communication with Miss Martineau, and that if I had, she is one of the last persons to whom I should speak as to a confidante.'[45]

So exercised was Marian by the rumour that she reiterated to Chapman on 30 October her request that he contradict the story whenever he could. 'Amongst her good qualities', she wrote tartly, 'we certainly cannot reckon zeal for other people's reputation. She is sure to caricature any information for the amusement of the next person to whom she turns her ear-trumpet.'[46] Mean though this reference to Harriet Martineau's deafness was, Marian was not mistaken in her character analysis. When Harriet heard in 1868 that Lewes was ill and likely to die, she wrote to a friend, 'What will she do? Take a successor, I shd expect.'[47]

Chapman, like the well-meaning friend he was, tried hard to counteract the falsehoods and excesses doing the rounds in London and beyond. He was in a difficult position, since he and the *Westminster Review* were already under fire from his Unitarian supporters – indeed James Martineau and W. B. Hodgson left him to found the *National Review* early in 1855[48] – and he was at the time close to Harriet Martineau, who was bailing him out financially. Chapman wrote on 4 October to George Combe in Edinburgh, confirming that Lewes and Marian had gone to the Continent together, Lewes's intention being to 'obtain material for his life of Goethe'.[49]

But Chapman was, of course, the last person who could help Combe recover from the shock of this news. Combe presumably knew about Chapman's not-so-private private life, and in any case he was already thoroughly infuriated with what he took to be a mixture of incompetence and sharp practice in Chapman's dealings over the *Westminster Review*. Chapman had told Lewes's Edinburgh friend Robert Chambers about Lewes and Marian, commissioning him to inform Combe. On 16 October Chapman wrote worriedly to Chambers about a story he seems to have started himself, presumably about her having fallen in love with *him*, a story which, though true, was hardly calculated to help her:

A word about Miss E. I am very anxious that what I *said* to you about *her especially*, should be regarded as strictly confidential. I mention this because Mr. Bray connected your name with a rumour about her; and I should be sorry to be thought disposed to disparage her. I only dropped the word I did because I felt that Lewes was not as you imagined almost alone to blame. Still I think him much the most blameworthy in the matter. Now I can only pray, against hope, that he may prove constant to her; otherwise she is *utterly* lost.

She has a noble nature which in good circumstances and under good influences would have shone out.[50]

The comment has a pious, even hypocritical, ring to it, the more so as Chapman himself had recently embarked on another seduction since the move from 142 Strand and the departure of Elisabeth Tilley in June 1854. He had fixed on Bessie Parkes's friend Barbara Leigh Smith, who lived near him in Blandford Square, as a desirable successor to Elisabeth.[51] But Chapman probably meant well; knowing that most people would be shocked by the news of Lewes and Marian, he intended to make sure she did not attract all the blame that would inevitably be cast on the affair.

Combe became very exercised about the story of Lewes and Marian, particularly as it related to Marian, whom his phrenological expertise had pronounced so admirable in every respect. His chief correspondent on the subject was Bray, to whom he wrote on 15 November saying he and his wife were 'deeply mortified and distressed', and asking whether there was 'insanity in Miss Evans's family; for her conduct, with *her* brain, seems to me like morbid aberration'.[52] Letters flew between Coventry and Edinburgh, in which both Bray and Combe proved themselves capable of holding illogical views of what was acceptable in sexual relations. Men with secret extra-marital relations might retain their respectability; women certainly could not; nor could men, like Lewes and Hunt, who did not keep their extra-marital activities secret.

Bray, like Chapman, tried to placate Combe, but he, too, acted somewhat in bad faith. He began by telling Combe on 8 October that Lewes and Agnes had 'not been man and wife to each other for some years', but he fudged the issue of the precise nature of the relationship between Lewes and Marian. Lewes needed to go abroad for his health, he wrote, and he 'offered to introduce [Marian] to friends of his in Germany and leave her there for 12 months, which is what she wished'. Bray pretended to think Marian 'guilty' only of imprudence and 'laying herself open to evil report'.[53] Cara had already written in similar vein to Combe's wife, suggesting that the relationship was merely a friendship and that Marian and Lewes simply had a common purpose in visiting Germany.[54] When this fiction could no longer be sustained, Bray assured Combe that 'my wife and Miss Hennell are sadly troubled about all this and wish me to say that Miss E's going had not their sanction, because they knew nothing at all about it'.[55]

Combe was not pacified; Bray wrote again on 28 October, quoting Marian's words to him about no one having a right to interfere with her conduct since she was independent, having long been separated by temperament and opinions from her brothers and sisters. Bray assured

Combe, as well he might, that Marian had been to her father 'the most devoted [daughter] I ever knew, and she is just as likely to devote herself to *one* other, in preference to all the world'. He added the well-meaning and no doubt sincere comment: 'I have known her for years and should always feel that she was better *by one half* than 99/100 of the people I have ever known.'[56]

All this was very fair as far as it went, but where was the justice or evenhandedness in Combe's remark on 15 November to Bray, whose own sexual history he had known since 1851, that Marian had taken a course of action which would 'degrade herself and her sex, if she be sane'? Or in his next sentence to the man he still counted as a friend despite knowing of his marital arrangements:

If you receive her into your family circle, while present appearances are un-explained, pray consider whether you will do justice to your own female domestic circle, and how other ladies may feel about going into a circle which makes no distinction between those who act thus, and those who preserve their honour unspotted?[57]

And what can we make of Bray's complacent reply, no matter how kindly he meant it, to the man to whom he had divulged his own secret:

I do not think that Miss Evans would admit that Lewes had a wife now, or has had for some years, and they may both of them intend to fulfil all the conditions that belong *naturally* to the marriage state. Mind I have no wish to defend the part she is taking – only I do not judge her. I don't think she is *mad*. She had organically, all the intellectual strength of a man and in feeling all the peculiar weaknesses of woman. I know she would prefer the close and devoted affection of one mind, to the ordinary and customary attentions of all the world besides i.e. if she were called upon to make her choice.[58]

It is hardly surprising that Marian was never again invited to play the stooge's part in Combe's Socratic dialogues in Edinburgh. Her relationship with the Brays, a much longer and deeper one, was not broken, though it took time and some hurt on both sides (at least as far as the women at Rosehill were concerned) before the warmth returned. The manner of Marian's beginning her new life exacerbated and complicated those changes which always take place when a member of a close circle marries outside that circle.

*

But of course Marian and Lewes were not married. Then and later stories circulated about 'blackguard Lewes' bolting 'with a –' and 'living in Germany with her' (the sculptor Thomas Woolner to William Bell Scott, as it happens an old friend of Lewes's youth, in October 1854); about 'Miss Evans, the infidel esprit forte, who is now G. H. Lewes's concubine' (Charles Kingsley to F. D. Maurice in 1857);[59] and so on. While Marian was generally judged the worse offender under the unspoken double standards of a large part of society, the affair raised lurid rumours about Lewes's undeniably colourful past and the precise nature of his and Agnes's relationships with the Hunts. There is, in fact, no firm evidence of Lewes's sexual activities outside marriage, though some bystanders assumed that as Agnes was to Hunt, so Mrs Hunt was to Lewes. Shirley Brooks, editor of *Punch*, noted in his diary in June 1873, after hearing of Thornton Hunt's death, 'Odd story about him, Geo. Lewes, & their respective & interchangeable wives.'[60]

There was also a story current among Marian's female friends Bessie Parkes and Barbara Leigh Smith that Lewes had at an unspecified time in the past seduced a young woman, who bore him a child. Mrs Gaskell was supposed to have found this child a foster mother.[61] This report can be neither verified nor denied with certainty. It is true that Mrs Gaskell not only disapproved of the Lewes 'marriage', but thought Lewes too 'soiled for a woman like her to fancy'[62] – but this may have been due more to her general sense of Lewes's free way of living, which he had never sought to hide, than to any particular information she had. If there had been a child, it is certain Lewes would have provided for it, as he did throughout his life for Agnes's four children by Hunt as well as his own three. A parallel story, which circulated long after Marian's death, that she, too, had a child, possibly by Chapman, can be emphatically denied.[63]

Barbara Leigh Smith, like Bessie Parkes, took no high moral line about Marian's conduct, as befitted her own circumstances and her honest, independent character. She was in the middle of her relationship with Chapman, which he hoped to make permanent, so much so that he argued in letters written to her in August and September 1855 that she should live openly with him in a house he would take for her while making provision in a separate establishment for his wife and children. Barbara might then 'look forward with joyous anticipation to becoming a Mother', for, despite Mrs Grundy, 'rely upon it we shall be happy yet'. 'Lewes and M. E. seemed to be perfectly so', he added complacently.[64]

Barbara was inclined by background and circumstances to do as Chapman suggested, since she was in possession of a private fortune, and had been brought up in equality with her brothers by a liberal father, Benjamin Leigh Smith, who was himself not married to her mother. She was the founder and leading spirit of a progressive Infants' School near her home which had no uniform, no punishment, and no catechism for the children. She was active in agitation for women's education, becoming in due course the co-founder of Girton College, Cambridge, and for Married Women's Property legislation. With Bessie Parkes she started and edited the *English Woman's Journal* in 1858.[65]

But despite the Smith family's unconventionalism, Barbara's father frowned on the idea of her living openly with Chapman. She must have had her own doubts about him too, for she allowed herself to be taken off by her brother for a holiday in Algiers, where she met and in 1857 married the eccentric French doctor and agitator for the abolition of slavery in Africa, Eugène Bodichon.[66]

For Bessie Parkes, as for Barbara, the problem about Marian's elopement with Lewes was not the scandalous nature of the relationship, but her distrust of Lewes (though of course that distrust arose out of the stories she had heard about his sexual freedom). Bessie had been given dark hints by her father that Lewes was 'an indifferent character' who had 'long been shaken from whatever hold he ever possessed on respectable domestic life; he was a clever man with a kind heart but never very well thought of '. He was witty, kind, honest, but 'a Comtean Atheist', and not moral. But though she acknowledged her prejudice against Lewes, she was happy for Marian's happiness, and she wrote robustly about the hypocrisy prevailing all round her:

Now when we remember the men who form illegal connexions sub rosâ – who do vile & bad things, & keep up a white washed character, I feel more lenient to that little Weimar home than others do.[67]

These are interesting comments indeed, being made in letters to Sam Blackwell, to whom she was then, and for some time on and off thereafter, engaged. Interesting, too, because she may well already have known what she undoubtedly knew later, that her own father was an unfaithful husband to her mother.[68] Joseph Parkes himself was sending long letters, as was his wife, from his Midlands home, warning Bessie not to damage her reputation by corresponding with Miss Evans, of whose 'folly, and I cannot but say *vice*' he had heard on a trip to London in September 1854. Lewes, he told Bessie, was '*morally* a *bad man*', being part of 'an odious history' with Thornton Hunt. Parkes predicted – and this was of course what all Marian's friends, male and female, feared – that Lewes would 'tire of & put away Miss Evans – as he has done others'. On his return to Birmingham in October, he found that the Lewes–Marian Evans affair was the talk of progressive circles there.[69]

To complicate matters further, part of Parkes's indignation related to the harm the scandal would do to the general liberal cause he and his Unitarian friends had in common with the Chapman–Lewes–Hunt, *Leader–Westminster Review* circle. As Combe did, he feared for the cause of progress. He knew men who had supported the *Leader* and the *Westminster* who would no longer do so because of the scandal. Indeed, Combe was one of these, writing to Bray in November that he intended to give up his subscription to the *Leader*.[70] Parkes was aware of Chapman's financial difficulties and the disaffection of his fellow Unitarians on the grounds of the *Westminster*'s apparent embracing of atheism, and the Marian–Lewes story now seemed the last straw: 'By this event partly, & Chapman's embarrassment, the Writing Corps are separating', as Parkes told Bessie.[71]

So the news of the Weimar couple was received with quivering fascination and disgust in England. James Martineau may have had it somewhere in his mind when he wrote his bad-tempered review of Marian's translation of Feuerbach's *Essence of Christianity* for the October number of the *Westminster*; he certainly let his impatience with atheism show in the periodical he was about to leave after the failure of his bid to take it over:

It is a sign of 'progress', we presume, that the lady-translator who maintained the anonymous in introducing Strauss, puts her name in the title-page of Feuerbach. She has executed her task even better than before: we are only surprised that, if she wished to exhibit the new Hegelian Atheism to English readers, she should select a work of the year 1840, and of quite secondary philosophical repute in its own country.[72]

Marian's own article, 'Woman in France: Madame de Sablé', appeared in the same number. It was her first full-length review in the *Westminster* since her article on Mackay's *Progress of the Intellect* in January 1851. Henry Crabb Robinson read it, as he read everything, and – ignorant of the identity of the author – pronounced it 'charming, acute, entertaining & yet wise'.[73] And so it is, though like the Mackay piece it contains a considerable amount of quotation and paraphrase from the work under review, Cousin's book on seventeenth-century women in France. Marian Evans's opinions on the subjects of marriage and woman's role in society cannot but be interesting in view of her own position. But now, as always, she was disinclined to shock, holding liberal, but not ultra-radical, views on the subject. Agreeing with Comte and Spencer, she points out the special 'class of sensations and emotions – the maternal ones', which distinguish woman from man:

The fact of her comparative physical weakness, which, however it may have been exaggerated by a vicious civilization, can never be cancelled, introduces a distinctively feminine condition into the wondrous chemistry of the affections and sentiments, which inevitably gives rise to distinctive forms and combinations.

She analyses the typical upper-class French marriage of the seventeenth century with a shrewd sense of what was good and what bad about it:

No wise person, we imagine, wishes to restore the social condition of France in the seventeenth century, or considers the ideal programme to be a *mariage de convenance* at fifteen, a career of gallantry from twenty to eight-and-thirty, and penitence and piety for the rest of her days. Nevertheless, that social condition had its good results, as much as the madly-superstitious Crusades had theirs.

In this case, the good result was the patronage of the arts shown by such women as Madame de Sablé, who kept a *salon* for literary and political discussions and the encouragement of men of genius. Moreover, she argues, women benefited too, by being 'admitted to a common fund of ideas, to common objects of interest with men; and this must ever be the essential condition at once of true womanly culture and of true social well-being'. As Marian had herself blossomed in the mainly male medium of Coventry and London, she could write with conviction of the good which arises out of intellectual intercourse between the sexes.

She ends her article on a note of hope for the future, based on the philosophical optimism she shared with Bray, Comte, Spencer, and Lewes, and surely encouraged too by her personal happiness with Lewes in Weimar:

Let the whole field of reality be laid open to woman as well as to man, and then that which is peculiar in her mental modification, instead of being, as it is now, a source of discord and repulsion between the sexes, will be found to be a necessary complement to the truth and beauty of life. Then we shall have that marriage of minds which alone can blend all the hues of thought and feeling in one lovely rainbow of promise for the harvest of human happiness.[74]

She and Lewes *were* happy, in spite of the trickle of news which reached them from London, causing them headaches and sleepless nights. They went to parties given by Liszt, who introduced them to Clara Schumann and the Russian composer Anton Rubinstein (whom George Eliot made the model for Klesmer in *Daniel Deronda*)[75] and heard three Wagner operas directed by him in the Court theatre. Marian described her response to Wagner's 'music of the future' in a striking phrase, coined to express her comic sense of inadequacy as a listener to *Lohengrin*. We must learn, she wrote in her worked-up journal account of 'Liszt, Wagner, and Weimar' in *Fraser's Magazine* in July 1855, 'to think of ourselves as tadpoles unprescient of the future frog'. Still, she adds in concession to her own failure to respond to Wagner's difficult harmonies, 'the tadpole is limited to tadpole pleasures; and so, in our state of development, we are swayed by melody'.[76]

Lewes was adapting a French farce, *The Fox Who Got the Grapes*, which he sent to London on 7 October. As they needed the money earned by such efforts, Marian 'partly condensed Liszt's art. On Meyerbeer' for the *Leader*, and she recorded with relief on 30 October the receipt of £15 from Chapman for her Madame de Sablé article.[77] They sent letters to, and received letters from, Robert Chambers and Arthur Helps, as well as Chapman and Bray. Many of these letters have disappeared, as has one from Chrissey sending 'melancholy news about her boy Robert'. Poor Robert had been 'very naughty – so naughty that he has had to leave his situation and they are determined to send him to sea', Marian told Bray cryptically on 12 November.[78] 'They' were Chrissey as advised by Isaac, to whom Marian had written asking him to pay her half-yearly income to Bray. (Robert died at sea less than six months later.[79]) Marian did not at this time tell any of her family about her decision to live with Lewes.

Lewes's work on his biography of Goethe went on apace, with Marian helping him in the task of translating extracts from Goethe's works for quoting in the book.[80] They read Goethe's works aloud to one another, and Lewes visited Goethe's daughter-in-law, Ottilie von Goethe, and Johann Peter Eckermann, who had been Goethe's secretary and who was now dying. Marian noted when she met him on 8 October that he was 'shattered in mind and body'.[81] Strauss had given Lewes a letter of introduction to Adolf Schöll, editor of Goethe's letters to Frau von Stein. Schöll called on Lewes and Marian on 8 August and took them to the Duke's summer residence, Schloss Belvedere, to see the suite of rooms, the 'Dichterzimmer', dedicated to Goethe, Schiller, and Wieland, with frescoes depicting scenes from their works.[82] They enjoyed roaming around Weimar and its environs, experiencing for themselves the places associated with Goethe.

After three months in Weimar they moved on to Berlin, where Lewes would have access to libraries and could talk to more acquaintances, editors, and scholars of Goethe and his works. Liszt invited them for a farewell breakfast on 1 November; on 3 November they caught a train for Berlin, arriving after an eight-hour journey at the Hôtel de l'Europe.[83]

As they had done in Weimar, Lewes and Marian spent the day after their arrival in Berlin looking for lodgings; they found a suitable house on Dorotheenstrasse, and moved in. The following morning, Sunday 5 November, they went out for a walk and met by chance one of the men Lewes had come to consult, the diplomat, *littérateur*, and collector of Goetheana, Karl August Varnhagen von Ense. Lewes knew him well, having visited Berlin twice before (the first time with an introduction from Carlyle), in 1838 and 1845. Varnhagen knew that Lewes was married, for he had received several cheerful letters following Lewes's wedding in February 1841 giving expression to his happiness with Agnes and announcing the births of his children as they occurred.[84] Now Varnhagen met Lewes with 'an Englishwoman, a Miss Evans', as he noted in his diary, 'who edits the *Westminster Review* and has translated Strauss's *Life of Jesus* and Feuerbach's *Essence of Christianity*'.[85]

For her part, Marian wrote in her journal that Varnhagen was 'a fine

looking courtly old man'. On his first visit to them on 7 November he
told them of 'his disappointment in Carlyle when after years of correspondence they at last met in the body'.[86] Carlyle had visited Berlin in
1852 to do research for his six-volume life of Frederick the Great, and
had complained about everything in Berlin, much to Varnhagen's disgust.[87] Lewes and Marian had the good sense not to complain, though
like Carlyle they found Berlin unattractive and German beds uncomfortable.[88] Marian told Chapman on 9 January 1855 that Berlin was
an ugly place, full of soldiers – '300,000 puppets in uniform' – but the
companionship of Lewes made it attractive to her: 'The day seems too
short for our happiness and we both of us feel that we have begun life
afresh – with new ambition and new powers.'[89]

Varnhagen opened his valuable library to Lewes, who visited him
several times over the next four months to consult and borrow books.
As the leading literary man of Berlin, his *salons* were attended by all sorts
of interesting people, whom Lewes and Marian met. Lewes renewed his
acquaintance with the literary hostess Henriette Solmar, and they met
various German scholars, including Professor Otto Friedrich Gruppe, a
polymath who combined 'talent, fertility, versatility' with 'an almost
childish naïveté in the value he attaches to poor jokes and other trivi-
alities'.[90] Marian wrote a brief account of Gruppe's book on 'The
Future of German Philosophy' in the *Leader* in July 1855, praising him
for abandoning the usual German abstractions, 'the attempt to climb to
heaven by the rainbow bridge of "the high *priori* road"' in favour of
humbly 'treading the uphill *à posteriori* path which will lead, not indeed to
heaven, but to an eminence whence we may see very bright and blessed
things on earth'.[91]

The people of most interest personally to Marian and Lewes were
Professor Adolf Stahr and his lover, the author Fanny Lewald. Though
Marian found them both full of ludicrous literary egotism – Fanny
Lewald had written a popular account of a trip she made to Britain in
1850, when she met the Carlyles, among other luminaries[92] – she was
interested in their situation. They had lived together for nine years. Stahr
was waiting for a divorce, and was able to marry Fanny on 6 February
1855, while Lewes and Marian were still in Berlin.[93]

In a lively letter to Bray on 12 November Marian recounted their
social activities, carefully pointing out once more how kindly she was
received by 'the best society of Berlin', i.e. Varnhagen and Fräulein

Solmar. They saw Lessing's *Nathan der Weise* at the theatre, and Marian was 'thrilled to think that Lessing dared nearly a hundred years ago to write the grand sentiments and profound thoughts' of religious tolerance in the play. She told Bray she liked the general tolerance of unorthodoxy in Germany, which went some way towards outweighing the disadvantages of German table manners and lack of wit: 'They put their knives in their mouths, write un-sit-out-able comedies and unreadable books.'[94]

She had some worries about home. Isaac was slow to pay Bray her half-yearly income as arranged, probably out of 'disinclination to accommodate me', as she told Bray. He was planning to call in some of her money to help Chrissey, so that her next instalment would be less than usual. She, too, wanted to help her sister. On 21 January 1855 she wrote to offer £10 towards her niece Emily's school bill.[95] Lewes was writing for the *Leader*, but his £20 a month for that went to Agnes and the children. He translated two French farces for money while in Germany, and Marian wanted to do another article for Chapman, but was too diffident to offer one, since he had not complimented her on 'Woman in France'.[96]

All their efforts were being put into the *Life of Goethe*, which Lewes had almost finished by the end of February, with Marian's help.[97] From 8 November 1854 she was also engaged on a translation from Latin of Spinoza's *Ethics*. The work was particularly congenial to her, as it had long been to Lewes, for Spinoza's clear, calm logic, his deduction of the moral life as a necessary corollary of human needs – the idea that our natural self-love is turned into love and duty towards others by our perception of the human fellowship we share with them. She worked hard, eventually completing over 650 pages of translation in February 1856.[98]

Spinoza had been persecuted for his pantheism, and vilified for his rationalist view of religion and philosophy. These aspects of his thought, forerunners of the religion of humanity of Comte and Feuerbach, had been as attractive to Goethe as to Lewes in his youth and to Marian when she began a translation of his *Tractatus Theologico-Politicus* in 1843. In the *Life of Goethe* Lewes dealt sympathetically with Goethe's youthful enthusiasm for Spinoza's clarity and disinterested morality, even revealing briefly his own excitement at hearing a passage from Spinoza as a young man.[99]

The translating of Spinoza thus went very well with the reading and writing and discussing of Lewes's work in progress on Goethe in the Dorotheenstrasse lodgings. Marian and Lewes had settled into a domestic pattern which would vary little for the rest of their lives. They generally researched, wrote, and translated in the mornings, then walked and visited museums in the afternoon. Those evenings which were not taken up by visiting friends or going to the theatre were spent at home reading chiefly Goethe and Shakespeare aloud, and looking at Lewes's manuscript as it grew. Back in England in March 1855, Marian recalled the 'happy months we spent at Berlin, in spite of the bitter cold which came on in January and lasted almost till we left':

How we used to rejoice in the idea of our warm room and coffee as we battled our way from dinner against the wind or snow! Then came the delightful long evenings in which we read Shakspeare, Goethe, Heine and Macaulay, with German Pfefferkuchen and Semmels [gingerbread and rolls] at the end.[100]

As with Spinoza, so with Shakespeare. Goethe had been obsessed with him, writing rhapsodic essays on his works and building into his novel *Wilhelm Meisters Lehrjahre* (*Wilhelm Meister's Apprenticeship*) not only a critical discussion of Shakespeare among the theatrical company Wilhelm joins, but a parallel, or pastiche, of the plot of *Hamlet* in Wilhelm's relationship with his absent father. When Lewes wrote his chapter on *Wilhelm Meister* he praised the criticism of *Hamlet* as 'still the best criticism we have on that wonderful play'.[101]

Of *Wilhelm Meister*, and more especially of *Die Wahlverwandtschaften* (*Elective Affinities*), Lewes gives an intelligent defence against charges of immorality, especially as regards the depiction of relationships between men and women. Lewes boldly praises 'the complete absence of all *moral verdict* on the part of the author' of *Wilhelm Meister*, in which characters lie, cheat, and behave promiscuously. Goethe neither moralizes nor wallows in the behaviour he presents: 'the Artist has been content to paint scenes of life, *without comment*', a stance which is justified in the story of how a weak young man has his character moulded and modified 'from self-culture to sympathy', all done in 'the artist's, not the preacher's way'.[102]

That Marian had an important input into the discussion of Goethe's novels we know from two sources. One is her 'Recollections of Berlin', in which she describes a discussion with Adolf Stahr about *Elective*

Affinities. Stahr called the novel's dénouement 'unvernünftig' (unreasonable). 'So, I said, were dénouements in real life very frequently: Goethe had given the dénouement which would naturally follow from the characters of the respective actors.'[103] The dénouement in question is the painful outcome of the helpless mutual attraction of two men and two women. Eduard and Charlotte, a married couple, invite Eduard's friends the Captain and Charlotte's young ward Ottilie to stay with them. A slow drama is played out in which, as Lewes says in his *Life of Goethe*, two of the characters – Eduard and Ottilie – represent Passion, recklessly falling in love and becoming completely absorbed in one another, 'like two children entering on a first affection'. By contrast, the other two, Charlotte and the Captain, represent Reason and Duty, subduing their mutual love 'with touching nobleness'.[104] Charlotte bears her husband's child, which drowns when in Ottilie's care. Ottilie pines away and dies of guilt, followed by Eduard. The end is melodramatic certainly, though in a strangely subdued way, given the self-control of Charlotte and the Captain and the disinterested tone of the narrator. Marian's remark about Goethe's consistency in his dénouement is therefore a shrewd one. It is 'unreasonable' in respect of the unreasonable pair, Ottilie and Eduard, but perfectly reasonable in respect of the other two.

The other evidence – if any were needed – that Lewes's *Life of Goethe* was enriched by intelligent discussions with his partner lies in the work itself. In the chapter on *Elective Affinities* Lewes quotes 'a dear friend of mine, whose criticism is always worthy of attention', in defence of the slow movement of the plot, with which the more volatile Lewes confesses his impatience.[105] In subsequent editions of the book, published in 1864 and 1875, Lewes proudly changed 'a dear friend' to 'a great writer, and one very dear to me'.

It is not only Lewes's defence of the representation of marriage and sexual relations in Goethe's novels which is of interest to us. Perhaps even more interesting, given his and Marian's situation, is his frank analysis of Goethe's liaisons in life. In his youth, Goethe loved and left Frederika Brion, for which he was much criticized. Lewes accepts that he was thoughtless to encourage Frederika. On the other hand:

He was perfectly right to draw back from an engagement which he felt his love was not strong enough properly to fulfil. It seems to me that he acted a more moral part in relinquishing her, than if he had swamped this lesser in a greater wrong, and escaped one breach of faith by a still greater breach of faith – a reluctant, because unloving, marriage . . . I am not forgetting the necessity of being stringent against the common thoughtlessness of youth in forming such relations; but I say that this thoughtlessness once having occurred, reprobate it as we may, the pain which a separation may bring had better be endured, than evaded by an unholy marriage, which cannot come to good.[106]

George Eliot would depict a similar dilemma (though with a different conclusion) in the Maggie–Stephen relationship in *The Mill on the Floss*, the novel in which she deposited a transposed version of her and Lewes's own difficult experience.

Then there is Goethe's marriage, and Lewes's treatment of it in his biography. When already established as court poet and privy councillor of Weimar, Goethe had scandalized bourgeois opinion by taking as his mistress Christiane Vulpius, a young woman of humble social position, who bore him his only child, August, in 1789. Society came to accept the liaison, but was shocked once again in 1806, when Goethe married Christiane in gratitude for her protection of him at the time of the Battle of Jena, the decisive Prussian battle of the Napoleonic Wars, when French soldiers entered his house. Lewes's restraint in discussing the marriage, and Weimar's response to it, is as impressive as his psychological insight and an understanding born of bitter experience in his own different, but not dissimilar, case:

The judgments of men are singular. No action in Aristotle's life subjected him to more calumny than his generous marriage with the friendless Phythia; no action in Goethe's life has excited more scandal than his marriage to Christiane. It was thought disgraceful enough in him to have taken her into his house (a *liaison* out of the house seeming, in the eyes of the world, a venial error, which becomes serious directly it approaches nearer to the condition of marriage); but for the great poet, the Geheimrath, actually to complete such an enormity as to crown his connection with Christiane by a legal sanction, *this* was indeed more than society could tolerate.[107]

'The judgments of men are singular.' And the judgements of women too, as Lewes and Marian knew they would find when they returned from Germany, where they were easily tolerated and accepted – perhaps partly because they were merely visitors, and so not perceived as a threat to the stability of society – to England, which was their home. On 11 March 1855 they set out in the snow for Cologne, then Brussels, then

Calais. On Tuesday 13 March they arrived in Dover, spending a night in a hotel, then taking lodgings in Sydney Place, where Marian stayed, translating Spinoza, while Lewes went up to London to settle his financial and family affairs and look for lodgings in the capital.

Marian's last words in her 'Recollections of Berlin', written on 27 March as she waited quietly for Lewes to call her up to London, convey in a subdued manner her apprehension about the new life on which she was about to embark in England:

English mutton, an English fire and an English bed were likely to be appreciated by creatures who had had eight months of Germany with its questionable meat, its stove-heated rooms and beds warranted not to tuck up. The taste and quietude of a first rate English hotel were also in striking contrast with the heavy finery, the noise, and the indiscriminate smoking of German inns. But after all, Germany is no bad place to live in, and the Germans, to counterbalance their want of taste and politeness, are at least free from the bigotry and exclusiveness of their more refined cousins.[108]

She and Lewes were under no illusion about the difficult social position they – and especially she – now held.

CHAPTER SIX

The Strong-minded Woman of the
Westminster Review *1855–6*

Having taken lodgings for Marian at 1 Sydney Place, Lewes left her in Dover while he went to London, where he had several matters to sort out before she could join him. Most importantly, he visited Agnes and the children in Kensington to settle their future. Agnes may have been in financial difficulties; a note about Lewes's finances made by George Eliot in 1878 records a debt in 1855 of £300.¹ Thornton Hunt, responsible for some of Agnes's children – three of her four by him had been born by this time – was not reliable when it came to contributing towards their upbringing. In December 1856 he and Lewes nearly came to blows over his failure to pay his share of Agnes's expenses.²

Lewes raised some cash – £39. 17s. od. – from selling his translation of a French farce, *The Cozy Couple*, to Charles James Mathews, manager of the Lyceum Theatre, with whom he had often collaborated on adaptations of French plays.³ He also got £2. 2s. od. for two articles published in the *Leader* in March. He was no longer the paper's literary editor, but he and Marian wrote several short reviews and articles during 1855, for which they were paid a guinea a time. Apart from her £90 a year from her father, Lewes and Marian had no income other than the amounts they could earn from journalism, mainly for the *Leader* and the *Westminster Review*. Marian's Weimar journal was written up to make two articles for *Fraser's Magazine*, for which Lewes had written several articles in the 1840s. 'Three Months in Weimar' appeared there in June and 'Liszt, Wagner, and Weimar' in July 1855, bringing in a welcome £14. os. od. Lewes, after some difficulty, sold the *Life of Goethe* to the publisher David Nutt. According to the contract, agreed in June, a print run of

1,500 was to be published, for which Lewes was paid £250 on publication at the end of October and a further £100 when the first 1,000 copies were sold.[4]

Marian spent an anxious month in Dover while Lewes was away grappling with these domestic and financial problems. She carried on with her translation of Spinoza, read Shakespeare and the *Nibelungenlied*, and wrote her recollections of Berlin. Her journal refers to frequent letters from Lewes, who must have known how vulnerable she felt, alone and waiting for his summons to go to London and brave the gossip there. As had happened at Weimar, she received on 9 April a 'painful letter' – we do not know from whom – which caused 'much depression, against which I struggled hard'.[5]

Only a few of her letters survive from this miserable month. On 16 March she had written bravely but distantly to Sara Hennell, to whom she could hardly confide her hopes and fears. She merely wrote that she was 'well and calmly happy' and hoping to hear how everyone at Rosehill was faring.[6] She replied on the same day to a letter from Bessie Parkes, expressing gratitude for Bessie's warmth, but warning her to 'believe no one's representations about me, for there is not a *single person* who is in a position to make a true representation'. To Bessie, too, she insists that her mind is 'deliciously calm and untroubled so far as my own lot is concerned'.[7]

By 4 April Lewes was on a visit to his sympathetic friend Arthur Helps in Hampshire, and Marian told Charles Bray that on his return she would join him in London to see *Goethe* and – she hoped – the Spinoza translation through the press, after which they would probably make 'a new flight to the south of Germany and Italy, for which we both yearn'.[8] This talk of escaping to the continent, only three weeks after returning from an eight-month stay in Germany, gives an inkling of Marian's anxiety about how she and Lewes would be received in London. A remark of Dickens's in a letter to Wilkie Collins on 4 April shows what literary London was saying. 'Do you know that Lewes is here again?' wrote Dickens; 'whether with any idea of emerging from what Carlyle calls the Pit of TOphet [*sic*], I can't say.'[9]

Lewes had found temporary lodgings in Bayswater, to which Marian came on 18 April. Chapman and Bessie Parkes visited, as did Rufa Hennell, a fact Marian made sure she reported to Bray for the benefit of Rufa's sisters-in-law Cara and Sara. She was too proud to risk a rebuff by inviting them all to visit, though she told Bray on 1 May that once she and Lewes were established at their new lodgings in East Sheen, 'a charming village close to Richmond Park', she hoped he would come and see them there. Rather than appeal to his affection for her as a reason for coming, she described the attractions of the place. Even as she issued this diffident invitation, she showed some apprehension, asking Bray not to '*mis*quote something I said two or three years ago, which something you seem to have converted into a supercilious, impertinent expression of disapprobation on my part'.[10] No doubt this was a disparaging remark she had made about Lewes before she had got to know him properly.

Marian had good reason to feel nervous about the meeting between these two men who knew her so well. Bray and Lewes were an incompatible pair, as was amply proved when Bray did visit East Sheen on 10 July. Though it was an occasion Marian eagerly desired, it turned out to be quite as awkward as she had anticipated with her finely-tuned pessimism. In her letter to Bray on 16 July, after his return to Coventry, she made a half-apology for some bad temper, explaining that both she and Lewes had been ill the day Bray visited. Lewes and Bray, both frank and assertive, had argued about the merits of phrenology, and Bray had upbraided Marian for deserting the cause. That Combe was invoked, whom Marian knew to have complained about 'the effect on his reputation of having introduced me to one or two friends',[11] made her particularly bitter. She defended herself and Lewes all the more staunchly because of Combe's pettiness:

I am not conscious of falling off from the 'physiological basis'. I never believed more profoundly than I do now that character is based on organization. I never had a higher appreciation than I have now of the services which phrenology has rendered towards the science of man. But I do not, and I think I never shall, consider every man shallow or unconscientious who is unable to embrace all Mr. Combe's views of organology and psychology – especially as some of the ablest men I have ever known are in that position of inability.

Her letter, though signed 'Yours affectionately', concludes with a proud remark intended to sting: 'I am glad to hear that you enjoyed the view from Richmond Hill and that you had thus some compensation for the trouble you took in coming to see us.'[12]

She could not fall back into the old relationship with her Coventry friends. Though she still loved them for what they had been to her in her unhappy youth, she had now outstripped them in opinions and experience as she had always done in intellectual force. She could not, and would not, remain subservient now that her circumstances made her less dependent on their support. Cara's reproachful silence and Sara's well-meaning but openly critical attitude to her relationship with Lewes hurt and irritated her. She persisted in writing to Sara in a tone which seemed to say, I know you disapprove of me; I wish you did not, as I crave your approval, but I think you are wrong and I refuse to beg forgiveness or understanding of my actions. Handicapped by her sense of what she had been to them and could never be again, she wrote letters she knew would be construed as cold and proud. What else could she do?

Cara's silence since writing her one letter in November 1854 to Berlin rankled most with Marian, who had also stopped writing, though she always sent her love to Cara in her letters to Bray and Sara. Now Cara wrote to know what Marian wanted her to do with some house-hold linen she had been keeping. 'Those dreadful sheets and pillow cases!' Marian wrote in reply on 4 September. 'Pray give them away if you won't use them, for I don't want them.' She grasped the opportunity offered by Cara's letter to explain, though not excuse, her relationship with Lewes, about which she assured her friend that she felt 'no levity' but was, on the contrary, 'profoundly serious'. Venting her anger at Combe's 'petty and absurd' concern for his own reputation, and telling Cara that she was 'unacquainted with Mr. Lewes's real character', she launched into an impassioned yet dignified explanation of her position:

No one can be better aware than yourself that it is possible for two people to hold different opinions on momentous subjects with equal sincerity and an equally earnest conviction that their respective opinions are alone the only true moral ones. If we differ on the subject of the marriage laws, I at least can believe of you that you cleave to what you believe to be good, and I don't know of anything in the nature of your views that should prevent you from believing the same of me. *How far* we differ I think we neither of us know; for I am ignorant of your precise views and apparently you attribute to me both feelings and opinions which are not mine. We cannot set each other quite right on this matter in letters, but one thing I can tell you in few words. Light and easily broken ties are what I neither desire theoretically nor could live for practically. Women who are satisfied with such ties do *not* act as I have done – they obtain what they desire and are still invited to dinner.[13]

It would be some years before Marian Evans, or Marian Lewes, as she had to remind friends like Bray and Bessie Parkes to call her when they wrote or visited, was invited to dinner as a matter of course. She suffered, as she knew she would, exclusion from mixed company; only the boldest women – Rufa, Bessie, Barbara Leigh Smith – issued and accepted invitations. And though many men did not object to visiting the Leweses, most did not take their wives with them or give general invitations in return. As Bessie Parkes wrote to Barbara in November 1863, by which time Marian was no longer the strong-minded woman known only in London's journalistic circles but the universally admired author of *Adam Bede*, *The Mill on the Floss*, *Silas Marner*, and *Romola*, public opinion was still a strong deterrent to normal social intercourse. 'For instance,' she wrote, 'Anthony Trollope goes there next week; but will he take his wife? and *so on*.'[14]

Marian's way of dealing with the undesirable consequences of her happy union with Lewes was to give out signals that she did not want or need ordinary social intercourse. Her position was impossible. Those who wished to have her friendship often felt rebuffed because she was, as Trollope said succinctly in 1874 to an acquaintance eager to meet George Eliot, 'somewhat difficult to know'.[15] But she can hardly be blamed for seeking to spare herself the humiliation of being excluded by people whose narrow-mindedness she disliked or whose hypocrisy she despised.

On the whole, Marian kept silent on such attitudes as they related to her life, preferring to be thought cold and proud rather than beseech forgiveness where she firmly believed she had done no wrong. In her novels she deposited her experience in complex and transformed ways, never putting any of her characters in a position exactly like her own, but setting up social and sexual dilemmas for heroines like Maggie Tulliver and Gwendolen Harleth which she shows to have no easy solution. In *The Mill on the Floss*, in which Maggie is thought by her acquaintances in St Ogg's to have eloped and had sexual relations with Stephen Guest, the narrator speaks out critically about the injustice of 'public opinion', in particular that part of it known as 'the world's wife', so ready to reach a damning judgement and so inclined to be harder on the woman than the man in such cases.[16]

Though Cara began to write again after receiving Marian's letter of 4 September, she and Marian were in no hurry to meet after the embarrassment of Bray's visit in July. Sara, however, did call when staying in London in July, but did not find the Leweses in. Marian wrote that she was 'sorry to miss you that last day that you called'.[17] In July she had sent Sara a letter she had received from Barbara Leigh Smith, saying, 'I think you will like to see such a manifestation of her strong noble nature. Burn it when you have read it.'[18] Barbara had undoubtedly written supporting Marian's right to live with whom she pleased, though at that time she disliked Lewes, thinking him too familiar and lacking 'the ordinary breeding in youth of what is called a gentleman', according to Bessie Parkes's daughter.[19] Barbara later came to like Lewes, and became Marian's closest and most understanding friend. This letter to Marian, which we may presume Sara Hennell burned as requested, was intended to cement her friendship with Marian, whom she had met through Bessie. In it she asked Marian to respond as a friend, and was clearly rewarded, for in her next letter, in January 1856, she addressed Marian as 'Dear Friend! (by your permission granted under your hand & seal August 1855)'.[20]

If Bray's visit was a disaster, Marian's relationship with Chapman, of whom Lewes also had a low opinion, flourished. She had reason to be grateful to him, not only because he stood by her, but also because he offered her regular work on the *Westminster Review* at a time when she and Lewes were struggling to get straight financially. While waiting in Dover in March, she received a letter from Chapman asking her to undertake the Contemporary Literature, or Belles Lettres, section of the *Review*, in which new literature was reviewed in brief. She received £12. 12s. od. a quarter for this work, beginning with the July 1855 number, and it was a relief to her to be able to rely on this regular income.

Chapman was useful in another way too. Though Lewes was temperamentally confident, optimistic, and generous, and thus bolstered her low self-confidence invaluably, it was gratifying for her to be deferred to by Chapman. He submitted for her scrutiny an article he had written for the *Westminster* on the position of women in ancient and barbaric societies. Marian responded thoroughly to his request for advice, no doubt glad to be able to exercise the commanding side of her nature, a side she consciously depressed in her relations and correspondence with others.

She certainly lectured him roundly on his faults of logic and style in a letter of 25 June, finding 'certain old faults' such as 'inexactness of expression, triads and duads of verbs and adjectives, mixed metaphors and a sort of watery volume that requires to be reduced by evaporation'.[21] Chapman was so cast down by the list of his faults which followed that she had to write again two days later, reassuring him that his article was worth publishing and that he ought not to be despondent.[22]

The need to earn her living and help Lewes with their housekeeping expenses and his support for Agnes – he paid her a minimum of £250 a year from now until his death in 1878, after which George Eliot continued the payment[23] – meant Marian now produced a rapid succession of reviews for the *Leader* and for the Belles Lettres section of the *Westminster*, as well as some substantial articles. A difference in tone can be detected between these essays and her earlier articles, such as the review of Mackay's *Progress of the Intellect* and the essay on women in France. Her writing now has a sharpness, a brilliance with a cutting edge, which is perhaps not unrelated to her feeling embattled socially and being in need of an outlet for her power. More positively, her confidence as a writer undoubtedly grew as a result of her emotional fulfilment with Lewes. His confidence and indifference to the criticism of others, so different from her own thin-skinnedness in this respect, as she admitted to Sara Hennell,[24] seem to have rubbed off on her a little. She found that she could be merciless, as she was towards the faults of composition in Chapman's article.

Her article on Lord Brougham's *Lives* of men of letters of the eighteenth century in the *Leader* in July is even rather too sharp. 'Literary lock and poker-making', 'third-rate biographies in the style of a literary hack', 'clumsy superfluities', are some of her remarks on Brougham's writing. And her alertness to hypocrisy in sexual matters has her accusing Brougham in a way she forbade herself, though strongly tempted, to do to some of her own acquaintances:

We had marked several other points for notice, especially that very remarkable criticism of Lord Brougham's on the *Nouvelle Heloïse*, in which he implies, that for a lover to remind his mistress that she had allowed him to kiss her, is to tell her what a 'forward, abandoned wanton she proved', and his supposition, that because Johnson was sometimes wandering all night in the streets with Savage he must necessarily have indulged in certain vices 'in their more crapulous form' (an unfortunate suggestion to come from the Brougham of Jeffrey's letters, who is described as 'roaming the streets with the sons of Belial').[25]

The difficulties of relations between men and women are prominent in another article in the *Leader* of 4 August. This time the subject was a book on Milton by Thomas Keightley. Marian singles out for discussion Milton's views on marriage and divorce. She deals with his argument in favour of divorce for those who have, in his words, 'unwarily, in a thing never practised before, made themselves the bondmen of a luckless and helpless matrimony'. Relating the argument to the topical case of Caroline Norton, who had recently appealed to the Queen over her estranged husband's refusal to pay her allowance (all her property and money having become his on their marriage), and to the bill then going before Parliament to amend the divorce laws, Marian robustly defends Milton's plea for divorce. To those who objected to Milton's pleading his own cause – he was unhappily married – along with the general one she replies with the pragmatic argument that 'if we waited for the impulse of abstract benevolence or justice, we fear that most reforms would be postponed to the Greek Kalends'.[26]

Certainly, marriage reform was slow to come in England in the nineteenth century. After much agitation, not least in the pages of the *Leader*, the Act of 1857 made divorce only slightly easier to obtain than before. There was still no equality between the sexes. Men could sue on the grounds of the wife's adultery alone, but women had to prove adultery plus cruelty or desertion or incest or bestiality. Married women still had no right to the wealth or property they brought to the marriage, or to any earnings they made, an injustice against which Barbara Leigh Smith was a strong campaigner, beginning with her pamphlet of 1854, *A Brief Summary, in Plain Language, of the Most Important Laws concerning Women*.[27] Though Marian wrote feelingly about the manifest injustice of Mrs Norton's case, Milton's plea on grounds of humanity and tolerance of human error rather than justice was closer to home for her, since Lewes and Agnes had agreed to allow one another sexual freedom in their marriage. Recognizing this, Lewes never complained or sought to blame Agnes for his inability to divorce her and marry Marian.

The position of women filled her mind during this first summer of her new life in London. The *Leader* for 13 October carries a short article on Margaret Fuller and Mary Wollstonecraft, a subject chosen at a time of 'dearth of new books', as she explains. Taking up her point in 'Woman in France' about the importance for both sexes of bringing women into touch with 'a common fund of ideas', she shows how both these remarkable women made the case for female equality on grounds not only of common justice but also of the desirability for men that their wives and partners should be educated to the same standard as men themselves. Marian adds her own striking metaphor to reinforce the case, one which would surface again in *Middlemarch* in relation to the unhappy marriage of Lydgate and Rosamond:

There is a notion commonly entertained among men that an instructed woman, capable of having opinions, is likely to prove an impracticable yoke-fellow, always pulling one way when her husband wants to go the other, oracular in tone, and prone to give curtain lectures on metaphysics. But surely, so far as obstinacy is concerned, your unreasoning animal is the most unmanageable of creatures, where you are not allowed to settle the question by a cudgel, a whip and bridle, or even a string to the leg. For our own parts, we see no consistent or commodious medium between the old plan of corporal discipline and that thorough education of women which will make them rational beings in the highest sense of the word.[28]

Marian felt a close affinity with Margaret Fuller and Mary Wollstonecraft, with their boldness, their honesty, their yearnings, and also their propensity to despair. Much later, in 1871, she tried to cheer up a friend by invoking the example of Mary Wollstonecraft and confiding that in her own case, too, 'hopelessness' had been 'all through my life, but especially in painful years of my youth, the chief source of wasted energy with all the consequent bitterness of regret',[29] adding that for Mary Wollstonecraft, as for herself, happiness had come after all.

As Marian was happy in her private life with Lewes, her writing career flourished. Reviews and articles of distinction came in rapid succession from her pen, the combined result of her wide reading, tenacious memory, and lively discussions with Lewes, who shared her intellectual breadth of interest and who had long made his living by reviewing on every subject under the sun. His chief interest in 1855 was natural history; his *Life of Goethe* has a long chapter on Goethe's contributions to biology and botany, and he spent many hours with Richard Owen in his laboratories at the Hunterian Museum and at his home near the Leweses in Richmond Park. Though Huxley and Darwin were soon to challenge Owen's reputation, he was in 1855 indisputably the leading scientist in Britain. Lewes reviewed his works and borrowed books from him for his own researches into animal life.[30]

We get some idea of the domestic happiness of the Leweses, whose personal relationship went so closely with their working partnership, from Marian's account to Bray in June of a typical day:

I think we like East Sheen better and better, and are happier every day – writing hard, walking hard, reading Homer and science and rearing tadpoles. I read aloud for about three hours every evening, beginning with Boswell's Johnson, or some such enjoyable book, not unfriendly to digestion, then subsiding into the dreary dryness of Whewell's History of the Inductive Sciences and winding up with Heine's wit and imagination. We breakfast at ½ past 8, read to ourselves till 10, write till ½ past 1, walk till nearly 4, and dine at 5, regretting each day as it goes.[31]

On 24 August 1855 Marian finished an article for the *Westminster Review* which has a claim to be her best. Lewes's son Charles later recorded that after reading this piece Lewes, during a walk in Richmond Park, told Marian that 'it convinced him of the true genius of her writing'.[32] The article, published in the October number of the *Review*, was 'Evangelical Teaching: Dr. Cumming', a scorching review of works on Biblical prophecy by Dr John Cumming, minister of the Scottish National Church in Covent Garden. In it Marian turns an intellectual searchlight on Cumming's narrow, bigoted Calvinism, exposing the unloveliness, the lack of logic, and the immorality of a fanatical adherence to a creed she had accepted in her own susceptible youth.

The article has one of the most arresting openings in all periodical literature. Though not rivalling in succinctness Francis Jeffrey's famous first sentence in the *Edinburgh Review* on Wordsworth's *Excursion* (1814) – 'This will never do' – it is a masterly catcher of the reader's attention and a promise of what is to follow:

Given, a man with moderate intellect, a moral standard not higher than the average, some rhetorical affluence and great glibness of speech, what is the career in which, without the aid of birth or money, he may most easily attain power and reputation in English society? Where is that Goschen of mediocrity in which a smattering of science and learning will pass for profound instruction, where platitudes will be accepted as wisdom, bigoted narrowness as holy zeal, unctuous egoism as God-given piety? Let such a man become an evangelical preacher; he will then find it possible to reconcile small ability with great ambition, superficial knowledge with the prestige of erudition, a middling morale with a high reputation for sanctity.[33]

What follows is a thorough routing of Cumming's arguments against Catholicism and atheism, his political interpretations of prophecy, the relish with which he consigns those who disagree with his theology to 'everlasting burning'. Cumming has no sympathy with those who have found themselves doubting and distressed. Marian quotes from *In Memoriam* Tennyson's line about one 'perplext in faith, but pure in deeds', a line which is closely followed by the more famous

> There lives more faith in honest doubt,
> Believe me, than in half the creeds.[34]

Cumming, she says, has no time for people (like her and so many others) who are 'craving light, yearning for a faith that will harmonize and cherish its highest powers and aspirations, but unable to find that faith in dogmatic Christianity'. Instead he assumes every doubter is 'hardened, conceited, consciously shutting his eyes to the light'.[35]

Indignation, personal experience, and a knowledge of all Cumming's learned sources and a great many more of which he is ignorant – these combine to call forth her clearest reasoning and a witty use of analogy:

As to the reading which he has prosecuted for fifteen years – *either* it has left him totally ignorant of the relation which his own religious creed bears to the criticism and philosophy of the nineteenth century, *or* he systematically blinks that criticism and that philosophy; and instead of honestly and seriously endeavouring to meet and solve what he knows to be the real difficulties, contents himself with setting up popinjays to shoot at, for the sake of confirming the ignorance and winning the cheap admiration of his evangelical hearers and readers. Like the Catholic preacher who, after throwing down his cap and apostrophizing it as Luther, turned to his audience and said, 'You see this heretical fellow has not a word to say for himself', Dr. Cumming, having drawn his ugly portrait of the infidel, and put arguments of a convenient quality into his mouth, finds a 'short and easy method' of confounding this 'croaking frog'.[36]

Having disposed of Cumming's pretensions to knowledge of his subject, the poverty of his logic in argument, and his injustice to his opponents, she turns to the moral harm of his doctrine. In Cumming's view there is no such thing as a spontaneously good action or feeling; all morality consists in acting 'for the glory of God'. The woman who had translated Feuerbach, agreeing completely with his philosophy of humanity, exposes the moral poverty of Cumming's creed:

The man who endures tortures rather than betray a trust, the man who spends years in toil in order to discharge an obligation from which the law declares him free, must be animated not by the spirit of fidelity to his fellow-man, but by a desire to make 'the name of God more known' ... A wife is not to devote herself to her husband out of love to him and a sense of the duties implied by a close relation – she is to be a faithful wife for the glory of God; if she feels her natural affections welling up too strongly, she is to repress them; it will not do to act from natural affection – she must think of the glory of God.[37]

Lewes was right to see in this essay evidence of his partner's literary genius. Her command of unusual but apt analogy, her sweeping sentence structure, her ability to shape the article dramatically, all these come into play in fruitful alliance with the intellectual mastery of her subject with which all who knew her were familiar. The excellence of the article was noticed by others too. Charles Bray wrote enthusiastically, keen to mend relations after his quarrel with Lewes:

My dear Marian,
 Mrs John Cash [Mary Sibree] read aloud to us the article on the 'Cumming' in the Westminster – We all said it must be yours, or we wd never guess again – No-one else *could* do it, altho' I shd be pleased to think that we had another person who could do it. *Tell us.*[38]

Bray added that he would like to 'come to Park Shot, or *anywhere* to see you', alluding to the Leweses' recent change of lodgings, on 3 October, to 8 Park Shot, Richmond, which would be their home for over three years and which would be the birthplace of 'George Eliot'. Marian replied, confessing that the article was hers, but asking him (forlorn hope) to keep the authorship a secret. It 'appears to have produced a strong impression', she wrote, 'and that impression would be a little counteracted if the author were known to be a *woman*'.[39] Particularly, as she may have suggested in the next sentence which has been heavily deleted and thereby rendered illegible, the free-thinking woman living outside marriage with Lewes.

With Marian, success gave confidence, but slowly. More excellent articles in the *Westminster Review* followed during 1856, until in September of that year, encouraged by Lewes, she first tried her hand at fiction. Much of her short reviewing at this time was of new novels, and we who know what she would shortly do as a novelist can watch with interest the critical standards she applies to the fiction of others. She noticed Kingsley's Elizabethan story *Westward Ho!* more than once, a practice common in those days of anonymous reviewing. In the *Leader* of 19 May 1855 she complained of Kingsley's using fiction to preach, and so turning his novel into an anti-Catholic tract:

It is as if a painter in colour were to write 'Oh, you villain!' under his Jesuits or murderers; or to have a strip flowing from a hero's mouth, with 'Imitate me, my man!' on it. No doubt the villain is to be hated, and the hero loved; but we ought to see that sufficiently in the figures of them. We don't want a man with a wand, going about the gallery and haranguing us. Art is art, and tells its own story.[40]

Her second notice, in the Belles Lettres section of the *Westminster* in July, takes this criticism further, in the process expounding a view of fiction which takes it for granted that literature should have a morally beneficial effect, be *utile* as well as *dulce*, but which requires that the message be subservient to the medium. Objecting to Kingsley's 'perpetual hortative tendency', his readiness to 'drop into the homily', she generalizes from his example:

If he would confine himself to his true sphere, he might be a teacher in the sense in which every great artist is a teacher – namely, by giving us his higher sensibility as a medium, a delicate acoustic or optical instrument, bringing home to our coarser senses what would otherwise be unperceived by us. But Mr. Kingsley, unhappily, like so many other gifted men, has two steeds – his Pegasus and his hobby: the one he rides with a graceful *abandon*, to the admiration of all beholders; but no sooner does he get astride the other, than he becomes a feeble imitator of Carlyle's *manège*, and attempts to put his wooden toy to all the wonderful paces of the great Scotchman's fiery Tartar horse.[41]

In the same number of the *Westminster* she moves on from Kingsley to review *Constance Herbert*, a new novel by Jane Carlyle's friend

Geraldine Jewsbury. Once more, her subject is an author's moralizing in fiction. This time she turns her attention to plots and dénouements, finding the so-called moral of the novel anything but moral. Her argument shows her applying to Geraldine Jewsbury's plot logic the same test by which she found Cumming's moral logic woefully lacking. If Cumming could praise a good action only if it was done for the glory of God, Geraldine Jewsbury preaches a high-sounding doctrine of renunciation which turns out on close scrutiny to be a sham, morally speaking:

This moral is illustrated in the novel by the story of three ladies, who, after renouncing their lovers, or being renounced by them, have the satisfaction of feeling in the end that these lovers were extremely 'good-for-nothing', and that they (the ladies) have had an excellent riddance. In all this we can see neither the true doctrine of renunciation, nor a true representation of the realities of life; and we are sorry that a writer of Miss Jewsbury's insight and sincerity should have produced three volumes for the sake of teaching such copy-book morality. It is not the fact that what duty calls on us to renounce, will invariably prove 'not worth the keeping'; and if it *were* the fact, renunciation would cease to be moral heroism, and would be simply a calculation of prudence.

Where Cumming offers the incentive of salvation, Geraldine Jewsbury hands out prizes to her characters this side of eternity. Marian will have none of this:

The notion that duty looks stern, but all the while has her hand full of sugar-plums, with which she will reward us by-and-by, is the favourite cant of optimists, who try to make out that this tangled wilderness of life has a plan as easy to trace as that of a Dutch garden; but it really undermines all true moral development by perpetually substituting something extrinsic as a motive to action, instead of the immediate impulse of love or justice, which alone makes an action truly moral.[42]

Marian touches magisterially here on a problem she herself would find difficulty with when she began writing novels rather than reviewing them. When parcelling out a future to her characters beyond the confines of the novel's story, she faced the same problem as Geraldine Jewsbury and others: whether to make this character or that happy in love, successful in marriage or career, and so on. Though the plots-in-progress of her novels are complex and open to different possibilities, the endings are, like any other writer's, single. Either Dorothea marries

Ladislaw or she does not; either Maggie lives or she dies. Moreover, it is difficult for the author to avoid seeming to reward or punish characters by choosing a particular ending for them.

It was a dilemma faced by all nineteenth-century novelists (many twentieth-century novels get round it by ending in flux, as it were), and which more than one resented. Dickens and Charlotte Brontë famously refused on occasion to decide on a single future for their heroes, Dickens with his alternative endings for *Great Expectations* (1860) and Charlotte Brontë in her extraordinary tantalizing *envoi* to *Villette* (1853). But such rebellions bring their own dissatisfactions. George Eliot would struggle to avoid crude examples of poetic justice, while seeking also to keep her novels from having unremittingly gloomy or tragic endings. The problem is peculiar to the novel form, since in drama we usually know whether we are about to see a tragedy or a comedy, and we adjust our expectations of poetic justice, or injustice, or reprieves for villains accordingly.

The same difficulty is tackled in another July article, her short *Leader* essay entitled 'The Morality of *Wilhelm Meister*', which arose out of her discussions with Lewes of Goethe's works and which was undoubtedly intended to draw attention to Goethe in advance of publication of Lewes's *Life of Goethe*. She was aware that Goethe's reputation in England, though nurtured by Carlyle in essays and translations in the 1820s, was that of a writer who lived an 'irregular' life and whose novels discuss and condone 'irregular' sexual relationships. (Carlyle had apologized for this in the preface to his translation of *Wilhelm Meister's Apprenticeship*, published in 1824, and had bowdlerized the text in places.[43]) Her answer is that there is no true morality in

the so-called moral dénouement, in which rewards and punishments are distributed according to those notions of justice on which the novel-writer would have recommended that the world should be governed if he had been consulted at the creation. The emotion of satisfaction which a reader feels when the villain of the book dies of some hideous disease, or is crushed by a railway train, is no more essentially moral than the satisfaction which used to be felt in whipping culprits at the cart-tail. So we dismiss the charge of immorality against *Wilhelm Meister* on these two counts – the absence of moral bias in the mode of narration, and the comfortable issues allowed to questionable actions and questionable characters.[44]

GEORGE ELIOT: A LIFE

It is partly an argument for realism: in life goodness is not invariably rewarded or evil punished. But Marian goes further, as well she might. For in life, and in novels by such writers as Goethe (and later George Eliot herself and Tolstoy, we might add), good and evil are not so easy to distinguish as in much fiction. What Marian values in Goethe is his recognition of this fact:

Everywhere he brings us into the presence of living, generous humanity – mixed and erring, and self-deluding, but saved from utter corruption by the salt of some noble impulse, some disinterested effort, some beam of good nature, even though grotesque or homely. And his mode of treatment seems to us precisely that which is really moral in its influence. It is without exaggeration; he is in no haste to alarm readers into virtue by melodramatic consequences; he quietly follows the stream of fact and of life; and waits patiently for the moral processes of nature as we all do for her material processes.

In fact, the 'large tolerance' of Goethe towards his characters is evidence of a 'moral superiority' in his novels.[45]

Not, we may add to this suggestive argument, that Goethe does not preach or ride hobby-horses. He does, but he lets his characters be, airing his principles generally rather than with specific reference to individuals and their actions. Tolstoy was to do this too, showing infinite tolerance for his 'mixed and erring' characters while unabashedly preaching his particular brand of religious belief or his particular view of history and its heroes, as in *War and Peace* (1869), without allowing those beliefs to dictate the turns of the plot or the narrator's attitude to his characters.

George Eliot's would be a different way. For her the organic unity of purpose and practice was important. She too shows tolerance of weak, selfish people in her novels, but her belief in a kind of determinism by which character carries its own consequences, or Nemesis, leads her in effect often to punish such characters by withholding happiness from them while seeing and sympathizing with the mitigating circumstances of their cases. Nevertheless, she appreciated an aspect of *Wilhelm Meister* of which interesting variations appeared in her own novels, namely the mixed nature of human character: 'The line between the virtuous and vicious ... is in itself an immoral fiction.'[46]

It is fitting that Marian should enunciate such an important idea about fiction in an article on Goethe. Love of Goethe's works was tied up with love of Lewes, and she was justifiably proud of his achievement in his biography. Who could have been better suited by temperament and experience than Lewes to write a truthful yet broad-minded biography of that complex man? Who better to follow him into the many fields of his activity – poetry, fiction, drama, actor-managing, criticism, science? Marian was proud of her husband's book and of its immediate success. She wrote to Bray on 21 November, 'I can't tell you how I value it, as the best product of a mind which I have every day more reason to admire and love.'[47]

The Life of Goethe sold over 1,000 copies within three months. A second edition was called for in 1864, and a third in 1875, followed by many reprints in America and Britain. The book made Lewes's reputation. Its dedicatee, Carlyle, helped to see it through the press in August, while Lewes took his three sons, Charlie (twelve), Thornie (eleven), and Bertie (nine), for a week's holiday in Ramsgate. (Marian stayed at home writing the article on Cumming; the boys knew nothing of her at this time.) Carlyle reported on its progress to Lewes, commenting favourably in his own way that the book 'promises to be a very good bit of Biography'.[48]

After publication Carlyle wrote to thank Lewes for sending him a copy and for dedicating it to him. The book was 'candid, well-informed, clear, free-flowing', he wrote flatteringly but by no means over-estimating what is still a wonderfully readable biography.[49] As one of the many admiring reviewers of the book, Robert Vaughan, wrote in the *British Quarterly Review*:

In the case of Mr. Lewes, the tastes and the acquirements thus requisite, are assembled together with a felicity somewhat rare in the annals of biography. He is himself a man of letters. An acute critic, he possesses, at the same time, no mean power of original production. His literary knowledge is extensive; his taste catholic. The masterpieces of the modern literature of Europe are familiar to him in their original languages. His mind is clear-sighted and singularly agile. Such characteristics fit him readily to enter into the cosmopolitan many-sidedness of Goethe.

Moreover, wrote Vaughan, surely clinching the argument for Lewes's excellence in the genre, the two volumes [in later editions a single volume] could all too easily have swelled to six. 'We shudder as we think of what we have escaped, and we style thrice-blessed Mr. Lewes's power of shelving the uninteresting.'[50]

The £250 Lewes received in October for his *Life of Goethe* took his total literary earnings for 1855 to £430. 13s. od., to which was added Marian's £119. 8s. od. for her articles in *Fraser's*, the *Westminster Review*, and the *Leader* during the year.[51] They could live adequately, if modestly, on what was left after Lewes had paid Agnes's debts and allowance. The Richmond lodgings were pleasant, but cramped; Marian later recalled that she and Lewes worked in the same small room, and that the scratching of Lewes's pen affected her nerves so much that it 'nearly drove her wild'.[52]

On 24 December Marian set off alone to pay a Christmas visit to Chrissey in Attleborough, while Lewes went to spend a few days, as usual at Christmas, with Arthur Helps. Marian's five days in the Midlands were, as might be expected, uncomfortable ones. Her relations knew nothing of Lewes, and were not sympathetic to her career in London. She may not have seen Isaac at all, and though she hoped Fanny Houghton would visit Attleborough while she was there, she replied resolutely to an invitation to spend a night with the Houghtons in Leamington on her way home that she planned to go straight to London from Nuneaton, not passing through Coventry or Leamington.[53] It follows that she did not visit her old friends at Rosehill. A tart paragraph in an otherwise friendly letter to Bray on 1 January 1856 reveals that she had been invited but – and the social significance was not lost on her – not by Cara:

I have never answered your note in which you invited me to call at your house on my way to my sister's. I am sure that note was written with the kindest intentions, but if you had thought twice you would have seen that I was not likely to take a journey twice as long as necessary and walk all through Coventry in order to make a call where I had only the invitation of the master of the house.[54]

We can imagine the relief with which she returned after this journey, fraught with hurt feelings and a sense of being in a false position towards her family and oldest friends, to the modest rooms she shared with Lewes in Richmond.

As if to neutralize the harsh expression of her hurt pride in her New Year letter to Bray, she made sure to thank Sara Hennell on 18 January for sending her the *Coventry Herald* review of Lewes's *Goethe*. She was pleased also to be able to enlist Sara's willing support for Barbara Leigh Smith's petition to Parliament about married women's property rights. Barbara had sent it to Marian, saying she already had the signatures of Harriet Martineau and Mrs Gaskell, as well as an MP and 'no Lord as yet but a distinct hope of one'.[55] Marian now sent it on to Sara, asking her to find some friends to sign it too, which Sara did with some enthusiasm.[56]

Marian took a warm interest – how could she not? – in the progress of the movement for women's rights and women's education. At the same time as she was raising support for Barbara's petition, she was urging Chapman to reject an article by another campaigner, Bessie Parkes's friend Matilda Hays, on the grounds that if it appeared in the *Westminster Review* it would do more harm than good to the cause, being 'feminine rant of the worst kind', full of 'undiscriminating Bosh' and 'bombastic stuff'. The subject was too important to be handled in this way: 'Pray admit nothing that touches on the Position of Women, that is not sober, well thought out, & expressed in good English.'[57]

Barbara received frequent small contributions to the women's cause over the years, but Marian would not be drawn into active or public agitation, though Barbara was a persistent and persuasive friend. The reason for her reticence does not need spelling out. It was the same reason which prompted her to ask Bray not to mention to anyone that she was the translator of Spinoza's *Ethics* when she finally completed the revision of her translation on 19 February.[58] She knew too well the view which would be taken in several quarters if she, in her circumstances, came forward in connection with a book on ethics. (She could not avoid provoking such a reaction when it became known that she was the author of the novels of George Eliot. Jane Carlyle was reported to have been astonished that Marian Evans of the *Westminster Review* had 'set up as a moralist' in her novels, and Henry Crabb Robinson confided to his diary his discomfiture that 'so admirable a book' as *Adam Bede* had been written by a woman whose history was 'unfortunate'.[59])

This caution to Bray about the Spinoza turned out to be unnecessary, as the translation was not in fact published. Lewes's otherwise unerring ability to negotiate an acceptable arrangement with publishers deserted

him on this occasion. He submitted the translation as his own to Henry
George Bohn, publisher of his 1853 book on Comte, relying on an
agreement he had made, or thought he had made, two years earlier with
Bohn's son that he would receive £75 for the work. A few angry letters
between him and Bohn in June 1856 ended in Lewes demanding the
return of the manuscript amid accusations and counter-accusations of
ungentlemanly behaviour. The translation lay unpublished until 1981.[60]

More incisive essays appeared, mainly on literary subjects, in the
Leader and the *Westminster Review* during 1856. Marian's critical-cum-
biographical article on Heine in the *Westminster* in January 1856, though
lacking the strong structure and sharp bite of the Cumming essay – it is,
after all, an appreciation rather than a scathing attack – gives a fine
account of the satirical heir of Goethe. The fact that Heine was both a
great lyrical poet, rivalling Goethe, and a wickedly witty polemical writer
encouraged her to ponder the nature of wit and humour in general and
to discuss German literature in this respect. She had fun at the expense
of the German sense of humour as she had met it in both the literature
and the people of that country, wondering aloud '*what* it can be that
produces ennui in a German'. Recalling an episode from her stay in
Berlin, she quotes an unnamed acquaintance who offered Proteus's joke
in *The Two Gentlemen of Verona* – 'Nod I? why that's Noddy' – as 'a
transcendent specimen' of Shakespearean wit.[61]

Heine is presented as a rare, perhaps unique, example of a witty
German. While French literature abounds in wit, which Marian defines
as ratiocinative, seizing on 'unexpected and complex relations', German
literature has more examples of humour, which 'associates itself with
the sympathetic emotions'. Some of the greatest writers – Marian cites
Shakespeare and Molière as fine examples – combine the two.[62] Having
set out these distinctions, Marian devotes most of the essay to illustrating by examples Heine's claim to a peculiar kind of witty humour. She
quotes his baffling irony in *Geständnisse* (*Confessions*, 1854), in which he
jokes painfully yet fancifully about his terrible illness, tuberculosis of the
spine, which had kept him bedridden since 1848, and from which he
finally died, mercifully, not long after this article was written. 'What
strange, deep pathos is mingled with the audacity of the following
passage', she writes, giving Heine's tongue-in-cheek recantation of his
former unbelief, in which he appears to decide that God does, after all,
exist. The proof is in his illness itself:

Alas! God's satire weighs heavily on me. The great Author of the universe, the Aristophanes of Heaven, was bent on demonstrating, with crushing force, to me, the little, earthly, German Aristophanes, how my wittiest sarcasms are only pitiful attempts at jesting in comparison with His, and how miserably I am beneath Him in humour, in colossal mockery.[63]

Marian wrote on Heine again, though more briefly, in August 1856, in the *Leader*, as well as in a short article for the newly founded *Saturday Review* in April.

With her thorough knowledge of the works of Heine and Goethe and her two translations of German higher criticism, Marian was, with Lewes, the leading interpreter of German culture in Britain. In July 1856 the *Westminster Review* carried another impressive essay on a German subject. Her long article, 'The Natural History of German Life', reviewed two books by the social historian Wilhelm Heinrich von Riehl. As she had done when writing about Heine, she once more took the opportunity to range widely in her discussion. Riehl's books were in the forefront of a new kind of history, the study of the middle and lower classes, the governed rather than those who govern. Because he could not find information about these classes in books, Riehl had set out to travel round Germany researching their economic and political history on the ground. He concluded that social change is necessarily a very slow business. Marian sums up his argument:

What has grown up historically can only die out historically, by the gradual operation of necessary laws. The external conditions which society has inherited from the past are but the manifestation of inherited internal conditions in the human beings who compose it; the internal conditions and the external are related to each other as the organism and its medium, and development can take place only by the gradual consentaneous development of both . . . As a necessary preliminary to a purely rational society, you must obtain purely rational men, free from the sweet and bitter prejudices of hereditary affection and antipathy; which is as easy as to get running streams without springs, or the leafy shade of the forest without the secular growth of trunk and branch.[64]

The language of development, of natural history, of the relation of organism to medium, was familiar to Marian in pre-Darwinian science and in the social philosophy of Herbert Spencer and Auguste Comte. She would use the new vocabulary of social science in her novels, and she would set her plots in times and places of political or philosophical upheaval – Renaissance Italy, England at the time of the first great Reform Bill of 1832 or earlier, when a predominantly agrarian society was giving way to industrialization at the end of the eighteenth century. Like Riehl, she accepted the slow pace of psychological and social change, understanding and even cherishing her characters' clinging to traditional beliefs and customs in the face of sometimes rapid political and industrial progress. Like him too, her instinct was to conserve what was valuable and rooted in human lives, though her conservatism was, of course, in tension with her personal history of rebellion against custom in the matter of religious belief and her defiance – albeit reluctant – of society's expectations about marriage and the relations between men and women. Her endorsement of Riehl's 'social-political-conservatism' is expressed with characteristic balance and vision:

He is as far as possible from the folly of supposing that the sun will go backward on the dial, because we put the hands of our clock backward; he only contends against the opposite folly of decreeing that it shall be mid-day, while in fact the sun is only just touching the mountain-tops, and all along the valley men are stumbling in the twilight.[65]

Extending the ideas she had expressed about Goethe's wide tolerance in his novels, she uses Riehl's history, too, as an opportunity to discuss the representation of the lower classes in fiction. In doing so, she gives expression to a theory of realism in art which she was very soon to put into practice. In the April number of the *Westminster Review* she had briefly noticed volume three of Ruskin's *Modern Painters*, declaring:

The truth of infinite value that he teaches is *realism* – the doctrine that all truth and beauty are to be attained by a humble and faithful study of nature, and not by substituting vague forms, bred by imagination on the mists of feeling, in place of definite, substantial reality.[66]

Now in the Riehl essay she invokes Ruskin again, agreeing with him that ideal representations of 'opera peasants' and 'lyric rustics' are undesirable. The true aim of the artist, 'whether painter, poet, or novelist, is the extension of our sympathies'. This is to be achieved not by idealizing, but rather by presenting the lower classes with all their faults, particular and generic, yet doing so with sympathy:

Art is the nearest thing to life; it is a mode of amplifying experience and extending our contact with our fellow-men beyond the bounds of our personal lot. All the more sacred is the task of the artist when he undertakes to paint the life of the People. Falsification here is far more pernicious than in the more artificial aspects of life. It is not so very serious that we should have false ideas about evanescent fashions – about the manners and conversation of beaux and duchesses; but it *is* serious that our sympathy with the perennial joys and struggles, the toil, the tragedy, and the humour in the life of our more heavily-laden fellow-men, should be perverted, and turned towards a false object instead of the true one.[67]

The argument is a sophisticated one, not merely a call for simple photographic realism or what Lewes later described as 'coat-and-waistcoat realism'.[68] We are to be brought by the artist into sympathy with flawed, sometimes stupid characters ('mixed and erring humanity') because we are to be made to see, as Spinoza and Feuerbach urge in their philosophies, that we belong to the same species, share our humanity with them. George Eliot's own early fiction sets out to achieve such an extension of our sympathies by imaginatively involving us in the difficulties of the lives she creates for her characters. The Riehl article expresses her embracing of the principle, while invoking Wordsworth and Scott as writers who embody it in their works.

Preparation for the Riehl essay took several weeks. Marian began reading for it on 29 April 1856.[69] Just over a week later, on 8 May, she and Lewes set off on a three-month visit to the seaside towns of Ilfracombe in Devon and Tenby in Wales, where Lewes collected and experimented on marine specimens for a successful series of papers, 'Sea-side Studies', which were published in *Blackwood's Magazine* from August 1856. The study of animal, particularly marine, life had become something of a craze among middle-class, and often clerical, amateurs in the 1850s. Charles Kingsley published *Glaucus: Or The Wonders of the Shore* in 1855; Philip Henry Gosse, famous as the father in Edmund Gosse's *Father and Son* (1907), was the author of several works on sea-anemones and other species; and William Broderip, to whom George Eliot referred in an extended metaphor in *The Mill on the Floss*, wrote *Leaves from the Notebook of a Naturalist* (1852). The Revd George Tugwell, a curate at Ilfracombe whom the Leweses now met, published his *Manual of the Sea-Anemones Commonly Found on the English Coast* later in 1856.

Indeed, Lewes and Tugwell teamed up, with Marian as the third member of the party, on some expeditions along the Ilfracombe shore. Lewes's lively opening chapter of his 'Sea-side Studies' describes the unlikely threesome setting forth in search of sea-anemones:

We are a lady and two men. The lady, except that she carries a landing-net, and has taken the precaution of putting on the things which 'won't spoil', has nothing out of the ordinary in her costume. We are thus arrayed: a wide-awake hat; an old coat, with manifold pockets in unexpected places, over which T. has slung a leathern case, containing his hammer, chisel, oyster-knife, and paper-knife; trousers warranted not to spoil; *over* the trousers are drawn huge worsted stockings, over which are drawn again huge leathern boots. T.'s are riding-boots, and reach his hip; mine are fisherman's boots, and come a few inches over the knee. The soles of both are well nailed, which is of material service in preventing our slipping so much on the rocks. Now these boots, with the worsted stocking peeping above, are not, it is true, eminently aesthetic. I will not recommend them as objects for the artist . . . Never mind, handsome is as handsome does.[70]

Their days were spent in hunting for specimens – how Marian's life had changed since her lonely seaside holiday in Broadstairs only four years before, when she ruefully compared her appearance to the jellyfish *Medusa* when writing to Spencer. Their evenings were passed in reading and writing, Lewes his *Blackwood* articles, Marian her Riehl, which she began 'with rather despairing prospects' on 13 May and finished on 5 June.[71]

On 29 May the Peace with Russia to mark the end of the Crimean War was celebrated at Ilfracombe with streamers, tea and cake, children's races, and fireworks and bonfires. This was 'a bit of primitive provincial life' which made Marian think 'of the times when such fires were lighted as signals to arm – the symbol of a common cause and a common feeling', as she wrote in her journal's 'Recollections of Ilfracombe'.[72] The observation, 'a bit of primitive provincial life', gives a hint that her wide reading – the recent study of Goethe, Heine, Ruskin, and Riehl, as well as the older acquaintance with Strauss, Feuerbach, Comte, Spinoza, and with Scott and Wordsworth – together with her present naturalizing with Lewes and Tugwell was preparing her for her new career as novelist. She came to it very slowly, diffidently, half re-luctantly, but inexorably. In her journal on 20 July, written in Tenby, she noted that since finishing the Riehl she had written little, 'done no *visible* work'. But, she added momentously, 'I have absorbed many ideas and much bodily strength; indeed, I do not remember ever feeling so strong in mind and body as I feel at this moment.' At last she articulated to herself her ambition and intention: 'I am anxious to begin my fiction writing.'[73]

As vital among her qualities as a novelist as her breadth of knowledge, the variety of her reading, and the collecting and observing of specimens, was her sensitivity, her acuteness of feeling. Though happy in her present life, she was alive to a past from which she was in part triumphantly, in part painfully cut off. Memories rose up. She wrote, strictly on business, to Isaac from Ilfracombe, asking him to deduct £5 from her half year's interest 'and give it to Chrissey towards helping to pay Emily's school bill'. She also asked him to send the remainder care of Chapman at King William Street, for of course Isaac must not know where, or with whom, she was living.[74] To Sara Hennell she described the 'pleasure – half melancholy – of recalling all the old impressions and comparing them with the new' at Tenby, which she had last visited in July 1843 with the Brays and Sara, and with Charles Hennell, now dead.[75]

The loss of certain female friendships as a result of her living with Lewes came home to her when she received a belated letter of support from Clementia Taylor. Marian replied in that subdued tone with which she always dealt with the social pain of her position. She thanked Mrs Taylor for her 'generous words' but declined to write in detail about her life:

I never write on private personal matters, unless it be a rigorous duty or necessity to do so. Some little phrase or allusion is misinterpreted, and on this false basis a great fabric of misconception is reared, which even explanatory conversations will not remove. Life is too precious to be spent in this weaving and unweaving of false impressions, and it is better to live quietly on under some degree of misrepresentation than to attempt to remove it by the uncertain process of letter-writing.[76]

Memories of her unhappy infatuation with Chapman also returned during this seaside visit. Barbara Leigh Smith wrote while Marian was at Ilfracombe, presumably telling her something about her recent relationship with Chapman and her subsequent ill health. Marian replied, sympathizing with her 'sorrows and renunciations'.[77] Barbara came to visit the Leweses at Tenby, staying from 12 to 16 July. It was an important meeting, clinching the friendship between the two women, which would remain very close, though Barbara spent half her time in Algiers after her marriage to Dr Eugène Bodichon in July 1857. Marian wrote in her journal that they enjoyed having Barbara with them, 'but were deeply touched to see that three years had made her so much older and sadder'.[78]

Barbara was exhausted by her propaganda work, and also by her struggles with her own feelings and with her family over her plan in September 1855 to live with Chapman as his mistress. She had been wooed by an extraordinary series of letters from Chapman while she was in Hastings in August and September 1855. He gave her detailed advice about her menstrual problems, seeking to persuade her that 'the fulfilment of your sexual life *may* prove the only permanent security of real health', and encouraging her to agree to bear him a child on the same grounds.[79] Thus he furthered his amorous cause with convenient, but not necessarily insincere, arguments about her health. Chapman's thinking on matters of feminine hygiene and sexual experience was not unusual at a time when many doctors and laymen were putting forward theories and statistics on the subject. Contraception, by the use of the condom and the (often erroneously understood) rhythm method, was increasingly practised and discussed during the 1850s.[80] Chapman told Barbara that if she preferred not to conceive immediately, 'we might avail ourselves of Riciborski's law for a time'.[81] He promised to study the matter.

Barbara's replies are lost, but Chapman's long letters indicate that she was willing to become his mistress, though anxious about her health and also about her father's opinion. Benjamin Leigh Smith's reaction was predictable, notwithstanding his own 'notorious cohabitation', in Barbara's words, with her mother, whom he had not married.[82] He told Barbara that if she wanted to practise free love she should go to America to do it. Chapman's letters leave it doubtful whether Barbara consummated the affair. Whatever happened when Chapman visited Hastings in September 1855, by July 1856 when she was with the Leweses in Tenby, the relationship was over. (Chapman, who had told Barbara in one of his letters that he was going to attend medical lectures and hoped to become a doctor, actually took his M.D. in 1857 and later practised and wrote books on medicine, specializing in women's illnesses.[83])

It appears that Barbara told something of this extraordinary story to Marian in Tenby, and that Marian in turn indicated to her impulsive, confiding friend that she and Lewes were sexually happy and that they practised some form of birth control, not thinking it right, in their circumstances, to have children.[84] Barbara wrote to Bessie Parkes from Tenby that though she had previously disliked Lewes, thinking him disreputable and rakish, she had revised her opinion now she had seen how happy he made Marian.[85]

Though aiming to begin her fiction writing at Tenby, Marian put it off until after their return to Richmond in August. She had undertaken to do two more big articles for Chapman, one on the eighteenth-century poet Edward Young, the other an essay on 'Silly Women's Novels' which she proposed to Chapman on 20 July.[86] She settled down to write about these while Lewes set off for Switzerland on 25 August. He had been wondering what to do about his two older sons' education, not being content to leave them at Bayswater Grammar School, where they were pupils. In April Marian had asked Bray if her old friend John Sibree, who took pupils, would agree to tutor them, and Lewes had written to Sibree himself saying he meant to take Charlie and Thornie to Germany in a year's time but would like to find them a tutor meanwhile.[87] Sibree declined, but the Brays sent information about Hofwyl, a school near Berne run on liberal principles, which some members of the Noel family had attended.[88] After making inquiries and deciding in favour of the school, Lewes took the two boys to Hofwyl, which he found beautifully situated and humanely run by the headmaster, Dr Müller, and his wife.[89]

'Silly Novels by Lady Novelists' appeared in the *Westminster Review* in October 1856. It is interesting as a statement of what makes some bad novels bad by a woman who enjoyed pretending to be a man in her career as anonymous reviewer and who would take a male pseudonym to protect her identity as a novelist. Though it may seem to be gratuitously unkind about the foibles of women writers, we know from our glances at Marian's striking career as a journalist, now about to come to a triumphant end, that she could be equally severe on men. She also makes it clear that she is not talking here about such excellent women novelists as the Brontë sisters or Mrs Gaskell.

As in the essay on Cumming, Marian opens this article with magnificent malice:

Silly novels by Lady Novelists are a genus with many species, determined by the particular quality of silliness that predominates in them – the frothy, the prosy, the pious, or the pedantic. But it is a mixture of all these – a composite order of feminine fatuity, that produces the largest class of such novels, which we shall distinguish as the *mind-and-millinery* species.[90]

In such novels the heroine is typically an heiress with a lord, a clergyman, and a poet vying for her love. She is a paragon:

Her eyes and her wit are both dazzling; her nose and her morals are alike free from any tendency to irregularity; she has a superb *contralto* and a superb intellect; she is perfectly well-dressed and perfectly religious; she dances like a sylph, and reads the Bible in the original tongues.

'The ideal woman in feelings, faculties, and flounces', she nevertheless marries the wrong man, but he soon dies, requesting his wife to marry the man she loves:

Before matters arrive at this desirable issue our feelings are tried by seeing the noble, lovely, and gifted heroine pass through many *mauvais moments*, but we have the satisfaction of knowing that her sorrows are wept into embroidered pocket-handkerchiefs, that her fainting form reclines on the very best uphol-stery, and that whatever vicissitudes she may undergo, from being dashed out of her carriage to having her head shaved in a fever, she comes out of them all with a complexion more blooming and locks more redundant than ever.[91]

This wonderfully witty essay proceeds through various sub-species of silly novel, showing particular contempt for examples of the '*oracular*' novel of religious or philosophical pretensions. Summing up her dis-satisfaction with what passes for an educated woman in the world of bad literature, she declares:

Take a woman's head, stuff it with a smattering of philosophy and literature chopped small, and with false notions of society baked hard, let it hang over a desk a few hours every day, and serve up hot in feeble English, when not required.[92]

In analysing so energetically what makes novels bad, Marian also gives an idea of the positive qualities required to make a good novel. What she christens the '*white neck-cloth* species', the Evangelical novel (legion in the mid-nineteenth century[93]), is a perversion of what should and could be an interesting kind of novel. 'The real drama of Evan-gelicalism – and it has abundance of fine drama for any one who has genius enough to discern and reproduce it – lies among the middle and lower classes.' Instead of showing exclusively genteel or upper-class leisured life, such a novel should aim to represent 'the working-day business of the world'.[94]

Here is the argument already aired in her articles on Ruskin and Riehl, now thrown down as a gauntlet which Marian herself was poised to pick up. Not that she wished to restrict the scope of the novel by making narrow prescriptions. On the contrary, any subject may be rendered interesting if the right talents are brought to it:

Like crystalline masses, it may take any form, and yet be beautiful; we have only to pour in the right elements – genuine observation, humour, and passion.[95]

On 22 September 1856, ten days after finishing 'Silly Novels', Marian Evans Lewes 'began to write "The Sad Fortunes of the Reverend Amos Barton", which I hope to make one of a series called "Scenes of Clerical Life"'.[96] Would she be mistress of the right elements – observation, humour, and passion?

CHAPTER SEVEN

The Birth of George Eliot:
Scenes of Clerical Life *1856–7*

Marian did not become George Eliot immediately. Though Lewes sent off the manuscript of 'The Sad Fortunes of the Rev. Amos Barton' to the publisher John Blackwood on 6 November 1856, and though Blackwood printed it in two parts in the January and February 1857 numbers of *Blackwood's Magazine*, it was not until 4 February 1857 that the name 'George Eliot' surfaced at all. Indeed, Blackwood had to resort until then to addressing the unknown writer as 'the Author of Amos Barton' and even 'My Dear Amos'.[1] The Leweses went to great, though ultimately unsuccessful, lengths to preserve first Marian's anonymity, then her pseudonymity, as a writer of fiction.

Of course the chief reason for the secrecy was Marian's understandable desire to have her work accepted on its merits and not in the full glare of curiosity and scandal surrounding her relationship with Lewes. The remarks called forth in several quarters by the eventual lifting of the incognito in June 1859 after the enormous success of *Adam Bede* showed her caution to be prescient enough. But she was also impelled to secrecy by her terrible diffidence, her fear that she would not succeed according to her own high standards. She to whom it was second nature to be merciless in penetrating the faults and pretensions of the writers whose works she reviewed could not but be harsh on her own efforts. On the other hand, her peculiar form of diffidence rendered her incapable of absorbing the criticism of others with equanimity; one remembers her ingenious special pleading to Sara Hennell from Geneva in October 1849: 'I want encouraging rather than warning and checking.'[2]

It was her weakness in this respect that made her require Lewes to screen her from adverse reviews of her work, or at any rate made her agree to Lewes's insistence that such criticism was bad for her. Undoubtedly she and Lewes were right about this. If he had not protected her, she might have given up writing altogether. As it was, every novel was wrestled into existence in spite of that despair against which Marian had always struggled, not always successfully, and against which she continued to fight, with Lewes and soon Blackwood enlisted on her side, all her life.

And so it was with the writing of 'Amos Barton'. Surely few first fictional births ever followed such a long gestation period. Marian had cogitated for years on the possibility of writing a novel. According to her journal entry of 6 December 1857, 'How I Came to Write Fiction', she had at an unspecified time in the past begun a narrative, 'an introductory chapter describing a Staffordshire village, and the life of the neighbouring farm houses', but 'as the years passed on I lost any hope that I should ever be able to write a novel, just as I desponded about everything else in my future life'.[3] Then she records how it came about that she overcame her fear of failure, and how Lewes became the manmidwife to her efforts.

According to her account, Lewes took on the role much more slowly and cautiously than might have been expected of such a shrewd and confident man. But then the combination of diffidence with such power of intellect and personality as hers may well have infected even her near-immune husband; and the fact that he, who had tried and triumphed in so many kinds of writing, had been least successful as a novelist may also have given him pause for thought. Marian's account is as follows:

My 'introductory chapter' was pure description though there were good materials in it for dramatic presentation. It happened to be among the papers I had with me in Germany and one evening at Berlin, something led me to read it to George. He was struck with it as a bit of concrete description, and it suggested to him the possibility of my being able to write a novel, though he distrusted – indeed disbelieved in, my possession of any dramatic power. Still, he began to think that I might as well try, some time, what I could do in fiction, and by and bye when we came back to England and I had greater success than he had ever expected in other kinds of writing, his impression that it was worthwhile to see how far my mental power would go towards the production of a novel, was strengthened. He began to say very positively, 'You must try and write a story', and when we were at Tenby he urged me to begin at once. I deferred it, however, after my usual fashion, with work that does not present itself as an absolute duty. But one morning as I was lying in bed, thinking what should be the subject of my first story, my thoughts merged themselves into a dreamy doze, and I imagined myself writing a story of which the title was – 'The Sad Fortunes of the Reverend Amos Barton'. I was soon wide awake again, and told G. He said, 'O what a capital title!' and from that time I had settled in my mind that this should be my first story. George used to say, 'It may be a failure – it may be that you are unable to write fiction. Or perhaps, it may be just good enough to warrant your trying again.' Again, 'You may write a chef-d'oeuvre at once – there's no telling.' But his prevalent impression was that although I could hardly write a *poor* novel, my effort would want the highest quality of fiction – dramatic presentation. He used to say, 'You have wit, description and philosophy – those go a good way towards the production of a novel. It is worth while for you to try the experiment.'[4]

If Lewes had such doubts – and he may have exaggerated them in an effort not to frighten Marian by seeming to expect too much, so ingeni-ous was she in finding reasons not to be hopeful, not to try – once he had brought her to the point of writing a story, he continued steadfastly in his difficult role of encourager. All his subsequent comments to Marian and to others were aimed at keeping her feelings as positive as possible about work done, work in hand, and work yet to be done. It is entirely appropriate that when she did choose a pseudonym, character-istically doing so only *after* her first story had been published and was deemed a success, it celebrated Lewes. She told John Cross that she fixed on George Eliot because 'George was Mr Lewes's Christian name, and Eliot was a good mouth-filling, easily-pronounced word.'[5]

The Edinburgh publisher John Blackwood was chosen as the man to send the story to because Lewes had contributed articles to *Blackwood's Magazine* intermittently since 1843, and had recently come to an agree-ment to publish 'Sea-side Studies' there. As Lewes noted in his journal retrospect of the year 1856:

I resumed also my contributions to *Blackwood* this year; which formed the proximate cause of Marian's introduction to fiction. We had long discussed the desirability of her trying her powers in that direction; & the temptation of appearing anonymously & successfully in *Blackwood* induced her to begin a series of tales.[6]

A better choice of publisher was never made. Blackwood was chief of the family firm, a thorough, shrewd, but honest businessman with reliable, if conventional, literary taste and an invaluable ability to exercise tact and patience with his authors. He was ably supported by his brother Major William Blackwood and by the manager of the London branch of the firm, Joseph Langford. Blackwood, though not prone to sudden enthusiasms, recognized the merit of 'Amos Barton' and said so. He did not gush, nor did he carp, and therefore his response was trusted by the critical, sensitive author he now found himself dealing with, if only indirectly.

Lewes had been careful to accompany the manuscript with a letter containing some remarks designed, discreetly, to predispose Blackwood in its favour. 'A friend' had asked him to submit it; he, Lewes, had doubted his friend's power before reading it, but had been pleasantly surprised. Such 'humour, pathos, vivid presentation and nice observation' had not been seen, he thought, since Goldsmith's *Vicar of Wakefield* and the novels of Jane Austen. Lest Blackwood be put off by the clerical aspect of the work, Lewes emphasized that the series of tales, of which 'Amos Barton' was the first, would illustrate 'the actual life of our country clergy about a quarter of a century ago; but solely in its *human* and not at all in its *theological* aspect'. On the other hand, in case the orthodox Church-and-State Blackwood should fear an attack on religion from a friend of the free-thinking Lewes, he was assured that 'the tone throughout will be sympathetic and not at all antagonistic'.[7]

This was no less than the truth. Though Marian was adept at critical analysis of clergymen like Cumming, whose creed was vicious, or the poet-clergyman Young, whom she attacked for his worldliness in her last big article for the *Westminster Review* in January 1857,[8] in her stories she showed tolerance towards a set of imperfect clergymen. A group of them appears in 'Amos Barton', and, as Blackwood was quick to notice, they are, 'with one exception', 'not very attractive specimens of the body'.[9] The exception, no more than a quick character sketch in the ten short chapters of 'Amos Barton', is the Revd Martin Cleves, who puts in a word at a clerical meeting intended to stifle malicious gossip about Amos. George Eliot gives him clerical talent, 'the wonderful art of preaching sermons which the wheelwright and the blacksmith can understand; not because he talks condescending twaddle, but because he can call a spade a spade'.[10]

She also lets this clergyman quietly enact the Feuerbachian idea of the sanctity of human rather than divine relations. When Amos's wife Milly dies after giving birth to her seventh child, Mr Cleves rides over to see if he can be of help to Amos. He gives comfort not by quoting scripture or creed, but by silently grasping Amos's hand, and so giving 'life-recovering warmth to the poor benumbed heart of the stricken man'.[11] George Eliot does not obtrude her humanism, here or elsewhere in the story, but an alert reader notices that what is valued about the good clergyman is his natural human goodness, not his clerical professions of faith.

Amos himself is not a good clergyman, and not a particularly good man. George Eliot boldly puts into practice her idea that fiction should present mixed and erring humanity, gaining by imaginative means the reader's understanding and sympathy for characters who are not immediately attractive. The narrator speaks out in the same voice as the erstwhile reviewer of Kingsley, Goethe, and Riehl. Stopping the narrative for a moment in chapter 5, he/she analyses Amos's character and demands our sympathy:

The Rev. Amos Barton, whose sad fortunes I have undertaken to relate, was, you perceive, in no respect an ideal or exceptional character; and perhaps I am doing a bold thing to bespeak your sympathy on behalf of a man who was so very far from remarkable, – a man whose virtues were not heroic, and who had no undetected crime within his breast; who had not the slightest mystery hanging about him, but was palpably and unmistakably commonplace; who was not even in love, but had had that complaint favourably many years ago. 'An utterly uninteresting character!' I think I hear a lady reader exclaim – Mrs Farthingale, for example, who prefers the ideal in fiction; to whom tragedy means ermine tippets, adultery, and murder; and comedy, the adventures of some personage who is quite a 'character'.[12]

Still sounding like the anonymous reviewer of 'Silly Novels', the narrator continues to persuade us:

Depend upon it, you would gain unspeakably if you would learn with me to see some of the poetry and the pathos, the tragedy and the comedy, lying in the experience of a human soul that looks out through dull grey eyes, and that speaks in a voice of quite ordinary tones. In that case, I should have no fear of your not caring to know what farther befell the Rev. Amos Barton, or of your thinking the homely details I have to tell at all beneath your attention. As it is, you can, if you please, decline to pursue my story farther; and you will easily find reading more to your taste, since I learn from the newspapers that many remarkable novels, full of striking situations, thrilling incidents, and eloquent writing, have appeared only within the last season.[13]

This rather aggressive pleading is a fault in art. George Eliot would learn to be more flexible, less anxious to argue her readers into acceptance of her stories and her views, though complete reticence or invisibility would never be her way, any more than it was Dickens's, or Thackeray's, or Hardy's. But even here, in her first story, in which we might expect some clumsiness, she has sufficient artistic instinct to postpone the preaching until after she has painted, almost without comment, the life of Amos in the first four chapters. She rather skilfully gives us first the gossip of some of Amos's parishioners, then a scene between Amos and his wife, then Amos in the work-house, and Amos in the company of the parasitic, come-down-in-the-world Countess Czerlaski, followed by a masterly summary of what the sceptical parish in general makes of 'the Countess, as she calls herself'.

Jane Austen does spring to mind, particularly *Northanger Abbey* with its setting up of Gothic melodramatic expectations, and its delight in puncturing these with mundane explanations. The Countess Czerlaski is a deliberately incongruous character to appear in the market town of Milby (based on Nuneaton). The local people distrust her, doubt her title, and think her relationship to her companion, Mr Bridmain, likely to be a disreputable one. But the narrator, intent on correcting the reader's taste for improbable characters and situations, reveals that the Milby mind has taken its suspicions too far. The Countess is really the half-sister of Mr Bridmain; she has no shady past, and is not a sham noblewoman, being an ex-governess who married a Count and was left a widow without a fortune. She is, says the narrator, 'a little vain, a little ambitious, a little selfish, a little shallow and frivolous, a little given to white lies'.[14]

That the Countess is the immediate cause, through selfishness and scandal, of Amos's downfall is, however, only partly her fault. George Eliot manages, for the first but by no means the last time, to show how a variety of causes converge to bring about misfortune. Amos's stupidity and vanity, Milly's passive goodness, Milby gossip, and Amos's unpopular Evangelical innovations in the church service, all play their part in the outcome.

It is hardly surprising to find that George Eliot sets her story in the Midlands of her youth, dating it back twenty-five years to the early 1830s, when she was growing up on the outskirts of Nuneaton, and deals with a subject – Evangelicalism – about which she had unparalleled knowledge from both her personal experience and her reading. Shepperton Church, a description of which opens the story, is recognizably Chilvers Coton Church, where she was baptized and where her father was an active member of the Parish Council. Amos Barton, too, is based, at least in terms of his circumstances if not his character, on the Revd John Gwyther, curate of Chilvers Coton from 1831 to 1841.

Gwyther's wife had died, like Milly Barton, after giving birth to her seventh child. Robert Evans, whose own wife had died only a few months before, told Francis Newdigate in November 1836 that he felt very sorry for Mr Gwyther: 'I do not know what he will do with such a family and so small an Income!'[15] As in the story, so in real life the absentee vicar of Chilvers Coton caused Gwyther to be removed so that he could place a relative in the curateship.[16]

Like Gwyther, Amos brings reforming measures to the church, and these are resented by many of his parishioners. George Eliot is completely at home in her Riehl-like observations of ordinary people's resistance to change. She also manages superbly the dialogue exchanges of her characters, in which they grumble miscellaneously about the hymns, the sermons, and the minister's dubious relationship with the Countess. This was the element – dialogue – which Lewes had wondered whether Marian would be able to add to her proven gifts of observation, description, analysis, and wit. It turned out that dialogue was George Eliot's forte, as critics from Henry James to F. R. Leavis were to observe.

Even in such a short story as 'Amos Barton', we get a foretaste of the brilliant humorous ventriloquism so abundant in her novels. Like her admired Walter Scott, she dares to give the flavour of local dialect in her characters' speech. From Scott, too, she learned to bestow a pleasing turn of the plot on a well realized minor character. Nanny, the maid-of-all-work in the hard-pressed Barton household, speeds the Countess's departure by some exasperated forthrightness to that idle unwanted guest:

'Is Mrs Barton ill?'

'Ill – yes – I should think she *is* ill, an' much you care. She's likely to be ill, moithered as *she* is from mornin' to night, wi' folks as had better be elsewhere.'

'What do you mean by behaving in this way?'

'Mean? why I mean as the missus is a-slavin' her life out an' a-sittin' up o'nights, for folks as are better able to wait of *her*, i'stid o' lyin' abed an' doin' nothin' all the blessed day, but mek work.'

'Leave the room and don't be insolent.'

'Insolent! I'd better be insolent than like what some folks is, – a' livin' on other folks, an' bringin' a bad name on 'em into the bargain.'

Here Nanny flung out of the room, leaving the lady to digest this unexpected breakfast at her leisure.[17]

The voice of the narrator is androgynous. It seems inclined to expect the reader to assume, as most early readers did, that the author is a man, with all the education and experience usually open only to men. Yet at the same time the voice clearly belongs to someone able to penetrate with equal fidelity the mysteries of the kitchen and the dairy, and the rituals of female visiting. It is like Scott combined with Jane Austen, Goldsmith with Charlotte Brontë. George Eliot is able to sound ironic, detached, wise, experienced, yet also caring, even passionate.

At last, as she turned thirty-seven, her unusual life bore its literary fruit. The early years of female friendship and piety, of self-analysis and self-restraint and of looking on critically at others, and the recent years of chiefly male company, educated, wide-ranging, sceptical, unorthodox; the emotional poverty of her youth and the fulfilment of her young middle age; and the paradox of her situation – the unusual freedom of her life choices so inextricably bound up with society's restrictions and exclusions – these losses and gains in her life combine wonderfully to make up the writer George Eliot.

Blackwood, knowing nothing of this, saw he had an unusual talent on his hands. He wrote to Lewes less than a week after receiving 'Amos Barton', declaring in his measured way, 'I am happy to say that I think your friend's reminiscences of Clerical Life will do.' He thought perhaps the author erred by explaining too much, rather than letting things 'evolve in the action of the story', and he viewed the 'windup', the hurried and short 'Conclusion', in which George Eliot sums up a future for her characters, as 'the lamest part of the story'.[18] But he recognized the humour, pathos, and power of the writing.

When Lewes replied that his 'clerical friend' was discouraged by these very mild (and fair) criticisms, Blackwood responded immediately to reassure the unknown author, whom he assumed from Lewes's phrase to be a clergyman, that he had a very high opinion of the story, so much so that he was willing to publish it without waiting to see the next tale in the series.[19] A letter came back thanking Blackwood for restoring the confidence of the 'shy, shrinking, ambitious' author and correcting the impression that he was a clergyman. 'I am not at liberty to remove the veil of anonymity', Lewes added. 'Be pleased therefore to keep the whole secret – and not even mention *my* negotiation or in any way lead guessers' to 'jump from me to my friend.'[20]

Lewes was probably aware of the near-transparency of this 'veil of anonymity', but he kept up the fiction as long as he could for the sake of Marian's feelings. If Blackwood guessed straight away that 'George Eliot' was Marian Evans Lewes, as he probably did, he was wise enough to keep the conjecture to himself. He would have trouble enough when the veil eventually came off nearly two years later. It was not until February 1858 that Marian and Lewes told him the secret when he visited them in Richmond; he wrote then to his wife that he had at last been introduced to George Eliot – 'a woman (the Mrs Lewes whom we suspected)'.[21] Two months earlier, in December 1857, Major William Blackwood had called, and Marian noted in her journal that 'it was evident to us when he had only been in the room a few minutes that he knew I was George Eliot'.[22] The Blackwoods kept silent, however, until Marian was ready to reveal her identity to them and shortly afterwards forced to reveal it to a public greedy to know the author of *Adam Bede*.

Blackwood paid her the compliment of beginning the January 1857 number of *Blackwood's* with the first part of 'Amos Barton'. He sent a cheque for £52. 10s. 0d. on 29 December 1856, a useful addition to the Leweses' finances, which were still not healthy. Lewes noted in his journal for 5 December that he had been 'agitated & distressed lately by finding Agnes £150 in debt mainly owing to T's [i.e. Thornton Hunt's] defalcations'. Lewes wrote angrily to Hunt, who sent him a challenge on 16 December. 'There is something ludicrous in the extravagance of this – A challenge from him to me, & on such grounds!'[23] Fortunately,

Lewes did not rise to the challenge. He presumably knew that Agnes was pregnant with her fourth child by Hunt, Mildred, who was born in May 1857.

On 4 December 1856 Marian finished the article on Young which she had begun in April but laid aside to do other work, including 'Amos Barton'. It was her last long article, written in her commanding journalistic style, anatomizing Young's pretensions to piety, his 'sycophancy and his psalmistry', his love of a lord and of the Lord, his taking orders late in life and 'choosing God for his "patron" henceforth'.[24] Chapman responded, with unconscious irony, by sending an extra £5 for the article and declaring that her articles were 'so uniformly excellent' that he intended to pay her henceforth 'at the rate of £12.12.0 per sheet'.[25]

Marian, who had no intention of writing any more articles if she could be successful in fiction, wrote back pleasantly and evasively, telling Chapman that the *Westminster Review* would 'always have the precedence with me over every other Review, both on the ground of old friendship & of the greater freedom which it gives to the expression of opinion'.[26]

On Christmas Day 1856, with Lewes away in Hampshire with Arthur Helps, Marian began the second of her 'Scenes of Clerical Life', 'Mr Gilfil's Love-Story'. She was heartened by Blackwood's judicious praise of 'Amos Barton' and by the comments he quoted to her from others. It was music to her ears to hear from him on 30 January 1857 that he had shown Thackeray the manuscript: 'I said to him "Do you know I think I have lighted upon a new Author who is uncommonly like a first class passenger."' Thackeray apparently commented favourably on the few pages he had read.[27] Much gratified, Marian replied (though to William, not John), giving her publishers a name to call her by:

Whatever may be the success of my stories, I shall be resolute in preserving my incognito, having observed that a *nom de plume* secures all the advantages without the disagreeables of reputation. Perhaps, therefore, it will be well to give you my prospective name, as a tub to throw to the whale in case of curious inquiries, and accordingly I subscribe myself, best and most sympathizing of editors,

Yours very truly,
George Eliot.[28]

More praise was to come. John Blackwood reported to 'My Dear George Eliot' on 10 February that he had received a letter from the writer and man-about-town Albert Smith, saying how moved he had been by Milly Barton's death; Blackwood commented that from Smith's account 'the luminaries of the Garrick generally seem to have mingled their tears with their tumblers over the death bed of Milly'. He added probingly, 'It will be great fun if you are a member of that society and hear yourself discussed.'[29] One wonders what feelings this remark aroused in Marian, who scarcely left her lodgings in Richmond except to walk in the park with Lewes. Of course, Lewes knew the Garrick Club set, and though he had curtailed his bachelorish social life since settling with Marian, he did go up to London sometimes to meet and dine with sociable friends like Thackeray, Richard Monckton Milnes, Carlyle, Herbert Spencer, and others. Spencer had returned to London in January 1857 after several months of travelling for his health. He often visited the Leweses at Richmond, sometimes with Chapman, sometimes alone.[30]

Lewes had returned from Vernon Hill with praise for 'Amos Barton' from the party gathered there over Christmas. Arthur Helps had said it was 'pestilently clever' and 'the women were charmed', as he reported to Blackwood on 11 February. Lewes also told Blackwood that he was planning another naturalizing trip, this time to the Scilly Isles, Guernsey, and Brittany. 'In the two latter places I have great hopes of having the company of Eliot', he added.[31] This was rather awkward, and it is highly likely that Blackwood saw through the subterfuge. However, he contented himself with replying, probably with tongue in cheek:

Generally contributors introducing their friends' M.S.S. to Editors assume the character of bores, but you are a noble and memorable exception. Are you going to confine yourself to the character of intermediaire at present?[32]

Lewes refused to be drawn, merely answering that he would send more articles of his own from the Scilly Isles for the *Blackwood's Magazine* series of 'New Sea-side Studies'.

It was just as well for Marian's peace of mind, as she struggled against headaches and 'general malaise'[33] to write 'Mr Gilfil's Love-Story', that she did not see two letters from Blackwood's London representative, Joseph Langford. On 27 January 1857 he asked Blackwood who the author of 'Amos Barton' was. 'Can you tell me? I have heard a hint that I dare not entertain and from no bad judge.'[34] London literary gossip seems already to have been speculating all too accurately. And not just London gossip. *Blackwood's Magazine* was read in the provinces too, and by one of those chances which make one think no coincidence in literature should ever be called far-fetched, Langford heard some news at which Marian would have shuddered. He wrote to Blackwood on 16 February:

I heard a curious thing about Amos Barton, namely that it is the actual life of a clergyman named Gwythir who at the time the incidents occurred lived at a place called, I think, Coton in one of the midland counties and who is now vicar of a small parish in Yorkshire. Indeed his daughter wrote to a lady, a friend of mine, telling her to be sure to read the story as it was their family history.[35]

If 'Amos Barton', which is only indirectly based on identifiable people and scenes, could be so quickly taken up and traced to a source which would eventually identify Marian as the author, 'Mr Gilfil's Love-Story' was almost a giveaway in this respect. Indeed, in one sense it is surprising that Marian, who had Lewes exercise all his ingenuity in keeping her identity even from her publisher, should have written in such revealing detail of the scenes of her Midlands home. While Lewes contrived to make Blackwood believe that it was the most natural thing in the world that his shy friend George Eliot would be sharing his working holiday and that George Eliot wished all his cheques to be paid into Lewes's bank account,[36] Marian laid herself open to discovery by the very simple means of writing about scenes she had known as a child.

On the other hand, she was only doing what came naturally, and moreover what she had always advised other writers to do, namely to draw on personal knowledge, to write authentically, to embed invented characters and episodes firmly in genuine remembered experience. Thus Mr Gilfil, another incumbent of Shepperton Church, but thirty years before Amos Barton, has an original, the Revd Bernard Gilpin Ebdell, who baptized Mary Anne Evans at Chilvers Coton. Ebdell, like Mr Gilfil, married the protégée of the local landowner and his wife. That landowner, Sir Christopher Cheverel in the story, is a portrait of the Sir Roger Newdigate whom George Eliot could not have known, since he died in 1806, but of whom she had heard from her father. And Cheverel Manor, lovingly described in chapter two of 'Mr Gilfil's Love-Story', is unmistakably the magnificent Gothicized Arbury Hall she used to visit with Robert Evans.[37]

In some respects, however, 'Mr Gilfil' is quite remote from Marian's own experience. It has more of a plot than 'Amos Barton', being longer, more worked out, less sketchy than its predecessor. Despite the direct scene painting, it is more fanciful too, flirting with melodrama. Caterina Sarti, the Italian protégée of the Cheverels, is a spoilt, petted, fiery, but disenfranchised figure – always called 'little monkey' by Sir Christopher and condescended to as a domestic pet by the family – who becomes so jealous in love that she seizes a dagger, intending to kill her faithless lover. As in 'Amos Barton', George Eliot deflects the high drama into a more everyday course, though here she does so at the expense of probability. Caterina finds her lover already dead of a heart attack. In an interesting foretaste of the moral dilemma of Gwendolen in *Daniel Deronda* – did she deliberately let her husband die, or was she trying to save him? – George Eliot has Mr Gilfil absolve Caterina of guilt. 'We mean to do wicked things that we could never do, just as we mean to do good or clever things that we could never do.'[38] But Caterina is not a successful creation; we can believe neither in her passion nor in her remorse.

There is once more some excellent dialogue. The story opens with that village gossip which George Eliot always hit off so well, exploiting it adroitly for purposes of exposition. The somewhat conventional faithless lover, Captain Wybrow, is a promising sketch for those young men, from Arthur Donnithorne in *Adam Bede* to Godfrey Cass in *Silas Marner* and Tito Melema in *Romola*, who do wrong from no very wicked motives, but are simply selfish, weak, and inclined to indolence, with disastrous consequences. Wybrow owes something to the plausible seducer Wickham in *Pride and Prejudice* and the plot and setting of 'Mr Gilfil' are reminiscent of *Mansfield Park*, which Marian and Lewes were reading together in February 1857.[39] But though George Eliot's wise irony resembles Jane Austen's, she deals with a wider social range and, unlike her predecessor, hints at dialect in the speech of her rustic characters. On the whole, however, 'Mr Gilfil's Love-Story' is less successful than its plainer predecessor, being in places more like those romances set in grand houses on which Marian had been so wittily severe in her essays.

Blackwood, quick to catch on to Lewes's remarks about the self-doubt of his new first-class passenger, was politely enthusiastic about 'Mr Gilfil'. He did, however, venture a criticism which Marian took to

THE BIRTH OF GEORGE ELIOT: SCENES OF CLERICAL LIFE

heart. On 30 April he wrote to Lewes, asking him to mention to George Eliot 'that I have some fear that he huddles up the conclusion of his stories too much'.[40] The very next day 'George Eliot' wrote back:

I will pay attention to your caution about the danger of huddling up my stories. Conclusions are the weak point of most authors, but some of the fault lies in the very nature of a conclusion, which is at best a negation.[41]

The third and longest story, 'Janet's Repentance', was begun on 18 April 1857 at St Mary's, on the Scilly Isles. It is an odd story, being too full of minor characters who, though well observed and given good robust speech as in the previous two, fill the space without having room to move, as it were. Here, if anywhere, is ample evidence that George Eliot needed, as Lewes declared to Blackwood in August, the 'larger canvas' of the full-length novel to allow 'his' talents proper scope.[42]

Though 'Janet's Repentance' is flawed in this way, there are some striking things about it. One is that the 'clerical' element is very strong. Where in 'Amos Barton' the fact of Amos's being a clergyman is significant but the main focus of the story lies in his non-clerical relationships, and in 'Mr Gilfil' the hero's profession is almost immaterial to the drama, here the clergyman, Mr Tryan, is seen from a doctrinal as well as a human point of view. George Eliot draws much more in this story on her personal acquaintance with clergymen and creeds ranging from orthodox Church of England through Evangelical to Independent and other dissenting sects.

The Nuneaton of her childhood is evoked in Milby, in which rival factions, the Evangelical Tryanites and the traditional anti-Evangelical party, come to blows against a background of other sects, such as the Independents of Salem Chapel. The familiar Marian Evans irony is deployed to show how confused and confusing the differences in opinion are for ordinary people who have to rub along together in daily life. An Anglican doctor does not refuse to cure dissenters, nor a general grocer object to selling them his wares, since, 'inasmuch as Congregationalism consumed candles, it ought to be supported'.[43]

More surprising than this tolerant irony is George Eliot's full and sympathetic description of Mr Tryan's religious beliefs. He saves the heroine, Janet Dempster, from drunkenness and despair by helping her to pray and keep faith in God's goodness, though it should be noted that she is helped as much by his personal kindness as by his expressions

177

of faith. No religious reader, either orthodox or dissenting, could be offended by 'Janet's Repentance', yet no agnostic would object to the narrator's assessment of the questions of doctrine from a neutral, humanist point of view:

Our subtlest analysis of schools and sects must miss the essential truth, unless it be lit up by the love that sees in all forms of human thought and work, the life and death struggles of separate human beings.[44]

George Eliot seems to have gained confidence from this experiment in writing about nuances of religious belief and how they operate in the 'press' of day-to-day life.[45] She certainly took a bold and triumphantly successful step in her next fictional enterprise, putting a Methodist minister, Dinah Morris, at the centre of *Adam Bede*. When her old friend François D'Albert Durade expressed surprise at the sympathetic tone towards religion in that novel, Marian replied that she had changed in the ten years since she stayed in Geneva. Then she had 'not yet lost the attitude of antagonism which belongs to the renunciation of *any* belief'; moreover, she had been 'very unhappy, and in a state of discord and rebellion towards my own lot'. Now she felt 'no antagonism towards any faith in which human sorrow and human longing for purity have expressed themselves'.[46] No one could have been better fitted than she was to render the inward experience of religious piety and at the same time to offer a detached, socio-philosophical view of it as a phenomenon of English life.

Another striking element in 'Janet's Repentance' is its remarkably accurate depiction of the psychology of a battered wife. Janet Dempster takes to drink as a defence against her drunken brutal husband. The scenes in which he intimidates her physically and psychologically, culminating in an episode in which he shuts her out of the house in her nightdress (not unlike an early chapter in D. H. Lawrence's *Sons and Lovers*), are powerfully done. She catches the helpless passivity of Janet, paralysed by her hopeless situation and irritating her husband to further rage by her dumb acceptance of it, and she analyses Dempster convincingly too:

And an unloving, tyrannous, brutal man needs no motive to prompt his cruelty; he needs only the perpetual presence of a woman he can call his own. A whole park full of tame or timid-eyed animals to torment at his will would not serve him so well to glut his lust of torture; they could not *feel* as one woman does; they could not throw out the keen retort which whets the edge of hatred.[47]

The Dempsters are based on a Nuneaton lawyer, James Buchanan, and his wife, a daughter of the Mrs Wallington whose school Marian attended and a close friend of Maria Lewis, through whom Marian knew the details of their unhappy marriage. When Blackwood complained that Dempster was 'rather too barefaced a brute' and asked the author to '*soften* your picture as much as you can', she replied defensively that 'the real Dempster was far more disgusting than mine; the real Janet alas! had a far sadder end than mine.'[48] Her memories of Mrs Buchanan's sufferings were mingled, no doubt, with her recent reading – in the week before she began 'Janet's Repentance' – of Elizabeth Gaskell's biography of Charlotte Brontë, in which the effect on the Brontë sisters of their brother Branwell's drunkenness and tyranny is unsparingly told.[49] She had probably also read Anne Brontë's *The Tenant of Wildfell Hall* (1848), which drew on Branwell's condition for the vicious husband, Arthur Huntingdon.

There is also a possibility – no more – that Marian knew about some disgrace in her own family to do with drunkenness. According to one story, an uncle of hers, George Evans, filled the position of black sheep of the family, becoming an alcoholic as a young man and disappearing from home.[50] Whatever the origins of the story, whether from her own experience, from hearsay, from her reading, or from a mixture of all these, Marian applied her fine knowledge of human psychology to give a masterly sketch of a dreadful marriage.

Blackwood's objections to 'Janet's Repentance' caused the familiar combination in Marian of shrinking hopelessness and aggressive defiance. She told him firmly on 11 June that she must 'let Dempster and Janet and the rest be as I *see* them', but she also thought it possible that she had failed to 'touch every heart among my readers with nothing but loving humour, with tenderness, with belief in goodness', in which case, she suggested, she should 'close the series for the Magazine *now*'.[51] Blackwood's reply saved the day: 'I do not fall in with George Eliots every day and the idea of stopping the Series as suggested in your letter gave me "quite a turn" to use one of Thackeray's favourite phrases.' He went further, appealing directly to his still unknown correspondent to consider him a friend and ally for the future:

The cordial tone of your letters gives me great pleasure, and after reading your last I should have liked very much to have shaken hands with you and expressed the hope which I now write that there are many years of happy friendly and literary intercourse before us.[52]

Blackwood's openness was rewarded, though still cautiously. Marian replied, thanking him for being such a generous editor. She then expressed in strangely subdued language a wish for the future: 'That that editor may one day become a personal friend is a prospect which I hope I may indulge without proving too sanguine.'[53]

The hesitancy of Marian's reply to Blackwood stemmed from her natural inclination to disbelieve in anyone's warmth towards her. Always her own first critic, she told Cara in October 1857, 'I can't help losing belief that people love me – the unbelief is in my nature and no sort of fork will drive it finally out.'[54] She had always felt like this; how much more acutely did she feel it now that her living with Lewes rendered her apart from those who had been, or might have become, friends. Cara herself, to whom Marian continued to write, and who sent occasional notes in return, did nothing, as far as we know, to speed the return of their personal friendship. She did not visit Marian in Richmond, though Charles Bray did, nor did she invite her and Lewes together to Coventry. Marian had declined the invitation sent to her by Bray alone to visit Rosehill at Christmas 1855; she seems to have been asked again for Christmas 1856, and once more declined, though less sharply than she had done the previous year.[55] She would never again sit under the acacia tree at Rosehill, for the Brays were retrenching, and moved out in March 1857, settling in the smaller Ivy Cottage in the grounds of the big house, which they sold to John Cash and his wife, the former Mary Sibree.[56]

Though Cara was slow to encourage a personal meeting with her old friend, a recently discovered letter to her from Marian suggests that she did write kindly in her occasional letters, now lost. The new letter is undated; someone, perhaps Cara, has written '1856' on the envelope. It may be that Cara had made the effort to write pleasantly about Lewes, whom she did not know and did not much want to know. At any rate, her letter brought forth the following softer than usual reply, in which Marian's earnest desire for a *rapprochement* with Cara mingles with a joyful expression of her happiness with Lewes:

Thank you, dear Cara, for your sweet letter, which was really something my soul thirsted for.

I know writing is a tax, but even a line now & then from your own self would seem something added to my life.

I think we are nearer to each other than we could ever have been before, for I am able to enter into your feelings & understand your life so much better. It is a great experience – this marriage! & all one's notions of things before seem like the reading of a mystic inscription without the key.

I can't tell you how happy I am in this double life which helps me to feel & think with double strength. I shouldn't say these things unless I loved you very dearly, as I do.

Ever your old yet new
Marian.[57]

As for future friendships, though Blackwood's prophecy proved correct, and a warm relationship did grow up between author and publisher, Marian's relationship with Lewes constituted here, too, a barrier for a time. Blackwood regretted the irregularity of her social position, worrying about the effect on sales of the public discovering who 'George Eliot' was. However, he did eventually, unlike some other good friends, introduce Marian to his wife.[58]

It was not entirely prickliness on her part that made her so cautious about professing friendship, for she had frequent experience of the awkwardness or evasion of others towards her. She had to explain to Cara in June 1857, writing from Jersey, where she and Lewes had gone instead of Brittany, that she had not invited Edward Noel to visit her, since she had no desire to put him, or anyone else, in a dilemma: 'I wish it to be understood, that I should never invite any one to come and see me, who did not ask for the invitation.'[59] In reminding Bessie Parkes once more not to call her Miss Evans, she gave a proud apology for having been the cause of a difficulty when Bessie had not known how to introduce her to a friend, and hoped that she might go on seeing Bessie 'without causing offence to any one'.[60] Her situation strikes us as intolerable, and it seemed so to her. Yet she had no choice but to tolerate it.

Family troubles during the spring and summer of 1857 also contributed to Marian's depression. The writing of 'Janet's Repentance' between April and October was achieved against a background of emotional upheaval about Chrissey and Isaac. In early April, while in the

Scilly Isles, she heard from Isaac's wife Sarah that one of Chrissey's children, Frances, had died of typhus fever, and that Chrissey and another daughter were seriously ill with the disease.[61] On 19 April Isaac sent a rare letter, informing her that Chrissey 'was worse and in great danger'. Though the news upset her, she seems not to have considered going to see Chrissey, pleading distance as an insurmountable barrier.[62] Instead, she asked Isaac to give £15 of her next half-yearly income to Chrissey for 'a change of air'.[63] By 2 May she had heard from Fanny Houghton that Chrissey and her daughter Katie were out of danger.[64]

That anxiety over, Marian now took a step which was both brave and belated. She wrote to Isaac and to Fanny Houghton, telling them of her relationship with Lewes. The wording of these letters, particularly that to Isaac, must have taken some pondering. In the end she opted for a description of her relationship which was truthful, making it obvious, without spelling out the fact, that she was not legally married:

My dear Brother

You will be surprized, I dare say, but I hope not sorry, to learn that I have changed my name, and have someone to take care of me in the world. The event is not at all a sudden one, though it may appear sudden in its announcement to you. My husband has been known to me for several years, and I am well acquainted with his mind and character. He is occupied entirely with scientific and learned pursuits, is several years older than myself, and has three boys, two of whom are at school in Switzerland, and one in England.

After asking Isaac to send her twice-yearly income to Lewes's bank account in future, she signs herself, 'dear Isaac, Your affectionate Sister Marian Lewes'.[65]

The next day Marian wrote to Chapman, 'My dear M. D.' (he having just got his degree), telling him she had taken 'a step which I have long been meditating – that of telling my brother and sister that I am married'. She gives no reason for deciding at this particular time to reveal her secret to her family; indeed, the reason is likely to have been her other secret, kept from Chapman as well as others, that of her authorship itself. Now that she had begun writing fiction, had taken on a pseudonym by which she hoped to become famous, had entered on her vocation, she found the confidence to face her family with her first secret, her liaison with Lewes. Chapman would no longer be needed as the conduit of letters from them to her, 'and you must henceforth remember that I am Mrs. Lewes to all my relatives'.[66]

This was uncharacteristically sanguine, for she would never be 'Mrs Lewes' to Isaac. Fanny Houghton, rather more tolerant than her half-brother, responded kindly, as Marian's grateful reply of 2 June indicates.[67] But Isaac did not write at all. On 9 June Vincent Holbeche, the Evans family solicitor and joint trustee with Isaac of Marian's inheritance, wrote that Isaac was so hurt at not having been told of her 'intention and prospects that he cannot make up his mind to write, feeling that he could not do so in a Brotherly Spirit'. Worse, Isaac wanted to know 'when and where you were married'.[68]

Marian's response to Holbeche was dignified: 'Our marriage is not a legal one, though it is regarded by us both as a sacred bond.'[69] Though not unexpected, Isaac's negative reaction was hurtful. Her journal has no entries between 30 May, the day on which she finished the first part of 'Janet's Repentance', and 22 June, when she wrote: 'My mind has been too intensely agitated and occupied during the last three weeks, for me to have energy left to make entries in my journal.'[70] (This confirms the impression given by her journals generally. Though by definition private, they do not contain expressions of her feelings at crises in her life, except such generalized accounts as this one. There were clearly some things too painful even for her journal.) She mentions having received a letter from Chrissey as well as Fanny. But Isaac prevailed on both his sisters not to write further. Marian put a brave face on this not unexpected outcome. She told Sara Hennell on 14 July, 'I dare say I shall never have any further correspondence with my brother, which will be a great relief to me.'[71]

'So now', she continued in her letter to Sara, 'there is nothing to be concealed from any one'. This was true as concerned her relationship with Lewes, but her circumstances were such that she continued – of necessity, she felt – to be in a false position towards everyone, since she was keeping her other big secret from friends as well as family. She could not help hinting oracularly at some work she hoped to do, expressing it as a compensation for the distress and disapproval her liaison with Lewes caused in others. Sara was told about the recent revelation to her family, and may have wondered at what followed:

If I live five years longer, the positive result of my existence on the side of truth and goodness will outweigh the small negative good that would have consisted in my not doing anything to shock others, and I can conceive no consequences that will make me repent the past.[72]

To Mary Cash she wrote in similar vein:

I feel, too, that all the terrible pain I have gone through in past years partly from the defects of my own nature, partly from outward things, has probably been a preparation for some special work that I may do before I die.[73]

Her friends were not yet enlightened, however, about the nature of this 'special work'.

It is characteristic of Marian that she should consider the writing of novels a vocation. Her special circumstances caused her to relate that sense of vocation to a personal life about which she felt no guilt, but which she was obliged, time and again, to vindicate to others. Those contemporaries who noticed and disliked what they felt to be sanctimoniousness in George Eliot's sober sense of the importance of her work – Eliza Lynn Linton referred to her 'assumption of special sacredness'[74] – might have tried imagining what life was like for her. She would have infinitely preferred not to be in a goldfish bowl, constricted and stared at, but it was her lot in life to be put there. Fame, which would soon be hers, brought the usual rewards in her case, but a great deal more of the attendant disadvantages than it did to most successful authors.

Just as Amos Barton was soon identified by Langford's connection in a remote corner of Yorkshire as the still living Revd John Gwyther, so Mr Tryan struck at least one reader of 'Janet's Repentance' as a portrait of the Revd John Jones, minister of Stockingford Church in Nuneaton from 1828 until his death in 1831. That reader was none other than Mr Jones's brother, who wrote to Blackwood in August 1857 after reading the first two parts of the story, saying they clearly 'alluded to his deceased Brother' and wondering who the author was.[75] The Revd John Jones, like Mr Tryan, had been an Evangelical reformer and had been subjected to public abuse. Marian's Evangelical friend and teacher, Maria Lewis, had been one of his supporters.[76] When Blackwood sent his brother's letter to Lewes, Marian replied, untruthfully, that Mr Tryan was 'not a portrait of any clergyman, living or dead'.[77] She was to find herself increasingly cornered by the curiosity which was the concomitant of her success as a writer, and she responded, against the grain, with untruths.

Her discomfort in this respect was made chronic by the appearance in June 1857 of a candidate for the authorship of the 'Scenes of Clerical Life'. Partly, it must be said, as a result of Marian's obduracy, this phantom continued for two full years to be the object of curious attention, at first in Yorkshire and the Midlands among those who had known the originals of her characters, then – astonishingly – in the Isle of Man, and finally in London and nationally in the pages of *The Times* itself. The first Marian heard was, ironically enough, from her half-sister Fanny. In the very letter in which Fanny acknowledged Marian's relationship to Lewes, she mentioned a rumour about the author of 'Scenes' – the last part of 'Mr Gilfil' being just published in the June number of *Blackwood's* – being a Mr Liggins. Marian wrote back disingenuously:

You are wrong about Mr. Liggins or rather your informants are wrong. We too have been struck with the 'Clerical Sketches', and I have recognized some figures and traditions connected with our old neighbourhood. But Blackwood informs Mr. Lewes that the author is a Mr. Eliot, a clergyman, I presume. *Au reste*, he may be a relation of Mr. Liggins's or some other 'Mr.' who knows Coton stories.[78]

Next came word from Blackwood that the *Manx Sun* of 4 July had attributed the stories to a Mr Liggers (later corrected to Liggins) who had once lived on the Isle of Man. Lewes joked heartily to Blackwood on 19 July:

G. E. begs me to send his kind regards. We were both amused with the divination of the Manx Seer and his friend Liggers. Quel nom! How can you wonder at the anonymous being desired, when its removal would disclose a somewhat antique Liggers who had sown his wild oats in Manx society, and was now subdued to the grave proprieties of Maga [nickname of *Blackwood's Magazine*]. Liggers would look well on a title page! Liggers's New Novel. / The Manx Cat./ By Joshua Liggers. / 3 vols. £1.11.6d.[79]

Soon Lewes and Marian stopped laughing. There *was* a Joseph (not Joshua) Liggins; he lived in the Midlands; unaccountably he allowed reports of his authorship to grow unchecked. By the summer of 1859 Florence Nightingale, Elizabeth Gaskell, and Dickens had entered the game of speculation about Liggins. At this point Lewes and Marian decided, not before time, that they would have less trouble if they revealed the author of *Scenes of Clerical Life* and *Adam Bede* to be Marian Evans Lewes.

It was a protracted saga, with a great many people becoming involved in claims and counter-claims. Twenty years later George Eliot transformed the episode into a fable in her last work, *Impressions of Theophrastus Such*. 'The Wasp Credited with the Honeycomb' is reworked from Aesop and adapted to the topic of the 'Mine and Thine in original authorship':

Several complimentary presumptions were expressed that the honeycomb was due to one or other admired and popular bird, and there was much fluttering on the part of the Nightingale and Swallow, neither of whom gave a positive denial, their confusion perhaps extending to their sense of identity; but the Owl hissed at this folly, arguing from his particular knowledge that the animal which produced honey must be the Musk-rat, the wondrous nature of whose secretions required no proof; and, in the powerful logical procedure of the Owl, from musk to honey was but a step.[80]

While the Liggins nonsense was going on, however, it was hard for Marian to see the joke. She and Lewes mishandled the business, wasting much energy in worrying about it and in putting off the inevitable lifting of the veil of anonymity.

The protracted stay away from Richmond came to an end in late July 1857, when Lewes and Marian returned from Jersey. They had been protected from snubs and gossip so far away from London, and they returned to find the Liggins affair becoming an increasing nuisance. But they also saw friends. Sara Hennell came to stay for a night on 31 July; Barbara Bodichon brought her husband to meet them on 4 August; Rufa Hennell, just married to Wathen Call, invited the Leweses to dinner (as Marian again made sure to tell Sara in a letter).[81] On 24 August Lewes left for a week's visit to Hofwyl to see Charlie and Thornie, and to take his youngest son, Bertie, to join them.[82]

While 'Janet's Repentance' was appearing in *Blackwood's* from July to November 1857, Marian negotiated with Blackwood for the three stories to be brought out in two volumes. Blackwood offered to print 750 copies, for which he would pay £120, 'a little less than ½ the clear profit supposing we sell the whole edition, which is of course no certainty'.

Marian accepted, but on Lewes's advice kept the copyright.[83] The final agreement, suggested by William Blackwood, was for a print run of 1,000, for which Marian was paid a total of £180.[84]

Scenes of Clerical Life appeared in two volumes in January 1858. Marian was apprehensive about its reception, but in her usual journal retrospect of the year on 31 December 1857 she expressed her pleasure at what she had done, allowing herself to hope a little too:

This time last year I was alone, as I am now, and dear George was at Vernon Hill. I was writing the Introduction to Mr. Gilfil's Love Story. What a world of thoughts and feelings since then! My life has deepened unspeakably during the last year: I feel a greater capacity for moral and intellectual enjoyment, a more acute sense of my deficiencies in the past, a more solemn desire to be faithful to coming duties, than I remember at any former period of my life. And my happiness has deepened too: the blessedness of a perfect love and union grows daily. I have had some severe suffering this year from anxiety about my sister and what will probably be a final separation from her – there has been no other real trouble. Few women I fear have had such reason as I have to think the long sad years of youth were worth living for the sake of middle age.

Our prospects are very bright, too. I am writing my new novel. G. is full of his 'Physiology of Common Life' which Blackwood has accepted with cordial satisfaction, and the first part, on 'Hunger and Thirst' appears in the Jan. No. of Maga.[85]

'I am writing my new novel.' On 17 October 1857 Marian had told Blackwood that the new work would be 'a country story – full of the breath of cows and the scent of hay'. A few days later her journal entry for 22 October reads: 'Began my new novel, "Adam Bede".'[86]

CHAPTER EIGHT

Provincial Life Revisited:
Adam Bede *1858–9*

On 5 January 1858 *Scenes of Clerical Life* appeared in two volumes. Three days earlier Lewes had returned from Vernon Hill with that day's *Times* in his pocket. It contained the first review of Marian's work. As she noted in her journal:

He had happened to ask a gentleman in the railway carriage coming up to London to allow him to look at the 'Times', and felt quite agitated and tremulous when his eyes alighted on the review. Finding he had time to go into town before the train started, he bought a copy there. It is a highly favourable notice, and as far as it goes, appreciatory.[1]

The reviewer, Samuel Lucas, professes himself 'most impressed' by this work by 'Mr. George Eliot – a name unknown to us'. He praises the author's 'combination of humour with pathos in depicting ordinary situations', invoking, aptly enough, Scott's comment on Goldsmith's *Vicar of Wakefield* that 'though each touch serves to show that he is made of mortal mould and is full of human frailties, the effect of the whole is to reconcile us to human nature'.[2]

Marian had asked for complimentary copies to be sent to Dickens, Thackeray, Tennyson, Ruskin, Froude, the Garrick Club's Albert Smith, and Jane Welsh Carlyle. Of the replies which survive, those from Dickens and Jane Carlyle are the most interesting. Dickens wrote enthusiastically about 'the exquisite truth and delicacy, both of the humour and the pathos', of the stories. He went on to guess that he was addressing a woman:

I have observed what seem to me to be such womanly touches, in those moving fictions, that the assurance on the title-page is insufficient to satisfy me, even now. If they originated with no woman, I believe that no man ever before had the art of making himself, mentally, so like a woman, since the world began.[3]

To Blackwood Dickens observed that 'all the women in the book are more alive than the men, and more informed from within', and he had 'not the faintest doubt' that a woman was the author of the episode in which Janet is shut out by her husband.[4] The example Dickens chooses has an added piquancy when one considers that he was to separate from his wife within a few months of writing this, shutting her out of his life with an ill-advised advertisement of his separation in his paper, *Household Words*, on 12 June. Jane Carlyle, noted for her sharp eye and even sharper tongue, wrote a brief riddle about the separation: 'When does a man really ill-use his wife?' To which the answer was: 'When he plays the Dickens with her.'[5]

Jane Carlyle's own letter of thanks for her copy of *Scenes* probably gave Marian even greater pleasure than Dickens's. She did not guess the sex of the author, though she saw the same excellences as Dickens did. Her ingenious solution to the mystery of authorship was to suppose the writer to be 'a man of middle age, with a wife from whom he has got those beautiful *feminine* touches in his book, a good many children, and a dog that he has as much fondness for as I have for my little Nero'. Moreover, she praised the work as 'full of tenderness and pathos without sentimentality, of sense without dogmatism, of earnestness without twaddle'.[6]

These responses were heartening for Marian as she proceeded with the writing of *Adam Bede*. As she had said self-knowingly to Blackwood in November 1857, she needed the 'sunshine of success', being 'as impressionable as I am obstinate, and as much in need of sympathy from my readers as I am incapable of bending myself to their tastes'.[7] More public praise came in the *Saturday Review* notice in May 1858, in which George Eliot was again commended for the humour, pathos, and truth to life of the stories. The reviewer gratifyingly quoted Ruskin on a good book 'always leading you to love or reverence something with your whole heart'.[8]

One of the most astute comments was one Marian never saw. Henry

Crabb Robinson, having discovered to his discomfort in 1859 that *Adam Bede* was by the Miss Evans whom he had liked but whose agnosticism and relationship with Lewes he deplored, belatedly sought out *Scenes of Clerical Life*. He was perplexed to find 'Janet's Repentance' 'very Evangelical in its tone', and related this example of an author's ability – which he half regretted – to 'write wisely and beautifully but without any actual belief in what themselves write' to the same phenomenon in Goethe, instancing the 'Confessions of a Beautiful Soul' in *Wilhelm Meister's Apprenticeship*.[9] Marian would have been flattered by the comparison, though irked by Robinson's opinion that such wisdom as hers and Goethe's smacked nonetheless of 'cant'.

The *Times* review and the responses of Dickens and Jane Carlyle compensated somewhat for the relatively slow sale of *Scenes of Clerical Life*. Though Mudie's circulating library immediately took 350 copies, sales stuck during January 1858, so that Marian became, as Lewes told Blackwood on 5 February, 'down in the mouth'. Blackwood replied soothingly that he thought nearly 800 copies had been sold and he was sure they would sell out soon.[10] He visited London at the end of February, and was invited to Richmond to be introduced at last to George Eliot. There was really no point in keeping the secret from him any longer, since Lewes and Marian were planning to go to Germany again for several months, and they could hardly go on with the transparent fiction that 'Eliot' was a friend who happened to spend long periods of time with Lewes in Scilly, Jersey, and now Munich and Dresden. Marian was relieved at having identified herself to Blackwood, who was 'kind', and who went away with the first thirteen chapters of *Adam Bede*.[11]

Even without the Liggins legend, which was soon to grow to unmanageable proportions, Marian was finding it hard to keep the secret from her friends. Her hatred of falsehood was in constant tension with her fear of failure and her shrinking dread of stirring up more gossip about her domestic life. She went to such trouble to save herself from that particular trouble that one wonders whether the deception was worth keeping up for another year and more. Rather as she had done to the Brays during the early days of her intimacy with Lewes, she let out hints and suggestions to selected friends, but always stopped short of telling the full truth. Chapman, of course, wondered why he had received no articles for the *Westminster Review* since the 'Young' in January

1857, though he often asked her to contribute. He knew she needed to earn a living; how was she doing it?

In February 1858 Bessie Parkes wrote asking Marian to contribute to the new periodical she was launching, with funding from Barbara Bodichon. This was the pioneering *English Woman's Journal*, which promoted the cause of employment and married property rights for women. Of course Marian supported the principles of the *Journal*, but she fobbed Bessie off, in the process giving a strong hint that she was engaged in other work:

I dare say you have not seen Mr. Chapman lately, or have not made any allusion to me in conversation with him, or he would have told you that I have not written for the Westminster since the last Christmas but one – that is, just a year ago – and that I have been obliged to say 'No' to all his requests for contributions. I have given up writing 'articles', having discovered that my vocation lies in other paths. In fact *entre nous*, I expect to be writing *books* for some time to come. Don't speak of that at all; but I tell you that you may not in the least misapprehend my negatives.[12]

The Brays, too, were wondering what she was doing. Her correspondence with both Charles and Sara had recently been going through a difficult patch. Marian and Lewes had been polite but critical of Sara's recent book, *Christianity and Infidelity* (1857). This work, setting out arguments on facing pages for and against Christianity, annoyed Marian, who saw both a weakness in logic and a choice of extracts and examples biased against non-belief – 'I think Infidelity cuts a very poor figure', she told Sara. But she was touched at receiving a copy in February 1857, inscribed to 'Dr. Pollian ab Achato suo fido', an allusion to the faithful friend of Aeneas and to Sara's old name for the learned young translator of Strauss.[13]

As for Bray, he had begun revising his *Philosophy of Necessity* for a new edition. He gave notice that he intended to attack the chapter on phrenology in Lewes's revised edition in 1857 of his *Biographical History of Philosophy*. Marian assured Bray in November 1857 that Lewes would 'not like you any the worse for cutting him up' (or, as she might have said more accurately, any the more for *not* cutting him up). But she still bristled on the subject which had caused her much anguish when Lewes and Bray had argued about it on their first meeting in July 1855, and she sharply reminded Bray that Lewes was not 'in sublime ignorance of what phrenologists say', as Bray seemed determined to believe. She defended Lewes's fairness towards positions he did not share, adding with that disconcerting cleverness of hers a comment on her own nature in this respect: 'The last refuge of intolerance is in not tolerating the intolerant – and I am often in danger of secreting that sort of venom.'[14]

Marian kept her letters steadfastly friendly throughout, being determined not to take or give offence unnecessarily. Cara softened sufficiently towards Marian's social position to invite her – and presumably Lewes too – to Coventry in March 1858. Marian thanked her warmly on 29 March, but pronounced it impossible, as they were about to set off for Munich.[15] Her alertness to the slightest nuance of Cara's demeanour towards her is shown by a note of 27 March which begins: 'Your letter was very sweet to me, coming spontaneously, not a propos of a parcel.' In the same note she recommended 'a lady of your acquaintance in whom I have a peculiar interest'. 'She will present herself to you shortly, with a note from my hand.'[16] This was a photograph of herself, which she had taken by the London photographer Mayall on 26 February, when Lewes, too, was photographed.[17]

At the same time, on 29 March, she wrote in the old satirical style to Bray, who had obviously been speculating that she was writing a novel. She found it easier to make a joke, turning the accusation of secret authorship on Bray himself, rather than tell a direct lie to the man she was not yet ready to reveal the truth to, especially as she knew too well how 'leaky' he was:

Apropos, when do you bring out your new poem? I presume you are already in the Sixth Canto. It is true, you have never told me you intended to write a poem, nor have I heard any one say so who was likely to know. Nevertheless, I have quite as active an imagination as you, and I don't see why I shouldn't suppose you are writing a poem, as well as you suppose that I am writing a novel, and when the second edition of your Philosophy of Necessity comes out, I shall consider that a surreptitious affair, got up by a pseudo-Charles Bray, the real one being deeply engaged on his epic.

Seriously, I wish you would not set false rumours, or any other rumours afloat about me. They are injurious. Several people, who seem to derive their notions from Ivy Cottage, have spoken to me of a supposed novel I was going to bring out.[18]

When Bray wrote back, presumably contritely, Marian relented, throwing out a largish hint after all: 'If I withhold anything from my friends which it would gratify them to know you will believe, I hope, that I have good reasons for doing so.'[19]

In fact, there was one friend who *had* been told the secret, and who was at present keeping it faithfully. Though Marian's journal makes no mention of what must have been a spontaneous gesture very soon after she began writing the first of the *Scenes of Clerical Life*, the recipient of the confidence remembered it in his meticulous way in his auto-biography. It was appropriate that, of all her friends, Marian should have told Herbert Spencer, with whom she had once been so intimately associated, who had been Lewes's closest friend, and who had brought Marian and Lewes together. In October 1856 Spencer was travelling for his health. He stopped in London on the way from Brighton to Paris, and spent an afternoon and evening in Richmond on 12 October.[20]

Spencer's memory of the occasion was that on this visit he had renewed an old suggestion of his that Marian should try writing fiction. She then told him 'that she had commenced, and had then in hand "The Sad Story [*sic*] of the Rev. Amos Barton": this confession being made under promise on my part of absolute secrecy'.[21]

The secret was still intact, but only just, in March 1858. Blackwood knew now, and told his wife, but not his London manager Langford. Blackwood was reliable, for, as he remarked to his wife, it was 'on all accounts desirable' to keep the authorship 'a profound secret'. Lewes had flattered him when he visited, telling him he did not think 'any other editor in the world would have been able to induce George Eliot to go on'. Blackwood recognized the flattery in this remark, but also took it as his due, which it undoubtedly was. Lewes, he said, was 'a monstrous clever fellow', and as for George Eliot, 'She is a most intelligent, pleasant woman, with a face like a man, but a good expression.'[22]

He went off with the first thirteen chapters of *Adam Bede*, writing to Lewes on 11 March that he thought 'Adam Bede all right, most lifelike and real', having read as much as he could on the train journey home to Edinburgh, and having 'felt very savage when the waning light stopped me as we neared the Scottish Border'.[23] He wrote again when he had read all thirteen chapters, mingling detailed praise with minor critical points, fearing 'the usual sad catastrophe' would result from Arthur Donnithorne's 'unfortunate attachment' to the dairy maid Hetty Sorrel, and asking how the story was to unfold.[24] Marian firmly refused to tell him, and he took her refusal in good part. Lewes once more praised his tact – 'for you perceive [George Eliot's] Pegasus is tender in the mouth, and apt to lay back his ears in a restive ominous style if even the reins be shaken when he is at work'.[25]

What Marian said in reply to Blackwood's curiosity is extremely interesting. She knew that her story, with its concentration on the birth of an illegitimate child to Hetty, the death – infanticide – of the baby, and the trial of Hetty, was liable to moral objections. Without revealing that this was the intended plot, she mounted a double defence in advance. One argument was general, theoretical, aesthetic, quite in line with what she had written about 'The Morality of *Wilhelm Meister*' before she herself had begun writing fiction. To Blackwood she now said, 'The soul of art lies in its treatment and not in its subject.'

The second defence was a practical one, which probably told Blackwood, though indirectly, exactly what the outcome of Arthur's unfortunate attachment to Hetty would be. Marian invoked Scott's *Heart of Midlothian*, also a story of illegitimate birth and child murder, and with a trial and eleventh-hour reprieve which Marian did not disdain to imitate:

The Heart of Midlothian would probably have been thought highly objectionable if a skeleton of the story had been given by a writer whose reputation did not place him above question. And the same story told by a Balzacian French writer would probably have made a book that no young person could read without injury. Yet what girl of twelve was ever injured by the Heart of Midlothian?[26]

Interestingly enough, she had contrasted Balzac, 'perhaps the most wonderful writer of fiction the world has ever seen', to Goethe in her essay on *Wilhelm Meister*, enunciating the paradox – so illuminating about Balzac's effect on his readers – that he 'drags us by his magic force through scene after scene of unmitigated vice, till the effect of walking among this human carrion is a moral nausea'.[27] Balzac's artistic realism is in this respect objectionable, unlike the less unremittingly sordid realism of Goethe and Scott and, she wishes to suggest to Blackwood, George Eliot. As Scott had done, so George Eliot too felt able by her handling of the subject of seduction and illegitimacy to render it acceptable to most readers, however youthful or fastidious.

On 7 March Marian made her will, using Chapman as a witness.[28] Lewes once more settled Agnes's debts, noting in his journal that she had overstepped her increased income by £184, and showing some bitterness at her lack of appreciation of his kindness: 'I fear she is quite *hardened*.'[29] Money was not quite as tight as it had been in previous years, though they were not yet well off. Lewes's accounts for the year 1857 show that he earned £433. 9s. 2d. from articles and from the reprints of his successful *Life of Goethe* and *Biographical History of Philosophy*. Marian had received £443. 0s. 0d. for *Scenes of Clerical Life*, first in *Blackwood's*, then in book form.[30]

They set off for Munich on 7 April 1858. Lewes wanted to consult the eminent scientists there for his *Physiology of Common Life*, a work which required more scholarly research than the popularizing, semi-amateur *Sea-Side Studies*. (*The Physiology of Common Life*, published by Blackwood in 1859, was translated into several languages, and became influential, particularly in Russia. Ivan Petrovitch Pavlov read it while studying at a theological seminary in 1863–4 and was so enthused by it that he turned from theology to physiology;[31] Dostoyevsky refers to it in the second chapter of *Crime and Punishment*, 1865–6.) Marian could continue writing *Adam Bede* as comfortably in Munich as she could in Richmond. Once more, they could live a more normal social life abroad than at home.

And they could be out of London, and out of England, while critics speculated about the new author who had appeared in the literary world. The escape from London was to become a regular occurrence when George Eliot's fame began in earnest, which it did after the publication, early the following year, of *Adam Bede*.

Lewes wrote to Blackwood on 14 April, announcing his and Marian's arrival in Munich, and giving a cheerful account of their search for lodgings, which they had at length found in Luitpoldstrasse:

We reached this place on Monday and have only just settled into our lodgings, the search after which seemed as little promising as that of the philosopher's stone. Imagine yourself in a semi desert of brick and mortar every other house appearing to be a palace (though most of them have lodgings to let) and with no better guide to vacant rooms than a scrap of paper pasted against a post (generally a long way off) informing you in illegible pot hooks that 'a solid gentleman' can find elegant rooms at such a place. In full persuasion of your solidity, you trudge to the spot indicated, and after being first sent here, then there, and finally back again you come perhaps to a dog kennel, or spitoon, which you are *not* ambitious of making your residence.[32]

On the way they had spent two days in Nürnberg, which Marian described in delighted detail in her journal. In the manner of Riehl, she mingled description with analysis, relating the physical features of the buildings she saw to the history of the people who had built them:

No sombre colouring, except the old churches: all was bright and varied, each façade having a different colour – delicate green, or buff, or pink, or lilac – every now and then set off by the neighbourhood of a rich reddish brown. And the roofs always gave warmth of colour with their bright red or rich purple tiles. Every house differed from its neighbour, and had a physiognomy of its own, though a beautiful family likeness ran through them all, as if the burghers of that old city were of one heart and soul, loving the same delightful outlines and cherishing the same daily habits of simple ease and enjoyment in their balcony windows when the day's work was done.[33]

They spent three months in Munich. Both were frequently ill, and Marian in particular found the climate depressing. But Lewes was otherwise in his element. Not only did he find himself fêted everywhere as the biographer of Goethe, but he had meetings with fellow scientists, including the anatomist Karl von Siebold and the celebrated chemist Justus von Liebig. He was invited to observe and assist in experiments in their laboratories, and was flattered to be introduced on one occasion as a 'professor from London'.[34] As Marian explained to Sara Hennell, Munich 'swarms with professors of all sorts – all gründlich [thorough], of course, and one or two of them great'.[35]

The professors' wives were happy to invite Mr and Mrs Lewes to dinner, as Marian also reported to Sara. Her pleasure in not being discriminated against was, however, slightly dulled by having on each occasion to 'sit on the sofa' all evening with the hostess, 'listening to her stupidities, while the men on the other side of the table are discussing all the subjects I care to hear about'.[36]

On 30 April they went to hear Prince Radziwill's music to *Faust*. 'Gretchen's second song, in which she implores help of the "Schmerz-ensreiche" [Mater Dolorosa] touched me a good deal', Marian wrote in her journal.[37] It might well do so, for in her writing she was even then building up to the seduction and pregnancy of Hetty, who has a strong affinity with Goethe's simple Gretchen, also seduced by a gentleman, and doomed to kill her child and be imprisoned for it. The song alluded to by Marian is that sung by Gretchen after her seduction by Faust when she is full of shame and dread. And Gretchen says, as Hetty might have said with equal right, 'Schön war ich auch, und das war mein Verderben' ('I was beautiful too, and that was my ruin').[38]

A month later, on 30 May, the Leweses were once more listening to music, this time Rossini's *William Tell,* and this occasion, too, had a connection with *Adam Bede.* In her journal account, 'The History of "Adam Bede"', written on 30 November 1858, she remembered how the fight between Adam and Arthur in chapter 27 came to her 'as a *necessity*' while she was listening to the opera that night.[39] Her frequent colds and headaches, and the large amount of social visiting she and Lewes did in Munich, meant that her writing went slowly, so that she had only got to the beginning of chapter 26 when they left Munich on 6 July for Dresden.[40]

Letters came from Blackwood, who agreed with Marian that it would be better not to consider publishing *Adam Bede* in *Blackwood's Magazine,* but to bring it out straight away as a book.[41] Blackwood sent encouragement, both about the probable issuing of *Scenes of Clerical Life* in a cheap edition and about the new novel in progress. He also told an anecdote which amused Marian, but undoubtedly gave her some pain too. As with Langford's early information about Gwyther and Amos Barton, so here coincidence played a strong part. Blackwood wrote about a recent visit to Epsom racecourse:

I was smoking my cigar and watching the betters in the enclosure in front of the Stand on the Derby day when I was accosted by Newdigate, the member for Warwickshire, who after some talk on politics etc. said, 'Do you know that you have been publishing a capital series of stories in the Mag., the Clerical Scenes, all about my place and County.' My disbelief availed nothing. He knew the author, a Mr. Liggers. This is I think the same unfortunate patronymic that the *Manx Cat* selected as the author's.[42]

Blackwood added that he found Newdigate 'a capital specimen of an honest high minded English gentleman and Squire'. He was, indeed, as Marian had reason to know, since this was Charles Newdigate Newdegate, MP for North Warwickshire, inheritor of the Arbury estate, and friend and employer of Isaac Evans. Marian merely replied that she knew he deserved the praise Blackwood had given him.[43]

Before leaving Munich Marian met Strauss for the second time, enjoying 'a quarter of an hour's chat with him', which she found much less painful than 'when I saw him in that dumb way at Cologne' in July 1854. Strauss spoke warmly of Dr Brabant, who had been 'his earliest English friend', as Marian told Sara.[44] She made no more sarcastic comments about the egotistical old doctor with whom she had once made a fool of herself. Slights and embarrassments and irritations took a long time to heal in her mind, but when they did she was generous, as she once more had occasion to be when she heard of George Combe's death in August. Though he had abruptly cut off relations with her and had let the Brays know that he thought Lewes a 'shallow, flippant man',[45] she now wrote that he was 'good and able, with the utmost that severity might make of his weaknesses'.[46]

After Lewes had spent a week at the end of June visiting his sons at Hofwyl, they packed up and went to Dresden, stopping at various tourist spots on the way. In Vienna they saw a room full of Rubens paintings, which added to the impression made by his works displayed in Munich. 'His are such real, breathing men and women – men and women moved by passions, not mincing and grimacing and posing in mere apery of passion!' she had written to Sara soon after her arrival in Germany.[47] After a day in Prague, where they visited the synagogue and Jewish cemetery, they settled in Dresden for six weeks.

Here Marian worked more steadily at *Adam Bede*, enjoying the 'long, quiet mornings' for her writing.[48] She and Lewes visited the art gallery several times, admiring the Holbeins and the 'rich collection of Flemish and Dutch pictures' of Teniers and others.[49] These were examples of that 'Dutch realism' which she had already invoked in her essays and in 'Amos Barton' and to which she alluded once more in chapter 17 of *Adam Bede*, written in Munich and entitled 'In Which the Story Pauses a Little'. Recapitulating the imputed horror of the 'lady reader' at finding that Amos Barton was no better, or better-looking, than the average, she argues in similar fashion with the supposed resistant reader of *Adam Bede*. 'Bless us', she writes, 'things may be lovable that are not altogether handsome, I hope?' Having referred to the 'precious quality of truthfulness' in many Dutch paintings, she continues, 'And so I come back to Mr Irwine [the flawed clergyman], with whom I desire you to be in perfect charity, far as he may be from satisfying your demands on the clerical character.'[10]

When the *Saturday Review* came to notice *Adam Bede* in February 1859, the reviewer took George Eliot to task for this chapter with its didactic reflections reminiscent of Fielding explaining one of his 'comic epic poems in prose', *Joseph Andrews* or *Tom Jones*:

The story of *Adam Bede* is supposed to have taken place fifty years ago, and one of the characters is a good, easy-going rector. That such a man, though not fervent in doctrinal controversies, and given to a little quiet sporting, might really be a good and useful man seems a very simple truth, and one that might be advanced without the slightest danger of affronting public opinion at this day. But the author of *Adam Bede* makes what he calls a pause in the story, and, in the language of Mause Headrigg [in Scott's *Old Mortality*], declares himself willing to 'bear testimony in the Grassmarket', and undergo any reasonable sort of martyrdom, while all that he really does is to emit the most harmless and inoffensive proposition.[11]

The anonymous reviewer has a point, but it is a point which arises out of George Eliot's very success. By the time we reach chapter 17 we are so engrossed in the characters and their doings, so accepting of the author's presentation of them, that we require no persuading to 'be in perfect charity' with them. As the reviewer had remarked at the beginning of this favourable notice, George Eliot 'has got into an original field of observation' and 'gives us something we have not had before'.[12] That there is no need for such an elaborate explanation of her procedures is a tribute to their complete success in practice.

Indeed, when one begins *Adam Bede* fresh from a reading of the interesting but slightly clumsy *Scenes of Clerical Life*, one is struck by the sudden expansive ease of the writing and the sureness of touch in plotting a larger, more complex story than there was room for in *Scenes*. If anything, Blackwood's remarks about the first thirteen chapters, though shrewd, seriously understate the promise they show. He runs through the opening scenes, finding them 'truly and graphically described', and praises the early delineations of character, particularly the comic ones. But his language uses no superlatives, and he murmurs a little about the amount of dialect, particularly in the speech of Lisbeth Bede, Adam's loving, complaining mother.[13]

Lewes, on the other hand, saw immediately how remarkable the novel was going to be. He encouraged Marian when work went slowly and she felt despondent; she read him chapters and parts of chapters as she wrote them, and he commented helpfully, suggesting one or two scenes, such as the fight in the wood between Adam and Arthur over Hetty, whom Arthur is seducing while Adam dreams of making her his wife after he has secured enough steady carpentry work to allow him to propose to her. Most of all, Lewes saw what a wonderful book was being written before his eyes, and was not to be put off by the author's doubts or the publisher's criticisms. No wonder Marian dedicated the manuscript, which Blackwood returned to her after publication, in this way:

To my dear husband, George Henry Lewes, I give this M.S. of a work which would never have been written but for the happiness which his love has conferred on my life. Marian Lewes. March 23. 1859.[14]

This dedication provides the best answer to all those who disapproved of the relationship or thought Lewes's influence on Marian detrimental to either her life or her writing or both.

George Eliot had promised Blackwood that her novel would be 'full of the breath of cows and the scent of hay'.[15] It was. Country life at the turn of the century is invoked with all its sights and smells, the fields and woods, the seasons and their rituals, from butter making to harvest supper. The narrator takes us into the dairy on a summer's day at Hall Farm in chapter 7, showing us one of the many 'scenes' in the novel, in which we are invited to share a vantage point with the narrator or one of the characters, a method borrowed from Scott but employed with less obvious stage management than in the Waverley novels.

The dairy is beautiful, and so is Hetty Sorrel, the dairy maid:

The dairy was certainly worth looking at: it was a scene to sicken for with a sort of calenture in hot and dusty streets – such coolness, such purity, such fresh fragrance of new-pressed cheese, of firm butter, of wooden vessels perpetually bathed in pure water; such soft colouring of red earthenware and creamy surfaces, brown wood and polished tin, grey limestone and rich orange-red rust in the iron weights and hooks and hinges. But one gets only a confused notion of these details when they surround a distractingly pretty girl of seventeen, standing on little pattens and rounding her dimpled arm to lift a pound of butter out of the scale.[16]

The character with whom we view the charms of Mrs Poyser's dairy, and Mrs Poyser's niece, is Arthur Donnithorne, the young man who is due to become Squire when his irritable grandfather dies, and who plans to bring in liberal reforms to help the tenants, with whom he is consequently 'a great favourite':

Every tenant was quite sure things would be different when the reins once got into his hands – there was to be a millennial abundance of new gates, allowances of lime, and returns of ten per cent.[57]

Things turn out differently, of course. With the knowing irony of a Fielding, the tolerant amusement of a Scott, and the quiet clever plotting of a Jane Austen, George Eliot tells her rather conventional story of youthful mistakes, lost chances, dashed hopes, shame and misery. More than any of her distinguished predecessors, however, she enters into the consciousness of a wide range of characters, from easy-going, 'open, generous' Arthur – who has 'committed an error which makes deception seem a necessity', so that, in George Eliot's fine phrase, 'duty was become a question of tactics' – to the upright but priggish and unforgiving Adam, the sweet-natured Methodist preacher Dinah Morris, and even the thoughtless beauty Hetty Sorrel herself.

In an unconventional handling of her conventional plot, George Eliot has Hetty's story take up most of the middle of the book. Where in *The Heart of Midlothian* Scott draws Effie Deans's pregnancy, childbirth, and child murder in one brief page, concentrating his narrative interest rather on the drama of the trial scene and Jeanie Deans's brave journey to London to ask the Queen for a pardon for her sister, George Eliot follows Hetty through the whole process, except the giving birth itself. Indeed, one reviewer was scandalized by the 'almost obstetric accuracy of detail', and another by what seemed like 'the rough notes of a man-midwife's conversations with a bride'. The writer in the *Saturday Review*, who made this last comment, expostulated, 'Let us copy the old masters of the art, who, if they gave us a baby, gave it us all at once.'[58]

In fact, George Eliot's bold discussion of Hetty's condition as she runs away from home to find Arthur is a good example of her putting into practice her creed of realism. Seductions, unwanted pregnancies, shame, running away – these things happen in communities, and always have done. Rural life is not all scenic beauty and happy families; Eden has its serpent. The idyll promised by the idea of cows and the sweet smell of hay is suggested in all its sensuousness, but it is a flawed idyll, as befits any story meant to be realistic rather than idealistic. George Eliot embodies the ideas she had expressed in her essays on Ruskin and Riehl, and she does so with great skill. In the manner of writers from Chaucer and Shakespeare to Scott and Wordsworth and Jane Austen, she catches the paradoxes of human life – the ugliness as well as the beauty, the unkindness as well as the neighbourliness, the necessary compromises in the individual's pursuit of happiness or goodness. Lisbeth Bede, one of her most expressive minor characters, puts it at its gloomiest: 'It's choice o' mislikins is all I'n got i' this world. One mossel's as good as another when your mouth's out o' taste.'[19]

Despite the objections of some reviewers, the stages of Hetty's pregnancy are not marked obtrusively. George Eliot, though she wishes to persuade her readers to the 'warts and all' theory of fiction, does not try to shock them into accepting it. She uses the calendar of the rural community's year to mark Hetty's adventures. It is June 1799 when Arthur sees Hetty in the dairy; his twenty-first birthday is celebrated on 30 July by the whole community, by which time he has succumbed to temptation; Arthur leaves to join the army getting ready to fight the French towards the end of August; Mrs Poyser notices Hetty has become more sober and less vain, and Adam observes a more experienced look in her eyes by Michaelmas (29 September) and the time of harvest home; and so on.

It is a commonplace of modern criticism of George Eliot to remark that she was vindictive towards female beauty in her novels. Rosamond Vincy in *Middlemarch* and Hetty in *Adam Bede* are usually cited, and Marian's own plainness is often adduced by way of explanation. While allowing an element of truth to this view – we know Marian was sensitive about her lack of beauty and had thought she might never have a man's love – we should see it as only a partial explanation. Nor is this sort of explanation applicable exclusively to George Eliot. After all, which great imaginative writer is not without a streak of venom towards some of his or her own creations? Tolstoy, perhaps, but certainly not Dickens or Jane Austen. Then, too, we might point out that female beauty is not always punished or disapproved of by George Eliot. There are many beautiful women in the novels towards whom she is charitable, and in whom she shows that it is possible for beauty to coincide with kindness and modesty, and not necessarily with vanity and shallowness.

Witness Dorothea, Romola, Maggie Tulliver, and in *Adam Bede* Dinah Morris, the character whose life is set in contrast to Hetty's.

It is truer to say that George Eliot appears to be in two minds about Hetty. There is loving, sensuous description of her beauty, for example in the surprisingly sumptuous picture of Hetty undressing in her bedroom in chapter 15. Her hair, her neck and arms, her round softness as she sits in her stays – no taboo makes George Eliot shy of using the word – looking in the mirror as we in turn look at her: all this is given fully.[60] She has the kind of beauty even other women love to look at; sharp Mrs Poyser cannot take her eyes off the girl, though she disapproves of her vanity and her lack of sympathy towards others.

If there is a problem with George Eliot's presentation of Hetty it has a more complicated foundation than a plain woman's need to punish imaginatively a pretty one. It is quite reasonable to suppose that a simple beauty might be self-centred and uncaring of others, as Hetty is. Mrs Poyser remarks pungently that 'things take no more hold on her than if she was a dried pea', and that she is 'no better nor a cherry wi' a hard stone inside it'.[61] But it is part of George Eliot's avowed function as a novelist to extend the reader's sympathy to embrace even dislikable characters, and with Hetty she both seeks our understanding of her ambitions, her hopes of Arthur, and her fear of discovery, and yet half withholds her own sympathy, reminding us constantly of Hetty's hardness, her 'little trivial soul'.[62]

Philosophically, George Eliot believed that human beings are determined by family likeness and social circumstance – what would later in the century be called heredity and environment – from which it follows logically that we should show tolerance towards people's faults. To understand all should be to forgive all. Morally, she believed in the necessity for individuals to strive to improve according to a humanist ethic not much different from the Christian ethic from which it derived. Temperamentally, she was impatient of faults in herself and others and found it hard to forgive. It is hardly surprising that tensions and inconsistencies should arise as she created her imaginative worlds out of this complex combination of elements.

Viewing matters in this light, we can see how it came about that Hetty should be represented as helpless and to be pitied, yet also, since she makes no effort at self-improvement, to be disapproved of, and finally – through the mechanism of the plot – to be punished. Yet this last element is complicated too. As George Eliot had said to Blackwood when he complained of her huddling up the conclusions of her first two stories, endings are difficult, being inevitably nothing more than negations. Hetty is punished, but that is only one possible ending. In fact, George Eliot's desire to be realistic, not to see through rose-tinted glasses, may well have impelled her towards a sad end for Hetty (though a counter-urge saw her succumb to Scott's device of the last-minute commutation of the sentence from death to transportation). For she based Hetty's story on a real trial and prison scene of a child murderer sentenced to death in Nottingham at the beginning of the century, a case known to her through her aunt Elizabeth Evans.

In her 'History of "Adam Bede"', written in her journal on 30 November 1858, Marian noted that the germ of the story was an anecdote told to her by her Methodist aunt during her visit to Griff in 1839, when 'it occurred to her to tell me how she had visited a condemned criminal, a very ignorant girl who had murdered her child and refused to confess'. Elizabeth Tomlinson, as she then was, had stayed all night praying with the girl, Mary Voce, and had heard her confess to the crime:

My aunt afterwards went with her in the cart to the place of execution, and she described to me the great respect with which this ministry of hers was regarded by the official people about the gaol. The story, told by my aunt with great feeling, affected me deeply, and I never lost the impression of that afternoon and our talk together; but I believe I never mentioned it, through all the intervening years, till something prompted me to tell it to George in December 1856, when I had begun to write the 'Scenes of Clerical Life'. He remarked that the scene in the prison would make a fine element in a story, and I afterwards began to think of blending this and some other recollections of my aunt in one story with some points in my father's early life and character.[63]

Dinah Morris, who performs the same office for Hetty – though Hetty, unlike Mary Voce in Nottingham in 1802, does not finally go to the gallows – is therefore based on Elizabeth Evans as far as her actions are concerned. But she is not a direct copy of the aunt. As if anticipating the rash of identifications which would begin as soon as *Adam Bede* was published, Marian noted in her journal that 'there is not a single *portrait* in "Adam Bede"; only the suggestions of experience wrought up into new combinations'.[64]

It was characteristic of George Eliot's method that she mingled elements of her aunt's story with others taken from her reading, in this case especially Robert Southey's *Life of Wesley*, from which she took notes. Dinah's open-air preaching and her habit of looking randomly in the Bible for practical guidance are examples; George Eliot also brings Wesley into a conversation Dinah has with Mr Irwine while Arthur is viewing Hetty in the dairy.[65] It may be, too, that she remembered hearing from the Sibrees how their father, John Sibree, an Independent minister in Coventry, had accompanied a criminal to his execution in 1820, preaching a sermon on the following Sunday to a congregation of – he claimed – six or seven thousand.[66]

The story and characters in *Adam Bede* are thus the products of Marian Evans's memories of her own childhood and youth, of her wide reading, and of her memories of anecdotes told to her by others. All the phases of her experience, of piety succeeded by scepticism, of family life with its companionship and its clashes of temperament, of the pleasures and pains of belonging to a close-knit community and the relief yet sense of loss following her exit from it, come into play and become, in her words, 'wrought up into new combinations'.

George Eliot's memory was, as a matter of fact, formidable. When Charles Bray found out she was the author of *Adam Bede*, he wrote to her admiringly but also mock-fearfully: 'You remember *everything* – which makes me horribly afraid of my "fore paws" & makes me pray "forgive us our sins & we forgive them that trespass against us".'[67] And Lewes told Mary Cash, when she visited Marian in 1873 for the first time in over twenty years and was amazed to find how well Marian remembered everything to do with the Sibree and Cash families: 'She forgets nothing that has ever come within the curl of her eyelash.'[68]

It was her extraordinary memory which, combined with her avowed adherence to realism in fiction and the additional interest aroused by the piquant mystery about the identity of 'George Eliot', led to her being plagued more than most authors by hunters of 'originals' for her books. Such originals existed, as they did for Dickens, say, but they were put into the alembic of memory, imagination, and association with other experiences, becoming in the process some of the most believable fictions in literary history. So successful is George Eliot in convincing readers that her characters are 'real' that we need to remind ourselves of the imaginative, creative, associative element which accompanies the reproductive, re-creating element so quickly seized on for comment by her contemporaries.[69]

Adam Bede himself is, understood in this way, in some respects 'like' Marian's father. 'Some points in my father's early life and character' appear, as she said in her description of how she came to write the novel. She repeated this to Sara Hennell in June 1859, when her friend had finally been told the secret of her authorship. Sara, unsettled and excited, immediately began relating news and gossip connected with *Adam Bede*. A Coventry acquaintance told her that Isaac had read the novel and declared that 'no one but his sister could write that book', and that there were 'things in it about his Father that she must have written'. In her reply Marian conceded that she had used 'things my father told us about his early life', but insisted that there was no 'portrait' of Robert Evans.[70]

We do not know precisely what the 'things' were. We do know that Adam has some of Robert Evans's characteristics – severity and uprightness amounting to priggishness, a respect for those above him socially but no fear of criticizing them when he disapproves of them, a thorough knowledge of his work and pride in doing things properly, an indispensable ability to work with both his hands and his head in all the matters of estate management. George Eliot uses her own knowledge of what her father knew and did, introducing us in the very first chapter, 'The Workshop', to the working-day life of a country carpenter and his colleagues.

Unusual as it was for a novel in 1859 to show characters actually at work, it was, as we know from her essays, part of George Eliot's idea of fiction that it should give an account of the daily life of the working, not just the leisured, classes. More unusual even than this is the portrait in the novel of a woman at work. Dinah's preaching and her going from house to house where she is needed to give support are not merely picturesquely mentioned in passing. They are what we see her doing. When Lisbeth Bede's husband is drowned, Dinah prays with her, talks to her, and, just as important, helps with the cooking and the cleaning. There is even a discussion in the book about the views of the Methodists on whether women should be allowed to preach. George Eliot puts to good use her knowledge that Wesley had given his blessing to women preaching in certain circumstances. She even raises, through Adam, the possibility that Dinah might continue with her work after marriage. In the Epilogue, set in 1807, seven years after the main action of the novel, Adam tells how, in spite of his having had no objection to her continuing, Dinah has given up preaching since the Methodist Conference [of 1803] decided against women preachers. His brother Seth points out, however, that Dinah could have 'left the Wesleyans and joined a body that 'ud put no bonds on Christian liberty',[71] which is in fact what Samuel and Elizabeth Evans had done.

Whether George Eliot's main motive was not to shock traditionalists by making Dinah a working mother, or whether she simply chose this ending for Dinah because she had to make a choice one way or the other, is impossible to know. For the first time, but not the last, she shows a female character striking out independently, but returning at the end to the orthodox role of wife and mother. Feminists then and now have been frustrated by her limiting end choices for her heroines.[72] We may speculate that what was operating was some combination of the urge to realism – the working woman was not the norm in 1859, let alone fifty years before – with a fear of alienating or scandalizing readers, and a temperamental timidity and adherence to convention despite the turns her own life had taken. Dinah has done her unusual work as a spinster; now she is married, she takes on the duties of a wife and mother. That George Eliot does not slavishly bow to convention is, however, indicated by her including the moment when Seth Bede puts forward a possible, more radical alternative. We should take warning that, of all novelists, George Eliot is not to be associated too simply with her endings; her opinions should not be read as arising directly out of the termination of her plots.

Adam Bede was written against a background of social and political events of great interest in terms of women's role in society. We have seen that Bessie and Barbara set up the *English Woman's Journal* in 1858. Much of its agitation was to do with female education, and with preparing bills to allow married women to keep their property. There was agitation, too, to extend the rights of women to sue for divorce following the Matrimonial Causes Act of 1857. Women were still at the mercy of their husbands, as was shown in June 1858, when Dickens separated from his wife, publicly blaming her for their domestic troubles. In the same month Bulwer Lytton had his admittedly troublesome but sorely provoked wife Rosina abducted and committed to an asylum, having long before deprived her unjustly of her children.[73]

The case for employment for women was often argued in terms of the 'surplus' of women among the population as shown by the census of 1851. Female emigration on a large scale was proposed as a solution to the problem in several articles in the 1850s and 1860s. W. R. Greg famously argued for it in a much reprinted essay, 'Why Are Women Redundant?' in the *National Review* (1862).[74] But Bessie Parkes and her colleagues maintained that the answer lay in opening up the world of work to women, since statistically so many of them could not rely on marriage for their financial support.

In 1858 Elizabeth Blackwell, the first female doctor, visited London to lecture and stimulate debate about women and the medical profession, which was still closed to them. Bessie published extracts from her lectures in the *English Woman's Journal*, and in June 1859 Barbara, on a visit from Algiers, took Elizabeth Blackwell to meet the Leweses, who were impressed by the 'energy, courage, and perseverance she had shown in studying medicine and taking a degree'.[75] Marian could not fail to be keenly interested in the efforts of such an exceptional woman. She was, after all, an exceptional woman herself. But her novels render in complex fashion the confusions and difficulties surrounding women – including the ordinary as well as the exceptional – and their lot. They have nothing of the manifesto about them.

Marian had written almost two thirds of *Adam Bede* in Germany between April and September 1858, and she finished the novel at Richmond on 16 November. Blackwood had already offered £800 for the copyright for four years, a good offer, which Marian readily accepted.[76] When he had read the concluding part of the manuscript in November, he wrote to congratulate the author on her success, adding, 'If the provincial dialect was not so exceedingly good, I would be inclined to say that there should be less of it.' This sounds quixotic, but is appropriate. There is a lot of dialect; it could well have been off-putting; in fact, George Eliot makes it fluent, amusing, believable, and not in the least tiresome. She replied to Blackwood that the dialect would need to be 'toned down' at the proof-correcting stage, admitting that she had found it 'impossible to keep it subdued enough in writing'. The toning down, amounting to no more than a few alterations in spelling such as 'yey' to 'ye' and 'al'ys' to 'allays', was duly done. Marian told Blackwood that Lewes had been her first and best guinea pig, 'being innocent of dialects' and therefore well placed to check for unintelligibility.[77]

Now all that remained was to await publication, which was at first planned for Christmas, but which Blackwood delayed for a month so that *Adam Bede* would not compete with Bulwer Lytton's new novel, *What Will He Do With It?*, which he was also bringing out.[78] But even before *Adam Bede* appeared, trouble about the authorship resumed. Spencer visited Richmond on 5 November, bringing 'the unpleasant news that Dr. Chapman had asked him point blank if I wrote the Clerical Scenes', as Marian noted in her journal.[79] She and Lewes were rather unreasonably angry with both Spencer and Chapman.

Marian wrote sharply to Chapman, rebuking him for circulating 'unfounded reports'. 'Should you like an old friend to speak idly of the merest hearsay on matters which you yourself had exhibited extreme aversion to disclose?' she asked him.[80] She also made it clear to Spencer that she regarded his refusal to lie on her behalf as treachery. Much later Spencer justified himself, a little fussily but not unreasonably, in his *Autobiography*:

I told them what had occurred, and was blamed for not giving a denial; the case of Scott being named as justifying such a course. Leaving aside the ethical question, however, a denial from me would have been futile. The truth would have been betrayed by my manner, if not otherwise. I have so little control over my features that a vocal 'No' would have been inevitably accompanied by a facial 'Yes'.

Spencer draws the simple, and no doubt correct, conclusion from this that 'a secret cannot safely be committed even to one in whom perfect confidence may be reposed'.[81]

Scott's example was regularly adduced by the Leweses, who were reading Lockhart's admiring *Life of Scott* during December, as an excuse for hanging on to Marian's anonymity, though they did so increasingly against the odds. As Marian reminded Blackwood on 1 December, Scott had given a direct contradiction when asked if he was the author of the Waverley novels, later justifying the lie in the 1829 preface to his works by making an analogy with an accused person in court who has the right to refuse to incriminate himself. Before long Lewes availed himself of this excuse to write to Chapman in February 1859 stating baldly that Marian had authorized him to say, 'as distinctly as language can do so, that she is not the author of "Adam Bede"'.[82]

Blackwood was just as keen that the secret should be kept, though his nervousness related solely to the possible adverse consequences for sales connected with Marian's marital status and not at all to fears that the novel would not be admired. Marian's anxiety ran more in the latter course, though she was also acutely aware that disapproval of her life might cloud the eyes of those who undertook to appraise her novel. She got so worked up as she awaited publication that she allowed Lewes to persuade her, 'against the grain', as she confessed, to write some sort of preface – now lost – which was rather ominously called a 'Remonstrance'.[83] Presumably it took critics to task in advance for prying into personalities and authorial secrets. Fortunately Blackwood kept his head as the Leweses were losing theirs, strongly advising against printing such a preface, and even chiding Lewes: 'It is not like so knowing a party as you to suggest so dangerous a preface as that proposed for G.E.'[84] No more was heard of the 'Remonstrance'.

In January 1859 Lewes and Marian began to look for a house to rent. They had been happy but cramped in their Richmond lodgings, and felt the need for more space. Their earnings had risen sufficiently to warrant a move to something larger. Lewes had earned over £460 in 1858 from articles and *Sea-Side Studies*, and Marian, with the £800 for *Adam Bede* and £30 for a German reprint of *Scenes of Clerical Life*, had nearly doubled her 1857 income and more than trebled that for 1856.[85] On 11 February they moved into Holly Lodge, a semi-detached house on Wimbledon Park Road in Wandsworth, a pleasant area south of the Thames.

Adam Bede was published in three volumes on 1 February 1859. Mudie took 500 copies at a 10 per cent discount, and another 230 copies were sold in the first few days. Blackwood told Lewes that his colleague George Simpson had shown a set of proofs to his brother, a cabinet maker, who declared that the writer must have been 'bred to the business or at all events passed a great deal of time in the workshop listening to the men'.[86] Lewes wrote back delightedly, putting his finger on the most salient characteristic of this work in which he had such faith:

GE was both greatly amused and greatly gratified at the Cabinet Maker's verdict. Having already been a clergyman of puseyite tendencies and large family, he is now a carpenter and doubtless will soon be a farmer and methodist. It is a great compliment when a writer's dramatic presentation is accepted as actual experience.[87]

'If the book is not a hit', he added, 'I will never more trust my judgement in such matters.'

It was a hit. After a relatively slow start, sales began to soar, particularly after the first favourable reviews appeared. The *Saturday Review* was the first to pronounce on 26 February 1859, and the reviewer was enthusiastic, apart from his doubts about Hetty's baby. The humour, observation, and realism of the unknown author received full praise, and Mrs Poyser was picked out, as she would be by every other reviewer, for particular mention as 'a really humorous creation'.[88] This was gratifying, though Marian was even more delighted by a second enthusiastic letter of thanks from Jane Carlyle, to whom she had once more sent a copy of her work. Reading the book was 'as good as *going to the country for one's health*', she wrote on 20 February; 'I found myself in charity with the whole human race when I laid it down.'[89]

This was just the kind of response George Eliot had hoped to elicit; and from now on the praise rolled in. Blackwood had sent a copy to Elizabeth Gaskell, who thanked him, intimating that she knew who the author was (i.e. Liggins), and praising Mrs Poyser's speeches – 'as good as a fresh blow of sea-air, and yet she is a true person, and no caricature'.[90] Mrs Poyser's sayings were quoted in every review, and they even equalled the feat of Dickens's Sam Weller, being mentioned in the House of Commons on 8 March. Charles Buxton, criticizing an action by the Foreign Secretary, the Earl of Malmesbury, partially excused him on the grounds that he had had 'much less information than was now before the House', and 'no doubt, now that the case could be seen as a whole, would wish that his conduct, as the farmer's wife said, in *Adam Bede*, could be "hatched over again, and hatched different"'.[91]

Mrs Poyser has a large repertoire of witty illustration. She finds an allusion or metaphor for every occasion, and is given a good deal of George Eliot's own sharpness of wit, particularly in the sustained passage at arms with the mean old landlord, Squire Donnithorne, who comes to propose an exchange of duties with a neighbouring tenant, and at the end of the novel in a battle of wits with the misogynist schoolteacher Bartle Massey. To the one she tells some home truths about his unpopularity with his tenants, as he hurries away, watched by an appreciative audience of 'two hilarious damsels' and a waggoner:

An' if I'm th' only one as speaks my mind, there's plenty o' the same way o' thinking i' this parish and the next to 't, for your name's no better than a brimstone match in everybody's nose – if it isna two-three old folks as you think o' saving your soul by giving 'em a bit o' flannel and a drop o' porridge. An' you may be right i' thinking it'll take but little to save your soul, for it'll be the smallest savin' y' iver made, wi' all your scrapin'.[92]

Her final word to the other, Mr Massey, in the verbal battle of the sexes, is another triumph:

I say as some folks' tongues are like the clocks as run on strikin', not to tell you the time o' day, but because there's summat wrong i' their own inside.[93]

Amusing as such speeches are when extracted, they are infinitely more interesting when read in their entirety and in context. George Eliot manages a feat with Mrs Poyser unusual in the annals of comic characters in fiction – she makes her more than just a sharp tongue. When her husband's niece Hetty is disgraced, Mr and Mrs Poyser feel that the shame attaches to them too. Their lives are blighted, and we believe just as much in Mrs Poyser's upset feelings as we do in her ready wit. As to the latter, George Eliot was rightly indignant when a reviewer supposed that Mrs Poyser's sayings were 'remembered proverbs'. 'I have no stock of proverbs in my memory', she told Blackwood, 'and there is not one thing put into Mrs Poyser's mouth that is not fresh from my own mint'.[94]

By 16 March Blackwood was reporting that the first run of just over 2,000 was nearly sold out and a second edition was therefore 'a certainty'. A third edition was required in May, when Mudie ordered another 200 copies urgently (and by telegraph), and very soon a fourth edition was under way. Lewes was exultant on hearing, on 9 July, that 5,000 copies had sold in a fortnight.[95] Before the year was out, more than 15,000 copies had been sold: over 3,000 in the three printings in three volumes at 31/6, and the rest in the cheaper two-volume edition at 12/–.[96]

Henry Crabb Robinson, who read everything and always had done since he was a young man in the 1790s responding to the early works of Godwin, Blake, Wordsworth, and Coleridge as they came out, read *Adam Bede*. In glorious unconsciousness of the identity of 'Eliot', he noted his progress with the book in March 1859. 'Its conversational style is admirable', he wrote on 10 March; on 16 March he praised its 'quiet humour'; a week later he had finished the book, and his opinion was that 'the novel will hold its place'. He set about telling his friends to read it, and on 16 April received 'a pleasing letter from the Provost of Eton (Hawtrey) thanking me for recommending him to read *Adam Bede*, which he praises as warmly as every one does, including Lady Byron, etc.'[97]

Everyone did read and admire it, particularly after the review in *The Times* on 12 April, which the writer, Eneas Sweetland Dallas, began with the striking words (a kind of obverse of Jeffrey's famous opening on Wordsworth's *Excursion*): 'There can be no mistake about *Adam Bede*. It is a first-rate novel, and its author takes rank at once among the masters of the art.'[98] Queen Victoria herself read the new novel everyone was talking about. 'How did you like "Adam Bede"?' she asked her daughter Vicky, who was living in Berlin, having married the Crown Prince of Prussia the previous year. 'People think it so very clever.'[99] She herself admired the book enough to recommend it to her uncle, King Leopold of Belgium, and to commission two paintings by Edward Henry Corbould of scenes from the novel. Quite in the spirit of George Eliot's contrasting of the two young women in *Adam Bede*, one picture represents Dinah preaching, the other Hetty making butter.[100]

The excitement and pleasure Marian felt at her success was tempered, as we might expect, by melancholy. This was in part due to her anxious temperament, which made her wonder if her next novel, which she had begun in January, could possibly be as good or as successful as *Adam Bede*. But there were other reasons for her to feel depression as well as elation. For one thing, the Liggins business revived with the publication of the novel. The day after *The Times* acclaimed the new genius, a 'Letter to the Editor' was printed in the paper, in which the Revd Henry Anders declared categorically that the author was 'Mr Joseph Liggins, of Nuneaton, Warwickshire'. Lewes swiftly replied with a letter of denial in the name of 'George Eliot' in *The Times* of 15 April.[101]

But the rumour would not die. Charles Bracebridge of Atherstone Hall, where Marian had dined with the Brays and Harriet Martineau in April 1845, joined in, persisting for months in the belief that Liggins was the author, and, worse, that Blackwood had cheated the poor man of the money due to him from the novel's success. William Blackwood wrote to *The Times* on 5 June accusing Liggins of false pretences, and on 25 June 'George Eliot' sent a second letter to the paper denouncing

Liggins as an impostor.[102] However, nothing availed until finally, at the end of June, Lewes and Marian bowed to the inevitable and lifted the incognito. Lewes wrote to Bray on 30 June to say so, knowing that Bray would lose no time in spreading the news in the Midlands.[103] Bray duly acquainted Bracebridge with the fact, and the Liggins myth at last began – though slowly and painfully – to fade.

Marian suffered perhaps more than was necessary from Liggins's passive persistence, and she certainly prolonged matters by her very efforts to scotch the myth. Because of it she had lost all her lingering warmth towards Chapman, and her relations with Spencer had cooled. As Lewes wrote bitterly to Bray when announcing that they were to keep the secret no longer, it was 'thanks (or no thanks) to Spencer' that the whole of the Garrick Club already knew the truth.[104] The Leweses found it hard to forgive Spencer, especially as they observed that he was jealous of the success of *Adam Bede*. 'He always tells us the disagreeable things he hears or reads of us and never the agreeable things', Lewes complained in his journal in March.[105]

When Blackwood, hearing that Marian liked pugs, arranged for his cousin to hunt 'in all the dog-fancying regions of London' till one was found and presented to her in July, she thanked him sincerely but sadly, telling him Pug had come 'to fill up the void left by false and narrow-hearted friends'. She added, 'I see already that he is without envy, hatred, or malice – that he will betray no secrets, and feel neither pain at my success nor pleasure in my chagrin.'[106]

It was not so much unkindness on Spencer's part that caused him to be cool with the Leweses as a lack of imaginative sympathy with Marian's anxiety about her authorship, Liggins, and the gossip which would once more erupt when the pseudonym was penetrated. Her isolation reinforced her inclination to despair and take offence. And another circumstance occurred at the time of *Adam Bede*'s publication and success which ensured that her happiness would not be unmingled with pain. Her sister Chrissey died of consumption on 15 March 1859.

Chrissey had been ill for some time. On 6 January she wrote to Isaac that her cough and breathing were 'very bad'. 'I was 45 Monday', she added forlornly, 'only 2 years younger than my Mother when she died.'[107] Marian knew nothing of Chrissey's illness, as none of the family had corresponded with her since she told them in 1857 of her relationship with Lewes. But towards the end of February 1859 Chrissey, knowing that she was dying, wrote to Marian, as the latter told Cara on 24 February, 'regretting that she ever ceased to write to me. It has ploughed up my heart.' Four days later Marian told Bray that she would visit Chrissey 'if she expresses a wish to see me', but that Lewes was not enthusiastic about her going.[108]

Lewes was, indeed, uncharacteristically uncharitable on the subject of Marian's family. He knew the effect their rejection had had on her, and now, seeing how she reacted to Chrissey's letter, he wrote in his journal, 'I almost wish the silence had never been broken. She had got used to that.'[109] Chrissey's daughter Emily wrote to say that Chrissey would love to see her sister, but feared the excitement would be too much for her. On 16 March Marian heard of her death.[110]

If Chrissey's death – with all its painful associations beyond the death itself – and Spencer's jealousy upset Marian, other friends reacted somewhat better to the news of her authorship. By May she had hopes of seeing Cara Bray at last, as the Brays intimated that they were coming to London in June and would like to see her. Marian wrote movingly to Sara on 21 May:

I should like to see her once more on this side Jordan, and as I am not likely ever to visit Coventry again, her flight hither is my only chance. It is surely nearly six years since I saw her!'[111]

Perhaps her experience of Cara's slowness to thaw lay behind a remark in *Adam Bede*. When disgrace comes to the Poysers, Mrs Poyser is less severe towards Hetty than her easy-going husband. The narrator comments: 'We are often startled by the severity of mild people on exceptional occasions', the reason being 'that mild people are most liable to be under the yoke of traditional impressions'.[112]

Cara did come to see her old friend in Wandsworth, and Marian chose that day, 20 June, to tell her three Coventry friends that she was George Eliot. In spite of the hints she had thrown out in letters, 'they seemed overwhelmed with surprize'. 'This experience', she noted, 'has enlightened me a good deal as to the ignorance in which we all live of each other.'[113] Actually, she had already shown her understanding of this to perfection in the scenes in *Adam Bede* in which Adam and Arthur talk at cross purposes, each intent on planning his own future, and Hetty's place in it, in ironic ignorance of the other's thoughts. But it is harder to see such things in our own lives than to perceive, or, in George Eliot's case, to create, them in the lives of others.

The Brays and Sara each responded characteristically to the news. Bray wrote after his return to Coventry that he was about to read the works of George Eliot for the second time. In September he praised *Adam Bede* as 'cram full of good sense & health, & wit & humour & good feeling & human nature – *No one* has done the like in my opinion in our age.'[114] Cara had been touched by the meeting with her old friend. She wrote warmly on 25 June:

Dear Marian, you know I was always a poor wooden thing at expressing what I feel, & I could not show the comfort your tender welcome after all these years gave me; & that you could confide to me some of your own precious thoughts, as you used to do. I am so glad to have a vivid impression of your life now, with its many lights & its one or two shadows, & to know the genial atmosphere & pleasant surroundings in which your thoughts spring & grow.

As the success of *Adam Bede* grew over the summer, Cara wrote again at the end of July, saying simply, 'Surely the gods could give no sweeter thing to mortal woman than such a success.'[115]

Sara's response was more complicated. Her own efforts at authorship were not successful; she was struggling with her next book, a vague, rambling, religious-without-religion tract which was published in 1860 with the title *Thoughts in Aid of Faith*. Charles Bray was unsympathetic – he 'will utterly sneer at what is entirely opposed to his notions', as Sara prophesied to Marian in April. Even Cara was not enthusiastic about this 'confession of faith', which Sara thought of calling 'Gleanings for the Garner of Faith' until gently dissuaded by Marian.[116] After hearing Marian's news, she was stunned – jealous, estranged, and left feeling foolish. She had been 'fancying you, as ten years ago, still interested in what we then conversed together upon – I was not sure that the writing that now occupied you was not the "Idea of a Future Life"'. Now she saw that her one sympathetic friend had 'floated beyond me in another sphere, and I remain gazing at the glory into which she has departed, wistfully and very lonely'.[117]

By September Sara had rallied sufficiently to write brightly about the success of *Adam Bede*. She asked Marian if she had seen the item in *Punch* 'quizzing a stupid prosy man, who "was much struck with Johnson's dictionary"', with the caption 'Did not know who had written

Adam Bede. Indeed hadn't heard of the book. Had heard of Adam Smith.'[118] The implication is that only a dolt had not by this time heard of *Adam Bede*.

Of all Marian's friends, Barbara Bodichon reacted best. She alone actually divined the secret for herself, not because of gossip, but because in April she read in Algiers some newspaper reviews with their extracts from *Adam Bede*, and she knew instinctively that the new novel was by her friend Marian Evans with her 'great big head and heart and her wise wide views'. No wonder Marian replied joyfully – 'God bless you, dearest Barbara' – and Lewes declared, 'You're a darling, and I have always said so!'[119]

Barbara's enthusiasm made her incautious. She had to be reminded that Marian was no longer 'Marian Evans'; 'that individual is extinct, rolled up, mashed, absorbed in the Lewesian magnificence!' wrote Lewes. And her feminism made her exult too robustly for Marian's feelings about the success of a woman 'whom they spit at'.[120] But still hers was a tremendous response. Barbara's sister Annie, an artist and feminist, also wrote of her delight at knowing '*you* as the author of the most inspiring novel of the age', and sent an amusing caricature of the egregious Liggins 'in the act of composing "Adam Bede"'.[121]

Once the secret was fairly out, Bessie Parkes too wrote of her pleasure at discovering 'that the Famous Unknown was my Marian':

Dearest Marian, remembering as I do, day after day, in which you used to say with a sort of despair, 'I have no creative power' it is with an amused delight that I see you taking all England by storm as you have done.[122]

George Eliot had indeed taken England by storm. 'Shall I ever write another book as true as "Adam Bede"?' she asked in her journal in April, when she knew that her fame was beginning.'[123] She was already under way with her next novel, which was to be, Lewes promised Blackwood on 21 April, 'a companion picture to Adam Bede; but this story is of an imaginative philosophical kind, quite new and piquant.'[124] The novel in progress was *The Mill on the Floss*.

CHAPTER NINE

More Provincial Life:
The Mill on the Floss *1859–60*

'I was delighted by an allusion in one of Lewes's notes to your being engaged in a new Tale', Blackwood wrote to George Eliot on 16 March 1859. 'Pray let me hear about this.'[1] Marian had decided in January that her new novel would include a flood; on 12 January she 'went into town', presumably to the London Library, 'and looked in the Annual Register for cases of *indundation*'. Her notebook contains several extracts from old volumes of the *Annual Register* describing the devastation wrought on villages along the River Tyne in Northumberland in November 1771 and in the countryside near Boston in Lincolnshire in November 1810.[2]

The novel that was to be *The Mill on the Floss*, though the title was not decided on till much later, did not proceed very quickly at first. She was distracted and held back by her usual doubts about the worth of her work in progress, and in addition by several external factors – the move to Wandsworth, Chrissey's illness and death, the excitement of seeing *Adam Bede* published, and the anxiety over authorship and Liggins. In connection with the latter, Marian wrote fiercely to Blackwood in April that while she would prefer to keep her incognito 'as long as I live', she would 'suffer no one to bear my arms on his shield'.[3]

She put aside her novel some time in late January or early February and began a short story instead. This was 'The Lifted Veil', begun 'one morning at Richmond, as a resource when my head was too stupid for more important work'.[4] At the end of March she rather diffidently offered Blackwood this 'slight story of an outré kind – not a *jeu d'esprit*, but a *jeu de melancholie*' for the magazine. On 29 April she sent him the completed 'dismal story'.[5]

For once Blackwood did not reply by return of post. On 18 May he sent page proofs of the story, which was published in 'Maga' in July, but he was unenthusiastic. Though it was 'a very striking story, full of thought and most beautifully written', he 'wished the theme had been a happier one' and thought she must have been 'worrying and disturbing' herself as she wrote it. Still, he was careful to add, not all readers were 'so fond of sweets as I am', and everyone would agree it was 'the work of a great writer'.[6]

It is indeed an uncharacteristic story for George Eliot to have written, or rather it has some of the elements familiar in her other writing, in particular her concern with the importance of love and sympathy between human beings and the inevitability of unhappiness resulting from wrongdoing, but in 'The Lifted Veil' these elements are present only in their negative aspects. Without humour, wit, or full characterization, the work represents a strangely dark voyage into the interior of one consciousness, that of the narrator, the miserable Latimer. This is the only example of a first person narrative in George Eliot's fiction, and the only one of her stories to deal with a subject related to the occult or pseudo-science. Latimer has the 'gift' of clairvoyance, but in his case it is an unwelcome one, a perversion of the creative faculty of the imaginative writer. On the first page he describes himself as 'cursed with an exceptional mental character'; on the last he faces a death he has anticipated with that 'curse of insight', that 'double consciousness' which has singled him out for an isolated, unhappy existence.[7]

The story has its literary historical interest, coming midway between Mary Shelley's *Frankenstein* (1818) and Stevenson's *Dr Jekyll and Mr Hyde* (1886), with both of which it shares a description of a morally dubious scientific experiment on human life. Latimer assists a medical friend, with whom he had studied at Geneva (where Frankenstein had studied electricity and galvanism), to perform a blood transfusion on a dead servant, who revives long enough to denounce Latimer's wife. Blackwood objected to this episode, blaming Lewes, 'our excellent scientific friend', whose 'experiments on some confounded animalcule' must have suggested it.[8] He may not have been very wide of the mark here, for Lewes was carrying out experiments on frogs during the early months of 1859, testing their reflexes and sensations. On 4 April he noted a novel occurrence in his journal:

This morning at breakfast Caroline, our servant, announced to me that the frog which was in the plate had nearly jumped out, & had frightened her. I assured her that its head was cut off. 'No indeed, sir', she said. 'I assure you it's quite lively, come & see, please sir.'[9]

In 'The Lifted Veil' the experiment comes right at the end, and, as Henry James pointed out in a brief notice of the story when it was reprinted in 1878, it has no necessary connection with the hero's second sight, which is the chief interest of the story.[10] Latimer has the misfortune to be able to see through all the 'ordinary indications of intonations and phrase and slight action' to the feelings and motivations of other people 'in all their naked skinless complication'. These feelings and motives are without exception unpleasant ones. Latimer is unloved, and sees it, which is torture to his 'morbidly sensitive nature perpetually craving sympathy and support'.[11] He marries the only person he meets whose motivation is not revealed to him; eventually she too becomes transparent to his second sight, and he sees that she hates him.

The story reads like a nightmare version of what Marian herself might have been if she had not discovered that she had the constructive genius of the novelist and the capacity to be loved. Herbert Spencer remembered that she had told him she was 'troubled by double consciousness – a current of self-criticism being an habitual accompaniment of anything she was saying or doing; and this naturally tended towards self-depreciation and self-distrust'.[12] In Lewes she had found the perfect mate to absorb and counteract the frightening aspects of this mental current. As Marian told Barbara Bodichon when the latter discovered the secret of authorship, Lewes was 'the prime blessing that has made all the rest possible to me – giving me a response to everything I have written, a response that I could confide in as a proof that I had not mistaken my work'.[13] Lewes performed this office of love over and over again, for the current of self-distrust never left her; indeed, as her fame increased, the anxiety increased too, lest she should fail to live up to past achievements.

It is not too much to suppose that Marian's feelings of resentment towards her family, particularly Isaac, played their part, even before the news of Chrissey's illness and death sharpened the pain as she was writing her story. She had already planned the plot of *The Mill on the Floss*, the story of love and misunderstanding between brother and sister. Isaac and her relations with him were painfully present to her early in 1859, blending with her social isolation and anxiety about authorship and revelation, and her disappointment in old friends, to make her indeed, as Blackwood saw, worried and disturbed.

And what if Lewes, her great support, should die? This horrible prospect was increasingly part of her anxiety. His health had been poor since she first knew him; in 1855, not long after their first return to England from Germany, he had fainted. She told Bray then that she had thought he was dead. Now in April 1859 he suddenly fainted again, and she was doubtless visited by another ghastly imaginative preview of her utter loneliness and unhappiness should he die.[14] 'The Lifted Veil' gives indirect fictional expression to such fears. Latimer is a negative version of herself.

The story draws on places she knew – in this case Geneva, Vienna, and Prague – and her relations with family and friends. It was also a product of her intellectual curiosity and wide reading. She was interested in, though sceptical of, mesmerism, phrenology, and clairvoyance. W. B. Hodgson had partially mesmerized her in 1844; Harriet Martineau believed in mesmerism instead of God; Bray was interested in it, and he was, as we know, a convinced phrenologist. George Combe had corresponded with Marian in 1852, complaining that the *Westminster Review* ignored 'such subjects as Mesmerism and Phrenology' in its pages, and sent her an account of experiments in the laboratory at Edinburgh University of the Professor of Chemistry, William Gregory, in which mesmerized patients described places they had never seen – a faculty Latimer in 'The Lifted Veil' also has.[15] Marian replied diplomatically, asserting that the majority of 'investigators' of mesmerism were 'anything but "scientific"', but allowing that the subject was interesting and ought to be given an airing if 'adequately treated'.[16] In her story she could use her knowledge and curiosity about the subject, allowing herself to conjure up imaginatively what she did not accept rationally.

The negativism and transparent depression of the tale worried Blackwood, and he never came to like 'The Lifted Veil', advising against including it in the 1866 edition of George Eliot's works. But he accepted it for 'Maga', where it appeared in July 1859, and he paid her £37. 10s. od. for it, carefully rejecting Lewes's surprising suggestion that the name 'George Eliot' be appended to it.[17] Meanwhile, to Blackwood's relief, Marian had resumed the new novel, which she was calling provisionally 'The Tullivers' or 'St Oggs on the Floss', on 27 April. She sent him the first part of the manuscript in June, and he expressed himself 'perfectly delighted with it'.[18] When he visited Wandsworth on 25 June he reported to his brother William that he liked her 'excessively', and Lewes too. 'It is most melancholy that their relations cannot be put straight.' He added that Marian had confessed 'to a most deep seated anxiety to get a large price' for the new novel, and that he felt sure he could agree.[19]

In fact relations between author and publisher were about to sink into an *impasse* and what could easily have been, but for their mutual good will and regard, a complete rupture. Money was one problem, as it so often is, and Marian needed no prompting to connect the size of an offer to her own sense of self-worth. The very success of *Adam Bede* caused her, and others, to think her next novel a most valuable commodity. And then Blackwood's anxiety about those relations which could not be 'put straight', and Marian's ultra-sensitivity to this anxiety in him, also got in the way of straight dealing between them.

The summer of 1859 was a difficult one, with Liggins being vociferously championed by Bracebridge and letters of denial having to be concocted for *The Times*. In June the Revd John Gwyther, alias Amos Barton, wrote to Blackwood saying he had felt 'pained' by the portrayal of him but was now only curious about the author, being sure that Mr Liggins, whom he had known slightly, was not 'equal to writing such a tale'. The Blackwoods thought Mr Gwyther should be acknowledged, and Marian duly wrote a rather chastened note, assuring him that there was a great deal of 'imagined addition' to the story she had heard about him, and that she had thought he was no longer alive.[20]

Though in June good news came in the form of a letter to the not yet unveiled author from Mrs Gaskell, saying she had been paid the greatest compliment of her life – 'I have been suspected of having written "Adam Bede"' – and though by October Blackwood had generously offered a second £800 for the novel in acknowledgement of its great success,[21] it seemed that no pleasure could be savoured long without some pain following hard on its heels, or even accompanying it.

Barbara Bodichon, who had been so generous in her delight at finding out the authorship, misjudged Marian's feelings enough to mix her joy with hurtful gossip. She wrote breathlessly in June, when she was visiting England, telling Marian what the people she met were saying about *Adam Bede* and the 'Mrs Lewes' who was now rumoured to be the author. Mrs Jones, wife of Lewes's friend, the designer of parts of the Crystal Palace, Owen Jones, was apparently agog with the news. But when Barbara tried to get her to agree to meet Marian, 'she seemed to feel fear'. 'Oh Marian, Marian, what cowards people are!' Barbara undoubtedly meant well, but she cannot have stopped to imagine how Marian would feel when she wrote:

I am so worried by people and invitations and parties got up for me that I think I shall say I am not married to Dr. Bodichon just to titter the people! they torment me so. You are right to get rid of the world.[22]

No doubt. But the pleasure of refusing invitations was not available to Marian. Lewes hurried to tell Barbara, '*entre nous*':

Please don't write or tell Marian anything *unpleasant* that you hear unless it is important for her to hear it. She is so very sensitive, and has such a tendency to dwell on and believe in unpleasant ideas that I always keep them from her. What other people would disregard or despise sinks into her mind. She knows nothing of this second postscript, of course.[23]

Even with the lifting of the veil at the end of June, done to stop the Liggins story, Marian had to bear innuendo and direct accusations that she and Lewes and Blackwood had deliberately started it in order to attract attention to *Adam Bede*. William Hepworth Dixon attacked her in the *Athenaeum* on 2 July as 'a clever woman with an observant eye and unschooled moral nature', a 'rather strong-minded lady, blessed with abundance of showy sentiment and a profusion of pious words, but kept for *sale* rather than for use'. The Liggins myth was 'a mystification, got up by George Eliot, as the showman in a country fair sets up a second learned pig to create a division among the penny paying rustics'.[24] This was despicable, but it sank into Marian's mind. It also shows that her morbid fear that general knowledge of her identity might lead to biased criticism of her work was not unfounded.

And so it went on. Dickens wrote warmly to 'My Dear Madam' in July, praising the 'World of Power' which *Adam Bede* revealed in addition to the qualities he had already admired in *Scenes of Clerical Life*. He was pleased to know his instinct about George Eliot being a woman had been right. In August he wrote again, expressing a desire to meet her and declaring in his vehement way that he had 'a horrible and unnatural desire upon me to see Liggins, whom, I am proud to remember I contemptuously rejected'.[25]

But to spoil such moments came ever more communications from and about Bracebridge, who, loth to drop Liggins altogether, started a new story to the effect that George Eliot had got much of her material from Liggins. Marian pointed out to Bray, who was corresponding with Bracebridge, and Lewes informed Bracebridge directly, that Mrs Lewes was the sole author of *Scenes of Clerical Life* and *Adam Bede*, and that they were wholly fictional works, only drawing on her early life and on people she knew in the sense that 'every work of fiction that appears' did.[26] By 30 September Lewes was writing to Bray that Marian was so upset by Bracebridge's nonsense – which he was publishing in the papers as well as writing in private letters – that 'she will leave England altogether I think if fools obtrude themselves more upon her'.[27]

The Leweses did go abroad briefly in July. Lewes paid his usual summer visit to his sons at Hofwyl, and this time Marian accompanied him to Switzerland. While he went to see the three boys, she stayed in Lucerne with some new friends, Richard and Maria Congreve, their close neighbours in Wandsworth. As Congreve was one of the leading disciples of Comte in England, positivism was a topic in which the two couples had a common interest, though since Congreve was an uncritical admirer of Comte's recent pseudo-religious writings and Lewes emphatically not, discussions were sometimes heated. Lewes had been one of Comte's first English champions with his *Leader* articles and his 1853 translation of *Comte's Philosophy of the Sciences*. Congreve had published in 1858 his translation of Comte's *Catechism of Popular Religion*, a work of alternative religion with creed and catechism which caused Lewes to distance himself from Comte. In Lucerne Lewes 'discussed positivism with Mrs C. & explained why I could not go on with Comte when he attempted to construct a cultus'.[28]

Though the two husbands were therefore wary of one another, Marian and Maria Congreve became very close friends indeed. Maria had met Marian once as a girl; she was the daughter of Dr John Bury, who had attended Robert Evans during his last illness in 1848–9. When the Leweses first came to live in Wandsworth early in 1859, Maria was happy to defy convention and call on them. She soon became the first of Marian's female worshippers, a younger woman who revered the woman Marian Lewes as well as the author George Eliot. Her friend-ship and adoration were particularly welcome, since her approach was made *before* she knew that Marian had written *Adam Bede*.[29]

When the Congreves went abroad for several months, Marian missed her new friend, writing vehemently in June that she wanted 'to get rid of this house – cut cables and drift about'. 'I dislike Wandsworth,' she told Maria, 'and should think with unmitigated regret of our coming here if it were not for you. But you are worth paying a price for.'[30] Marian was careful not to let Lewes's disagreement with Congreve over Comte get in the way of her friendship with Maria. As she wrote to Bray when Bracebridge's antics were making her almost ill: 'I have had heart-cutting experience that opinions are a poor cement between human souls'.[31]

While Marian stayed in Lucerne, Lewes set off on 13 July to see his sons. He had a delicate mission to perform. Since Charles, the oldest, was nearly seventeen and would soon leave school, Lewes had been thinking about his future. In May he had asked Blackwood for advice about 'putting Charley into the publishing business', an idea Blackwood advised against.[32] Whatever career was finally decided on, Charles would have to come home from Switzerland, and Lewes intended him to live with him and Marian, not with Agnes in Kensington. This, of course, meant that the boys would have to be told about the state of Lewes's relations with Agnes and about Marian.

Lewes's journal for 13 July gives a brief account of his discussions with Charles, Thornie, and Bertie at Hofwyl:

Dined at the school. Coffee and fruit in the drawingroom, followed by cigar in the shade. The boys then accompanied me to the wood and there lying on the moss I unburthened myself about Agnes to them. They were less distressed than I had anticipated and were delighted to hear about Marian.

On 15 July Lewes heard Charles play the piano – he would soon be playing duets with Marian – and swam in the lake with the boys. 'Our talk mainly about the domestic changes, and future arrangements', he noted.[33] The next day he left the boys to rejoin Marian in Lucerne.

Poor boys. They continued to write their letters home to 'Mamma', the mother whom they never saw while they were at Hofwyl and who did not write to them very often.[34] Now they began, prompted by Lewes, to write also to Marian, addressing her as 'Dear Mother'. Lewes had been able to tell them that she was the author of *Adam Bede*, the fame of which had already reached Hofwyl. When fifteen-year-old Thornie wrote his first letter to Marian on 18 August, he assured her that 'Charlie and I both like A.B. very much'.[35] Charles was to spend one more year at school before returning to England. Though the boys were relatively happy at Hofwyl, where the discipline was more relaxed than at many an English public school, they were undoubtedly homesick. Lewes was a loving if distant father, visiting once a year and writing them cheerful letters, in which he took an interest in their school doings, and their lives were no worse than those of their contemporaries with more conventional backgrounds, who also saw very little of their parents, especially their fathers. Nevertheless, one feels sorry for them.

The Switzerland trip lasted less than two weeks. In late August the Leweses again escaped the London summer and the Liggins–Bracebridge bother, spending a few days in Wales (where they saw someone reading *Adam Bede* at a remote railway station[36]), then making for Weymouth in Dorset, travelling via Lichfield, so that Marian could visit Chrissey's two daughters, Emily and Katie, at their boarding school there.[37] Emily was soon reading *Adam Bede* and writing to tell 'dear Aunt Pollie' how much she liked it.[38] Marian's correspondence with her teenage niece was the only contact she had at this time with any of her family. As with Lewes's sons, the news about her authorship was helpful in bridging the awkward gap created by the Agnes–Lewes–Marian relationships. In Lichfield she and Lewes stayed at the Swan Hotel, where Marian had stopped with her parents when returning from a visit to her Evans relations in 1826.

One reason for this journey was Marian's need to look at rivers and mills in order to get a strong mental picture of a location for *The Mill on the Floss*. An obliging miller showed them round his property near Weymouth, but the setting was not right for the idea she had already formed.[39] Late in September they set off for Lincolnshire, visiting Newark and Gainsborough in search of mills. Lewes noted in his journal that the trip was taken 'on artistic grounds, Polly wanting to lay the scene of her new novel on the Trent'. She found this expedition 'fruitful'.[40] Since the flood she had in mind was to be a tragic, climactic one at the end of the novel, it was all the more important for a writer of her observant, realistic inclination to have clear in her mind the whole

1. Robert Evans, miniature by Carlisle, July 1842

2. Mary Ann Evans, watercolour by Cara Bray, 1842

3. Griff House, engraving from J. W. Cross's *Life of George Eliot*, published by William Blackwood and Sons, 1885

4. View of Coventry, watercolour, *c.* 1847

5. Charles Bray, photograph, date unknown

6. Cara Bray, *née* Hennell, miniature by Sara Hennell, 1833

7. Rosehill, Coventry, engraving from Cross's *Life of George Eliot*

8. Sara Hennell, watercolour by Cara Hennell, 1833

9. Dr John Chapman, oil on canvas by J. J. Benjamin Constant, c. 1885

10. Marian Evans, portrait by François D'Albert Durade, 1850

11. Herbert Spencer, photograph, 1858

12. Agnes Lewes, G. H. Lewes, and Thornton Hunt, pencil sketch by
William Makepeace Thackeray, *c.* 1848

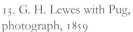
13. G. H. Lewes with Pug, photograph, 1859

14. View of Weimar, lithograph, *c.* 1850

15. Recently discovered manuscript letter from George Eliot to Cara Bray, probably written in 1856

16. George Eliot, sketch by Samuel Laurence, 1860 (misdated 1857)

To my dear husband, George Henry Lewes,
I give this MS. of a work which would
never have been written but for the
happiness which his love has conferred
on my life.

Marian Lewes

March 23. 1859

The first volume was written at Richmond, the second at
Munich & Dresden, the third at Richmond again. The
work was begun on the 22°: October 1857, & finished on
the 16th November 1858. A large portion of it was
written twice, though often scarcely at all altered in
the copying; but other parts only once, & among these
the description of Dinah & a good deal of her sermon,
the love-scene between her & Seth, "Hetty's world", most
of the scene in the Two Bedchambers, the talk between Arthur
& Adam, various parts in the second volume which I can recal
less easily, & in the third, Hetty's journeys, her confession, & the cottage
scenes.

17. Page from the manuscript of *Adam Bede*, 1859, showing
dedication to Lewes

Popular idea of George Elliott, in the act of composing "Adam Bede".

18. Caricature of Liggins writing *Adam Bede*, by Anne Leigh Smith, 1859

Two scenes from *Adam Bede*, watercolours by Edward Henry Corbould. Commissioned by Queen Victoria, 1861

19. 'Dinah Morris preaching on Hayslope Green'

20. 'Hetty Sorrel and Captain Donnithorne in Mrs Poyser's Dairy'

21. Agnes Lewes, photograph,
date unknown

22. Charles Lewes, photograph,
c. 1864

23. Thornton Lewes, photograph,
c. 1861

24. George Eliot's application for a reader's ticket at the
British Museum, 1861

25. Illustration to *Romola*, chapter 39, by Sir Frederic Leighton, 1863

26. (*Above*) The drawing room
at the Priory, Regent's Park,
engraving from Cross's *Life of
George Eliot*

27. Barbara Bodichon, portrait
by unknown artist

28. George Eliot, etching by
Paul Rajon, 1884, from a
photograph taken in 1858

29. The Heights, Witley, engraving after a sketch by Helen Allingham from
Cross's *Life of George Eliot*

30. Group including John Walter Cross (seated on right), photograph, date unknown

31. No. 4 Cheyne Walk, Chelsea, engraving from Cross's *Life of George Eliot*

32. George Eliot, drawing by Princess Louise on her concert
programme, 1877

physical setting of mill, river, and surrounding countryside in which to embed her symbolic catastrophe.

Marian was still far from finishing the novel, however. On 16 October she told Blackwood that she had completed the first volume of 'Sister Maggie', as it was then being called. This first third of the novel covers the childhood of Maggie and Tom Tulliver and Tom's time away at school, and lays the foundations of Mr Tulliver's financial problems and fatal illness. Marian sought expert help with the complicated legal and financial position in which she puts Mr Tulliver concerning his dispute over the water needed for the mill. On 6 October she asked Joseph Langford to recommend a lawyer who could help her avoid 'legal blunders'. Langford suggested Henry Sheard, who not only helped her with the details of Mr Tulliver's lawsuit and subsequent insolvency, but also became Marian's and Lewes's solicitor for the purpose of drawing up their wills in November.[41]

All was not well between her and Blackwood. She did not send him what she had written of the novel so far. On 21 September he had written with an offer of £3,000 for the right to publish it in 'Maga' and for the copyright for four years. This was a much higher offer than the £800 originally given for *Adam Bede*, and acknowledged the success of that novel, for which Blackwood had volunteered an extra £800 in recognition of its sales.[42] But Blackwood added a remark which riled Marian in her raw sensitivity about the lifting of the incognito and the Liggins–Bracebridge persecution. He proposed to print the novel in *Blackwood's Magazine* without the author's name, a practice which was quite usual. Marian, however, read in this proposition an anxiety and reluctance on Blackwood's part about putting the name 'George Eliot' in his magazine.

Though Blackwood was careful not to indicate this in his letters to her, she was not altogether wrong in the inference she drew. The correspondence between the two Blackwoods and their colleagues at this time refers nervously to the damage likely to be done to sales and to the reputation of 'Maga' and the firm of Blackwood now that all the world knew that George Eliot was 'Mrs Lewes' or, as Dixon had sneered in the *Athenaeum*, the 'strong-minded woman' who was living with Lewes.[43]

There was more to divide them even than this. Blackwood knew that, to weigh against the disadvantage of George Eliot's being known to be Marian Lewes, there was the considerable advantage of George Eliot's being such a successful author. This was reflected in the offer he made for *The Mill on the Floss*. But he was wise enough to know that Marian might be offered even larger sums by rival publishers. And she was. Dickens was on the lookout for a novel to appear in his new periodical *All the Year Round*, which he had set up after dissolving *Household Words* and breaking his connection with his publishers Bradbury and Evans in anger at their failure to insert a statement about his separation from his wife in *Punch*, of which they were also the publishers.[44] He accordingly laid siege to George Eliot.

First he came to dinner at Wandsworth on 10 November to meet the author he had admired from the days of *Scenes of Clerical Life*. 'We had a delightful talk about all sorts of things,' Lewes noted in his journal of this meeting with Dickens, whom he had first known twenty-three years before.[45] Then Dickens wrote to say *A Tale of Two Cities*, currently being serialized in *All the Year Round*, was soon to finish, to be followed by Wilkie Collins's *The Woman in White*, which he calculated would last about eight months. Would Mrs Lewes write a story to follow Collins in summer 1860? Dickens would send his sub-editor W. H. Wills to agree 'any terms perfectly satisfactory' to Marian, who could keep the copyright and negotiate with any publisher of her choice to reprint the story.[46]

Marian was flattered, but replied that '*Time* is an insurmountable obstacle' to Dickens's proposition.[47] Meanwhile the Blackwoods and their assistants suspected that she had 'sold herself to the highest bidder', thinking the tempter was probably 'that fallen angel C. D.'[48] Not to be outdone, Bradbury and Evans, former publishers of the fallen angel and proprietors of *Once a Week*, a new magazine in direct competition with *All the Year Round*, also approached George Eliot. They did so through Lewes, who was asked in November to write for the magazine; on 1 December they offered £4,500 for George Eliot's new novel, 'i.e. for publication in "Once a Week" and for two subsequent editions', as she noted.[49]

Yet another two literary magazines were established at this time, *Macmillan's Magazine*, the first number of which appeared on 1 November 1859, and the *Cornhill Magazine*, launched in January 1860 by the publisher George Smith with Thackeray as editor and the first part of a Trollope novel, *Framley Parsonage*, as the opening piece of fiction. On 27 October 1859 Lewes received a visit from Smith, who asked him to write a series of papers on natural history for the *Cornhill*.[50] 'Studies in Animal Life' duly appeared there in 1860, being published as a book in 1862 by the firm of Smith, Elder. Smith may already have had his eye on George Eliot as a possible catch. He was prepared to pay very large sums; Trollope received £1,000 for *Framley Parsonage*, twice as much as he had previously been offered for a novel.[51] No wonder the Blackwoods were worried, since they had a magazine to keep running against these newcomers with their famous names, as well as a publishing firm.

When Marian rejected his offer of £3,000 in a cool letter of 22 September, John Blackwood was naturally annoyed. He was conscious of having 'discovered' her, encouraged her, and shown her financial generosity. Blackwood had liked her, and though he knew Lewes was a sharp man of business in his dealings with publishers, he rather liked him too. Sensibly he merely told Marian on 14 October that *Adam Bede* was still selling well and that he was 'very sorry indeed that you cannot entertain our proposal for the new Tale'. 'I hope Maggie gets on as gloriously as she promised', he added pleasantly.[52] Privately, however, he was disappointed, both personally and as a matter of business. On 27 October he sent £400 for *Adam Bede*, promising more in January, in order to give her 'a further pecuniary share in the triumph of Adam'. Marian's letter of thanks was perfunctory, making Blackwood feel quite 'savage'.[53]

George Simpson in the Edinburgh office wrote to Joseph Langford in London that 'Mr John' was 'excessively sore on the subject'. 'His enthusiasm about GE was extraordinary, and his feeling of sympathy for his [*sic*] unfortunate position most heartfelt', wrote Simpson, whose own view – he had not met Marian – was that George Eliot was 'inordinately greedy' and expected 'some wonderful price from a Routledge or Smith Elder and Co'.[54]

Greed, or a sense of rising worth and a desire to capitalize on it, did come into it, as is usual on these occasions. Lewes was hard-headed and inclined to get as much as he could for Marian, and she was not impervious to the prospect of being comfortably off. She also, of course, saw large offers as homage to her genius, and was not immune to that testimony either. But she would have accepted Blackwood's offer for the sake of continuity and pleasant relations and justice to him, were it not for her hurt feelings. It is interesting to speculate on whether she would have said yes to the £4,500 offer which came from Bradbury and

Evans on 1 December. As it happens, after a few awkward letters between her and Blackwood, she had taken courage the very day before
this offer arrived and written a long letter of explanation and inquiry to
the man she had hailed as the best of publishers.

It was clear, she wrote, that there had been a misunderstanding between them. She told Blackwood his proposal of 21 September to
publish the novel in 'Maga' without the name George Eliot had 'seemed
to me (rendered doubly sensitive by the recent withdrawal of my incognito)' part of 'a depreciatory view that ran through your whole letter, in
contrast with the usual delicacy and generosity of your tone'. She was
also offended that he and the Major had taken the Bracebridge business
so lightly, and that they had laughed off another nuisance in the form of
an advertisement by an unscrupulous publisher, Newby, of *Adam Bede,
Junior: A Sequel.* Instead of putting a disclaimer in *The Times,* as she and
Lewes wished them to do, the Blackwoods, who privately thought the
Leweses were making too much fuss about this 'sequel' – after all, the
same thing had happened to Dickens after *Pickwick Papers*[55] – had
inserted a paragraph in the *Athenaeum,* a paper which, as she not
unreasonably pointed out, had 'grossly insulted' her.

Marian had inferred from these circumstances that Blackwood's feelings towards her had changed and that he no longer really wished to
publish her work. She also thought she had the right to 'seek not less
than the highest reasonable advantage' from her work, and the sum and
conditions offered by Blackwood had not met her sense of what was
appropriate. However, she regretted that her acknowledgement of his
generosity in giving her extra money for *Adam Bede* had appeared 'curt
and unresponsive', and announced, truthfully enough, that she much
preferred 'permanent relations to shifting ones'.[56] The letter combines
openness with pride, apologetic regret with self-righteousness. She
meant it to clear the air and, thanks to Blackwood's easy personality, it
did.

Blackwood thought things over and confided in William before replying. William believed she had made her case fairly, on the whole, and
pointed out to John that because of her relationship with Lewes there
would always be some 'disagreeables' attaching to their publishing her
books, but that it was worth the risk.[57] John agreed. He wrote to George
Eliot the next day, explaining on his side that the proposal to print the
story anonymously in the magazine was 'our usual custom', but accept-

ing that she felt sensitive on that point. 'My opinion', he continued, 'is that George Eliot has only to write her book quietly without disturbing herself about what people are saying, and she can command success.' He proposed coming to see her and Lewes when he was in London the following week to work out 'a fair sum for Maggie'.[58]

Oddly enough, this conciliatory letter was written not from Edinburgh, but of all places from Arbury Hall, where Blackwood was the weekend guest of Charles Newdigate Newdegate. 'I need not describe this fine quaint old place to you, of all people in the world.' No indeed. Marian was even then putting the finishing touches to Book III (halfway through the second volume) of *The Mill on the Floss*, the part in which Maggie and Tom thwart one another constantly – 'You are always so harsh to me, Tom', says Maggie in chapter 5 of this book.[59] With Isaac's unkindness to her much in her mind, she contented herself with replying to Blackwood on 5 December: 'I congratulate you on having seen that fine old place, Arbury. You must have passed by my brother's house, too – my old, old home.'[60]

Blackwood visited Holly Lodge on 7 December. He discussed terms and left with the first half of *The Mill on the Floss* after 'a very long and on the whole very satisfactory interview'. Lewes had suggested publishing it in shilling numbers, which he calculated would make a profit of £5,000 on 10,000 copies, but Blackwood and Marian were not in favour of that mode of publishing. 'Lewes is much the keener of the two', Blackwood told his brother, and Marian was more inclined to accept whatever Blackwood thought a fair offer. She seemed to him to have 'got over her worry' and 'had not the vexed anxious look which was generally painfully visible'.[61] Blackwood found the manuscript 'wonderfully clever', if slow in exposition, and on 14 December he made his second formal offer – £2,000 for 4,000 copies in three volumes at 31/6 and payment at the same rate for every copy sold beyond the 4,000, plus £150 per thousand for any subsequent edition at 12/– and £60 per thousand for any cheap 6/– edition. This offer was graciously accepted.[62]

Relieved of anxiety about publication, Marian did as Blackwood had advised and got on quietly with finishing her novel. Christmas was spent with the Congreves. On 12 January 1860 Herbert Spencer came to dinner.[63] He had redeemed himself by sending a generous letter at the end of September 1859 about *Adam Bede*, which he said came up to his ideal of a work of art, high praise from one so 'constitutionally given to fault finding', as he candidly confessed himself to be. Marian had responded immediately to this overture of friendship and his 'precious words' about her work.[64]

Her other old friend, John Chapman, was not forgiven, however. When he wrote on 16 January, asking permission to reprint her five big articles from the *Westminster Review* of 1855–6, and proposing to share profits with her, Lewes replied in a letter which is now lost. 'Squashed that idea', wrote Lewes in his journal, and we can guess that the letter was brief and brutal.[65]

The novel's title was still a problem, a reflection of the difficulty of singling out one among many important strands in the plot. 'Sister Maggie', appropriate to the first half, which deals with the pleasures and pains of Maggie's life with her beloved but 'Rhadamanthine' (i.e. severely judgemental) brother,[66] seemed less so now that George Eliot had brought Maggie into adulthood and into love relations with Philip Wakem and Stephen Guest. Lewes favoured 'The House of Tulliver, or, Life on the Floss', which, with its allusion to the House of Atreus in Greek tragedy, gives a clue to the strong element of family tragedy in the novel. Mr Tulliver goes to law in a dispute over water, loses his case, becomes insolvent, and has to work for the lawyer Wakem whom he blames for his misfortune; he is compared by the narrator to Oedipus, whose will is also overborne by 'external fact'.[67] In the end Blackwood came up with the title *The Mill on the Floss*, which he thought both appropriate and 'poetical'. Marian replied willingly on 6 January, '"The Mill on the Floss" be it then!'[68]

By 7 February Lewes was sending Blackwood corrected proofs of the first volume (Books I and II) and promising the manuscript of the second (Books III to V), with the now familiar comment, 'There never *was* so diffident and desponding an author, since the craft first began!'[69] Blackwood resumed his old habit of sending back encouraging comments and lots of praise mingled with mild criticism, and letting her know that reading her novel as it came in instalments from her pen was a privilege and an excitement for him and his family. After reading most of the last volume, which George Eliot had warned him would provoke his 'lasting enmity' because it was tragic, he responded that, on the contrary, he had been obliged several times to 'start from my seat and walk to the Major's adjoining room exclaiming "By God she is a *wonderful* woman".[70]

On 22 March George Eliot finished the novel about which Blackwood was so genuinely excited, writing the last eleven pages, in which Maggie and Tom drown in the flooded river, 'in a furor'.[71] She had been, as she told Barbara Bodichon, crying herself 'almost into stupor, over visions of sorrow' as she brought her tragedy to a close,[72] and on 24 March, two days after it was completed, she and Lewes set off for Italy, determined not to repeat the mistake of waiting at home to see what the critics made of it. 'All England', wrote Lewes proudly to his son Charles, was 'on tiptoe with expectation' about the new novel.[73] But of course all England now knew who George Eliot was, and some unpleasant reviews might be expected.

In fact, the novel, published on 4 April, was generally well received. It sold 6,000 copies in two months, and though less successful than *Adam Bede*, brought George Eliot a total of £3,685 by the end of 1860, including the rights to an American reprint and German and Dutch translations.[74] The reviewers admired the observation, wit, and humour they had liked in *Adam Bede*, and several lingered over the unsurpassed early scenes of the childhood joys and sorrows of Maggie and Tom. Dallas in *The Times* was once more intelligent and positive, beginning his review with one of his striking opening sentences: '"George Eliot" is as great as ever.' Like other reviewers, he thought her description of childhood 'unique' in its sympathetic detail: the passion over equal shares in a jam tart, the fishing trip, the disobedience of fussy adult orders, and the arguments which Tom resolves by punishing and excluding Maggie, and Maggie by fleeing to the attic in tears to attack or caress her old doll.[75]

Here was the same truth to ordinary life which had been the hallmark of *Adam Bede*, but transposed to a consistently minor key. Though Maggie's Dodson aunts are wonderfully comic creations with their decided views on jam-making and dinner hours, and their love of fine china and bonnets, they and their houses have none of the pastoral charm of Mrs Poyser and her kitchen. One of them, Aunt Pullet, is a marvellously observed example of an excessively house-proud farmer's wife. When the Tulliver children visit her, she sends the maid out with dusters for their shoes, for 'Mrs Pullet's front-door mats were by no means intended to wipe shoes on: the very scraper had a deputy to do its dirty work.'[76] Another, Aunt Glegg, is comically quarrelsome, mean with money, and careful not to wear her best clothes, or even her second best, when visiting the Tulliver household, where she distrusts the cooking and the draughts:

One would need to be learned in the fashions of those times [i.e. the late 1820s] to know how far in the rear of them Mrs Glegg's slate-coloured silk gown must have been, but from certain constellations of small yellow spots upon it, and a mouldy odour about it suggestive of a damp clothes-chest, it was probable that it belonged to a stratum of garments just old enough to have come recently into wear.[77]

The aunts are wonderful, but they are not lovable, being constantly in dispute with one another, or their husbands, or Mr Tulliver, or the world in general. They represent in comic mode the kind of embattled striving and thwarting in which Tom and Maggie are tragically engaged. As Dallas, among others, noted, 'everybody in this tale is repelling everybody, and life is in the strictest sense a battle.'[78]

The reason is not far to seek. Where *Adam Bede* drew on people and episodes George Eliot had known chiefly at one remove – she knew her Methodist aunt only through a few visits, and Adam Bede only resembles her father in so far as he shares his occupation and is what Robert Evans might be *imagined* to have been like as a young man, a period of his life not known personally to the youngest daughter of his middle age – *The Mill on the Floss* is more directly autobiographical. Maggie and Tom are versions of Mary Ann and Isaac Evans. In 1829, when the opening of the novel is set, Maggie is ten and Tom thirteen, the same ages as their originals had then been. Maggie adores but irritates and resents Tom, as Mary Ann did Isaac.

In writing of Tom's 'saturnine sternness' when he undertakes to work to pay off his father's debts and win back the mill, of this 'character at unity with itself' which is 'strong by its very negations', George Eliot has in mind Isaac's hard unimaginative rectitude.[79] Family life had indeed been a battle for her; she had been at odds with her father and Isaac, and was finally estranged from all her relations. The sorrow and bitterness of her state of exile from her family was further intensified during the writing of the novel by the contrition and death of Chrissey.

A passage in *Adam Bede* refers to Adam and his querulous mother as follows:

Family likeness has often a deep sadness in it. Nature, that great tragic dramatist, knits us together by bone and muscle, and divides us by the subtler web of
our brains; blends yearning and repulsion; and ties us by our heartstrings to the
beings that jar us at every movement.[80]

The Mill on the Floss illustrates this melancholy view fully. Parent and
child, brother and sister, in the Dodson and Tulliver families, seem
doomed to check one another with 'that family repulsion which spoils
the most sacred relations of our lives'.[81]

Greek tragedy inspired the symbolic, tragic structure of the novel, its
ironic twists of plot, its compelling use of coincidence, the exile and
rejection of Maggie, and the reconciliation of Maggie and Tom, clasp-
ing one another at the moment of death after being bitterly divided in
life. Psychologically, this ending is, as critics have noticed, a piece of
wish fulfilment.[82] Unlike her author, Maggie is forgiven, even sanctified,
by the brother she loves but despises, being, to adapt what Marian had
said of herself, intolerant of his intolerance, but also in need of his
approval.

Though the climax of the novel is the well paced, skilfully rendered
scene of the flood, with Maggie and Tom as the principals, it is pre-
ceded by a separate catastrophe which has only a tenuous connection
with the death of the brother and sister. The third volume, consisting of
Books VI and VII, introduces Stephen Guest, the young man who
sweeps Maggie off her feet, into a boat, and down the Floss towards
what appears to be an illicit sexual relationship. This turn of events
caused some outrage among the critics. Bulwer Lytton in a letter, Richard Holt Hutton in the *Spectator*, and in his quiet way Blackwood – the
novel's first reader apart from Lewes – all pointed out the imbalance in
structure which resulted from this new relationship and the prominence
it is given in the third volume.

George Eliot herself knew before any of them made the point that
the last volume had 'the material of a novel compressed into it'. She
later confessed that she had been 'beguiled by love of my subject' in the
first two volumes into an '*epische Breite*' (epic breadth) which 'caused a
proportionate want of fullness in the treatment of the third, which I
shall always regret'.[83] It is interesting to hear her talk of love of her
subject – the chiefly painful episodes of childhood – for in this respect
she is like Wordsworth, whom she invokes indirectly in the novel. Like

him, she believes in the importance of childhood memories and their
rootedness in a particular place and landscape; like him, she takes a
philosophically optimistic view of the role of the past in 'building up
the being that we are'. Yet as in Wordsworth's *Prelude*, the memories she
calls up are mostly shot through with guilt or fear or regret:

> Fair seed-time had my soul, and I grew up
> Fostered alike by beauty and by fear.[84]

Though she talks of Maggie and Tom passing out through the 'golden
gates' of childhood, the feeling of that childhood has been in its observed details far from golden.[85]

But structural imbalance was not the only problem for critics.
Maggie finds herself in love with Stephen when she is half promised
to the deformed Philip Wakem (whom she loves in a pitying way), and
Stephen is unofficially engaged to Maggie's cousin, Lucy Deane. They
are victims of 'the laws of attraction', mutually and irresistibly drawn
to one another. The chapter 'Illustrating the Laws of Attraction' alludes to Goethe's *Die Wahlverwandtschaften* (*Elective Affinities*), which we
know she had read and admired, as she also did the 'Goethean' novels
of helpless sexual attraction by George Sand, *Jacques* (1834) and *Con-
suelo* (1842).[86]

In the chapter 'Borne Along by the Tide' Stephen and Maggie drift in
a boat until they have gone too far to return to St Ogg's that day.
Stephen argues that they were fated to love one another, that the 'natural law' of mutual desire 'surmounts every other', to which Maggie
retorts, 'If the past is not to bind us, where can duty lie?'[87] Though
George Eliot brings Maggie back in obedience to that sense of duty, she
gives Stephen's argument due weight. It is not necessarily wrong to
follow passion, she suggests, but it can certainly be problematic: 'The
great problem of the shifting relation between passion and duty is clear
to no man who is capable of apprehending it'; we have 'no master key
that will fit all cases'.[88] This is a brave authorial remark, rendered the
more piquant by the writer's own sexual choice, different from Maggie's
but equally problematic.

Critics found themselves confused. Would Maggie, headstrong but
generous, have fallen for Stephen in this way? Some thought it improbable, unrealistic. Others conceded that fine girls do fall in love with
young coxcombs, but was it right to show this in a novel? Then again,

Stephen Guest begins as an arrogant young gentleman; has there been time for George Eliot to persuade us that he grows into someone with a mind and conscience as well as good looks and a diamond ring? How to take the episode morally, as well as in terms of its realism, puzzled the critics.

As so often, Blackwood was first to give a simple but salient response to the chapter 'Borne Along by the Tide'. While not yet possessing the rest of the novel, he asked its author 'why the devil' she had 'put Maggie into a position where she would be more than human if she did not come to grief'.[89] George Eliot returned no answer. If she had, she would undoubtedly have said that Maggie was, of course, only human, and that dilemmas such as hers, to which there is no ready solution, may and do occur. She had a bitter awareness that this was true in her own life. There were innumerable occasions on which she was reminded of the irregularity of her own position, as when her well-meaning admirer Elizabeth Gaskell wrote frankly in November 1859, 'I wish you *were Mrs. Lewes*.'[90] So did she, fervently, but that was impossible.

The fictional solution for Maggie was in a single sense happier than the solution, or non-solution, with which Marian was living. Maggie is reconciled to her brother, and dies happy. But on the other hand she does not consummate her love with Stephen, she is socially disgraced, and she does, after all, die. It seems that the transposed, or displaced, emotional matter concerning George Eliot's relations with Isaac and with Lewes could only be dealt with in tragic terms. Greek tragedy could be invoked, but for the classical notion of a clash between the individual and a mysterious external fate George Eliot substituted a very modern view of nature, the 'great tragic dramatist' which knits us together but also divides us from one another. The tragic arena is family life and the difficult business of choosing a mate, and the intellectual context for the drama is provided by the most advanced thinking in nineteenth-century history and science.

The narrator of *The Mill on the Floss* is a Riehl-like figure, a natural historian who looks at a community of the recent past and comments on the mixture of continuity and change within it, on 'the onward tendency of human things' and the 'historical advance of mankind'[91] – shades of the philosophical optimism of Comte or Spencer – yet also on the individual failures and losses suffered by this or that person who, through a combination of elements internal and external, is unable to adapt to changing circumstances. Mr Tulliver is the prime example: a respectable but limited miller and farmer, wastefully and futilely going to law to try to stop changes which are inevitable. As so often in the novel, George Eliot reaches for a scientific metaphor to describe Mr Tulliver:

Certain seeds which are required to find a nidus for themselves under unfavourable circumstances have been supplied by nature with an apparatus of hooks, so that they will get a hold on very unreceptive surfaces. The spiritual seed which had been scattered over Mr Tulliver had apparently been destitute of any corresponding provision, and had slipped off to the winds again from a total absence of hooks.[92]

The first part of this could be Darwin writing in *The Origin of Species*, which was published in November 1859, when George Eliot was just over half-way through writing her novel. Both Darwin and George Eliot discuss the unseen laws of nature which underlie the process Darwin calls 'inheritance and the complex action of natural selection, entailing extinction and divergence of character'.[93] The Dodson aunts are presented with all their generic family resemblance and their individual divergences. Family life is a microcosmic illustration of the 'struggle for life' alluded to in Darwin's title, the full glory of which is *The Origin of Species by Means of Natural Selection, or The Preservation of Favoured Races in the Struggle for Life*. Uncannily, *The Mill on the Floss* fictionalizes the concerns of Darwin's epoch-making book without being directly influenced by it.

Of course George Eliot and Lewes began reading Darwin's book as soon as it came out. If anything, they undervalued it from familiarity with what was known as 'the Development Theory', the doctrine of evolution which had been presented in some form or other for over half a century by writers such as Goethe, Lamarck, and more recently Robert Chambers in his *Vestiges of Creation* (1844). Lewes himself was working in the field, not only writing *The Physiology of Common Life* and *Studies in Animal Life*, but also sending scientific papers to be read out at the annual meetings of the British Association for the Advancement of Science. He reviewed Darwin's works, and was one of his earliest supporters and admirers.[94] On 23 November 1859 Marian noted that she had begun reading *The Origin of Species*; two days later she told Bray: 'It makes an epoch'; a week after that she wrote to Barbara Bodichon that

though ground-breaking and bound to be influential, the book produced in her 'a feeble impression compared with the mystery that lies
under the processes'.[95]

The slightly negative tone of this response arises surely out of
George Eliot's sense that on the *human* level, at least, the doctrine of
development – though she subscribed to it as did Comte, Spencer, Mill,
and Lewes – involved insoluble problems morally and emotionally.
Darwin could view the struggle for life among plant and animal species
with equanimity: 'Let the strongest live and the weakest die.'[96] But how
could George Eliot see her human creations in this neutral way? Animal
and plant analogies provided her with a rich stock of metaphor and
simile for her novel: seeds with hooks, beavers building dams, Mrs
Tulliver as a cackling hen or a goldfish for ever trying to swim 'beyond
the encircling glass' in her cross-purposes relationship with her husband.[97] But the science of other species could not explain the mystery
which lies under the processes, human and social, which she is so adept
at presenting and analysing.

The Mill on the Floss sets tragedy against comedy, intractableness
against progress, confusion against clarity. George Eliot yearned as
much as anyone for certainty, but her intelligence and her experience
told her that certainty was not to be had in the matters of most importance to most human lives.

Marian's female friends responded interestingly to *The Mill on the Floss*.
Sara Hennell saw that Maggie was a version of her author's younger
self, with her propensity to rush upstairs and burst into tears when
upset, and her long unhappiness and loneliness while living with her
father. Marian had given Sara her copy of Thomas à Kempis's *De
Imitatione Christi*, in which she had found consolation during her father's
last months. In the novel Maggie goes through a period of renouncing
all claims to personal happiness, strengthened by her reading of the
same work. Sara thought, astutely enough, that Marian's 'sympathetic
suffering with Maggie' led to some imbalance, or loss of control, at the
end of the novel.[98]

Barbara Bodichon, whose father had recently died, responded particularly to the family tragedy of the Tulliver family. She also appreciated, as did her sisters Bella and Annie, the particularly *female* suffering
of Maggie. 'It touches our private experience', she told Marian.[99] She

may have been thinking of her struggles with herself and her father over her love affair with Chapman, but also probably of Maggie's frequent complaints about the limitations on the possibility of action for women.

Though this strong element of the plot becomes rather submerged in the love problems at the end, it is prominent during Maggie's girlhood. She is the cleverer of the two Tulliver children, but it is Tom who is sent to school to learn Euclid and the classics, a torture for such a practical, unacademic boy. The view of the older Tullivers is that money spent on education is wasted on a girl. 'An over 'cute woman's no better nor a long-tailed sheep', says Mr Tulliver. 'She'll fetch none the bigger price for that.' Mr Wakem puts it even more brutally: 'We don't ask what a woman does – we ask whom she belongs to.'[100]

Time and again Maggie expresses her frustration. When Mr Tulliver is ill and financially ruined, Tom goes out to work while Maggie has to sit at home sewing and bearing with her father's terminal depression and her mother's constant complaints. Tom demands that she give up seeing Philip Wakem, her only link with the world outside the family circle; she replies that he has no pity. 'You are a man, Tom, and have power, and can do something in the world.' The narrator speaks for Maggie and for all girls and women who have felt constricted by the traditional passive role of watching and waiting while the men act:

While Maggie's life-struggles had lain almost entirely within her own soul, one shadowy army fighting another, and the slain shadows for ever rising again, Tom was engaged in a dustier, noisier warfare, grappling with more substantial obstacles, and gaining more definite conquests. So it has been since the days of Hecuba, and of Hector, Tamer of horses: inside the gates, the women with streaming hair and uplifted hands offering prayers, watching the world's combat from afar, filling their long, empty days with memories and fears: outside, the men in fierce struggle with things divine and human, quenching memory in the stronger light of purpose, losing the sense of dread and even of wounds in the hurrying ardour of action.[101]

If there were not so much else going on in the novel, it would count as the kind of feminist work Barbara and her sisters and Bessie Parkes would have liked their friend to write – the story of a girl doomed to a life of lost opportunities because of her sex. That story does lie within the larger structure, but is not fully developed, though the theme of injustice to women is sounded once more with some force when Maggie returns from her fateful boat trip with Stephen to a society inclined to be much harsher on Miss Tulliver – 'a designing bold girl' – than on 'poor Mr Stephen Guest'. 'A young man of five and twenty is not to be too severely judged in these cases', the world's wife indulgently declares.[102] The double standard was thoroughly familiar to Marian, who was still not overwhelmed with invitations to dinner. She spoke from the heart when she told Blackwood on 3 April that she hoped Rome would 'at last chase away Maggie and the Mill from my thoughts', for 'she and her sorrows have clung to me painfully'.[103]

The Leweses spent a full three months away from home. This trip was both an escape from the literary criticism and social constrictions of England and a middle-class Victorian version of the traditional 'grand tour' of the Italian cities and their treasures. Lewes and Marian took in the sights of Rome, Naples, Florence, and Venice, and other cities, visiting museums, churches, and galleries wherever they went. It was also their last time alone together for the foreseeable future. On their return to England at the beginning of July they would have with them Charles, whom they were to bring from Hofwyl to share their home in Wandsworth. Marian had only met him briefly the previous summer. How well would he settle in with them? What effect would the presence of a seventeen-year-old boy have on the quiet routine to which she and Lewes were accustomed?

Marian wrote lengthy 'Recollections of Italy 1860' in her journal, describing the places, people, and paintings she saw. She may have anticipated that she might draw on her impressions in future novels, as in the event she did, using Florence for *Romola*, Rome for Dorothea's honeymoon in *Middlemarch*, Genoa for a crisis in *Daniel Deronda*. She also took the opportunity to note the paradox that seeing a place one has long heard about and looked forward to visiting is bound to involve some anxiety and disappointment, even when, as she found with Venice, the reality actually meets or even exceeds expectation. Wordsworth had captured in the *Prelude* the complex experience of first coming to London with 'bold imaginations' of 'golden cities', to look at last 'upon the living scene'.[104] In the same spirit Marian described a version of the anxious, critical other consciousness she had described to Spencer when she now found herself contemplating the cities of Italy she had looked forward to seeing for years:

One great deduction to me from the delight of seeing world-famous objects is the frequent double consciousness which tells me that I am not enjoying the actual vision enough, and that when higher enjoyment comes with the reproduction of the scene in my imagination I shall have lost some of the details, which impress me too feebly in the present because the faculties are not wrought up into energetic action.[105]

Rome, where they stayed for most of April, disappointed them at first with its ugly modern streets, and Marian anticipated the rest of her stay with 'some dejection at the probable relations our "Rome visited" was to bear to our "Rome unvisited"'.[106] They had arrived just in time for Holy Week, and found the ceremonies 'wearisome' and 'empty', as Dorothea Casaubon was also to do. Interestingly, the heathen Lewes was more affronted by 'Papal Rome' – 'very odious; built on shams', he wrote on 18 April, his forty-third birthday – than his formerly evangelical companion. Marian even knelt to be blessed by the Pope, remembering, as she told Maria Congreve, 'what Pius VII said to the soldier – that he would never be the worse for the blessing of an old man'. Still, she too found the Holy Week ceremonies 'a melancholy, hollow business' and was 'not conscious of improvement from the Pope's blessing', as she added drily.[107]

Ancient Rome thrilled them more than Catholic Rome, and so also did the small English corner. For of course they visited the graves of Shelley and Keats in the Protestant Cemetery, where thoughts of the free-thinking, free-loving Shelley's detractors, 'the unloving cavillers of the world', not unnaturally arose in Marian's sensitive sympathizing mind.[108]

Everywhere they went they took an interest in the ordinary people going about their business. Lewes, scornful of the indifference and haste with which a priest gabbled his annual Easter blessing of their landlord's house, was touched by the reverence with which the landlord and his wife themselves looked on as the conjugal bed was blessed. They and their children 'timidly peeping in made a pretty picture which the sham of the priest alone spoiled'.[109] During a brief stop in Leghorn on the way to Rome they had watched a congregation coming out of the synagogue, noting 'varied types from the rich merchant to the meagre, bent drudge'.[110] And in Naples they were most struck by the everyday objects collected from the ruins of Pompeii and Herculaneum:

linen just rinsed, a loaf of bread with the baker's name imprinted on it, ropes, keys, walnuts, oil, children's toys, 'all the familiar objects of familiar life', as Lewes put it in his journal.[111]

At Florence, where they settled in the middle of May for three weeks, they made the acquaintance of Anthony Trollope's brother Tom. Marian was accepted and invited as Lewes's wife in this Trollope household. As was their custom, the Leweses visited all the sights and read avidly about Florence, its famous sons, and its art. Marian valued the cathedral and campanile the more because she could view them from Dante's 'accustomed seat' in a nearby piazza, and she climbed Galileo's tower 'for the sake of looking out over the plain from the same spot as the great man looked from more than two centuries ago'. In the same spirit they visited Michelangelo's house, preserved by his descendants.[112] Lewes was reading a life of Savonarola, the Dominican monk and martyr of the late fifteenth century who had tried to reform the Church, and it occurred to him 'that his life and times afforded fine material for an historical romance'. 'Polly', he noted in his journal, 'caught at the idea with enthusiasm.'[113]

The result, eventually, was *Romola*, George Eliot's only historical novel placed outside England and set more than sixty years in the past. All the well-known Victorian novelists were interested in historical romance, influenced to a man (and woman) by Scott. Dickens's *Tale of Two Cities* had just been serialized in *All the Year Round*; Thackeray's *Henry Esmond* (1852) was set in the England of Queen Anne's time; Trollope's *La Vendée* (1850) in France in the 1790s; and, closer to George Eliot's new interest, Tom Trollope was publishing *Filippo Strozzi* in 1860 and during the 1860s wrote several more novels with Italian themes. Once George Eliot had decided that fifteenth-century Florence was to be the setting of her new novel, she turned to Tom for advice on linguistic and historical questions.

After Florence came Venice, then, on 21 June, a journey through the Alps to Switzerland. Marian had written to Mrs Bell, erstwhile nurse to Lewes's children, who was staying at Holly Lodge looking after Pug, asking her to prepare the house for their return with Charles.[114] It was fixed that Thornie was to leave Hofwyl a few months later. He was a headstrong, charming, irreverent boy (very like his father as a young man), whom they did not choose to have living with them in Wandsworth. Charlie, by contrast, was 'the most entirely lovable human animal of seventeen and a half, that I ever met with or heard of', as Marian told Bray after their return.[115]

Their plan for Thornie was that he should finish his education in lodgings at Geneva. On their way home they visited Marian's old friends the D'Albert Durades – François was translating *Adam Bede* into French, and Marian now authorized him to do *The Mill on the Floss* as well[116] – and Lewes almost came to an arrangement for Thornie to lodge with them. In the end Lewes decided that he could not afford D'Albert Durade's terms for Thornie, and began to think of Edinburgh instead. With Blackwood's help, Thornie was settled in October at the High School there, lodging with a classics teacher, George Robertson, and his family. Thornie contemplated life in Edinburgh with likeable but somewhat alarming high spirits. He wrote from Hofwyl in September, 'I am already (in imagination) an Edinburgh student, kicking up rows, and attacking the peelers [i.e. the police], the most poetic parts of student life.'[117]

As for Charles, Lewes took the advice of Anthony Trollope, the most famous employee of the Post Office, and put him in for the Civil Service examination. Charles triumphed, coming top of the poll in August, and became a clerk in the Post Office.[118] Wandsworth was too far away from central London, where Charles was to work, and so the Leweses set about finding another house. Towards the end of September they moved to Harewood Square near Regent's Park, then in December they took a house in the adjoining Blandford Square, where Barbara Bodichon lived when in England and where Chapman had lived for a time after moving from 142 Strand in the summer of 1854.

Though she had not much liked Wandsworth, Marian considered the move into London something of a sacrifice. She wrote in her journal of 17 December that they had rented the house at 16 Blandford Square for three years, 'hoping by the end of that time to have so far done our duty by the boys as to be free to live where we list'. For her own part, she 'languished sadly for the fields and the broad sky'.[119]

During August George Eliot sat for her first portrait since D'Albert Durade had drawn her in Geneva eleven years before. Samuel Laurence, who had lived with his wife in a sort of commune in Bayswater with Thornton and Kate Hunt in the 1840s, where Lewes and Agnes had been frequent visitors, was the artist.[120] Marian was as unenthusiastic about being painted at the age of forty as she had been at thirty; she was worried about work, being in the early stages of research for the Italian novel and doubtful if it would ever be written.[121] As had happened the previous year, when she wrote 'The Lifted Veil' to give vent to negative feelings while planning *The Mill on the Floss*, so now she wrote another 'slight Tale' called 'Mr David Faux, confectioner', which Lewes thought 'worth printing', according to her journal for 27 September.[122]

But either she did not think it worth printing, or she was still feeling sensitive about Blackwood's dislike of 'The Lifted Veil', for she did not offer the new story to him. This clever but unredeemedly negative tale of a deceitful confectioner, aptly named Faux, who is exposed by his innocent idiot brother, was not published until July 1864, when George Smith printed it in the *Cornhill Magazine* under the revised title 'Brother Jacob'. It illustrates in stark and economical terms the theme of so many of her larger fictions, namely 'the unexpected forms in which the great Nemesis hides herself'.[123] Like 'The Lifted Veil', it is sardonic and remarkable for the complete absence of family or conjugal love be-tween any of the characters.

When Laurence's portrait was completed in September, Lewes did not like it, but Blackwood, thinking it captured the 'pensive sad look' which had struck him the first time he saw her, bought it to hang in his office in Edinburgh.[124] Marian told Blackwood about the progress of the portrait on 28 August. In the same letter she mentioned her plan to write a historical novel set in Florence, but indicated a wish to write 'another English story' first. She had not yet got the English Midland countryside out of her system. On 28 November she noted in her journal that she was engaged in writing a story which 'thrust itself between me and the other book I was meditating. It is "Silas Marner, the Weaver of Raveloe".'[125]

CHAPTER TEN

Realism and Romance:
Silas Marner *and* Romola *1861–3*

Charles's arrival and the move into London at the end of 1860 turned out to be a good thing for Marian in many respects. As Lewes confessed in his journal in January 1861, he and Marian had 'looked forward with some misgivings to having him always with us, but he has been a comfort & delight, & never occasioned us any anxiety'.[1] For Charles's sake they began to go out more. They took him to hear the *Messiah* at St James's Hall in December 1860, to a Beethoven concert in February, and a Mendelssohn concert and the opera in April. Marian now met Lewes's mother, who lived not far away in St John's Wood with her irascible husband, Captain Willim.[2] The Leweses also entertained at home more frequently than before. Trollope became a good friend; on 20 November 1860 he came to dinner, and the same evening Arthur Helps arrived with the news that Queen Victoria had told him how much she admired George Eliot's novels.[3]

There were even signs that here and there Marian was becoming more acceptable socially, though progress was naturally fitful and problematic. Trollope was delighted to visit the Leweses, but though his brother and sister-in-law in Florence could invite Marian into their home without fear, Trollope and his wife Rose did not ask her to their home at Waltham Cross in Hertfordshire. Indeed, Trollope employed some ingenuity when inviting Lewes to have dinner and spend the night there in April 1861. He wrote to say he had some friends 'who will like to meet you'. That it might be clear without spelling it out that only Lewes was meant, he added adroitly, 'Of course a man who comes here sleeps here.' Lewes went on 15 April.[4]

About the same time as this routine, if delicate, rebuff to Marian occurred, she was invited to visit Clementia Taylor, the MP's wife and progressive spirit who had written in 1856 'with generous consideration and belief at a time when most persons who knew anything of me were disposed (naturally enough) to judge me rather severely', as Marian now wrote appreciatively.[5] She declined, however, to visit Mrs Taylor. Her sense of how intolerable it would be to her pride to be thought to covet invitations which might not be forthcoming rendered her unhappily incapable of accepting those few which actually were. Her only way of coping, of keeping some control over her own social life, was to make a self-sacrificing rule never to pay visits at all. She was cutting off her nose to spite her face, but that was preferable to putting herself forward and constantly courting snubs, enough of which came her way despite the care she took to avoid them. She simply told Clementia that she never paid visits, but was happy to receive them from friends.[6]

Not that she felt she had many friends. When writing to Blackwood in September 1860 she had fallen naturally into a negative turn of phrase which indicates how much of a torture her situation could be to her. Wondering who wrote the review of her works in the *North British Review* in August, she confided to Blackwood that 'it is so unmixed in its praise that if I had any friends, I should be uneasy lest a friend should have written it'.[7] How typical in its fastidiousness is that hypothetical 'uneasy', and how sad the admission, albeit exaggerated, of friendlessness. Such brave, even wilful, stoicism is evident again in a letter of December 1860 to Barbara Bodichon, like Blackwood one of the few friends – for she did have some – with whom she felt able to be relatively unguarded in correspondence. Barbara had become interested in Catholicism, as had Bessie Parkes, who finally converted in 1864. In her letter to Barbara, Marian wrote sympathetically, with the same understanding she showed in her novels, about the need felt by so many people to turn for comfort to the 'forms and ceremonies' of religion; for herself, however, she felt, unconsciously hitting on the same phrase as her contemporary Marx, that it was best 'to *do without opium*'.[8]

In the same letter to Barbara, Marian touched on 'that matter broached by your friend Mrs. Brodie'. This seems to have been the exploration of whether it was possible for Lewes to divorce Agnes, if not in England then somewhere abroad. 'We have consulted a barrister, very accomplished in foreign and English law,' Marian wrote, but 'he pronounces it *impossible*'. Clearly Lewes had set the inquiry on foot because his teenage sons were now returning to England to become adults in a society which would not know how to place them. Lewes wished to avoid saddling them with the disadvantage of being caught in a situation still scandalous, though no longer new. Marian wrote bravely:

I am not sorry. I think the boys will not suffer, and for myself I prefer excommunication. I have no earthly thing that I care for, to gain by being brought within the pale of people's personal attention, and I have many things to care for that I should lose – my freedom from petty worldly torments, commonly called pleasures, and that isolation which really keeps my charity warm instead of chilling it, as much contact with frivolous women would do.[9]

Her charity is more evident in the large-heartedness of her books and in what we know to have been a mutually loving relationship with Lewes and increasingly also with his sons, than in her correspondence, where, as here, her pain finds expression in rather cold, because feignedly unconcerned, remarks. Doing without opium, whether in the form of religious consolation or social acceptance, was a lonely and difficult business.

Meanwhile, George Eliot was writing *Silas Marner*, which she finished on 10 March, six months after the idea had suggested itself to her. The novel is remarkable for its successful marriage of realism and romance, the historical and the legendary, for the exquisite blend of humour and pathos, and for its structural tautness. Being less than half the length of her first two novels, it lacks their large cast of characters, and their expansiveness of speech and narrative. What it lacks in scope, however, it makes up for in intensity and close patterning.

The plot is single, though it consists of the mirrored destinies of two men, Silas Marner, the lonely weaver, and Godfrey Cass, the son of the local squire. Silas is restored to life and love by finding and caring for the golden-haired child Eppie on the spot where he used to keep his gold coins; Godfrey self-interestedly denies his relationship to Eppie, and thereby unwittingly dooms himself to a life of fatherlessness.[10] Of course it is the author who acts as providence, or Nemesis, by making Godfrey childless in his marriage to Nancy, whom he had feared to lose if he divulged his previous marriage to Eppie's unfortunate mother. But we accept the patterning of poetic justice, as we accept imaginatively George Eliot's plot exploitation of superstition about weavers, ghosts, and the mysterious, seemingly agentless, theft of Silas's gold without giving intellectual assent to such superstition.

Here is a finely told tale illustrating that Nemesis she had recently invoked in 'Brother Jacob', but in this case, as she promised Blackwood in February 1861, the Nemesis is 'a very mild one'. Godfrey Cass suffers in due proportion to his act of moral cowardice, but his ending is not tragic. As he says ruefully to his faithful wife, 'I wanted to pass for childless once, Nancy – I shall pass for childless now against my wish.'[11] The other strand of the story, Silas's, is touching and in the end happy, illustrating, as George Eliot also told Blackwood, 'the remedial influences of pure, natural human relations'.[12]

Wordsworth, whose spirit lurked in *The Mill on the Floss*, particularly in the childhood scenes and in the narrator's reverential comments about the influence of our early life on later feelings and actions, is directly invoked in *Silas Marner*. The novel is prefaced by three lines from Wordsworth's pastoral poem from the second edition of *Lyrical Ballads*, 'Michael' (1800):

> A child, more than all other gifts
> That earth can offer to declining man,
> Brings hope with it, and forward-looking thoughts.

The ageing shepherd Michael, who fathers a child late in life, finds his daily life and work renewed –

> from the Boy there came
> Feelings and emanations – things which were
> Light to the sun and music to the wind;
> . . . the old Man's heart seemed born again.[13]

So it is with Silas Marner. The embittered exile from the community makes a natural movement of nurturing towards the toddler who finds her way into his cottage, and by awakening memories of a past he had blocked out, she returns him to humanity. George Eliot writes concisely but movingly, as she does throughout this wonderful short novel. She exploits the fact of the weaver's shortsightedness by turning the arrival of Eppie – how she got there by crawling away from her opium-dosed and dying mother we know, though Silas does not – into a natural miracle:

Turning towards the hearth, where the two logs had fallen apart, and sent forth only a red uncertain glimmer, he seated himself on his fireside chair, and was stooping to push his logs together, when, to his blurred vision, it seemed as if there were gold on the floor in front of the hearth. Gold! – his own gold – brought back to him as mysteriously as it had been taken away! He felt his heart begin to beat violently, and for a few moments he was unable to stretch out his hand and grasp the restored treasure. The heap of gold seemed to glow and get larger beneath his agitated gaze. He leaned forward at last, and stretched forth his hand; but instead of hard coin with the familiar resisting outline, his fingers encountered soft warm curls. In utter amazement, Silas fell on his knees and bent his head low to examine the marvel: it was a sleeping child – a round, fair thing with soft yellow rings all over its head.

Eppie reminds him of his little sister, of his old home, long left behind under the bitterness of a false suspicion of theft. He now finds himself open to 'a hurrying influx of memories'. The child

stirred fibres that had never been moved in Raveloe – old quiverings of tenderness – old impressions of awe at the presentiment of some Power presiding over his life; for his imagination had not yet extricated itself from the sense of mystery in the child's sudden presence, and had formed no conjectures of ordinary natural means by which the event could have been brought about.[14]

It *is* a mystery, a chance occurrence, but it is also natural and explicable. Here, if anywhere, George Eliot embodies her interest in, and insight into, the mystery that lies under the process of life she had invoked on reading Darwin's *Origin of Species*.

The story of Silas's bringing up of Eppie is beautifully told. As Lewes assured Blackwood, who was afraid there would be too much sadness in the last third of the novel, what was to come was 'almost all pure sunshine & poetry'.[15] In the spirit of 'Michael', George Eliot shows Eppie creating 'fresh and fresh links between his life and the lives from which he had hitherto shrunk continually into narrower isolation'. She needs his attention, and he needs – and is offered on all sides – help from his neighbours; she 'warmed him into joy because she had joy'.[16] Feuerbachian community spirit, Wordsworthian restoration of joy through a child and through closeness to nature, and the equally Wordsworthian notion of gain for loss (Eppie for gold), work unobtrusively through the story.

The realistic lower-class country setting of sixty years ago blends perfectly with the 'legendary tale' which George Eliot always spoke of as coming to her as an inspiration, prompted, appropriately, by memory. She told Blackwood in February that the idea came to her quite suddenly, 'suggested by my recollection of having once, *in early childhood*, seen a linen-weaver with a bag on his back' (my italics).[17] Her shrewd reader Henry Crabb Robinson noticed, as he avidly read the novel in the Athenaeum Club when it came out, that not only was it Wordsworthian, but it had an affinity with Coleridge's 'Ancient Mariner' too. On reaching the point where Silas finds Eppie and refuses to let anyone else have her, he wrote, 'And he too will be saved, I see; it is to him what the blessing of the animals [i.e. the water-snakes] is to the Ancient Mariner.'[18]

Robinson hit on something here, for George Eliot's novel seems poised between the complementary modes of Wordsworth and Coleridge as explained by the latter in his account of the origin of their joint volume of *Lyrical Ballads* (1798 and 1800) in chapter 14 of his *Biographia Literaria* (1817). Famously, Coleridge declared that his own aim had been to take 'persons and characters supernatural, or at least romantic' and bestow on them 'a human interest and a semblance of truth sufficient to procure for these shadows of imagination that willing suspension of disbelief for the moment, which constitutes poetic faith'. Wordsworth's task had been to 'give the charm of novelty to things of every day, and to excite a feeling analogous to the supernatural, by awakening the mind's attention from the lethargy of custom, and directing it to the loveliness and the wonders of the world before us'.[19]

Silas Marner shares with the Ancient Mariner an almost legendary quality, and the things which happen to him are incomprehensible to him and seem symbolic and romantic to us; with Michael he shares an ordinariness, and sorrows and blessings which have an everyday source and existence while partaking of the mysterious, the archetypal, and the sacramental. 'Natural Supernaturalism', a phrase used by Carlyle in *Sartor Resartus* (1836), the book which Marian had so admired as a young woman, comes to mind too as appropriate to the ethos of *Silas Marner*.[20]

Other legendary echoes and parallels are with *Pilgrim's Progress*, the story of the Prodigal Son (on which 'Michael' also draws), *The Winter's Tale* with its sixteen-year gap and discovery of the lost daughter Perdita, and the fairy tale *Cinderella*, though in this case inverted, since Eppie refuses to be raised from her lowly status to that of 'princess' when Godfrey belatedly seeks to adopt the daughter he had once denied. The accent on family life, disrupted and disintegrated for Silas when he is a young man, and restored to him in middle and old age, also carries interesting modulated echoes of George Eliot's own experience of love lost and denied, exile from the family, and love found in another place in middle age.

The one aspect about Marian's life with Lewes about which no evidence remains, as far as I know, is how much, if at all, she regretted that her anomalous position dictated childlessness for her. We should be cautious about equating her feelings directly with those expressed with reference to any one of her characters. After all, like Shakespeare and Tolstoy, and like her own perverted creative artist Latimer, she could think herself into the skin, and under it, of a wide variety of human types and individuals of either sex. Still, one's attention is drawn to a sentence describing the 'one main thread of painful experience' running through the married life of Godfrey Cass's wife Nancy, a woman happy with her husband but unhappy in her childlessness:

This excessive rumination and self-questioning is perhaps a morbid habit inevitable to a mind of much moral sensibility when shut out from its due share of outward activity and of practical claims on its affections – inevitable to a noble-hearted, childless woman, when her lot is narrow. 'I can do so little – have I done it well?' is the perpetually recurring thought; and there are no voices calling her away from that soliloquy, no peremptory demands to divert energy from vain regret or superfluous scruple.[21]

The one great difference between Nancy and the woman who wrote so understandingly about her situation is the very fact of the creative genius which made such writing possible.

George Eliot finished writing *Silas Marner* on 10 March 1861, and it was published on 2 April. She and Lewes were preparing to take flight once more to Florence, where Marian wanted to continue the research for *Romola* which *Silas Marner* had interrupted. On 19 April they set off, leaving Charles in charge of the house, but not of Pug, who had been lost a few months before.[22] Blackwood kept them informed of the novel's sales. 7,500 copies were printed in the first month; by the end of the year something over 8,000 had been sold in one volume at 12/–, bringing George Eliot £1,600.[23]

The critical response was quietly favourable. All the reviewers praised the verisimilitude and humour of the scenes at the Rainbow Inn, particularly in chapter 6, where the assembled villagers discuss their everyday concerns until interrupted by the exciting news of the theft of Silas's gold. Dallas in *The Times* once more saluted the charm and truth to life of George Eliot's writing. Richard Holt Hutton declared in the *Economist* that 'the conception is as fine as the execution is marvellous', and likened the Rainbow Inn chapters to the public house scenes in Shakespeare's *Henry IV* plays.[24] Blackwood had written: 'You paint so naturally that in your hands the veriest earthworms become most interesting perfect studies in fact.' And perhaps most gratifying of all, Thornie wrote from Edinburgh that he enjoyed the novel so much that when he reached the last page, he 'almost got angry at there being no more of it'.[25]

Inasmuch as Marian could feel relaxed and content about any of her works, she could feel so about *Silas Marner*. It was produced with less despair than any of its predecessors or successors; its publication was attended with no unpleasant feelings between her and Blackwood; there was no Liggins to worry about; and none of the critics invoked the vision of the author as a strong-minded woman of dubious morals. This was due, no doubt, partly to the lack of opportunity afforded by the story for scandalized comment about gynaecological handbooks and sexual errors, and partly to the fact that readers and critics were becoming used to the difficult idea that a woman with unconventional religious views and unconventional domestic arrangements could write novel upon novel full of sympathy, humour, and genius.

In Florence she and Lewes settled down to a routine of sightseeing, looking at bookstalls, and 'poking into the curiosities of old Florence', as Lewes told Charles on 17 May.[26] With Tom Trollope they visited the monastery at Camaldoli, where they saw in the guest book the signature of Wordsworth, who had visited in 1837. Marian rode part of the way there, giving Lewes a shock when her horse fell on the edge of a precipice. Countrywoman as she was, Marian was 'neither hurt nor shaken'.[27] On 14 June they returned to London, having visited Bertie, now almost fifteen, in Switzerland on the way.

The preparation for writing *Romola* went slowly. One reason was anxiety about Lewes's health. He was constantly ill during the summer, with headaches and an alarming loss of weight. Marian felt guilty about her own despondency when she saw Lewes 'so constantly cheerful even in ill health, so perfect in temper and in the external estimate of facts, without any perceptible influence of changing moods!'[28] Actually, Lewes's eternal optimism did flag from time to time; he had confessed to Blackwood in March: 'I cannot help *occasionally* being made anxious by her persistent depreciation of what she writes.' He therefore valued the more Blackwood's positive responses – 'When you come to my aid, I rally again.'[29] But he never let Marian see that her depression had its insidious effect even on him, and the reason for this was also vouchsafed in a confessional moment to Blackwood. Telling him how much Marian loved his sons, and how Charles worshipped her, he explained:

Among the many blessings that have come to me late in life this of seeing the perfect love between her and the children is one of the greatest; perhaps because it was one of the rocks ahead. Having had no domestic life for many years I now have such domestic happiness as can be given to few.[30]

In September they spent ten days or so in Malvern, so that Lewes could try Dr Gully's famous water cure. He had begun to fear that his illness – unspecified but with symptoms which included headaches, loss of appetite, weakness, and loss of weight – might be fatal.[31] Apart from the worry about his health, and about Thornie's future – it was decided that he should take the Civil Service examination for India – Marian was more than usually despairing about her work. By November she was on the point of giving up her 'Italian novel' altogether.[32]

She had confessed to Blackwood, who visited on 15 June, that she always needed to hear her characters talking. Lisbeth Bede's speech, she told him, had been suggested by hearing her father revert to a Derbyshire dialect when in the company of his brothers. She was worried because she could not hear Savonarola and the other characters of her new novel, since, of course, they spoke in an Italian, not an English, dialect, and an obsolete one at that.[33] Her journal during her preparation for *Romola* makes dismal reading, haunted as it is, day after day, by the 'demon despair', which she knew to be destructive, but against which she felt powerless 'whenever an old work is dismissed and a new one is being meditated'.[34]

Lewes was patiently, though anxiously, waiting for her to stop researching and begin writing, but in November she applied, in the name Marian Evans Lewes and with Owen Jones as her sponsor, for a reader's ticket at the British Museum, since the London Library could not meet her need for books about medieval costumes, among other things.[35] When Blackwood announced he was coming to visit in December – bringing his wife for the first time – Lewes asked him to help 'make her begin'. 'When you see her,' he instructed Blackwood, 'mind your care is to discountenance the idea of a Romance being the product of an Encyclopaedia.'[36]

Still Marian went on saturating herself in the life and times of Savonarola, hoping that she would come to feel at home imaginatively in that milieu, as she had succeeded in doing with English rural life from the 1790s to the 1820s. She was also correcting proofs of all her works to date for a new cheap edition Blackwood was bringing out.[37] Despite Lewes's weakness and her own dejection, they were entertaining a lot, settling into a routine of letting friends know that they would always be welcome for dinner and music on Saturday evenings. Spencer came, as did Barbara and Bessie, and Lewes's old friend from the *Leader* days, Edward Pigott. The artist Frederic Burton, who was to paint the most famous portrait of George Eliot in 1865, also became a regular Saturday evening visitor. On 3 October they took delivery of a grand piano, on which she and Charlie played duets.[38]

Another distraction from work was their having Thornie with them in September, 'our noisy hopeful', as Marian called him, or Caliban, as the Blackwoods, who often invited him to their Edinburgh home, had christened him. He was friendly with Willie, the son of Major Blackwood, who now began to take the place of his father in the family business, since the Major had died, aged forty-eight, in April. Thornie caused the Blackwood uncle and nephew to chuckle over an adventure he had one night in December on coming home late from the theatre. His landlord, Mr Robertson, locked him out, and when Thornie remonstrated with him the next day, he 'made his shoeleather acquainted with my posterity', as Thornie recounted with relish to his father. 'You need not ask me what I did; I did what you would have done in my place – knocked him down.'[39]

Taking courage from the idea of a new year and a fresh start, Marian finally started writing *Romola* on 1 January 1862.[40] From now until 9 June 1863, when she finished the novel, the writing was a torture to her. Her journal, often reduced during this period to short single-sentence entries, testifies to despair, headaches, and 'unfruitful' days and weeks as far as writing was concerned. We cannot be sure that she wrote fewer letters than usual during the eighteen months of writing *Romola*, but it is certainly the case that relatively few survive from this, the most miserable, period of her happy married life.

Though it seems she nowhere acknowledged it directly, we can infer that she realized that *Romola* was not as successful as her previous works. The finished novel is full of wonderful things, as we shall see, but Henry James's concise comment – 'It smells of the lamp'[41] – sums up the reason for its relative failure as a piece of imaginative literature. Marian knew she had over-prepared,[42] but she soldiered on in that fluctuation of mind familiar to many a writer, forever running the whole gamut from complete faith in the importance and worth of the work in hand to absolute certainty about its uselessness.

She and Lewes, surprisingly, made the torment worse by agreeing to bring out this novel in serialized form. She had published *Scenes of Clerical Life* monthly in *Blackwood's Magazine*, but they were stories, not novels, and in any case serialization did not begin until 'Amos Barton' was complete and 'Mr Gilfil's Love-Story' already begun. She had flirted with, but resisted, the idea of printing *Adam Bede* and *The Mill on the Floss* in *Blackwood's*, not liking to put herself into the yoke – which more self-confident and faster writers like Dickens and Thackeray sometimes kicked against – of writing against the clock.[43] She did not even consider serializing *Silas Marner*, all along conceiving it as a one-volume novel.

It was not *Blackwood's Magazine* which serialized *Romola*, though George Eliot and Blackwood had both expected that it would be. As she had almost done with *The Mill on the Floss*, she now allowed herself to accept an offer from another publisher. On 27 February George Smith called and offered an unprecedented £10,000 to publish *Romola* in twelve monthly parts in the *Cornhill Magazine*, followed by a three-volume edition. 'It is the most magnificent offer ever yet made for a novel', wrote Lewes in his journal.[44] And so it was. Bradbury and Evans's offer of £4,500 for a George Eliot novel in December 1859 now looked paltry by comparison, as did the serial and volume offer Smith had made in July 1861 to Wilkie Collins, a then unsurpassed £5,000.[45]

Lewes's excited journal entry of 27 February continues with an account of Marian's characteristic reaction to Smith's amazing offer: 'Polly, as usual was disinclined to accept it, on the ground that her work would not be worth the sum!' Another problem, and one which weighed so heavily with Marian that by 1 March the deal with Smith seemed to be out of the question, was that Smith wanted to begin serializing *Romola* in April or May, to follow Trollope's *Framley Parsonage*, which was coming to an end.[46] Marian knew this was impossible, since she had written only sixty pages, or approximately three chapters, during January and February. 'I cannot consent to begin publication until I have seen nearly to the end of the work', she wrote firmly on 1 March.[47]

In the end, however, she did consent to do so. Smith visited again on 8 April, proposing to publish the novel in weekly numbers at sixpence each, but when George Eliot read the first few chapters to him a month later he realized that it would not be suitable for cutting up into such small parts. On 19 May it was agreed that *Romola* should be published in twelve monthly instalments in the *Cornhill*, beginning in July, then as three volumes. The agreed payment was rather less than the stupendous amount of £10,000, but at £7,000 was still the largest sum yet paid for a novel.[48]

Lewes was also made a magnificent offer by the open-handed Smith. Thackeray was giving up the editorship of the *Cornhill Magazine*, and Smith offered the position to Lewes, who declined because of his poor health and his desire to get on with his work on Aristotle and the history of science. However, he agreed to be Smith's 'literary adviser' or 'consulting editor' at 'the pleasant salary of £600 a year!' as he told Charlie.[49] For *Romola* George Eliot was to be paid in monthly instalments of £583. 6s. 8d. 'on delivery of each portion of the Manuscript'.[50] Marian's earning power had increased greatly since she and Lewes had returned to England together only seven years before. Her salary from articles for the whole of 1855 had been £119. 8s. od., less than a quarter of her monthly earnings from *Romola*. (Lewes's income in 1855 was £430. 13s. od.; in 1862 it was £639. 14s. od.[51])

Smith lost money on *Romola*, which sold less well than *Adam Bede*, *The Mill on the Floss*, and *Silas Marner*, for which the level-headed Blackwood had paid much less. Indeed, Smith also lost on Collins's *Armadale* and on other works for which he paid higher sums than any other publisher. He could afford such losses because of the extraordinary success of his overseas trading in commodities ranging from medical supplies for the Crimea to telegraphic equipment for India. In 1872 he was to make more than a million out of mineral water, when he bought up the Apollinaris spring in Germany.[52]

Of course, Blackwood could not, and would not, compete with his extraordinary rival. George Eliot wrote to him on 19 May, when agreement had been reached with Smith, saying she had received an offer 'which I suppose was handsomer than almost any terms ever offered to a writer of Fiction'. She had accepted, but had ensured that the copyright would revert to her after six years 'so that my new work may then be included in any general edition' – such an edition being likely to be brought out by Blackwood, publisher of all the other works.[13]

Once more Blackwood remained calm. His reply is a model of courtesy. 'My dear Madam', he wrote:

I am of course sorry that your new Novel is not to come out under the old colours but I am glad to hear that you have made so satisfactory an arrangement.

Hearing of the wild sums that were being offered to writers of much inferior mark to you, I thought it highly probable that offers would be made to you, and I can readily imagine that you are to receive such a price as I could not make remunerative by any machinery that I could resort to.

He added that he had enjoyed their 'successful enterprises together and much pleasant correspondence and I hope we shall have much more'.[14]

Blackwood may be forgiven for venting himself privately to Langford about 'the conduct of our friends in Blandford Square' and 'the voracity of Lewes', but he said that he had resolved not to fuss – 'quarrels especially literary ones are vulgar'. He mildly agreed to insert an advertisement in *Blackwood's Magazine* which read 'A New Novel by the Author of "Adam Bede" Will Be Commenced in the Next Number of the Cornhill Magazine'.[15] Marian expressed her regret at leaving him, both in her journal on 23 May and face to face when Blackwood visited on 17 June. Blackwood reported the occasion to his nephew with some satisfaction at the moral victory he felt he had achieved:

She said that 'under all the circumstances she had felt that she must accept the enormous offer that had been made – that she could never feel to another publisher as she felt towards me – that pleasure to her was gone in the matter and she did not feel sure now whether she had acted right' – whether she meant this last as towards me or as wisely regarding herself I could not tell. She also said that she 'hoped another time would arise', apparently meaning that she would then show how strong her feeling was. I did not wish any *confidences* nor in her peculiar circumstances to hit her, so merely looked her full in the face and shaking hands said, 'I'm fully satisfied that it must have been a very sharp pang to you' and came away.[16]

Opinions may legitimately vary about whether George Eliot was being disloyal or simply prudent in accepting Smith's offer. As her own village wiseacre Mr Macey of the Rainbow Inn in *Silas Marner* put it:

There's allays two 'pinions; there's the 'pinion a man has of himsen, and there's the 'pinion other folks han on him. There'd be two 'pinions about a cracked bell, if the bell could hear itself.[17]

There can only be one opinion, however, about the effect that writing such an ambitious novel for serialization had on George Eliot, even with the starting date postponed to July. The pressure to write to order, combined with the weight of knowledge that more money had been invested in her effort than in the history of fiction writing, as well as the consciousness that she was diverging from the area of her proven success – provincial England – was hardly conducive to peace of mind in a woman of her physical and psychological constitution. Small wonder that she later told Cross about the writing of *Romola*: 'I began it a young woman – I finished it an old woman.'[18]

While negotiations with Smith were going on, rumours about 'George Eliot's next novel' began to do the rounds. When 'Salem Chapel', a new work in the series 'The Chronicles of Carlingford', set in a country town and dealing with the rivalries between High Church, Evangelicalism, and Dissent, began in the pages of *Blackwood's Magazine* in February 1862, Bessie Parkes's *English Woman's Journal* put two and two together and made George Eliot the author of this work. Sara Hennell wrote in April assuming her to be so, and received a frosty reply: 'I am NOT the author of the Chronicles of Carlingford. They are written by Mrs. Oliphant, author of "Margaret Maitland" etc. etc. etc.' Marian had suffered so much when trying to hold on to her anonymity that now, having abandoned it, she would 'never, I believe, write anonymously again'.[19]

It was not simply that she shuddered at the reminder of Liggins and the treachery of Spencer and Chapman; she was also offended that her friend should think she had written stories which, she believed, 'represented the Dissenters in a very different spirit from anything that has appeared in my books', as she told Sara. She refrained from adding that

Mrs Oliphant's talent for fiction writing was far inferior to her own, though she no doubt thought Sara's critical sense rather blunt on that score. In June she wrote to Bessie asking her to correct the misstatement in the *English Woman's Journal* about her supposed authorship of the Carlingford stories.[60] The story she *was* writing was about to begin serialization, but not, of course, in 'Maga'.

The first part of *Romola*, starting in the *Cornhill Magazine* in July, consisted of the 'Proem', a prologue establishing the time and place (Florence in 1492), and the first five chapters. The artist Frederic Leighton had been engaged to illustrate each number, and Marian was delighted with his drawings. 'He is an invaluable man to have because he knows Florence by heart', she told Sara in July.[61] The opening number was no sooner published than Anthony Trollope sent her an encouraging letter, praising the descriptions of Florence – 'little bits of Florence down to a door nail, and great facts of Florence up to the very fury of life among those full living nobles' – for their wonderful energy and accuracy. He gently warned her, however, not to 'fire too much over the heads of your readers', and his expression of 'wonder and envy' at the 'toil' she must have undertaken 'in getting up your work' may have been a polite way of suggesting that there had perhaps been too much of it.[62]

She had indeed 'got up' the complicated history of that time of change and restlessness, when there existed in Florence, as she writes in the Proem, a

strange web of belief and unbelief; of Epicurean levity and fetichistic dread; of pedantic impossible ethics uttered by rote, and crude passions acted out with childish impulsiveness; of inclination towards a self-indulgent paganism, and inevitable subjection to that human conscience which, in the unrest of a new growth, was filling the air with strange prophecies and presentiments.[63]

The novel opens at the time of the death of Lorenzo de Medici, when a struggle is under way between those, like Romola's father, who support Lorenzo's revival of classical learning and his interest in the new science of Copernicus and the explorations of Columbus, and the followers of the Dominican monk Savonarola, who attempts to reform the Church from within by appeals to mysticism and miracle. Among these groups are many sub-factions, and a web of espionage and the self-promotion of several mercenary individuals renders the plot complex. George Eliot manages the many strands very well, though, like Scott, she resorts to simple coincidence rather often to bring her characters into the desired contact and conflict. Savonarola is the chief historical figure in the novel, a man both heroic and martyred, and yet fanatical, ambitious, and compromised by the intrigues he embraces, believing, as he does, that 'the cause of my party *is* the cause of God's kingdom'.[64] The plot brings the most important invented figures, Tito Melema and Romola Bardi, into contact with Savonarola.

Tito appears suddenly in Florence, a young Greek who has been shipwrecked, and who fascinates everyone he meets with his honeyed voice and his 'hyacinthine locks', an echo of Milton's description of Adam in Book IV of *Paradise Lost*, itself alluding to Homer's description of Ulysses in the *Odyssey*, Book VI.[65] His past is mysterious, and in order to flourish in Florence as a translator, secretary, ambassador, and eventually as a double agent working impartially for both the Mediceans and the supporters of Savonarola, he denies that part of his past which involves duty.

In a superb working out of the Nemesis George Eliot had shown operating in the disgrace of Arthur Donnithorne and the childlessness of Godfrey Cass, those other young men of easy conscience, Tito is pursued round Florence by a 'ghost', his adopted father whom he has abandoned to slavery. Like Judas or Peter, Tito, when confronted by the crazed old Baldassarre while he is supping with a powerful employer in the Rucellai Gardens, denies him. 'There is a traitor among you', says Baldassarre; 'he left me in slavery; he sold gems that were mine, and when I came again, he denied me.' Tito risks all and denies him once more with an easy lie. George Eliot comments:

Nay, so distinct sometimes is the working of a double consciousness within us, that Tito himself, while he triumphed in the apparent verification of his lie, wished that he had never made the lie necessary to himself – wished he had recognised his father on the steps – wished he had gone to seek him – wished everything had been different. But he had borrowed from the terrible usurer Falsehood, and the loan had mounted and mounted with the years, till he belonged to the usurer, body and soul.[66]

Tito marries Romola, the beautiful daughter of a blind old scholar with an antipathy to Savonarola and to the mystical mummery associated with him. In several scenes between husband and wife George

Eliot shows her wonderful ability, realized most fully in *Middlemarch*, to represent in painful dialogue the successive stages of a marriage begun in hope and ending in conflict and despair. Scrupulous, upright Romola discovers the duplicity of her husband, whose very quality of accommodating himself to the interests of others had attracted her to him in the first place. When they clash, Tito seeks to command her with kisses, but 'she was too much agitated by the sense of the distance between their minds to be conscious that his lips touched her'.[67]

Later, when Romola has become aware of his deception and dereliction of duty, she accuses him of never being open with her. George Eliot notes their disharmony, which has similarities with that she had described so feelingly between Tom and Maggie Tulliver or that she was yet to create between Lydgate and Rosamond in *Middlemarch*:

But Romola's touch and glance no longer stirred any fibre of tenderness in her husband. The good-humoured, tolerant Tito, incapable of hatred, incapable almost of impatience, disposed always to be gentle towards the rest of the world, felt himself becoming strangely hard towards this wife whose presence had once been the strongest influence he had known. With all his softness of disposition, he had a masculine effectiveness of intellect and purpose which, like sharpness of edge, is itself an energy, working its way without any strong momentum. Romola had an energy of her own which thwarted his, and no man, who is not exceptionally feeble, will endure being thwarted by his wife. Marriage must be a relation either of sympathy or of conquest.[68]

This strand of the novel is finely done, but it is stretched out rather thinly, getting lost for long periods while George Eliot deals with the busy, bustling life of Florence and its barbers, mountebanks, sellers of trinkets, monks, spies, artists, and politicians. Here, though she applies tremendous skill to make her fifteenth-century Florence come alive – using the arrival of a stranger, Tito, to introduce us naturally to the streets and squares and their people, and setting up episodes on feast days with their processions and local customs much as she had employed the events and dates of the farming year in *Adam Bede* – she cannot avoid a sense of clutter. Fifteenth-century Florence is much stranger to her readers in 1862, and now, than early nineteenth-century rural England. Too much needs explaining to a modern, largely Protestant English readership.

As for the idiom, or idioms, of Florentine speech in palace, monastery, garret, and marketplace, George Eliot fails where success was hardly possible. She could not, and we cannot, hear her characters speak in their full naturalness. One of her greatest successes had been to make us believe in ordinary people like the regulars at the Rainbow Inn in *Silas Marner*. In *The Mill on the Floss* we do not doubt her sureness of touch, as when she has Mr Tulliver use an expression with which we may not be familiar, but in which we have instant faith: 'That's the fault I have to find wi' you, Bessy', he tells his wife in chapter 2; 'if you see a stick in the road, you're allays thinking you can't step over it.'[69]

For her Florentine talk, however, she made the mistake of learning Italian phrases and idioms and translating them into an English no one ever spoke. One such phrase is 'A bad Easter and a bad year to you, and may you die by the sword!', which she seems to have borrowed from Boccaccio's *Decameron*. Another uses a metaphor relating to the Italian custom of catching migrating birds with large nets – 'to go a-hunting with a fine net to catch reasons in the air, like doctors of law' – a phrase adapted from a Tuscan proverb.[70] Such phrases have no resonance, no life. Where in the other novels humour arises genially out of the speech of the supporting characters, in *Romola* a kind of heavy quaintness is the result. As Richard Holt Hutton noticed in his review in the *Spectator*, the 'Florentine buzz' is not successful; 'its allusions are half riddles, and its liveliness a blank to us'.[71]

Not only did George Eliot write the novel in the midst of headaches and depression; she sometimes came near to missing her deadlines. On 30 September 1862 she noted in her journal that she was not yet at the end of the part due to be published in December.[72] Lewes, also in ill health, was sufficiently worried to 'mislay' a letter of Sara Hennell's in September in which someone's critical remarks about *Romola* were quoted. He told Sara that he kept all bad criticisms from Marian, since if she saw them she would give up once and for all.[73]

For this practice (which was actually less firm and fixed than Lewes wanted Sara to believe) both Lewes and George Eliot were later attacked. It was customary after their deaths to suggest that her writing suffered in the later novels for her being shielded from criticism which might have helped her. The very Mrs Oliphant with whom George Eliot was at pains not to be confused wrote of the disadvantages (as well as some advantages) which arose out of Lewes's thus keeping her in a sort of 'mental greenhouse'. Her own circumstances were very different as a young widow with children to raise and debts to clear.[74] Though Marian did see or hear some adverse criticism of her work, it is true that she was so easily put off by it that Lewes sought to shield her from what he thought she could not stand. It was a weakness in her, and novel-reading posterity owes Lewes a debt of gratitude for having pandered to it.

In his letter to Sara, Lewes pointed out that 'Englishmen of high culture', including F. D. Maurice, Bulwer Lytton, and Trollope, had written 'wonderful eulogies' of *Romola*. Browning, too, wrote warmly in August 1863, when serialization came to an end and the novel appeared in three volumes, calling *Romola* 'the noblest and most heroic prose-poem that I have ever read'.[75] Browning was likely to be an especially receptive reader, having recently returned to England after the death in Florence in July 1861 of Elizabeth Barrett Browning, whose poems of Italian liberation written there, *Casa Guidi Windows* (1851), Marian read, or re-read, while writing *Romola*.[76]

The Florence conjured up, with partial success, in *Romola* was known to, and rendered by, Browning himself in some of his most famous dramatic monologues, poems like those spoken by the Florentine artists Fra Lippo Lippi and Andrea del Sarto in the collection *Men and Women* (1855). It is interesting to compare the robust speech of Browning's speakers with that in *Romola*. There is a similar use of non-resonant translated foreign idiom, as when the prior in 'Fra Lippo Lippi' says rather flatly, 'Lose a crow and catch a lark'. But on the whole Browning chooses a kind of Shakespearean–Websterian language as well as the familiar English iambic pentameter metre, thus suggesting the strangeness of fifteenth-century Florence while retaining a rhythm and language familiar to the book-reading and theatre-going English reader. (He does, however, resort to the odd 'Zooks', a staple of historical romance scrupulously avoided by George Eliot.) Browning paid his first call on the Leweses in December 1862, and was soon a good friend and regular visitor.[77]

Romola was well received by the critics, despite their disappointment that there was no lush English countryside and no Mrs Poyser in it. Complaints were made, usually quite respectfully, about the air of the historical guide book which pervades the work, but George Eliot's understanding of flawed human nature, and her portrayal of Tito in particular, were praised. Hutton remarked that Romola herself was 'a shade more modernized than the others' and 'several shades less indi-vidual'.[78] This is a fair comment. She is a generalized, and at the end idealized, version of Maggie Tulliver, feminist in feeling but submitting herself to her sense of duty to others. It is hard to believe in her conversion by Savonarola, except in the merely human, non-religious aspect of his influence over her. She finishes the novel a secular Madonna, believed by the inhabitants of an Italian plague village to be the Virgin Mother herself, but helping them in a purely Feuerbachian effort of human sympathy.

Hutton wrote to George Eliot, who replied interestingly to his criti-cism – this being a notable, if rare, example of her awareness of, and ability to tackle, adverse criticism when it came from a reader who engaged seriously with her work and was largely sympathetic towards her efforts:

You have seized with a fulness which I had hardly hoped that my book could suggest, what it was my effort to express in the presentation of Bardo and Baldassarre; and also the relation of the Florentine political life to the devel-opment of Tito's nature. Perhaps even a judge so discerning as yourself could not infer from the imperfect result how strict a self-control and selection were exercised in the presentation of details. I believe there is scarcely a phrase, an incident, an allusion, that did not gather its value to me from its supposed subservience to my main artistic objects. But it is likely enough that my mental constitution would always render the issue of my labour something excessive – wanting due proportion.

As often happens, criticism from another here provoked a reply from the author which is as astute about her successes and failures as the comments of any severe reader could be. She went on:

It is the habit of my imagination to strive after as full a vision of the medium in which a character moves as of the character itself. The psychological causes which prompted me to give such details of Florentine life and history as I have given, are precisely the same as those which determined me in giving the details of English village life in 'Silas Marner', or the 'Dodson' life, out of which were developed the destinies of poor Tom and Maggie. But you have correctly pointed out the reason why my tendency to excess in this effort after artistic vision makes the impression of a fault in 'Romola' much more per-ceptibly than in my previous books.[79]

Smith had commissioned *Romola* in an effort to stop the slide in sales of the *Cornhill Magazine* from the initial 110,000 in early 1860 to nearer 70,000 in January 1862.[80] Blackwood's nephew William could not help gloating on 12 July 1862 that sales were still going down, 'and no fresh stir from Romola'. A week later he added that as the first part of *Romola* had not boosted sales, Smith was going to start a new Trollope novel as well. *The Small House at Allington* duly began to appear alongside *Romola* in September 1862. A year later, when the three-volume edition of George Eliot's novel was slow to sell, John Blackwood himself admitted to 'a pious feeling that things are wisely ordered'.[81] He had kept in touch, writing from time to time with details of sales of the novels he had published and the odd small cheque in royalties for them.[82]

Though Marian was exhausted after eighteen months of writing and worrying, she and Lewes did not go abroad as usual after publication. They contented themselves with two weeks on the Isle of Wight in June 1863, returning on 29 June to welcome Thornie, who came from Edinburgh to take the second set of exams for the Indian Civil Service, and Bertie, who arrived in London from Hofwyl on 28 July.[83] All three boys were now at home, and all three were the cause of anxiety to Lewes.

In the summer of 1862 Trollope had written frankly and kindly to warn Lewes that Charles was not doing well at the Post Office, and would not be promoted from the most junior clerk unless he made an effort to work more quickly and efficiently. Lewes had been dashed by the news, but Charles's willingness to improve had saved the situation.[84] Now Thornie failed his exam and refused to revise for another two years to retake it. As Lewes noted in his journal on 21 August 1863:

He refused for a long while to choose any other career, having set his mind on going out to Poland to fight the Russians. The idea of his enlisting in a guerrilla band, and in such a cause was too preposterous, and afflicted us greatly. But for some time we feared that he would set us at defiance and start. Finally, he consented to join Bertie in Algiers and learn farming.[85]

Bertie, being the least academically accomplished of the three, was put into farming, but not in the end in Algiers. He was to go to Natal, after serving an apprenticeship on a farm in Scotland. Lewes wrote to the son of his old Edinburgh friend, Robert Chambers, asking him if he could recommend a farming family called Stoddart, of whom he had heard. 'Are they sour and calvinistic or calvinistic and sweet?'[86]

The adventurous Thornie went straight to Natal, without Scottish or other apprenticeship. Barbara Bodichon had some acquaintances there, to whom she wrote on his behalf. On 16 October he set off, 'in excellent spirits', with 'a first-rate rifle and revolver' – which he would find himself using – and 'a smattering of Dutch and Zulu', as Marian told Sara Hennell.[87] Bertie went to Lanarkshire.

Lewes and Marian were also on the move. They had decided to invest some of their now considerable wealth in buying a house of their own. On 21 August they paid £2,000 for the Priory, a large house on the outskirts of Regent's Park. The designer Owen Jones was brought in to modernize and decorate the house, and in the first week of November the Leweses moved in.[88] As Charles was to be twenty-one on 24 November, they gave a combined coming-of-age and housewarming party. A further cause for celebration was Charles's promotion at the Post Office.[89]

Among the guests were Spencer, the painter Burton, Dallas of *The Times*, Pigott, Owen Jones, and Trollope. Some women came – Clementia Taylor, Barbara's friend Elizabeth Malleson and her sister, and Cara Bray's London cousin Mary Marshall – but neither Trollope nor Owen Jones was accompanied by his wife.[90] Bessie Parkes was invited, but she managed to excuse herself on the grounds of a previous engagement. She wrote to Barbara Bodichon in terms she could not use to Marian:

She has written to ask me to go to Charleys birthday evening next week; but I cant go to an evening party there without worrying my Father & Mother; & I was thankful to be going out of town for a few days, to Kate Webber, as a real excuse.[91]

Unlike Barbara, Bessie had not revised her ill opinion of Lewes, coloured by the (unverified) story she had heard of Mrs Gaskell having years before found foster parents for an illegitimate child fathered by Lewes. She now expostulated to Barbara:

Rightly or wrongly the wretched little man has continued to damn himself so completely in public opinion, that it makes it more difficult to frequent *his* house than dear Marian's. You remember what Mrs Noel said to you; & Mrs Gaskill [*sic*] said just the same thing to me, only much more strongly. I dont think Lewes deserves the whole of it; at all events not now since Marian took him in hand; but there is the fact of the public opinion, and it creates a double difficulty, especially for an unmarried woman.

And finally, 'Anthony Trollope goes there next week; but will he take his wife?'[92]

Questions of that kind would meet increasingly with the answer 'Yes', but progress was slow. Marian now shared with Dickens the position of most successful novelist in England. She was universally admired. She was wealthy enough to own a large house. Now forty-four – for she celebrated her own birthday only two days before Charles – she had lived quietly, faithfully, and respectably with Lewes for nearly ten years. All these facts weighed with others in her gradual rehabilitation in the eyes of society. Her critics, after the piece of nasty scandal-mongering by Dixon in his review of *Adam Bede*, now always paid her the respect due to a novelist of genius, whatever the details of her personal life. Yet her own friend, the radical feminist Bessie Parkes, could still write so unfairly of Lewes, and could still worry about what 'the world's wife' would say if she attended a party at the Priory.

CHAPTER ELEVEN

Politics and Poetry:
Felix Holt *and* The Spanish Gypsy *1864–8*

Writing *Romola* had so exhausted George Eliot that she was in no hurry to begin another novel immediately. As Lewes confided in his journal soon after the three-volume edition was published, it had been 'flatly received by the general public'. Sales of only just over 1,700 copies of this edition in the first year after publication confirmed Lewes's early impression.[1] However, he and Marian were bolstered by the enthusiasm of what he called 'the élite', meaning the literary intelligentsia, who included Tennyson, Browning, John Duke Coleridge, great-nephew of the poet and later Lord Chief Justice of England, Richard Monckton Milnes (later Lord Houghton), the Trollope brothers, and the Revd F. D. Maurice, Principal of the Working Men's College. All of these had conveyed their admiration of *Romola*, both for its positive moral influence and for its caring attention to the history of Italy, a nation now struggling into freedom and much supported emotionally, rhetorically, and financially by a large section of the British middle class and establishment.

Indeed, when the patriot Garibaldi visited England in April 1864, he was acclaimed not only by the masses who turned out at Southampton to greet his arrival, but also by senior ministers in the Government. Both Lord John Russell and Lord Palmerston entertained him, and the Prince of Wales visited him, much to Queen Victoria's annoyance. She wrote to Russell on 13 April, expressing regret at 'the extravagant excitement respecting Garibaldi' and advising the Government to be careful about receiving him in an official capacity: 'Brave and honest though he is, he has ever been a revolutionist leader.'[2] To her daughter Vicky she wrote, after Garibaldi's departure, of 'the incredible folly and imprudence of your thoughtless eldest brother going to see him without my knowledge!'[3]

Lewes and Marian went to see him too. On Lewes's forty-seventh birthday, 18 April, they hired a carriage and pair and drove to the Crystal Palace at Sydenham to watch 'the working classes present their deputations to him – one among the many public triumphs he is now receiving from England', as Lewes noted. Owen Jones had got tickets for them. For Marian the occasion was of the kind she liked to create in her novels, a meeting of the private and the public event. While observing and sharing the crowd's excitement in the presence of an historic figure, she was also able to savour a personal pleasure and success. F. D. Maurice, whom she greatly admired, and who had sent her an 'exquisite' letter of praise about *Romola*, came forward to be introduced to her.[4]

That Maurice should show her this courtesy was gratifying. Lewes had written to George Smith in the summer of 1863 about his praise of *Romola*: 'What a noble letter it was for a clergyman, an old man, and a celebrated man to write to a woman frowned on by the world, precisely on the grounds of morality!'[5] Maurice's sister, the widow of Archdeacon Julius Hare, had also written warmly about *Romola*, and had invited Marian to visit her. Breaking her proud rule of abstinence, Marian did go to see Mrs Hare, and was much upset by her death in March 1864. On Mrs Hare's first writing kindly to her, Marian had commented to Sara Hennell with an allusion to her social position with Lewes:

These things *entre nous*. I tell them you because I know you feel an interest in certain relations between conduct and religious belief which have been much urged on my notice by the experience of the last eight years.[6]

With the move to the Priory in November 1863, the Leweses began to entertain more lavishly. No expense had been spared on decorations and furnishings, the whole of which had been in the hands of Owen Jones, the foremost designer and interior decorator of the day. Jones even cast his artistic eye over Marian herself, who reported with amusement to Maria Congreve, then in Florence, that had she been able to attend the housewarming party, she would have seen 'an affectionate but dowdy friend of yours, splendid in a grey moire antique – the consequence of a severe lecture from Owen Jones on her general neglect of personal adornment'.[7]

Their social circle grew larger. Sunday afternoon was the time they liked to receive visitors. Jones came, and Pigott, Spencer, Browning, Trollope, and Burton were regular guests. A few wives accompanied their husbands, but Marian was careful only to invite those she felt sure would not refuse. Bessie Parkes asked to bring her friend Isa Craig, Secretary of the National Association for the Promotion of Social Science, but when the two women did visit together in 1864, Bessie complained to Barbara Bodichon about the masculine atmosphere at the Priory. 'I am sorry to say there were 3 gentlemen there, Owen, Herbert Spencer, and Burton the artist', she wrote. 'I did not mind the two first, but I did mind the last, fearing he would go away and talk of having seen Isa there.' Though Bessie was prejudiced against Lewes, and liable therefore to exaggerate the discomfort Marian felt in company, there is undoubtedly some acuity in her next remark to Barbara:

It *was* so sad to see Marian sitting alone with 4 men when we entered the room. Isa and I brought in quite a wholesome atmosphere of womanhood and I read in Marian's expressive face that she felt it. She left the men and came and sat close to my good little Isa, looking at her with eager loving eyes, in a sort of thirsty manner which went to the depths of my heart. Doubtless it is so long since she has seen a new woman worth seeing.[8]

Marian's own reticent entry in her journal of 30 January 1864 is rather poignant in this respect. 'We had Browning, Dallas and Burton to dine with us', it reads, 'and in the evening a gentleman's party.'[9]

In the spring of 1864 Marian's nephew Robert Evans wrote twice to announce the deaths first of his father, her half-brother Robert, then of Henry Houghton, husband of her half-sister Fanny. She replied sympathetically, expressing her warmth of feeling towards those relations who had ceased to communicate with her. To Robert's wife, Jane, she wrote that she 'cherished the memory that we had one dear Father whom we both venerated', and hoped for a meeting one day which 'would be a very sweet renewal of the past'. Jane Evans was touched enough to reply, telling Marian that the last book her husband had held in his hands was *Adam Bede*.[10]

Lewes's much disliked stepfather, Captain Willim, also died at this time, and Lewes spent a lot of time during February and March visiting his mother, arranging for the funeral, and settling Mrs Willim's affairs. His health and spirits were rather low. On New Year's Day 1864 his retrospect of the past year recorded 'a chequered year'. He had earned £1,083 in 1863, more than in any previous year, but that was mainly for editorial work on the *Cornhill Magazine* rather than original writing. There had been 'much trouble about the two boys; much bother about the new house', but also 'continued happiness with the best of women'. Thackeray had died suddenly on Christmas Eve 1863 at the age of fifty-two. Lewes attended his funeral at Kensal Green on 31 December, at which more than a thousand people turned up.[11]

But new friendships were being made, and one of them appeared to promise an opportunity for a fresh literary venture by George Eliot. Theodore Martin, writer and translator from German, was also at Thackeray's funeral, and he returned home with Lewes to be introduced to Marian. On 7 January he brought his wife, the actress Helen Faucit, and as a result of this visit Lewes made a 'skeleton' of a five-act play with Helen Faucit in mind for the heroine's part. He turned to Marian, suggesting that she work out a drama on his outline. Her interest was fired, though she did not begin at this time.[12]

As Helen Faucit was to appear in several Shakespeare plays at Glasgow at the end of March, the Leweses somewhat surprisingly arranged to travel there to see her act. They stayed in the same hotel as the Martins, getting to know and like them. Bertie was learning farming only a few miles away, so they combined their theatrical trip with a visit to him.[13] Edinburgh was also only twenty or thirty miles away, but they did not go to see Blackwood, who in happier times would have been delighted to entertain them.

Not that relations with Blackwood had been broken off. Occasional notes about business matters were exchanged, and Lewes used the move to the Priory as an excuse to write a chattier letter than usual. On 9 November 1863 he sent their new address, described the upheaval of moving, and told Blackwood about Thornie's exam failure, his mad plan to fight with the Poles, and recent departure to Natal 'to seek his fortune & shoot elephants instead of Russians'.[14] Blackwood had taken a keen interest in Thornie, generously inviting him to spend the Christmas of 1861 at Strathtyrum, his country estate outside Edinburgh, where he could golf and shoot fowl to his heart's content.[15]

As ever, Blackwood answered promptly and pleasantly, wishing

Thornie well and predicting that 'a clever active young fellow like him may probably do better on his own hook than in the routine of any government service'. He finished his letter on just the right note of interest in Marian, steering expertly between the Scylla of indifference and the Charybdis of eagerness: 'What are you both about? I hope G.E. is thinking of something new.'[16] Correspondence was resumed, though it was naturally intermittent, since no new work was on the stocks, and therefore no publisher being considered by George Eliot.

Her feelings towards both her publishers were rather guilty. She had left Blackwood, who had been so generous with encouragement, extra royalties in the early days, the voluntary return of her manuscripts and copyrights, the gift of Pug, and his hospitality to Thornie. And though she had sometimes been irked by his criticism of details in the novels as he read them, she had been stimulated too, and had positively fed on his admiration of her successes. Her relationship with Smith seems to have been entirely different. He was a man of business, who did not presume (or care) to enter into discussions or appreciations of his authors' works. Though he was sociable, introducing his wife to Marian and always writing kindly, there was no growth of friendship between them. Marian's guilt towards Smith related to the loss to him from the poor sales of *Romola*. To offer some recompense, she gave him her story 'Brother Jacob' for publication without payment in the *Cornhill Magazine*, where it appeared in July 1864.[17]

Frederic Burton had become one of the most frequent guests at the Priory. Unsurprisingly, he asked Marian if he could paint her. Aware of her lack of beauty, displeased with Laurence's portrait and with the photographs she had reluctantly had taken, Marian hesitated. She and Lewes asked Helen Faucit to show them copies of the portrait Burton had done of her, and they went to look at a recent picture of his on a subject from Norse legend which they thought 'divine', as Marian told Sara Hennell on 30 April.[18] They liked Burton so much that they decided, rather on the spur of the moment, to go to Italy with him, as Marian also told Sara.

On 4 May the three set out, Charles staying behind at the Priory in charge of their new dog, a bulldog called Ben. (Lewes told Blackwood of this newcomer in a letter of 8 March, adding with singular lack of tact that he had wanted to call him Savonarola, but had decided that

name would be 'too much of a mouthful when one was angry'. As if to
placate Blackwood, he added quickly, 'You will admire him, I'm sure!'[19])

This Italian trip lasted six weeks, most of the time being spent in Venice.
The Leweses did not visit Florence this time, nor did they do very much
reading. For the first time Marian was not preparing for, writing, or
recovering from a novel. This was pure holiday, made up of sightseeing
and viewing paintings with Burton's expert eye to add new interpretations to the Leonardos, Titians, Tintorettos and others they looked at
in churches and galleries. They went to theatre and opera, and were able
to stay in the same Venice hotel, the Hôtel de la Ville overlooking the
Grand Canal, where they had stayed in 1860. Lewes suffered from
headaches and nausea, almost fainting one day in Milan, where they
spent a few days on the way to Venice.[20]

From Venice Lewes wrote to Charles on 18 May, describing idyllic
floatings in gondolas down the Grand Canal, and telling him of an
encounter with 'three *gamins* who chaffed us into the pleasurable weakness of giving them *soldi*. One of these boys reminded your mother and
me greatly of Thornie.'[21] Before leaving for Italy they had received three
letters from the irrepressible Thornie, whom Marian described to D'Albert Durade as 'at once amiable and troublesome, easy and difficult to
manage'.[22]

Thornie had sent them a hilarious account of the voyage, on which
he edited a newspaper, acted in farces, and shocked his fellow passen-
gers with his evolutionary opinions. His first letter from on board the
Damietta tells his father that he has been 'set down as an Atheist and a
fool':

You remember explaining to me that the human child in an early stage has a
tail, well, when I informed the Damiettans of this it created a roar of laughter,
nobody would believe it, and the consequence is, that there are constant allusions to my tail.[23]

Once arrived in Natal, Thornie had set about using his letters of
introduction from Barbara Bodichon, Pigott, and Bulwer (now Sir
Edward Bulwer Lytton), and looking out for 'some coffee planter,
where I can learn the business, and get my board and lodging in return
for my work'.[24]

When Lewes and Marian got back to the Priory on 20 June, they were met by Charles with the news of his engagement to Gertrude Hill, granddaughter of the medical and sanitary reformer Thomas South-wood Smith, whom Lewes had known as a young man moving in London's radical circles. The news 'startled us at first', Lewes wrote in his journal; it 'made Polly happy, and me rather melancholy – the thought of marriage is always a solemn and melancholy thought to me'.[25] Marian wrote cheerfully to D'Albert Durade that 'our "boy" Charles in this his twenty-second year has become engaged to a young lady, for whom we had observed that he had a growing penchant, but who we suspected would hardly fall in love with our amiable bit of crudity.' 'That', she continued, 'was a mistake, a parental notion', for 'she *has* fallen in love with him, and it is very pretty to see their fresh young happiness'.[26]

On 29 June Marian gave her first sitting to Burton, having finally decided that she liked him and his paintings enough to trust him. This was to be 'positively' the last time anyone would paint her, she told Barbara Bodichon in August. Lewes had seen the work so far, and was 'in raptures with it'.[27] Marian sat to Burton on several occasions, the last being on 22 July 1865. His portrait, which was shown at the Royal Academy in 1867, and given in 1883 to the National Portrait Gallery by Burton, who was then Director of the National Gallery,[28] was reckoned by those who knew George Eliot to be the best likeness.

Burton's portrait, though showing as melancholy a George Eliot as Laurence's disliked portrait of 1860, suggests more depth of character and gives fuller expression to the sitter's best physical features – her abundant hair and her expressive, if heavy, eyes. The consensus of contemporary opinion about George Eliot's appearance was that her face was long, mannish, equine, but attractive when animated in conversation. Henry James's description to his brother William after a visit to the Leweses in 1878 is representative: 'The great G.E. herself is both sweet and superior, and has a delightful expression in her large, long, pale equine face.'[29]

By others who knew her she was said to look like George Sand, her fellow jolie-laide female novelist with a male pseudonym, or like Wordsworth (also equine), John Locke, Dante, Cardinal Newman, or her 'own' Savonarola. She had described his 'high nose and large under lip' in chapter 65 of *Romola*, having seen the 'very striking portrait' of him by Fra Bartolommeo in the Accademia in Florence in May 1860.[30]

Dante and Savonarola were invoked by several of her friends and acquaintances. Tom Trollope thought Savonarola's 'particularly unbalanced countenance' looked like 'a strong caricature of hers', while she also bore some resemblance to portraits of Dante, 'who though stern and bitter-looking, was handsome'.[31] And Browning, who like Tom Trollope had been resident in Florence and knew the busts and portraits there of both Dante and Savonarola, was reported as saying grandly of George Eliot, 'She has the nose of Dante, the mouth of Savonarola, and the mind of Plato.'[32] No doubt some fancifulness was involved in such comparisons, though it seems intellectually appropriate that writers like Locke, Wordsworth, and Newman should have come to some people's minds, and thematically appropriate, in the wake of *Romola*, that Dante and Savonarola arose in others'.[33]

À propos of Newman, George Eliot was reading his autobiographical *Apologia Pro Vita Sua* in July 1864, a defence of his conversion to Catholicism in answer to an attack on him by Kingsley. She told Sara Hennell she felt indignant at the latter's 'arrogance, coarse impertinence and unscrupulousness' and was moved by Newman's work as 'the revelation of a life – how different in form from one's own, yet with how close a fellowship in its needs and burthens – I mean spiritual needs and burthens'.[34] Her remark is interesting, showing once more that though she had converted to unbelief and had not wavered from it for over twenty years, she shared her fellow creatures' longing for spiritual comfort and support.

The novels all allow for religious belief and endorse it where it is seen to aid or guide sympathetic action. Indeed, *Romola* is, as regards its heroine's progress, an odyssey from unbelief, through flirtation with mysticism, to a kind of respiritualized secular humanism. Comte, whom she had re-read while preparing to write *Romola*, Feuerbach, and Spinoza continued to feed into George Eliot's thinking on religion and its substitutes. Though she never returned to Christianity in any of its denominations, she remained interested in forms of worship, as her correspondence with Maria Congreve, Bessie Parkes, and Barbara Bodichon demonstrates. In 1861 she had begun to visit various places of worship accompanied by Charles Lewes or by Barbara when she was in London, and was able to appreciate 'the simple pregnant, rhythmical English of those Collects and of the Bible' with which she had been so inward in her youth.[35]

In December 1865 George Eliot spelt out her complex attitude to the Church of England in an explanatory letter to her daughter-in-law Gertrude Lewes, who had married Charles in March in the Rosslyn Hill Unitarian Chapel in Hampstead. Gertrude's sister, Octavia Hill (later founder of the National Trust), had asked about her background and views, to which she now replied:

I was brought up in the Church of England, and never belonged to any other religious body. I care that this should be known, not at all on personal grounds, but because, as I have been, and perhaps shall be, depicting dissenters with much sympathy [she is thinking of the Revd Rufus Lyon in *Felix Holt*, which she was then writing] I would not have it supposed that the sympathy springs from any partiality of association.

This much to set the record straight as to her background. She continued with an interesting statement about her divided feelings *now* towards the Church of England:

As to its origin historically, and *as a system of thought*, it is my conviction that the Church of England is the least morally dignified of all forms of Christianity i.e. all considerable forms dating from the Reformation; but as a portion of my earliest associations and most poetic memories, it would be more likely to tempt me into partiality than any form of dissent.[36]

The remark is of a piece with her assertion about opinions being a poor cement in human relations. As Adam Bede puts it when proposing to Dinah Morris, 'Feeling's a sort o' knowledge.'[37] And as she wrote in an article, 'The Influence of Rationalism', in May 1865, large minds are apt to be divided on the question of tradition because, 'while they have attacked its misapplications, they have been the more solicited by the vague sense that tradition is really the basis of our best life'.[38]

As far as her own work was concerned, she was in July 1864 in a state of 'horrible scepticism'. 'Shall I ever be good for anything again? – ever do anything again?' she asked in her journal.[39] The idea of writing a drama had slowly taken root in her mind, and she had begun reading about Spain with the notion of setting her drama on the theme of the clash of cultures at 'that moment in Spanish history when the struggle with the Moors was attaining its climax'. The original seed sowed itself during the visit to Venice with Burton, when George Eliot was struck by an Annunciation, said to be by Titian, in the Scuola di San Rocco, which made her think of writing about the problems facing an ordinary young woman 'chosen to fulfil a great destiny'.[40]

By 6 September she had made a start on the work, which would eventually be *The Spanish Gypsy*. But her journal records halting progress, and, despite encouragement from Lewes, a 'sticking in the mud' at the end of Act II in November.[41] On 21 February 1865, Lewes took drastic action, so overwrought had she become. 'George has taken my drama away from me', she recorded.[42]

Both Marian and Lewes, especially Lewes, suffered from headaches and weakness. In August 1864 Lewes was getting thinner and thinner, Marian told Sara Hennell.[43] He tried riding lessons, and took the waters at Harrogate in September and again at Malvern in October.[44] In his usual helpful way, he was brushing up his Spanish by reading *Don Quixote* so that he could encourage Marian and discuss her work with her.[45] But she was in danger of doing what she had done when preparing for *Romola* – compensating for the foreignness of her topic by over-researching.

In December there was talk of a new periodical which would be liberal but independent of party. Trollope was involved in setting it up; its chief innovations were to be the freedom of individual contributors from editorial or political control, and the signing of articles at a time when all other periodicals carried mainly unsigned pieces. This new venture was the enormously influential *Fortnightly Review*, which Trollope skilfully persuaded Lewes to edit, though his friend was understandably reluctant on account of his wretched health.

Lewes had voluntarily given up his consultative role on the *Cornhill Magazine* in October because of its falling circulation, and had sighed with relief at 'a tie loosened', though he regretted the loss of the salary.[46] But Trollope urged him to edit the *Fortnightly*, praising his expertise in editorship and appealing to his personal friendship. Lewes accepted on condition that there should be a sub-editor to share the work.[47] The first number appeared on 15 May 1865, with Lewes as editor at £600 a year and John Dennis as sub-editor.

Having taken on this new responsibility, Lewes found himself busy during the early months of 1865 preparing the Prospectus for the *Fortnightly Review*, writing letters to potential contributors, and doing more dining out than was good for his health. The new periodical was founded to take account of impending political changes. Parliamentary debates on further electoral reform were taking place, and it was clear that a second great Reform Act would be passed sooner or later, extending the franchise beyond the £10 householders who had joined the electoral register on the passing in June 1832 of the first Reform Act. This Act, though momentous, had left eighty per cent of men, and all women, still without the vote.[48]

Lewes's plans for the *Fortnightly*, supported by Trollope, who was a liberal-minded Tory, and another founder, the Liberal MP Henry Danby Seymour, were for the periodical to espouse the cause of reform in general without making party political points. In a letter to Seymour on 13 January Lewes borrowed from Comte (and perhaps also from Coleridge in his influential *On the Constitution of Church and State*, 1830) the motto 'Progress and Order' to describe the attitude he hoped the *Review* would adopt. His Prospectus, drafted in March, stated the principle of diversity, both in the subjects covered – literature, art, science, philosophy, and politics – and in the points of view expressed by contributors. But, Lewes added:

It must not be understood from this that the REVIEW is without its purpose, or without a consistency of its own; but the consistency will be one of tendency, not of doctrine; and the purpose will be that of aiding Progress in all directions. The REVIEW will be liberal, and its liberalism so thorough as to include great diversity of individual opinion within its catholic unity of purpose.[49]

Under Lewes's genial editorial guidance, the *Fortnightly Review* quickly became associated with progressive thinking in all fields. He himself wrote on literary matters and on science, and soon established a regular feature, 'Causeries', in which he gave a masterly round-up of the state of current affairs, putting to good use his omnivorous interest in the culture, politics, science, and literature not just of Britain but also of Europe. Other contributors included the scientists T. H. Huxley, John Tyndall, and Sir John Herschel; Walter Bagehot's famous work on the English constitution first appeared serially in the *Fortnightly*, as did Trollope's novel *The Belton Estate*.

Marian also helped give the first number a good send-off by agreeing to write 'The Influence of Rationalism', a review of William Lecky's history of the influence of rationalism in Europe. In accordance with the periodical's policy of carrying only signed articles, her review appeared over the signature 'George Eliot'. The article discusses in particular Lecky's account of the decline in belief in witchcraft, and while she partly endorses Lecky's view that such superstitions have been outgrown, she characteristically notices that on the one hand it was possible for a seventeenth-century thinker such as Sir Thomas Browne to be both intellectually sophisticated and a believer in witches, and on the other it was possible for 'enlightened' men and women of the 1860s to believe they saw the famous Daniel Home – Browning's 'Mr Sludge, "The Medium"' in the 1864 poem of that name – floating in the air at fashionable *séances* in London salons.[50]

Progress was an idea associated inseparably in her mind with mixed conditions, involving some loss as well as some gain. She had not shifted her position from that expressed in her *Westminster* article on Riehl in 1856, namely that while it would be foolish to attempt to halt progress by putting back the hands of the clock, it was equally fatuous to pretend or suppose that dawn was broad midday.[51]

Marian wrote two other articles in 1865, also to help Lewes, who had agreed to be consulting editor of a new venture of George Smith's, the *Pall Mall Gazette*. Both short pieces appeared in the paper in March. One, 'A Word for the Germans', debunks the clichéd notion of the heaviness and obscurity of German scholarship. 'No one in this day really studies any subject without having recourse to German books', particularly in the fields of history, natural science, and Biblical criticism, and John Bull should beware of ready but ignorant ridicule in these matters.[52] The other, 'Servants' Logic', is a rather heavy piece highlighting the inevitable two opinions on questions of housekeeping, the above-stairs opinion and the below-stairs opinion.[53]

On 29 March, a month after Lewes had taken away her half-finished drama, Marian at last wrote in her journal, 'I have begun a Novel'.[54] Her interest in the starting up of the *Fortnightly Review*, in the parliamentary debates on reform, in the distress of the ribbon weavers of Coventry, about whom the Brays kept her informed, and in the events during the run-up to the general election of July 1865, bore fruit in this work, *Felix Holt, The Radical*, set at the time of the 1832 Reform Act. She threw herself into the kind of reading she had done for *Adam Bede* and *The Mill on the Floss* – the *Annual Register* for 1832, a history of Puritanism, William Blackstone's famous *Commentaries on the Laws of England*, and the tragedies of Aeschylus.⁵⁵ Since the date chosen for her novel fell within her own lifetime, she could also call on her childhood memories of living in a rural but coal-mining and ribbon-weaving area during the last great period of public agitation for parliamentary and electoral reform.

Work went slowly, but her usual journal comments about progress are less completely hopeless than they had been for *Romola*, even expressing a grim humour, as when she wrote on 23 July 1865, 'I am going doggedly to work at my novel, seeing what determination can do in the face of despair.'⁵⁶ The election in July returned Palmerston's Liberal ministry to power, and when Palmerston died on 18 October at the age of eighty, Russell took over as Prime Minister with Gladstone as Leader of the House of Commons. Both were advocates of Reform, which therefore came a step closer, though Russell's first Bill of 1866 was defeated with the help of some of his own party who voted against it with the Conservatives. On 27 April 1866 Gladstone made the speech in which he famously asserted that though the House might reject this Bill, 'You cannot fight against the future. Time is on our side.'⁵⁷

George Eliot could therefore not have chosen a more topical subject for her novel than radicalism, reform, and the problems associated with them. As Lewes said to Blackwood at the time of the Gladstone speech, it was a pity *Felix Holt* was not quite ready to be published, for 'just in the thick of the reform discussion so many good quotable "bits" would be furnished to MPs'.⁵⁸ Blackwood agreed, telling Langford that George Eliot's politics were 'excellent' and her sayings would be 'invaluable in the present debate'. He had already written to her, cheerfully telling her how good her politics appeared to him, a Tory. 'As far as I see yet,' he said, having read two thirds of the novel, 'I suspect I am a radical of the Felix Holt breed, and so was my father before me.'⁵⁹

George Eliot had returned, without fuss on either side, to her old publisher. Lewes approached Blackwood on 18 April, when the novel was well over half written – no more deadline horrors of the *Romola* kind were to be risked – asking him if he was interested in making an offer for the copyright for five years of this 'novel of English Provincial Life just after the passing of the Reform Bill in '32'. He wanted Blackwood to reply without seeing the manuscript, 'which would involve too much delay'.⁶⁰ Blackwood answered quickly and pleasantly, was sure the novel would be 'first rate', but insisted on seeing 'a volume or so' in accordance with his usual practice. He promised to give an answer within a couple of days of receiving the manuscript, and indicated that he would probably offer between £4,000 and £5,000.[61]

In this way Blackwood kept his freedom to judge for himself, while indicating his high expectations of a new novel by George Eliot and his willingness to offer more for a novel of hers than he had ever done previously. He could not and would not match Smith's amounts, and in any case had a shrewd idea that Smith had lost money on *Romola*. Smith himself recalled much later that George Eliot offered *Felix Holt* to him, making it clear that she expected £5,000 for it. According to Smith, he read the manuscript and concluded 'it would not be a profitable venture'.[62]

George Eliot's and Lewes's surviving letters and journals contain no references to Smith as a possible publisher of *Felix Holt*. Perhaps Smith was misremembering, as he often did in his recollections; on the other hand, Marian may have shrunk at first from risking a snub from Blackwood, or she may have felt she owed Smith first refusal, or she may have thought Smith would offer £5,000 but Blackwood not. We cannot be sure about her precise motives (very probably mixed in any case) or movements. Whatever they were, the fact is that she now returned to her old friend and best of publishers.

Blackwood's enthusiasm about *Felix Holt* related particularly to the return to home ground – the richly observed Loamshire of the early novels – to the array of well observed minor characters with their sharp sayings, and to the panoramic view of middle England at a time of change and confusion. 'Surely such a picture or rather series of pictures of English Life, manners, and conversation never was drawn', Blackwood wrote to Langford in April.[63]

The 'condition of England' novel had flourished fifteen or twenty years before with such novels as Thackeray's *Vanity Fair*, Mrs Gaskell's *Mary Barton* and *North and South*, Kingsley's *Alton Locke*, and Dickens's *Bleak House* and *Hard Times*. Now with *Felix Holt* George Eliot took a momentous social and political change in the recent history of Britain and followed a group of characters through it. The Introduction, a masterly piece of social history in the wide manner of Scott, shows her formidable grasp both of the broader picture of political attitudes and major national events and of the confusions and paradoxes which were to be found in particular parts of the country, among particular political parties, and among those who belonged to no party at all.

As she says in chapter 3, 'There is no private life which has not been determined by a wider public life.'[64] She uses this statement of fact to justify bringing together for plot purposes individuals who in a different political climate would scarcely have come into contact with one another. In this case she unrepentantly brings the son of the working class, the self-taught demagogue Felix Holt, into the same political arena as Harold Transome, heir (or apparent heir) to the landed estate of Transome Court and Radical candidate for Parliament.

Where in *Romola* the scene-setting had been laborious, and the effort of making the strange seem imaginatively familiar to the reader a comparative failure, here George Eliot sails through her Introduction with ease. She is helped by the fact that her readers were more familiar with the subject matter, particularly in 1866, when agitation for a second dose of reform naturally appealed to the precedent of 1832. And she was herself completely at home, drawing once more on her own experience and memories, and on a lifetime's reading in social, political, and religious history which had thoroughly woven itself into her experience.

Her method of exposition is to take the year 1831, just before the passing of the first Reform Act, and to imagine a coach journey through the 'central plain' of England with an obligingly talkative coachman to point out the landmarks on the way. By this means she begins with a general historical and geographical sweep, a looking back and a looking round, then gradually brings into focus the particular landscape and its inhabitants who are to be the actors in the drama to follow. This looking back is done from a modern viewpoint, with full awareness of the changes wrought between 1831 and 1866. The tone is correspondingly capacious.

The first paragraph of the Introduction suggests nostalgia for the loss of a gone but still remembered age. There is an echo of Wordsworth's line in the 'Immortality Ode' about the loss 'of splendour in the grass, of glory in the flower':

Five-and-thirty years ago the glory had not yet departed from the old coach-roads; the great road-side inns were still brilliant with well-polished tankards, the smiling glances of pretty barmaids, and the repartees of jocose ostlers; the mail still announced itself by the merry notes of the horn; the hedge-cutter or the rick-thatcher might still know the exact hour by the unfailing yet otherwise meteoric apparition of the peagreen Tally-ho or the yellow Independent; and elderly gentlemen in pony-chaises, quartering nervously to make way for the rolling swinging swiftness, had not ceased to remark that times were finely changed since they used to see the pack-horses and hear the tinkling of their bells on this very highway.[65]

We are scarcely given time to savour this (double) vision of a departed golden age, however, for the second paragraph reminds us of the distinct disadvantages to many of living in those unreformed times with their 'pocket boroughs, a Birmingham unrepresented in parliament and compelled to make strong representations out of it, unrepealed corn laws, three-and-sixpenny letters, a brawny and many-breeding pauperism, and other departed evils'.[66]

By this we are given to understand that reform had been badly needed, and that those who urged it deserved support, yet it was of necessity a mixed and partial business, both in terms of the motives of the agitators and in terms of its effects. George Eliot, who in a letter of 1868 described the bent of her own mind as 'conservative rather than destructive',[67] puts some less than revolutionary rhetoric into the mouth of her radical Felix Holt. He calls himself 'a Radical – yes; but I want to go to some roots a good deal lower down than the franchise'. When making a speech to the local miners he distinguishes between the dangerous power of the masses 'to do mischief – to undo what has been done with great expense and labour, to waste and destroy', and a rather vaguely conceived positive power of self-improvement, to be attempted with or without the vote.[68]

If this is radicalism, it is of the conservative kind George Eliot admired in the social history of Riehl. She believed, with Gladstone, that there was no fighting against the future; she aligned herself with the progressives of her generation in most matters; but she was as disinclined as any diehard Tory to relish sudden or – especially – violently achieved change. Education was to precede enfranchisement. No wonder Blackwood thought her politics in *Felix Holt* were excellent.

The polling-day riot George Eliot describes in her novel, based on her memories of Nuneaton in December 1832 and on some recent reading in *The Times* and the *Annual Register* about election disturbances in that first election following the Reform Act of June 1832,[69] is a somewhat tame affair. She is hampered by the awkwardness of having Felix *appear* to lead the rioters (for which he is prosecuted) while in fact he is trying to divert the mob from theft, fire, and murder.

Describing a riot was a tricky undertaking for novelists. Scott was able to do it from a safe historical distance, and his heroes are always bystanders. Dickens in *Barnaby Rudge* (1840) and *A Tale of Two Cities* (1859) succeeded because of his genuine fascination with violence and his rhetorical ingenuity. In *A Tale of Two Cities* he turns the crowds forcing entry into the Bastille into 'a living sea', a resistless and anonymous force of nature bursting its bounds.[70] In *Barnaby Rudge* Newgate Prison itself seems to come alive, and the battle is between the released force of the fire, 'seen sporting and toying with the door' and the door itself, which finally loses: 'The door sank down again: it settled deeper in the cinders – tottered – yielded – was down!'[71] The people who set these events in motion have faded into the background.

With Felix at the heart of her riot, George Eliot could not manage the scene in this way. Besides, her imagination was not excited, as Dickens's was, by the sheer force exerted by a crowd out of control. She may have been politically more radical than Mrs Gaskell or Kingsley or Disraeli or even Dickens, but she distrusted public disorder as much as any of them.

Despite these difficulties, and the fact that Felix Holt himself is, as Henry James said, 'a fragment', the product of an idea for a hero which fails to become credibly embodied, the 'broad picture of midland country life' is magnificently achieved, as James also saw. George Eliot 'bears you along' with 'a kind of retarding persuasiveness', particularly in the Introduction, which James rightly thought incomparable.[72] Her very success in this respect, however, involved her in difficulties of construction. She wanted to set against this wonderfully realized public background the individual tragedy of an embittered woman, Mrs Transome. The mechanism she employed to link Mrs Transome's misery, caught between her insensitive son and the family lawyer who is the father of that son, with the Felix Holt–Esther Lyon plot was an extraordinarily intricate legal arrangement of entails and settlements of the Transome estate and the mystery of unknown or exchanged identities.

Perhaps the complications of Chancery in *Bleak House* or the elaborate mystery surrounding the identity of John Harmon, alias John Rokesmith, in Dickens's most recent novel, *Our Mutual Friend* (1865), encouraged George Eliot to attempt something comparable. But the whole point about the Jarndyce v. Jarndyce case in *Bleak House* is that no one can understand it – Chancery is a deadening, obfuscating, money-eating institution. As for the Harmon plot in *Our Mutual Friend*, as Stephen Gill has pointed out, it is 'the albatross about Dickens's neck' in that novel. It is so complicated that it impedes progress and requires pages of explanation to unravel the mystery, which is in the end not interesting enough to warrant such elaboration.[73]

George Eliot writes very differently from Dickens, or for that matter from Wilkie Collins, with his excruciatingly complex legal twists, but it is striking that *Felix Holt* uses the same kind of plot mechanisms of mistaken identity, inheritance, and blackmail as Dickens's and Collins's novels of the early 1860s. Certainly there is too much complication about Esther Lyon's entitlement to the Transome estate, which comes into force only on the death of the old bill-sticker Tommy Trounsem. (Surely Hardy had the Transome–Trounsem connection at the back of his mind when writing about the D'Urberville–Durbeyfield business in *Tess of the D'Urbervilles*, published in 1891.) So troublesome was the legal problem, indeed, that George Eliot asked the Comtist lawyer and contributor to the *Fortnightly Review*, Frederic Harrison, for help with its details. Thus she could be sure that her legal plot was defensible *as law*; unfortunately, accuracy in that respect did not guarantee it imaginative life.

Felix Holt has some fine scenes of strong dialogue, including encounters between individuals who dislike or misunderstand one another. Some of these scenes are comic, some painful; often comedy and painfulness are skilfully blended, as in the scenes involving the quaint Independent minister, Rufus Lyon. George Eliot invokes a 'cynical sprite' who would make fun of Mr Lyon's innocently boring Scripture-laden talk and its (non) effect on the urbane but soulless Harold Transome. She herself plays that cynical sprite, then smartly changes the point of view, reminding us how shallow Transome's expressions of interest in human rights are beside Mr Lyon's peculiarly expressed but utterly sincere concern for others.[74] When she is describing individuals thwarting or misunderstanding one another she is as superb as she is at rooting them in a vividly realized time and place. Plot complexities and a problem in rendering her ideal, radical-but-not-too-radical hero make

Felix Holt less successful than her previous English novels, but it is so in proportion as its scope is more ambitious.

Felix Holt was finished on 31 May 1866. Now that Lewes had heavy editorial duties on the *Fortnightly Review*, he was less free than before to drop everything and escape to the continent with Marian, but they did set off for a visit to the Low Countries and Germany on 7 June, leaving Blackwood to oversee sales and send them news of the critical reception of the novel. Sales were, in fact, slow, but Blackwood was soothing, pointing to the generally favourable reviews and the steady trickle of copies going to Mudie's and the bookshops, and blaming the political upheaval at home and abroad in the summer of 1866 for the sluggishness of sales. He lost money on *Felix Holt*, which had sold fewer than 5,000 copies by December, but he was too gentlemanly even to hint this.[75]

By going abroad for June and July, the Leweses missed some excitement which proved the timeliness of *Felix Holt*. On 23 July there was a riot in Hyde Park after the failure of the Reform Bill in Parliament and the resignation of Russell's ministry. They found themselves travelling in Germany just when Austria and Prussia went to war over Schleswig and Holstein, so that wherever they went they saw troops massing and found that 'war and rumours of war' were frightening away their fellow tourists.[76] They returned home on 2 August after visiting the cities of Holland and Belgium, admiring their favourite Flemish paintings, and seeking out the Portuguese synagogue in Amsterdam for its association with Spinoza, about whom Lewes had written at length in the *Fortnightly* in April.[77]

While they were away, Frederic Harrison sent a long letter describing his dream that George Eliot might write a poem or drama to illustrate Positivism in 'the home, the school, the temple, the workroom', a work which would give embodiment to Comte's vision of a secular but pseudo-religious society with its saints, its calendar, its Temples of Humanity.[78] George Eliot's reply reveals that, while she could never have the form or content of a work dictated to her, and would not espouse Comtism systematically, she had some sympathy with, and attraction to, Harrison's idea. She told him on 15 August that she had always tried to 'make certain ideas thoroughly incarnate' in her works. But she warned, with an awareness that she was not immune from failure in this respect, against the danger of lapsing 'from the picture to the diagram'.[79] *Romola* had suffered from insufficient incarnation of ideas, as had *Felix Holt*, though to a lesser extent. Her next completed work would too. She confided to Harrison on 15 August that she had taken up her half-finished verse drama, or dramatic poem, *The Spanish Gypsy*.

She and Lewes now planned a journey to the south of France for a few months for the sake of Lewes's health. But first they saw Bertie off for Natal on 9 September, where he was to join Thornie in a new farming venture.[80] Lewes also had to persuade Trollope to release him from the editorship of the *Fortnightly Review*, which he was finding too much for his health, though he enjoyed the work. Trollope was reluctant to let his friend go, but accepted the necessity. Lewes resigned as editor in December 1866, and was succeeded by John Morley.[81]

On 21 December Blackwood made an offer of £1,000 for the copyright of all the novels to date, which he intended bringing out in an illustrated edition in sixpenny numbers. He told George Eliot firmly that he would rather not include the two stories 'The Lifted Veil' and 'Brother Jacob', of which he had not changed his opinion that, though clever, they exhibited 'a painful want of light'.[82] George Eliot did not demur.

The Leweses set off on 27 December 'on our journey to the South, for the sake of George's health, which has been continually declining', as Marian noted in her journal.[83] His symptoms were headaches, nausea, and severe dyspepsia, but despite the long journeys and uncomfortable beds, Lewes improved enough for them to risk going further south and into Spain. Marian had secretly wished to be able to visit the scenes she was struggling to make real in her drama, so they decided to brave the hazards they had heard about – the hardships of Spanish roads, hotels, insects, and smells – and set off at the end of January 1867 for San Sebastián, Barcelona, and the southern territory of *The Spanish Gypsy*, Málaga, Granada, Córdoba, and Seville. Marian reported to Frederic Harrison from Granada that the 'horrors of Spanish hotels and cookery' had been greatly exaggerated. Even the sixteen-hour journey uphill from Málaga to Granada in a diligence pulled by ten mules was not too much for their 'rickety bodies'.[84]

They were thrilled with Granada, and with the astonishing Moorish fortress, the Alhambra, which, despite the vandalism inflicted on it after the expulsion of the Moors in 1492, was a true wonder of the world.

Their friend Owen Jones had visited the Alhambra in 1834 and executed detailed plans and drawings of it, which he published in two volumes in 1842 and 1845. His own work, both in interior decorating and in his design for various courts for the Crystal Palace, showed the influence of the Arabic forms and ornaments to be seen in the Alhambra, the last great example of Moorish art in Europe. Lewes noted that the work of restoration going on there was 'vastly inferior to that by Owen Jones at Sydenham'. He also described his and Marian's feelings about walking among the ancient glories of the long-departed Moors. 'The difference of religion & of race makes the antiquity seem so much the greater.' Marian drank in the strangeness. On 22 February she and Lewes even dared to visit some of the gypsies who lived (as their successors still live) in holes in the mountains around Granada, all in the cause of absorbing the atmosphere for *The Spanish Gypsy*.[85]

From Granada George Eliot wrote to Blackwood, giving him the first hint that she was writing a work 'the subject of which is connected with Spain'. He replied that he was curious to hear about it: 'Is it a Romance?' To this she returned the not unhumorous answer, 'The work connected with Spain is not a Romance. It is – prepare your fortitude – a poem.' She sweetened this pill with an additional hint about 'private projects about an English novel'.[86] But she was reluctant to let him see the manuscript of the poem, and he had to persuade her to let him begin printing the first part of the work at the end of November.[87]

Though Marian and Lewes returned home on 16 March, and she settled down to recasting and completing her Spanish work, it was to be more than a year before she finished it. Her own and Lewes's poor health made for slow progress; they found themselves undertaking more journeys in search of health, spending two weeks on the Isle of Wight in early July, and going on another long trip abroad at the end of July. This was a revisiting of some of the German towns they had first stayed in thirteen years before, when they had just set up together as Mr and Mrs Lewes. George Eliot told Emanuel Deutsch, an Orientalist at the British Museum with whom she and Lewes had recently become friendly, that they were 'renewing past joys', particularly in Ilmenau, the little town associated with Goethe, and hence with Lewes's biography and the happy days they had spent researching it.[88]

Their relationship, Marian's position (or non-position) in society, and indeed the position of women generally – these questions, never far below the surface of her consciousness, became uppermost again during 1867. On 5 May they went to hear Richard Congreve give the first in a series of lectures on Positivism, and found themselves mingling with 'a considerable audience – about 75, chiefly men – of various ranks, from lords and MPs downwards, or upwards, for what is called social distinction seems to be in a shifting condition just now', as Marian told Sara Hennell on 13 May, alluding to the readings of the amended Reform Bill going on at that time.[89]

Among the lords were Lewes's friend Lord Houghton, and Lord and Lady Amberley (parents of Bertrand Russell), who were Liberal in politics and liberal in social matters. Lewes introduced Marian to Lady Amberley, who accepted an invitation to lunch. This certainly represented a shift in social conditions, though Lady Amberley was clearly a little awestruck at her own daring. She wrote in her diary after meeting Marian that 'the correct etiquette about Lewes and George Eliot appears to have been somewhat undecided'.[90]

Two weeks after this encounter between the Lady and the erstwhile strong-minded woman, John Stuart Mill made a famous speech in the House of Commons, seeking to add a significant amendment to Gladstone's new Reform Bill. On 20 May he moved to change 'man' to 'person' in the Bill's provision for extending the franchise. He spoke of half the population – the female half – being unrepresented, though many of them owned property, managed estates, and paid taxes, and some were teachers of the nation's children. He invoked the injustice suffered by Elizabeth Garrett, the first woman to study medicine in England, who found the doors of the medical profession firmly closed against her.[91] His amendment was, of course, defeated at a time when many Tories were still trying to stop the extension of the franchise to some working *men*.

George Eliot could not fail to be interested in the question. She told Clementia Taylor, who supported Mill, that she thought his speech 'sober and judicious', but she skilfully avoided giving even verbal support to the cause, preferring to focus on the need for women to be educated equally with men. To Sara Hennell she was more open, and more reactionary, expressing her belief that the women's suffrage agitation was 'an extremely doubtful good'.[92]

One reason for her disappointing lack of enthusiasm for women's suffrage undoubtedly was her innate caution and conservatism about the extension of the suffrage generally. Felix Holt was, as we have seen, a very tame reformer, not at all in a hurry to secure votes for the colliers of Loamshire. Blackwood knew he was safe in asking her in November 1867, after Disraeli had delivered a speech to the working men of Edinburgh, to write an 'address to the Working Men on their new responsibilities', the Reform Bill having been passed in July.[93] She obliged with 'Address to Working Men, by Felix Holt', which was published in *Blackwood's Magazine* in January 1868. In it Felix, quite in character, lectures the new voters about their 'heavy responsibility', the sanctity of doing work well, the 'dependence of men on each other', the organic, slow-growing nature of society and culture, and the need for 'the preservation of order'.[94] It is a fine, sombre piece of secular preaching, not the work of one throbbing with a sense of the need to effect change urgently and wholesale.

In the same spirit George Eliot replied to some lobbying by Mill's supporter and Lewes's successor at the *Fortnightly Review*, John Morley. Here woman's nature and function are adduced as a reason for caution with a conservatism which George Eliot found in Comte and Spencer and Darwin, as well as in older political thinkers:

I would certainly not oppose any plan which held out any reasonable promise of tending to establish as far as possible an equivalence of advantages for the two sexes, as to education and the possibilities of free development. I fear you may have misunderstood something I said the other evening about nature. I never meant to urge the 'intention of Nature' argument, which is to me a pitiable fallacy. I mean that as a fact of mere zoological evolution, woman seems to me to have the worse share in existence. But for that reason I would the more contend that in the moral evolution we have 'an art which does mend nature' – an art which 'itself is nature'. It is the function of love in the largest sense, to mitigate the harshness of all fatalities. And in the thorough recognition of that worse share, I think there is a basis for a sublimer resignation in woman and a more regenerating tenderness in man.[95]

Polixenes' speech to Perdita in Act IV, scene iv of *The Winter's Tale* is quoted here in support of a view which, if looked at from the point of view of George Eliot's own life and choices, seems all wrong with its unmistakable allusion to woman's special function as wife and mother. But then it was precisely because her life was unusual (and not entirely willingly so) that she refused to found an opinion on the basis of it. As she put it to Morley, 'The peculiarities of my own lot may have caused me to have idiosyncracies rather than an average judgment.'

The less happy George Eliot was about promoting votes for women, the more keen she was to support their education. Emily Davies therefore found her a very willing listener when she sought in November 1867 to interest her in the founding of a college for women, to be attached to Cambridge and 'get their Degrees if possible'. George Eliot replied that the subject was one on which she felt '*no doubt*, and I shall rejoice if the idea of a college can be carried out'.

It was carried out, with Barbara Bodichon as chief financial contributor, though her name was kept off the committee because of her prominence as a campaigner for women's suffrage. Emily Davies knew that the scheme, which was realized two years later with the founding of Girton College, needed support from men who might withhold it if the educational cause became mixed up with the suffrage question.[96] Marian gave money for the Girton project, but in relatively small amounts – £50 in March 1868, for example – partly out of a natural carefulness with money, partly because she did not wish to be too visible as a supporter of any public cause.[97]

George Eliot worked on slowly at *The Spanish Gypsy*, which she finished on 29 April 1868. What had begun three and a half years before as an attempt at drama had now become a 'dramatic poem' with scenes of dialogue mingled with a linking narrative, the whole written in blank verse apart from the odd scene in prose and some lyrics sung by Juan, a poet-musician, in the style of traditional Spanish ballads.

It seems that George Eliot wrote the original Act I in prose, then tried her hand at blank verse for Act II, which she drafted in November 1864. *Felix Holt* intervened, then she took up her drama again on 30 August 1866, deciding on 15 October to recast it in verse. From then on, all her references to its progress are to her 'poem', though she wrote at least one scene in prose first, as her journal entry for 10 January 1868 shows.[98] The final work is a rather hybrid creature, more a narrative poem with some of the dialogue set out as in a play than a verse drama, and divided not into Acts but into five books of irregular length.

Blackwood received the instalments with equanimity, describing the poem as 'grand', but not entering with his usual gusto into discussion of it. He offered £300 for an edition of 2,000 copies, promising a royalty on any further copies which might be required.[99] It was nothing like what she could command for a novel, but as Blackwood said, 'There are no certainties in publishing.' Something over 3,000 copies were sold in the first year, bringing George Eliot £350, and the American publisher Ticknor and Fields paid £400 for 8,000 copies sold in the United States.[100]

Early responses and reviews were polite, even positive, though Frederic Harrison, who was sent a copy in gratitude for his legal help with *Felix Holt*, and who had urged George Eliot to write a poem, was embarrassed in his delayed reply of 11 November for something enthusiastic to say. To his friend Edward Beesly he wrote on first receiving the poem in May that he was 'afraid it is a fiasco', particularly in its mixing of narrative and drama.[101]

The poem is not as bad as that, but it can hardly be called a success. The blank verse is ponderous and unvaried, like a distant and effortful imitation of Shakespeare and Milton without the spring and rhythm and music of those authors. Browning and Tennyson are probable models too. Tennyson had published his dramatic poem *Enoch Arden* in 1864, and Browning's dramatic monologues were well known to George Eliot, as was the fact that he was at work on a dramatic poem even longer than *The Spanish Gypsy*, his retelling of a seventeenth-century Italian murder story, *The Ring and the Book*, published in twelve books in 1868–9.[102] Neither of these works counts as its author's best effort, but Tennyson's verse always sings and Browning can personify and ventriloquize in a more robust and varied way than George Eliot could manage.

The heroine, Fedalma, on finding she is the daughter of Zarca, king of the despised race of gypsies, faces a choice not unlike Maggie Tulliver's. She must renounce either her new-found father, her race, and a duty to lead that race out of hostile Spain into Africa, or her love for Duke Silva, who has proposed to her, thinking her a Spanish Catholic like himself. Fedalma chooses, or rather has the choice made for her by a deep feeling of duty and belonging. She renounces Silva and rejoins her race. Tragedy results from the gypsies' alliance with the Moors who take the town Duke Silva is defending. Fedalma's father is killed by Silva, leaving her to lead her people, which she does in a spirit of stoicism:

> I am but as the funeral urn that bears
> The ashes of a leader.[103]

Duke Silva, ashamed of having been used by Zarca in the attack on the Spanish fortress, goes on a pilgrimage to Rome to atone for his sins.

Personal choice and sacrifice are here set in the context of the 1490s, when Catholic Spain expelled the Moors, with the gypsies also exiled as an alien and inferior race. As with *Romola*, set in the same period, the context is remote and the required exposition therefore too busy, while the characters remain mere sketches. In the end, however, the chief fault lies in the failure of the poem to sound like poetry. One example of a speech no better or worse than most others is Fedalma's lament on leaving Silva to fulfil her fate, while she wishes she knew something of his feelings:

> Oh, I am sick at heart. The eye of day,
> The insistent summer sun, seems pitiless,
> Shining in all the barren crevices
> Of weary life, leaving no shade, no dark,
> Where I may dream that hidden waters lie;
> As pitiless as to some shipwrecked man,
> Who gazing from his narrow shoal of sand
> On the wide unspecked round of blue and blue
> Sees that full light is errorless despair.[104]

There is a leadenness about such lines, and even a curious lack of conviction about her metaphors, usually one of the great strengths of her fiction. As one of her best contemporary critics, Richard Holt Hutton, said, 'Verse to her is a fetter, and not a stimulus.' Henry James asked his readers to imagine what it would be like if Tennyson 'were to come out with a novel' or George Sand 'were to produce a tragedy in French alexandrines'.[105]

George Eliot clung to Lewes's praise, and to the expressions of admiration which came from friends. She consoled herself for the doubts expressed by some reviewers and the sluggish sales to general readers by quoting Balzac to Blackwood in July: 'When I want the world to praise my novels, I write a drama: when I want them to praise my drama, I write a novel.'[106] In November she meditated writing a poem on the subject of Timoleon, the Corinthian who liberated Syracuse from tyranny in the fourth century BC. This plan she mentioned only once more, in her journal of 1 January 1869, when she listed as her tasks for the year 'A Novel called Middlemarch, a long poem on Timoleon, and several minor poems'.[107]

Thus, casually, and in what we can with hindsight see to have been an otherwise unpromising list, does George Eliot make the first mention of the work by which she is now best known, the novel thought by many to be the greatest Victorian novel, and by not a few to be both the finest English novel of any period and one of the greatest of European novels.

CHAPTER TWELVE

Writing Middlemarch
1869–72

It seems odd to us now, playing the role of a knowing posterity, that George Eliot might have written a long poem about Timoleon and might not have written *Middlemarch*. We have the single but mighty advantage of hindsight over her, for in 1869, as she cogitated her new novel of English life, work went as slowly and haltingly, as doubtingly and despairingly, as it had done on *Romola* or *The Spanish Gypsy*. Ill health, domestic troubles, changes of mind, loss of nerve leading to two separate beginnings for the novel – these are the story of 1869 and 1870.

Her research into Greek history and culture for the long poem on Timoleon went on intermittently until September 1869, when the subject disappears from her notebooks and journal. But progress on *Middlemarch*, first conceived as the story of Lydgate's arrival as a reforming doctor in the country town shortly before the debating of the Reform Bill of 1832, also halted before the end of 1869. The second beginning, the story of Dorothea Brooke, occupied the end of 1870, and some time early in 1871 George Eliot had the brilliant idea – though she had no faith then in its brilliance – of joining the Lydgate–Featherstone–Vincy–Middlemarch plot and the 'Miss Brooke' plot to make one novel, *Middlemarch: A Study of Provincial Life*.¹

But early in 1869 George Eliot was still far from sure about her next big work. At this time she wrote two short poems, 'Agatha' and 'How Lisa Loved the King'. The first, a semi-dramatized account of a visit by a countess to the cottage of Agatha, an old peasant woman and secular saint – 'half grandame and half saint' – was based on a similar visit Marian and Lewes had made in the company of the Gräfin von

Baudissin when they journeyed to the Black Forest in the summer of 1868.[2] The American publisher James Fields came to the Priory on 13 May 1869 to propose an American edition of George Eliot's works, and he offered her £300 for 'Agatha', which appeared in the *Atlantic Monthly* in August.[3] It is an index of George Eliot's fame and the pulling power of her name that she could earn more in 1869 for this slight poem than she had made in a year of writing excellent but anonymous articles in the *Westminster Review* fifteen years before.

Blackwood paid a more realistic £50 for the second short poem of 1869, 'How Lisa Loved the King', which was published in *Blackwood's Magazine* in May. This was a rhymed story of the faithful love of a subject for her king, adapted from Boccaccio's *Decameron*. George Eliot managed on occasion a telling rhyme and an appropriately Keatsian cadence – Keats having written poems on subjects from Boccaccio – as in the lines

> As if the soul within her all on fire
> Made of her being one swift funeral pyre.

But she was also capable of sinking to such lines as the following, in which she tells of the king's visit to

> The Tuscan trader's daughter, who was sick,
> Men said, it was a royal deed and catholic.[4]

On 3 March Marian and Lewes set out on their fourth visit to Italy, knowing it might be their last long trip for some time to come. Lewes's mother, now over eighty, was ailing and relied on frequent visits from her only surviving son. And they were also awaiting, in some trepidation, the arrival of Thornie, who had undertaken the long trip home from Natal in circumstances which gave cause for concern. On 6 January 1869 Lewes had received a letter from Thornie which, as he wrote tersely in his diary, 'made me very miserable. Went into the city to send him £250.'[5]

Thornie had written the letter on 12 October 1868. It is a most moving document. Beginning with a story of a failed speculation into which he and Bertie had entered, involving a plan to sell blankets to the Maguta tribe in return for ivory – the kind of scrape one might expect two adventurous young men to get into – it modulates into a terrible tale. Thornie the scapegrace asks his father to lend them £200 to cover the losses incurred on their business venture. He then moves to a second request for money:

I had hoped to have been able to come home to England with the proceeds of the trip but 'l'homme propose et Dieu dispose'. The fact is this, that with this stone in the kidney and other internal complications, for there is something serious besides the stone, I am gradually wasting away. I eat almost nothing, nothing but delicacies tempt me, and those we can't afford. I can't do a stroke of work of any sort, I can hardly stoop to touch the ground, I can't sit up for half an hour, all I can do is lie down, then get up and walk about for half an hour, then lie down again. Every evening about sundown when the paroxysms come on, I can hardly turn myself over, and if I want to sit up, I must push myself up with my hands, from my shoulder blades downwards I am power-less; and I have a sort of shooting compression of the chest, which makes breathing difficult, and makes me shout with pain. And as this lasts usually for 2 to 3 hours, and sometimes there is more or less pain all night long, so that I get no sleep, and sometimes I have slight attacks in the day time – you can fancy that my life is not a pleasant one. In fact if I were 50 instead of 24, I should have quietly walked some fine day over our waterfall; but while there is youth there is hope; and I hope and trust that a trip to England, to consult one or two of the best doctors may do me good; the change and sea voyage would probably do me good, but at any rate I should like to know from the best medical authorities, whether any thing can be done for me, whether I am to remain a cripple all my life, in short, what my future is to be. I know this trip, seeing physicians etc, perhaps undergoing some operation will cost a great deal of money, but – que voulez vous. It is my last chance in life, and you are the only person I can apply to, so I don't hesitate to make the application.[6]

Lewes immediately sent him the money for the journey. On 9 January he told Thornie's old friend Blackwood the news, adding, 'The vision of him haunts me incessantly.'[7]

The Italian trip lasted two months, and took in many cities, including Florence, where they stayed with Tom Trollope, and Rome, which they enjoyed much better than they had in Holy Week in 1860. 'It seems splendid to us now', wrote Lewes in his journal on 6 April, 'the change being obviously due to the brighter weather & the more moderate expectations.'[8]

It was in Rome, on 18 April, Lewes's fifty-second birthday, which both he and Marian had 'entirely forgotten', that they met a young man whose future was to be curiously connected with theirs. This was John

Cross, twenty-nine-year-old son of Anna Cross, a widow whom Lewes had met in October 1867, when on a short walking tour in Surrey with Herbert Spencer. The Cross family, which Lewes had noted 'worshipped' George Eliot, lived in Weybridge.[9] John was a banker who had been working in New York but returned to England in 1869. He became a frequent visitor at the Priory, and the Leweses often went to Surrey to see him and his mother and sisters. Cross also became their financial adviser, handling their increasing investments. There was nothing curious about this development, but surely no one could have dreamt that he would one day marry George Eliot, or that he would write the well-meaning biography of her which contributed decisively to a slump – albeit temporary – in her reputation.

Lewes and Marian came home on 5 May, somewhat refreshed though still anxious. Three days later, on Saturday 8 May, they returned from a visit to Mrs Willim to find, to their astonishment, that Thornie had arrived much earlier than expected. He had lost four stones in weight, and 'from a fine muscular fellow' had become 'piteously wasted', as George Eliot told Blackwood on 11 May. Lewes's diary records that he was 'dreadfully shocked to see him so worn'.[10] Poor Thornie was unable to stand or walk; he rolled on the floor in agony.

It happened that on Sunday 9 May, the day after Thornie's sudden arrival, the young American writer Henry James came to the Priory with two American friends, Grace Norton and Sara Sedgwick, who had already visited the Leweses in January and knew that Sunday afternoon was the regular visiting time.[11] The Americans stumbled into a crisis. Thornie was in agony, and Lewes dashed off to a chemist for morphine. James wrote to his father the next day telling him that 'the one marvel as yet, of my stay, is having finally seen Mrs Lewes, tho' under sadly infelicitous circumstances'. He goes on with the cool observation that George Eliot was 'magnificently ugly' but utterly charming in the talk she held with her visitors – rather a heroic feat in the circumstances, we might think. 'Behold me literally in love with this great horse-faced bluestocking', writes James, before going on to reveal that Lewes's son, 'an extremely pleasant looking young fellow of about twenty four, lay on the drawing-room floor, writhing in agony from an attack of pain in the spine to which he is subject'.[12]

The next few months were a waking nightmare for Thornie, and for Lewes and Marian, as they struggled to deaden the pain with doses of morphine and to cheer the boy who had been so lively and who was now dying slowly of tuberculosis of the spine, the terrible disease that had kept Heine on his 'mattress-grave' in Paris for several years before he died.

The summer was spent fluctuating between hope and despair. One of the Queen's physicians, James Paget, was called in, but he found both diagnosis and treatment difficult. On 18 May Agnes Lewes came, at Lewes's summons, to sit with her son. Charles and Gertrude had been abroad when Thornie came home, and had not been told about his illness. When Charles saw his brother on 1 June, he fainted from shock.[13] Their friends rallied round, Barbara Bodichon being particularly supportive. 'She comes twice a-week to sit with Thornie, and she is wonderfully clever in talking to young people', Marian told Maria Congreve.[14]

Occasionally Thornie seemed to improve. He was carried out on to the lawn on hot days, and at the end of July Paget thought he might recover. But less than three weeks later Marian was writing to a new friend, Emilia Pattison, the young wife of the Rector of Lincoln College, Oxford, that she was 'in danger of forgetting that there is enjoyment, as well as suffering, in the world'. Thornie's case now seemed hopeless, and Marian indulged in a rare piece of confession mingled with vehemence and a kind of negative pride:

In proportion as I profoundly rejoice that I never brought a child into the world, I am conscious of having an unused stock of motherly tenderness, which sometimes overflows, but not without discrimination.[15]

The false note she seems to strike here must have arisen from the strain, not unlike that she had endured when nursing her father, of looking after a beloved family member who seems likely to die, though whether sooner or later is clear to no one. She described the situation to Cara Bray on 21 August: 'We feel utterly in the dark as to the probabilities of his case, and must resignedly accept what each day brings.'[16]

By 11 October Lewes saw that Thornie was 'drifting away'. He died peacefully on 19 October, 'still a boy, though he had lived for 25 years and a half', as Marian wrote in her journal. 'This death', she added, 'seems to me like the beginning of our own.'[17] Thornie was buried in Highgate Cemetery. We do not know if Agnes attended the funeral, since both Lewes's and Marian's journals break off for several weeks at this point. For months Lewes had hardly done any research towards his big work of psychology and physiology, *Problems of Life and Mind*, so taken up was he in nursing Thornie, keeping Agnes informed, and visiting his mother. He and Marian went off, completely exhausted, to Limpsfield in Surrey to recuperate.

George Eliot had done more work over the summer than might have been expected in the circumstances. Fifty pages, or three chapters, of the Lydgate–Featherstone–Vincy story had been completed by 11 September. Ten days later Marian asked Maria Congreve to get her 'some information about provincial Hospitals, which is necessary to my imagining the conditions of my hero'. She was reading and taking notes about the history of medicine and medical colleges, but she was naturally distracted, and felt unconfident about her story.[18]

In July she had written eleven connected sonnets, 'Brother and Sister', forming a brief narrative of her childhood relationship with Isaac. The poems are technically uninteresting, but the subject matter reveals Marian's preoccupation with family relationships. Some episodes remind us of *The Mill on the Floss*. There is a fishing expedition on which the little sister fears brotherly chastisement for not concentrating but instead receives unmerited but delicious praise for landing a catch, and a brief mention of meeting a gypsy who startled her at play. A close echo of the *Prelude* comes in Sonnet V:

> Thus rambling we were schooled in deepest love,
> And learned the meanings that give words a soul,
> The fear, the love, the primal passionate store,
> Whose shaping impulses make manhood whole.

The last sonnet chronicles the separation, and she speaks daringly for both her brother and herself – 'our souls still yearning in divorce' – though she was in fact completely in the dark about Isaac's feelings towards her after nearly twenty years of separation. Still, she ends on an affirmative note:

> But were another childhood-world my share
> I would be born a little sister there.[19]

The poems were first published by Blackwood in a volume of her poetry in 1874.

In the last weeks of Thornie's illness she began another poem, 'The

Legend of Jubal', which seems to be a displaced expression of her anxiety about her writing past, present, and future. Jubal, the descendant of Cain, creates music for his race, inventing the lyre. He goes on his travels, returning home as an old man hoping for praise and thanks for his gift. His people fail to recognize him and turn him away, though they sing praises to his name:

> The immortal name of Jubal filled the sky,
> While Jubal lonely laid him down to die.

The worst of it is, not that his people doubt his identity, but that he comes to doubt it himself. Jubal

> Shrank doubting whether he could Jubal be,
> And not a dream of Jubal.[20]

George Eliot was a prey, like other writers, and indeed like many a person with past achievements to live up to, not only to doubts about whether she would ever again match her past successes, but, worse, to an irrational inclination to doubt whether she really had written *Adam Bede* and the rest of the novels. 'The Legend of Jubal' was published in May 1870 in both *Macmillan's Magazine* and the *Atlantic Monthly*.

Christmas 1869 was spent quietly with Charles and Gertrude in Hampstead. They went to hear the Unitarian service at Rosslyn Chapel, then walked over Hampstead Heath to visit Thornie's grave in Highgate Cemetery.[21] Life went on quietly after that, with Lewes's health giving increasing cause for anxiety. He fainted in February 1870, and went off for a few days with Spencer to the Isle of Wight to recover.[22] On 6 March Dickens came to lunch. He too looked 'dreadfully shattered', as George Eliot remembered on 13 June, when she heard of his death.[23]

On 14 March the Leweses set out for Germany once more. They were both lionized in Berlin, where they met 'Princes, Professors, Ambassadors, and persons covered with stars and decorations', as Lewes told his mother in a letter of 28 March. At one social event 'the American Ambassador and myself were the only undecorated persons there'. 'As Talleyrand said of Castlereagh at the Congress of Vienna "the absence of decoration was a distinction".'[24] Lewes visited laboratories, hospitals, and lunatic asylums in connection with his physiological and psychological researches. They heard Wagner's *Tannhäuser*, concluding that 'the music of the future' was not for them; they had not evolved beyond the tadpole stage of appreciation George Eliot had noted on their first German visit in 1854–5.[25] The publisher Franz Duncker got them tickets to attend the Reichstag on 24 March, where they heard Bismarck speak, though only briefly, in a debate on the currency.[26]

After several weeks in Berlin, Marian and Lewes went to Vienna, where they were met by Bulwer Lytton's son Robert, who worked at the British Embassy there. Once more they moved in glittering literary, scientific, and political society, before leaving for Salzburg and Munich, and home on 6 May.[27]

The Sunday afternoons, interrupted during Thornie's illness the previous summer, began again on their return. Imperceptibly it had become acceptable to visit *and* to invite George Eliot in mixed company. Lord and Lady Houghton, Lord and Lady Amberley, Mr and Mrs Beesly, Edward and Georgiana Burne-Jones, Mark and Emilia Pattison, among other married couples of rank or high professional standing, now sought George Eliot's company. The Pattisons invited both Leweses to Oxford at the end of May, where they met, among others, Matthew Arnold's niece Mary Arnold, later the best-selling novelist Mrs Humphry Ward. She remembered George Eliot's 'long, pallid face, set in black lace', her 'low clear voice' talking of Spain, and above all her 'evident wish to be kind to a young girl'.[28]

Though Charles Eliot Norton, the American visitor and friend of Henry James, wrote after visiting the Leweses in January 1869 that George Eliot was still 'not received in general society, and the women who visit her are either so émancipée as not to mind what the world says about them, or have no social position to maintain',[29] his remark was really behind the times. Norton may have been exaggerating his impression for the sake of a good story to tell his correspondent. There is in any case some evidence that American society was in general more puritanical than English. The covering up of piano legs, so fixed in the public mind now as 'Victorian', was originally an American practice. Lewes's friend, the naturalist Richard Owen, had complained in 1856 to John Murray, publisher of the *Quarterly Review*, about American squeamishness and 'the Yankee nether-clothing of the pianoforte legs'.[30]

From about the time of *Romola*, which was received so reverently by so many respectable people, George Eliot had proved through her books that she was no frivolous woman seeking to undermine public morality. And those who met her were uniformly struck by her serious air and her devoted wifehood and motherhood in her domestic relations with Lewes and his sons. American and English admirers alike, both men and women, not only came seeking admittance at the Priory; they also wrote admiring, even adoring, letters.

Among the younger men who had recently got to know the Leweses were three who assiduously cultivated George Eliot, asking her advice in matters to do with their careers and with their spiritual and emotional troubles. One was Oscar Browning, a master at Eton, who invited Lewes and Marian to spend a day with him in June 1867, and who confided in George Eliot in 1875, when he was dismissed under suspicion of making homosexual advances to pupils. She was supportive – we do not know how closely Browning confided in her – becoming almost confessional herself in her effort to encourage him: 'Perhaps the most difficult heroism is that which consists in the daily conquests of our private demons, not in the slaying of world-notorious dragons.'[31] In her own case this meant constant efforts to shake off hopelessness, to keep down pride, and not to let resentment at the injustice of her position as Lewes's partner, not wife, spoil the happiness she had gained by entering into that partnership.

The second young man who warmed to her kindness was Emanuel Deutsch of the British Museum. He showed the Leweses round the new exhibits at the Museum in May 1867, and a few months later asked George Eliot's advice when writing an article on the Talmud for the *Quarterly Review*. He was soon visiting the Priory regularly to give her lessons in Hebrew, an activity which bore rich fruit in *Daniel Deronda*.[32]

Deutsch was an enthusiast for a Jewish homeland; when he visited Palestine in 1869 he wrote that all his 'wild yearnings' had been fulfilled. In May 1868 he confided in George Eliot some doubts about his future and his calling, to which she replied that he should not distrust his vocation: 'I believe in it still, though I am the least hopeful of mortals both in my own affairs and in those of any one who is dear to me.'[33] Deutsch and his experience, including his painful decline and death from cancer in 1873, were etched in George Eliot's mind as she wrote about Daniel Deronda and his Jewish mentor Mordecai in her last novel.

Clifford Allbutt was the third young man who turned to George Eliot. A young doctor in Leeds, an idealist whose chance reading of

Comte while an undergraduate in Cambridge had made him look to science and the socially useful occupation of medicine, Allbutt made Lewes's acquaintance at a meeting of the British Medical Association in Oxford in the summer of 1868. In September 1868 both Leweses visited him in Leeds.[34]

It was in a letter to Allbutt that George Eliot declared the bent of her mind to be more conservative than destructive. She also explained to him that her books were based on her 'conviction as to the relative goodness and nobleness of human dispositions and motives'. Allbutt received one of the fullest expressions of opinion she ever gave about her vocation, no doubt drawn from her in the context of thinking about his obviously admirable and important profession:

And the inspiring principle which alone gives me courage to write is, that of so presenting our human life as to help my readers in getting a clearer conception and a more active admiration of those vital elements which bind men together and give a higher worthiness to their existence; and also to help them in gradually dissociating these elements from the more transient forms on which an outworn teaching tends to make them dependent.[35]

A few months later George Eliot responded to a confidence Allbutt had placed in her, possibly having to do with problems in his long engagement. Once more her reply is as revealing as any of her recorded statements about her philosophy and about her profession:

My keen sympathy with your present suspense makes me long that you should share my reliance on those old, old truths which shallow, drawing-room talk contemptuously dismisses as 'commonplaces', though they have more marrow in them, and are quite as seldom wrought into the mental habits as any of the subtleties that pretend to novelty. Never to beat and bruise one's wings against the inevitable but to throw the whole force of one's soul towards the achievement of some possible better, is the brief heading that need never be changed, however often the chapter of more special rules may have to be re-written.[36]

Here is a clear definition of her intellectual position, intermediate between optimism and pessimism, accepting the physical and social laws of life as proposed by Darwin, Spencer, and Comte, but intent on avoiding a passive fatalism, particularly with regard to moral questions, in the face of these inexorable laws. She draws on arguments she had found congenial in Spinoza and Feuerbach about the need to recognize and will the good of one's fellow human beings, to use one's sympathetic imagination as a co-member of the human species in order to promote the well-being of others, to temper egoism with altruism. The Oxford English Dictionary credits her with the first use of the word 'meliorism' to describe this philosophical position, quoting from a letter she wrote to the philosopher and psychologist James Sully in January 1877.[37] But her letter to Allbutt of December 1868, without using the word, already defines its meaning.

Once again, while writing in general terms to Allbutt, she also drew a personal inference. Her own tendency had always been mentally to 'beat and bruise' her wings against undesirable inevitabilities such as her plain looks, her temperamental and ideological clashes with her brother and father, the lack of active opportunities for an intelligent young woman. 'I know', she confided in Allbutt, 'through the experience of more than two thirds of my life the immense difficulty, to a passionate nature, of attaining more than a fitful exercise' of the required resignation. 'And especially I know (what you hint at) the blighting effect on the sympathies of an unsatisfied yearning for a supreme engrossing affection.'[38]

Young women sought George Eliot's advice and consolation too, and with the most congenial of these she was, in turn, a little confessional. Maria Congreve, who had looked up to her before knowing she was the author of *Adam Bede*, continued in her warm friendship. To her George Eliot wrote frankly in December 1870 of her own 'strong egoism' which had caused her so much melancholy and was traceable to a 'fastidious yet hungry ambition'.[39]

Two of her friends, Emilia Pattison and Georgiana Burne-Jones, were admiring young women with difficult marriages. We do not know how detailed their confidences were, but as with Oscar Browning she was sympathetic to their troubles, promising Emilia Pattison, for example, that she would 'talk over all affairs of the heart' when she saw her.[40]

Because Mrs Pattison's husband Mark was much older than she was, because she did not love him, lived separately from him much of the time, and – though George Eliot did not live long enough to know this – married again soon after his death in 1884, and because Mark Pattison was at work in the early 1870s on a life of the seventeenth-century French classical scholar Isaac Casaubon, it was thought by many that George Eliot based *her* Mr Casaubon on Pattison.[41] We know, however, that after *Scenes of Clerical Life*, in which a few portraits of real people appeared, and which caused her such problems with Gwyther, Liggins, and Bracebridge, she never again used an acquaintance as a direct model for a main character. Besides, she would hardly portray Mark Pattison as Mr Casaubon and still expect to remain friends with him. That is not to say, of course, that people she knew did not contribute in a myriad ways to her fictional creations, making with her wide reading and her large capacity for invention a rich mixture from which she fashioned her highly particularized characters and their circumstances.

American women wrote to George Eliot too. Some were famous, like Harriet Beecher Stowe, who asked about her religious views. George Eliot corrected her correspondent's impression that she had embraced pantheism. That belief, she replied, 'could not yield a practical religion, since it is an attempt to look at the universe from the outside of our relations to it (that universe) as human beings.'[42]

Others who approached her were comparatively obscure, like Harriet Peirce, wife of a Harvard lecturer, who wrote from Cambridge, Massachusetts. As an ambitious young married woman dissatisfied with merely domestic duties, she looked to George Eliot for sympathy. Again George Eliot was moved to personal confession, though her diffidence kept her from doing more than merely sketch her history in reply to Mrs Peirce's first letter in September 1866:

I was too proud and ambitious to write: I did not believe that I could do anything fine, and I did not choose to do anything of that mediocre sort which I despised when it was done by others. I began, however, by a sort of writing which had no great glory belonging to it, but which I felt certain I could do faithfully and well [i.e. translation].[43]

In August 1869 Mrs Peirce wrote again. This letter, unlike her first, has survived. It is worth quoting from to show how intense, passionate, sentimental, and unashamedly loving one woman, not evidently lesbian, could be towards another in the later nineteenth century. Mrs Peirce begins:

Dearest –
You will not be bored by another love-letter – a little one? It is three whole years since I wrote to you before, and you sent me such a grave, kind, precious little answer. O how wise thou art! Where didst thou learn it all?[44]

Jane Carlyle wrote and received such letters from women too. The patterns of female friendship at this time were many, but a predominant one was the idolatrous love of an unmarried woman for an older married one, such as Geraldine Jewsbury's for Jane Carlyle, and Edith Simcox's for George Eliot from their meeting in 1872. Edith's feelings *were* sexual, as her autobiography shows, but she accepted that George Eliot's were not. As has often been noted, George Eliot attracted the adoration of several women, a fact which is hardly surprising given her – somewhat problematic – status as a role model, the general veneration in which she was held, and the intelligent handling in her novels of situations which could be seen to belong to 'The Woman Question', though her more clear-sighted friends were rightly aware that her novels were not fictionalized propaganda.

Many women, married or not, had close relationships with other women, and in the days before Freud identified sexuality as the basis for all relationships they could talk and write unashamedly of their love for one another, as could members of the same family, for that matter. Some women had romantic, and possibly sexual, relationships, like Henry James's sister Alice, who lived with her friend Katherine Loring in what was known and accepted in society as a 'Boston marriage'.[45]

Barbara Bodichon's sister Annie lived with a female friend in Rome. Of the women who had collaborated with Barbara and Bessie Parkes on the *English Woman's Journal*, some lived in relationships with other women. Matilda Hays, for example, was the long-term companion of Lady Monson, who left her husband almost immediately after her marriage. Eliza Lynn Linton, also separated from her husband, took a younger woman to live with her in the 1870s. They, too, gravitated towards Rome, where Matilda Hays was then living in a group of English and American female artists and actresses.[46] Of these partnerships some were sexual, some probably not.

In other words, relationships between women existed along a spectrum from shared sexual lives to loving but asexual friendships, much as they do today. The difference is that the language of love was much more widely used in the nineteenth century than it is now for female friendships which have no sexual element. We should bear this in mind as we see George Eliot become increasingly involved in friendships and correspondences which seem odd to our more liberated yet more suspicious and more easily embarrassed sensibilities.

Harriet Peirce's letter to George Eliot continued with extravagant expressions of love and of jealousy that so many of her townspeople – 'the Nortons, Harry James Jr' – had met her idol, while she had not. 'Darling,' she went on, 'The Spanish Gypsy made me sad, it was so noble: the poetry was so beautiful, but must noble women always fail? Is there no sumptious [*sic*] flower of happiness for us?'[47] George Eliot's reply to this, if she sent one, has not survived.

Mrs Peirce's question about noble women was prophetic of the response to Dorothea's relative failure to achieve her ambitions in *Middlemarch*. George Eliot's answer would have been, we can be sure, a meliorist one. But this is to anticipate, since in August 1869, when Harriet Peirce wrote, Dorothea had not yet been created. Suffice it to say that ideas about women's function, rights, and duties were prominent as George Eliot cogitated her great novel. She herself had thought long and hard on these questions, and had aired them in her essays fifteen years before, as well as in her novels, particularly *The Mill on the Floss* and, more distantly because of the fifteenth-century setting, *Romola*.

Now public events were catching up with George Eliot and her fellow liberals. In October 1869 all Barbara Bodichon's and Emily Davies's hard work came to fruition with the opening in Hitchin, Hertfordshire, of Girton College. George Eliot and Lewes donated copies of their books to the library of the new college.[48] The Married Women's Property Bill, for which Barbara had long campaigned, was brought in during 1869, becoming law in 1870; John Stuart Mill's ground-breaking work, *The Subjection of Women*, appeared in 1869; and the first great Education Act, advocating universal elementary education, was passed in 1870, a by-product being the opening up of the teaching profession to large numbers of women.

A new Working Women's College, on the model of the Working Men's Colleges which had been in existence for some years, was being planned by one of George Eliot's acquaintances, Elizabeth Malleson. George Eliot pledged a modest annual two guineas for its support. When Elizabeth Garrett Anderson opened her Hospital for Women on Euston Road in 1872, Marian and Lewes subscribed, sending their two guineas each year to that cause too.[49]

Lewes's diary for 13 July 1870 noted that Marian had had an idea for a dramatic sketch: 'Woman's triumph – losing her voice & obliged to sink into insignificance.' This was 'Armgart', a short dramatic poem on that topical subject, woman's lot. George Eliot finished it in September.[50] Though it peters out in a weak ending, this is the strongest of George Eliot's shorter poems, rising to counterpointed eloquence in places as it dramatizes the fate of Armgart, the successful opera singer whose voice is ruined.

Armgart is that thing of horror to so many men, that thing George Eliot had confessed to Mrs Peirce that she had been, a proud and ambitious woman. Graf Dornberg, who wants to marry her, thinks 'too much ambition has unwomaned her'.[51] His proposal of marriage requires her to renounce her career, since

> A woman's rank
> Lies in the fulness of her womanhood:
> Therein alone she is royal.

To which Armgart replies that if Nature decrees that women should be wives and – uniquely – mothers, Nature has also in her case given her a voice and the ambition to use it:

> I am an artist by my birth –
> By the same warrant that I am a woman:
> Nay, in the added rarer gift I see
> Supreme vocation.[52]

She further declares:

> The man who marries me must wed my Art –
> Honour and cherish it, not tolerate.

And when the Count replies bitterly that such a man has not yet lived, she returns a strong, if scornful, reply:

> Seek the woman you deserve,
> All grace, all goodness, who has not yet found
> A meaning in her life, nor any end
> Beyond fulfilling yours. The type abounds.[53]

Armgart falls prey to a throat disorder; her wonderful voice is wonderful no more. Friends urge her to marry now. She talks bitterly of her refusal to sink into ordinariness, to succumb to 'The Woman's Lot: A Tale of Everyday'. Her female cousin points out the unpleasant pride of this, referring to her own role as satellite to the queenly Armgart, which the latter had been happy to accept. Armgart crumbles, and the poem ends with her seeking a humble life as a singing teacher.[14]

The problem of what a woman is to do remains unsolved. George Eliot must have thought while writing this poem how lucky she had been to find a man who was happy to 'wed her Art' when her vocation became clear. But then, as she always said, her own case was peculiar, for the main choice, that between motherhood and a profession, was one she did not really have to make. It may well have been a sacrifice for her to renounce having children, but it was one demanded of her not by the fact of her wishing to pursue her writing career – the one profession capable of being combined with wifehood and motherhood in any case, as was proved by Elizabeth Gaskell and Margaret Oliphant – but by the social pressures of her position with Lewes. The concerns aired in 'Armgart' touched on George Eliot's own experience, of course, but were not its direct expression.

The same is true of the story George Eliot began at the beginning of November 1870, 'Miss Brooke'. Dorothea is at once introduced as 'a marriageable girl' with an unusually theoretical mind and noble aspirations, these being elements in her character which, as the narrator remarks ironically in what eventually became the first chapter of *Middlemarch*, 'tended to interfere with her lot, and hinder it from being decided according to custom, by good looks, vanity, and merely canine affection'.[15]

By 31 December George Eliot had written a hundred pages of her story. She noted in her end-of-year journal that 1870 had been a year of illness and slow progress but also of feeling 'unspeakably happy, loving and beloved'.[16] She and Lewes had been pleased to hear in September of Bertie's engagement to Eliza Harrison, the daughter of an English colonist in Natal. Since Thornie's death, they had worried about him being alone so far away.[17] At home, Lewes's mother had died on 10 December, sitting peacefully in her chair.

Like most English people from Queen Victoria down, George Eliot followed with interest the progress of the Franco-Prussian War, begun in July 1870. Britain took a neutral position, but sympathy was at first with the Prussians until accounts of Prussian cruelty at the siege of Paris in December swung public opinion towards the French. Lewes wrote to Adolf Stahr and his wife Fanny Lewald in September that he and Marian felt 'bound by many a grateful thought to German friends and to the German people', but that they also pitied the sufferings of the French.'[58] By January 1871 George Eliot was describing the war as 'hellish' and declaring her loss of sympathy with the Germans: 'No people can carry on a long fierce war without being brutalized by it, more or less.'[59]

The momentous joining of her two stories into one novel, *Middlemarch*, went unrecorded in George Eliot's journal, which has very sparse entries for the year 1871. On 19 March she records having reached page 236 of her novel, and is afraid she has 'too much matter'.[60] Nevertheless, she was now set on her complex interlocking plots, with the first link occurring in chapter 10 when Dorothea's uncle Mr Brooke invites to dinner not only the country gentry belonging to his own circle but also the chief people – i.e. men – of middle-class Middlemarch. Here Mr Vincy the manufacturer and mayor, his brother-in-law the Evangelical bank manager Mr Bulstrode, and the lawyers and doctors of the town mingle with their social superiors from the surrounding county.

George Eliot's anxiety about the volume of matter she had in her mind grew till Lewes found a way of accommodating her need for more than the usual three-volume format. On 7 May he asked Blackwood to consider a new mode of publishing which would circumvent the circulating libraries, with their reliance on three-volume novels, and make people '*buy* instead of borrowing'. The plan, taken, Lewes said, from the example of Victor Hugo's long work *Les Misérables*, was to bring the novel out in eight parts at two-monthly intervals, each part costing five shillings.[61] The first part would be called 'Miss Brooke' and would consist of chapters 1 to 12, dealing mainly with Dorothea and her engagement to Casaubon, but introducing Lydgate, the Vincy family, and their rich old uncle Featherstone.

Blackwood agreed to try the experiment (though he had declined a similar suggestion made twenty years before by Bulwer Lytton for his overlength work, *My Novel*[62]), and also accepted Lewes's suggestion that George Eliot should be paid a royalty of two shillings on every copy sold of each five-shilling part.[63] Book I was to appear at the beginning of December.

Lewes's separate negotiations with the American publisher Osgood & Co. caused Blackwood some annoyance, since the novel was to appear there in weekly instalments, beginning in November. Blackwood naturally feared that copies of the first of these short instalments would travel back to Britain and steal the thunder of the larger parts appearing at two-monthly intervals here. On the other hand, he accepted that the expectation and excitement this would create around *Middlemarch* might enhance its British sales. He stuck admirably to his principle of not quarrelling with his author, or even with his author's shrewd husband-cum-business manager.[64]

This principle, of which Blackwood was justly proud, was in his mind in the summer of 1871 for another reason. Edinburgh was celebrating the centenary of Scott's birth, and Blackwood gave a speech at the dinner on 15 August. In it he alluded to Scott's well-known stormy relations with his publishers. Blackwood was able to say that his own experience with his authors was not like this; his authors were among his dearest friends. As he wrote with pardonable vanity to Lewes in September, 'I had the feeling myself that nobody could have said what I did, and said it so truly.'[65] Lewes had already told William Blackwood that Marian, on reading a copy of Blackwood's speech, had cried out at this passage about his authors being his friends, 'I am sure it was *their* fault if they were not so.'[66]

She and Lewes had hoped to be in Edinburgh themselves for the Scott celebrations, but her health was too precarious; in the autumn of 1871 she had a serious intestinal disorder. But she had been touched and honoured to be invited.[67] When a new correspondent began to write to her in August she found herself telling him that her 'worship' of Scott was intimately connected with her memory of life with her father after Chrissey and Isaac had left home:

I was able to make the evenings cheerful for him during the last five or six years of his life by reading aloud to him Scott's novels. No other writer would serve as a substitute for Scott, and my life at that time would have been much more difficult without him.[68]

The new correspondent was Alexander Main, a young man who lived in Arbroath on the east coast of Scotland. Main wrote rapturous praises of *Romola* and *The Spanish Gypsy*, and soon asked if he could compile a volume of extracts from George Eliot's works, illustrating her wit and wisdom. Blackwood, who published the work in January 1872, was amused by the idolatry of the young man, who was soon nicknamed 'the worshipper of genius' and 'the Gusher' in the Blackwood office.[69] But he was careful to keep this sardonic merriment from George Eliot, who was not inclined to laugh at Main's reverence for her genius. Lewes, who once upon a time would have made fun too, encouraged Main because he saw how Marian's confidence was boosted by his adoration. It was Lewes who first suggested the title of Main's work, *Wise, Witty, and Tender Sayings of George Eliot*.[70]

Whatever his views of Main and of George Eliot's weakness in soaking up Main's gushing, Blackwood saw well enough the strength of her genius in *Middlemarch*. On 31 May he visited the Leweses at Shottermill, near Haslemere in Surrey, where they had taken a cottage for several months while Owen Jones supervised alterations at the Priory. He left with the manuscript of Book I ('Miss Brooke'), which he thought 'filled to overflowing with touches of nature and character that could not be surpassed'.[71]

On receiving Book II, 'Old and Young', which sets up multiple tensions between Dorothea, her older husband, and his second cousin, the young Will Ladislaw, and among the younger Vincys and their uncle Featherstone, whose fortune Fred Vincy hopes to inherit, Blackwood wrote on 20 July, 'You are like a great giant walking among us.' His admiration for her sureness of touch in presenting all sorts and conditions of men – and women – knew no bounds. 'Where did you hear those horsey men talking?' he asked, referring to the horse-dealers who get the better of Fred Vincy – for all his expensive university education – in the sale of his horse.[72]

As the eight instalments of the novel appeared between December 1871 and December 1872 – the last three Books coming at monthly instead of two-monthly intervals – Blackwood and others found themselves marvelling more and more at George Eliot's imaginative inwardness with so many kinds of people and so many walks of life. Lewes reported to Alexander Main in December 1872 that Sir James Paget had been astonished at her command of medical detail:

He could not understand how the author had not had some direct personal experience – it seemed to him that there must have been a biographical foundation for Lydgate's career. When I told him that she had never even known a surgeon intimately, and had no acquaintance in any degree resembling Lydgate, he said it was like 'assisting at the creation – a universe formed out of nothing!'

While the medical men are surprised at the medical fidelity the lawyers are expressing their astonishment at the ingenuity and correctness of the Law. And all of us wonder at the insight into Soul![73]

The consensus was that this was George Eliot's greatest novel, though many readers still loved *Adam Bede* best for its pastoral charm and some found the conclusion of *Middlemarch* too pessimistic for their liking. But all agreed that its publication marked an epoch in English literature and the history of the novel. As with *Adam Bede*, to which he had responded freshly and admiringly when he knew nothing of its author, so now, as he read each instalment of the manuscript, Blackwood was a reliable indicator of what the public's response would be. In September he reported that his wife and daughter had read Book VII and felt excited to be 'ahead of the rest of the world'.[74]

Such testimony to the real excitement aroused by *Middlemarch* as came from Blackwood, from Main, and from other friends, kept Marian going through renewed intestinal illness and the usual authorial despair. As she told Blackwood after reading his praise of Book III, all the enthusiasm was wonderful, but of course the book was not yet finished. 'I am thoroughly comforted as to the half of the work which is already written – but there remains the terror about the *un*written', she wrote.[75]

A month later, on 13 February, the heroic Lewes told Blackwood that she was very low. 'Reading "Felix Holt" the other morning made her *thin* with misery,' he wrote graphically. She felt she 'could never write like that again and that what is now in hand is rinsings of the cask! How battle against such an art of ingeniously self-tormenting?'[76] How indeed?

Lewes's way, which perhaps confirmed George Eliot in her bad habit of indulging in despair but which certainly encouraged her better habit of transcending it triumphantly, was explained in a letter to a new correspondent at this time. Elma Stuart was a young widow living in France with her son. In January 1872 she sent a carved book-slide and letter, thus beginning a feverishly adoring correspondence which lasted till George Eliot's death. Elma booked the plot next to George Eliot's grave in Highgate Cemetery, where she was buried in 1903 with the inscription 'Elma Stuart, whom for 8½ blessed years George Eliot called by the sweet name of "Daughter"'.[77] George Eliot replied pleasantly to her first letter on 1 February 1872; on the same day Lewes wrote too, explaining his principle of protecting George Eliot from both direct criticism and direct praise of her work, though of course he actually filtered the latter through to her in large quantities.

The problem for Lewes was twofold. George Eliot was only too ready to believe adverse criticism and, Armgart-like, think of giving up altogether if she could not do exceptional work. But if praise came in too strong doses, particularly while a book was still being written, the burden of her readers' high expectations might have the same un-desirable end result. Lewes's explanation to Elma Stuart might sound equivocating, even disingenuous, but it gives a true picture, I believe, of the complex personality of the woman he lived with, for whom un-certainty about her work was a condition of life:

She has long passed beyond that stage of authorship in which *praise* – public or private – is regarded as the desirable end; and indeed very little praise of the direct kind ever reaches her, for I rigidly exclude all public criticism from her sight, and when friends or acquaintances are disposed to be complimentary they are turned over to me, who have stomach for any amount of eulogy on her (it can't hurt *me*, you know!)

But while she is at once sceptical of praise and averse to be constantly 'chewing the cud' by having her works talked about to her, she is proportion-ately affected by *sympathy*, and grateful for all acknowledgment of influence such as your letter so sweetly expresses.[78]

As for *Middlemarch*, the work she feared represented mere 'rinsings of the cask', Blackwood's prophecy in his end-of-year letter on 31 Decem-ber 1872 that its publication 'will be one of the events by which 1872 will be remembered' was fully realized.[79] The novel set a limit, as Henry James wrote in his review of *Middlemarch* in 1873, 'to the development of the old-fashioned English novel'.[80]

Reading *Middlemarch* is an extraordinary experience. All human life is there, and George Eliot shows great architectonic skill in bringing to-gether the disparate elements of her plots and sub-plots, in revealing the 'stealthy convergence of human lots', the 'slow preparation of effects from one life on another' which she invokes in chapter 11.[81] This is done partly in terms of discoveries about a character's past life or certain connections which are found to exist through previous mar-riages and surprising wills and codicils to wills. Such complex inventions are an important element of the plot, as they are of Dickens's comparable panoramic masterpiece, *Bleak House*.

Thus Will Ladislaw turns out to be not only the grandson on his father's side of Mr Casaubon's aunt, a fact which is known from the beginning, but also the grandson on his mother's side of a Mrs Dunkirk who was the first wife of Mr Bulstrode before he came to Middlemarch. Since Bulstrode's second wife is Harriet, sister of the mayor Mr Vincy and therefore aunt of Rosamond and Fred, this brings Will, the eternal outsider of the novel, into connection with the heart of Middlemarch. The process by which Will and the rest of Middlemarch find out this relationship to Bulstrode involves the unmasking of the latter's guilty past. When Bulstrode is consequently brought low, so also is Lydgate, another incomer to Middlemarch, because Lydgate and Bulstrode are partners in the management of the Fever Hospital, because Lydgate is married to Rosamond Vincy, and because Bulstrode has lent him money.

Such plot connections and discoveries do much more than contribute to a good story, satisfying the reader's desire for mystery and revelation, important though that function is. When George Eliot talks in chapter 11 of the hidden connections between people, she has particularly in mind the not yet apparent link of human sympathy between her two chief centres of consciousness, Dorothea of the original 'Miss Brooke' story and Lydgate of the original Middlemarch story. Dorothea is as yet unaware that Lydgate will need help in his trouble. Later, when she has endured an unhappy marriage to Mr Casaubon and recognizes Lydgate's similar marital misery, she seeks, despite class distinctions, unkind rumours, and the disapproval of her cautious, haughty friends, to help him clear his name. Having 'beaten and bruised her wings against the inevitable' in the form of Mr Casaubon's cold, miserable, egotistical jealousy, Dorothea enacts in her kindness to Lydgate that attempt to 'achieve some possible better' which George Eliot had enunciated to Clifford Allbutt as her living creed.

Dorothea thus carries in her fully realized fictional self and circumstances George Eliot's long-meditated philosophical and moral ideal. What makes *Middlemarch* a morally inspiring rather than moralistic novel in connection with Dorothea, however, is the complete imaginative vision George Eliot has, and holds, of her. Unlike Romola, she is not an ideal, remote figure. She lives and breathes and commits errors; she is laughed at, criticized, pitied, and admired. She suffers and survives, and her heroism towards Lydgate is as believable as her naïve notion at the beginning that because Mr Casaubon is a scholar and not garrulous, he is therefore a deep thinker and an admirable man, or her belief that it would be a great thing to marry a modern Milton or Hooker (both of whom had notoriously unhappy marriages).

For his part, Lydgate, while still a newcomer with bright ideas for reforming the medical provision in Middlemarch, initially takes no interest in Dorothea, whom he thinks after their first meeting 'a little too earnest' for a woman. George Eliot renders his thought processes with a neutrality instinct with anticipatory irony:

The society of such women was about as relaxing as going from your work to teach the second form, instead of reclining in a paradise with sweet laughs for bird-notes, and blue eyes for a heaven.[82]

This careless thinking about the ideal function of a wife works in Lydgate to make him susceptible to marriage with Rosamond, a woman who appears all softness and feminine beauty, but who has her own strong desires, which turn out to be tragically incompatible with Lydgate's.

Both Lydgate and Dorothea are exquisitely rendered compounds of character reacting to circumstances, making their marital mistakes through a combination of innate tendencies to illusion and stubbornness and the limitation imposed by the petty but tenacious conventions of society, 'the hampering threadlike pressure of small social conditions', as George Eliot describes the Middlemarch environment with reference to Lydgate.[83] For Dorothea, the problem has to do chiefly with her gender: what can a woman *do* in life? For Lydgate, it has to do with the difficulties of carrying through reforms in a society 'as slow to be set on fire as a *stomach*', as Marian had written pungently eighteen years before when discussing the probable reaction in England to her translation of Feuerbach's revolutionary *Essence of Christianity*.[84]

To take Lydgate first. He is a much more successfully rendered reformer than Felix Holt, since he is not required to be ideal in respect of character or opinions, nor does he have to become involved in a 'major' event such as a riot. On the contrary, Lydgate's gradual succumbing to failure as he alienates his fellow medical practitioners, partly through their jealousy, slowness to accept new ideas, and anxiety about losing patients, partly through his own tactlessness and pride, and partly through the confused thinking of the general Middlemarch mind as to the benefits and results of one prescription or diagnosis rather than another, with rumour and ignorance speeding the passage of (mis)-information from person to person – all this, gradually built up and viewed from every conceivable point of view, is infinitely more satisfying and exciting, in ways now moving, now ironic, now comic, now tragic, than any more ostensibly exciting single event such as a riot could be.

In this respect *Middlemarch* is that very rare thing: a successful historical novel. In fact, it is so successful that we scarcely think of it in terms of that sub-genre of fiction. Here, as in no other novel, the historical period – in this case the years 1829 to 1832 – has been thoroughly absorbed and made indissoluble from, yet subordinate to, the lives and fates of individual characters. George Eliot's remark in chapter 3 of *Felix Holt* about private lives being determined by a wider public life finds its complete embodiment in *Middlemarch*. We are so involved imaginatively in Lydgate's particular struggles with the recalcitrant surgeons and apothecaries, complicated by his mistaken notions about women and money, that the whole social and intellectual background to his struggles comes alive too.

George Eliot's reading of source material was, as ever, thorough, but her incorporation of the material was more complete, more admirably invisible, as it were, than had been the case with *Romola* or even *Felix Holt*. She studied the early numbers of the *Lancet*, founded in 1823 by the radical Thomas Wakley, who argued for rationalization of the medical profession, which was characterized at that time by appallingly low standards. There was great ignorance and much rivalry between the different ranks: physicians – the highest ranking members, who scarcely ever practised surgery or dispensed drugs – surgeons, apothecaries, and general practitioners such as Lydgate. But Lydgate, unlike his Middlemarch rivals, has studied in Edinburgh and Paris, the two centres of advanced thinking about medicine in the 1820s.

Edinburgh produced most of the medical pioneers of the nineteenth century – Joseph Lister; Robert Liston, who first used ether in surgery at University College Hospital in London in 1846, but who had studied and practised in Edinburgh; James Syme; and James Simpson, first user of chloroform in 1847.[85] It was in Edinburgh in the late 1820s that the surgeon Robert Knox bought corpses for dissection from the notorious Burke and Hare, who were found guilty of murdering vagrants to keep Knox supplied. Burke was hanged in January 1829 after Hare had turned Crown witness. George Eliot puts her knowledge of the famous case to perfect use. Lydgate asks permission to do an autopsy – a new, daring, and much disputed procedure which only became legal in 1832 – on a Mrs Goby. What is more natural than that Middlemarch opinion, already suspicious of the arrogant newcomer, should leap to conclusions:

There would be no limits to the cutting-up of bodies, as had been well seen in Burke and Hare with their pitch-plaisters – such a hanging business as that was not wanted in Middlemarch![86]

Lydgate's use of the microscope and the stethoscope, following recent innovations among Parisian doctors and scientists, is equally a matter for reactionary opinion to chew over.[87] George Eliot shows her complete mastery of the subject, and, more importantly, of its possibilities in a novel about complex human relationships, when she adds to the ignorant suspicion of Lydgate's methods among some Middlemarchers the equally ignorant support won by his successful diagnoses among grateful but woefully untrained patients. Lydgate is as embarrassed by his defenders as he is irritated by his opponents.

Lewes said to Mary Cash, née Sibree, in 1873 that George Eliot forgot nothing that came 'within the curl of her eyelash'.[88] She forgot nothing, and she adapted her experiences in a myriad ways. Thus she shows Minchin and Sprague, the two rival physicians already established in Middlemarch, as bitter enemies who nevertheless combine against Lydgate and his innovations.[89] Had not Susanna Chapman and Elisabeth Tilley, natural rivals for the attentions of Chapman, banded together to expel Marian Evans when she arrived at 142 Strand and threatened to monopolize those attentions?

And though George Eliot had presumably never attended a committee meeting of a Board of Health, she manages wonderfully to convey the bickering and manoeuvrings of the group which meets with momentous results in Middlemarch. In chapter 18 Lydgate arrives late and is required to give the casting vote in the appointment of a new chaplain to the Fever Hospital financed by Bulstrode and run by himself. Whichever way he votes, he will make enemies. This superbly narrated episode rests on the sure foundation of George Eliot's intelligence, understanding of human nature, and wide reading. It may also owe something of its flavour to youthful conversations with her father, who, as a member of the parish council under the chairmanship of the Revd John Gwyther, had known such manoeuvres during the appointment of a treasurer in 1834.⁹⁰

Her inwardness with hospital politics emanated from reading progressive works on medicine such as *A Treatise on Fever* (1830) and other works by Thomas Southwood Smith. She also had access, we know, to first-hand information about Smith's career as a medical reformer from Lewes and from Smith's granddaughter Gertrude Lewes.⁹¹ Charles Bray, too, may have contributed to the sure touch with detail in the book. He had direct experience of sitting on the board of the Provident Dispensary established in Coventry in 1830, when none of the resident doctors would have anything to do with it, and may have discussed the problems of the Dispensary with Marian in the 1840s.⁹²

As with medical reform, so with other important movements of the late 1820s – George Eliot took them as grist to her mill. The political reform movement provides Will Ladislaw with employment on the radical newspaper the *Trumpet*; it adversely affects Mr Vincy's manufacturing business, with unfortunate results for Rosamond's dowry. With the candidacy of Mr Brooke for a reforming Parliament, the old class distinctions of 'middle England' (suggested in the very title of the novel) begin to be broken down. The gentry are brought into new relations with manufacturing Middlemarch, as at the 'miscellaneous' dinner party given by Mr Brooke in chapter 10.⁹³ At this party the men of Middlemarch – bankers, lawyers, doctors, and the wealthier tradesmen – discuss the beauty and character of Miss Brooke, while the county women, Lady Chettam and the rector's wife Mrs Cadwallader, talk about the other centre of interest, Lydgate, and his new methods in diagnosis.

This dinner party with its several conversations, all rendered with wit and precision, performs many functions, for *Middlemarch*, though diffuse and panoramic, as its subtitle, *A Study of Provincial Life*, signals, is admirably economical in the multiple uses to which George Eliot puts a single episode such as this. Gentry and middle class meet together, making 'fresh threads of connection' as society undergoes change in the face of political reform.⁹⁴ County comes together with town, but no improbably sudden transformation occurs, for only the *men* of Middlemarch are present at the party. Mr Brooke, 'always objecting to go too far, would not have chosen that his nieces should meet the daughter of a Middlemarch manufacturer', Rosamond Vincy.[95]

Themes are struck which resonate throughout the novel: medical affairs, marriage (Dorothea's in particular), and the position of women. This last topic is dealt with indirectly, in the rather unpleasant weighing up of Dorothea's qualities by the jocular men of Middlemarch. They discuss her as if she were a horse about to run a race, betraying a pitifully low opinion of woman's function, and one which reflects back badly on their intelligence: 'A fine woman, by God!' 'Not my style of woman', and 'There should be a little devil in a woman' make up the sum of opinion among these red-faced middle-aged men.[96]

Such careless remarks jar in the ears of the reader, who knows that Dorothea aspires, however naïvely and vaguely, to do good in the world, mistakenly thinking that marriage to Mr Casaubon will give her the necessary freedom and opportunity. She is under an illusion. Her marriage to Casaubon is foolish, Quixotic, funny in a desperate way. The caustic Mrs Cadwallader, George Eliot's 'organ of depreciation', as Richard Holt Hutton called her,[97] points out the absurdity of Dorothea's marrying a middle-aged pedant whose life has been spent researching the 'Key to all Mythologies', trying to prove that 'all the mythical systems or erratic mythical fragments in the world were corruptions of a tradition originally revealed'.[98]

Mrs Cadwallader jokes about his coat of arms – 'three cuttle-fish sable, and a commentator rampant', and about his blood: 'Somebody put a drop under a magnifying-glass, and it was all semicolons and parentheses.' Her frank view of Mr Casaubon's potential as a sexual partner is that marriage to him is 'as good as going to a nunnery'. When Sir James Chettam, the disappointed suitor, exclaims in horror that Casaubon 'has one foot in the grave', Mrs Cadwallader answers in a flash, 'He means to draw it out again, I suppose.'[99]

This is wickedly funny, but George Eliot, having created the joke through her character, lets the wit work in the reader's mind in a complex mingling with sympathy and admiration for Dorothea, who after all is seeking, albeit gropingly, to break out of the stultifying role of the wife who is merely a wife, doing as all 'sane people' do, which is simply 'what their neighbours do'. In the first chapter George Eliot surveys Dorothea's unusual character – Puritan, narrowly educated, inclined to self-righteousness, yet generous, spontaneous, intent on doing good, though with little idea of how to set about it. In the absence of careers for women, her only hope is to marry someone whose work she can share. In this spirit she chooses Casaubon.

George Eliot looks at the question from all sides. In the course of a characteristic paragraph she shifts the point of view until the reader – assumed for maximum effect to be a man with the usual opinions about marriage – finds that his comfortable established notions have been subtly undermined by an ironic and surprising plea in favour of Dorothea in all her absurdity:

And how should Dorothea not marry? – a girl so handsome and with such prospects? Nothing could hinder it but her love of extremes, and her insistence on regulating life according to notions which might cause a wary man to hesitate before he made her an offer, or even might lead her at last to refuse all offers. A young lady of some birth and fortune, who knelt suddenly down on a brick floor by the side of a sick labourer and prayed fervidly as if she thought herself living in the time of the Apostles – who had strange whims of fasting like a Papist, and of sitting up at night to read old theological books! Such a wife might awaken you some fine morning with a new scheme for the application of her income which would interfere with political economy and the keeping of saddle-horses: a man would naturally think twice before he risked himself in such fellowship. Women were expected to have weak opinions; but the great safeguard of society and of domestic life was, that opinions were not acted on. Sane people did what their neighbours did, so that if any lunatics were at large, one might know and avoid them.[100]

Middlemarch is full of such passages of intellectual surprise. George Eliot, with her deep understanding of people's limitations and prejudices, presents these with sympathy, but turns the bright light of her sceptical, comparing intelligence on them too, so as to widen her reader's sympathies through understanding. To this end she uses irony and the shifting perspective, as in the paragraph just quoted, and she also introduces certain metaphors which illustrate the narrator's role as observer, as student of human nature and its conditions.

In chapter 6 she talks of applying, metaphorically speaking, a strong microscopic lens to Mrs Cadwallader's matchmaking, thereby revealing 'a play of minute causes producing what may be called thought and speech vortices to bring her the sort of food she needed'. It is in the same spirit of scientific observation that chapter 27 opens with the parable of the mirror:

Your pier-glass or extensive surface of polished steel made to be rubbed by a housemaid, will be minutely and multitudinously scratched in all directions; but place now against it a lighted candle as a centre of illumination, and lo! the scratches will seem to arrange themselves in a fine series of concentric circles round that little sun. It is demonstrable that the scratches are going everywhere impartially, and it is only your candle which produces the flattering illusion of a concentric arrangement, its light falling with an exclusive optical selection. These things are a parable. The scratches are events, and the candle is the egoism of any person now absent – Miss Vincy, for example.[101]

In this way George Eliot moves between consciousnesses, now getting under the skin of her fictional creations and rendering their sensibilities with the finest accuracy of detail, now standing back and observing their mistaken judgements, their petty selfishnesses, their partial understanding of themselves and others. Even the odious Mr Casaubon, with his facial moles, his noisy way of consuming soup, his stiff little speeches, and his shutting Dorothea out of the things that most concern him, is understood and pitied. 'Why always Dorothea?' is the famous opening to chapter 29, when the Casaubons have returned from their disastrous honeymoon in Rome. 'Was her point of view the only possible one with regard to this marriage?'

In spite of the blinking eyes and white moles objectionable to Celia, and the want of muscular curve which was morally painful to Sir James, Mr Casaubon had an intense consciousness within him, and was spiritually a-hungered like the rest of us.[102]

With that turn of her authorial attention, that all-inclusive pronoun 'us', George Eliot works her creative magic. By the time of Mr Casaubon's (admittedly convenient) death, we have come to feel pity for the 'damp despondency' of his 'uneasy egoism', his scholar's fear of critical ridicule from his peers, and his growing jealousy of his young cousin Will Ladislaw, all bright curls and sunny smiles in contrast to his ageing raylessness.[103]

Middlemarch convinces us that George Eliot, like Shakespeare, could enter imaginatively into the consciousness of every kind of human being. But there is good reason to think that she understood Casaubon particularly well. His temperament is an exaggerated version of her own; he is a witty but feeling satire on herself. Here is strong egoism, a 'fastidious yet hungry ambition', pride and self-doubt, and the terrible experience of 'laborious uncreative hours' spent in paralysing fear of a 'chilling ideal audience',[104] all known to the author as well as to her creation.

When Harriet Beecher Stowe asked her – what was she thinking of? – if Mr Casaubon was a portrait of Lewes, George Eliot responded frankly to the ludicrousness of this suggestion:

Impossible to conceive any creature less like Mr. Casaubon than my warm, enthusiastic husband, who cares much more for my doing than for his own, and is a miracle of freedom from all author's jealousy and all suspicion. I fear that the Casaubon-tints are not quite foreign to my own mental complexion. At any rate I am very sorry for him.[105]

George Eliot is sorry for Casaubon, but she is sorrier for Dorothea, married as she is to his helpless but smothering negativeness. Tolstoy famously opened *Anna Karenina*, begun the year after *Middlemarch* was published, with the proposal that all happy families are alike, but unhappy families are unhappy in different ways. He proceeds to illuminate the point with portraits of some more or less unhappy marriages. George Eliot does the same. Marvellous as the portrayal of the Casaubon marriage is, that of the Lydgate–Rosamond marriage is even more wonderful. Henry James in his rather uneven review of the novel thought that the 'most perfectly successful passages in the book' were 'those painful fireside scenes between Lydgate and his miserable little wife'. 'There is nothing more powerfully real than these scenes in all English fiction, and nothing certainly more *intelligent*.'[106]

James was right, though he may not have gone far enough when he limited his remark to English fiction. George Eliot is unmatched in her extraordinary ability to render dialogue upon dialogue, sometimes witty, sometimes tense, sometimes painful, sometimes amusing to the reader but not to the participants. There are dozens of strong conversations in *Middlemarch* – that between Mr Vincy and Mr Bulstrode, the chalk-and-cheese brothers-in-law, in chapter 13, for example; all the scenes featuring Mr Brooke and Mrs Cadwallader; those between Fred and Rosamond in chapters 11 and 12; the discussions, laced with professional rivalry, between doctors and lawyers; the conversations between

Dorothea and her husband, with his habit of giving an affirmative answer in a peculiarly negative tone of voice – but the strongest of all are the many painful conversations which mark the dreadful downward progress of the Lydgates' marriage.

Having begun with the foolish and arrogant expectation that Rosamond will provide adoration, rest, sweet music, and soothing beauty in the home when he returns from a hard day at the hospital, Lydgate has to learn that she has her wishes too, and that too often these do not tally with his. Time and again he loses his temper and leaves her self-righteously but quietly determined to do as she likes. 'What she liked to do was to her the right thing', and Lydgate finds that 'affection did not make her compliant'. Between them there is 'that total missing of each other's mental track, which is too evidently possible even between persons who are continually thinking of each other'.[107]

George Eliot shows that the physical attraction of two people can be strong, while temperamentally they are incompatible. Rosamond's cool thwarting of Lydgate's efforts to save money in order to pay the debts they have carelessly incurred leads him – in a beautifully appropriate metaphor – to survey her 'as if he were looking for symptoms'.[108]

Though most of the author's sympathy lies with Lydgate, whose marital mistake 'was at work in him like a recognized chronic disease'[109] (note the metaphor again), and whose energies are dissipated, so that he fails in his ambition to be a discoverer, a path-breaker in the profession, there is a sense of Rosamond's misery too. She is selfish, inflexible, narrow-minded, but some of the fault lies in her limited education and some in the fact that as a decorative young wife – the very thing Lydgate had thought he wanted – she has nothing to do.

Like Maggie Tulliver, like her admirable opposite Dorothea, Rosamond has no life outside the home, as even Lydgate recognizes after yet another degrading argument about money. He has 'a life away from home, and constant appeals to his activity on behalf of others'.[110] Not that Rosamond herself articulates this difference, or shows a desire to work. But George Eliot raises on her behalf as well as that of the aspiring Dorothea the pressing question of what a woman can do.

Thorough feminists were, and are, dissatisfied with the answer *Middlemarch* appears to give to that question. Dorothea must accept that her vocation, which she has never quite been clear about, except with respect to her plan for new cottages for the local farm workers, is to be reduced to being the supportive wife of 'an ardent public man', as her second husband Will Ladislaw sets out to be. The narrator strikes a pessimistic, or as George Eliot would have it, a melioristic note in the Finale, with its forward look to the future lives of the characters. 'Many who knew her', we are told, 'thought it a pity that so substantive and rare a creature should have been absorbed into the life of another' and be known only as a wife and mother.[111] Yet Dorothea's 'finely-touched spirit had still its fine issues, though they were not widely visible', says the even-handed, non-committal narrator.

The final sentence of the novel balances positives against negatives in a measured, finely calibrated way:

But the effect of her being on those around her was incalculably diffusive: for the growing good of the world is partly dependent on unhistoric acts; and that things are not so ill with you and me as they might have been, is half owing to the number who lived faithfully a hidden life, and rest in unvisited tombs.[112]

The question may be asked why Dorothea has to end up living a hidden life. Florence Nightingale, for one, pointed out that there was a woman 'close at hand, in actual life', an idealist and 'a connection of the author's, who has managed to make her ideal very real indeed'.[113] She meant Octavia Hill, sister of Gertrude Lewes, who was putting her public housing project into practice in London.[114] Florence Nightingale might equally have had herself in mind, or for that matter the author of *Middlemarch*, as an example of a woman who achieved the goal she set herself.

We might speculate about the reasons why George Eliot made Dorothea fail, but we ought to remember that Lydgate, too, fails, though he is a man with all the advantages that entails. Society must take some of the blame for his failure, at least, since it is not ready for his progressive approach to medicine. And Dorothea is restricted by social conditions too. She suffers, before her marriage, during it, and even in her wealthy widowhood, from 'the gentlewoman's oppressive liberty' which is no liberty at all, since she can do nothing without the approval of the men in her circle.[115]

In the end, however, we should remember that *Middlemarch* is a novel, an imaginative construct replete with paradox and multiple possibilities, not a position paper on the Woman Question or any other Question. It is too large, too complex, too great, too gloriously able to embrace the varying point of view, to be reducible to an argument on behalf of one group or another, though of course women and their relative powerlessness are undeniably at the questioning heart of this greatest of novels.

CHAPTER THIRTEEN

A New Departure:
Daniel Deronda 1873–6

Lewes had hoped that each part of *Middlemarch* would sell up to 10,000 copies. He was disappointed to find that sales were nearer 5,000 for each of the eight parts, though Blackwood thought this sale a good one. By December 1872 George Eliot had earned about £4,000. The four-volume edition, published in the same month at 42/–, and reprinted during 1873 in a cheaper format, sold another 3,000 or so copies. But the real success of the book, commercially speaking, came with the corrected one-volume edition, published at 7/6 in 1874. This edition sold 10,000 in several printings during 1874, and by 1879 more than 30,000 copies of the novel, including foreign editions, had been sold. George Eliot had earned about £9,000.[1]

George Eliot was glad of the opportunity to make corrections for the 1874 one-volume edition. In spite of Sir James Paget's admiration of her grasp of medical detail, she had blundered in describing the effect on Lydgate's eyes of his brief resort to opium during his troubles, and she now put this right.[2] She also made a subtle but significant change to the penultimate paragraph of the novel. The passage refers back to the Prelude, in which St Teresa of Avila is invoked as a type of the successful aspiring woman. While Teresa was born into a society in which it was possible, if exceptional, to reform a religious order, the Prelude predicts that Dorothea will be a less fortunate modern Teresa, born with 'a certain spiritual grandeur ill-matched with the meanness of opportunity' available and destined to be 'foundress of nothing'.[3]

This melancholy prediction from the Prelude is taken up in the Finale, in the original version of which George Eliot wrote of a society which 'smiled on propositions of marriage from a sickly man to a girl less than half his own age', as well as one which neglects to educate women out of their 'motley ignorance'.[4]

Critics were quick to exclaim that society, in the form of Dorothea's family and friends, certainly did *not* smile on her marriage to Mr Casaubon. Richard Holt Hutton pointed out reasonably enough, in his review of the four-volume edition in the *Spectator* of 7 December 1872, that this attempt to 'represent the book as an elaborate contribution to the "Woman's" question' was a mistake, 'meting out unjust measure to the entirely untrammelled imaginative power which the book displays'.[5] George Eliot saw the point, and dropped the passage in the 1874 edition. She retained a reference to society's partial responsibility for Dorothea's failure to do great things, but restricted it to the statement that the medium in which a Teresa could perform her 'ardent deeds' is 'for ever gone'.[6]

Though reviews of *Middlemarch* were enthusiastic and admiring, George Eliot could not help being disappointed by what Lewes let her see or hear of them. She told a Swiss admirer, Charles Ritter, in February 1873 that though *Middlemarch* had made 'a deep impression' and though its critics were 'as polite and benevolent as possible', none had satisfied her thirst for 'the word which is the reflection of one's own aim and delight in writing', 'the word which shows that what one meant has been perfectly seized, that the emotion which stirred one in writing is repeated in the mind of the reader'.[7]

This may sound greedy and ungrateful, in view of the almost universal acceptance by reviewers that *Middlemarch* was the finest novel of the age. Yet when one reads a selection of the reviews immediately after reading the novel itself, it is hard not to sympathize with George Eliot. For all their respect, the critics carp and snap at details; most pursue an appreciation of the main characters, often finding fault with the characterization of Will Ladislaw (George Eliot too soft on him) and Rosamond (George Eliot too hard on her). These judgements are not completely unjustified, but they are woefully inadequate as responses to the overwhelming excellence of the novel, even in passages where Will is let off the hook or Rosamond has the screw turned once too often on her selfishness.

Still, *Middlemarch* did take hold of its readers' imaginations, as both sales in the first two years after publication and personal responses to

George Eliot amply proved. Lewes was stopped by excited friends when he went to the London Library in January 1873; he reported to Black-wood that Pigott, Huxley, and other worthies of the Athenaeum Club were full of enthusiasm about the novel.[8] Letters from admirers poured in, and a new worshipper, Edith Simcox, who reviewed *Middlemarch* in the *Academy* in January 1873, became a dedicated Sunday visitor.

Edith was a gifted woman, sometimes embarrassing George Eliot with her importunate love, but liked and encouraged by Lewes, whom she in turn revered for his perfect love of his partner. And she did more than just hang around the Priory worshipping her idol. In 1875 she and a friend founded a shirtmaking firm for women workers, run-ning it on co-operative principles. Edith represented the Union of Shirt and Collar Makers at the Trades Union Congress held in Glasgow in October 1875, one of the first two women delegates to attend a Congress.[9]

George Eliot gave encouragement, and sometimes financial support, to an increasing number of women who were actively exploiting new possibilities in the wake of the recent reforms in the laws governing the education and property of women. She followed with interest the career of Octavia Hill and another young acquaintance, Jane Senior, who in January 1873 became the first woman to be appointed a Government Inspector. When Mrs Senior submitted her Parliamentary report on the education of girls in pauper schools the following year, George Eliot praised its 'fullness, clearness, and wisdom of suggestion'. She also commiserated with her friend's difficulties with prickly officials: 'As the old professor considered Sir Humphry Davy "a verra troublesome fellow" in chemistry, so a clear-eyed ardent practical woman may be found very troublesome as an inspector.'[10]

This Dorothea who *had* found a public role, despite opposition, was given a glimpse of George Eliot's innate caution in political matters. Her sensitivity to her own social position coincided with an ingrained conservatism, for all that it co-existed with intellectual and tempera-mental rebelliousness. The result was that she kept out of practical politics. 'Though I saw a great deal of the Poor in my early youth,' she told Mrs Senior in May 1874, 'I have been for so many years aloof from all practical experience in relation to them, that I am conscious of my incompetence to judge how far it would be wise to use existing arrangements rather than to try and supersede them.' Then, sounding like her father in his reports on poor tenants on the Newdigate Estate forty years before:

Do what one will with a pauper system it remains a huge system of vitiation, introducing the principle of communistic provision instead of provision through individual, personal responsibility and activity.[11]

She wrote in the same vein to Clementia Taylor in July 1874, praising her work in collaboration with Madame Belloc – for Bessie Parkes was now married and the mother of Hilaire Belloc – helping poor work-house girls. 'You see', she wrote, 'my only social work is to rejoice in the labour of others.'[12]

Her own youth was brought back even more forcibly to her mind at this time, for in April 1874 she and Lewes were visited at the Priory by Edith Griffiths, the eldest daughter of Isaac Evans. Edith was the first of his children to approach her aunt; she did so presumably without her father's knowledge. On 9 May George Eliot thanked Edith for some photographs she had sent of Griff House, still Isaac's home and formerly her own. 'Dear old Griff', she wrote; 'I seem to feel the air through the window of the attic above the drawing room, from which when a little girl, I often looked towards the distant view of the Coton "College" [i.e. the workhouse].'[13]

George Eliot's response to the change of ministry which occurred in February 1874 would have pleased her father and brother. Gladstone and the Liberals went out, and Disraeli came in with the first Conservative majority since 1841. 'Do you mind about the Conservative majority?' she asked Barbara Bodichon. 'I don't.'[14] But she and Lewes went on supporting the cause of social, educational, and medical reform. Lewes's list of their donations to charity at the end of 1873 is dominated, after regular gifts to family members – Agnes and her children, Bertie and his wife and baby daughter (called Marian), Lewes's sister-in-law Susanna and her son Vivian – by such progressive causes. They gave to Elizabeth Garrett Anderson's Hospital for Women, to the College for Working Women, to Girton, to Octavia Hill 'for distribution', and £50 to Cara Bray to help her publish a children's book intended to teach kindness to animals, Cara being a passionate member of the Society for the Prevention of Cruelty to Animals.[15]

Lewes's diary also records their ever-increasing investments in canal, railway, and gas companies in Britain and America. John Cross, with his banking experience in New York, was asked to invest the income from *Middlemarch* in American railway companies of his choosing.[16] George Eliot was now a rich woman, a fact which she and Lewes acknowledged by acquiring in December 1873 that grand symbol of wealth, a carriage of their own with the hire of 'man, horse, harness, and standing room for £140 a year'.[17]

These two, married in fact but not in law, originating from the non-professional middle class, and both without the benefits, social and intellectual, of a university education, now rode in a carriage and visited with the fashionable and the learned. Both Cambridge in the shape of Frederic Myers, Fellow of Trinity College and supporter of higher education for women, and Oxford in the person of Benjamin Jowett, Master of Balliol College, invited them to visit in the summer of 1873.

The trip to Cambridge in May 1873 was memorable for two reasons. George Eliot wrote a poem, 'A College Breakfast-Party', for her volume of poems the following year, a versified symposium of views about faith, science, God, love, and duty which probably draws on a breakfast which Myers held for her at Trinity. Questions about 'the social Ought' and its difficult relation to 'the individual claim' are raised, though in the – for George Eliot – straitjacket form of blank verse such questions have an unfortunate sonority and pomposity which was absent from their successful embodiment in the life of *Middlemarch*.[18]

Even more unfortunate for George Eliot's reputation in some quarters – particularly after her death, when acquaintances of both the worshipping and the irreverent sort, as well as some of the sort who first worshipped in her presence then sneered in her absence, took up their pens – was the wise saw attributed to her by Frederic Myers in a famous essay written soon after her death. Everybody has heard it, or heard of it. Myers wrote, thinking either of this visit or of another in May 1877:

I remember how, at Cambridge, I walked with her once in the Fellows' Garden of Trinity, on an evening of rainy May; and she, stirred somewhat beyond her wont, and taking as her text the three words which have been used so often as the inspiring trumpet-calls of men, – the words *God, Immortality, Duty*, – pronounced, with terrible earnestness, how inconceivable was the *first*, how unbelievable the *second*, and yet how peremptory and absolute the *third*. Never, perhaps, have sterner accents affirmed the sovereignty of impersonal and unrecompensing Law. I listened, and night fell; her grave, majestic countenance turned toward me like a Sibyl's in the gloom; it was as though she withdrew from my grasp, one by one, the two scrolls of promise, and left me the third scroll only, awful with inevitable fates. And when we stood at length and parted, amid that columnar circuit of the forest-trees, beneath the last twilight of starless skies, I seemed to be gazing, like Titus at Jerusalem, on vacant seats and empty halls, – on a sanctuary with no Presence to hallow it, and heaven left lonely of a God.[19]

Perhaps George Eliot did say what Myers reports her as saying; it certainly accords with her views. But she would have protested, with justice, at the way Myers has written up the speech, presenting her as an Evangelist of a new and gloomy Gospel. 'Taking as her text' suggests clergymen and pontification. 'Terrible earnestness' is Myers's impression. Her 'countenance' (not face); 'like a Sibyl' (what does a Sibyl's face look like?); 'in the gloom' (seeming to apply to George Eliot's speech as well as to the weather conditions in which she made it) – all these are calculated expressions, metaphorical and exaggerated, as is the further fanciful reference to the scrolls, suggesting Revelation, Apocalypse, a prophecy of doom. What a heavy weight Myers makes George Eliot bear. He is the first of many to apply the term 'Sibyl' to her, a term which so easily dismisses her from the ranks of ordinary humanity, not to mention excluding from view her considerable ability as a humorist.

If George Eliot's earnestness, and her very position as leading novelist of the day, made her liable to this kind of caricature, it should be pointed out that Myers, unlike others who employed the vocabulary of the high priestess or Sibyl, was not being intentionally comic at her expense. He was an admirer who nevertheless resented what he later called 'the mechanical theory of the Universe, the reduction of spiritual facts to physiological phenomena', to which she subscribed. Myers, who had also become agnostic for the same reasons as George Eliot, still needed a belief in something more than the here and now.

Myers was not the only man of his generation to resent and struggle against Darwinism and agnosticism, even while he honestly embraced them. Along with his Cambridge colleagues Henry Sidgwick and Edmund Gurney, both of whom knew and admired George Eliot, he founded in 1882 the Society for Psychical Research, believing that one could gain entrance to 'the Unseen' through clairvoyance, hypnotism, hallucination.[20] The movement was partly prophetic of Freud's experiments and discoveries, partly mixed up with the charlatanry of table-rapping and calling up of spirits at the *séances* which were fashionable in the 1860s and 1870s.

The Leweses coincided with Myers, and with Charles Darwin himself, at one such *séance* at the London home of Erasmus Darwin in January 1874. Lewes and Marian 'left in disgust' when the medium insisted on complete darkness.[21] Though George Eliot was respectful of the needs of others for some kind of faith, 'tricksy spirits' and charlatans who made money as mediums earned her scorn, as she carefully explained to Harriet Beecher Stowe, who had described in 1872 a 'weird and Brontëish' conversation she believed she had held with the spirit of Charlotte Brontë.[22]

If she was impatient with the spirit manifestations claimed by tricksters, George Eliot was not at all so with the beliefs of those who strove after some genuine but ideal object. In this fact lies, at least in part, the explanation of the otherwise surprising plan which began to form in her mind during 1873. This was her decision to concentrate the story of her next 'big book' on the aspirations of idealistic Jews to achieve in practice their vision of establishing a community in a Jewish homeland.

Emanuel Deutsch was a man with such a vision, but he did not live to see its fulfilment. In December 1872 he had set off once more for the East, having been given sick leave from the British Museum to go searching for respite, if not recovery, from cancer.[23] In May 1873 Deutsch died in Alexandria, released at last from his painful and hopeless life. He was undoubtedly in George Eliot's mind when she began to think, a month later, about her next work. The first mention of *Daniel Deronda* comes in Lewes's diary on 29 June 1873, where it appears as 'novel & play Deronda'.[24]

George Eliot had tried to comfort Deutsch in July 1871 by reminding him that 'it has happened to many to be glad they did not commit suicide, though they once ran for the final leap, or as Mary Wollstonecraft did, wetted their garments well in the rain hoping to sink the better when they plunged'.[25] Mordecai in *Daniel Deronda* shares with Deutsch a fatal illness and a desire for a Jewish homeland. His sister Mirah prepares to commit suicide in the Thames, as Mary Wollstonecraft did, by wetting her cloak.[26]

The Leweses were in Fontainebleau when they discussed this new work, which fortunately developed into a novel, not a play. A month later they had moved to Frankfurt, where they bought books on Jewish subjects and attended the synagogue. The first two weeks of August 1873 saw them in Bad Homburg, a spa they had first visited the previous September, when they had observed the gamblers gathered round the gaming tables at the casino. Marian had been struck then by the degraded nature of the scene, with 'hateful, hideous women staring at the board like stupid monomaniacs', as she told Anna Cross.

She had noticed in particular the great-niece of Byron playing obsessively, her 'fresh young face' incongruous among the 'hags and brutally stupid men around her'.[27] Lydgate had already been shown gambling feverishly and desperately on his own play at billiards at the Green Dragon in Middlemarch; in *Daniel Deronda* George Eliot called on her memory of the scene at Homburg to show Gwendolen Harleth playing the tables at the sophisticated European casino of Leubronn.

Once more George Eliot had set herself an ambitious task of preparation for a novel. She got deep into reading books of Hebrew poetry and Jewish history and scripture. On 5 November 1873 she gave Blackwood the first inkling that she was 'slowly simmering towards another big book', but she offered him no clue as to its subject.[28] Work was slow and hard because of the research, the anxiety about following the success of *Middlemarch*, the usual despair, and more than usual illness. Toothache, eye strain, and on 3 February 1874 the first of many painful attacks of kidney stone, the illness from which she would finally die, meant that by the end of 1874 she was less than a quarter of the way through the writing.[29]

Lewes was ailing too. Throughout their visit to France and Germany in July and August 1873 he suffered from deafness. George Eliot reported on 1 January 1874 that he was 'thinner than ever', though still showing his 'wonderful elasticity and nervous energy'.[30] The first volume of his *Problems of Life and Mind*, on which he had been working for several years, was published in January 1874 by Trübner & Co. It sold remarkably well. But Lewes had had his famous elasticity sorely tested by Blackwood, who had agreed to publish the work, even setting it up in print, but had pulled back at the last minute in May 1873, saying he could not publish a work which 'grated' so much on him in its treatment of religious faith.[31]

Blackwood saw in the book scorn for religion where Lewes intended only to lay out different modes of thinking. Lewes was annoyed at the waste of time and irritated by Blackwood's misunderstanding of his tone, but he wrote to say he was willing to treat the matter as buried, assuring Blackwood that nothing had changed in their relationship.[32] Ironically, he and Blackwood had slipped into the habit of calling *Problems* the 'Key to All Mythologies', with Lewes even joking about leaving an unfinished volume for his faithful Dorothea to see through the press after his death. Blackwood had written amusedly, before seeing the contentious first volume, that 'if the lamented Casaubon had written it' he would have insisted on his publishing at his own risk.[33]

On their return from France and Germany at the end of August 1873, Marian and Lewes heard that Lewes's old friend and partner Thornton Hunt had died. He was sixty-two, and had spent his whole life in busy but unremunerative newspaper journalism. Lewes now met Agnes in town to help her redeem the insurance policy Hunt had taken out for her.[34] This meant that Agnes was from now on more comfortably off, but Lewes continued his regular payments to her, as well as sending gifts from time to time for her children by Hunt.

In 1873 Lewes also sent money to his son Bertie: £50 to buy a piano and £25 for the baby Marian. He and George Eliot were pleased that Bertie was happily married, but worried to hear at the end of the year that his finances were precarious and he himself was unwell. Bertie's infrequent letters are short, awkward, almost the letters of a young stranger. He wrote on 29 October 1873 to thank Lewes for the money, promised to write more often, gave a staccato account of his farming business, and asked dutifully about his father's writing. Ominously, he remarked on his neuralgia, his having become 'quite a skeleton', and his being unable to sleep for pain.[35]

Bertie was following, in his quieter, less articulate and charming way, in the path of his brother Thornie. His death came on 29 June 1875. He had left his wife on their farm to go to Durban to see a doctor, and he died, aged twenty-nine, knowing that Eliza had borne him a second child, named George Herbert, in May.[36] Bertie did not live to see his son. After his death his young wife set about corresponding shyly with the famous namesakes of her two children, the parents-in-law on whom she now relied absolutely.

Charles, himself not strong physically, wanted to go to Natal to bring Eliza and the children back, but Lewes dissuaded him. As George Eliot told Sara Hennell, they were now 'naturally the more solicitous about

Charles, the only one left'. All the boys, she added, seemed to have 'inherited an untrustworthy physique' from their father.[37] Lewes himself had a foretaste of death on 14 December 1875, when he 'felt a strange pressure inside the ears accompanied by inability to move or speak. Thought paralysis had come on or Death.'[38]

Lewes was putting all his efforts into his ambitious work on the interaction of mind and body. Volume II of *Problems of Life and Mind* was published early in 1875, and he was working steadily on the next volume. He was also, more than ever, giving the necessary boost to George Eliot's confidence as she continued with *Daniel Deronda*. As had been the case for some years, she found it easier to make progress when they escaped from London and the burden – albeit a pleasurable one – of the Sunday *salons*, in order to spend four or five months in the country. The summer of 1874 was passed near Redhill in Surrey, from where George Eliot told the patient Blackwood that she was 'brewing' her 'big book with more or less (generally less) belief in the quality of the liquor which will be drawn off'.[39]

Getting away from London had always been desirable to Marian, who flourished in the country; it was becoming more than ever so since the publication of *Middlemarch*. For all her semi-reclusiveness and Lewes's well-known protectiveness, she was increasingly vulnerable to unwanted visitors and correspondents. As with all celebrities, members of the public felt they had an automatic right of access to her, as if she had been a museum or gallery. Moreover, because her novels were indisputably moral in tendency, sharing with readers a philosophical outlook embodied in the story, many thought their rights extended to receiving long replies, wise answers to their eager questions, and detailed responses to unsolicited gifts of their own poems or essays or novels.

One such correspondent was Marie Howland of New Jersey, who in May 1874 sent George Eliot her 'significant' work of fiction, *Papa's Own Girl*, demanding that George Eliot read and admire it, as was surely to be expected from one whom *she*, Marie Howland, was proud to 'honor and love'. George Eliot told Anna Cross about her long letter 'desiring my opinion' of this work, 'without a suspicion that I could have any reason for not eagerly devouring it'. She was inclined not to answer the letter, on the grounds that it seemed 'to indicate a self-estimate in no need of consolation'.[40]

The instinct for self-preservation shown here came to the fore again a few months later with reference to her own immediate family. She was in friendly contact with one or two members of the younger generation of Evanses. Her niece Emily Clarke, Chrissey's daughter, had long been a correspondent, and Marian's feelings towards her were warm, for her own and her mother's sake. In September 1874 she and Lewes went to Brighton to see Emily, who was teaching there.[41] A week or so later Marian received a letter from Robert Evans, son of her half-brother Robert. He was also well disposed towards her, and she towards him, since he had written kindly in 1864 to tell her of his father's death. Now Robert suggested that his aunt, George Eliot's half-sister Fanny Houghton, might be ready to meet the younger sister who had so shocked the Evans family, first by her refusal to attend church, and then – much more seriously for Fanny – by her relationship with Lewes.

George Eliot replied that while she appreciated Robert's good intentions, it was 'too late' for such a meeting. Fanny had ceased to communicate in 1857, and had never since sent 'the slightest sign of remembrance'. 'Those who willingly renounce a friendship cannot after a long lapse of years recover it at a given moment.'[42] As people often do, George Eliot found it hard to forgive the hurtful actions of her own generation, while as if in mitigation of her unforgivingness in that direction, she warmly welcomed the friendship of the next generation.

Besides, as she told Robert, he might be mistaken in his supposition that Fanny would want to see her. In this respect, her negative instinct may well have been right. Certainly Fanny's response to hearing of her brilliant sister's death in 1880 was less than understanding. She dwelt at length in a letter to Isaac of January 1881 on 'Mary Ann's' unfortunate position and the consequent embarrassment to the family. With all the certainty of complete ignorance she further declared of Lewes: 'That man spoiled her life.'[43]

In 1874 George Eliot was already enjoying – if that is the word – glimpses of the kind of thing that would be said and written after her death. The importunate author of *Papa's Own Girl*, writing in May, alluded to her having sat at the feet of Herbert Spencer.[44] She had presumably read a biographical volume such as the one deliciously entitled *Men of the Time*, which had an entry on George Eliot in every edition from 1862.[45] Each new edition of the work added to the number of mistakes in the entry, according to which she was, by the time the 1875 edition appeared, the daughter of a *poor* clergyman, the adopted daughter of a *rich* clergyman, the pupil of Herbert Spencer, and the intimate friend of John Stuart Mill.[46]

No wonder she shuddered at the thought of what biographers would do to her after her death. Not only could she see such hashes being made of the simplest (and least controversial) details of her life while she was still alive and able to correct them, but she and Lewes were reading at this time an example of what happens to a great writer once he is dead. The third volume of John Forster's *Life of Dickens* (1872–4) had just been published. George Eliot told Blackwood she was saddened by the 'melancholy aspect' of Dickens's later years with their 'feverish pursuit of loud effects and money'. (There was nothing in the biography about the much more troublesome business of Dickens's relationship with the actress Ellen Ternan.)

But worse almost than the unattractive but undeniable facts themselves was their being paraded for all to read:

Is it not odious that as soon as a man is dead his desk is raked, and every insignificant memorandum which he never meant for the public, is printed for the gossiping amusement of people too idle to re-read his books?

Then, quoting Tennyson:

> He gave the people of his best:
> His worst he kept, his best he gave.[47]

If George Eliot shivered at the thought of her life being left in the unsafe hands of future biographers, Tennyson was even more alarmed, as the poem from which she quotes, 'To —, After Reading a Life and Letters' (1849), amply shows. Stanzas four and five give full expression to the writer's fear and advance resentment of posterity's curiosity:

> For now the Poet cannot die,
> Nor leave his music as of old,
> But round him ere he scarce be cold
> Begins the scandal and the cry:

> 'Proclaim the faults he would not show:
> Break lock and seal: betray the trust:
> Keep nothing sacred: 'tis but just
> The many-headed beast should know.'

The biographer's reply might be that 'the best', in the form of the writer's works, survives biography, while 'the worst', in the form of the life, or aspects of the life recoverable by biography, is usually no worse than the worst that could be said or written of anyone. This defence could hardly be expected to offer much consolation to the subject, perhaps. Yet the desire to write, and to read, biography arises in the first place out of admiration for the achievements of that subject. Of course George Eliot's books are her 'best'. Just because they are so, we are interested in the life from which they emerged.

And, though the biographer necessarily feels uncomfortable at George Eliot's metaphor of raking the desk for memoranda not meant for the public eye, an interest in such rakings is not, as she proposes in her letter to Blackwood, automatically a *substitute* for reading, or re-reading, the works. The topic is one on which, one suspects, the subject and the biographer could never be in complete agreement, unless they were one and the same person.

Daniel Deronda was published, like *Middlemarch*, in eight parts. After some discussion with Blackwood it was agreed that these should come out monthly, rather than every two months, and the new novel duly appeared between February and September 1876, George Eliot keeping always two or three months ahead of publication. This meant she was less harassed and frightened about getting behind with copy than she had been when writing *Middlemarch*.

But she was nervous. She knew that in taking on the large task of presenting Jewish history and prophecy, and of creating a group of contemporary Jewish characters ranging from East End pawnbrokers to the philosophical visionary and scholar Mordecai, she was doing something which might not succeed either as art or in the favour of her readers who, she foresaw, would groan at the departure from their beloved English provincial life. As she wrote in her journal on 12 April 1876: 'The Jewish element [which came mainly in the parts of the novel not yet published] seems to me likely to satisfy nobody.'[48]

George Eliot's anxiety took the extreme, if understandable, form of fearing to let her manuscript out of her hands. Blackwood's nephew William reported to his uncle on 21 April 1875 that when he visited in the hope of being given the first volume to take back to Edinburgh, he witnessed 'one of the most striking scenes' of his life. 'If you had seen her face of horror and fright and meek expression', he told Blackwood, 'you would have been startled.' 'She seemed just to tremble at the idea of the M.S. being taken from her as if it were her baby.'[49] William thought she would let it go when he visited again a few days later. But though he and Langford called on 25 April,[50] the manuscript was not yet given up.

Blackwood, meanwhile, having heard about his nephew's visit on 21 April, wrote to George Eliot from Edinburgh the very next day in his prompt, soothing, but remarkably uncloying way:

My Dear Mrs Lewes

Willie tells me he has had a long and most interesting visit at the Priory, the only drawback to which was that you were complaining of not feeling well and being depressed. I have seen that depression on you before at periods when other authors would have been crowing and flapping their wings without the solid reason which I am sure you have for doing so. I am quite elated at the prospect of Willie bringing down so large a portion of your new Novel and I feel your sending the M.S. to me in this way as a thing to be proud of. Curiously enough I was walking about with Theodore Martin yesterday when talking about you and Lewes; he mentioned how devoted the Queen was to your works, especially Adam Bede. So I told him how you had given me the M.S. of the first volume of Adam with strict injunctions not to read it until I could do so quietly at home and how I utterly disobeyed orders by peeping into the first pages on the top of the omnibus where Lewes deposited me at Kew and fastening upon it the moment I left King's Cross next morning until I finished my reading with delight before I reached Newcastle when night was setting in.[51]

Blackwood's winning reference to the success of *Adam Bede*, to his own excitement on reading it, and, implicitly, to the great moment for both author and publisher which had accompanied the handing over of that manuscript on Sunday 28 February 1858 in the rented rooms in Richmond – namely, the moment when she revealed herself to him as George Eliot[52] – did its work. On 18 May Blackwood himself had lunch with the Leweses, and left with the first part of *Daniel Deronda* in his hands.[53]

As usual, his response was brisk and encouraging. He sat up most of the night reading, and wrote immediately to congratulate the author on her success.[54] More than ever before Blackwood was an important precursor of the reading public in his response. Like them, he reacted heartily to a good story, interesting characters, and any amount of wit and wisdom on the part of the author. He was the true British reader, liking to see familiar things well done, suspicious of excess of any kind, yet aware that George Eliot had already succeeded with her previous novels in getting him to accept certain things against which his principles and prejudices would normally have cried out in protest.

Thus he had long ago accepted that her clergymen would not be patterns of behaviour; nor would they be seen much going about their strictly clerical duties, still less praying or having their relationship to God alluded to. Mr Gascoigne in *Daniel Deronda* is another shrewd portrait of a limited clergyman. He is shown as not dislikeable but not in the least admirable, being intent on the acquisition for his niece Gwendolen of wealth, land, and a good family name through her marriage with Grandcourt, while knowing of certain rumours about Grandcourt's sexual past and moral ruthlessness.

George Eliot goes further in this novel than in any of the others. Mr Gascoigne is, in fact, a debased version of the cleric, rendered exclusively in terms of his material greed and class snobbery and not at all as one who sees as his vocation the cure of souls. Though not vicious, he is the clerical equivalent of the undoubtedly vicious Grandcourt, that masterly negative and extreme type of the degenerate aristocrat.

Blackwood had learned, too, to accept what in a less intelligent, less responsible author would have been completely unacceptable to him, namely, the bold presentation of the sexual element in the relations between men and women. There had been the indirectly but potently suggested history of Hetty's pregnancy in *Adam Bede*, not to mention the sensuous scenes in the wood which made the pregnancy possible. There had been Maggie's dilemma over Stephen, Godfrey Cass's hidden marriage and fatherhood of Eppie, Tito's 'marriages' to both Romola and Tessa, and Mrs Transome's guilty secret of adultery with Mr Jermyn. *Middlemarch* had brilliantly shown the physical attraction between Lydgate and Rosamond and, more problematically, between Dorothea and Ladislaw, an attraction of which Will Ladislaw, at least, is fully aware long before the convenient death of the inconvenient Mr Casaubon.

Now George Eliot's two main protagonists, Gwendolen and Daniel, have a relationship which looks for all the world – and *to* the world – like an adulterous affair. Indeed, Gwendolen is in love with Deronda, and he, in a reprise of Maggie's emotional situation, is 'in love' both with her and with Mirah, the Jewish girl he has saved from suicide. George Eliot stretches her understanding – and ours – of the complexity and contradictoriness of human emotions and motives more in *Daniel Deronda* even than in *Middlemarch*.

In one of the many astonishing scenes between Gwendolen and Grandcourt – the proposal scene – she tackles the question of what love between two human beings can be said to be. In this case Grandcourt's chief motivation is the challenge of taming and conquering a spirited, masterful girl, as if she were a horse to be broken in, and Gwendolen's is a confused mixture of a desperate desire to avoid the fate of governessing for herself and genteel poverty for her mother and sisters, a dislike of being touched and caressed, and a disgusted awareness of Grandcourt's relationship with Mrs Glasher, on whom he has fathered four children.

That there is nothing ordinarily recognizable as love on either side here only renders the whole question more complex and interesting. Grandcourt, often described in terms of an inert reptile, a sleepy lizard, or 'neutral' alligator, exercises his negative spell on Gwendolen, who intends to reject him:

She spoke with dignity and looked straight at Grandcourt, whose long, narrow, impenetrable eyes met hers, and mysteriously arrested them: mysteriously, for the subtly-varied drama between man and woman is often such as can hardly be rendered in words put together like dominoes, according to obvious fixed marks. The word of all work Love will no more express the myriad modes of mutual attraction, than the word Thought can inform you what is passing through your neighbour's mind. It would be hard to tell on which side – Gwendolen's or Grandcourt's – the influence was more mixed. At that moment his strongest wish was to be completely master of this creature – this piquant combination of maidenliness and mischief: that she knew things which had made her start away from him, spurred him to triumph over that repugnance; and he was believing that he should triumph. And she – ah, piteous equality in the need to dominate! – she was overcome like the thirsty one who is drawn towards the seeming water in the desert, overcome by the suffused sense that here in this man's homage to her lay the rescue from helpless subjection to an oppressive lot.[55]

Despite her repugnance, Gwendolen has 'a momentary phantasmal love for this man who chose his words so well', and she accepts him.

His subsequent brutality to her, his breaking her in, is one of the most powerful and painful developments in all fiction.

The difficulty of deciding on the rights and wrongs of actions and motives is embodied in the dénouement of this dreadful marriage. Grandcourt drowns in the sea near Genoa, and Gwendolen, who has wished his death, thinks she may have contributed to it. She tells Deronda, her mentor and secular confessor:

I don't know how it was – he was turning the sail – there was a gust – he was struck – I know nothing – I only know that I saw my wish outside me.

In the confusion of the moment, as she confusedly remembers it, Grandcourt called for a rope to be thrown to him, 'and I held my hand, and my heart said, "Die!" – and he sank.'[56] The impossibility of being certain of cause and effect in relation to one's own motives recalls *Middlemarch* and the dilemma of Lydgate when Raffles dies under his care, and Bulstrode's equivocation about whether to let Raffles be given alcohol against Lydgate's orders. In *Daniel Deronda* George Eliot prepares for Gwendolen's crisis as early as chapter 4, when, prophetically employing a nautical metaphor, she says of the play of contrary tendencies in a character: 'A moment is room wide enough for the loyal and the mean desire, for the outlash of a murderous thought and the sharp backward stroke of repentance.'[57]

George Eliot, more than most novelists, makes it her vocation not only to show character in action, but to interpret it in all its complexity. She is also of all authors the one most eloquent on the point that all interpretation is approximate, liable to error. Gwendolen interprets Grandcourt's silences and short drawlings as rich in meanings flattering to herself, as Dorothea had interpreted Mr Casaubon's stiff speeches as delightful learnedness. All George Eliot's characters are engaged in interpreting the signs emanating from their fellow creatures, whether words, looks, gestures, or actions, and it is in the nature of things that they often misinterpret these.

People are enigmas to one another. Yet interpretation must go on, despite the pitfalls. As the narrator of *Middlemarch* says in connection with Fred Vincy's futile attempt not to be outwitted by the horse dealers of the town:

Scepticism, as we know, can never be thoroughly applied, else life would come to a standstill: something we must believe in and do, and whatever that something may be called, it is virtually our own judgment.[18]

Interpreting phenomena is an activity doomed to partial failure but necessary to human life.[19]

In making Grandcourt the most negative, least energetic, least alive example of the class to which he belongs, George Eliot adds her critical voice to those of Carlyle in *Sartor Resartus*, Thackeray in *Vanity Fair*, and Dickens in *Bleak House*. All had depicted the English aristocracy at its most worthless – hunting, shooting, fishing, and putting in occasional stupid, lazy appearances in Parliament. All wished the institution as dead in fact as it was morally, though all, of course, made the personal acquaintance of individual members of the aristocracy whom they would except from the general anathema.

Grandcourt is a sinister degenerate, while other members of his class are merely silly. Mr Bult, 'the expectant peer', is a calculated caricature with entrenched, inherited political opinions and 'the general solidity and suffusive pinkness of a healthy Briton on the central table-land of life'.[60] George Eliot sets him up as a suitor for the hand of the heiress Catherine Arrowpoint; against him she ranges the eccentric Herr Klesmer. Composer and music tutor, a genius with opinions not tempered in their expression by awe of his social betters or the desire to be polite, Klesmer is 'a felicitous combination of the German, the Sclave, and the Semite, with grand features, brown hair floating in artistic fashion, and brown eyes in spectacles'.[61]

He is a little ridiculous in his earnestness and unabashed sentiment about the arts. But George Eliot cunningly sets him against insular pink Britishness in order to show up the worthlessness of the latter. Klesmer wins the argument about the importance of music beyond its social usefulness as an after-dinner amusement; his aspirations for an international accord in politics, if vague, look admirable beside Mr Bult's commercial and imperial outlook on Africa and the South Seas; and, against the odds, he wins the girl.

The Jewish Klesmer, one character we know she modelled in part on someone she knew – Anton Rubinstein, whom she had met in Weimar in 1854 and would meet again in May 1876 at a musical party given by Nina Lehmann, daughter of Lewes's old friend Robert Chambers[62] – is used strategically in *Daniel Deronda*. George Eliot introduces him in the early chapters to prepare the reader's mind favourably, or at least not unfavourably, for the two characters who carry the intellectual freight of the work, Daniel himself and the learned Mordecai, who, as Daniel finds out, is Mirah's brother. Through these characters and their spheres of action George Eliot builds up a radical alternative vision to the non-vision which characterizes British institutional life.

It is Jewish, idealistic, serious, religious. The ailing Mordecai, steeped in Old Testament prophecy and Hebrew teaching, seeks a friend to carry out in the East his political dream of founding a Jewish community, separate from non-Jews yet communicating with them, in a Palestinian homeland. It is a remarkable fictional prophecy of the influential work twenty years later of the Zionist Theodor Herzl, author of *Der Judenstaat: Versuch einer modernen Lösung der Judenfrage* (*The Jewish State: Attempt at a Modern Solution to the Jewish Question*), published in German and English in 1896. There is an interesting foretaste, too, of some elements of the distinction made in 1887 by Ferdinand Tönnies between *Gemeinschaft* (community) and *Gesellschaft* (society). In his *Gemeinschaft und Gesellschaft* Tönnies defines the first as organic, traditional, and religious, and the second as urban, heterogeneous, deracinated.[63]

Here, it seems, is George Eliot's answer to those who had criticized *Middlemarch* for its pessimistic representation of society and the fate of admirable individuals caught in society's tight mesh. Here is a novel with a forward thrust, a positive vision – positive in both the ordinary and the Comtian sense of renewing society in a post-Christian era. But it puzzled readers then, and may puzzle us still. Why must we turn our backs on British society in order to find a positive future? Is there no renewal from within? And why does an agnostic, one who respects the need for religious belief in others but repudiates it for herself, set out, without irony, a religious ideal? Moreover, is the history of Judaism any less fraught with superstition, narrowness, exclusiveness than that of Christianity? Certainly when she had translated Feuerbach in 1854 George Eliot had agreed with his analysis of Judaeo-Christian authority as pernicious in many respects, not least on the question of egotistical exclusiveness.

It is true that Mordecai and Daniel stress not Jewish exclusiveness so much as 'separateness and communication',[64] the cherishing of a precious heritage without the need in future for secrecy and the misunderstandings with the Gentile communities which have followed in the past from Jews existing in small groups, isolated and only more or less tolerated within larger Christian societies. Still, it is surprising to find George Eliot engaging so deeply with a vision she did not – could not – actively share.

Her intellectual curiosity, her genuinely transnational interests and a concomitant dissatisfaction with average British insularity in cultural, social, and political matters, and her desire to penetrate imaginatively a new and different community from those she had previously depicted, combined to make her try this altogether new subject. (New, that is, with the exception of Disraeli, by an interesting irony Conservative Prime Minister of insular Britain while *Daniel Deronda* was being written. In his earlier manifestation as novelist, Disraeli had created in *Coningsby* (1844) the romantic idealized Jew, Sidonia, with his insistence on the culture of the race and its importance as a precursor of Christianity.)

A reply to a query from Harriet Beecher Stowe in October 1876 gives vent to George Eliot's frustration with the thoughtless but insidious anti-semitism she has observed:

Can anything be more disgusting than to hear people called 'educated' making small jokes about eating ham, and showing themselves empty of any real knowledge as to the relation of their own social and religious life to the history of the people they think themselves witty in insulting? They hardly know that Christ was a Jew. And I find men educated at Rugby supposing that Christ spoke Greek. To my feeling, this deadness to the history which has prepared half our world for us, this inability to find interest in any form of life that is not clad in the same coat-tails and flounces as our own lies very close to the worst kind of irreligion. The best that can be said of it is, that it is a sign of the intellectual narrowness – in plain English, the stupidity, which is still the average mark of our culture.[65]

A few days later she wrote to Blackwood that she had wanted in *Daniel Deronda* to 'widen the English vision a little'.[66]

The choice of the Jewish ideal for her subject had one advantage which she may not have articulated to herself. It liberated her from certain difficulties she would have faced had she tried to envisage a better British society in this, her only work set in the near-present, rather than the past. She shrank from party politics, as well as from systematic

Positivism. By choosing a vision which was hers only by imaginative adoption, she avoided being harnessed to any cause closer to home, whether Comtist, Marxist, universal suffragist, feminist, or any other. Unlike Disraeli, who had openly declared in the 1849 preface to *Coningsby* that he had chosen the novel form as the best means of 'scattering his suggestions' and 'influencing opinion', George Eliot was artist first, opinion-former second, and party politician not at all. As she said to one correspondent in January 1876, 'My writing is simply a set of experiments in life.'[67]

Experiments in form too. George Eliot offers a motto to the first chapter which alerts us to the question of chronology and beginnings. The motto has reference both to the form a narrative may take and to the enlarged time scale to be envisaged within the novel that follows:

Men can do nothing without the make-believe of a beginning. Even Science, the strict measurer, is obliged to start with a make-believe unit, and must fix on a point in the stars' unceasing journey when his sidereal clock shall pretend that time is at Nought. His less accurate grandmother Poetry has always been understood to start in the middle; but on reflection it appears that her proceeding is not very different from his; since Science, too, reckons backwards as well as forwards, divides his unit into billions, and with his clock-finger at Nought really sets off *in medias res*. No retrospect will take us to the true beginning; and whether our prologue be in heaven or on earth, it is but a fraction of that all-presupposing fact with which our story sets out.[68]

Then follows the famous opening – 'Was she beautiful or not beautiful?' – the question asked about Gwendolen by Deronda, who is watching her play at the gaming tables of the fictional European resort of Leubronn. The two meet fleetingly but significantly, whereupon Gwendolen is summoned home by a letter from her mother informing her of the family's financial ruin. Her return is the signal for the narrative to go back and fill in Gwendolen's life up to the time of the stay in Leubronn. George Eliot shows great organizational skill in this novel of forward-looking and backward-looking, the very technique serving the overall purpose of stretching our imaginations to accept the fitful interaction, the separateness yet communication, between the Jewish characters clustered around Deronda and the English gentry and Wessex aristocracy of Gwendolen's world.

Her skill has not always been fully recognized. Contemporary reviewers were inclined to separate the 'English part' from the 'Jewish part', usually approving enthusiastically of the first and more or less regretting the second. In a letter to Barbara Bodichon of October 1876 George Eliot expressed her irritation with those who 'cut the book into scraps and talk of nothing in it but Gwendolen'. 'I meant everything in the book to be related to everything else there', she stated firmly.[69]

When F. R. Leavis gave George Eliot a very high place in the history of fiction in *The Great Tradition* (1948), he too expressed reservations about *Daniel Deronda*, proposing, to his later regret and recantation, that a good novel about Gwendolen Harleth could be extracted from it by 'cutting away' the Deronda part.[70] But George Eliot's claim to have written a much more tightly connected whole than was generally recognized is justified. Though the two chief centres of consciousness, Gwendolen and Daniel, are apart for much of the time, a metaphorical vocabulary is quietly but repeatedly used to connect them.

In the second chapter Deronda redeems a necklace Gwendolen has pawned after losing at roulette, and returns it to her. Thereafter the vocabulary of loss and gain, of gambling, and of redemption recurs in meanings and contexts both literal and metaphorical, in relation to episodes in both their lives. The gamble of Gwendolen's acceptance of Grandcourt, the 'gain' she thereby makes out of the loss to Mrs Glasher, her viewing Daniel as her secular redeemer, are such elements. So are Daniel's relations with Mirah, whose life he saves, and with Mordecai, whom he replaces as a missionary, and the depiction of the losses and gains involved in Daniel's discovery of his Jewishness from his mother, who has also gambled, weighing the advantages for herself of a career as a singer over motherhood and the advantages for her son of being brought up as an English gentleman over living as a Jew.

Ironic and inverted parallels also abound. Daniel saves Mirah from drowning; Gwendolen lets her husband drown. Grandcourt, like a much more dark and dangerous Darcy, arrives among the Wessex gentry as the 'prefigured stranger'[71] in the minds of all the local families with marriageable girls – how similar to the social satire of *Pride and Prejudice* the early part of *Daniel Deronda* is, yet how indicative of a different perspective, a going far beyond the perfect observation of polite English society. A cruel mockery of a marriage is the result of the elegant wooing of Grandcourt and Gwendolen, not a fraught but finally fairy-tale romance like that between Darcy and Elizabeth Bennet in Jane

Austen's novel. The phrase 'prefigured stranger', employed ironically with reference to Grandcourt, is picked up without irony to refer to Deronda, 'the prefigured friend' of whom Mordecai dreams and whom he sees one evening rowing on the Thames.[72]

Daniel, glad to discover his Jewishness, is to carry out the mission for the dying Mordecai, marrying Mirah, because love and duty coincide there. Daniel's role in the novel is an extension of that sketched for Will Ladislaw in *Middlemarch*. It is a difficult type to make flesh – one about whose birth and antecedents there is some mystery, a semi-outsider, a young man unfixed in terms of his career who has to be shown as rather indeterminate, because his sphere of action is postponed beyond the action of the novel. Much less immediately attractive or interesting than a strong but flawed heroine such as Dorothea or Gwendolen, or a strong but flawed hero like Lydgate, Daniel is more like a Wilhelm Meister, an insipid youth to whom things happen for most of the plot.

George Eliot tries to make us inward with Daniel, for, unlike Goethe with his hero (or Scott with his young men), she does not want us to find him insipid. But as Richard Holt Hutton rather shrewdly said in his *Spectator* review in September 1876, for most of the novel we are 'rather being prepared to make acquaintance with Deronda than actually making acquaintance with him'.[73] Robert Louis Stevenson burst out in a letter of 1877 against 'that melancholy puppy and humbug Daniel Deronda', the 'Prince of Prigs: the literary abomination of Desolation in the way of manhood'.[74] More temperately, Leslie Stephen thought Deronda, like Stephen Guest in *The Mill on the Floss*, too much a woman's hero.[75]

If Deronda made readers feel dissatisfied, Mordecai made them truly uncomfortable. Blackwood was the first to express, however diplomatically, his difficulty on reading Book V, entitled 'Mordecai', in which we are taken into the world of Jewish culture and history, and shown Mordecai's aspirations. 'Of Mordecai', Blackwood wrote evasively, 'I feel that it would be presumptuous to speak until one has read more.'[76] George Eliot replied that she had expected him to feel doubtful. Her aim, she said, was to achieve 'an outline as strong as that of Balfour of Burley', the stern fanatical Presbyterian in Scott's *Old Mortality*.[77]

The example of *Old Mortality* is adduced in the novel itself, when Daniel's friends are preparing to be introduced to Mordecai, 'whose conversation would not be more modern and encouraging than that of Scott's Covenanters'.[78] Mazzini, too, the Italian patriot who had won the hearts of so many English people, despite his fanaticism and broken English, is invoked as a hook to help the reader get a grip on Mordecai.[79]

If we are forced to admit that none of this ultimately makes Mordecai live in our imaginations, we must add in justice to George Eliot's achievements that he fails by the very highest standards of fictional representation, standards raised to astonishing and unprecedented heights by George Eliot herself. It is because she managed a Dorothea, a Lydgate, a Gwendolen, and a Grandcourt that her less successfully realized creations dissatisfy us as much as they do. Balfour of Burley is no such failure, though he is as eccentric and preachy as Mordecai, because the fictional company he keeps scarcely ever touches the heights regularly inhabited by George Eliot's protagonists.

Blackwood, tipped off by Lewes that Marian had been 'damped' by his difficulty with Mordecai, swiftly wrote in praise of Book VI, 'She is *A Magician*.'[80] This was a much-needed tonic to her as she continued writing her novel. It was more than diplomacy on Blackwood's part, however, for when Joseph Langford muttered about Mordecai, Blackwood told him: 'She is so great a giant that there is nothing for it but to accept her inspirations and leave criticism alone.'[81]

In October 1876, with *Daniel Deronda* now published in full – the eight parts sold over 7,500 copies each – George Eliot wrote a letter of gratitude to her old friend and publisher. Unfortunately it has been lost, but Blackwood's reply survives:

Tears came into my eyes, and I read the passage at once to my wife who was sitting beside me when I received the letter. I look upon such expressions coming from you, as the very highest compliment that a man holding the position I do could receive, and I shall keep the letter for my children as a memorial that their father was good for something in his day. You are too good about my poor letters which I always felt to be too meagre and too few but I do look back upon our correspondence with pride and pleasure.[82]

George Eliot earned over £4,000 from the sales of the novel in parts, receiving the same royalty of 2/– per copy sold as she had for *Middlemarch*.[83] By the end of October Blackwood had negotiated to publish a complete edition of the novels, the Cabinet Edition, at first proposing an advance of £4,000, but agreeing to George Eliot's preferred method of payment by royalty on each volume sold. He confided to his nephew that it was just as well to agree to this, since 'it would have been a long time for £4,000 to come back'.[84] Though he did not indicate the fact to George Eliot, or presumably to anyone outside the firm, Blackwood seems not to have made a profit out of publishing George Eliot's novels, universally admired though they were.[85] Sales were good, but not exceptional.

What was exceptional, as Blackwood saw from her first novel to her last, was George Eliot's fictional genius. He was happy to have fostered it, fulfilling that always necessary function of the publisher to the top of his bent, as George Eliot's paradoxical strengths and weaknesses of temperament repeatedly required him to do. The fact of her writing that lost letter of gratitude, and Blackwood's modest, emotional reply, suggest an almost valedictory element in the relationship between author and publisher. Perhaps she felt more than the usual exhaustion after finishing a large book, with more than the usual disbelief that she would ever do another. Though they continued in their old relationship for the few years both had left to live, she did not, in fact, write another novel. Who knows what would have been her subject, and what its mode of treatment, if she had?

CHAPTER FOURTEEN

Last Years 1877–80

When Marian had finished writing *Daniel Deronda* in early June 1876, she and Lewes resorted once more to foreign travel for respite both from the writing and from people's responses to the published work. They planned to go to Italy, but by the time they reached Aix-les-Bains both were ill and they could not face further travel and the heat of an Italian summer. Instead, they spent several weeks at various resorts in Switzerland and the Black Forest, returning home on 1 September to mountains of post. As George Eliot wrote gloomily to Blackwood from Ragatz in Switzerland, Charles Lewes was sending them news after 'reading or sifting our letters and letting us know the obliging propositions of American editors (and English) to furnish the public with our biographies etc'. 'Doubtless', she added, 'the biographies will be given whether we furnish the facts or not – and we certainly shall not.'[1]

Meanwhile, she and Lewes were living quietly as tourists, choosing the least frequented places they could find and keeping deliberately out of reach of the world, though the world sometimes impinged on them, as when Lewes read in *The Times* of the recent deaths of two formidable women whose careers had at least symbolic connections with George Eliot's own. George Sand had died on 8 June, Harriet Martineau on 27 June.[2]

The pile of letters which awaited them at the Priory included an enthusiastic appreciation from the Principal of Jews' Theological College in London, Dr Hermann Adler, of the 'fidelity with which some of the best traits of the Jewish character have been depicted' in *Daniel Deronda*.[3] Many more such letters followed from Jewish readers at home and abroad. All were gratified at the dignity of her Jewish characters, and many were astounded at her knowledge of their history and religion. Lewes had written to Blackwood the previous year: 'You are surprised at her knowledge of the Jews? But only learned Rabbis are so profoundly versed in Jewish history and literature as she is.'[4] George Eliot was buoyed up by the generous response of these readers; it compensated in part for the 'repugnance or else indifference towards the Jewish part' shown by many non-Jewish readers.[5]

A rumour began to circulate about this time – thanks to some of the more reckless American visitors and their wretched biographies, furnished with facts or not, which George Eliot so resignedly deplored – that Lewes himself was Jewish. He put his finger on the reason in a letter to Richard Owen in December 1876:

Is it not psychologically a fact of singular interest that she was never in her life in a Jewish family, at least never in one where Judaism was still a living faith and Jewish customs kept up? Yet the Jews all fancy she must have been brought up among them; and in America it is positively asserted that *I* am of Jewish origin![6]

As clergymen, doctors, and lawyers had previously seen their professions portrayed with such an inward grasp of detail in George Eliot's fiction that they thought the author must either be, or be intimate with, one of them, so now Jewish readers assumed she must have had close contact with someone Jewish. Who closer to her than Lewes? Many non-Jewish readers also took up the notion, sometimes with a rather unpleasant tone. Lewes's erstwhile Bohemianism, his dark, vivacious looks and gestures, his not having been to a university, even the fact that he had acted the part of Shylock in the provinces in 1849, were taken by some contemporaries, and by more recent critics too, as indications of a Jewish origin.

Mathilde Blind, who published the first biography of George Eliot in 1884, a year before Cross's appeared, called Lewes 'the Wandering Jew', though she may have meant only that he was rootless in his youth. The printer Henry Vizetelly remembered Lewes in his memoirs of 1893 as 'a mean-looking little man of a decidedly Jewish type'; and more recently Richard Ellmann wrote vaguely in his book of biographical speculations in 1973 about Lewes's 'Jewish associations' and about his having played Shylock.[7]

And was there not a rumour running through society in *Middlemarch* that Ladislaw – taken by many to be modelled on Lewes – had on one side of the family a 'Jew pawnbroker' for a grandfather?[8] George Eliot is proved almost too astute about human nature in this instance. As in *Middlemarch* she shows how an uninformed gossiping remark about Ladislaw is taken up and passed on as fact, so Lewes now came in for the same treatment by association both during and after his lifetime. Not that he minded. He saw in the attribution to him of a Jewish background to which he could not lay claim yet another indication of his partner's all-inclusive imaginative success. 'What a stupendous genius it is!' he had enthused to Blackwood on the subject of her ability to capture the Jewish, as she had already captured the clerical and the medical, way of life.[9]

At the end of November 1876 they at last found the country house they had long searched for among the woods and lanes of Kent and Surrey. John Cross accompanied them on 29 November to Witley, near Haslemere in Surrey, where they saw and fell in love with the Heights, an imposing red brick house set in several acres, with a sweeping, south-facing view over a beautiful wooded valley. They bought it straight away for just under £5,000, intending to give up the Priory and settle there permanently.[10] This they did not in the end do, for after an experimental and idyllic summer at Witley in 1877, they decided reluctantly that it would not be warm enough for 'us chilly people' in the winter, and that they should keep their 'nest in town', as George Eliot told Clementia Taylor the following November.[11]

Various alterations and decorations were set in motion to make the Heights habitable for the summer months, and meanwhile Lewes and Marian settled down to another busy winter of socializing, despite a real deterioration in the health of both. Marian explained to an American correspondent, Elizabeth Phelps, that though she would like to cross the Atlantic to see friends there, Lewes's health forbade such a long sea voyage. She added: 'It is this that hinders me from carrying out my longing to go to the East', a longing she had first hoped to fulfil in 1874 when cogitating *Daniel Deronda*.[12]

Lewes worked quietly at the fourth volume of *Problems of Life and Mind*; Volume III, *The Physical Basis of Mind*, had come out at the beginning of 1877. But he continued to get weaker and thinner, though both he and Marian were more worried about her excruciating attack of kidney stone in February 1877.[13] They were nevertheless seen regularly at the popular Saturday afternoon concerts at St James's Hall, where Marian fell victim to more than one amateur artist among her fellow music lovers. Laura Alma-Tadema drew her on one of these occasions, as did Queen Victoria's fourth daughter, Princess Louise, executing a head and shoulders sketch on her programme on 16 March 1877.[14]

Two months later, on 15 May, Lewes and Marian met Princess Louise at a party given by the Liberal MP George Goschen, who had been First Lord of the Admiralty under Gladstone from 1871 to 1874, and was to be Chancellor of the Exchequer in a later administration under Lord Salisbury in the 1880s. Princess Louise asked particularly to be introduced to George Eliot. John Bright and T. H. Huxley were also there, and Lewes recounted the scene for Elma Stuart's benefit in the context of telling her in July that Gertrude had given birth to her third child:

Charles and Gertrude have got another daughter – we wanted a grandson, but the superior powers thought otherwise. Perhaps they thought with Huxley, in this sense. The other day at dinner Madonna was talking with Bright about woman's suffrage, and the Princess interposed with, 'But you don't go in for the superiority of women, Mrs. Lewes?' 'No.' – 'I think', said Huxley, 'Mrs. Lewes rather teaches *the inferiority of men*.'[15]

Richard Wagner and his wife Cosima, daughter of Liszt, were also in London during May. The Leweses invited them to the Priory, and attended several of Wagner's concerts and rehearsals, making no references now to their inability to appreciate his music.[16]

They paid their now annual visit to Jowett in Oxford in May, followed by the usual few days at Cambridge, during which time the servants moved their things down to Surrey, where they intended to 'camp experimentally' for four or five months.[17] Their neighbours at Witley were Sir Henry and Lady Holland; Tennyson had a summer residence a short coach ride away at Blackdown. Apart from making and receiving visits from these neighbours, and from the Cross family not far away in Weybridge, they meant to live a quiet life, but a very comfortable one. They had with them their servants, including the coachman, who brought up from the station their orders for fresh fish from the fishmonger at Waterloo Station every Wednesday and Saturday. Blackwood was invited to lunch on one of these days to share the fish.[18]

When Blackwood came, he thought the view over the Surrey countryside even finer than that from Richmond Hill. Lewes called it Paradise, and Blackwood took the opportunity to say to George Eliot that 'something should be born here'; the answer 'was in the nature of assent', he told his nephew on 25 June.[19] Blackwood meant a novel, of course, though he knew how exhausted George Eliot had increasingly become after each work was finished, and how long she took to simmer and brew before producing anything new.

Two or three short sketches for novels date probably from this time. One was the merest scribble on the back of a card calendar for 1876, using names recalled from her stay in the pension Plongeon in Geneva nearly thirty years before. A second fragment, rather longer than this, suggests another novel of English life set at the beginning of the nineteenth century and concerning the lives of some families living in 'our rich Central plain'. Robert Evans's career is remembered once more in the few sentences devoted to one Richard Forrest, 'not an ordinary tenant farmer', but 'a man of weight in his district' who 'in some quarters was held more of a power – in other words was more grumbled at by people who did ill for themselves – than the master of Longwater himself'.[20]

It is likely, however, that George Eliot knew she would write no more fiction. She was acutely aware of poor health and advancing age (though she was not yet fifty-eight in the summer of 1877), and she dreaded putting herself through another prolonged period of anxiety and depression. John Cross, who set up a net on the lawn at Witley and taught both Leweses to play tennis, received a telling reply to some question or hint of his about her next work. 'My dearest Nephew', she wrote – Cross was so addressed by Lewes too –

Which would you choose? An aunt who lost headaches and gained flesh by spending her time on tennis and Badminton, or an aunt who remained sickly and beckoned death by writing more books? Behold yourself in a dilemma! If you choose the plump and idle aunt, she will declare that you don't mind about her writing. If you choose the pallid and productive aunt she will declare that you have no real affection for her. It is impossible to satisfy an author.[21]

Her last journal entry of the year, on 31 December, takes a farewell not only of 1877, but of the journal itself, which was now full. It does more. George Eliot looks back on her career as reflected in the journal, and faces the consequences for the future of her past achievements as an author. The entry reads like a farewell to her art:

Today I say a final farewell to this little book which is the only record I have made of my personal life for sixteen years and more. I have often been helped by looking back in it to compare former with actual states of despondency from bad health or other apparent causes. In this way a past despondency has turned to present hopefulness. But of course as the years advance there is a new rational ground for the expectation that my life may become less fruitful. The difficulty is, to decide how far resolution should set in the direction of activity rather than in the acceptance of a more negative state. Many conceptions of works to be carried out present themselves, but confidence in my own fitness to complete them worthily is all the more wanting because it is reasonable to argue that I must have already done my best.[22]

At the beginning of 1878 London University opened its degrees to women; it was the first university to do so. George Eliot wrote to Barbara Bodichon on 17 January rejoicing at the news, and expecting Barbara to be pleased too at this sign of progress.[23] No doubt Barbara *was* pleased, though she would have been forgiven for regretting that Cambridge was so slow in this respect, despite the example of Girton College, which had moved from Hitchin to the outskirts of Cambridge in 1873. It was well into the present century before either Oxford or Cambridge awarded degrees to women.[24]

In her letter to Barbara George Eliot also mentioned Edison's new invention, the phonograph, 'which can report gentlemen's bad speeches with all their stammering', and which captured Tennyson reading his poetry, but not, alas, George Eliot reading her fiction. A few weeks later the Leweses had another brush with the future when they went into town 'to have the Telephone explained and demonstrated' at Bell's Telephone Office.[25]

For such ailing people, they undertook once more a formidable amount of entertaining and visiting during the spring of 1878. They attended the wedding of Tennyson's son Lionel at Westminster Abbey on 28 February, and were to be seen at concerts and dinners with fashionable people in the world of the liberal aristocracy, the arts, and the sciences. At the Goschens' house on 31 May they met the Crown Prince and Princess of Germany, Frederick William and Queen

Victoria's eldest daughter Vicky, who asked them to visit if they ever returned to Berlin.[26]

On 16 April 1878, slipped in with references to a musical party at Frederic Leighton's, is a mention in Lewes's diary that 'Polly read her m.s.'[27] This was not the new novel hoped for by the Blackwoods – 'When may we look forward to seeing or hearing of another fascinating book from Mrs Lewes?' wrote William Blackwood to Lewes on 16 May[28] – but her set of short essays-cum-character sketches, *Impressions of Theophrastus Such*. When Blackwood received the manuscript in November, he was surprised, not having heard much about it from the author. 'From the way she spoke I knew she was not idle', he told Langford on 24 November, 'but the M.S. came without beat of drum and you may guess my pleasure and surprise.' The essays 'seem desperately good, full of wit and wisdom'.[29]

So they are, though the wit is almost always subdued or bitter, and the wisdom a little heavily expressed. The character sketches – a disillusioned scholar, a social flatterer, an 'old-young coxcomb' who cannot believe he has got older and is no longer an amazingly precocious youth, and various other types of vain and self-deluded humanity – show George Eliot's habitual ironic intelligence and honest awareness of human conceit and smallness. Several, including that of Theophrastus himself, are partial self-portraits, if exaggerated or distorted ones. But they often leave a dull and bitter taste, being mere sketches of human limitations such as a Casaubon, a Tito, or a Bulstrode would have been if they had not been imaginatively embedded in a fully realized community and engaged in the shifting and dramatic interaction of a plot.

In short, it is in the nature of the minor genre to which *Theophrastus Such* belongs to lack plot, development, drama, light and shade, movement and feeling. What George Eliot elects to do here she does well, but none of her readers, from Blackwood on, could rejoice that she had chosen to do this rather than give them another novel.

Biographically, the Theophrastus essays are interesting. The last one, 'The Modern Hep! Hep! Hep!' – the title echoes the cry of the Crusaders on their mission to convert non-Christians, and was used by anti-Jewish rioters in Germany earlier in the century[30] – extends the effort in *Daniel Deronda* to 'widen the English vision' with regard to Jews. The first, 'Looking Inward', is a scrupulous self-description by Theophrastus, a bachelor with a 'cowardly shrinking from a candid opinion' of his works, a man who is his own fiercest critic, liking to 'keep the scourge in my own discriminating hand', but who knows that he may nevertheless be more conceitedly egotistical than truly self-critical.[31] Herbert Spencer, Mr Casaubon, and George Eliot herself come to mind in this connection.

In 'Looking Backward' George Eliot returns in the person of Theophrastus to her Midlands childhood. One cannot doubt the personal note at the end of this essay:

I cherish my childish loves – the memory of that warm little nest where my affections were fledged. Since then I have learned to care for foreign countries, for literatures foreign and ancient, for the life of Continental towns dozing round old cathedrals, for the life of London, half sleepless with eager thought and strife, with indigestion or with hunger; and now my consciousness is chiefly of the busy, anxious metropolitan sort.

Theophrastus goes on to talk of the many 'voluntary exiles' who have gone forth 'when they would willingly have kept sight of the familiar plains, and of the hills to which they had first lifted up their eyes'.[32] The author, too, was one of these.

We may also detect something personal in 'A Too Deferential Man', the sketch of one Hinze (equivalent of Tom, Dick, or Harry), described bitingly as a 'complimentary ape'. This man visits Felicia, a 'clever woman', and turns her, against her will, into a version of the Delphic Sibyl. He poses questions and elicits answers 'on the changes of Italian travel, on the difficulty of reading Ariosto in these busy times, on the want of equilibrium in French political affairs, and on the pre-eminence of German music'. She, 'in dread lest she should seem to be playing the oracle', becomes 'somewhat confused, stumbling on her answers rather than choosing them':

But this made no difference to Hinze's rapt attention and subdued eagerness of inquiry. He continued to put large questions, bending his head slightly that his eyes might be a little lifted in awaiting her reply.
'What, may I ask, is your opinion as to the state of Art in England?'[33]

The scene contains a mild but heartfelt plea – doomed not to be heeded, of course – from the woman who received visitors at the Priory on Sunday afternoons, perceived in equal measure as a goddess to be worshipped and as a sacrificial victim to be made fun of in a hundred letters and memoirs published when she was safely dead. *Impressions of Theophrastus Such*, though it contains this indirect attempt to prevent both worship and sacrifice, unfortunately added grist to the mill of the inevitable generation of iconoclasts which reacted in the 1890s to too reverent a view of the great George Eliot.

The image of a humourless high priestess grew among those who only read *about* her, or who had dim memories of *Middlemarch* being pessimistic, *Daniel Deronda* heavy, *Theophrastus Such* sibylline, and her later letters – as published selectively by Cross in his 1885 biography – sombre and self-righteous. George Eliot fell victim to a strong but not always fair reaction against 'the Novel-with-a-Purpose' (W. E. Henley, 1890); she was accused of an 'utter absence of feeling for form' (Arnold Bennett, 1896), and a 'lack of imagination' and 'predominance of intellect' (W. C. Brownell, 1901) – as if she had not triumphantly proved the compatibility, rather than opposition, of these two faculties. And from the leading critic of the turn of the century, George Saintsbury, came the remark in 1895 that the novels after *Silas Marner* were 'studies of immense effort and erudition not unenlightened by humour, but on the whole dead'.[34]

The fault lay equally with those who worshipped her. These people were as blind and deaf to her humour, her imaginative range, and her skill in plotting as were her detractors. Myers with his picture of an admirable but gloomy Sibyl, Cross with his awe of his wife's learning, the Comtians with their desire to appropriate her as their secular priestess and prophet, all were busily spinning the collective web of George Eliot's reputation as oracular wise woman.

In June 1877 Frederic Harrison had once more urged her to be the Poet of Positivism, which in a sense she already was, since her poem 'O May I Join the Choir Invisible', published in 1874 with her other poetry, had been used by Richard Congreve in a recent address to the Positivist School.[35] She had replied to Harrison with a combination of gratification and evasion – how else could she respond? – writing of the 'terrible pressure of disbelief' in her duty or right to speak oracularly on matters of faith.[36]

She was certainly not keen to contribute directly to the construction of a liturgy for Positivism. But of course she could not stop Congreve or Harrison or anyone else from appropriating her works to their own ends. 'O May I Join the Choir Invisible' *is* a kind of secular hymn, expressing the desire to live on after death 'in minds made better' by her presence, and to be associated, as she associated Dorothea at the end of *Middlemarch*, with 'a good diffused' in this world rather than with the personal spiritual afterlife of the Christian faith.[37]

The summer of 1878 was spent at the Heights. It was only the Leweses' second residence in their Surrey paradise, and it was their last. Blackwood was hoping they would visit him in his own golfing Eden at St Andrews, but George Eliot wrote on 30 July to say that Lewes was too unwell to contemplate the journey.[38] Blackwood, himself in ill health, tried to persuade them that the change would do Lewes good, to which Lewes himself replied in tones reminiscent of his sons writing home from Africa. 'You do not realise my state', he wrote starkly. 'If I could even read an amusing book for three hours I should consider myself strong enough to come. But I can't work at all, – and can't read for more than an hour.' With characteristic lack of self-pity, he ended the letter with the assurance that 'we look forward eagerly to better luck next year'.[39] He probably knew it was not to be.

But Marian did not see, or did not dare to recognize, that Lewes was dying. Throughout the summer she told friends about his biliousness, gout, cramps, and headaches, but she wrote too that he was 'as joyous as ever' in their lovely surroundings.[40] John Cross, whose mother was also in her last illness, visited when he could, later recording both Lewes's sudden bouts of pain and his 'extraordinary buoyancy of spirits' as soon as the pain was gone.[41] At the end of October the Leweses visited Cross's brother-in-law William Hall on his estate at Six Mile Bottom near Newmarket. Also there was Turgenev, whom Lewes had first met in Berlin in 1839, and who had visited the Priory several times during his trips to London in recent years.[42]

In mid-November Lewes and Marian went to Brighton for a few days to see Emily Clarke and to be out of the way while the servants got the Priory ready for their return to London.[43] In Brighton Lewes suffered from piles – 'very bad', as he noted laconically in his diary.[44] Back in London, they went to the Saturday concert on 16 November, where they heard music by Mozart and Schubert. 'Came home feeling very unwell', Lewes noted.

Though he was 'much worse' the next day, Lewes saw his nephew Vivian, who brought his fiancée Constance to lunch. Lewes's sister-in-law Susanna had asked for his help, since Constance's parents were

GEORGE ELIOT: A LIFE

against the marriage. Lewes, who had helped support Susanna financially since his brother Edward's death at sea in 1855, wrote to Constance's father to urge him to recognize the engagement.[45] He was also still busy in his role as Marian's agent, writing on 21 November to Blackwood what was probably his last letter. Appropriately, it sends a new George Eliot manuscript – *Theophrastus Such* – with the suggestion that if Blackwood likes it, it will make a 'handsome volume' at 10/6. The last sentence puts his concern for Marian above his anxiety about himself: 'She is pretty well, but horribly anxious about me.'[46]

Lewes had spent the last few days and nights in agony. Sir James Paget visited almost daily. By 25 November Marian was facing her worst fears. On that day she wrote briefly to Blackwood, saying Lewes was 'sadly ill' and suggesting that publication of *Theophrastus Such* could be deferred for a time. She also wrote to Barbara, confessing, 'I have a deep sense of change within, and of a permanently closer companionship with death.'[47]

Lewes died shortly before six o'clock on the evening of Saturday 30 November 1878. He was sixty-one. Charles was there, and immediately set about informing friends. Paget certified the cause of death as enteritis, but, as Charles told one of Lewes's oldest friends from the *Leader* days, Edward Pigott, he had a cancer which would have become more and more painful, 'and would have carried him off within six months'.[48] The funeral, which Marian was too distraught to attend, took place at Highgate on Wednesday 4 December. Dr Sadler of the Rosslyn Chapel presided over the simple Unitarian service, and Lewes was buried in the dissenters' part of Highgate Cemetery.

Charles Lewes, John Cross, Trollope, George Smith, the Burne-Joneses, and Frederic Harrison and his wife were among the mourners. Joseph Langford represented Blackwood, who had intended to make the journey from Edinburgh to support George Eliot as 'about the oldest and truest' friend she had, but in the end his own ill health forced him to change his mind.[49]

Also at Highgate was another old, though of late years more distant, friend. Breaking his rule of not attending funerals because his beliefs were 'at variance with those expressed in burial-services', Herbert Spencer made his way to the Cemetery on 4 December to pay tribute to his old friend. He had known both Lewes and Marian longer than anyone else, having been the close companion of both in the early 1850s and the means of bringing them together.

Spencer, recognizing the constancy and devotion of Lewes and Marian, which 'exceeded that of any married pair I have known',[50] wrote some moving words to the woman who had once fixed her longings on him and who had subsequently found her affection returned so magnificently by Lewes. Crusty old bachelor as he was, Spencer made a heroic imaginative leap when writing his letter of condolence on 5 December:

I can but dimly conceive what such a parting must be, even in an ordinary case. Still more dimly can I conceive what it must be in a case where two lives have been so long bound together so closely, in such multitudinous ways. But I can conceive it with clearness enough to enable me to say, with more than conventional truth, that I grieve with you.[51]

Kind letters of sympathy and support, and of praise for Lewes's vitality, wit, intelligence, and versatility came from many. Jowett, Browning, Tennyson, Burne-Jones, Mark Pattison, Turgenev, and Robert Lytton, now Viceroy of India, were among those who sent their private tribute. In due course obituaries in the papers and journals added public tributes and assessments, the most moving and best representation of the man and his work being that by Trollope in the *Fortnightly Review*, of which Lewes had been the first editor. Trollope praised Lewes the journalist and critic, Lewes the popularizer of philosophy, Lewes the biographer of Goethe, Lewes the scientific philosopher in his last years. He also celebrated the man:

To me it has often been a marvel that he should have lived and worked, and thoroughly enjoyed his life, – as he did with a relish beyond that of most healthy men, – when I have observed the frailness of his physical nature.[52]

Lewes had enjoyed life, and had been the chief creator of happiness for Marian and of an environment in which she was encouraged, against heavy odds, to write her novels under the name George Eliot. Her younger relations sent letters of condolence. Emily Clarke wrote to her 'dearest Aunt Polly': 'He whom you have lost was so loving and tender hearted. God help you to bear it.' Isaac Evans did not break his silence, but his wife Sarah wrote a single sentence: 'My heart aches for you in your sad bereavement.'[53] God, whom her niece had invoked, could not help Marian to bear it, since she did not believe in God. Charles stayed with her at the Priory, telling Bessie Belloc on 6 December that she could not bring herself to see anyone else. 'She is strong', he wrote, 'in the determination to try and carry out the work my dear Father left behind him.'[54]

What Marian had dreaded had come about. Lewes had died first. Unlike Dorothea, who refused to finish the worthless work of her distrustful husband, George Eliot willingly took on the task of revising and preparing for the press the last two volumes of *Problems of Life and Mind*. Not only did she feel it a loving duty to her un-Casaubonlike husband, but it gave her a reason to go on living from day to day.

In his prompt letter of condolence, written from Paris on 3 December 1878, Turgenev had hoped she would 'find in your own great mind the necessary fortitude to sustain such a loss! All your friends, all learned Europe mourn with you.'[55] The following weeks and months brought letters from all parts of the world to confirm Turgenev's words. Friends called and left their cards. For nearly two months Marian received no one except Charles, who, ever the son of his father, took over all the correspondence and arrangements. She kept busy by going through Lewes's notes, immersing herself in his discussions of the relations between psychological and physiological aspects of human motivation and action, and of the derivation of a moral sense from emotions and instincts.[56]

The work was congenial to her, who was as well versed in the areas covered by the work as Lewes himself. She finished the fourth volume, *The Study of Psychology*, in time for publication by Trübner in May 1879, and the final volume, *Mind as a Function of the Organism*, before the end of the year. Some of Lewes's scientific acquaintances offered their assistance. The Cambridge physiologist Dr Michael Foster wrote in January offering to help her with 'any physiological point'.[57]

Foster's kindness, and that of other scientists, including Clifford All-butt, who wrote movingly of the importance of Lewes's works on physiology and their influence on young scientists,[58] emboldened her to put to them a plan to found a lectureship or studentship in Lewes's name. After discussions with Foster, who with his Cambridge colleague Henry Sidgwick came to the Priory on 9 March 1879, a Studentship in Physiology was decided on. Huxley joined Sidgwick and other scientists as a Trustee; the George Henry Lewes Studentship was to be held at Cambridge, because of its superior facilities; it was open to young scientists working in laboratories – 'the way he [i.e. Lewes] would have liked to work', as Marian told Barbara Bodichon[59] – with tenure for three years.

Marian put up £5,000 to fund the Studentship, which was open to both men and women.[60] The first Student, Dr Charles Roy, was appointed in October 1879. He became a Fellow of the Royal Society in 1884, and held the Chair of Pathology at Cambridge. The first successful woman, Winifred Parsons, held the Studentship for a year in 1918–19.[61] Marian was able to help, by endowing this scheme, many a young striving Lydgate, and eventually a few young Dorotheas, who wished to pursue physiological or medical research. Lewes had never had free access to a laboratory – though Richard Owen had sometimes let him share his facilities – but, amateur though he was, his work, and his enthusiasm and clarity in describing his work, encouraged many young people, the most famous of whom was Pavlov, to take up physiological research.

George Eliot was experiencing the same feelings as those expressed by Queen Victoria after the death of Prince Albert in December 1861. She had read the Queen's *Leaves from the Journal of Our Life in the Highlands from 1848 to 1861*, edited by Lewes's old friend Arthur Helps in 1868, commenting then in a letter to Helps:

I think I have read the Queen's Journal with more sympathy because I am a woman of about the same age, and also have my personal happiness bound up in a dear husband whose loss would render my life a series of social duties and private memories.[62]

Like Victoria, George Eliot found herself unable to see people; like Victoria, she filled her diary with verses from Tennyson's great sequence of mourning poems, *In Memoriam* (1850). She also noted, in January 1879, an exquisite stanza from Heine's *Buch der Lieder* (*Book of Songs*, 1827) which she had singled out for praise in her article on Heine in the *Westminster Review* in 1856 as an expression of 'pure feeling breathed in pure music':

> Anfangs wollt' ich fast verzagen
> Und ich glaubt' ich trug es nie,
> Und ich hab' es doch ertragen, –
> Aber fragt mich nur nicht, wie.

Her own translation of the lines went: 'At first I was almost in despair, and I thought I could never bear it, and yet I have borne it – only do not ask me *how*.'[63]

Work on *Problems* and the Studentship was the one positive thing, but even here, as so often in her life, there was a special painfulness – beyond the loss of Lewes – to be borne. The money needed for the Studentship was in a bank account in Lewes's name, and she could not draw it out until she had changed her name by deed poll to Lewes, the name she had ached to be able to take, and had wanted to be known by, since 1854. Now she took it after Lewes's death. Charles Lewes and John Cross were the witnesses in January 1879 to her signing herself, with an interesting reversion to her old Christian names, 'Mary Ann Evans Lewes'.

Before this, she had had to go through the ordeal of proving Lewes's will, made on 21 November 1859. Lewes had left the copyright of his works to his sons, and everything else to 'Mary Ann Evans, Spinster'. Underneath the will is written by the registrar 'Proved at London 16th December 1878 on the Oath of Mary Ann Evans Spinster the sole Executrix to whom Admin. was granted.'[64] Blackwood's manager, George Simpson, expressed his pity for her on this occasion. 'Could not the possibility of such a trial have been provided against?' he asked on 27 January 1879 on hearing that she had had to prove the will in court.[65]

Marian, or Mary Ann, Lewes, as she so belatedly was – we must assume, I think, that she had not legally changed her name earlier because of her feelings of justice towards Agnes, and did so now only in order to become mistress of her own money and property – lived on quietly. During the first few months of 1879 she read through Lewes's journals and his early works, including his book on Spanish drama (1846) and 'my darling's first article on Goethe' (1843).[66] Her kidney attacks returned at the end of January, and Sir James Paget was called in.[67]

She dreaded company, but slowly began to see her closest friends. The first to be admitted was John Cross, who came on 23 February. Herbert Spencer called the same day; 'did not see him', she wrote in her diary.[68] Cross could help her with her complicated financial affairs. During the next few months she more than once called him in to help her resist some begging letters and requests for money, including personal appeals from Lewes's nephew Vivian, and a request from Bessie Belloc for £500, presumably for an educational cause.[69]

Cross's mother had died on 9 December 1878. He had taken up Dante's *Divine Comedy* soon after, struggling with the Italian. Marian offered to help him, and together they read Dante to help distract them from their grief. As she continued to mourn Lewes throughout the spring and summer of 1879, reading his works, visiting his grave, and even experiencing, in defiance of her rationalist beliefs, some spiritual visitation – '*His presence came again*', she wrote in her diary on 28 May[70] – she was becoming ever closer to Cross. His description of their relationship in *George Eliot's Life* is understandably reticent:

Her sympathetic delight in stimulating my newly awakened enthusiasm for Dante, did something to distract her mind from sorrowful memories. The divine poet took us into a new world. It was a renovation of life.[71]

It was, in fact, the story of Abelard and Eloisa in reverse, hingeing on the seductive charm of the teacher–pupil relation, with the woman as teacher and the man as pupil. Some letters between them have been lost or destroyed, so that the reader of George Eliot's letters is less prepared for the shock of reading her letter to Cross of 16 October 1879 than he or she might otherwise have been. We are shocked, and embarrassed too, but only partly because what we read is an awkward love letter from a woman of nearly sixty to a man twenty years her junior. Part of our unease comes surely from a sense of obtruding our outsiders' eyes into the private sadness, grief, love, and embarrassment of someone with emotional needs as demanding as our own, the expression of which we would hate to think of being read by strangers 'with hard curiosity' just as much as George Eliot did.[72]

The letter begins: 'Best loved and loving one – the sun it shines so cold, so cold, when there are no eyes to look love on me.' Marian addresses Cross as 'thou', talks of his tenderness and goodness, touches on business matters and lawn tennis, and finishes with a quotation from the *Aeneid* and an allusion to Dante:

Why should I compliment myself at the end of my letter and say that I am faithful, loving, more anxious for thy life than mine? I will run no risks of being 'inexact' – so I will only say 'varium et mutabile semper' but at this particular moment thy tender

Beatrice.[73]

Cross wanted to marry her. Over the next few months she agonized about what to do. If she had been unable to confide in her closest friends in 1853 when contemplating living with Lewes as his wife, now she was equally alone in her deliberations. Her friends in 1880 were likely to be shocked, angered, or hurt if she married Cross.

What would Charles think, and all Lewes's friends – Pigott, Spencer, Trollope, for example? And the Positivists, who believed in perpetual widowhood? The Congreves, Harrisons, and Beeslys would feel let down, though in justice they would have to admit, as Harrison eventually did in a letter to Cross, that since George Eliot had never declared herself a member of the Positivist Church, she could hardly be expected to hold herself bound by its rules.[74] Worse was the thought of how her female friends would view the marriage, from the self-confessedly idolatrous Edith Simcox, Elma Stuart, and Maria Congreve to Georgiana Burne-Jones, Barbara Bodichon, and – still in her thoughts for old times' sake – Cara and Sara, for whom this would be the second great shock administered by their brilliant and wayward friend of nearly forty years.

Beyond these circles of family and friends, who might be expected to react with the pain of jealousy or resentment, was a larger crowd in the intermediate distance. People who knew George Eliot from visits to the Priory, from correspondence, from the worlds of literature, journalism, publishing, politics, art, and music – such people might find this marriage disturbing, even ridiculous, given the age difference between the husband and the wife. What would feminists make of it? And the less visible, but more numerous, ranks of those who read and admired her novels?

Numbers of people had disapproved of the strong-minded woman who had chosen to live with Lewes, and had been slowly persuaded by the evident love and faithfulness of their union, and greater numbers still by the moral complexion of her works, that her choice had not been immoral. Now they would be required to adjust their notions once more, to make room in their imaginations for a love between Lewes's 'widow' and a man young enough to be what she and Lewes had always called him, her nephew. And her remaining siblings? Would Isaac unbend, or would his disapproval of his sister be deepened by the embarrassment of such a marriage? And Fanny Houghton?

Marian told no one. She had seen *Theophrastus Such* through the press, nearly withdrawing it in March 1879 out of lack of confidence, but Blackwood had persuaded her that it was good enough to go forward.[75] Three printings were necessary on publication in June. George Eliot managed a smile at the remark of one acquaintance of Charles who told him that 'Theophrastus was a higher order of book and *more difficult to write* than a novel.' Reporting this to William Blackwood on 12 June, she added wryly, 'Wait long enough, and every form of opinion will turn up.'[76]

In April 1879 Bertie's wife and children arrived in England, having left Natal for good. George Eliot was continuing to support them, but their meeting was not happy. Eliza made demands which George Eliot considered unreasonable; at the same time she found fault with everything in England, being used to receive deference as a white woman in Africa, however poor. George Eliot wrote with bitter humour to Elma on 18 June that 'the African daughter-in-law is going on better, and becoming more reconciled to our non-colonial inferiority.' Eliza was living near Charles and Gertrude, who found little Marian a place at the kindergarten attended by their daughters.[77]

In one sense George Eliot was returning to the land of the living. Her brief diary entries show that she gradually received more friends – Maria Congreve in March, Edith Simcox in April, Barbara Bodichon, who came to stay with her at the Heights on 29 September for a few days.[78] In another sense, especially as the first anniversary of Lewes's death approached, she seemed closer than ever to death herself. Her fine old friend, Lewes's fellow encourager of her genius, John Blackwood, died on 29 October 1879. 'He has been bound up with what I most cared for in my life for more than twenty years', she told Charles when she knew he was dying.[79]

Though by this time she knew of Cross's desire to marry her, and had written her 'Beatrice' letter of love to him, part of her wanted to die soon and be buried next to Lewes. In this spirit she wrote in her diary on Saturday 29 November:

Reckoning by the days of the week, it was this day last year my loneliness began. I spent the day in the room where I passed through the first three months. I read his letters, and packed them together, to be buried with me. Perhaps that will happen before next November.[80]

In this way she made sure that the prying eyes of posterity would not see Lewes's letters to her.

On 17 December she copied Emily Brontë's poem 'Remembrance' into her diary. The first stanza reads:

> Cold in the earth – and the deep snow piled above thee
> Far, far removed, cold in the dreary grave!
> Have I forgot, my only love, to love thee,
> Severed at last by Time's all-severing wave?

After George Eliot's death, a rumour was started, and soon embellished and enlarged, to the effect that she had endured a crisis while going through Lewes's papers, that she had discovered evidence of his unfaithfulness, and that her feelings had changed from loving grief to repulsion. Oscar Browning, to whom she had been so kind during his troubles at Eton, set the rumour going. In January 1881 he told Henry James, who told his sister Alice in a letter, that George Eliot 'went back on' Lewes when she found something 'which caused her to wish to sink him in oblivion'. James added that he thought the notion 'Browningish and fabulous',[81] as indeed it was, though of course it was the rumour which flourished and his doubts about its authenticity which sank into oblivion as others took up the story. How, we might ask, could Browning possibly know such a thing? He was not a confidant of George Eliot, whom he had in any case not seen since he was, with Turgenev, among the guests at Six Mile Bottom in October 1878, a month before Lewes's death.[82]

But of course the story was scandalous and interesting enough to bear repeating. Eliza Lynn Linton also picked it up from Oscar Browning, who subsequently dropped hints in his *Life of George Eliot* (1890). In her autobiography, published in 1899, Eliza declared that she did not 'for one instant' believe that George Eliot had 'discovered proofs of Lewes's infidelity'.[83] As with Henry James, however, she was giving currency to the story even as she denied its truth. Nearly a century later the gossip was recycled once more.[84]

Among the Positivists, Frederic and Ethel Harrison, who did not like the marriage to Cross, privately told friends that they believed George Eliot had 'got tired of Mr Lewes & had liked Mr Cross before he died'. Edward Beesly, recounting this to Herbert Spencer in December 1880, hastened to add that he did not believe it himself, and that though he, too, disliked second marriages, he saw reasons enough to explain why George Eliot had taken the step:

Loneliness, a longing to have her real name & position like other & inferior women, gratitude to the warmhearted man who wanted to give her name & home & everything, – affection for him of a right & good kind: Why are not these enough?[85]

Why not indeed?

At the end of March 1880 Marian went to Weybridge to stay with the Cross family. After her return to London she saw Sir James Paget, who reassured her about her health. 'My marriage decided', she wrote in her diary on 9 April. The next day she went to look at 4 Cheyne Walk in Chelsea, the imposing house on the Thames embankment into which she and Cross would move after their honeymoon abroad.[86]

Marian was extremely nervous, writing to Cross's sister Eleanor about the mixture of feelings she was experiencing. Touchingly, she began by saying, 'You can hardly think how sweet the name Sister is to me', a name she had not been called by 'for so many, many years'. Then she talked of being loved and welcomed by the whole Cross family, and of 'your Brother's great gift of love to me'. 'Yet I quail a little', she went on, 'in facing what has to be gone through – the hurting of many whom I care for.'[87] This letter was written on 13 April. The next day she wrote again to Eleanor Cross that she had 'often wished that my life had ended a year ago'. 'But now what remains of it must have a new consecration in gratitude for the miracle of his love.' She confessed, in the midst of this tussle of pessimism and optimism, of the desire for death and the hope of a new life, to feeling 'terrified'.[88]

As before she had dropped inadequate hints to the Brays of her intentions of going abroad with Lewes – mentioning Labassecour but not her travelling companion – so now she wrote to Elma Stuart saying she was going away and asking Elma to trust her 'when I act in a way which is thoroughly unexpected'.[89] She faced one difficult personal interview. On 30 April she told Charles Lewes, who reacted warmly, like the generous man he was, as she reported with relief to Eleanor Cross.[90]

Charles undertook to tell those whom Marian shrank from seeing. While she wrote on 5 May, the eve of the wedding, to Cara Bray, Barbara Bodichon, Georgiana Burne-Jones, and William Blackwood, telling them of her plans and asking for their understanding, she left Charles to inform Edith Simcox, Maria Congreve, and Clementia Taylor, all of whom would be upset.

Charles's positive reaction to the news gave her courage. Nor was it simulated or exaggerated for her sake. He was genuinely pleased. Soon after the marriage, he met Annie Ritchie, Thackeray's daughter, who had also married a man nearly twenty years her junior. George Eliot had commented on Annie's marriage in August 1877 that the age gap was 'bridged hopefully by his solidarity and gravity'.[91] Now Annie Ritchie wrote to her husband that Charles had told her he owed everything to George Eliot, that his father 'had no grain of jealousy in him', and that George Eliot had told him 'if she hadn't been human with feelings and failings like other people, how could she have written her books'.[92]

The explanation, which was good enough for Charles, should be good enough for us, as should George Eliot's remark to Georgiana Burne-Jones, that 'explanations of these crises, which seem sudden though they are slowly dimly prepared, are impossible'.[93] She had so often experienced, and so intelligently dramatized in her fiction, the difficulties of human relationships, the sense of human nature obeying laws yet the awareness of 'the mystery that lies under the processes', as she had written on reading Darwin's *Origin of Species* in 1859.[94]

On Thursday 6 May 1880, at 10.15 am, Marian was married to John Cross at St George's, Hanover Square. The Cross family attended, as did Charles Lewes, who in an appropriate reversal of the usual arrangements gave his stepmother away.[95] It was a Church of England ceremony, presumably at the request of the Crosses. The wedding journey, which lasted ten weeks, took the couple to Amiens, Paris, then south to Italy, where they spent some time in Verona and Padua, finally arriving at their chief destination, Venice, on 2 June.

Marian's friends expressed their understanding in their different ways. Georgiana Burne-Jones wrote, with difficulty, that she was still 'the old loving Georgie' in spite of the change. Barbara Bodichon, independent as ever, exclaimed that she would have married Marian herself if she had been a man, adding, 'All love is so different that I do not see it unnatural to love in new ways.'[96] Charles, knowing George Eliot would be anxious for news of her other friends, reported cheerfully that the difficult trio, Edith, Maria, and Clementia, were all very sympathetic, though the latter two were 'evidently quite unprepared for it'.[97] Edith's autobiography makes it clear that the idea of George Eliot marrying 'the fatal Johnny', as she had been calling him since noticing that he was the favourite Priory visitor of both Lewes and Marian, had already crossed her mind.[98]

Emily Clarke, Marian's loyal niece, wrote warmly of the 'welcome surprise', and wished her aunt happiness.[99] Another member of the Evans family was told the news in a deliberately indirect way. The last communication Isaac Evans had sent to his sister was a letter from his solicitor saying he would have no more contact with her. Now Marian instructed her solicitor to write to Isaac's, informing him of her marriage. The news was duly passed on to Isaac.[100] She was too proud to write directly to her brother, and perhaps wanted him to feel the humiliation of hearing from a solicitor, but at the same time it was a gesture of reconciliation; it was important to her that her brother be informed of her legal marriage. She sought his approval, though she despised his reasons for having so long withheld it.

Isaac replied. On 17 May he wrote from Griff:

My dear Sister

I have much pleasure in availing myself of the present opportunity to break the long silence which has existed between us, by offering our united and sincere congratulations to you and Mr Cross.

He signed himself 'Your affectionate brother'.[101]

When she received the letter, Marian wrote from Milan on 26 May in the spirit of Maggie Tulliver and the sister in the 'Brother and Sister' sonnets. 'It was a great joy to me to have your kind words of sympathy,' she began, 'for our long silence has never broken the affection for you which began when we were little ones.' The letter finishes with a signature which movingly combines her childhood Christian names with her new married surname: 'Always your affectionate Sister, Mary Ann Cross'.[102] No doubt it was right that each should be forgiving and forgiven, though that the cause should be the mere fact of a legal marriage and a new name is surely a pity.

John Cross's feelings for Marian were reverential. Even allowing for the worshipful nature of his correspondent Elma Stuart, we must take as genuine his expression in a letter to her on 11 May of delight that he had been 'united for life with her who has for so long been my ideal', and of his sense of 'the high calling' of the marriage.[103] It is an unusual reason for marrying, but by no means an impossible one. Henry James commented amusedly after George Eliot's death that she 'would have killed' Cross with her 'intellectual pace – all Dante and Goethe, Cervantes and the Greek tragedians'. He also reported Cross himself as saying that 'it was a carthorse yoked to a racer'.[104]

However amusing the marriage was to some observers, both husband and wife had reason to expect happiness from it. They wrote cheerful letters back to Cross's sisters, and to Charles, to whom Marian often mentioned her previous journeys with Lewes, 'the beloved Pater'.[105] But perhaps inevitably the honeymoon put strains on two people who had comfortably filled the roles of aunt and nephew to one another, of genius and admirer, of teacher and pupil. On 16 June, while they were staying at the Hôtel de l'Europe on the Grand Canal in Venice, Cross suffered some kind of fit or derangement. He jumped from their hotel room into the Grand Canal.

Hard facts are few, and rumour – as so often in George Eliot's life – both vague and colourful. In his biography of George Eliot, Cross himself dealt with the incident with understandable reticence, merely saying that a combination of 'continual bad air' from the drains, the extreme heat, and exhaustion from sightseeing made him 'thoroughly ill'.[106] The only direct source of information, George Eliot's Venetian diary, becomes monosyllabic at this point, merely recording that on Wednesday 16 June a Dr Ricchetti was called in, and on 18 June a second doctor, Cesare Vigna, came to see Cross. The entry for Saturday 19 June reads tersely:

Dr. Vigna twice. Better. Wrote to the girls [Cross's sisters]. Sent Telegram. Willy [Cross's brother] arrived in the evening.[107]

At home, Edith Simcox heard a rumour that Cross had caught typhoid fever at Venice and might die. On 10 July she called on Charles Lewes, anxious to know how Cross and Marian were, but Charles and his family were holidaying at Witley. The next day Edith went to Weybridge to ask Eleanor and Florence Cross about their brother, and was assured that he was not in danger, but very weak. The sisters told her they had been worried about John before the marriage – 'he was so worn and ill'. 'He had to continue all his business to the last' because Marian 'would not let anyone be told and he shrank from the responsibility', Edith reported in her autobiography.[108]

After George Eliot's death, rumours multiplied. Lord Acton, who had met her and Lewes at Tennyson's house in April 1878, later noted – on whose authority is not known – some details:

At Venice she thought him mad, and she never recovered the dreadful depression that followed. Sent for Ricchetti, told him that Cross had a mad brother. Told her fears. Just then, heard that he had jumped into the Canal.[109]

Whether there *was* madness in the Cross family is not clear, but there is evidence that John Cross himself suffered from bouts of depression both before and after his marriage. In March 1882 Edith Simcox heard from his protective sisters that he was ill and that they had forbidden him all emotional excitement, attributing his anxiety to the strains of writing his biography of George Eliot.[110] We have seen that Cross himself told Henry James soon after George Eliot's death that, intellectually speaking, he was a mere carthorse yoked to a racer; others thought so too, and inferred that his leap into the Grand Canal was motivated by fear of his formidable wife.

Underlying some comments is the unspoken assumption that a forty-year-old bachelor, known to have been very close to his widowed mother, may also have been escaping from the physical demands of his older wife. Typical of such remarks is that by Walter Sichel in 1923:

It was rumoured that after a prolonged course of Dante at Venice he had cast himself into the Grand Canal and begged the gondoliers not to rescue him.[111]

A recent novel, *Johnnie Cross* (1983), by Terence De Vere White, builds on the same notion. Inevitably, perhaps, the marriage, the honeymoon, and the canal incident attracted gossip of this kind, which can in the nature of things be neither fully confirmed nor fully discounted.

The Venice episode is likely to appear funny, sad, fantastic, alarming in different measure according to the point of view of the observer. It was not funny for Cross and Marian, who left Venice, accompanied by William Cross, for the cooler climate of Austria and Germany. They came home on 26 July, going straight to Witley to recuperate. Marian's own health immediately gave way. At the end of September she suffered a return of her kidney trouble. After a brief trip to Brighton in October, she stayed quietly at Witley, while Cross made almost daily trips to London to arrange for the removal of furniture from the Priory to Cheyne Walk.[112]

On 15 November, still at Witley, Marian wrote to her old friend D'Albert Durade, commiserating with him on the death of his wife, whom she had been grateful to be allowed to call Maman in the lonely days in Geneva after the death of her father.[113] By 29 November the removal of furniture was not quite complete, but Marian and Cross left the Heights, the summer paradise which she found too cold in winter, and camped briefly in Bailey's Hotel in Kensington. They finally moved into 4 Cheyne Walk on 3 December.[114]

The second anniversary of Lewes's death had passed without her being able to visit his grave, so feeble was her health and so cold the weather. She had written to Charles on 23 November, worrying about Lewes's grave becoming 'lost among the new ones round it', and wondering if a higher railing could be erected round it to stop it disappearing from view.[115]

Her own birthday – she was sixty-one on 22 November – was too bound up with Lewes's last illness and death to be a matter for celebration. But she received her usual birthday letter from Sara Hennell; this, and a request from the irrepressible Charles Bray for a photograph of Cross, ensured that they were two of the last people to receive a letter from her. It was appropriate, as was her smiling response to her old friend Bray's characteristic request for information about her new husband:

Mr. Cross has no photograph of himself. But I think you would be satisfied with his coronal arch which finishes a figure six feet high. If his head does not indicate fine moral qualities, it must be phrenology that is in fault.[116]

On 17 December Bessie Belloc was invited to lunch the following week with the Crosses in their new home. Herbert Spencer, too, received an invitation on 18 December. Marian had been re-reading his work on sociology. Spencer went to see his old friend on Sunday 19 December, when he found her 'looking worn' but not otherwise unwell.[117] It was fitting that she should see these two old friends, Bessie and Spencer, who, though less close to her in late years, had been warm supporters when she was the unknown Marian Evans of the *Westminster Review* causing a scandal by going off to Germany with Lewes.

George Eliot died at 10 pm on 22 December 1880, after a severe
throat infection had been added to her worsening kidney disease. Cross
wrote to Georgiana Burne-Jones to tell her that 'my great wife and your
dear friend died tonight'; she had died quietly, but with a 'frightful
suddenness' which 'has entirely stunned me'. He was left alone after less
than three weeks in the new house they had 'meant to be so happy in'.[118]
How would England mourn the death of this greatest of novelists and
most controversial of women?

EPILOGUE

The burden of arranging for the funeral of the greatest writer, and the greatest woman, of the age fell on Cross, though Charles Lewes once more proved invaluable with his help. A short delay occurred in fixing the date because, as Charles told William Blackwood on 24 December, there was 'a movement on foot for burial in the Abbey, and it may be possible for you to get some influential Edinburgh signatures'.[1]

Herbert Spencer, Henry Sidgwick, Burne-Jones, and John Tyndall were among those who supported Cross in petitioning the Dean of Westminster for her to have a place in Poets' Corner. As Tyndall put it, if the Dean agreed, 'the verdict of the future will be that Dean Stanley has enshrined a woman whose achievements were without parallel in the previous history of womankind'.[2] This was undeniable.

But George Eliot proved to be in death, as in life, a controversial figure. John Morley and Huxley, both admirers of her genius, argued that it would be inappropriate for a person 'whose life and opinions were in notorious antagonism to Christian practice' to be buried in a Christian church.[3] This view, which has its obvious logic, prevailed. George Eliot was not buried in Westminster Abbey, though a hundred years after her death a memorial tablet was finally laid on the floor of Poets' Corner by George Eliot lovers. It is still possible to wonder about the fittingness of her being commemorated in this way, but that has less to do with the awkwardness and nonconformity of George Eliot herself, and more to do with the contradictory status of the Abbey as both a Christian church and a secular pantheon for the commemoration of the great in the realms of politics, the arts, and literature. Inasmuch as

Westminster Abbey *is* such a pantheon, George Eliot belongs there as surely as any of the other great men and women who are buried or commemorated there.

If it was a pity that burial in the Abbey was not granted, and an opportunity for publicly celebrating the greatness of George Eliot thus denied, it was nevertheless fitting that she should be buried, after all, in Highgate Cemetery, near Lewes, the man who had brought her happiness and enabled her genius to flourish. A great many joined the service on Wednesday 29 December, led, as two years before at Lewes's funeral, by Dr Sadler, who quoted from her poem 'O May I Join the Choir Invisible'. Spencer, Pigott, Robert Browning, Frederic Burton, Millais, Beesly, Harrison, Huxley, Lionel Tennyson, George Goschen, Morley, William Blackwood, Alice Helps, Elizabeth Garrett Anderson, and Edith Simcox were among the crowd.[4] Oscar Browning was there too. He noticed a stranger among the chief mourners, 'tall and slightly bent, his features recalling with a striking veracity the lineaments of the dead'.[5] It was Isaac Evans, come to attend the funeral of his brilliant sister.

Mary Ann Evans, Marian Evans, Marian Lewes, Mary Ann Cross, and above all George Eliot – the woman known by these different names had always been difficult to categorize. Her genius, her pride, her sensitivity, and her diffidence had ensured that her life was a complex but fruitful and extremely interesting one. The conjunction of her particular character and genius with the particular circumstances in which she found herself with regard to her family and the most important relationships of her life meant that pleasures and pains were, for her, more than usually mingled.

Inquiring, sceptical, even rebellious by nature and intellect, she was also conservative, timid, self-doubting. She shocked family and friends more than once with her actions – losing her faith and refusing to attend church, pursuing a journalistic career in London, living with a married man, and finally marrying a man so much younger than herself – but her desire was always to please, to conciliate, to conform if she could. In her novels she dramatized these and similar paradoxes in a variety of ways, skilfully and sympathetically putting difficult choices before her characters and showing their human frailty and the sometimes disastrous consequences of dubious actions undertaken out of mixed and confused motives. As she said to Charles Lewes in explanation of her own – by no means clear or easy – decision to marry John Cross, if she had not been human with feelings and failings like other people, how could she possibly have written those novels?

After her death there were immediate tributes to her greatness. But her reputation as a novelist began to decline around the turn of the century, and her life was thought by many to have been rather dull, though it may be pointed out that this view co-existed with a contradictory sense that her life had been shockingly unprincipled, or at least unorthodox. Cross's *Life*, published in 1885 after much hard work and lengthy negotiations with the ultra-sensitive Herbert Spencer and the touchy and conservative Isaac Evans,[6] unfortunately and unintentionally set the tone for the relative neglect of George Eliot which followed.

Cross's aim was, of course, to preserve his wife's dignity; to that end he all but expunged John Chapman from the record, and omitted or altered all the irreverent, idiomatic, sharp, witty, and aggressive passages from George Eliot's letters and journals. As William Hale White immediately recognized when he read the *Life*, the Marian Evans he had known at 142 Strand in the early 1850s had been obliterated by her anxious husband. 'I do hope', he wrote in the *Athenaeum* in November 1885, that 'in some future work, the salt and spice will be restored to the records of George Eliot's entirely unconventional life.'[7]

Virginia Woolf, F. R. Leavis, Barbara Hardy, David Carroll and other critics and commentators have ensured that George Eliot's reputation as a great novelist – an imaginative and witty one – has been restored and enhanced. Through his fine edition of the Eliot and Lewes letters and his fair-minded documentary biography of George Eliot, Gordon Haight brought the life back into visibility and made a vast amount of material available to others who, like the present biographer, are fascinated by the works and the life of this wonderful woman.

George Eliot's life was a truly extraordinary one, and her literary achievement matchless. St Teresa had 'found her epos in the reform of a religious order'; Dorothea, though foundress of nothing, had an incalculably diffusive effect on those around her, as the Prelude and Finale of *Middlemarch* tell us. George Eliot's special contribution was to write novels of great range, vision, humour, and passion, a truly wonderful 'set of experiments in life'.

NOTES

INTRODUCTION

1. Charles Dickens to John Chapman, 3 May 1852, *The Letters of Charles Dickens*, ed. Madeleine House, Graham Storey, Kathleen Tillotson et al., 8 vols. so far (Oxford, 1965–), VII, 907 (Pilgrim Edition).
2. Henry Crabb Robinson Diary, 4 May 1852, *Henry Crabb Robinson On Books and their Writers*, ed. Edith J. Morley, 3 vols. (London, 1938), II, 716.
3. Herbert Spencer, *An Autobiography*, 2 vols. (London, 1904), I, 393.
4. GE to Charles and Cara Bray, 5 May 1852, *GEL*, II, 23–4.
5. See Charles Bray, *Phases of Opinion and Experience during a Long Life* (London, 1884), p. 74.
6. George Combe Journal, 29 August 1851, *GEL*, VIII, 27.
7. See Spencer, *Autobiography*, I, 393, 394.
8. Bessie Rayner Parkes Belloc, *In a Walled Garden* (London, 1895, reprinted 1900), pp. 17–18.
9. William Hale White, *Athenaeum*, No. 3031 (28 November 1885), p. 702. GE appears as 'Theresa' in *The Autobiography of Mark Rutherford* (London, 1881, reprinted with an introduction by Don Cupitt, 1988). See also W. H. Stone, *Religion and Art of William Hale White* (Stanford, California, 1954), p. 193.
10. Eliza Lynn Linton, *My Literary Life* (London, 1899), p. 95. See also Nancy Fix Anderson, *Woman Against Women in Victorian England: A Life of Eliza Lynn Linton* (Bloomington, Indiana, 1987).
11. Spencer, *Autobiography*, I, 396.
12. *Middlemarch*, ed. Rosemary Ashton (Harmondsworth, 1994), p. 9 (chapter 1).
13. See Rosemary Ashton, *Little Germany: Exile and Asylum in Victorian England* (Oxford, 1986, reprinted 1989), p. 16.
14. GE to Sara Hennell, 18 January 1854, *GEL*, II, 137.

15. See Michael Mason, *The Making of Victorian Sexuality* (Oxford, 1994), pp. 171–2.
16. Anthony Trollope to W. M. Thackeray, 15 November 1860, *The Letters of Anthony Trollope*, ed. N. John Hall, 2 vols. (Stanford, California, 1983), I, 128.
17. See A. J. Youngson, *The Scientific Revolution in Victorian Medicine* (London, 1979), and Roy and Dorothy Porter, *In Sickness and in Health: The British Experience 1650–1850* (London, 1988).
18. See GE to Clifford Allbutt, August 1868, *GEL*, IV, 472.

CHAPTER ONE: *A Warwickshire Childhood 1819–41*

1. See Olive Cook, *The English Country House* (London, 1974, reprinted 1984), p. 198.
2. GE to Charles Bray, 30 September 1859, *GEL*, III, 168.
3. A large bundle of letters from Robert Evans to Francis Newdigate, some with draft replies by Newdigate scribbled on the back, is in the Warwickshire County Record Office (WCRO).
4. 'Looking Backward', *Impressions of Theophrastus Such* (1879, reprinted with introduction and notes by Nancy Henry, London, 1994), p. 20.
5. Robert Evans to Francis Newdigate, 20 October 1833, MS WCRO.
6. Robert Evans to Francis Newdigate, 1 July 1836, ibid.
7. *Theophrastus Such*, pp. 22–3.
8. Ibid., pp. 24–6.
9. Ibid., p. 23.
10. See Henry Crabb Robinson Diary, 24 March 1832, *Henry Crabb Robinson On Books*, I, 405; Robert Southey to Walter Savage Landor, 14 April 1829, *The Life and Correspondence of the Late Robert Southey*, ed. C. C. Southey, 6 vols. (London, 1849–50), VI, 44.
11. See *Coventry Herald and Observer*, 23 December 1832; J. W. Cross, *George Eliot's Life as Related in Her Letters and Journals*, 3 vols. (Edinburgh and London, 1885), I, 27.
12. See *Coventry Herald*, 4 January 1833; 'Occurrences at Nuneaton', 21 December 1832, an anonymous diary of events at Nuneaton, MS Nuneaton Library; and S. Parkinson, *Scenes from the 'George Eliot' Country* (Leeds, 1888), pp. 83–4.
13. See Geoffrey Best, *Mid-Victorian Britain 1851–75* (London, 1971), p. 55.
14. Robert Evans to Francis Newdigate, 13 September 1834, MS WCRO.
15. *Pickwick Papers* (1837), chapter 13.
16. Robert Evans to Francis Newdigate, 31 July 1837, MS WCRO.
17. *Theophrastus Such*, p. 24.
18. Robert Evans to Francis Newdigate, 5 March 1834, MS WCRO.

NOTES

19. Robert Evans to Francis Newdigate, 6 July 1834, ibid.

20. See GE's sequence of sonnets, 'Brother and Sister', written in 1869 and published in *The Legend of Jubal, and Other Poems* (1874).

21. Cross, I, 14.

22. GE to Maria Lewis, 16 March 1839, *GEL*, I, 22.

23. Ibid., I, 16.

24. Isaac Evans's letters to Charles Newdigate Newdegate are in WCRO.

25. GE Journal, 25–31 August 1859, MS Yale.

26. GE to Sara Hennell, 7 October 1859, *GEL*, III, 174.

27. Robert Evans to Francis Newdigate, 15 December 1833, MS WCRO.

28. Robert Evans to Francis Newdigate, 12 April 1835, ibid.

29. Edith Simcox Autobiography, 12 June 1885, K. A. McKenzie, *Edith Simcox and George Eliot* (Oxford, 1961), p. 129.

30. Robert Evans Journal, 22 November 1829, *GEL*, I, lxxii.

31. Cross, I, 157.

32. John Sibree and M. Caston, *Independency in Warwickshire: A Brief History of the Independent or Congregational Churches in that County* (Coventry and London, 1855), p. 267.

33. See William Mottram, *The True Story of George Eliot in Relation to 'Adam Bede'* (London, 1905), pp. 111, 116, 147, 249. Mottram was the grandson of Samuel and Robert Evans's sister Ann.

34. *Our Times* (June 1881), quoted Cross, I, 24ff.

35. GE School Notebook, Gordon S. Haight, *George Eliot: A Biography* (Oxford, 1968, reprinted 1969), p. 554.

36. See Rosemary Ashton, *The Life of Samuel Taylor Coleridge: A Critical Biography* (Oxford, 1996), p. 383.

37. MS Yale, part quoted in Haight, p. 554.

38. GE to Maria Lewis, 6 January 1836, *GEL*, I, 3.

39. See Robert Evans Journal, 31 December 1835, *GEL*, I, 3n; Robert Evans to Francis Newdigate, 22 January 1836, MS WCRO.

40. GE to Maria Lewis, 6 January 1836, *GEL*, I, 3.

41. Correspondence between Robert Evans and Francis Newdigate, 29 December 1835 – 23 January 1836, MSs WCRO.

42. Robert Evans to Francis Newdigate, 19 April, 1 October 1835, ibid.

43. See Haight, pp. 24, 30.

44. Ibid., p. 21.

45. Robert Evans to Francis Newdigate, 22 February 1836, MS WCRO.

46. Robert Evans to Chrissey Evans, 17 April 1836, MS Nuneaton Library.

47. See OED; Richard D. Altick, *The Presence of the Present: Topics of the Day in the Victorian Novel* (Columbus, Ohio, 1991), p. 780.

48. Robert Evans Journal, 25 December 1836, Haight, p. 21.

49. GE to Sara Hennell, 7 October 1859, *GEL*, III, 175.

50. Ibid.

51. *Middlemarch*, p. 392 (chapter 39).

52. GE to Maria Lewis, 26 May 1838, *GEL*, I, 4.

53. GE to Maria Lewis, 18 August 1838, ibid., I, 6.

54. Ibid., I, 7.

55. Cross, I, 39–40.

56. GE to Maria Lewis, 20 May 1839, *GEL*, I, 25, 26.

57. GE to Maria Lewis, 6–8 November 1838, ibid., I, 12.

58. GE to Maria Lewis, 16 March 1839, ibid., I, 21, 23.

59. GE to Maria Lewis, 4 September 1839, ibid., I, 29.

60. GE to Martha Jackson, 9 October 1838, ibid., I, 9.

61. GE to Maria Lewis, 6–8 November 1838, ibid., I, 13.

62. GE to Maria Lewis, 1 October 1840, and to Sara Hennell, 4 February 1849, ibid., I, 68, 275.

63. GE to Maria Lewis, 17 July 1839, ibid., I, 27 and n.

64. GE to Maria Lewis, 4 September 1839, ibid., I, 30.

65. GE to Maria Lewis, 17 July 1839, ibid., I, 27.

66. GE to Elizabeth Evans, 5 March 1839, ibid., I, 19.

67. Robert Evans Journal, 1 November 1839, ibid., I, 33n.

68. GE to Maria Lewis, 22 November 1839, ibid., I, 35.

69. *Coventry Herald*, 23 December 1831.

70. GE to Maria Lewis, 13 March 1840, *GEL*, I, 40–41.

71. GE to Maria Lewis, 12 August 1840, ibid., I, 64.

72. GE to Maria Lewis, 27 October 1840, ibid., I, 71.

73. GE to Maria Lewis, February 1840, 1 October 1840, ibid., I, 38, 69.

74. GE to Maria Lewis, 30 March and 28 May 1840, ibid., I, 46–7, 51.

75. Cross, I, 44. Isaac's wife told Cross the story after GE's death.

76. GE to Samuel and Elizabeth Evans, 9 March 1841, *GEL*, I, 83.

77. GE to Samuel and Elizabeth Evans, 5 December 1840, ibid., I, 73.

78. GE to Martha Jackson, March 1841, ibid., I, 86.

79. GE to Maria Lewis, 8 March 1841, ibid., I, 82.

CHAPTER TWO: *Coventry, Rebellion and* The Life
of Jesus *1841–6*

1. GE to Maria Lewis, 23 October 1841, *GEL*, I, 117.

2. See the useful family tree of the Newdigate family in Marghanita Laski, *George Eliot and Her World* (London, 1973), p. 119.

3. Isaac Evans to Charles Newdigate Newdegate, 22 November 1855, MS WCRO.

4. Isaac Evans to Charles Newdigate Newdegate, 7 February 1880, MS
   Nuneaton Library; quoted Kathleen Adams, *Those of Us Who Loved Her:
   The Men in George Eliot's Life* (Warwick, 1980), p. 30.
5. See Alice Lynes, *George Eliot's Coventry* (Coventry, 1970), p. 21; Sibree and
   Caston, *Independency in Warwickshire*, p. 120.
6. Mary Sibree gave her account in Cross, I, 155–6.
7. GE to Martha Jackson, 21 May 1841, *GEL*, I, 93.
8. Robert Evans Journal, 11 April 1841, Haight, p. 34.
9. GE to Samuel Evans, 2 October 1841, *GEL*, I, 113.
10. See Mary Sibree's account, Cross, I, 156.
11. GE to Maria Lewis, 12 August 1841, *GEL*, I, 102.
12. Ibid., I, 115, 126n.
13. GE to Maria Lewis, 16 October 1841, ibid., I, 116.
14. GE to Maria Lewis, 13 November 1841, ibid., I, 120–21.
15. GE to Maria Lewis, 18 February and 27 May 1842, ibid., I, 126, 140.
16. Edith Simcox Autobiography, 12 June 1885, McKenzie, pp. 129–30.
17. Her copy is in the G. H. Lewes Library, a collection of Lewes's (and GE's)
    books deposited by Lewes's son Charles in the Dr Williams's Library,
    London.
18. See Bray, *Phases of Opinion*, p. 76. Cross, I, 92, says they met once at Mrs
    Pears's house in May 1841, but if they did, there is no other record of it,
    and the friendship between GE and the Brays certainly did not begin until
    her visit to them on 2 November 1841.
19. Charles C. Hennell, *An Inquiry Concerning the Origin of Christianity* (London,
    1838, 2nd edition 1841), Preface to the First Edition, p. iv.
20. Ibid.
21. Ibid., pp. 476, 477, 483, 489.
22. Ibid., pp. xi–xii and n.
23. Analysis of Hennell's *Inquiry* done by GE for the Analytical Catalogue of
    Chapman's publications, quoted Cross, I, 102. The MS of Strauss's
    German preface, dated Stuttgart, 25 November 1839, is in Coventry City
    Libraries.
24. Cara Bray to Revd Edward Gibson, 6 July 1845, MS Coventry.
25. Cara Bray's Commonplace Book is in the Coventry City Libraries.
26. Tennyson, 'Crossing the Bar' (1889), printed at Tennyson's request at the
    end of all editions of his poetry.
27. Cara Bray to Frances Power Cobbe, 21 May 1895, MS Huntington
    Library; Frances Power Cobbe to Cara Bray, nd, MS Coventry.
28. Martha Barclay (*née* Jackson) to Charles Lewes, 3 June 1884, MS Yale.
29. Bray, *Phases of Opinion*, pp. 50, 82.
30. Ibid., p. 76.

31. Ibid., pp. 69–70.
32. See Robert E. Schofield, *The Lunar Society of Birmingham: A Social History of Provincial Science and Industry in Eighteenth-Century England* (Oxford, 1963).
33. Cross, I, 160.
34. Bray, *Phases of Opinion*, pp. 21, 51, 87; see also Lynes, *George Eliot's Coventry*, pp. 14, 21, 27–8.
35. Bray, *The Philosophy of Necessity*, 2 vols. (London, 1841), I, i, 250–51.
36. Ibid., II, 492.
37. Bray, *Phases of Opinion*, pp. 64, 142; Lynes, *George Eliot's Coventry*, p. 28.
38. Quoted by Bray himself, *Phases of Opinion*, p. 101.
39. Edith Simcox Autobiography, 12 June 1885, McKenzie, p. 131.
40. Bray, *Phases of Opinion*, p. 73.
41. GE to Elizabeth Pears, 28 January 1842, and to Maria Lewis, 18 February 1842, *GEL*, I, 125, 127.
42. See *GEL*, I, 129n, 131n.
43. GE to Robert Evans, 28 February 1842, ibid., I, 129 and n.
44. Ibid., I, 129.
45. Ibid., I, 128–30.
46. GE to Cara Bray, 12 March 1842, ibid., I, 131; Cross, I, 104.
47. Cara Bray to Mary Hennell, 17 March 1842, *GEL*, I, 132.
48. GE to Cara Bray, 20 April 1842, ibid., I, 138.
49. Ibid., I, 138n, 133.
50. GE to Elizabeth Pears, 31 March 1842, ibid., I, 134; Cross, I, 113.
51. Mary Sibree's second account given to Cross, and published as an Appendix to the second edition of *George Eliot's Life* (London, 1886), I, 397, 398; *GEL*, I, 132n.
52. See *GEL*, I, 144n.
53. Ibid., I, 140 and n, 141n.
54. GE to Sara Hennell, 30 August 1842, ibid., I, 144.
55. GE to Sara Hennell, 16? September 1842, ibid., I, 147. Cara Bray gave the portrait to the National Portrait Gallery in 1899.
56. GE to Francis Watts, 4 July 1842, ibid., I, 142; Mary Sibree's account, Cross (1886), I, 398–9.
57. Cara Bray's engagement diary notes that Rufa Brabant arrived on 7 October, and Charles Hennell on 8 October, MS Coventry.
58. See Coleridge to Robert Brabant, December 1815, *Collected Letters of Samuel Taylor Coleridge*, ed. Earl Leslie Griggs, 6 vols. (Oxford, 1956–71), IV, 614.
59. Rufa told her story to John Chapman, who recorded it in his diary, 27 June 1851, Gordon S. Haight, *George Eliot and John Chapman* (London, 1940, reprinted 1969), p. 186.
60. See *GEL*, I, 153 and n; Cara Bray's Commonplace Book, MS Coventry.

61. See *GEL*, I, 158n.

62. Cara Bray to Sara Hennell, 22 February 1843, ibid., I, 156–7.

63. GE to Cara Bray, 8 and 20 November 1843, ibid., I, 164, 165.

64. GE to Cara Bray, 24 November 1843, ibid., I, 167.

65. Chapman's diary, 27 June 1851, Haight, *George Eliot and John Chapman*, pp. 185–6.

66. Eliza Lynn Linton to Herbert Spencer, 27 November 1885, MS BL (Add MS 65,530, f. 39); quoted with the names omitted in George Somes Layard, *The Life of Mrs Lynn Linton* (London, 1901), p. 251.

67. Eliza Lynn Linton, *The Autobiography of Christopher Kirkland*, 3 vols. (London, 1885), I, 288–9.

68. See *GEL*, I, 176n.

69. Cara Bray to Sara Hennell, 30 March 1845, ibid., I, 184.

70. GE to Sara Hennell, 6 April 1845, ibid., I, 185–6.

71. Cara Bray to Herbert Spencer, 29 January 1886, MS BL (Add MS 65,530, f. 42).

72. Cara Bray to Sara Hennell, 6 April 1845, *GEL*, I, 186.

73. Ibid., I, 172n, 175n.

74. Ibid., I, 171n.

75. Cara Bray to Sara Hennell, 14 April 1845; GE to Sara Hennell, 16? April 1845, ibid., I, 187 and n.

76. GE to Sara Hennell, March? 1846, ibid., I, 208–9.

77. GE to Sara Hennell, May? 1846, ibid., I, 216. See Rosemary Ashton, *The German Idea: Four English Writers and the Reception of German Thought 1800–1860* (Cambridge, 1980, reprinted London, 1994), pp. 147–53.

78. David Friedrich Strauss, *The Life of Jesus, Critically Examined* [translated by Mary Ann Evans], 3 vols. (London, 1846), I, ix–x.

79. Ibid., I, 108–21.

80. GE to Sara Hennell, 4 March 1846 and nd [1845], *GEL*, I, 207, 203.

81. Cara Bray to Sara Hennell, 14 February 1846, ibid., I, 206.

82. GE to Sara Hennell in two letters of April? 1846, ibid., I, 213, 215.

83. Haight, p. 59.

84. Bray, *Phases of Opinion*, p. 75. The cast of GE's head was destroyed after Cross's death, *GEL*, I, 178n.

85. See Cara Bray to Sara Hennell, 22 February 1843, *GEL*, I, 157.

86. Cara Bray to Rufa Hennell, 28 July 1844, ibid., I, 180.

87. *Life and Letters of William Ballantyne Hodgson*, ed J. M. D. Meiklejohn (Edinburgh, 1883), p. 364.

88. See Cara Bray to Sara Hennell, 19 April 1845, *GEL*, I, 188.

89. Sara Hennell to her mother, 10 October 1845, ibid., I, 199–200n.

90. Sara Hennell to her mother, 29 October 1845, ibid., I, 201.

91. Cara Bray's Commonplace Book, MS Coventry.

92. GE to Charles and Cara Bray, 1 June 1846, *GEL*, I, 219.

93. Cara Bray's engagement diary, 10 June 1846, MS Coventry.

94. GE to Cara Bray, 25 May 1845, and to Sara Hennell, 27 May 1845, *GEL*, I, 193, 194.

95. Census information, courtesy of the late Gordon S. Haight.

96. George Combe Journal, 18 September 1851, deciphered and quoted by Gordon S. Haight, 'George Eliot's Bastards', in *George Eliot: A Centenary Tribute*, ed. Gordon S. Haight and Rosemary T. VanArsdel (London, 1982), p. 5.

97. See Kathleen Adams, *Those of Us Who Loved Her*, pp. 52ff.

98. John Chapman Diary, 27 June 1851, Haight, *George Eliot and John Chapman*, pp. 184–5.

99. Bray, *Phases of Opinion*, pp. 125–6. For a detailed study of Victorian discussions of the subject see Michael Mason, *The Making of Victorian Sexuality*.

100. *Middlemarch*, p. 619 (chapter 61).

CHAPTER THREE: *Father's Illness and Death; Interlude in Geneva 1847–50*

1. GE to Charles Bray, 21 October 1846, *GEL*, VIII, 12–14.

2. GE to Mary Sibree, 10 May 1847, ibid., I, 234–5.

3. GE to Martha Jackson, 16 December 1841, ibid., I, 122–3.

4. See Cara Bray, Commonplace Book, MS Coventry; GE to Sara Hennell, 23 May 1846, *GEL*, I, 218.

5. GE to Sara Hennell, 9 October 1843, *GEL*, I, 162.

6. Sara Hennell to her mother, 25 September 1846, ibid., I, 223n.

7. *Coventry Herald*, 17 July 1846.

8. Ibid., 4 December 1846, reprinted *Essays of George Eliot*, ed. Thomas Pinney (New York, 1963), p. 17.

9. Ibid., pp. 23–5.

10. GE to Sara Hennell, 5 November 1846, *GEL*, I, 225.

11. Ibid., I, 225 and n.

12. Cara Bray to Sara Hennell, 3 January 1847, ibid., I, 230n.

13. GE to Sara Hennell, 28 February 1847, ibid., I, 231.

14. Sara Hennell to her mother, 20 June 1847, ibid., I, 235n.

15. GE to Sara Hennell, 16 September 1847, ibid., I, 236.

16. Ibid., I, 237.

17. Quoted in Cross, I, 151.

18. GE to Sara Hennell, 13 October 1847, *GEL*, I, 240.

NOTES

19. GE to Sara Hennell, 1 February 1848, ibid., I, 243–4.
20. GE to Sara Hennell, 27 November 1847, ibid., I, 241.
21. GE to John Sibree, 11 February 1848, ibid., I, 245–8.
22. GE to John Sibree, February 1848, ibid., I, 250.
23. GE to John Sibree, 8 March 1848, ibid., I, 254.
24. See David Goodway, *London Chartism 1838–1848* (Cambridge, 1982).
25. GE to John Sibree, 8 March 1848, *GEL*, I, 255, 256.
26. A. J. Youngson, *The Scientific Revolution in Victorian Medicine*, pp. 68–9.
27. Cara Bray to Sara Hennell, 15 April 1848, *GEL*, I, 256–7.
28. Cara Bray to Sara Hennell, 30 April 1848, ibid., I, 259n.
29. GE to John Sibree, 14? May 1848, ibid., I, 261.
30. GE to Sara Hennell, 4 June 1848, ibid., I, 264.
31. GE to Charles Bray, 5 June 1848, ibid., I, 265 and n.
32. GE to Charles Bray, 11 June 1848, ibid., I, 268.
33. *GEL*, I, 271n.
34. GE to Sara Hennell, 9 February 1849, ibid., I, 277.
35. Ibid., I, 277–8.
36. GE to Sara Hennell, 9 February 1849, and May 1849, ibid., I, 276, 277.
37. Cara Bray to Sara Hennell, 11 September 1848, ibid., I, 272.
38. GE to Charles Bray, May 1849, ibid., I, 283–4.
39. GE to Charles and Cara Bray, 30 May 1849, ibid., I, 284.
40. Haight, p. 68; *GEL*, II, 178n.
41. J. A. Froude, *The Nemesis of Faith* (London, 1849, reprinted with an introduction by Rosemary Ashton, 1988).
42. J. A. Froude to A. H. Clough, 28 February 1849, *The Correspondence of Arthur Hugh Clough*, ed. Frederick L. Mulhauser, 2 vols. (Oxford, 1957), I, 246–7.
43. *Coventry Herald*, 16 March 1849, reprinted in *George Eliot: Selected Critical Writings*, ed. Rosemary Ashton (Oxford, 1992), p. 15.
44. Cara Bray's engagement diary, MS Coventry.
45. GE to Cara Bray, 10 July 1860, *GEL*, III, 321.
46. Cross, I, 208.
47. GE to Charles and Cara Bray, 28 August 1849, *GEL*, I, 301–2.
48. Ibid., I, 290n.
49. GE to Fanny Houghton, 4 October 1849, ibid., VIII, 18.
50. GE to Charles and Cara Bray, 24 October 1849, ibid., I, 316.
51. GE to Sara Hennell, 26 October 1849, ibid., I, 320.
52. GE to Sara Hennell, 18 April 1849, and to Charles and Cara Bray, 4 December 1849, ibid., I, 280 and n, 321 and n.
53. Rosemary Ashton, *G. H. Lewes: A Life* (Oxford, 1991), p. 44.
54. GE to Charles and Cara Bray, 20 September 1849, *GEL*, I, 310.

55. Ibid., I, 307.
56. GE to Charles and Cara Bray and Sara Hennell, 22 December 1849, ibid., I, 324.
57. GE to Charles and Cara Bray, 4 October 1849, ibid., I, 312.
58. GE to Charles and Cara Bray, 13 September 1849, ibid., I, 306.
59. GE to Charles and Cara Bray, 11 October 1849, ibid., I, 315.
60. GE to Charles and Cara Bray, 28 August 1849, ibid., I, 302–3.
61. GE to Fanny Houghton, 6 September 1849, ibid., I, 304; IX, 338.
62. GE to Charles and Cara Bray, 28 August 1849, ibid., I, 301.
63. Ibid., I, 302.
64. GE to Charles and Cara Bray, 20 September 1849, ibid., I, 310.
65. Ibid., I, 303, 312, 330; Bray, *Phases of Opinion*, p. 89.
66. GE to Fanny Houghton, 9 February 1850, *GEL*, IX, 338.
67. Ibid., III, 187; GE to Fanny Houghton, 9 February 1850, and to Charles and Cara Bray, 4 December 1849, ibid., I, 328, 322.
68. The original was sold to the National Portrait Gallery in 1905 by M. D'Albert Durade's son. One copy is in Coventry City Libraries, one in the Bibliothèque Publique et Universitaire in Geneva, and the third has recently been discovered in the William Andrews Clark Memorial Library at the University of California Los Angeles, see *Newsletter* of UCLA Center for 17th- and 18th-Century Studies, no. 25 (Spring 1995).
69. See GE to François D'Albert Durade, 20 March 1875, *GEL*, VI, 129.
70. GE to Fanny Houghton, 30 March 1850, and to Sara Hennell, 11 April 1850, ibid., I, 333, 335.
71. GE to Cara Bray, 24 April 1850, ibid., I, 336; IX, 338.
72. Cara Bray's engagement diary, MS Coventry. No GE letters survive between 24 April and 30 November 1850.
73. *Westminster Review* (January 1851), *Essays*, p. 30.
74. Ibid., pp. 30–31.
75. GE to Charles and Cara Bray, 30 November 1850, *GEL*, I, 337.

CHAPTER FOUR: *Marian Evans in London:*
142 Strand 1851–3

1. *GEL*, I, 334–5n.
2. Dickens, *Bleak House* (London, 1853), chapter 16.
3. *Punch*, XXIII (25 September 1852), 139, and XXIX (21 July 1855), 27.
4. Spencer, *Autobiography*, I, 399.
5. See Chapman Diary, 27 June 1851, Haight, *George Eliot and John Chapman*, p. 185.

6. Eliza Lynn Linton, *My Literary Life*, p. 92.

7. Spencer, *Autobiography*, II, 33; [William Hale White], *The Autobiography of Mark Rutherford*, ed. Cupitt, p. 107.

8. See *George Eliot and John Chapman*, p. ix. Haight publishes the diary, and explains and restores the deleted passages where possible, by means of studying photographic enlargements. He thinks Chapman himself may have deleted the passages soon after writing them.

9. *George Eliot and John Chapman*, p. 123.

10. She first signed herself 'Marian Evans' in a letter to Chapman of 4 April 1851, *GEL*, I, 348.

11. Spencer, *Autobiography*, II, 33.

12. *George Eliot and John Chapman*, pp. 30, 54–5.

13. GE to Charles and Cara Bray, 28 January and 15 February 1851, *GEL*, I, 343 and n, 345.

14. Chapman Diary, 20 May 1851, *George Eliot and John Chapman*, p. 168.

15. GE to Charles and Cara Bray, 15 February 1851, *GEL*, I, 346. Haight assumes that Lewes reviewed Harriet Martineau's book in the *Leader*, see *GEL*, II, 122–3n, but Henry Crabb Robinson in an unpublished diary entry of 19 November 1851 ascribes it with certainty to GE, MS Dr Williams's Library.

16. Bessie Rayner Parkes Belloc, *In a Walled Garden*, p. 3.

17. GE to Charles and Cara Bray, 28 January 1851, *GEL*, I, 341–3.

18. Henry Crabb Robinson Diary, 8 February 1851, *Henry Crabb Robinson On Books*, II, 707.

19. *In a Walled Garden*, p. 3.

20. *Henry Crabb Robinson On Books*, II, 707.

21. *Leader*, 1 March 1851, p. 202.

22. Ibid., 8 March 1851, pp. 227, 228.

23. Henry Crabb Robinson Diary, 10 November 1851, MS Dr Williams's Library.

24. Chapman Diary, 8 January 1851, *George Eliot and John Chapman*, p. 129.

25. Chapman Diary, 9, 11, 12 January 1851, ibid., pp. 129–31 and n.

26. Ibid., pp. 125, 217, 205.

27. Ibid., p. 131.

28. Ibid., pp. 133–4.

29. Ibid., pp. 135–6.

30. Chapman Diary, 18 February 1851, ibid., pp. 141–2.

31. Chapman Diary, 24 March 1851, ibid., p. 147.

32. Chapman Diary, 11 January 1851, ibid., p. 130.

33. Chapman Diary, 19 January 1851, ibid., pp. 133–4.

34. See Ashton, *G. H. Lewes*, p. 329.

35. Chapman Diary, 12 January 1851, *George Eliot and John Chapman*, p. 131.
36. Haight, p. 71.
37. See Chapman Diary, 28 April and 21 June 1851, *George Eliot and John Chapman*, pp. 160, 182.
38. GE to John Chapman, 9 May 1851, *GEL*, I, 350.
39. Cara Bray's engagement diary, MS Coventry.
40. Chapman Diary, 27 and 30 May, 5 June 1851, *George Eliot and John Chapman*, pp. 171, 172, 175.
41. GE to John Chapman, 9 June 1851, *GEL*, VIII, 23.
42. *George Eliot and John Chapman*, p. 205.
43. GE to John Chapman, 12 June 1851, *GEL*, VIII, 24.
44. GE to John Chapman, 1 August 1851, ibid., 356–7.
45. Chapman Diary, 14 and 15 August 1851, *George Eliot and John Chapman*, pp. 201–2.
46. Chapman Diary, 16 August 1851, ibid., p. 202.
47. George Combe Journal, 29 August 1851, *GEL*, VIII, 27, 28.
48. Chapman Diary, 13 September 1851, *George Eliot and John Chapman*, p. 210.
49. George Combe to John Chapman, 7 December 1851, *GEL*, VIII, 33.
50. *Leader*, 20 September 1851, pp. 897–8.
51. Chapman Diary, 23 September 1851, *George Eliot and John Chapman*, p. 213.
52. GE to Cara Bray, 3 October 1851, and to Charles Bray, 4 October 1851, *GEL*, I, 363, 364.
53. Spencer, *Autobiography*, I, 360–2.
54. Ibid., I, 200–201.
55. Spencer, letter of 15 April 1851, ibid., I, 369.
56. GHL Journal, 28 January 1859, MS Yale.
57. Herbert Spencer to his father, 3 October 1851, *The Life and Letters of Herbert Spencer*, ed. David Duncan (London, 1908), p. 63.
58. See Ashton, *G. H. Lewes*, for a full discussion of Lewes's life and work.
59. Chapman Diary, 6 October 1851, *George Eliot and John Chapman*, p. 217.
60. GE to Charles Bray, 8 October 1851, *GEL*, I, 367.
61. Thomas Carlyle to Robert Browning, 10 October 1851, *Letters of Thomas Carlyle to John Stuart Mill, John Sterling, and Robert Browning*, ed. Alexander Carlyle (London, 1923), p. 288. For GE and Carlyle see Gordon S. Haight, 'The Carlyles and the Leweses' in *Carlyle and his Contemporaries: Essays in Honor of Charles Richard Sanders*, ed. John Clubbe (Durham, North Carolina, 1976), pp. 181–204.
62. GE to Sara Hennell, 13 October 1851, *GEL*, I, 368–9.
63. Chapman Diary, 21 September 1851, *George Eliot and John Chapman*, p. 213.
64. GE to Sara Hennell, 24 November 1851, and to Cara Bray, 27 November 1851, *GEL*, I, 376, 377.

65. *Westminster Review* (January 1852), *Essays*, pp. 49, 50. Dr Arnold's friend was John Keble.

66. GE to Cara Bray, 27 May 1852, *GEL*, II, 29.

67. GE to Cara Bray, 5 June 1852, ibid., II, 33.

68. See *George Eliot and John Chapman*, pp. 50–53.

69. George Combe to John Chapman, 7 December 1851, *GEL*, VIII, 33.

70. GE to Sara Hennell, 21 January 1852, ibid., II, 4, 5.

71. GE to Cara Bray, 28 February 1852, and to Clementia Taylor, 27 March 1852, ibid., II, 12, 15 and n.

72. GE to Charles and Cara Bray and Sara Hennell, 2 February 1852, ibid., II, 9.

73. Bessie Rayner Parkes to Barbara Leigh Smith, 6 and 27 March 1852, MSs Girton College, Cambridge (Bessie Rayner Parkes Collection).

74. GE to Clementia Taylor, 27 March 1852, *GEL*, II, 15.

75. Henry Crabb Robinson Diary, 12 February 1852, MS Dr Williams's Library.

76. GE to Sara Hennell, 21 April 1852, *GEL*, II, 19.

77. GE to Cara Bray, 30 March 1852, ibid., II, 16.

78. Spencer, *Autobiography*, I, 399.

79. Herbert Spencer to Edward Lott, 23 April 1852, ibid., I, 395.

80. GE to Herbert Spencer, 21 April 1852, *GEL*, VIII, 42.

81. GE to Charles and Cara Bray, 27 April 1852, ibid., II, 22.

82. GE to Sara Hennell, 29 June 1852, ibid., II, 40.

83. Spencer instructed his trustees to deposit the letters after his death with the British Museum, with the strict instruction that they should not be opened until 1985, MS BL (Add MS 65,530). The Trustees of the British Museum in fact allowed Haight to publish them in Vol. VIII of *GEL* in 1978.

84. Dickens, *Bleak House*, chapter 19.

85. GE to Herbert Spencer, 8? July 1852, *GEL*, VIII, 50–51.

86. GE to Herbert Spencer, 16? July 1852, ibid., VIII, 56–7.

87. GE to Herbert Spencer, 29? July 1852, ibid., VIII, 61.

88. Anthony Trollope, *He Knew He Was Right* (1869), chapter 94.

89. See *George Eliot and John Chapman*, p. 56.

90. GE to Charles Bray, 14 July 1852, *GEL*, II, 43–4. There is a huge correspondence between Chapman, Combe, and Bray in the Combe Papers, MSs National Library of Scotland, some of which Haight published in Vol. VIII of *GEL*.

91. Charles Bray to George Combe, 20 July 1852, *GEL*, VIII, 58.

92. GE to Cara Bray, 19 August 1852, ibid., II, 51.

93. GE to Fanny Houghton, 22 August 1852, ibid., II, 52.

94. See the early chapters of Ashton, *G. H. Lewes*.

95. GE to Charles Bray, 23 June 1852, *GEL*, II, 37.

96. R. K. Webb, *Harriet Martineau: A Radical Victorian* (London, 1960), p. 304.

97. GE to Charles Bray, 18 September 1852, *GEL*, II, 56.

98. GE to Charles and Cara Bray, 22 November 1852, ibid., II, 68.

99. GE to Charles and Cara Bray, 7 October 1852, ibid., II, 59.

100. GE to Charles and Cara Bray, 21 October 1852, ibid., II, 62.

101. GE to Charles and Cara Bray, 13 November 1852, ibid., II, 67.

102. GE to George Combe, 21 December 1852, ibid., VIII, 68.

103. GE to Charles and Cara Bray and Sara Hennell, 31 December 1852, ibid., II, 75.

104. GE to Charles Bray, 24 January 1853, and to Charles and Cara Bray, 26 February 1853, ibid., II, 83, 90.

105. GHL to F. O. Ward, [Spring 1853], *The Letters of George Henry Lewes*, ed. William Baker, 2 vols. (Victoria, British Columbia, 1995), I, 227.

106. George Bernard Shaw, *Saturday Review*, 20 June 1896 and 5 June 1897, reprinted in *Our Theatres in the Nineties*, 3 vols. (London, 1932), II, 161, III, 155.

107. See Ashton, *G. H. Lewes*, pp. 69–75.

108. GE to Herbert Spencer, 8? July 1852, *GEL*, VIII, 51.

109. See Ashton, *G. H. Lewes*, pp. 46–50.

110. William Baker, *The Libraries of George Eliot and George Henry Lewes* (Victoria, British Columbia, 1981), p. 43.

111. GHL, *A Biographical History of Philosophy*, 4 vols. in 2 (London, 1845–6), IV, 250.

112. Thomas Adolphus Trollope, *What I Remember*, 2 vols. (London, 1887), II, 299.

113. GE to Sara Hennell, 28 March 1853, to Charles and Cara Bray, 11 April 1853, and to Cara Bray, 16 April 1853, *GEL*, II, 94, 97, 98.

114. GE to Sara Hennell, 1 October and 25 November 1853, ibid., II, 118–19 and n, 127.

115. GE to John Chapman, 2 December 1853, ibid., II, 130.

CHAPTER FIVE: *Life with Lewes: Weimar and Berlin 1854–5*

1. GE to Charles and Cara Bray, 26 February 1853, *GEL*, II, 89.

2. GE to John Chapman, 19 December 1853, ibid., II, 133.

3. GE to John Chapman, December 1853, in Rosemary Ashton, 'New George Eliot Letters at the Huntington', *Huntington Library Quarterly*, LIV (Spring 1991), 120.

4. GE to Sara Hennell, 6 February 1854, *GEL*, II, 141.

5. Ludwig Feuerbach, *The Essence of Christianity*, translated by Marian Evans (London, 1854, reprinted New York, 1957), p. 271 (chapter 27).

6. GE to Charles and Cara Bray, 19 February and 11 April 1853, *GEL*, II, 88, 97.

7. GE to Fanny Houghton, December 1853, and to Charles and Cara Bray, 19 May 1854, ibid., II, 134, 157.

8. GE to George Combe, 3 March 1854, ibid., VIII, 104.

9. GE to Sara Hennell, 3 June 1854, ibid., II, 159.

10. See *GEL*, II, 50n, 163; VIII, 115n.

11. GE to Cara Bray, 18 April 1854, ibid., II, 150.

12. GE to Sara Hennell, 3 June 1854; GHL to Charles Bray, 25 June 1854, ibid., II, 160, VIII, 112.

13. GE to Charles Bray, 14 April 1854, ibid., II, 149.

14. GE to Charles Bray, 27 May 1854, and to Sara Hennell, 10 July 1854, ibid., II, 158, 165.

15. GE to Cara Bray, 15 February 1853, ibid., II, 87.

16. GE to Sara Hennell, 10 July 1854, ibid., II, 165.

17. Herbert Spencer, *Principles of Biology*, 2 vols. (London, 1864–7, reprinted 1890), I, 444–5.

18. GE to Charles and Cara Bray and Sara Hennell, 19 July 1854, *GEL*, II, 166.

19. GE Journal, 20 July 1854, MS Yale.

20. GE to John Chapman, 6 August 1854, *GEL*, VIII, 116.

21. GE to Charles Bray, 16 August 1854, ibid., II, 171.

22. GHL to Charles and Thornie Lewes, ibid., VIII, 120.

23. GE, 'Recollections of Weimar 1854', written 30 November 1854, MS Yale.

24. Ibid.

25. See Ashton, *G. H. Lewes*, pp. 126–8.

26. 'Recollections of Weimar', MS Yale.

27. Ashton, *G. H. Lewes*, pp. 81–2.

28. GE to John Chapman, 6 August 1854, *GEL*, VIII, 115.

29. GE to John Chapman, 30 August 1854, ibid., II, 173.

30. GE to Charles Bray, 16 August 1854, ibid., II, 170.

31. GE to Bessie Parkes, 10 September 1854, ibid., II, 173.

32. GE Journal, 10 August 1854, ibid., II, 170.

33. GE to Charles Bray, 16 August 1854, ibid., II, 171.

34. See *GEL*, I, 345 and n, 364.

35. Sara Hennell to GE, 20 October 1854, MS Coventry (acquired 1993).

36. GE to Charles Bray, 16 October 1854, *GEL*, II, 178, 179; IX, 341.

37. Sara Hennell to GE, 20 October 1854, MS Coventry.

38. GE to Sara Hennell, 31 October 1854, *GEL*, II, 181, 182.

39. Sara Hennell to GE, 15 November 1854, ibid., II, 186.

40. GE to John Chapman, 6 August 1854, ibid., VIII, 116; GE Journal 11 and 13 October 1854, MS Yale.

41. GHL to Thomas Carlyle, 19 October 1854, *GEL*, II, 176, 177.

42. Thomas Carlyle to Edward Fitzgerald, 19 October 1854, MS Cambridge University Library.

43. *GEL*, II, 177n.

44. Sir Charles Gavan Duffy, *Conversations with Carlyle* (London, 1892), p. 222.

45. GE to John Chapman, 15 October 1854, *GEL*, VIII, 124.

46. GE to John Chapman, 30 October 1854, ibid., II, 180.

47. Harriet Martineau to Henry Reeve, 17 November 1868, Webb, *Harriet Martineau*, p. 14.

48. Henry Crabb Robinson's diary for November–December 1854 is full of references to Hodgson, Martineau, Greg and others leaving the *Westminster Review* and starting the *National Review*, MSs Dr Williams's Library.

49. John Chapman to George Combe, 4 October 1854, *GEL*, VIII, 122.

50. John Chapman to Robert Chambers, 16 October 1854, ibid., VIII, 125–6.

51. See *George Eliot and John Chapman*, p. 88.

52. George Combe to Charles Bray, 15 November 1854, *GEL*, VIII, 129.

53. Charles Bray to George Combe, 8 October 1854, ibid., VIII, 122–3.

54. Cara Bray to Cecilia Combe, 23 September 1854, ibid., VIII, 119.

55. Charles Bray to George Combe, 18 October 1854, ibid., VIII, 126.

56. Charles Bray to George Combe, 28 October 1854, ibid., VIII, 128, 129.

57. George Combe to Charles Bray, 15 November 1854, ibid., VIII, 130.

58. Charles Bray to George Combe, 19 November 1854, ibid., VIII, 131.

59. Thomas Woolner to William Bell Scott, 4 October 1854, ibid., II, 176; Charles Kingsley to F. D. Maurice [1857], Robert Bernard Martin, *The Dust of Combat: A Life of Charles Kingsley* (London, 1959), p. 181.

60. Shirley Brooks Diary, 25 June 1873, MS London Library.

61. Bessie's daughter Marie Belloc Lowndes, unpublished notes on her mother's life, MS Girton.

62. Elizabeth Gaskell to George Smith, 2 November 1857, *The Letters of Mrs Gaskell*, ed. J. A. V. Chapple and Arthur Pollard (Manchester, 1966), p. 587.

63. *Diaries and Letters of Marie Belloc Lowndes 1911–1947*, ed. Susan Lowndes (London, 1971), p. 99.

64. John Chapman to Barbara Leigh Smith, 29 August and 14 and 17 September 1855, *George Eliot and John Chapman*, pp. 89, 91.

65. Sheila R. Herstein, *A Mid-Victorian Feminist: Barbara Leigh Smith Bodichon* (New Haven, Connecticut, 1985), pp. 61, 170ff., 134.

66. *George Eliot and John Chapman*, pp. 91–2.

67. Bessie Parkes to Sam Blackwell, [12 September 1854] and 28 September 1854, MSs Girton.

68. Marie Belloc Lowndes, *I, Too, Have Lived in Arcadia* (London, 1941), p. 39.

69. Joseph Parkes to Bessie Parkes, 1, 5, and 14 October 1854, MSs Girton.

70. George Combe to Charles Bray, 15 November 1854, *GEL*, VIII, 129.

71. Joseph Parkes to Bessie Parkes, 1 October 1854, MS Girton.

72. *Westminster Review*, LXII (October 1854), 559.

73. Henry Crabb Robinson Diary, 14 October 1854, MS Dr Williams's Library.

74. 'Woman in France: Madame de Sablé', *Westminster Review* (October 1854), *Essays*, pp. 53, 57, 80, 81.

75. GE Journal, 18 September and 28 October 1854, MS Yale; *GEL*, IX, 177 and n.

76. 'Liszt, Wagner, and Weimar', *Fraser's Magazine* (July 1855), *Essays*, p. 103.

77. GE Journal, 1, 7, and 30 October 1854, MS Yale.

78. GE to Charles Bray, 12 November 1854, *GEL*, II, 184.

79. GE to Charles Bray, 23 June 1855, ibid., II, 204.

80. GE Journal, 4 October 1854, MS Yale.

81. GE Journal, 29 September and 8 October 1854, ibid.

82. GE Journal, 8 August 1854, and 'Recollections of Weimar', ibid.

83. GE Journal, 1, 3 November 1854, ibid.

84. See T. H. Pickett, 'George Henry Lewes's Letters to K. A. Varnhagen von Ense', *Modern Language Review*, LXXX (July 1985), 513–32.

85. Varnhagen Diary, 5 November 1854, *Aus dem Nachlass Varnhagen's von Ense, Tagebücher*, ed. Ludmilla Assing, 15 vols. (Leipzig, 1861–70, Berlin, 1905), XI, 300.

86. GE Journal, 7 November 1854, MS Yale.

87. Varnhagen Diary, 1 October 1852, *Tagebücher*, IX, 374.

88. 'Recollections of Berlin 1854–5', written at Dover, 27 March 1855, MS Yale.

89. GE to John Chapman, 9 January 1855, *GEL*, VIII, 134.

90. 'Recollections of Berlin', MS Yale.

91. *Leader*, 28 July 1855, *Essays*, p. 153.

92. 'Recollections of Berlin', MS Yale.

93. GE Journal, 6 February 1855, ibid.

94. GE to Charles Bray, 12 November 1854, *GEL*, II, 184, 185.

95. GE Journal, 21 January 1855, MS Yale. The letter itself is lost.

96. GE to Sara Hennell, 22 November 1854, *GEL*, II, 188, 189.

97. GE Journal, 25 February 1855, MS Yale.

98. Benedict de Spinoza, *Ethics*, translated by George Eliot, ed. Thomas Deegan (Salzburg, 1981), p. v.

99. GHL, *The Life and Works of Goethe*, 2 vols. (London, 1855), I, 281, 283.

100. 'Recollections of Berlin', MS Yale.
101. GHL, *Life of Goethe*, II, 213.
102. Ibid., II, 210, 212.
103. 'Recollections of Berlin', MS Yale.
104. GHL, *Life of Goethe*, II, 376.
105. Ibid., II, 379.
106. Ibid., I, 144.
107. Ibid., II, 356.
108. 'Recollections of Berlin', MS Yale.

CHAPTER SIX: *The Strong-minded Woman of the*
Westminster Review *1855–6*

1. See 'G. H. Lewes's Literary Receipts', *GEL*, VII, 383 (Appendix II).
2. See Ashton, *G. H. Lewes*, pp. 178–9.
3. Ibid., pp. 83, 161.
4. Ibid., p. 161.
5. GE Journal, 9 and 10 April 1855, MS Yale.
6. GE to Sara Hennell, 16 March 1855, *GEL*, II, 194.
7. GE to Bessie Parkes, 16 March 1855, ibid., II, 195–6.
8. GE to Charles Bray, 4 April 1855, ibid., II, 197.
9. Dickens to Wilkie Collins, 4 April 1855, *Letters*, Pilgrim Edition, VII, 586.
10. GE to Charles Bray, 1 May 1855, *GEL*, II, 199.
11. GE to Cara Bray, 4 September 1855, ibid., II, 214.
12. GE to Charles Bray, 16 July 1855, ibid., II, 210.
13. GE to Cara Bray, 4 September 1855, ibid., II, 214.
14. Bessie Parkes to Barbara Bodichon, 18 November 1863, MS Girton.
15. Trollope to Rhoda Broughton, 26 October 1874, *Letters of Anthony Trollope*, II, 632.
16. *The Mill on the Floss*, ed. A. S. Byatt (Harmondsworth, 1979), Book 7, chapter 2, 'St Ogg's Passes Judgment'.
17. GE to Sara Hennell, 13 September 1855, *GEL*, II, 217.
18. GE to Sara Hennell, 21 July 1855, ibid., II, 211.
19. Marie Belloc Lowndes, in an unpublished volume of biography of her mother, MS Girton. Marie Lowndes also discusses Barbara's and Bessie's relations with GE and opinions of Lewes in an unpublished correspondence with Gordon S. Haight in 1942, MSs Yale.
20. Barbara Leigh Smith to GE, 14 January 1856, MS Yale.
21. GE to John Chapman, 25 June 1855, *GEL*, II, 206.
22. GE to John Chapman, 27 June 1855, ibid., II, 208.

23. See GE's note on GHL's accounts, ibid., VII, 383 (Appendix II).
24. GE to Sara Hennell, 28 July 1855, ibid., II, 212.
25. 'Lord Brougham's Literature', *Leader*, 7 July 1855, *Essays*, pp. 138, 139, 142.
26. 'Life and Opinions of Milton', *Leader*, 4 August 1855, ibid., pp. 156–7.
27. See O. R. McGregor, *Divorce in England: A Centenary Study* (London, 1957), pp. 17–18; Lee Holcombe, 'Victorian Wives and Property', in *A Widening Sphere: Changing Roles of Victorian Women*, ed. Martha Vicinus (Bloomington, Indiana, 1977), pp. 8–9.
28. 'Margaret Fuller and Mary Wollstonecraft', *Leader*, 13 October 1855, *Essays*, p. 203.
29. GE to [Emanuel Deutsch], 7 July 1871, *GEL*, V, 160.
30. See GHL to Richard Owen, September 1855, ibid., VIII, 142. For an excellent account of Owen's career, see Nicolaas A. Rupke, *Richard Owen: Victorian Naturalist* (New Haven, Connecticut, 1994).
31. GE to Charles Bray, 17 June 1855, *GEL*, II, 202–3.
32. Cross, I, 384.
33. 'Evangelical Teaching: Dr. Cumming', *Westminster Review* (October 1855), *Essays*, pp. 159–60.
34. Tennyson, *In Memoriam* (1850), stanza xcvi, lines 11–12.
35. *Essays*, p. 173.
36. Ibid., p. 174.
37. Ibid., p. 186.
38. Charles Bray to GE, 13 October 1855, MS Yale.
39. GE to Charles Bray, 15 October 1855, *GEL*, II, 218.
40. '*Westward Ho!*', *Leader*, 19 May 1855, p. 475.
41. '*Westward Ho!*', *Westminster Review* (July 1855), *Essays*, pp. 126–7.
42. '*Constance Herbert*', *Westminster Review* (July 1855), ibid., pp. 134, 135.
43. See Ashton, *The German Idea*, pp. 82–7.
44. 'The Morality of *Wilhelm Meister*', *Leader*, 21 July 1855, *Essays*, p. 145.
45. Ibid., pp. 146–7.
46. Ibid., p. 147.
47. GE to Charles Bray, 21 November 1855, *GEL*, II, 221.
48. Thomas Carlyle to GHL, 7 August 1855, ibid., VIII, 141.
49. Thomas Carlyle to GHL, 3 November 1855, ibid., VIII, 145. See also Ashton, *G. H. Lewes*, pp. 162–8.
50. *British Quarterly Review*, XXIII (April 1856), 468–9.
51. See *GEL*, VII, 358, 373 (Appendix I, Appendix II).
52. Cross, I, 385.
53. GE to Fanny Houghton, 28 December 1855, *GEL*, II, 223.
54. GE to Charles Bray, 1 January 1856, ibid., II, 224.
55. Barbara Leigh Smith to GE, 14 January 1856, MS Yale.

56. See GE to Sara Hennell, 18 and 28 January and 19 February 1856, *GEL*, II, 225, 227.

57. GE to John Chapman, 1 February 1856, Ashton, 'New George Eliot Letters at the Huntington', p. 122.

58. GE Journal, 19 February 1856, MS Yale.

59. See Duffy, *Conversations with Carlyle*, p. 222; Henry Crabb Robinson Diary, 17 July 1859, *Henry Crabb Robinson On Books*, II, 786.

60. See *GEL*, VIII, 156–60. The translation was edited by Thomas Deegan (Salzburg, 1981).

61. 'German Wit: Heinrich Heine', *Westminster Review* (January 1856), *Essays*, pp. 221, 222.

62. Ibid., pp. 218, 219, 220.

63. Ibid., p. 245.

64. 'The Natural History of German Life', *Westminster Review* (July 1856), ibid., p. 287.

65. Ibid., p. 299.

66. 'Art and Belles Lettres', *Westminster Review* (April 1856), *Selected Critical Writings*, ed. Ashton, p. 248.

67. 'The Natural History of German Life', *Essays*, p. 271.

68. GHL, 'The Principles of Success in Literature', chapter 2, *Fortnightly Review*, I (1 June 1865), 187.

69. GE Journal, 29 April 1856, MS Yale.

70. 'Sea-side Studies', *Blackwood's Magazine*, LXXX (August 1856), 190.

71. GE Journal, 13 May and 5 June 1856, MS Yale.

72. 'Recollections of Ilfracombe', 8 May–26 June 1856, *GEL*, II, 248.

73. GE Journal, 20 July 1856, MS Yale.

74. GE to Isaac Evans, 27 May 1856, *GEL*, VIII, 155, 156.

75. GE to Sara Hennell, 29 June 1856, ibid., II, 256.

76. GE to Clementia Taylor, 8 June 1856, ibid., II, 254.

77. GE to Barbara Leigh Smith, 13 June 1856, ibid., II, 255.

78. GE Journal, 20 July 1856, MS Yale.

79. John Chapman to Barbara Leigh Smith, 29 August and 1 September 1855, MSs Yale. For accounts of Chapman's relationship with Barbara, see *George Eliot and John Chapman*, and Herstein, *A Mid-Victorian Feminist*.

80. See Mason, *The Making of Victorian Sexuality*, p. 171; Patricia Anderson, *When Passion Reigned: Sex and the Victorians* (New York, 1995), p. 121.

81. John Chapman to Barbara Leigh Smith, 17 September 1855, MS Yale.

82. Herstein, *A Mid-Victorian Feminist*, p. 10.

83. See John Chapman to Barbara Leigh Smith, 15 September 1855, MS Yale; *George Eliot and John Chapman*, p. 98.

84. Margaret Crompton, 'Prelude to Arcadia: The Early Life and Friendships

of Bessie Rayner Parkes', unpublished TS, pp. 115–16, MS Girton; Marie Lowndes to Gordon S. Haight, 6 July and 31 August 1942, MSs Yale.

85. Marie Lowndes to Gordon S. Haight, 31 August 1942, MS Yale. Mrs Lowndes paraphrases Barbara's letter to her mother, telling Haight that she has destroyed the original.

86. GE to John Chapman, 20 July 1856, *GEL*, II, 258.

87. GE to Charles Bray, 1 April 1856, ibid., II, 235; GHL to John Sibree, 2 April 1856, ibid., VIII, 152.

88. See GE to Sara Hennell, 6 April 1856, ibid., II, 236 and n.

89. See GE to Charles Bray, 5 September 1856, ibid., II, 262.

90. 'Silly Novels by Lady Novelists', *Westminster Review* (October 1856), *Essays*, p. 301.

91. Ibid., pp. 302, 303.

92. Ibid., p. 310.

93. See Robert Lee Wolff, *Gains and Losses: Novels of Faith and Doubt in Victorian England* (London, 1977).

94. 'Silly Novels', *Essays*, pp. 318, 302.

95. Ibid., p. 324.

96. GE Journal, 22 September 1856, MS Yale.

CHAPTER SEVEN: *The Birth of George Eliot:* Scenes of Clerical Life 1856–7

1. See John Blackwood to GE, 29 December 1856 and 30 January 1857, *GEL*, II, 284, 290.

2. GE to Sara Hennell, 4 October 1849, ibid., I, 312.

3. GE Journal, 6 December 1857, ibid., II, 406.

4. Ibid., II, 406–7.

5. Cross, I, 431.

6. GHL Journal, 7 January 1857, MS Yale.

7. GHL to John Blackwood, 6 November 1856, *GEL*, II, 269.

8. 'Worldliness and Other-Worldliness: The Poet Young', *Westminster Review* (January 1857), *Essays*, pp. 335–85.

9. John Blackwood to GHL, 12 November 1856, *GEL*, II, 272.

10. *Scenes of Clerical Life* (1858), ed. David Lodge (Harmondsworth, 1973), p. 93.

11. Ibid., p. 109.

12. Ibid., p. 80.

13. Ibid., p. 81.

14. Ibid., pp. 78–9.

15. Robert Evans to Francis Newdigate, 10 November 1836, MS WCRO.

16. See Haight, p. 217; Laski, *George Eliot and Her World*, p. 55.
17. *Scenes of Clerical Life*, pp. 102–3.
18. John Blackwood to GHL, 12 November 1856, *GEL*, II, 272.
19. GHL to John Blackwood, 15 November 1856, and John Blackwood to GHL, 18 November 1856, ibid., II, 273, 275.
20. GHL to John Blackwood, 22 November 1856, ibid., II, 277.
21. John Blackwood to Julia Blackwood, 1 March 1858, ibid., II, 436.
22. GE Journal, 10 December 1857, MS Yale.
23. GHL Journal, 5 and 16 December 1856, ibid.
24. 'Worldliness and Other-Worldliness', *Essays*, pp. 341, 349.
25. John Chapman to GE, 15 January 1857, *GEL*, VIII, 163.
26. GE to John Chapman, 15 January 1857, Ashton, 'New George Eliot Letters at the Huntington', pp. 122–3.
27. John Blackwood to GE, 30 January 1857, *GEL*, II, 291.
28. GE to William Blackwood, 4 February 1857, ibid., II, 292.
29. John Blackwood to GE, 10 February 1857, ibid., II, 293.
30. See GE to Sara Hennell, 26 January 1857, ibid., II, 290 and n.
31. GHL to John Blackwood, 11 February 1857, ibid., II, 295.
32. John Blackwood to GHL, 13 February 1857, ibid., II, 296.
33. GE Journal, 11 February 1857, MS Yale.
34. Joseph Langford to John Blackwood, 27 January 1857, *GEL*, II, 298n.
35. Joseph Langford to John Blackwood, 16 February 1857, ibid., II, 298.
36. See GHL to John Blackwood, 26 April 1857, and John Blackwood to GE, 8 June 1857, ibid., II, 321 and n, 345.
37. See Haight, pp. 220–21.
38. *Scenes of Clerical Life*, p. 235.
39. GE Journal, 1 February 1857, MS Yale.
40. John Blackwood to GHL, 30 April 1857, *GEL*, II, 323.
41. GE to John Blackwood, 1 May 1857, ibid., II, 324.
42. GHL to John Blackwood, 9? August 1857, ibid., II, 378; IX, 342.
43. *Scenes of Clerical Life*, p. 259.
44. Ibid., p. 322.
45. Ibid.
46. GE to François D'Albert Durade, 6 December 1859, *GEL*, III, 230–31.
47. *Scenes of Clerical Life*, p. 335.
48. GE to John Blackwood, 11 June 1857, *GEL*, II, 347.
49. According to her Journal, GE began *The Life of Charlotte Brontë* (1857) on 9 April and finished it on 16 April 1857, MS Yale.
50. See Kathleen Adams, *Those of Us Who Loved Her*, p. 7.
51. GE to John Blackwood, 11 June 1857, *GEL*, II, 348.

52. John Blackwood to GE, 14 June 1857, ibid., II, 352, 353.

53. GE to John Blackwood, 16 June 1857, ibid., II, 353.

54. GE to Cara Bray, 30 October 1857, ibid., II, 397.

55. See GE to Charles Bray, 2 December 1856, ibid., II, 279.

56. See GE to Sara Hennell, 24 February 1857, and to Mary Cash, 6 June 1857, ibid., II, 302, 343.

57. GE to Cara Bray, nd [1856], MS Herbert Art Gallery and Museum, Coventry (MS acquired in January 1996).

58. See GE Journal, 23 December 1861, MS Yale.

59. GE to Cara Bray, 5 June 1857, GEL, II, 339.

60. GE to Bessie Parkes, 24 September 1857, ibid., II, 384, 385.

61. See GE to Cara Bray, 5 April 1857, ibid., II, 314.

62. Ibid.; GE Journal, 22 April 1857, MS Yale; GE to Fanny Houghton, 3 May 1857, GEL, VIII, 169.

63. GE to Isaac Evans, 16 April 1857, GEL, II, 317.

64. GE Journal, 2 May 1857, MS Yale.

65. GE to Isaac Evans, 26 May 1857, GEL, II, 331–2.

66. GE to John Chapman, 27 May 1857, ibid., VIII, 171.

67. GE to Fanny Houghton, 2 June 1857, ibid., II, 336.

68. Vincent Holbeche to GE, 9 June 1857, ibid., II, 346.

69. GE to Vincent Holbeche, 13 June 1857, ibid., II, 349.

70. GE Journal, 22 June 1857, MS Yale.

71. GE to Sara Hennell, 14 July 1857, GEL, II, 364.

72. GE to Sara Hennell, 5 June 1857, ibid., II, 342.

73. GE to Mary Cash, 6 June 1857, ibid., II, 343.

74. Eliza Lynn Linton to Herbert Spencer, 27 November 1885, MS BL, part quoted in Layard, Life of Mrs Lynn Linton, p. 252.

75. William Pitman Jones to Messrs Blackwood, 12 August 1857, GEL, II, 375.

76. Haight, p. 9.

77. GE to John Blackwood, 18 August 1857, GEL, II, 375.

78. GE to Fanny Houghton, 2 June 1857, ibid., II, 337.

79. GHL to John Blackwood, 19 July 1857, ibid., II, 366.

80. Impressions of Theophrastus Such, pp. 88, 97.

81. GE Journal, 31 July and 4 August 1857, MS Yale; GE to Sara Hennell, 21 September 1857, GEL, II, 382.

82. GE Journal, 24 August 1857, MS Yale.

83. John Blackwood to GE, 28 October 1857; GE to John Blackwood, 30 October 1857, GEL, II, 393–4, 395.

84. See GE to John Blackwood, 11 December 1857, ibid., II, 411 and n.

85. GE Journal, 31 December 1857, MS Yale.

86. GE to John Blackwood, 17 October 1857, *GEL*, II, 387; GE Journal, 22 October 1857, MS Yale.

CHAPTER EIGHT: *Provincial Life Revisited:*
Adam Bede *1858–9*

1. GE Journal, 2 January 1858, *GEL*, II, 415–16.
2. *The Times*, 2 January 1858, in *George Eliot: The Critical Heritage*, ed. David Carroll (London, 1977), pp. 61, 62.
3. Charles Dickens to GE, 18 January 1858, *GEL*, II, 423, 424.
4. Charles Dickens to John Blackwood, 27 January 1858, ibid., II, 427, 428.
5. Jane Welsh Carlyle Notebook, *New Letters and Memorials of Jane Welsh Carlyle*, ed. Alexander Carlyle, 2 vols. (London, 1903), II, 115.
6. Jane Welsh Carlyle to GE, 21 January 1858, *GEL*, II, 426, 425.
7. GE to John Blackwood, 7 November 1857, ibid., II, 400.
8. *Saturday Review*, 29 May 1858, in *Critical Heritage*, pp. 67, 70.
9. Henry Crabb Robinson Diary, 18 and 21 August 1859, *Henry Crabb Robinson On Books*, II, 789–90.
10. See Haight, p. 247; GHL to John Blackwood, 5 February 1858, *GEL*, II, 432; John Blackwood to GE, 10 February 1858, ibid., II, 433.
11. GE Journal, 28 February 1858, *GEL*, II, 435–6.
12. GE Journal, 2–3 February 1858, ibid., II, 430; GE to Bessie Parkes, 3 February 1858, ibid., II, 431. For the *English Woman's Journal* see *Barbara Leigh Smith Bodichon and the Langham Place Group*, ed. Candida Ann Lacey (London, 1987).
13. See GE to Sara Hennell, 9 October 1856, 2 March 1857, 24 February 1857, *GEL*, II, 265–6, 304, 301. GE's inscribed copy is in Dr Williams's Library.
14. GE to Charles Bray, 9 and 15 November 1857, *GEL*, II, 402, 403.
15. GE to Cara Bray, 29 March 1858, ibid., II, 443.
16. GE to Cara Bray, 27 March 1858, ibid., VIII, 199–200.
17. See GE Journal, 26 February 1858, MS Yale.
18. GE to Charles Bray, 29 March 1858, *GEL*, II, 442–3.
19. GE to Charles Bray, 31 March 1858, ibid., II, 444.
20. GE Journal, 12 October 1856, MS Yale.
21. Spencer, *Autobiography*, I, 492.
22. John Blackwood to Julia Blackwood, 1 March 1858, *GEL*, II, 436.
23. John Blackwood to GHL, 11 March 1858, ibid., VIII, 197.
24. John Blackwood to GE, 31 March 1858, ibid., II, 446.

25. John Blackwood to GHL, 2 April 1858; GHL to John Blackwood, 3 April 1858, ibid., II, 447, 448.

26. GE to John Blackwood, 1 April 1858, ibid., VIII, 201.

27. 'The Morality of *Wilhelm Meister*', *Essays*, p. 146.

28. GE Journal, 7 March 1858, MS Yale.

29. GHL Journal, March 1858, ibid.

30. See *GEL*, VIII, 359–60, 374–5 (Appendix I and II).

31. See Ivan Petrovitch Pavlov, *Lectures on Conditioned Reflexes*, translated and edited by W. Horsley Gantt, 2 vols. (London, 1928, reprinted 1963), I, 13.

32. GHL to John Blackwood, 14 April 1858, *GEL*, II, 448–9.

33. GE Journal, 14 April 1858, MS Yale.

34. GHL Journal, 3 May 1858, ibid.

35. GE to Sara Hennell, 10 May 1858, *GEL*, II, 452.

36. Ibid., II, 454.

37. GE Journal, 30 April 1858, MS Yale.

38. See the shrine and prison scenes of Goethe's *Faust*, Part One (1808).

39. 'History of "Adam Bede"', GE Journal, 30 November 1858, *GEL*, II, 504.

40. Ibid.

41. GE Journal, 4 May 1858, MS Yale.

42. John Blackwood to GHL, 23 May 1858, *GEL*, II, 457, 458.

43. GE to John Blackwood, 28 May 1858, ibid., II, 459.

44. GE to Sara Hennell, 28 July 1858, ibid., II, 472.

45. See GE to Sara Hennell, 22 September 1856, ibid., II, 264.

46. GE to Sara Hennell, 5 September 1858, ibid., II, 479.

47. GE to Sara Hennell, 17 April 1858, ibid., II, 451.

48. GE Journal, 30 November 1858, ibid., II, 504.

49. 'Recollections of our Journey from Munich to Dresden', GE Journal, 27 October 1858, MS Yale.

50. *Adam Bede*, ed. Stephen Gill (Harmondsworth, 1980), pp. 223, 225 (chapter 17).

51. *Saturday Review*, 26 February 1859, in *Critical Heritage*, p. 76.

52. Ibid., p. 73.

53. John Blackwood to GE, 31 March 1858, *GEL*, II, 444, 445.

54. *GEL*, III, 40n. The MS of *Adam Bede* is in the British Library.

55. GE to John Blackwood, 17 October 1857, *GEL*, II, 387.

56. *Adam Bede*, p. 127 (chapter 7).

57. Ibid., p. 130.

58. *Examiner*, 5 March 1859, and *Saturday Review*, 26 February 1859, in *Critical Heritage*, pp. 11, 76.

59. *Adam Bede*, p. 166 (chapter 11).

60. Ibid., p. 195 (chapter 15).

61. Ibid., pp. 384, 385 (chapter 31).

62. Ibid., p. 386.

63. *GEL*, II, 502.

64. Ibid., II, 503.

65. See *George Eliot: A Writer's Notebook 1854–1879, and Uncollected Writings*, ed. Joseph Wiesenfarth (Charlottesville, Virginia, 1981), pp. 24–7. For Dinah Morris and Elizabeth Evans see also Valentine Cunningham, *Everywhere Spoken Against: Dissent in the Victorian Novel* (Oxford, 1975), pp. 153–7.

66. See Sibree and Caston, *Independency in Warwickshire*, p. 75.

67. Charles Bray to GE, 18 September 1859, MS Yale.

68. Mary Cash's account, in the second edition of Cross (1886), I, 412 (Appendix).

69. The rage for identification continued after GE's death. In 1898 Lady Newdigate-Newdegate published the correspondence of her ancestor Sir Roger Newdigate under the title, taken from 'Mr Gilfil's Life-Story', *The Cheverels of Cheverel Manor*; in 1905 a grandson of Robert Evans's sister Ann wrote over-systematically about the Evans family, finding a host of originals for *Adam Bede*, see William Mottram, *The True Story of George Eliot in Relation to 'Adam Bede'*.

70. Sara Hennell to GE, 26 June 1859; GE to Charles and Cara Bray and Sara Hennell, 27 June 1859, *GEL*, III, 98, 99.

71. *Adam Bede*, p. 583 (Epilogue).

72. For discussions of GE and feminism, see in particular Jenni Calder, *Women and Marriage in Victorian Fiction* (London, 1976), pp. 121–58; Elaine Showalter, *A Literature of Their Own: British Women Novelists from Brontë to Lessing* (Princeton, New Jersey, 1977); Gillian Beer, *George Eliot*, Key Women Writers series (Brighton, 1986).

73. See John Sutherland, *Victorian Fiction: Writers, Publishers, Readers* (London, 1995), pp. 62, 71–3.

74. See Mason, *The Making of Victorian Sexuality*, p. 238; A. James Hammerton, 'Feminism and Female Emigration 1861–1886', in *A Widening Sphere*, p. 52ff.; Lucia Zedner, *Women, Crime, and Custody in Victorian England* (Oxford, 1991), pp. 63–4.

75. GHL Journal, 26 June 1859, *GEL*, III, 102–3n.

76. GE Journal, 4 November 1858, ibid., II, 492–3n.

77. John Blackwood to GE, 23 November 1858; GE to John Blackwood, 25 November 1858, ibid., II, 499, 500 and n.

78. GE Journal, 30 November 1858, ibid., II, 504–5.

79. GE Journal, 5 November 1858, ibid., II, 494n.

80. GE to John Chapman, 5 November 1858, ibid., II, 494.

81. Spencer, *Autobiography*, II, 38.

82. GE to John Blackwood, 1 December 1858; GHL to John Chapman, 12 February 1859, *GEL*, II, 505 and n, III, 13.

83. GE to John Blackwood, 22 December 1858, ibid., II, 509.

84. John Blackwood to GHL, 31 December 1858, ibid., II, 513.

85. See *GEL*, VII, 360, 375 (Appendix I and II).

86. John Blackwood to GHL, 4 February 1859, ibid., III, 8–9.

87. GHL to John Blackwood, 5 February 1859, ibid., III, 10.

88. *Saturday Review*, 26 February 1859, in *Critical Heritage*, p. 74.

89. Jane Welsh Carlyle to GE, 20 February 1859, *GEL*, III, 17, 18.

90. Elizabeth Gaskell to John Blackwood, 9 March 1859, ibid., VIII, 224, 225.

91. Hansard's *Parliamentary Debates*, third series, CLII (3 February–10 March 1859), 1507.

92. *Adam Bede*, p. 394 (chapter 32).

93. Ibid., p. 569 (chapter 53).

94. GE to John Blackwood, 25 February 1859, *GEL*, III, 25.

95. John Blackwood to GE, 16 March 1859, ibid., III, 33; William Blackwood to GE, 5 May 1859, ibid., III, 65 and n; GHL Journal, 9 July 1859, ibid., III, 118n.

96. Ibid., III, 234–5n; see also J. A. Sutherland, *Victorian Novelists and Publishers* (London, 1976), p. 190.

97. Henry Crabb Robinson Diary, 10, 16, 22 March, 16 April 1859, *Henry Crabb Robinson On Books*, II, 782, 783.

98. *The Times*, 12 April 1859, in *Critical Heritage*, p. 77.

99. Letter of 29 June 1859, *Dearest Child: Letters between Queen Victoria and the Princess Royal 1858–1861*, ed. Roger Fulford (London, 1964), p. 198.

100. See Haight, pp. 335, 336.

101. See *GEL*, III, 48, 50.

102. Ibid., III, 74–5, 93.

103. GHL to Charles Bray, 30 June 1859, ibid., VIII, 237.

104. Ibid.

105. GHL Journal, 24 March 1859, ibid., III, 49n.

106. GE to John Blackwood, 30 July 1859, ibid., III, 124.

107. Chrissey Clarke to Isaac Evans, 6 January 1859, ibid., VIII, 222.

108. GE to Cara Bray, 24 February 1859, and to Charles Bray, 28 February 1859, ibid., III, 23, 27.

109. GHL Journal, 24 February 1859, ibid., III, 24n.

110. See GE to Cara Bray, 8 March 1859, and to Sara Hennell, 21 March 1859, ibid., III, 30, 38.

111. GE to Sara Hennell, 21 May 1859, ibid., III, 71.

112. *Adam Bede*, p. 459 (chapter 40).

113. GE Journal, 20 June 1859, *GEL*, III, 90n.
114. Charles Bray to GE, 26 June 1859, ibid., III, 95; Charles Bray to GE, 18 September 1859, MS Yale.
115. Cara Bray to GE, 25 June and 24 July 1859, MSs Yale.
116. Sara Hennell to GE, 14 April 1859, MS Yale; GE to Sara Hennell, 15 April 1859, *GEL*, III, 48.
117. Sara Hennell to GE, 26 June 1859, *GEL*, III, 95–6.
118. Sara Hennell to GE, 5 September 1859, MS Yale.
119. Barbara Bodichon to GE, 26 April 1859; GE and GHL to Barbara Bodichon, 5 May 1859, *GEL*, III, 56, 63, 64.
120. GHL to Barbara Bodichon, 5 May 1859; Barbara Bodichon to GE, 26 April 1859, ibid., III, 65, 56.
121. Annie Leigh Smith to GE, 29 June 1859; GE to Barbara Bodichon, 23 July 1859, ibid., VIII, 237, 239 and n.
122. Bessie Parkes to GE, 17 August 1859, ibid., VIII, 241.
123. GE Journal, 17 April 1859, MS Yale.
124. GHL to John Blackwood, 21 April 1859, *GEL*, III, 55.

CHAPTER NINE: *More Provincial Life:* The Mill on
the Floss *1859–60*

1. John Blackwood to GE, 16 March 1859, *GEL*, III, 33.
2. GE Journal, 12 January 1859, ibid., III, 33n; *George Eliot: A Writer's Notebook*, pp. 36–8.
3. GE to John Blackwood, 29 April 1859, *GEL*, III, 60.
4. GE Journal, 26 April 1859, ibid., III, 60n.
5. GE to John Blackwood, 31 March and 29 April 1859, ibid., III, 41, 60.
6. John Blackwood to GE, 18 May 1859, ibid., III, 67.
7. *The Lifted Veil*, ed. Beryl Gray (London, 1985), pp. 1, 66. The story was first published in *Blackwood's Magazine* in July 1859, then first collected in the Cabinet Edition of GE's works in 1878.
8. John Blackwood to GE, 18 May 1859, *GEL*, III, 67.
9. GHL Journal, 4 April 1859, MS Yale.
10. Henry James, *Nation* (April 1878), in *A Century of George Eliot Criticism*, ed. Gordon S. Haight (London, 1966), p. 131.
11. *The Lifted Veil*, pp. 21, 22.
12. Spencer, *Autobiography*, I, 396.
13. GE to Barbara Bodichon, 5 May 1859, *GEL*, III, 64.
14. See GE to Charles Bray, 1 May 1855; GHL Journal, 29 April 1859, ibid., II, 199; III, 61.

15. See B. M. Gray, 'Pseudo-Science and George Eliot's "The Lifted Veil"', *Nineteenth-Century Fiction*, XXXVI (March 1982), 410.

16. GE to George Combe, 8 April 1852, *GEL*, VIII, 41.

17. John Blackwood to GE, 21 December 1866, and 8 July 1859, ibid., IV, 322; III, 112. See also GHL to John Blackwood, 13 June 1859, ibid., III, 83.

18. GE Journal, 27 April 1859, ibid., III, 88n; John Blackwood to GE, 20 June 1859, III, 88.

19. John Blackwood to William Blackwood, 25 June 1859, ibid., III, 94.

20. John Gwyther to the Blackwoods, 13 June 1859; GE to John Gwyther, 15 June 1859, ibid., III, 83–4, 85.

21. Elizabeth Gaskell to GE, 3 June 1859; John Blackwood to GE, 27 October 1859, ibid., III, 74, 190.

22. Barbara Bodichon to GE, 28 and 30 June 1859, ibid., III, 103, 107.

23. GHL to Barbara Bodichon, 30 June 1859, ibid., III, 106.

24. *Athenaeum*, 2 July 1859, ibid., III, 109n.

25. Charles Dickens to GE, 10 July and 6 August 1859, ibid., III, 114; VIII, 240.

26. GE to Charles Bray, 19 September 1859; GHL to Charles Holte Bracebridge, 19 September 1859, ibid., III, 115–17, 158–60.

27. GHL to Charles Bray, 30 September 1859, ibid., VIII, 245.

28. GHL Journal, 18 July 1859, MS Yale. For an account of Comte and his English disciples, see T. R. Wright, *The Religion of Humanity: The Impact of Comtean Positivism on Victorian Britain* (Cambridge, 1986).

29. See *GEL*, III, 62 and n.

30. GE to Maria Congreve, 8 June 1859, ibid., III, 79.

31. GE to Charles Bray, 5 July 1859, ibid., III, 111.

32. GHL Journal, 27 May 1859, ibid., III, 73–4.

33. GHL Journal, 13 and 15 July 1859, ibid., III, 115–16.

34. See Ashton, *G. H. Lewes*, pp. 181–2, 201.

35. Thornie Lewes to GE, 18 August 1859, *GEL*, VIII, 242. See also GHL to John Blackwood, 22 July 1859, ibid., III, 117.

36. GHL Journal, 26 August 1859, MS Yale.

37. GHL Journal, 3 September 1859, *GEL*, III, 142.

38. Emily Clarke to GE, 20 October 1859, ibid., VIII, 250.

39. GHL Journal, 5 September 1859, ibid., III, 148.

40. GHL Journal, November 1859, ibid., IX, 345.

41. GE to Joseph Langford, 6 and 10 October 1859, ibid., III, 173, 180. See also ibid., III, 212n.

42. John Blackwood to GE, 21 September 1859, ibid., III, 161.

43. See William Blackwood to John Blackwood, 18 October 1859; Joseph Langford to John Blackwood, 23 November 1859, ibid., III, 188, 221n.

44. Ibid., III, 205n.
45. GHL Journal, 10 November 1859, ibid., III, 197.
46. Charles Dickens to GHL, 14 November 1859, ibid., III, 203.
47. GE Journal, 18 November 1859, ibid., III, 205.
48. George Simpson to Joseph Langford, 16 November 1859, ibid., III, 204–5.
49. GHL Journal, 15 November 1859; GE Journal, 1 December 1859, ibid., III, 204, 233n.
50. GHL Journal, 27 October 1859, ibid., III, 189.
51. See Jenifer Glynn, *Prince of Publishers: A Biography of the Great Victorian Publisher George Smith* (London, 1986), p. 125.
52. John Blackwood to GE, 14 October 1859, *GEL*, III, 182, 183.
53. John Blackwood to GE, 27 October 1859; GE to John Blackwood, 28 October 1859; John Blackwood to William Blackwood, 30 October 1859, ibid., III, 190, 191, 192.
54. George Simpson to Joseph Langford, 3 November 1859, ibid., III, 194.
55. See John Blackwood to William Blackwood, 28 October 1859, ibid., III, 191n.
56. GE to John Blackwood, 30 November 1859, ibid., III, 217, 218, 219.
57. William Blackwood to John Blackwood, 1 December 1859, ibid., III, 220, 221.
58. John Blackwood to GE, 2 December 1859, ibid., III, 222, 223.
59. *The Mill on the Floss*, ed. A. S. Byatt, p. 319 (Book III, chapter 5).
60. GE to John Blackwood, 5 December 1859, *GEL*, III, 224.
61. John Blackwood to William Blackwood, 7 December 1859, ibid., III, 232, 233.
62. John Blackwood to William Blackwood, 12 December 1859; John Blackwood to GE, 14 December 1859; GE to John Blackwood, 20 December 1859, ibid., III, 233, 235, 236.
63. GE Journal, 16 January 1860, MS Yale.
64. Herbert Spencer to GE, 30 September 1859; GE to Herbert Spencer, 2 October 1859, *GEL*, VIII, 246, 247.
65. John Chapman to GE, 16 January 1860; GHL Journal, 18 January 1860, ibid., VIII, 257 and n.
66. *The Mill on the Floss*, p. 107 (Book I, chapter 6).
67. Ibid., p. 198 (Book I, chapter 13).
68. GE to John Blackwood, 3 January 1860; John Blackwood to GE, 6 January 1860; GE to John Blackwood, 6 January 1860, *GEL*, III, 240, 244, 245.
69. GHL to John Blackwood, 7 February 1860, ibid., III, 258.
70. GE to John Blackwood, 23 February and 20 March 1860, ibid., III, 264–5, 276.

71. GE to John Blackwood, 22 March 1860, ibid., III, 278.

72. GE to Barbara Bodichon, 6 March 1860, ibid., III, 271.

73. GHL to Charles Lewes, 17 March 1860, ibid., III, 275.

74. See *GEL*, VII, 360 (Appendix I).

75. *The Times*, 19 May 1860, in *Critical Heritage*, pp. 131, 136.

76. *The Mill on the Floss*, p. 148 (Book I, chapter 9).

77. Ibid., p. 109 (Book I, chapter 7).

78. *Critical Heritage*, p. 133.

79. *The Mill on the Floss*, p. 407 (Book V, chapter 2).

80. *Adam Bede*, pp. 83–4 (chapter 4).

81. *The Mill on the Floss*, p. 423 (Book V, chapter 2).

82. See F. R. Leavis, *The Great Tradition* (London, 1948), pp. 39–40; Barbara Hardy, '*The Mill on the Floss*', in *Critical Essays on George Eliot*, ed. Barbara Hardy (London, 1970), pp. 42–58.

83. GE to John Blackwood, 3 April and 9 July 1860, *GEL*, III, 285, 317.

84. Wordsworth, *The Prelude* (1850), Book I, lines 301–2.

85. *The Mill on the Floss*, p. 270 (Book II, chapter 7). See Rosemary Ashton, *The Mill on the Floss: A Natural History* (Boston, Massachusetts, 1990), pp. 75–7.

86. See GE to Sara Hennell, 9 February 1849, *GEL*, I, 277–8. For a discussion of George Sand and GE see Patricia Thomson, *George Sand and the Victorians: Her Influence and Reputation in Nineteenth-Century England* (London, 1977).

87. *The Mill on the Floss*, pp. 601–2 (Book VI, chapter 14).

88. Ibid., pp. 627, 628 (Book VII, chapter 2).

89. John Blackwood to GE, 7 March 1860, *GEL*, III, 272.

90. Elizabeth Gaskell to GE, 10 November 1859, ibid., III, 197.

91. *The Mill on the Floss*, p. 363 (Book IV, chapter 1).

92. Ibid., p. 366.

93. Charles Darwin, *The Origin of Species* (1859), ed. J. W. Burrow (Harmondsworth, 1986), p. 171.

94. See Ashton, *G. H. Lewes*, pp. 192–4, 243–5.

95. GE to Charles Bray, 25 November 1859, and to Barbara Bodichon, 5 December 1859, *GEL*, III, 214 and n, 227. For George Eliot and Darwin see Gillian Beer, *Darwin's Plots: Evolutionary Narrative in Darwin, George Eliot and Nineteenth-Century Fiction* (London, 1983) and Sally Shuttleworth, *George Eliot and Nineteenth-Century Science* (Cambridge, 1984).

96. Darwin, *Origin of Species*, p. 263.

97. *The Mill on the Floss*, p. 134 (Book I, chapter 8).

98. Sara Hennell to GE, 28 June 1860, MS Yale. GE's copy of the *De Imitatione Christi* is now in Coventry City Libraries.

99. Barbara Bodichon to GE, 13 June 1860, MS Yale.

100. *The Mill on the Floss*, pp. 60, 542–3 (Book I, chapter 2; Book VI, chapter 8).

101. Ibid., pp. 450, 405 (Book V, chapter 5; Book V, chapter 2).

102. Ibid., p. 621 (Book VII, chapter 2).

103. GE to John Blackwood, 3 April 1860, *GEL*, III, 285.

104. Wordsworth, *Prelude* (1850), Book VII, lines 83, 142, 144.

105. GE Journal, 'Recollections of Italy 1860', MS Yale.

106. See GE to Maria Congreve, 4 April 1860, *GEL*, III, 286; 'Recollections of Italy 1860', MS Yale.

107. GHL Journal, 18 April 1860, MS Yale; GE to Maria Congreve, 6 April 1860, *GEL*, III, 288.

108. GE, 'Recollections of Italy 1860', MS Yale.

109. GHL Journal, 7 April 1860, ibid.

110. GE, 'Recollections of Italy 1860', ibid.

111. GHL Journal, 5 May 1860, *GEL*, III, 291.

112. GE, 'Recollections of Italy 1860', MS Yale.

113. GHL Journal, 21 May 1860, *GEL*, III, 295.

114. GE to Martha Bell, 8 June 1860, ibid., III, 304.

115. GE to Charles Bray, 14 July 1860, ibid., III, 324.

116. GE to François D'Albert Durade, 28 June 1860, ibid., III, 309.

117. GHL Journal, 6 October 1860; Thornie Lewes to GHL, 11 September 1860, *GEL*, III, 352; VIII, 270–71.

118. GHL Journal, 15 August 1860; Anthony Trollope to GHL, 9 August 1860, ibid., III, 331; VIII, 269.

119. GE to François D'Albert Durade, 6 December 1860; GE Journal, 17 December 1860, ibid., III, 363, 362n.

120. See *GEL*, III, 307n.

121. GE to John Blackwood, 28 August 1860, ibid., III, 339 and n.

122. GE Journal, 27 September 1860, MS Yale.

123. *Brother Jacob* (1864), ed. Beryl Gray (London, 1989), p. 55. For criticisms of the story see Beryl Gray's afterword and Peter Allen Dale, 'George Eliot's "Brother Jacob": Fables and the Physiology of Common Life', *Philological Quarterly*, LXIV (Winter 1985), 17–35.

124. John Blackwood to Joseph Langford, 10 September 1860, *GEL*, III, 343.

125. GE Journal, 28 November 1860, ibid., III, 360.

CHAPTER TEN: *Realism and Romance:* Silas Marner *and*
Romola *1861–3*

1. GHL Journal, 1 January 1861, MS Yale.

2. See *GEL*, III, 372 and n.

3. GE Journal, 28 November 1860, ibid., III, 360.
4. Anthony Trollope to GHL, 7 April 1861, ibid., VIII, 279; GHL Journal, 15 April 1861, ibid., VIII, 281–2n.
5. GE to Clementia Taylor, 1 April 1861, ibid., III, 396.
6. GE to Clementia Taylor, 6 April 1861, ibid., III, 397–8.
7. GE to John Blackwood, 27 September 1860, ibid., III, 351.
8. GE to Barbara Bodichon, 26 December 1860, ibid., III, 366.
9. Ibid., III, 366–7.
10. Q. D. Leavis suggests a parallel with *A Tale of Two Cities*, in which Dr Manette, the obsessive shoemaker 'buried alive' for eighteen years in the Bastille, is 'returned to life' when he is found by his golden-haired daughter Lucie, *Silas Marner*, ed. Q. D. Leavis (Harmondsworth, 1944, reprinted 1981), p. 25n.
11. *Silas Marner*, p. 236 (chapter 20).
12. GE to John Blackwood, 24 February 1861, *GEL*, III, 382.
13. Wordsworth, 'Michael', lines 200–203.
14. *Silas Marner*, pp. 167, 168 (chapter 12).
15. GHL to John Blackwood, 28 February 1861, *The Letters of George Henry Lewes*, II, 22.
16. *Silas Marner*, p. 184 (chapter 14).
17. GE to John Blackwood, 24 February 1861, *GEL*, III, 382.
18. Henry Crabb Robinson Diary, 18 April 1861, *Henry Crabb Robinson On Books*, II, 801.
19. Coleridge, *Biographia Literaria*, ed. James Engell and W. Jackson Bate, *The Collected Works of Samuel Taylor Coleridge*, Bollingen series, 16 vols. in progress (London, 1969–), VI: 2 (1983), 6–7.
20. See GE to Martha Jackson, 16 December 1841, *GEL*, I, 122–3. 'Natural Supernaturalism' is the title of Book III, chapter 8 of *Sartor Resartus*. See also M. H. Abrams, *Natural Supernaturalism: Tradition and Revolution in Romantic Literature* (New York, 1973).
21. *Silas Marner*, p. 215 (chapter 17).
22. See GE Journal, 1 January 1862, *GEL*, IV, 3n.
23. See GHL Journal, 4 May 1861; John Blackwood to GE, 23 September 1861, ibid., III, 410n, 453.
24. *The Times* (29 April 1861), and *Economist* (27 April 1861), in *Critical Heritage*, pp. 179, 175.
25. John Blackwood to GE, 19 February 1861; Thornton Lewes to GE, 6 April 1861, *GEL*, III, 379; VIII, 280–81.
26. GHL to Charles Lewes, 17 May 1861, ibid., III, 414.
27. GHL Journal, 4 June 1861, ibid., III, 424.
28. GE to François D'Albert Durade, 26 August 1861, ibid., III, 448.

29. GHL to John Blackwood, 6 March 1861, ibid., III, 387.
30. GHL to John Blackwood, 28 May 1861, ibid., III, 421.
31. GHL Journal, 18 September 1861, ibid., III, 451n.
32. GE Journal, 6 November 1861, MS Yale.
33. John Blackwood to Julia Blackwood, 15 June 1861, *GEL*, III, 427.
34. GE Journal, 19 June 1861, ibid., III, 428.
35. See GE to Joseph Langford, 27 March 1861, ibid., III, 394 and n. The record of her application on 14 November 1861 is in the British Museum.
36. GHL to John Blackwood, 14 December 1861, *GEL*, III, 474.
37. GE Journal, 29 September 1861, ibid., III, 462n.
38. GE Journal, 3 October 1861, MS Yale.
39. Thornton Lewes to GHL, 22 December 1861; John Blackwood to William Blackwood junior, 23 December 1861, *GEL*, VIII, 295; III, 474.
40. GE Journal, 1 January 1862, ibid., IV, 3n.
41. *Atlantic Monthly* (May 1885), in *Critical Heritage*, p. 500.
42. Works on Florentine art, history, politics, and society which GE read in 1861 are listed in Cross, II, 235–6.
43. See Carol A. Martin, *George Eliot's Serial Fiction* (Columbus, Ohio, 1994), pp. 20–24.
44. GHL Journal, 27 February 1862, *GEL*, IV, 17–18.
45. See John Sutherland, Introduction to Wilkie Collins, *Armadale* (Harmondsworth, 1995), p. xxix.
46. GHL Journal, 1 March 1862, *GEL*, IV, 19.
47. GE Journal, 1 March 1862, MS Yale.
48. GHL Journal, 8 April and 17 May 1862, *GEL*, IV, 24, 33.
49. GHL Journal, 8 April 1862; GHL to Charles Lewes, 10 May 1862, ibid., IV, 24, 31.
50. Memorandum of Agreement between Smith, Elder and GE, 21 May 1862, ibid., VIII, 301.
51. See *GEL*, VII, 373, 377–8 (Appendix II).
52. See Glynn, *Prince of Publishers*, pp. 114, 140, 190–91.
53. GE to John Blackwood, 19 May 1862, *GEL*, IV, 34–5.
54. John Blackwood to GE, 20 May 1862, ibid., IV, 35–6.
55. John Blackwood to Joseph Langford, 25 May 1862, ibid., IV, 38 and n.
56. GE Journal, 23 May 1862; John Blackwood to William Blackwood, 18 June 1862, ibid., IV, 36n, 44.
57. *Silas Marner*, p. 98 (chapter 6).
58. Cross, II, 255.
59. GE to Sara Hennell, 23 April 1862, *GEL*, IV, 25.
60. GE to Bessie Parkes, [June 1862], ibid., IV, 44.
61. GE to Sara Hennell, 14 July 1862, ibid., IV, 49.

62. Anthony Trollope to GE, 28 June 1862, ibid., VIII, 303, 304.

63. *Romola*, ed. Andrew Sanders (Harmondsworth, 1980), p. 48 (Proem).

64. Ibid., p. 578 (chapter 59).

65. Ibid., p. 75 (chapter 3).

66. Ibid., pp. 421, 425 (chapter 39).

67. Ibid., p. 352 (chapter 32).

68. Ibid., p. 492 (chapter 48).

69. *The Mill on the Floss*, p. 57 (Book I, chapter 2).

70. *Romola*, pp. 59–60, 416 (chapters 1 and 39). See Andrew Brown's excellent notes to the Clarendon Edition of *Romola* (Oxford, 1993), pp. 598, 655, to which I am indebted for the identification of Florentine idiom.

71. *Spectator* (18 July 1863), in *Critical Heritage*, p. 199.

72. GE Journal, 30 September 1862, MS Yale.

73. GHL to Sara Hennell, 12 September 1862, *GEL*, IV, 58.

74. Margaret Oliphant, *Autobiography and Letters*, ed. Mrs Harry Coghill (Edinburgh, 1899), p. 5. See also Elisabeth Jay, *Mrs Oliphant: A Fiction to Herself* (Oxford, 1995).

75. Robert Browning to GE, 2 August 1863, *GEL*, IV, 96.

76. GE Journal, 19 February 1862, ibid., IV, 15.

77. GE Journal, 16 December 1862, MS Yale.

78. *Spectator* (18 July 1863), in *Critical Heritage*, p. 204.

79. GE to Richard Holt Hutton, 8 August 1863, *GEL*, IV, 97.

80. See Glynn, *Prince of Publishers*, p. 127.

81. See R. F. Anderson, '"Things Wisely Ordered": John Blackwood, George Eliot, and the Publication of *Romola*', *Publishing History*, XI (1982), 26, 27.

82. See John Blackwood to GE, 20 November 1862, *GEL*, IV, 63.

83. GE Journal, 28 July 1863, ibid., IV, 94.

84. Anthony Trollope to GHL, 15 May 1862; GHL Journal, 17 May 1862, ibid., VIII, 300; IV, 34.

85. GHL Journal, 21 August 1863, ibid., IV, 102.

86. GHL to Robert Chambers junior, 21 August 1863, ibid., VIII, 312.

87. GE Journal, 26 September 1863; GE to Sara Hennell, 16 October 1863, ibid., IV, 107, 109.

88. GHL Journal, 13 November 1863, ibid., IV, 112.

89. GE to François D'Albert Durade, 28 November 1863, ibid., IV, 118.

90. GHL Journal, 24 November 1863, ibid., IV, 115.

91. Bessie Parkes to Barbara Bodichon, 18 November 1863, MS Girton.

92. Ibid.

CHAPTER ELEVEN: *Politics and Poetry:* Felix Holt *and*
The Spanish Gypsy *1864–8*

1. GHL Journal, 22 August 1863, *GEL*, IV, 102 and n.
2. Queen Victoria to Earl Russell, 13 April 1864, *Letters of Queen Victoria*, second series, ed. George Earle Buckle, 3 vols. (London, 1926–8), I, 169.
3. Queen Victoria to the Crown Princess of Prussia, 27 April 1864, *Dearest Mama: Letters between Queen Victoria and the Crown Princess of Prussia 1861– 1864*, ed. Roger Fulford (London, 1968), p. 324.
4. GHL Journal, 18 April 1864, MS Yale.
5. GHL to George Smith, [?August 1863], *Letters of George Henry Lewes*, II, 46.
6. GE to Sara Hennell, 23 August 1863, and to Clementia Taylor, 3 March 1864, *GEL*, IV, 104, 134–5.
7. GE to Maria Congreve, 28 November 1863, ibid., IV, 116.
8. Bessie Parkes to Barbara Bodichon, [?December 1864], Margaret Crompton, 'Prelude to Arcadia', pp. 159–60, TS Girton College. See also GHL Journal, 25 December 1864, *GEL*, IV, 172.
9. GE Journal, 30 January 1864, *GEL*, VIII, 316n.
10. See GE to Robert Evans junior, 2 February 1864, and to Jane Evans, 12 February 1864; Jane Evans to GE, 15 March 1864, ibid., IV, 130–31, 134; VIII, 316–17.
11. GHL Journal, 1 January 1864, ibid., IV, 126.
12. GHL Journal, 8 February 1864, ibid., IV, 132.
13. GHL Journal, 4 April 1864, MS Yale.
14. GHL to John Blackwood, 9 November 1863, *Letters of George Henry Lewes*, II, 51.
15. See John Blackwood to GHL, 28 November 1861, MS Blackwood Papers, National Library of Scotland.
16. John Blackwood to GHL, 10 November 1863, *GEL*, IV, 112–13.
17. See *GEL*, IV, 157n; George Smith to GE, 3 May 1864, ibid., VIII, 318.
18. GHL Journal, 6 March 1864, MS Yale; GE to Sara Hennell, 30 April 1864, *GEL*, IV, 147.
19. GHL to John Blackwood, 8 March 1864, *Letters of George Henry Lewes*, II, 57.
20. GHL Journal, 9 May 1864, MS Yale.
21. GHL to Charles Lewes, 18 May 1864, *GEL*, IV, 151.
22. GE to François D'Albert Durade, 28 November 1863, ibid., IV, 117.
23. Thornton Lewes to GHL, 14 November 1863, MS Yale.
24. Thornton Lewes to GHL, 28 January 1864, MS Yale. See also GE to Barbara Bodichon, 4 April 1864, *GEL*, IV, 141.

25. GHL Journal, 23 June 1864, *GEL*, IV, 154n.

26. GE to François D'Albert Durade, 24 June 1864, ibid., IV, 154.

27. GE to Barbara Bodichon, 12 August 1864, ibid., VIII, 321.

28. See *GEL*, VIII, 321n.

29. Henry James to William James, 1 May 1878, *Letters of Henry James*, ed. Leon Edel, 4 vols. (London, 1974–84), II, 172.

30. *Romola*, p. 622 (chapter 65); GHL Journal, 22 May 1860, MS Yale.

31. Tom Trollope, *What I Remember*, II, 296–7.

32. See T. H. S. Escott, *Platform, Press, Politics and Play: Being Pen and Ink Sketches of Contemporary Celebrities* (Bristol, 1895), p. 257.

33. GE is compared to Locke by Robert Buchanan, *A Look Round Literature* (London, 1887), p. 220; to Wordsworth by Kate Field, see Lilian Whiting, *Kate Field: A Record* (London, 1899), p. 397; to Cardinal Newman by Charles Kegan Paul, *Biographical Sketches* (London, 1883), p. 162.

34. GE to Sara Hennell, 13 July 1864, *GEL*, IV, 158, 159.

35. See GE to Sara Hennell, 2 and 30 July 1861, ibid., III, 433, 442.

36. GE to Gertrude Lewes, 21 December 1865, ibid., IV, 213, 214.

37. *Adam Bede*, p. 553 (chapter 52).

38. GE, 'The Influence of Rationalism', *Fortnightly Review* (15 May 1865), *Essays*, p. 409.

39. GE Journal, 17 July 1864, MS Yale.

40. GE, 'Notes on the Spanish Gypsy and Tragedy in General', Cross, II, 42.

41. GE Journal, 10 November 1864, *GEL*, IV, 167.

42. GE Journal, 21 February 1865, ibid., IV, 179n.

43. GE to Sara Hennell, 28 August 1864, ibid., IV, 160–61.

44. See ibid., IV, 162, 166, 167.

45. See GE to Sara Hennell, 2 October 1864, ibid., IV, 165.

46. GHL Journal, 2 October 1864, ibid., IV, 165–6.

47. GHL Journal, 30 December 1864, ibid., IV, 173. See also Anthony Trollope to GHL, 24 December 1864, ibid., VIII, 327.

48. See Linda Colley, *Britons: Forging the Nation 1707–1837* (London, 1992), pp. 346–9.

49. GHL to Henry Danby Seymour, 13 January 1865, *GEL*, VIII, 332; GHL, Prospectus for *Fortnightly Review*, March 1865, ibid., VIII, 335, 336.

50. GE, 'The Influence of Rationalism', *Fortnightly Review* (15 May 1865), *Essays*, p. 401 and n.

51. 'The Natural History of German Life', *Westminster Review* (July 1856), ibid., p. 299.

52. 'A Word for the Germans', *Pall Mall Gazette* (7 March 1865), ibid., p. 389.

53. 'Servants' Logic', *Pall Mall Gazette* (17 March 1865), ibid., pp. 391–6.

54. GE Journal, 29 March 1865, *GEL*, IV, 184.

55. GE Journal, 10 May, 7 June, 2 August 1865, MS Yale.

56. GE Journal, 23 July 1865, *GEL*, IV, 197.

57. Hansard's *Parliamentary Debates*, 3rd series, vol. 183 (London, 1866), p. 152.

58. GHL to John Blackwood, 25 April 1866, *GEL*, VIII, 374.

59. John Blackwood to Joseph Langford, 26 April 1866, and to GE, 26 April 1866, ibid., IV, 247, 246.

60. GHL to John Blackwood, 18 April 1866, ibid., VIII, 373.

61. John Blackwood to GHL, 20 April 1866, ibid., IV, 241.

62. Ibid., IV, 240n.

63. John Blackwood to Joseph Langford, 26 April 1866, ibid., IV, 247.

64. *Felix Holt, The Radical*, ed. Peter Coveney (Harmondsworth, 1972), p. 129 (chapter 3).

65. Ibid., p. 75 (Introduction).

66. Ibid.

67. GE to Clifford Allbutt, August 1868, *GEL*, IV, 472.

68. *Felix Holt*, pp. 368, 399 (chapters 27 and 30).

69. GE to John Blackwood, 27 April 1866, *GEL*, IV, 248. See also Fred C. Thomson, Introduction to the Clarendon Edition of *Felix Holt* (Oxford, 1980), pp. xv–xvi.

70. Dickens, *A Tale of Two Cities*, ed. George Woodcock (Harmondsworth, 1970), pp. 245, 240.

71. Dickens, *Barnaby Rudge*, ed. Gordon Spence (Harmondsworth, 1973), pp. 581, 584 (chapter 64).

72. Henry James, *Nation* (16 August 1866), in *Critical Heritage*, pp. 275, 276.

73. Stephen Gill, Introduction to *Our Mutual Friend* (Harmondsworth, 1971), p. 22.

74. *Felix Holt*, p. 276 (chapter 16).

75. See John Blackwood to GE, 18 June, 10 September, 13 December 1866, *GEL*, IV, 275, 307, 318 and n.

76. GHL to Charles and Gertrude Lewes, 15 July 1866, ibid., IV, 284.

77. GE to Sara Hennell, 10 August 1866, ibid., IV, 298.

78. Frederic Harrison to GE, 19 July 1866, ibid., IV, 287. See Wright, *The Religion of Humanity*, pp. 30–39.

79. GE to Frederic Harrison, 15 August 1866, *GEL*, IV, 300.

80. GE to John Blackwood, 6 September 1866, ibid., IV, 305.

81. See Anthony Trollope to GHL, 9 November 1866, ibid., VIII, 387.

82. John Blackwood to GE, 21 December 1866, ibid., IV, 322.

83. GE Journal, 27 December 1866, MS Yale.

84. GE to Frederic Harrison, 18 February 1867; GHL to Charles Lewes, 18 February 1867, *GEL*, IV, 344, 345.

85. GHL Journal, 17, 18, and 22 February 1867, MS Yale.

86. GE to John Blackwood, 21 February 1867; John Blackwood to GE, 20 March 1867; GE to John Blackwood, 21 March 1867, *GEL*, IV, 347, 353, 354, 355.

87. John Blackwood to GE, 29 November and 6 December 1867, ibid., IV, 402, 403.

88. GE to Emanuel Deutsch, 13 August 1867, ibid., IV, 384.

89. GE to Sara Hennell, 13 May 1867, ibid., IV, 363.

90. Lady Amberley Diary, 5 May 1867, ibid., VIII, 399n.

91. Hansard's *Parliamentary Debates*, 3rd series, vol. 187 (London, 1867), pp. 817–29.

92. GE to Clementia Taylor, 30 May 1867, and to Sara Hennell, 12 October 1867, *GEL*, IV, 366, 390.

93. John Blackwood to GE, 7 November 1867, ibid., IV, 395.

94. GE, 'Address to Working Men, by Felix Holt', *Blackwood's Magazine* (January 1868), *Essays*, pp. 417, 419, 420, 425.

95. GE to John Morley, 14 May 1867, *GEL*, VIII, 402.

96. GE to Emily Davies, 16? November 1867, ibid., IV, 399; Emily Davies to Barbara Bodichon, 20 November 1867, ibid., VIII, 409–10 and n. See Rita McWilliams-Tullberg, 'Women and Degrees at Cambridge University, 1862–1897', in *A Widening Sphere*, pp. 117–45.

97. GE to Emily Davies, 4 March 1868, *GEL*, VIII, 414.

98. GE Journal, 4 November 1864, ibid., IV, 167; GE Journal, 30 August and 15 October 1866, 10 January 1868, MS Yale.

99. John Blackwood to GE, 22 April and 2 May 1868, *GEL*, IV, 431, 435.

100. See *GEL*, IV, 480 and n; VII, 362 (Appendix I).

101. Frederic Harrison to GE, 11 November 1868, ibid., IV, 485; Frederic Harrison to Edward Beesly, May 1868, MS LSE (Harrison Papers).

102. See GE to John Blackwood, 9 November 1867, *GEL*, IV, 396–7.

103. GE, *The Spanish Gypsy*, *The Works of George Eliot*, Cabinet Edition (Edinburgh and London, 1878), p. 369 (Book V).

104. Ibid., p. 251 (Book III).

105. Richard Holt Hutton, 'George Eliot as Author', in *Essays on Some of the Modern Guides of English Thought in Matters of Faith* (London, 1887), p. 238; Henry James, '*The Spanish Gypsy*', *North American Review* (October 1868), in *A Century of George Eliot Criticism*, p. 55.

106. GE to John Blackwood, 30 July 1868, *GEL*, IV, 464.

107. GE Journal, 22 November 1868 and 1 January 1869, ibid., IV, 490; V, 3.

CHAPTER TWELVE: *Writing* Middlemarch *1869–72*

1. For a lucid account of the writing of *Middlemarch* see David Carroll, Introduction to *Middlemarch*, Clarendon Edition (Oxford, 1986). See also Jerome Beaty, *'Middlemarch' from Notebook to Novel* (Urbana, Illinois, 1960).

2. 'Agatha', *Atlantic Monthly* (August 1869), reprinted in *The Legend of Jubal, and Other Poems*, Cabinet Edition, p. 63. See also GE to Countess Ida von Baudissin, 4 February 1869, *GEL*, V, 11.

3. See GHL Diary, 13 May 1869, ibid., V, 34.

4. 'How Lisa Loved the King', *Blackwood's Magazine* (May 1869), *The Legend of Jubal, and Other Poems*, pp. 153, 168. See John Blackwood to GE, 18 February 1869, *GEL*, V, 15.

5. GHL Diary, 6 January 1869, ibid., V, 4n.

6. Thornton Lewes to GHL, 12 October 1868, ibid., VIII, 433–4.

7. GHL to John Blackwood, 9 January 1869, ibid., V, 4.

8. GHL Journal, 6 April 1869, MS Yale.

9. See GHL Journal, 19 October 1867, *GEL*, IV, 393; GHL Journal, 18 April 1869, MS Yale.

10. GE to John Blackwood, 11 May 1869; GHL Diary, 8 May 1869, *GEL*, V, 35, 33.

11. See GHL Diary, 31 January 1869, MS Yale.

12. Henry James to his father, *Henry James Letters*, I, 116, 117.

13. GHL Diary, 18 May and 1 June 1869, *GEL*, V, 40n, 36n.

14. GE to Maria Congreve, 26 May 1869, ibid., V, 41.

15. GE to Emilia Pattison, 10 August 1869, ibid., V, 52.

16. GE to Cara Bray, 21 August 1869, ibid., V, 53.

17. GHL Journal, 11 October 1869; GE Journal, 19 October 1869, ibid., V, 59n, 60.

18. GE Journal, 11 and 21 September 1869, MS Yale.

19. 'Brother and Sister', *The Legend of Jubal, and Other Poems*, pp. 201, 207.

20. 'The Legend of Jubal', *Macmillan's Magazine* (May 1870), ibid., pp. 38, 37.

21. GHL Diary, 25 December 1869, *GEL*, V, 74n.

22. GHL Diary, 17 and 28 February 1870, ibid., V, 79n.

23. GE to John Blackwood, 7 March 1870; GE to Sara Hennell, 13 June 1870, ibid., V, 81, 102.

24. GHL to Elizabeth Willim, 28 March 1870, ibid., V, 83.

25. GHL Journal, 25 March 1870, ibid., V, 85n.

26. GE to Maria Congreve, 3 April 1870, ibid., V, 87.

27. GHL to Charles Lewes, 23 April 1870, ibid., V, 91.

28. Mrs Humphry Ward, *A Writer's Recollections*, 2 vols. (London, 1918), I, 145–6.

29. Charles Eliot Norton to G. W. Curtis, 29 January 1869, *GEL*, V, 7.

30. See Richard Owen to John Murray, 29 December 1856, Rupke, *Richard Owen*, p. 227.

31. GE to Oscar Browning, 23 June 1867 and 2 March 1875, *GEL*, IV, 368; VI, 126. For Browning's dismissal from Eton see H. E. Wortham, *Oscar Browning* (London, 1956), pp. 100–149.

32. See GHL Journal, 21 May 1867, *GEL*, IV, 365n; Haight, p. 470.

33. Haight, p. 470; GE to Emanuel Deutsch, 23 May 1868, *GEL*, IV, 446. For Deutsch see Viscountess Strangford, *Literary Remains of the Late Emanuel Deutsch* (London, 1874).

34. See *GEL*, IV, 471–2n.

35. GE to Clifford Allbutt, August 1868, ibid., IV, 472.

36. GE to Clifford Allbutt, 30 December 1868, ibid., IV, 499. For Allbutt see H. D. Rolleston, *Sir Thomas Clifford Allbutt* (London, 1929).

37. GE to James Sully, 19 January 1877, *GEL*, VI, 333–4 and n. The OED has 1858 as the date of the first use of 'meliorist', in John Brown's *Horae Subsecivae*.

38. GE to Clifford Allbutt, 30 December 1868, *GEL*, IV, 499.

39. GE to Maria Congreve, 2 December 1870, ibid., V, 125.

40. GE to Emilia Pattison, 5 September 1872, ibid., V, 304. For Emilia Pattison, later Emilia Dilke, see Betty Ellen Askwith, *Lady Dilke* (London, 1969). For Edward Burne-Jones's unfaithfulness to Georgiana see Penelope Fitzgerald, *Edward Burne-Jones: A Biography* (London, 1975).

41. See Haight, pp. 448–50, 563–5, for the arguments for, and especially against, this identification.

42. GE to Harriet Beecher Stowe, 8 May 1869, *GEL*, V, 31.

43. GE to Harriet Peirce, 14 September 1866, ibid., VIII, 384.

44. Harriet Peirce to GE, 2 August 1869, ibid., VIII, 461.

45. See Lilian Faderman, *Surpassing the Love of Men: Romantic Friendship and Love Between Women from the Renaissance to the Present* (New York, 1981), pp. 190–203.

46. See Anderson, *Woman Against Women in Victorian England*, pp. 155–7. See also correspondence between Marie Lowndes and Gordon S. Haight, June–September 1942, MSs Yale.

47. Harriet Peirce to GE, 2 August 1869, *GEL*, VIII, 463.

48. GE to Emily Davies, 18 November 1869, ibid., VIII, 468.

49. GE to Elizabeth Malleson, 20? July 1869, and to Elizabeth Garrett Anderson, 31 October 1871, ibid., VIII, 460; V, 209 and n.

50. GHL Diary, 13 July 1870; GE Journal, 27 October 1870, ibid., V, 119 and n.

51. 'Armgart', *Macmillan's Magazine* (July 1871), *The Legend of Jubal, and Other Poems*, p. 76 (scene i).

52. Ibid., pp. 95, 98 (scene ii).
53. Ibid., pp. 104, 105 (scene ii).
54. Ibid., pp. 124, 138 (scene v).
55. *Middlemarch*, ed. Rosemary Ashton, p. 8 (Book I, chapter 1).
56. GE Journal, 31 December 1870, *GEL*, V, 127.
57. See GE to Cara Bray, 12 September 1870, ibid., V, 114.
58. GHL to Adolf and Fanny Stahr, 1 September 1870, ibid., VIII, 486–7.
59. GE to Sara Hennell, 2 January 1871, ibid., V, 131–2.
60. GE Journal, 19 March 1871, ibid., V, 137.
61. GHL to John Blackwood, 7 May 1871, ibid., V, 146.
62. See John Sutherland, 'Eliot, Lytton, and the Zelig Effect', *Victorian Fiction*, pp. 107–13.
63. John Blackwood to GHL, 6 September 1871, *GEL*, V, 182–3.
64. John Blackwood to GHL, 9 October 1871, ibid., V, 199–200.
65. John Blackwood to GHL, 18 September 1871, ibid., V, 189.
66. GHL to William Blackwood, [September? 1871], ibid., V, 182.
67. See GHL to Charles Lewes, 26 April 1871, ibid., V, 144.
68. GE to Alexander Main, 9 August 1871, ibid., V, 175.
69. See John Blackwood to William Blackwood, 24 October and 2 November 1871, ibid., V, 205, 212.
70. GHL to Alexander Main, 29 September 1871, ibid., V, 194.
71. John Blackwood to GE, 2 June 1871, ibid., V, 148.
72. John Blackwood to GE, 20 July 1871, ibid., V, 167.
73. GHL to Alexander Main, 5 December 1872, ibid., V, 337–8.
74. John Blackwood to GE, 7 September 1872, ibid., V, 306.
75. GE to John Blackwood, 18 January 1872, ibid., V, 237.
76. GHL to John Blackwood, 13 February 1872, ibid., V, 246.
77. See *GEL*, I, lxxvii.
78. GHL to Elma Stuart, 1 February 1872, ibid., V, 244–5.
79. John Blackwood to GE, 31 December 1872, ibid., V, 352–3.
80. Henry James, *Galaxy* (March 1873), *Critical Heritage*, p. 359.
81. *Middlemarch*, p. 95 (Book I, chapter 11).
82. Ibid., pp. 93, 95 (Book I, chapters 10 and 11).
83. Ibid., p. 180 (Book I, chapter 18).
84. GE to Sara Hennell, 18 January 1854, *GEL*, II, 137.
85. See Youngson, *The Scientific Revolution in Victorian Medicine*, pp. 12–14, 30, 54, 70; Lilian R. Furst, 'Struggling for Medical Reform in Middlemarch', *Nineteenth-Century Literature*, XLVIII (December 1993), 341–61.
86. *Middlemarch*, p. 443 (Book V, chapter 45).
87. Ibid., pp. 147–9 (Book II, chapter 15).
88. Cross (1886), I, 412 (Appendix).

89. *Middlemarch*, p. 182 (Book II, chapter 18).

90. See Robert Evans to Francis Newdigate, 31 March 1834, MS WCRO.

91. See William Baker, *The George Eliot–George Henry Lewes Library: An Annotated Catalogue of Their Books at the Dr Williams's Library, London* (London,
   1977), p. 190; *George Eliot's 'Middlemarch' Notebooks: A Transcription*, ed.
   John Clark Pratt and Victor A. Neufeldt (London, 1979), pp. 58–9.

92. Bray, *Phases of Opinion*, p. 87.

93. *Middlemarch*, p. 88 (Book I, chapter 10).

94. Ibid., p. 95 (Book I, chapter 11).

95. Ibid., p. 90 (Book I, chapter 10).

96. Ibid., p. 89.

97. Richard Holt Hutton, *Essays*, p. 235.

98. *Middlemarch*, p. 24 (Book I, chapter 3).

99. Ibid., pp. 56–7, 71, 59, 58 (Book I, chapters 6 and 8).

100. Ibid., p. 9 (Book I, chapter 1). Barbara Hardy deals with matters of form,
    structure, and irony in *Middlemarch* in *The Novels of George Eliot: A Study in
    Form* (London, 1959, revised 1963) and *Particularities* (London, 1982). See
    also David Lodge, '*Middlemarch* and the Idea of the Classic Realist
    Text', in *The Nineteenth-Century Novel: Critical Essays and Documents*, ed.
    Arnold Kettle (London, 1981).

101. *Middlemarch*, pp. 60, 264 (Book I, chapter 6; Book III, chapter 27).

102. Ibid., p. 278 (Book III, chapter 29).

103. Ibid., pp. 211, 209 (Book II, chapter 21).

104. Ibid., p. 86 (Book I, chapter 10).

105. GE to Harriet Beecher Stowe, October? 1872, *GEL*, V, 322.

106. Henry James, *Galaxy* (March 1873), *Critical Heritage*, p. 357.

107. *Middlemarch*, pp. 585, 586, 587 (Book VI, chapter 58).

108. Ibid., p. 656 (Book VII, chapter 64).

109. Ibid., p. 591 (Book VI, chapter 58).

110. Ibid., p. 666 (Book VII, chapter 65).

111. Ibid., p. 836 (Finale).

112. Ibid., p. 838.

113. Sir Edward Cook, *The Life of Florence Nightingale*, 2 vols. (London, 1913),
    I, 97.

114. See Gillian Darley, *Octavia Hill: A Life* (London, 1990).

115. *Middlemarch*, p. 274 (Book III, chapter 28).

CHAPTER THIRTEEN: *A New Departure:* Daniel
Deronda *1873–6*

1. See Introduction to *Middlemarch*, Clarendon Edition, pp. lix-lxii; Haight,
   p. 443.
2. See GE to Sir James Paget, 7 December 1872, *GEL*, IX, 66.
3. *Middlemarch*, pp. 3, 4 (Prelude).
4. Ibid., p. 852 (Notes).
5. Richard Holt Hutton, *Spectator* (7 December 1872), *Critical Heritage*, p. 307.
6. *Middlemarch*, p. 838 (Finale).
7. GE to Charles Ritter, 11 February 1873, *GEL*, V, 374.
8. GHL to John Blackwood, 8 January 1873; GHL Diary, 7 January 1873,
   ibid., V, 365 and n.
9. See McKenzie, *Edith Simcox and George Eliot*, pp. 26–7, 38. See also Gillian
   Beer, *George Eliot*, pp. 182–3.
10. GE to Jane Senior, 24 January 1873 and May 1874, *GEL*, V, 372; VI, 46.
11. GE to Jane Senior, May 1874, ibid., VI, 46–7.
12. GE to Clementia Taylor, 1 July 1874, ibid., VI, 65.
13. GE to Edith Griffiths, 9 May 1874, ibid., VI, 45–6 and n.
14. GE to Barbara Bodichon, 9 February 1874, ibid., VI, 14.
15. GHL Diary 1873, MS Yale; GE to Cara Bray, 29 May 1874, *GEL*, VI, 52.
16. GHL to John Cross, 19 January 1873, *GEL*, IX, 71 and n.
17. GHL Diary, 21 November and 9 December 1873, ibid., V, 469n.
18. 'A College Breakfast-Party' (April 1874), *The Legend of Jubal, and Other
    Poems*, pp. 231, 232, 260.
19. F. W. H. Myers, 'George Eliot', *Century Magazine* (November 1881), re-
    printed in Myers, *Essays*, 2 vols. (London, 1883), II, 268–9. Haight thinks
    Myers refers to the May 1877 visit, see *GEL*, VI, 380n.
20. F. W. H. Myers, 'Autobiographical Fragment', *Collected Poems,* ed. Eveleen
    Myers (London, 1921), pp. 2, 14, 18.
21. GHL Diary, 16 January 1874, *GEL*, VI, 6n.
22. GE to Harriet Beecher Stowe, 24 June 1872, ibid., V, 280 and n.
23. See GE to Emilia Pattison, 16 December 1872, ibid., V, 344 and n.
24. GHL Diary, 29 June 1873, *GEL*, V, 425n.
25. GE to Emanuel Deutsch, 7 July 1871, ibid., V, 160–61.
26. *Daniel Deronda*, ed. Barbara Hardy (Harmondsworth, 1967), p. 230 (Book
    II, chapter 17).
27. GE to Anna Cross, 25 September 1872, and to John Blackwood, 4 Octo-
    ber 1872, *GEL*, V, 312, 314.
28. GE to John Blackwood, 5 November 1873, ibid., V, 454.
29. See GHL Diary, 31 December 1874, ibid., VI, 91n.

30. GE Journal, 1 January 1874, ibid., VI, 3.

31. John Blackwood to GHL, 24 May 1873, ibid., V, 410.

32. GHL to John Blackwood, 25 May 1873, ibid., V, 413, 414.

33. GHL to John Blackwood, 13 July 1872; John Blackwood to GHL, 17 January 1873, ibid., V, 291, 369.

34. GHL Diary, 28 August, 21 October, and 3 November 1873, MS Yale.

35. Herbert Lewes to GHL, 29 October 1873, *GEL*, IX, 106, 107.

36. See GE to Barbara Bodichon, 13 August 1875, ibid., VI, 161.

37. GHL Diary, 10 August 1875, MS Yale; GE to Sara Hennell, 20 November 1875, *GEL*, VI, 191.

38. GHL Diary, 14 December 1875, MS Yale.

39. GE to John Blackwood, 16 June 1874, *GEL*, VI, 58.

40. GE to Anna Cross, 14 June 1874, ibid., VI, 56 and n.

41. GHL Diary, 16 September 1874, MS Yale.

42. GE to Robert Evans, 26 September 1874, *GEL*, IX, 134, 135.

43. Fanny Houghton to Isaac Evans, 28 January 1881, MS Kathleen Adams.

44. Marie Howland to GE, 30 May 1874, *GEL*, VI, 56n.

45. Ibid., III, 429n.

46. See GE to George Bancroft, 15 July 1874, ibid., VI, 68 and n.

47. GE to John Blackwood, 20 February 1874, ibid., VI, 23.

48. GE Journal, 12 April 1876, ibid., VI, 238.

49. William Blackwood to John Blackwood, 21 April 1875, ibid., VI, 136.

50. GHL Diary, 25 April 1875, MS Yale.

51. John Blackwood to GE, 22 April 1875, *GEL*, VI, 137.

52. See GE Journal, 28 February 1858, ibid., II, 435–6.

53. See John Blackwood to Julia Blackwood, 19 May 1875, ibid., VI, 143.

54. John Blackwood to GE, 20 and 25 May 1875, ibid., VI, 143, 144–5.

55. *Daniel Deronda*, p. 346 (Book III, chapter 27).

56. Ibid., p. 761 (Book VII, chapter 56).

57. Ibid., p. 72 (Book I, chapter 4).

58. *Middlemarch*, p. 240 (Book III, chapter 23).

59. See David Carroll, *George Eliot and the Conflict of Interpretations* (Cambridge, 1992).

60. *Daniel Deronda*, p. 283 (Book III, chapter 22).

61. Ibid., p. 77 (Book I, chapter 5).

62. See GHL to Nina Lehmann, 8 May 1876, *GEL*, IX, 176–7.

63. See Suzanne Graver, *George Eliot and Community: A Study in Social Theory and Fictional Form* (Berkeley, California, 1984); Bernard Semmel, *George Eliot and the Politics of National Inheritance* (Oxford, 1994).

64. *Daniel Deronda*, p. 791 (Book VIII, chapter 60).

65. GE to Harriet Beecher Stowe, 29 October 1876, *GEL*, VI, 302.

66. GE to John Blackwood, 3 November 1876, ibid., VI, 304.

67. GE to Joseph Payne, 25 January 1876, ibid., VI, 216.

68. *Daniel Deronda*, p. 35 (Book I, chapter 1).

69. GE to Barbara Bodichon, 2 October 1876, *GEL*, VI, 290.

70. F. R. Leavis, *The Great Tradition*, p. 137. For a refutation of Leavis see Elinor Shaffer, *'Kubla Khan' and The Fall of Jerusalem: The Mythological School in Biblical Criticism and Secular Literature 1770–1880* (Cambridge, 1975), pp. 225 ff.

71. *Daniel Deronda*, p. 145 (Book II, chapter 11).

72. Ibid., p. 550 (Book V, chapter 40).

73. Richard Holt Hutton, *'Daniel Deronda'*, *Spectator* (9 September 1876), *Critical Heritage*, p. 368.

74. Robert Louis Stevenson to Arthur Martin, December 1877, *The Letters of Robert Louis Stevenson*, ed. Bradford A. Booth, 6 vols. so far (New Haven, Connecticut, 1994–), II, 228.

75. Leslie Stephen, *George Eliot* (London, 1902), p. 190.

76. John Blackwood to GE, 24 February 1876, *GEL*, VI, 221–2.

77. GE to John Blackwood, 25 February 1876, ibid., VI, 223.

78. *Daniel Deronda*, p. 627 (Book VI, chapter 46).

79. Ibid., p. 595 (Book VI, chapter 42).

80. GHL to John Blackwood, 27 February 1876; John Blackwood to GHL, 2 March 1876, *GEL*, VI, 224, 227.

81. See *GEL*, VI, 262n.

82. John Blackwood to GE, 12 October 1876, ibid., VI, 294.

83. See John Blackwood to GE, 12 July 1876, ibid., VI, 273. For editions and sales see Clarendon Edition of *Daniel Deronda*, ed. Graham Handley (Oxford, 1984), pp. xxiii–xxiv, xxxiii–xxxvi.

84. John Blackwood to William Blackwood, 6 November 1876, *GEL*, VI, 305n.

85. This can be inferred from the Blackwood inventory drawn up on 29 October 1879, on John Blackwood's death, MS NLS (Blackwood Papers). I am indebted to John Sutherland for this information.

CHAPTER FOURTEEN: *Last Years 1877–80*

1. GE to John Blackwood, 6 July 1876, *GEL*, VI, 266.

2. Ibid., VI, 266 and n.

3. GE to John Blackwood, 2 September 1876, ibid., VI, 275.

4. GHL to John Blackwood, 1 December 1875, ibid., VI, 196.

5. GE Journal, 1 December 1876, ibid., VI, 314.

6. GHL to Richard Owen, 24 December 1876, in Revd Richard Owen, *The Life of Richard Owen*, 2 vols. (London, 1894), II, 232.

7. Mathilde Blind, *George Eliot* (London, 1884), p. 112; Henry Vizetelly,

Glances Back Through Seventy Years, 2 vols. (London, 1893), I, 351; Richard Ellmann, *Golden Codgers: Biographical Speculations* (London, 1973), p. 30.

8. *Middlemarch*, p. 719 (Book VII, chapter 71).

9. GHL to John Blackwood, 1 December 1875, *GEL*, VI, 196.

10. GHL Diary, 29 November 1876; GE Journal, 11 December 1876, ibid., VI, 313, 314. The Heights is now an old people's home.

11. GE to Clementia Taylor, 10 November 1877, ibid., VI, 417.

12. GE to Elizabeth Phelps, 16 December 1876, ibid., VI, 318, 319 and n.

13. GHL Diary, 23 February 1877, ibid., VI, 345.

14. The Alma-Tadema sketch is in the National Portrait Gallery; Princess Louise's is at Yale.

15. GHL to Elma Stuart, 12 July 1877, *GEL*, VI, 394.

16. See GE to Edward Burne-Jones, 8 May 1877, ibid., VI, 368, 373.

17. GE to Elma Stuart, 27 May 1877, ibid., VI, 377.

18. See GHL to John Cross, 10 June 1877, and to John Blackwood, 20 June 1877, ibid., VI, 386, 388.

19. John Blackwood to William Blackwood, 25 June 1877, ibid., VI, 390.

20. See William Baker, 'A New George Eliot Manuscript', in *George Eliot: Centenary Essays and an Unpublished Fragment*, ed. Anne Smith (London, 1980), pp. 11, 13. The fragment is at King's School, Canterbury.

21. GE to John Cross, 6 November 1877, *GEL*, VI, 415.

22. GE Journal, 31 December 1877, ibid., VI, 439–40.

23. GE to Barbara Bodichon, 17 January 1878, ibid., VII, 6.

24. See McWilliams-Tullberg, 'Women and Degrees', in *A Widening Sphere*, pp. 120, 129.

25. GHL Diary, 21 March 1878, *GEL*, VII, 16 and n.

26. GHL Diary, 31 May 1878, ibid., VII, 28–9.

27. GHL Diary, 16 April 1878, ibid., VII, 21.

28. William Blackwood to GHL, 16 May 1878, ibid., VII, 26.

29. John Blackwood to Joseph Langford, 24 November 1878, ibid., VII, 82.

30. See *Theophrastus Such*, pp. 183–4.

31. Ibid., pp. 13, 6.

32. Ibid., pp. 26–7.

33. Ibid., p. 51.

34. *A Century of George Eliot Criticism*, pp. 161, 169, 179, 167.

35. Frederic Harrison to GE, 12 June 1877, *GEL*, IX, 194.

36. GE to Frederic Harrison, 14 June 1877, ibid., VI, 387.

37. 'O May I Join the Choir Invisible' (1867), in *The Legend of Jubal, and Other Poems*, pp. 301, 303.

38. GE to John Blackwood, 30 July 1878, *GEL*, VII, 45.

39. GHL to John Blackwood, 6 August 1878, ibid., VII, 50.

40. GE to Barbara Bodichon, 15 October 1878, ibid., VII, 71.

41. Cross, III, 334.

42. See GHL to Charles Lewes, 15 October 1878, *GEL*, VII, 73.

43. GE to Elma Stuart, 15 November 1878, ibid., VII, 76–7.

44. GHL Diary, 11 November 1878, MS Gabriel Woolf (owner of GHL's Diary for 1878).

45. GHL Diary, 31 October 1878, MS Gabriel Woolf.

46. GHL to John Blackwood, 21 November 1878, *GEL*, VII, 78–9.

47. GE to John Blackwood, 25 November 1878, and to Barbara Bodichon, 25 November 1878, ibid., VII, 83, 84.

48. Charles Lewes to Edward Pigott, 1 December 1878, ibid., IX, 244.

49. John Blackwood to Joseph Langford, 1 and 2 December 1878, ibid., VII, 85.

50. Spencer, *Autobiography*, II, 318–19.

51. Herbert Spencer to GE, 5 December 1878, *GEL*, VII, 87.

52. Anthony Trollope, 'George Henry Lewes', *Fortnightly Review*, XXV new series (1 January 1879), 23, 21–2.

53. Emily Clarke to GE, 2 December 1878; Sarah Evans to GE, 5 December 1878, *GEL*, IX, 244, 247.

54. Charles Lewes to Bessie Belloc, 6 December 1878, ibid., VII, 87.

55. Ivan Turgenev to GE, 3 December 1878, ibid., IX, 247.

56. For a detailed discussion of GE's work of completion and revision, see K. K. Collins, 'G. H. Lewes Revised: George Eliot and the Moral Sense', *Victorian Studies*, XXI (1978), 463–92.

57. GE Diary, 2 January 1879, MS New York Public Library (NYPL).

58. Clifford Allbutt to GE, 19 January 1879, *GEL*, VII, 97.

59. GE to Barbara Bodichon, 8 April 1879, ibid., VII, 128.

60. See GE to Barbara Bodichon, 2 July 1879, ibid., VII, 177 and n.

61. See E. M. Tansey, 'George Eliot's Gift to Medicine', *Transactions of the Medical Society of London*, CIV (1988), 15–24.

62. GE to Arthur Helps, 12 January 1868, *GEL*, IV, 417.

63. GE, 'German Wit: Heinrich Heine', *Westminster Review* (January 1856), in *Essays*, p. 249 and n; GE Diary, January 1879, MS NYPL.

64. GHL's will, Somerset House.

65. See *GEL*, III, 212–13n; IX, 346.

66. GE Diary, 4, 7, and 8 February 1879, MS NYPL.

67. GE Diary, 6 February 1879, *GEL*, VII, 100n.

68. GE Diary, 23 February 1879, ibid., VII, 107n.

69. See GE to John Cross, 22 April 1879, ibid., VII, 138 and n.

70. GE Diary, 28 May 1879, ibid., VII, 152.

71. Cross, III, 359.

72. See GE to Cara Bray, 28 November 1880, *GEL*, VII, 341.

73. GE to John Cross, 16 October 1879, ibid., VII, 211–12.

74. Frederic Harrison to John Cross, 6 May 1880, ibid., VII, 272.

75. GE to John Blackwood, 25 March 1879; John Blackwood to GE, 1 April 1879, ibid., VII, 122, 125.

76. GE to William Blackwood, 12 June 1879, ibid., VII, 165.

77. GE to Elma Stuart, 18 June 1879, ibid., VII, 169.

78. See *GEL*, VII, 117n, 202; IX, 261.

79. GE to Charles Lewes, 27 October 1879, ibid., VII, 217.

80. GE Diary, 29 November 1879, ibid., VII, 227.

81. Henry James to Alice James, 30 January 1881, *Henry James Letters*, II, 337.

82. See Oscar Browning, *Life of George Eliot* (London, 1890), p. 130.

83. Eliza Lynn Linton, *My Literary Life*, p. 101.

84. See Marghanita Laski, *George Eliot and Her World*, p. 112.

85. Edward Beesly to Herbert Spencer, 27 December 1880, MS UCL (Beesly Papers).

86. GE Diary, 9 and 10 April 1880, *GEL*, VII, 259.

87. GE to Eleanor Cross, 13 April 1880, ibid.

88. GE to Eleanor Cross, 14 April 1880, ibid., VII, 260.

89. GE to Elma Stuart, 23 April 1880, ibid., VII, 263.

90. GE to Eleanor Cross, 30 April 1880, ibid., VII, 267.

91. GE to Barbara Bodichon, 2 August 1877, ibid., VI, 398.

92. Annie Ritchie to Richmond Ritchie, 24 May 1880, ibid., VII, 284.

93. GE to Georgiana Burne-Jones, 5 May 1880, ibid., VII, 269.

94. GE to Barbara Bodichon, 5 December 1859, ibid., III, 227.

95. GE Diary, 6 May 1880, ibid., VII, 270.

96. Georgiana Burne-Jones to GE, 6–7 May 1880; Barbara Bodichon to GE, 8 May 1880, ibid., VII, 272, 273.

97. Charles Lewes to GE, 13 May 1880, MS Kathleen Adams.

98. Edith Simcox, Autobiography, 7 January 1878 and 7 May 1880, *GEL*, IX, 212, 308.

99. Emily Clarke to GE, 6 May 1880, ibid., IX, 306.

100. Thomas Holbeche to Isaac Evans, 7 May 1880, ibid., IX, 307.

101. Isaac Evans to GE, 17 May 1880, ibid., VII, 280.

102. GE to Isaac Evans, 26 May 1880, ibid., VII, 287.

103. John Cross to Elma Stuart, 11 May 1880, ibid., VII, 276.

104. Henry James to Alice James, 30 January 1881, *Henry James Letters*, II, 337.

105. See GE to Charles Lewes, 12 August 1880, *GEL*, VII, 312.

106. Cross, III, 407–8. Phyllis Rose points out that Venice had had a similar effect on others, including Byron and Alfred de Musset, *Parallel Lives: Five Victorian Marriages* (London, 1984), p. 302.

107. GE Diary, 16–19 June 1880, *GEL*, VII, 300.
108. Edith Simcox Autobiography, ibid., IX, 314.
109. See Haight, pp. 509, 544.
110. Edith Simcox Autobiography, McKenzie, p. 122.
111. See *GEL*, VII, 301n.
112. GE Diary, 1–14 November 1880, ibid, VII, 331.
113. GE to François D'Albert Durade, 15 November 1880, ibid., VII, 333.
114. GE Diary, 29 November and 3 December 1880, ibid., VII, 341, 342.
115. GE to Charles Lewes, 23 November 1880, ibid., VII, 338.
116. GE to Charles Bray, 4 December 1880, ibid., VII, 342.
117. GE to Bessie Belloc, 17 December 1880, and to Herbert Spencer, 18 December 1880, ibid., VII, 347, 348 and n.
118. John Cross to Georgiana Burne-Jones, 22 December 1880, and to Elma Stuart, 23 December 1880, ibid., VII, 350, 351.

EPILOGUE

1. Charles Lewes to William Blackwood, 24 December 1880, MS NLS (Blackwood Papers).
2. See Haight, pp. 548–9.
3. Ibid., p. 549.
4. See Edith Simcox Autobiography, 29 December 1880, *GEL*, IX, 324.
5. Oscar Browning, *Life of George Eliot*, pp. 138–9.
6. Letters between Cross and Spencer about the *Life* are in the British Library (Add MS 65,530) and the Beinecke Library at Yale. Letters from Cross to Isaac Evans are in the Nuneaton Library.
7. *Athenaeum*, No. 3031 (28 November 1885), 702.

BIBLIOGRAPHY

I. MANUSCRIPT SOURCES

I have consulted the large collection of George Eliot (and G. H. Lewes) manuscripts in the Beinecke Rare Book and Manuscript Library of Yale University. The collection includes originals or copies of all the surviving GE and GHL journals and diaries, and a large number of letters from, to, and about GE and GHL.

The next largest collection of materials I have consulted is in the National Library of Scotland, Edinburgh. GE's and GHL's letters to and from John Blackwood and his colleagues are in the Blackwood Papers; other relevant collections in the NLS include the George Combe Papers.

I have been indebted to the late Gordon S. Haight for miscellaneous manuscript materials (see individual footnotes for details); also to Mrs Kathleen Adams of the George Eliot Fellowship for MS letters of the Evans family; and to Gabriel Woolf for GHL's MS Diary for 1878.

Other libraries whose unpublished material relating to GE I have consulted are:

Henry W. and Albert A. Berg Collection, New York Public Library (GE's diary for 1879).

British Library (Herbert Spencer Papers, Add MS 65,530).

British Library of Political and Economic Science, London School of Economics (Frederic Harrison Papers).

British Museum (GE's application for a Reader's Ticket).

Cambridge University Library (Edward Fitzgerald Papers).

Coventry City Libraries (Cara Bray's engagement diary and Commonplace Book, Sara Hennell's MS letters to GE, David Friedrich Strauss's Preface to German edition of Charles Hennell, *Inquiry Concerning the Origin of Christianity*).

Girton College, Cambridge (Bessie Rayner Parkes Collection).

Henry E. Huntington Library, San Marino, California (Cara Bray's MS letters to Frances Power Cobbe).

Herbert Art Gallery and Museum, Coventry (GE MS letter to Cara Bray).

John Murray Archives, London (George Smith Papers).

London Library (Shirley Brooks Diary).

Nuneaton Library (Robert and Isaac Evans MS letters; Anonymous Diary, 'Occurrences at Nuneaton', 1832).

Somerset House (GHL and GE wills).

University College London (UCL) Library (Edward Spencer Beesly Papers).

Warwickshire County Record Office (WCRO), Warwick (Robert and Isaac Evans MS letters).

Dr Williams's Library, London (Henry Crabb Robinson MS Diary; GHL Annotated Library).

2. BOOKS AND ARTICLES

Abrams, M. H., *Natural Supernaturalism: Tradition and Revolution in Romantic Literature* (New York, 1973).

Adams, Kathleen, *Those of Us Who Loved Her: The Men in George Eliot's Life* (Warwick, 1980).

Altick, Richard D., *The Presence of the Present: Topics of the Day in the Victorian Novel* (Columbus, Ohio, 1991).

Anderson, Nancy Fix, *Woman Against Women in Victorian England: A Life of Eliza Lynn Linton* (Bloomington, Indiana, 1987).

Anderson, Patricia, *When Passion Reigned: Sex and the Victorians* (New York, 1995).

Anderson, R. F., '"Things Wisely Ordered": John Blackwood, George Eliot, and the Publication of *Romola*', *Publishing History*, XI (1982).

Ashton, Rosemary, *G. H. Lewes: A Life* (Oxford, 1991).

—— *The German Idea: Four English Writers and the Reception of German Thought 1800–1860* (Cambridge, 1980, reprinted London, 1994).

—— *The Life of Samuel Taylor Coleridge: A Critical Biography* (Oxford, 1996).

—— *Little Germany: Exile and Asylum in Victorian England* (Oxford, 1986, reprinted 1989).

—— *The Mill on the Floss: A Natural History* (Boston, Massachusetts, 1990).

—— 'New George Eliot Letters at the Huntington', *Huntington Library Quarterly*, LIV (Spring 1991).

Askwith, Betty Ellen, *Lady Dilke* (London, 1969).

Baker, William, *The George Eliot–George Henry Lewes Library: An Annotated Catalogue of Their Books at the Dr Williams's Library, London* (London, 1977).

—— *The Libraries of George Eliot and George Henry Lewes* (Victoria, British Columbia, 1981).

—— 'A New George Eliot Manuscript', *George Eliot: Centenary Essays and an Unpublished Fragment*, ed. Anne Smith (London, 1980).

Beaty, Jerome, *'Middlemarch' from Notebook to Novel* (Urbana, Illinois, 1960).

Beer, Gillian, *Darwin's Plots: Evolutionary Narrative in Darwin, George Eliot and Nineteenth-Century Fiction* (London, 1983).

—— *George Eliot*, Key Women Writers (Brighton, 1986).

Belloc, Bessie Rayner Parkes, *In a Walled Garden* (London, 1895, reprinted 1900).

Best, Geoffrey, *Mid-Victorian Britain 1851–75* (London, 1971).

Blind, Mathilde, *George Eliot* (London, 1884).

Bray, Charles, *Phases of Opinion and Experience during a Long Life* (London, 1884).

—— *The Philosophy of Necessity*, 2 vols. (London, 1841).

Browning, Oscar, *Life of George Eliot* (London, 1890).

Buchanan, Robert, *A Look Round Literature* (London, 1887).

Buckle, George Earle (ed.), *Letters of Queen Victoria*, second series, 3 vols. (London, 1926–8).

Calder, Jenni, *Women and Marriage in Victorian Fiction* (London, 1976).

Carlyle, Jane Welsh, *New Letters and Memorials of Jane Welsh Carlyle*, ed. Alexander Carlyle, 2 vols. (London, 1903).

Carlyle, Thomas, *Letters of Thomas Carlyle to John Stuart Mill, John Sterling, and Robert Browning*, ed. Alexander Carlyle (London, 1923).

Carroll, David, *George Eliot and the Conflict of Interpretations* (Cambridge, 1992).

—— (ed.), *George Eliot: The Critical Heritage* (London, 1977).

Clough, Arthur Hugh, *The Correspondence of Arthur Hugh Clough*, ed. Frederick L. Mulhauser, 2 vols. (Oxford, 1957).

Coleridge, Samuel Taylor, *Collected Letters of Samuel Taylor Coleridge*, ed. Earl Leslie Griggs, 6 vols. (Oxford, 1956–71).

—— *The Collected Works of Samuel Taylor Coleridge*, Bollingen Series, 16 vols. in progress (London, 1969–).

Colley, Linda, *Britons: Forging the Nation 1707–1837* (London, 1992).

Collins, K. K., 'G. H. Lewes Revised: George Eliot and the Moral Sense', *Victorian Studies*, XXI (1978).

Cook, Sir Edward, *The Life of Florence Nightingale*, 2 vols. (London, 1913).

Cook, Olive, *The English Country House* (London, 1974, reprinted 1984).

Cross, J. W., *George Eliot's Life as Related in her Letters and Journals*, 3 vols. (Edinburgh and London, 1885; reprinted with additions, 1886).

Cunningham, Valentine, *Everywhere Spoken Against: Dissent in the Victorian Novel* (Oxford, 1975).

Dale, Peter Allen, 'George Eliot's "Brother Jacob": Fables and the Physiology of Common Life', *Philological Quarterly*, LXIV (Winter 1985).

Darley, Gillian, *Octavia Hill: A Life* (London, 1990).

Darwin, Charles, *The Origin of Species* (London, 1859, reprinted with an introduction by J. W. Burrow (Harmondsworth, 1986).

Dickens, Charles, *Barnaby Rudge*, ed. Gordon Spence (Harmondsworth, 1973).

—— *The Letters of Charles Dickens*, Pilgrim Edition, ed. Madeleine House, Graham Storey, Kathleen Tillotson et al., 8 vols. so far (Oxford, 1965–).

—— *A Tale of Two Cities*, ed. George Woodcock (Harmondsworth, 1970).

Duffy, Sir Charles Gavan, *Conversations with Carlyle* (London, 1892).

Eliot, George, *Adam Bede*, ed. Stephen Gill (Harmondsworth, 1980).

—— *Brother Jacob*, ed. Beryl Gray (London, 1989).

—— *Daniel Deronda*, ed. Barbara Hardy (Harmondsworth, 1967).

—— *Daniel Deronda*, ed. Graham Handley, Clarendon Edition (Oxford, 1984).

—— *Essays of George Eliot*, ed. Thomas Pinney (New York, 1963).

—— [trans.], *The Essence of Christianity*, by Ludwig Feuerbach (London, 1854).

—— [trans.], *Ethics*, by Benedict de Spinoza, ed. Thomas Deegan (Salzburg, 1981).

—— *Felix Holt, The Radical*, ed. Peter Coveney (Harmondsworth, 1972).

—— *Felix Holt, The Radical*, ed. Fred C. Thomson, Clarendon Edition (Oxford, 1980).

—— *George Eliot: A Writer's Notebook 1854–1879, and Uncollected Writings*, ed. Joseph Wiesenfarth (Charlottesville, Virginia, 1981).

—— *The George Eliot Letters*, ed. Gordon S. Haight, 9 vols. (New Haven, Connecticut, 1954–5, 1978).

—— *George Eliot's 'Middlemarch' Notebooks: A Transcription*, ed. John Clark Pratt and Victor A. Neufeldt (London, 1979).

—— *Impressions of Theophrastus Such*, ed. Nancy Henry (London, 1994).

—— *The Legend of Jubal, and Other Poems* (Edinburgh and London, 1874).

—— [trans.], *The Life of Jesus, Critically Examined*, by David Friedrich Strauss, 3 vols. (London, 1846).

—— *The Lifted Veil*, ed. Beryl Gray (London, 1985).

—— *Middlemarch*, ed. Rosemary Ashton (Harmondsworth, 1994).

—— *Middlemarch*, ed. David Carroll, Clarendon Edition (Oxford, 1986).

—— *The Mill on the Floss*, ed. A. S. Byatt (Harmondsworth, 1979).

—— *Romola*, ed. Andrew Sanders (Harmondsworth, 1980).

—— *Romola*, ed. Andrew Brown, Clarendon Edition (Oxford, 1993).

—— *Scenes of Clerical Life*, ed. David Lodge (Harmondsworth, 1973).

—— *Selected Critical Writings*, ed. Rosemary Ashton (Oxford, 1992).

—— *Silas Marner*, ed. Q. D. Leavis (Harmondsworth, 1944, reprinted 1981).

—— *The Spanish Gypsy* (Edinburgh and London, 1878).

Ellmann, Richard, *Golden Codgers: Biographical Speculations* (London, 1973).

Escott, T. H. S., *Platform, Press, Politics and Play: Being Pen and Ink Sketches of Contemporary Celebrities* (Bristol, 1895).

Faderman, Lilian, *Surpassing the Love of Men: Romantic Friendship and Love Between Women from the Renaissance to the Present* (New York, 1981).

Fitzgerald, Penelope, *Edward Burne-Jones: A Biography* (London, 1975).

Froude, J. A., *The Nemesis of Faith* (London, 1849, reprinted with an introduction by Rosemary Ashton, 1988).

Fulford, Roger (ed.), *Dearest Child: Letters between Queen Victoria and the Princess Royal 1858–1861* (London, 1964).

—— (ed.), *Dearest Mama: Letters between Queen Victoria and the Crown Princess of Prussia 1861–1864* (London, 1968).

Furst, Lilian R., 'Struggling for Medical Reform in Middlemarch', *Nineteenth-Century Literature*, XLVIII (December 1993).

Gaskell, Elizabeth, *The Letters of Mrs Gaskell*, ed. J. A. V. Chapple and Arthur Pollard (Manchester, 1966).

Glynn, Jenifer, *Prince of Publishers: A Biography of the Great Victorian Publisher George Smith* (London, 1986).

Goodway, David, *London Chartism 1838–1848* (Cambridge, 1982).

Graver, Suzanne, *George Eliot and Community: A Study in Social Theory and Fictional Form* (Berkeley, California, 1984).

Gray, B. M., 'Pseudo-Science and George Eliot's "The Lifted Veil"', *Nineteenth-Century Fiction*, XXXVI (March 1982).

Haight, Gordon S., 'The Carlyles and the Leweses', *Carlyle and his Contemporaries: Essays in Honor of Charles Richard Sanders*, ed. John Clubbe (Durham, North Carolina, 1976).

—— (ed.), *A Century of George Eliot Criticism* (London, 1966).

—— *George Eliot: A Biography* (Oxford, 1968, reprinted 1969).

—— *George Eliot and John Chapman* (London, 1940, reprinted 1969).

—— 'George Eliot's Bastards', *George Eliot: A Centenary Tribute*, ed. Gordon S. Haight and Rosemary T. VanArsdel (London, 1982).

Hammerton, A. James, 'Feminism and Female Emigration 1861–1886', *A Widening Sphere: Changing Roles of Victorian Women*, ed. Martha Vicinus (Bloomington, Indiana, 1977).

Hardy, Barbara, '*The Mill on the Floss*', *Critical Essays on George Eliot*, ed. Barbara Hardy (London, 1970).

—— *The Novels of George Eliot: A Study in Form* (London, 1959, revised 1963).

—— *Particularities* (London, 1982).

Hennell, Charles C., *An Inquiry Concerning the Origin of Christianity* (London, 1838, 2nd edition 1841).

Herstein, Sheila R., *A Mid-Victorian Feminist: Barbara Leigh Smith Bodichon* (New Haven, Connecticut, 1985).

Hodgson, William Ballantyne, *Life and Letters of William Ballantyne Hodgson*, ed. J. M. D. Meiklejohn (Edinburgh, 1883).

Holcombe, Lee, 'Victorian Wives and Property', *A Widening Sphere: Changing Roles of Victorian Women*, ed. Martha Vicinus (Bloomington, Indiana, 1977).

Hutton, Richard Holt, *Essays on Some of the Modern Guides of English Thought in Matters of Faith* (London, 1887).

James, Henry, *Letters of Henry James*, ed. Leon Edel, 4 vols. (London, 1974–84).

Jay, Elisabeth, *Mrs Oliphant: A Fiction to Herself* (Oxford, 1995).

Karl, Frederick, *George Eliot: A Biography* (London, 1995).

Lacey, Candida Ann (ed.), *Barbara Leigh Smith Bodichon and the Langham Place Group* (London, 1987).

Laski, Marghanita, *George Eliot and Her World* (London, 1973).

Layard, George Somes, *The Life of Mrs Lynn Linton* (London, 1901).

Leavis, F. R., *The Great Tradition* (London, 1948).

Lewes, George Henry, *A Biographical History of Philosophy*, 4 vols. in 2 (London, 1845–6).

—— *The Letters of George Henry Lewes*, ed. William Baker, 2 vols. (Victoria, British Columbia, 1995).

Linton, Eliza Lynn, *The Autobiography of Christopher Kirkland*, 3 vols. (London, 1885).

—— *My Literary Life* (London, 1899).

Lodge, David, '*Middlemarch* and the Idea of the Classic Realist Text', *The Nineteenth-Century Novel: Critical Essays and Documents*, ed. Arnold Kettle (London, 1981).

Lowndes, Susan (ed.), *Diaries and Letters of Marie Belloc Lowndes 1911–1947* (London, 1971).

—— *I, Too, Have Lived in Arcadia* (London, 1941).

Lynes, Alice, *George Eliot's Coventry* (Coventry, 1970).

McKenzie, K. A., *Edith Simcox and George Eliot* (Oxford, 1961).

McWilliams-Tullberg, Rita, 'Women and Degrees at Cambridge University, 1862–1897', *A Widening Sphere: Changing Roles of Victorian Women*, ed. Martha Vicinus (Bloomington, Indiana, 1977).

Martin, Carol A., *George Eliot's Serial Fiction* (Columbus, Ohio, 1994).

Martin, Robert Bernard, *The Dust of Combat: A Life of Charles Kingsley* (London, 1959).

Mason, Michael, *The Making of Victorian Sexuality* (Oxford, 1994).

Mottram, William, *The True Story of George Eliot in Relation to 'Adam Bede'* (London, 1905).

Myers, F. W. H., *Collected Poems*, ed. Eveleen Myers (London, 1921).

—— *Essays*, 2 vols. (London, 1883).

Newdigate-Newdegate, Lady, *The Cheverels of Cheverel Manor* (London, 1898).

Oliphant, Margaret, *Autobiography and Letters*, ed. Mrs Harry Coghill (Edinburgh, 1899).

Owen, Revd Richard, *The Life of Richard Owen*, 2 vols. (London, 1894).

Parkinson, S., *Scenes from the 'George Eliot' Country* (Leeds, 1888).

Paul, Charles Kegan, *Biographical Sketches* (London, 1883).

Pavlov, Ivan Petrovitch, *Lectures on Conditioned Reflexes*, translated and edited by W. Horsley Gantt, 2 vols. (London, 1928, reprinted 1963).

Pickett, T. H., 'George Henry Lewes's Letters to K. A. Varnhagen von Ense', *Modern Language Review*, LXXX (July 1985).

Porter, Roy and Porter, Dorothy, *In Sickness and in Health: The British Experience 1650–1850* (London, 1988).

Robinson, Henry Crabb, *Henry Crabb Robinson On Books and their Writers*, ed. Edith J. Morley, 3 vols. (London, 1938).

Rolleston, H. D., *Sir Thomas Clifford Allbutt* (London, 1929).

Rose, Phyllis, *Parallel Lives: Five Victorian Marriages* (London, 1984).

Rupke, Nicolaas A., *Richard Owen: Victorian Naturalist* (New Haven, Connecticut, 1994).

Schofield, Robert E., *The Lunar Society of Birmingham: A Social History of Provincial Science and Industry in Eighteenth-Century England* (Oxford, 1963).

Semmel, Bernard, *George Eliot and the Politics of National Inheritance* (Oxford, 1994).

Shaffer, Elinor, *'Kubla Khan' and The Fall of Jerusalem: The Mythological School in Biblical Criticism and Secular Literature 1770–1880* (Cambridge, 1975).

Shaw, George Bernard, *Our Theatres in the Nineties*, 3 vols. (London, 1932).

Showalter, Elaine, *A Literature of Their Own: British Women Novelists from Brontë to Lessing* (Princeton, New Jersey, 1977).

Shuttleworth, Sally, *George Eliot and Nineteenth-Century Science* (Cambridge, 1984).

Sibree, John and Caston, M., *Independency in Warwickshire: A Brief History of the Independent or Congregational Churches in that County* (Coventry and London, 1855).

Southey, Robert, *The Life and Correspondence of the Late Robert Southey*, ed. C. C. Southey, 6 vols. (London, 1849–50).

Spencer, Herbert, *An Autobiography*, 2 vols. (London, 1904).

—— *The Life and Letters of Herbert Spencer*, ed. David Duncan (London, 1908).

—— *Principles of Biology*, 2 vols. (London, 1864–7, reprinted 1890).

Stephen, Leslie, *George Eliot* (London, 1902).

Stevenson, Robert Louis, *The Letters of Robert Louis Stevenson*, ed. Bradford A. Booth, 6 vols. so far (New Haven, Connecticut, 1994–).

Stone, W. H., *Religion and Art of William Hale White* (Stanford, California, 1954).

Strangford, Viscountess, *Literary Remains of the Late Emanuel Deutsch* (London, 1874).

Sutherland, John, *Victorian Fiction: Writers, Publishers, Readers* (London, 1995).

—— *Victorian Novelists and Publishers* (London, 1976).

Tansey, E. M., 'George Eliot's Gift to Medicine', *Transactions of the Medical Society of London*, CIV (1988).

Thomson, Patricia, *George Sand and the Victorians: Her Influence and Reputation in Nineteenth-Century England* (London, 1977).

Trollope, Anthony, *The Letters of Anthony Trollope*, ed. N. John Hall, 2 vols. (Stanford, California, 1983).

Trollope, Thomas Adolphus, *What I Remember*, 2 vols. (London, 1887).

Uglow, Jennifer, *George Eliot* (London, 1987).

Varnhagen von Ense, Karl August, *Aus dem Nachlass Varnhagen's von Ense, Tagebücher*, ed. Ludmilla Assing, 15 vols. (Leipzig, 1861–70, Berlin, 1905).

Vizetelly, Henry, *Glances Back Through Seventy Years*, 2 vols. (London, 1893).

Ward, Mrs Humphry, *A Writer's Recollections*, 2 vols. (London, 1918).

Webb, R. K., *Harriet Martineau: A Radical Victorian* (London, 1960).

White, William Hale, *The Autobiography of Mark Rutherford* (London, 1881, reprinted with an introduction by Don Cupitt, 1988).

Whiting, Lilian, *Kate Field: A Record* (London, 1899).

Wolff, Robert Lee, *Gains and Losses: Novels of Faith and Doubt in Victorian England* (London, 1977).

Wortham, H. E., *Oscar Browning* (London, 1956).

Wright, T. R., *The Religion of Humanity: The Impact of Comtean Positivism on Victorian Britain* (Cambridge, 1986).

Youngson, A. J., *The Scientific Revolution in Victorian Medicine* (London, 1979).

Zedner, Lucia, *Women, Crime, and Custody in Victorian England* (Oxford, 1991).

INDEX

Page numbers in *italic* refer to passages of particular significance.

Disraeli, Benjamin, 59, 64, 285, 332, 348
Dixon, William Hepworth, 223, 227, 268
Dostoyevsky, Fyodor, 195
Dover, 134, 135
Dresden, 198
Duncker, Franz, 303

East Sheen, 137, 144
Ebdell, Revd Bernard Gilpin, 175
Eckermann, Johann Peter, 128
Economist, 90, 91, 253
Edinburgh, 54–5, 102, 313
  and *Middlemarch*, 319–20
Edinburgh Review, 81, 105, 144
Edison, Thomas, 359
Education Act (1870), 7, 309
Eichhorn, Johann Gottfried, 47, 51

ELIOT, GEORGE (1819–80)
appearance, *275–6*
  Bessie Parkes on, 4, 82
  in Cara Bray's portrait, 46
  Eliza Lynn on, 49, 82
  GE on, 59, 70, 270–71
    at Geneva, 71
    at Broadstairs, 99, 158
    in Germany, 113
  in D'Albert Durade's portrait, 74
  Chapman on, 88
  Blackwood on, 192
  photograph of, 192
  in Laurence's portrait, 245, 275
  in Burton's portrait, 275
  Henry James on, 275, 299
characteristics
  conservatism, 6, 207, 305, 331–2, 381
  depression, 30, 35
    Charles Bray on, 43
    when caring for father, 64, 65, 67
    in Geneva, 69, 71
    in Dover, 136
    about her writing, 165, 200, 220–21,
      232, 245, 254, 255–6, 259, 263,
      277, 278, 281

  about Chrissey, 181–2, 214–15
  about Liggins, 213–14, 224, 227
  in 'Lifted Veil', 219, 220–21
  diffidence, 164, 165, 220, 254, 381
  egotism, 27, 30, 32, 306, 324–5, 333,
    361
  impulsiveness, 49, 50, 83
  independence, 4–5, 53, 70
  intelligence, 3, 49, 54, 66, 89–90, 97,
    121
  intolerance (temperamental), 25, 30,
    76, 203
  piety, 19, 20–21, 22, *26–30*, 35
  pride, 40, 44, 62, 72, 99–100, 116–17,
    381
  rebelliousness, 6, 45, 178, 248, 307, 381
  self-criticism, 26, 30, 32, 72, 164, 180,
    189, 220, 306, 325
  self-righteousness, 184, 230, 333, 361,
    362
  scepticism, 4–5, 8, 25, 69, 345–6, 381
  sensitivity, in childhood and youth:
    18–19, 20, 32
    to criticism, 72, 141, 164, 189, 194,
      316
    about her relationship with GHL,
      159, 164, 181, 222, 223, 237, 247
  'strong-minded woman', 58, 119, 123,
    253, 290, 370, 378
  tolerance, intellectual and religious, 25,
    76, 167, 177–8, 203, 276, 335
  unconventionality, 5–6, 49, 97–8, 100,
    207, 253, 370, 374, 379, 380,
    382
  wit, *57–9*, 61, 71, 98, 99, 106, 211–12,
    233–4, 253, 259, 322, 360
childhood
  at Griff, 12, 16–17
  and *Mill on the Floss*, 103, 220–21, 231,
    234
  and *Felix Holt*, 281
  and 'Brother and Sister' sonnets, 301,
    375
  and *Theophrastus Such*, 361

Feuerbach, Ludwig – *contd*
  and *Scenes of Clerical Life*, 168
  and *Daniel Deronda*, 347
Fielding, Henry, 199, 201
Fields, James, publisher, 297
Fitzgerald, Edward, 118
Florence:
  GE and GHL visit (1860), 241, 243,
    275; (1861), 252, 253; (1869), 298
  and *Romola*, 241, 243, *260–63*
Foleshill, Coventry:
  GE lives at (1841–9), 20, 31, 32, 33, 34,
    44–5, 73
Forster, John, 340
Fortnightly Review, 286, 287, 291
  GHL edits, 278–80, 287, 288
  and Reform, 279
  GE publishes 'Influence of
    Rationalism' in, 279–80
  obituary of GHL in, 365
Foster, Michael, 366
Franco-Prussian War, 311–12
Franklin, Mary and Rebecca, 18, *20–22*, 24,
  29, 34, 36, 46
Fraser's Magazine:
  GHL and, 105
  GE's articles in, 113, 127, 135, 152
Frederick William, Crown Prince of
  Germany, 360
Freud, Sigmund, 112, 308, 334
Froude, James Anthony, 41, 68–9, 81, 92,
  188

Gall, Franz Joseph, 91
Garibaldi, Giuseppe, 269–70
Garrick Club, 174, 188, 214
Gaskell, Elizabeth, 5, 153, 161, 179
  and GE's relationship with GHL,
    123, 237, 267
  and Liggins, 185
  and *Adam Bede*, 211, 222
  GE compared to, 282, 285, 311
Geneva, 65, 87, 164
  GE at, 68, *70–74*, 244, 358

Genoa, 241, 345
GHL Studentship, 366–7
Girton College, 7, 124, 292, 309, 332
Gladstone, William Ewart, 281, 290, 332,
  357
Goethe, Johann Wolfgang von, 57, 158,
  376
  Tasso, 31
  Wilhelm Meister, 47, 131
  GE's *Leader* article on *Wilhelm Meister*,
    149–50, 168, 194
  GE and *Faust*, 60, 114, 196–7
  GE and *Die Wahlverwandtschaften*, 60,
    131–2, 156
  GHL's *Life* of, 102, 104, 106, 113, 114,
    128–33, 143, 289
  Crabb Robinson compares GE to, 190
  and *Adam Bede*, 194, 196–7
  and *Mill on the Floss*, 236, 238
  and *Daniel Deronda*, 351
Goethe, Ottilie von, 128
Goldsmith, Oliver, 167, 171, 188
Goschen, George, 357, 359, 381
Granada, 288–9
Great Exhibition (1851), 78, 89, 90, 93
Greg, William Rathbone, 81, 90, 93, 208
Griff, near Coventry:
  GE's childhood and youth at, 12, 16–
    17, 24, 31–2, 33
  GE's Methodist aunt visits, 24–5, 30,
    204
  Isaac settles at, 31, 33
  GE visits, 45, 74
  Blackwood and, 231
  GE gets photograph of, 332
  Isaac writes to GE from, 375
Griffiths, Edith (*née* Evans, GE's niece),
  332
Gruppe, Otto Friedrich, 129
Gurney, Edmund, 334
Gwyther, Revd John:
  and 'Amos Barton', 170, 175, 184, 197,
    222, 307
  and Robert Evans, 170, 321

INDEX

Rosehill (Charles and Cara Bray's house
 in Coventry):
 GE visits, 3, 41–2, 48, 75, 83, 87, 101,
  112
 Charles Bray describes, 41–2
 Spencer visits, 41, 98, 101
 Dr Brabant visits, 47
 1851 Census and, 55
 Emerson visits, 66
 Chapman and, 75, 79, 87
 GE declines invitation to, 152, 180
 sold to Cashes, 180
Rosslyn Hill Unitarian Chapel, 277, 302,
 364
Rousseau, Jean Jacques, 5, 60, 66–7, 71,
 141
Royal Academy, 275
Royal Society, 82
Rubinstein, Anton, 127, 346
Ruskin, John, 188, 189
 GE on, 156, 158, 163, 202
Russell, Lord John, 269, 287

Sadler, Dr Thomas, 364, 381
St George's, Hanover Square, 374
St James's Hall, 357
Saintsbury, George, 362
Sand, George:
 GE reads, 57, 64
 GE on, 67
 GE compared to, 96–7, 236, 275,
  294
 and Mill on the Floss, 236
 dies, 354
Saturday Review, 155, 189, 199, 201, 211
Savonarola, Girolamo, 275, 276
 see also ELIOT, GEORGE: writings:
 Romola
Sayn-Wittgenstein, Princess Carolyne,
 115
Schiller, Johann Christoph Friedrich, 31,
 47
Schleiermacher, Friedrich, 38, 90
Schöll, Adolf, 128

Scott, Walter,
 GE compared to, 8, 21–2, 170–71, 243
 GE admires, 28, 54, 157, 158, 313
 GE reads aloud to father, 65–6, 313
 and Adam Bede, 194, 199, 200, 201, 202,
  204
 and secrecy, 209
 and Romola, 261
 and Felix Holt, 282
 and Daniel Deronda, 351–2
Scott, William Bell, 123
Senior, Jane, 331
Shakespeare, William:
 GE compared to, 6, 202, 252, 293, 324
 GE reads, 28, 31, 131
 Merry Wives of Windsor, 64, 94
 Othello, 114
 Hamlet, 131
 Two Gentlemen of Verona, 154
 Silas Marner and, 251, 253, 291
Sheard, Henry, 227
Shelley, Mary, 219
Shelley, Percy Bysshe, 92, 242
Sibree, John, 19–20, 34, 46, 205
Sibree, John junior, 34, 47, 63–5, 161
Sibree, Mary (later Cash):
 friendship with GE, 19, 34, 42, 46, 47,
  50, 57, 184
 GE criticizes, 72
 praises GE's article on Cumming, 146
 buys Rosehill, 180
 on GE's memory, 205, 320
Sidgwick, Henry, 334, 366, 380
Simcox, Edith:
 discusses GE with Maria Lewis, 18–
  19, 36, 43
 friendship with GE, 308, 371
 and Middlemarch, 331
 and GE's marriage to Cross, 370, 374,
  375, 376–7
 attends GE's funeral, 381
Simpson, George, 210, 229, 368
Simpson, James, 9, 65, 319
Smith, Albert, 174, 188